HISPANIC FOLK MUSIC OF NEW MEXICO

AND THE SOUTHWEST

HISPANIC FOLK MUSIC OF NEW MEXICO AND THE SOUTHWEST

A Self-Portrait of a People

---

by John Donald Robb

UNIVERSITY OF OKLAHOMA PRESS

NORMAN

Also by John Donald Robb

Hispanic Folksongs of New Mexico (Albuquerque, 1954)

Library of Congress Cataloging in Publication Data

Main entry under title:

Hispanic folk music of New Mexico.

   Principally unacc. melodies; the songs have Spanish words with English translations.
   Bibliography: p.
   Discography: p.
   Includes index.
   1. Hispanic American folk music—New Mexico.   I. Robb, John Donald, 1892–
M1668.4.H52   784.7'5   78–21392
ISBN 0–8061–1492–4

To Harriet

who for over fifty years has played
the role of the perfect wife without
missing a cue

Peasant music is the outcome of changes wrought by a natural force whose operation is unconscious. . . . For this reason the individuals of which it consists—the single tunes are so many examples of high artistic perfection. In their small way, they are as perfect as the grandest masterpieces of musical art. They are, indeed, classical models of the way in which a musical idea can be expressed in all its freshness and shapeliness—in short in the very best possible way, in the briefest possible form and with the simplest of means. On the other hand, the favourite national or popular art songs contain, beside a few interesting tunes, so many musical commonplaces, that their value remains far lesser than that of peasant music in the narrower sense of the term.

Béla Bartók, *Hungarian Folk Music*

CONTENTS

ILLUSTRATIONS

PREFACE

Mankind has always been attracted to elemental things. We live among the seeming humdrum of prosaic things, usually unaware of the incredible richness of those "things" and the equally incredible richness of the popular vocabulary with which we name them. One tires of the famous or infamous, the doings of the great, the exceptional, the rich, the powerful. It is relaxing to be among simple, unpretentious people, to share their vivid experience of life as reflected in folk music.

Years ago in Minnesota I came under the spell of such music. My mother in the 1890's sang, "Can she bake a cherry pie, Billy Boy, Billy Boy," and father, a veteran of Shiloh and Vicksburg, would sing "Blue-eyed, bonny, bonny Eloise, the Belle of the Mohawk Vale." A decade later when I was a teenaged youth we would drive in a ranch wagon behind a team of horses to the county seat for the Old Settlers' Reunion on the Fourth of July. There, to fascinating fiddle tunes, slim-waisted cowboys danced with the young goddesses from the ranches on a cottonwood platform erected in front of the county courthouse. This was beauty to my adolescent eyes and ears. And so I was "hooked."

Years later, in 1941, when I moved to the Southwest, I found the folk tradition still alive in the villages but fast fading away. I started recording and studying what I found.

The present work is a supplement to and expansion of my earlier book, *Hispanic Folksongs of New Mexico*, and a number of articles and record albums that are listed in the Bibliography and the Discography. It aspires to be a panoramic survey of the traditional Hispanic folk music of the Southwest from an observation post in New Mexico. In rereading my earlier writings, I find little that needs to be changed. I would now place more emphasis on the erosion of the Spanish tradition as it has been filtered through and modified by the Mexican, Indian, and Anglo cultures in the New World. In particular I would emphasize the contribution from Mexico, richer in the number of items that can be identified than that of Spain, although the latter tradition is more basic, like a strong foundation, almost invisible, on which the visible rests.

In this book I have broadened the field of my reporting by including more references to the music of the southwestern states neighboring New Mexico, especially California, Arizona, Colorado, and Texas. I have supplied examples of forms that I have not previously dealt with, together with many additional texts and melodies that add perspective to the forms discussed in my earlier book and that altogether constitute a sizable anthology. Finally I have provided additional analysis and discussion of the southwestern environment and the personalities involved in its music.

Most of the literature published in this country dealing with the Hispanic folk music of the Southwest has concentrated on the literary and linguistic aspects of the subject. If the music is reproduced in any fashion, it is usually in the form of transcriptions by someone other than the author, and rarely is there any adequate discussion of the music itself. It seems strange, at least to a musician, that scholarly works dealing with folk music have often taken the music for granted. Notable exceptions are Terrence Hansen's fine article on the *corridos* of southern California, which appeared in 1959 in *Western Folklore*, and Richard B. Stark's *Music of the Spanish Folk Plays in New Mexico*. In most Spanish and Mexican folk-music literature the melody is usually printed with the words of at least one verse, a practice I have adopted for this book.

Omitting the music, it might be argued, would help keep alive the process of aural transmission and the consequent changes and variations that make true folk music a living tradition. But education, especially musical education, tends to turn the young toward different modes of musical expression that are dependent on the written score and thus to destroy the old tradition, in whose formation, one must admit, musical illiteracy played a part. It was not a bad part, however, for it placed a premium on spontaneity and led to the development of a great treasury of timeless melody. If, as some believe, the aural tradition is dying out with the old men and women who were its carriers, the intervention of scholars is a good thing, the only thing in fact that could rescue its beauties from oblivion.

Because my approach is primarily that of a musician, I have tried in my writings to present a musical point of view and have included transcriptions of the melodies as well as discussions of the music itself.

I have paid special attention to the matter of cross referencing because, for me, studies like this are roughly proportionate in interest and value to the interrelationships established, each one of which gives added meaning to the examples affected. These relationships may be of one melody or text to another, of a text to a melody or vice versa, of either to a publication or work of folk art, such as a *bulto* or *retablo*, of a text to historical events great or small, and so forth. The cross-referencing process thus becomes analogous to weaving, the individual strands being fashioned into a more or less tightly knit fabric that acquires its texture, its pattern, and its color from the particular admixture of strands involved. I can testify that the subject becomes constantly more engrossing as one explores these relationships.

Cross referencing has revealed a very large number of interrelationships among the examples in this volume. I have identified many of them. There must, however, be many more that further study would reveal. The mere comparison of titles discloses some of them. The comparison of first lines, of other lines, or of entire verses discloses others. To identify them all would be an interminable process and is beyond the practical scope of this investigation.

The transcription and translation of the song texts have sometimes presented difficulties. When the song text had to be deciphered from a recording, it was sometimes impossible to determine just what words the singer was singing. When the transcriptions were based in part on reference to handwritten notebooks, there were many words not to be found in any dictionary, including words of colloquial use well understood by the people of the particular region but unintelligible without their assistance. There were also misspellings so misleading as to compel reliance on the context for a guess at the exact meaning. I have added punctuation marks when it seemed necessary. At other times I have reproduced the texts sans punctuation. For the convenience of the English-speaking reader, the English style of capitalization has been used for the Spanish song titles as well as for their English translations.

In addition there was the difficulty of translating Spanish expressions into English when a literal translation would make no sense whatever. Furthermore, my translations of identical passages, made at different times over a period of some thirty years, sometimes differ considerably. The arduous and time-consuming labor of comparing these word for word in order to arrive at one theoretically correct solution seemed better left for those primarily interested in the linguistic study of the texts, particularly since some of them are susceptible to varying interpretations.

Most of the translations are free in the sense that I have tried, while preserving the meaning of the original, to bring that meaning over in intelligible, unstrained English. In a few instances I have followed the rhyming and rhythmic patterns of the original, for, although this practice sometimes makes a faithful translation more difficult, it does permit the text to be sung in English to the melody of the song. I feel this more than compensates for the deficiencies of translation. In fact, had time permitted, I would have preferred to make such translations of all the song texts.

In a number of instances the informants have sung only a few of the verses of a lengthy song but have later supplied me with the complete text. Likewise, they have sometimes omitted verses or sung them in a different order from the corresponding texts, repeated lines or entire verses, or made other minor changes. These irregularities, particularly the repetitions, are so frequent and so unpredictable that, though I may have sometimes pointed them out in the case of individual songs, to do so in detail would be unrewarding.

Sometimes, however, repetitions are obviously employed purposefully to give emphasis or, in choruses and refrains, to provide bridges and contrast between the successive verses. At other times they seem to be the result of a whim, a lapse of memory, or a rotelike duplication of the way the singer first learned the song. Such repetitions lend an air of casualness. They also tend to reassure the listener hearing a song for the first time that he heard it correctly or to make clear what was obscure the first time through. Incidentally, repetition often helps the person transcribing a text from a recording to verify what he has written.

I have avoided the temptation to "fix up" a garbled text just because a more intelligible one has been found elsewhere. My position has been that the sources, the texts, even though garbled, must be reported as they are.

A preponderant number of references to specific songs and dances are to items contained in my own collection. The reasons are simple. This is the material with which I am most familiar, and it is extensive enough to cover almost the entire field. Furthermore, these recordings have been readily accessible to me, and that is not true of much of the published or unpublished material of others.

John Donald Robb
Albuquerque, New Mexico

ACKNOWLEDGMENTS

Although most of the transcriptions and translations are mine, I owe a debt of gratitude, first, to my many informants listed in the index of my collection of recordings and in particular to those who have made major contributions, including Edwin Berry, Vicente F. Gallegos, the late Próspero S. Baca, and the late Francisco S. Leyva; to those who have edited my work and who have in the process corrected many of my errors; to those whose writings I have consulted; and to the Rockefeller Foundation, whose generous grant made it possible for me to engage others to assist in the organization of materials for this publication, and particularly to Norman Lloyd, formerly of that foundation.

Since 1942, when I first started collecting and recording folk songs in the Southwest, I have had the assistance of so many other friends and colleagues that neither my memory nor my records hold all their names. Nevertheless, I wish to acknowledge my indebtedness to the following, whose contributions I do remember, for help generously given: my colleagues, T. M. Pearce, the late Arthur L. Campa, the late Joaquín Ortega, Rubén Cobos (who has read and helpfully criticized the song texts), Robert Duncan, Alex Chávez, Marshall Nason, the late León F. Márquez, and Sabine Ulivarrí, all of the University of New Mexico; my former secretaries, Mrs. Jackie Schlegel, Mrs. Jean Ross Silvola, Mrs. Bea Capelli, and the late Mrs. Lynn M. Barker; Mrs. Edna Westfall, Mrs. Frank C. Hibben, the late United States Senator Joseph M. Montoya, Mr. and Mrs. Gilberto Espinosa, the late Miss Erna Fergusson, and the late Mrs. Lolita Pooler; my former students, who have executed many projects with and for me, and in particular Max Lare, Murray Feldman, and the late William R. Fisher; the following, who have worked for me under the Rockefeller grant, Mary Margaret Barela, Susan Blatz, Rosslyn Smith, the Reverend Alfred Trudeau, Baker Morrow, Cipriano Griego, Isadora Sandoval, and Mary Wicker, who has copied and recopied the manuscript and given editorial assistance; Lawrence D. Wheeler, who has copied all the musical examples and song settings; and finally a special acknowledgment to my assistant Rowena Rivera, who has been invaluable in the completion of this work.

I also wish to acknowledge with thanks, but without prejudice as regards material in the public domain, permission granted by institutions and individuals to reproduce song texts and melodies from their publications or collections. These include the University of California Press, Berkeley, for excerpts from articles that have appeared in *Western Folklore* ("Corridos in Southern California," Terrence L. Hansen, 1959; "The Music of Los Pastores," John D. Robb, 1957; "The Matachines Dance," John D. Robb, 1961), the Southwestern Museum in Los Angeles, for a number of recordings made in California in 1904 and 1905 by Charles F. Lummis; Vincent Acosta and Doris Seibold, for permission to record and use several songs recorded by them and deposited in the archives of folk music of the University of Arizona, and Frances Gillmor, of that university, for permission to make the recordings; the Consejo Superior de Investigaciones Científicas in Madrid, Spain, for permission to reproduce a number of song texts and melodies from the *Cancionero Popular de la Provincia de Madrid* (Matos 8a); the Instituto de Investigaciones Estéticas of the Universidad Autónoma de México, for permission to use song texts and melodies from Vicente T. Mendoza's unpublished manuscript, "Estudio y Clasificación de la Música Tradicional Hispánica en Nuevo México"; the Texas Folklore Society, for the use of several examples from their publications; and finally the following collectors for permission to use items from their collections: Alex Chávez, Rubén Cobos, Terrence Hansen, Peter Hurd, Ralph Steele Boggs, Vicente F. Gallegos, T. M. Pearce, and the late Arthur L. Campa.

I want to acknowledge with my hearty thanks the expert editorial work of Julie Harrison Blissert, who not only made the solutions of the editorial problems seem simple, but gave me the eerie feeling that E. B. White himself was clarifying and strengthening my prose.

A feeling of sadness comes over me as I write in these pages the names of my friends the singers, all of them illumined by their love of music and life. Many of them have gone to their rest. Others I have lost track of. Some few I am still in contact with. But to all of them I wish this book to be a memorial.

EXPLANATION OF FORMAT

Each example used in this work is designated by an alphanumeric symbol representing the section in which the example appears and the number of the example within that section. For instance, the section dealing with the *romance* is designated Section A. The first example in that section is A1. If there are one or more variants of the same example or closely related examples, they are designated A1a, A1b, and so on. There are instances where two or more songs having the same title or first line are entirely different songs; such songs are given different numbers.

A formal heading introduces each example and provides up to seven pieces of information about the song or melody, in this order: title, bibliographical source, name of the informant, age of the informant, place of recording, year of recording or other date representing a minimum age of the song, and name of the collector. When one (or more) of these facts is unknown, as is frequently the case, that slot is simply omitted (rather than filled with "informant unknown," or "year unknown"). Further notes sometimes follow this heading, referring the reader to other similar or contrasting songs and melodies. Thus the first example is described in the following heading:

A1. *Canción del Fraile* (Song of the Friar)
R13, Francisco Chávez, age 43, and Juan Morales, age 40?, La Jara, N.Mex., 1944, Robb. Cf. Matos 8a, Parte Musical, p. 80.

Translated, the heading reads: This is example number A1; its title is *Canción del Fraile*, or, in English, *Song of the Friar*; it is number 13 in the J. D. Robb Collection of Folk Music Recordings; it appears here as sung by Frank Chávez, forty-three years of age, and Juan Morales, about forty years of age. It was recorded at La Jara, New Mexico, in 1944 by J. D. Robb. Compare it with an example in Matos' *Cancionero Popular de la Provincia de Madrid*, Volume I (see Bibliography under Matos 8a), Musical Portion at page 80.

The bibliographical source is usually indicated in the heading by an abbreviation. I have referred to items of my own collection by using a capital R followed by the serial number of the item in my collection, as R137; or, in the case of series B of that collection, RB137. (To avoid confusion, there is no Section R in this volume.) Other sources are usually listed in the Bibliography or Discography and are ordinarily referred to in the heading by the abbreviated code name shown in parentheses at the end of each entry (Baca 1, Boyd 1c, Campa 2, and so on).

References in Section A to Matos 8a are confusing because the words and melody of the same song may be separately listed in Matos' book under Parte Musical and under Parte Literaria, with different item and page numbers. The two parts are at least to some extent cross-referenced by Matos, however.

The Mendoza manuscript (Mendoza 9d) consists similarly of a literary part—fifteen manila folders, with consecutively numbered pages, containing song texts and comments—and a musical part—five notebooks of melody transcriptions. In referring to the literary part, I have simply given the page number (for example, Mendoza 9d, p. 25). When citing the musical transcriptions, I have given the number of the notebook and the page (for example, Mendoza 9d, notebook 4, p. 2).

Cross referencing is indicated by the abbreviation Cf. following immediately after the heading of the particular song text or melody, as shown above.

References to the author's volume of Field Trip Reports, consisting of notes made at the time of the recording and containing comments given by the informants, are abbreviated with the initials FTR and the date of the report (for example, FTR 6/7/49).

In the song texts, when a line terminates with a bracket and the word *Bis* (twice), it means that the line is repeated by the singer.

When a *coro* (chorus) or *refrán* (refrain) is repeated, the repetition is indicated by the word *Coro* or *Refrán* in the Spanish song text, and by the word *Chorus* or *Refrain* in the English version.

In most instances where no musical example appears with the song, the reason is that it was not recorded; that is, only the text was collected. Certain of the examples, however, are intended to be spoken, and have no music. These have been noted in the comments accompanying the songs.

HISPANIC FOLK MUSIC OF NEW MEXICO

AND THE SOUTHWEST

INTRODUCTION

Deep among the mountains and valleys of the American Southwest lie the villages of the descendants of the Spanish conquerors. Here, incredibly, still live a people whose family language is Spanish, who still dance the *matachines* dance on feast days, who perform the Christmas play *Los Pastores* (The Shepherds), and who give the Virgin Mary and the saints such pet names as La Tañita de Galisteo and San José del Cadillal. And here at social gatherings and on ceremonial occasions they sing and play music of the age-old Hispanic tradition.

A Japanese observer has written of the United States:

In travel to New York I crossed quite a few states, but their towns, their shops, their people or other features looked so much alike that my friends' kind explanations about the places we were passing by or through were rather boring. Of course there were different states, yet they were trifling as compared with the uniformity which existed by their side. Taken as a whole, industrialized America seems to be losing its variety and its charm accordingly.

One potent answer to this somewhat superficial observation is found in the villages of the Southwest, particularly in their traditional music and customs. So rich is the variety of this music that a native of Tierra Azul, a tiny New Mexico settlement, could sing for me the famous Penitente chant *Por el Rastro de la Cruz* (01) and then casually respond to a different version that I sang for him with the comment, "Oh, that's the Chimayó tune," correctly identifying a village some thirty miles away. In fact the second version was the tune that Juan Ortega, of Chimayó, had sung for me two years earlier (O1d).

Certainly these villages, unknown to the superficial observer of the United States, supply a great deal of the variety and charm that the Japanese visitor found to be lacking. Each village has its own patron saint, and most of them observe the saint's day with appropriate fiestas. Many of them have their own local customs and superstitions, such as a procession on the saint's day to the spring that supplies the water of the village, or fear of the powers of the local *bruja* (witch). All possess their own, often beautiful, natural setting. Some retain their own native crafts, such as the wood carving of *santos* (saints) by Jorge López of Córdova, New Mexico, and the weaving by the Ortega family in nearby Chimayó. There are villages—of which Abiquiu, New Mexico, is said to be one—settled by *genizaros*, Indians who adopted the Spanish traditions and mode of living. There are villages where the houses are of adobe, the most readily available building material, and others where the villagers have built houses of stone salvaged from the ruins of abandoned missions.

Everywhere there is music, and much of it is music composed by a villager telling of happenings in the village or glorifying local heroes. Poems, recited without music, also commemorate village heroes. One of these (B55) is the *corrido* of José Apodaca, the leader of the *matachines* dancers of the village of San Antonio in Bernalillo County, New Mexico.

The songs collected in a particular village may consist of any of the types discussed in this book or perhaps even of other types. However, the songs of each village usually include certain songs of strictly local origin, often about tragic events such as floods. Even when they are not of local inspiration or origin, songs often take on local characteristics, as in *Por el Rastro de la Cruz*, mentioned above. My collection contains more than 140 songs recorded by singers from one village alone—Tomé, New Mexico—and many of them deal with local persons and events. In Appendix B I have identified a number of songs associated with particular villages.

THE NATURE OF FOLK MUSIC

Many years ago I defined folk music as music that bears the characteristic imprint not of any single individual but rather of the thoughts and emotions of a people united by such ties as language, religion, nationality, and residence (Robb 13, p.1). I see no reason to modify that definition, but I would like to discuss the characteristics of this music in greater detail. Of course each poem or tune was originally composed by an individual, although the composer's name is usually lost to us. It would be ridiculous to say that a folk song, accepted as such, ceased to be a folk song simply because someone subsequently discovered the name of the author.

Again a folk song is one that has been adopted by the folk culture. It is handed down by ear and not in written notation, although not infrequently the words are written down in notebooks. Occasionally some of the fleeting musical versions are frozen into notation by scholars, as in my own collection. But as a result of transmission by ear, true folk music is constantly changing and proliferating into many versions.

Many of the best folk songs are old. I cannot, however, accept the view held by some that a folk song must be a hundred years old to deserve that title. Some songs that I should call folk songs have undoubtedly lived, died, and been forgotten in the course of a hundred years. With age, however, the process of change has had time to operate, so that many people have contributed to the form of the song, and as a result it reflects the spirit of the people rather than merely that of an individual. Melody and rhythm are its principal elements. Folk music usually embodies traditional elements of the folklore of the people, or at any rate their attitudes toward life.

In *An Outline History of Music*, Karl Nef wrote:

John Meier . . . sees the chief characteristic of the folk song to be the fact that the mass views it as its own, treats it freely by altering it, whether by additions, omissions or otherwise. When the mass at large in this manner assumes overlordship over a song, when a song has become "popular" in the sense of having become current among the people, then it has become a genuine folk song, no matter by whom it was created. In this way songs by master poets and by professional composers have also become actual folk songs. [Nef, p. 38]

Process of Change. There is no final or fixed form of a true folk song, for each time it is sung it assumes a slightly, or even greatly, varied form in a continuous evolution. It therefore grows like the branches of a tree with many twigs and leaves, each of which is in its own way unique. A true folk song must have the vitality to survive and be remembered. By a process akin to natural selection certain types tend to survive and others die out, like the *décima* in New Mexico. Whatever other changes take place, folk songs tend to revert to a cultural norm. In their evolution, difficult or arty elements are weeded out, and there is a trend toward a simplicity that marks some examples with a surprising perfection and beauty (for a fuller discussion of this process, see Robb 13, pp. 1–2).

One of the interesting experiences of the folk-song hunter is the encounter with variants of a song previously collected, for each variant throws light not only upon its geographical diffusion but also upon the process by which a song is transmuted from a personal creation by some author into the portrait of a people. As my experience in collecting has increased, I have adopted more and more the practice of asking my informants whether they know particular songs in the hope of adding to my stock of variants.

Nature of Performance. While the performance of folk music as a rule is crude, this very crudity gives it a raw power that is lacking in the performances of professional entertainers who sing what they call folk music. The sincerity of grief that is heard in a Penitente *alabado* more than makes up for the absence of trained voices. Likewise the gusto and vigor of the fiddlers makes up for their sometimes scratchy bowing.

Improvement and Degeneration. My colleague T. M. Pearce first called my attention to the fact that, because of a singer's faulty memory, misunderstanding of unfamiliar words, and similar reasons, the song texts sometimes degenerate into garbled and unintelligible versions. The same seems to be true of the literary form, the rhyming pattern, and so forth. However, a strange fact emerges: although the melodies constantly change, they tend rather to *improve* as the personal idiosyncrasies of the singer get rubbed off in the long course of aural transmission. Extraneous elements, like the occasional inclusion of clichés of contemporary popular music, are incongruous. There seems to be an intuitive faculty at work in the musicians, a feeling of what is appropriate to the style of the region or cultural tradition.

ORIGINS AND INFLUENCES

The Hispanic folk music of the American Southwest has many roots, not merely those found in Spain itself. The Spanish and Mexican roots are the tap roots. And yet the folk music of our Southwest is a living cultural entity different from any of its sources. It is a thing apart, having dropped off parts of its original dress and added elements from other sources.

An instance of such elimination is the simple melodies originally composed for mariachi bands in Mexico with alternating vocal solos and instrumental interludes, including flamboyant trumpet solos. These songs sometimes survive in the Southwest without any instrumental accompaniment and with none of the extroverted flamboyance, sometimes approaching brashness, of the Mexican original. Instead they tend to be characterized, like the *canción Palomita Que Vienes Herida* (C14), by a softness and tenderness remote from their origins.

Of course the colorful street calls still heard in Spain[1] and Mexico are no longer heard in the Southwest, for itinerant street venders have almost completely disappeared from the North American scene. On the other hand, one of the characteristic song types of the region, the *indita*, has come about by the addition of elements borrowed from American Indian music.

Although true folk music comes, through

[1] See Y3, the street call of a scissors grinder played on the pan pipes and recorded in Seville, Spain, in 1970. See also Y2, a very similar scissors grinder's street call played on the same instrument, which I recorded in Oaxaca, Mexico, in 1952.

Street calls were once a colorful adjunct of life in the United States. They were still a part of the daily experience in Minneapolis when I was growing up there between 1892 and 1911. The hand-organ man with his monkey, the scissors grinder, and others were frequent visitors.

In 1962, a year I spent in San Salvador, in the Republic of El Salvador in Central America, I found that the tradition was still very much alive and that the street calls of the shoemaker, the ventriloquist purveying entertainment, and others were well known to the householder.

aural transmission and the inevitable modifications that result, to reflect the qualities of a people rather than an individual, it is clear that some individual starts the process. Some folk songs can be identified as having been at their inception popular songs, as in the case of *Susanita* (M1), which turns out to be an almost completely transformed version of the famous Stephen Foster song *Oh! Susannah*. In his celebrated treatise on *Hungarian Folk Music*, Béla Bartók states that practically every recent European peasant music arose under the influence of some kind of "national" or "popular" art music (Bartók, p. 1). But it is relatively rare that the melodies can be traced back to a specific origin, a fact that has prompted some to include anonymity as a part of the definition of folk music.

Spanish Folk Music. The following description of Spanish folk music by M. García Matos, one of Spain's leading collectors, illustrates the indebtedness of our southwestern music to that of Spain, for practically every word of the quotation could be taken as an accurate description of the traditional Hispanic music of New Mexico and the Southwest:

The predominant literary form of Spanish folklore is the quartet of octosyllabic verses, the uneven verses giving the rhyme, a form which appeared toward the sixteenth century. Next came in order of its importance the one called seguidilla, which is also of four verses of which the first and third are heptasyllabic and the second and fourth are pentasyllabic. Born according to all the information we have from the fifteenth century, they at times form a tercet in which the odd verses furnish a new rhyme and are of five syllables, the others having seven. . . . Numerous songs . . . have their tone based on the classical diatonic modes . . . it would not be conjecturing to suppose that many of them must have been influenced by the Roman domination over Spanish culture. Nearly all the Greek modes or Greek-Roman modes are present in the melodies, the Doric and Phrygian and their respective Hypodoric and Hypophrygian flexions being those which appear most frequently . . . free rhythm and heterometry —changing measure— are as frequent as the rhythm of the single measure. All these characteristics including . . . frequently embellished notes of brief or rapid emission . . . are, as we now shall state, constant in the Spanish folklore in the majority of the regions. . . . We shall finish by saying that Spanish folklore is substantially monodic of one single voice, even when it is performed by a

5

choir or group. But in the northern regions, it is usually sung by a duo by thirds which in a sporadic way is found in other zones. [Matos 8d, Introduction]

Indian Influence. Since the Spanish settlers came into a country already occupied by North American Indians, it is only natural that the music of the newcomers should be influenced by that of their Indian neighbors. The most conspicuous result was the emergence of a type of song known as the *indita* (see Section F). There were marriages between Spaniards and Indians and in these interracial families some persons grew up under the influence of the two cultures that were blended in them.

Reciprocal Influences. Underlying the various types of Hispanic folk music in the Southwest is a vast network of customs, crossing back and forth over racial, religious, national, and temporal boundaries, some of which tend to appear, fade, and reappear in the village life of the area. The dying out of such observances as the *matachines* dances and their revival from time to time is a case in point. It is known that these dances are of ancient origin; that they have taken on the coloration of Indian adaptations, as well as the more traditional Hispanic traits; that they die out and reappear; that sometimes, as at Tortugas, New Mexico, they appear with purely Indian dances, as well as with different versions of the *matachines* itself; and that at other times, as at Jémez, New Mexico, they appear in two distinct versions—a Spanish version with fiddle and guitar imported from a nearby Spanish village and an Indian version with Indian music, chorus, drums, and costuming, which nevertheless follows generally the plot, the dance evolutions, and other aspects of the traditional *matachines* dance (see Section W).

Internal Evidence of Age or Origin. Not infrequently in the song texts themselves there are clues to the age of a song. The most conspicuous forms of which this is true are the *corrido* and the related form of the *indita*. It is customary for both forms to set forth in the very first stanza the year, and often the month and the exact day, of the happenings described in the song. For instance, in the *Corrido de la Muerte de Antonio Maestas* (I17) the first verse gives the date as July

5, 1889. This date is accurately repeated in all the variants with one exception, in which the singer transposed the last two numbers so that the year appears as 1898. When I asked one informant why a song had been written and circulated so widely about the death of this young man, a cowboy, he replied that the man came from a very fine family and the song was "very accurate." One of my informants told me that this song was composed for the family of the dead man by Higinio V. Gonzales, a well-known *poeta* of the era. (For more about Gonzales, see Robb 13c.) Another song, *El Tecolote* (The Owl, I10–10g), has an owl taking exercises "with the troops of Santa Anna," who was, of course, the commanding general of the Mexican troops in the war of 1846–48. In its humorous tone, its animal subject, and its reference to the bad habit of drinking, it reminds one of the Mexican soldiers' song of 1917, *La Cucaracha* (The Cockroach), the bad habit there being the smoking of marijuana.

Among the internal evidence of antiquity may be included the use of modal scales, *musica ficta* (Robb 13, pp. 6–8), and use of obsolete words (for example, *reses* instead of *vacas* in the *corrido* about Antonio Maestas mentioned above). Songs containing references to kings or nobility or sword play usually turn out to be *romances* of an early date; references to automobiles and telephones suggest the twentieth century; wagon trains, the nineteenth. In many cases the dates set forth in the songs confirm such conjectures.

There is some evidence that the Easter religious observances in New Mexico villages and the southwestern Christmas play *Los Pastores*, along with their accompanying music, are derived from the European mystery plays, which persisted in the Old World to the sixteenth century. One of these religious plays, *Adam and Eve*, was enacted in Mexico City in 1532, before the final decline of the plays in Europe (Campa 2c).

Historical Evidence. Hypotheses about the origin of songs of more recent provenance can sometimes be verified or rejected in the light of the known facts of history. In certain cases, as for instance in the popular melodies taken over by the folk musicians, written records give evidence of the dates of origin of the style (waltz, polka, and so on) or even of the particular melody.

Original poems in Spanish were in years past published in various Spanish language newspapers (a practice that is being revived in certain student newspapers in universities of the Southwest, such as the *Candle* of New Mexico Highlands University in Las Vegas, New Mexico). Some of these poems were the texts of songs that have become folk songs by reason of their nature, popularity, and long usage. The minimum age of certain folk songs can be established by reference to old files of these newspapers. Among them are *La Voz del Pueblo* and *El Independiente* of Las Vegas, New Mexico, editions of which dating as far back as 1894 still exist. Another, *El Nuevo Mexicano*, of Santa Fe, New Mexico, also exists in editions dating as far back as 1892. A complete text of *Don Simón*, several versions of which are included in this volume, was published in *El Independiente* of Las Vegas, New Mexico, on November 2, 1895, establishing a minimum age of over eighty years and permitting comparison with examples recorded almost a half century later (L1–L1c). That it is in fact considerably older is suggested by Vicente T. Mendoza's comment to me that it was originally a part of a *zarzuela*.

Song texts may also be found in the handwritten notebooks of singers and poets. I have been permitted to make copies of several of these for the University of New Mexico Library. One of them is dated 1901. These notebooks reveal, for instance, that the *décima* was a very popular form around the turn of the century.

Geographical Considerations. A good many songs can be traced back to the geographical area in which they originated. The first European colonizers of the American Southwest were Spaniards who came from Mexico, and many folk songs that cannot be traced to Spain or to local origins came from Old Mexico, whose influence is very strong. When collecting songs, I often ask informants if they know a specific song that I already have in other versions. On one trip to Mexico such questions provided in quick succession three songs (R1265, R1266, R1267) that I had previously collected in the Southwest (C14, R19, C48). While it is of course possible that these songs actually originated in the United States, it is more logical to theorize that they came from or by way of Old Mexico. First, the flow of civilization until about 1825 was from south to north. Second, the Mexican versions are more nearly complete and more developed, whereas the songs collected in New Mexico are simpler and thus presumably further removed from the original source.

It is possible that these songs could be traced to their actual authors through *cancioneros* published in Mexico or the works of Mexican scholars. In fact one of the three songs mentioned above, *El Muchacho Alegre* (C48), appears in Vicente Mendoza's *Lírica Narrativa de México—El Corrido* in a version collected in the Mexican state of Michoacán in 1939 (Mendoza 9e, p. 289). Both melody and text are identifiable as being from a common source with that of my examples, though with substantial variations. In the same book Mendoza includes as *corridos* of Mexican origin a number of the songs mentioned in this book as part of the Hispanic heritage of the Southwest.

In my early years of collecting I was assured by various persons that there was no real Hispanic folk music of American origin and that it all came from Spain or Mexico. Incredulous, I determined to find out for myself whether that could be true. It was, therefore, with a sense of elation that I was able after considerable research to identify the *Corrido de la Muerte de Antonio Maestas* (I17) as the first *corrido* I had collected that was of undeniable New Mexican origin (see Robb 13a). Since then a good number of these songs of American origin have been identified (see Appendix B).

My New Mexico informants learned many songs in other states where they had gone to herd sheep or work on the railroads or in the mines. There are examples from Arizona (R1189), California (R460), Colorado (R208), Idaho (C75), Texas (R2412), Utah (R268), and Wyoming (B47). A number of *romances* and other folk songs have been identified by Espinosa, Campa, Mendoza, Cobos, and others as foreign in origin, although circulating in the Southwest. Examples are *Delgadina* (A2) from Spain, *Canción del Fraile* (A1) from France, *Adiós Muchachos* (C66) from Argentina, *Mi Gallo Tuerto* (R827) from Venezuela, and of course, a host of songs like *Heráclio Bernal* (B12) from Mexico (for more on songs of Spanish origin, see Campa 2, chapters 2 and 4).

Kansas appears in some songs because Spanish-speaking vaqueros sometimes went along with the trail herds from Texas or New Mexico to the rail head, which at the time was in Kansas (see *Los Vaqueros de Kansas*, I18). The composers, however, were usually from the border states of the Southwest—California, Arizona, New Mexico, Texas, and Colorado.

Anglicisms in Southwestern Spanish. For better or worse, people of differing ethnic backgrounds living in proximity, especially in the intimacy of village life, are influenced by each other and react on one another in ways ranging from the extreme of hatred and murder to the opposite of love and marriage. One manifestation of this influence and interaction is the conscious or unconscious linguistic imitation of each by the other. Whether the imitation is based on mutual or one-sided admiration or is merely the unconscious result of being subjected to the repetition of the same stimulus or impression depends on the particular case.

I have discussed elsewhere how southwestern spoken and written English is permeated with Spanish words—lariat, rodeo, corral, chaps, remuda, arroyo, hombre, coyote, chili, and gringo (see, under Discography, Robb 13t). These are accepted as perfectly natural additions to the English vocabulary.

However, the reverse process by which English words are incorporated into southwestern Spanish is regarded with something akin to horror by scholars, perhaps because such words usually undergo a "sea change" in the process, such as bizarre spelling or the addition of Spanish suffixes which tend to give them a ludicrous appearance. I refer to such words as *Crismes* (Christmas), *junque* (junk), *trucke* (truck, used instead of *camión*), *baybito* for little baby (see B26, verse 10), *drenaje* for drainage (B29, verse 7), *dipo* for depot (B47a, verse 2), *juisque* for whiskey (D7, verse 5), and many others.

Acclimatization of the Melodies. While lyrics can be traced, it seems impossible to be precise about the origins of most of the melodies. With the exception of compositions by known composers like Vicente Saucedo, Luis Martínez, and Eduardo Gallegos, all of whom have composed songs that have been widely sung by folk musicians, most of the melodies are anonymous. Some are borrowed from other songs and sung with new words. A clear example of such borrowing is *El Crucifijo*, in which the singer simply borrowed from the Anglo-American culture the traditional tune *Auld Lang Syne*. The study of variants reveals, however, that the constant process of change tends to create a new regional type of melody irrespective of the actual origin. Throughout my field trip reports are comments by old men and women that they learned this or that song when they were very young from a friend or relative; this information often pushes the date far enough back for the aural tradition to have brought about very radical changes toward the regional style.

When a folk musician sings or plays a melody that originated in another culture, he always changes it in one subtle way or another. In fact he cannot help doing so. Of the countless examples of this practice let me refer to just a few from my own collection: a fiddle tune (R212) that turns out to be a strangely familiar and yet strangely altered version of the Civil War tune *The Girl I Left Behind Me*; an Indian melody sung with Spanish words by David Frescas, who is of half-Indian and half-Spanish-American blood (F22); the song *Adiós a Guaymas* (C69), an almost unrecognizable version of *Home, Sweet Home*; and *Canción del Fraile* (A1), an adopted version of the French folk song *Marlborough Went Forth to War*.

I have gone about the task of searching for melodic origins and age in various ways. It has been my routine practice to ask the singer when and where he learned the song. Sometimes the answers are indefinite, but they usually furnish evidence at least of the minimum age of the melody. The characteristics of the melody itself add their quota of evidence and often are easily identifiable as belonging to a certain class, such as the *alabado* or the *corrido*. Long experience enables students of folk music to memorize hundreds of the more important melodies and the style of others, such as the *matachines* dances, and thus to piece together the story of their origins and use.

The New Mexico *alabados* and *matachines* dance tunes are special cases. The former, according to Juan B. Rael, are of Spanish, Mexican, and local origin (Rael, pp. 18–19).

However, they have circulated by ear long enough to have become a New Mexico type distinct from any other that I have encountered elsewhere in the world. This is true also of the *matachines* dance tunes. There is evidence of foreign origin for two of the dances of the so-called Aztecas of Tortugas, New Mexico—*La Cruz* (W101) and *Los Enanos* (W107). According to my informant, Leonardo ("Lalo") Pacheco, his own father brought *La Cruz* from Zacatecas in Old Mexico, while *Los Nanos* (The Dwarfs) is from Xochimilco, Mexico, where he said, "there is a tribe of dwarfs." The *matachines* dances of New Mexico seem to have evolved into a regional type different from the Aztecas dances, featuring fiddle and guitar (rather than fiddle and drum) or even fiddle alone. The dances of the Aztecas resemble more closely the dances of the Indios of Saltillo, Mexico (R1242–1251) in the use of the instrumental combination of fiddle and drum (on the origin of the *matachines* dance, see Robb 13e).

For all practical purposes I think that we may assume that all the *alabados* and *matachines* dances of New Mexico owe more to the process of evolution that has taken place there over a long period of time than to any foreign influence, although the latter are similar in style to some of the dances of Old Mexico. I would suppose that the same is probably true of most of the old songs having to do with weddings, wakes, or *velorios*, and other ritualistic events.

The voluminous anthologies of Vicente T. Mendoza and other publications contain so many variants of song texts and melodies (many of which are sung in the border states as well as in Mexico) that to trace and compare these connections or even to cross-reference them all is beyond the scope of the present work. It would, itself, be a fascinating subject for research. It seems clear that it would reveal a great many songs common to both regions and delineate more clearly the influence of Mexican music on our own.

It would be foolhardy for me to claim to have done more than scratch the surface of the subject of origins. The paucity of written evidence often compels one to rely on internal evidence found in the song texts themselves, on hunches derived from the peculiar inflection or sound of a melody, or on comments, often unreliable, from the musicians themselves. An example of internal evidence is the second and third verses of the *alabanza Milagros de San Antonio* (P12), which raise a suspicion that this may be a fragment of a *romance* from Portugal. But for most of the examples we have no proof of origin, which makes it all the more interesting when evidence or even hints of a song's origin do turn up.

FORMS

The basic form of most of the song texts is strophic; that is, they consist of a series of stanzas or verses sung to the same tune. The most common form of each verse is the *copla*, a stanza or verse of four octosyllabic lines with the second and fourth rhyming. Other forms, such as the *décima*, are exceptional although formerly of frequent occurrence. An *estribillo*, or refrain, interpolated between verses is not uncommon. Other forms are the *seguidilla*, characterized by alternate lines of five and seven syllables (see Matos' description of the *seguidilla* quoted on p. 5), and the verse of eight lines, or double *copla*. Generic names such as *alabado* are commonly used in New Mexico to refer to a large range of religious songs. In the interest of clearer understanding I use it to refer to unmetered songs characterized by a florid style of singing reminiscent of plainsong and relating to the passion of Christ (other types of religious songs are classified and described in Part II).

The relatively few basic forms permit of a number of variants, such as the repetition of the last line or the last two lines of a *copla* (see *Rubén Leyva*, B18), the beginning or termination of each verse with the same line, the beginning or ending of each line with the same word (see *A Que No Me Lleva el Río*, E18, and *A Nuestra Señora de Guadalupe*, V8), the employment of lines of different numbers of syllables from those mentioned above, and the substitution of assonance (the coincidence of vowel sounds) for complete rhyme. (For a clarifying explanation of the verse forms of the *romance*, *décima*, *glosa* [*décima glosada*], and *seguidilla*, and of the schemes of rhyming and assonance such as the *espinela*, see "Poetic Forms Used in Los Pastores," Stark 16, pp. 347–52.)

Hybrid Forms. The song texts frequently refuse to fit smoothly into the defined forms.

A song text, for example, might fall equally well into either of two classifications or else lie in a no man's land between them. There are explanations for this, one of which is that the singers are sometimes unfamiliar with the definitions. Another may be the inventiveness of the singers.

The *décima*, *La Severiana* (D4), for instance, could in some versions equally well be classified as a *relación* or as a *décima*, and the *Cuando de Pecos* (H1) as a mixture of *décima*, *cuando*, and *indita*. Another hybrid form is the *indita*, in which, as I have said, elements of Hispanic or Mexican folk music are blended with Indian elements. The examples of the *indita* in Section F illustrate this blending.

Formal Construction. A rather charming scheme is found in some songs in which the same words are employed in each verse or in each of a series of verses with the exception of certain critical words appropriate to the changing action of the song. A good example is *Delgadina* (A2). In addition to the interpolation of a refrain between the verses, this *romance* reveals the following structure:

A. Verses 1–5: Incestuous proposal of the king to his daughter Delgadina, its rejection, and his revenge, the imprisonment of Delgadina.

B. Verses 6–8: Delgadina's appeal to her sister.
Verses 9–11: Delgadina's appeal to her brother.
Verses 12–14: Delgadina's appeal to her mother.
Verses 15–17: Delgadina's appeal to her father.

C. Verses 18–21: Delgadina's salvation by death and the damnation of the king.

The song is in three well-defined parts, as indicated. Each set of verses in part B repeats the identical framework of words with only those variations appropriate to the changing scenes. An element of unity is supplied by the recurrent theme of gold—the sister combing her golden hair, her brother playing with marbles of gold, her mother donning golden slippers, her father sitting on cushions of gold. All these elements of art indicate that this old *romance* has been handed down in a form not too far removed from the original, for many other versions of *Delgadina* have no such interesting form.

Another song with a similar structure is the *relación Leonor* (D6). I have given the words of the verses in this song with certain word spaces left blank. In each blank I have inserted a number in parentheses. Below the text following these numbers, respectively, I have listed the words supplied by the singer of this particular variant. Obviously a singer with a little imagination could expand the song indefinitely simply by thinking up new words to insert in the blanks.

En un (1) _____ muy la-la-la-la-la-la-la-la-la-la-largo
se paseaba un (2) _____
(3) _____ las (4) _____
de mi querida Leonor.

In a very large _____
There passed by a _____
_____ the _____
Of my beloved Lenore.

The words inserted in the three verses are as follows:

(1) *llano* (plain), *bosque* (forest), *río* (river)
(2) *cantador* (singer), *cazador* (hunter), *pescador* (fisherman)
(3) *cantando* (singing), *buscando* (hunting for), *pescando* (fishing for)
(4) *mañani-ti-ti-ti-ti-ti-ti-ti-ti-ti-ti-tas* (morning songs), *venadi-ti-ti-ti-ti-ti-ti-ti-ti-ti-tos* (little deer), *pescari-ti-ti-ti-ti-ti-ti-ti-ti-tos* (little fish)

Another song with a similar formal plan is *Cuatro Palomitas Blancas* (C39).

It is interesting to observe the occurrence of similar patterns in the folk music of other cultures. A Negro spiritual from Florida (R1305) goes like this:

I got a ———— in dat land,
I got a ———— in dat land,
I got a ———— in dat land,
Where I'm gwine.

In each verse is inserted the name of father, mother, brother, and so forth, each being repeated three times. This is simplicity carried almost to the ultimate—almost but not quite, for there are touching Negro spirituals that not long ago were sung in my hearing by the choir of the Church of God in Christ in Albuquerque, New Mexico, in which the song texts consisted of the reiteration of just one phrase—"God is not dead," or "If nothing else works try Jesus."

Another type of formal construction is a *copla* in which the first two lines are repeated in reverse order. An example is *Rosita* (C85), the fourth verse of which is as follows:

Cuando esa rosa te pones
haces mi amor derribar;
haces mi amor derribar
cuando esa rosa te pones.

When you wear that rose
You make my love pour out;
You make my love pour out
When you wear that rose.

Another song with this pattern is *El Sombrerito* (C71).

Variety of Forms. It may be a surprise to some that there are so many different forms of Hispanic folk songs current in the Southwest and so many different types within a particular form. The *décima* with its many subcategories is a good example of such types within a form. We are, in fact, in the presence of the continuation of an ancient tradition, which over the centuries has evolved and handed down these forms. It has become second nature for the composers of new songs to write their song texts and melodies within the traditional forms. The departure from tradition would probably be considered by the folk as a bizarre intrusion of a sort of personality cult.

Differing forms may, however, emerge from a common source when their preexisting differences have finally been recognized and defined, as in the *alabado* and *alabanza* (see Sections O and P). The only new forms that have emerged are, in reality, not intrusions but mergers of existing traditional forms. The *indita* is a perfectly natural marriage of two cultures, the Indians' culture and that of the Spanish invaders. The *alabado* appears to have evolved from the plainsong tradition, cut loose from its moorings as a learned art.

So the feeling of the folk, it seems to me, has without any formulation created an invisible pressure upon the troubadours to hand on the traditional forms and not to go off on individualistic excursions. The originality is thus limited to the contents of the song texts and to new arrangements of melodies within a predetermined style. This is still a very large field of action.

Responsorial Singing. Responsorial singing —that is, singing in which the verses are sung by a leader and the chorus or refrain or even alternate verses are sung in response by a group—is a part of folk tradition in the Southwest. It is observable in *Las Posadas* (The Lodgings), a sort of prelude to the Christmas play *Los Pastores*, and also in Easter services of the Penitentes during Holy Week. The responses of the group or congregation are made impressive by their reiteration, after each verse sung by the leader, of such simple but powerful messages as this, from one of the Penitente ceremonies: "Danos Señor una buena muerte" (Give us, O Lord, a good death). Responsorial singing, as well as responsorial speaking or reading, has of course for centuries been part of the Christian ritual, as well as a practice of primitive and folk musicians in many parts of the world. In the Southwest it possesses its own characteristic flavor whose quality must be experienced to be felt.

Overriding of Time Value, Accent, and Elision. In singing, the time values, normal accents, or elisions employed in spoken Spanish are often ignored or overridden in favor of the accentuation required by the music. What Curt Sachs says of poets seems to apply as well to the singers of the folk songs with which we are dealing:

Poets disfigure and level the logical accents obligatory to making ourselves understood in talk between man and man; they replace the free, expressive rhythm of spoken phrases by stereotype patterns of long and short or strong and light; they supplant the natural flow of speech by artificial arrangements of words that often wrong the rules of grammar and syntax; they even replace common by uncommon words that none would use in ordinary speech. Art denaturalizes nature in order to raise it to a higher, or at least a different, plane. [Sachs, p. 31]

For one example of the abnormal prolongation of the time value of a single syllable, see the first syllable of the *alabado Por el Rastro de la Cruz* (O1), where the time value of the syllable *por* is enlarged to accommodate the several notes of the melisma to which it is sung.

For an illustration of an ignored or overridden accent, see the word "Jesús" in the fourth verse of *Bendito Sea Dios* (S2). The spoken accent on the second syllable is overridden in the version as sung by an accent on the first syllable of the word. Another instance is found in the second verse of *Salgan, Salgan, Salgan* (T4) in which the second line is written "Católicos pechos" but is sung with the accent on the first syllable, not the second, of the word "Católicos."

When two words occur in succession, the first ending in a vowel and the second beginning with a vowel, the two vowels are counted and sung as one syllable. This is the form of elision most often encountered. An example of an overridden elision is found in the sixth verse of *O Jesús, O Buen Pastor* (S1). There the words "Yo en" in the first line are sung to separate notes and the elision is ignored. The late Myron Schaeffer, an exceptionally acute observer, devotes two paragraphs to the demonstration of this practice in the Panamanian *mejorana*, a first cousin of our southwestern *décima* (Schaeffer 14, p. 30).

The Copla. This is a four-line verse, the first two lines of which are frequently, if not normally, separated from the others by a semicolon; each of the divisions, consisting of two lines when the *copla* is in its pure form, expresses a complete thought. The simplicity of this form makes it particularly popular with the composer who wishes to improvise verses. The *copla* is, perhaps, the most pervasive of all the forms of Hispanic folk music that circulate in the Southwest, and yet, paradoxically, it is employed in so many other different types of songs that it seemed better for the purposes of this publication to avoid grouping all the *coplas* in a separate category.

Mendoza has written very interestingly about the dissemination of the *copla* in the Southwest, particularly in New Mexico (Mendoza 9d, Parte Literaria, pp. 216–347). He has observed that in this state there are *coplas* of a pure Spanish type and *coplas* of a type influenced from the south, meaning, I assume, particularly Mexico. Among the *coplas* which he includes in the category of those in the authentic Spanish style are certain examples of the *Entrega de Novios*, certain improvised verses *(Coplas de Circunstancias*, N7), and the *Vals Chiqueado* (N1). And among those which he describes as showing southern influence are the songs *Sierra Nevada* (B46), *Cuatro Palomitas Blan-*

cas (C39), *Don Simón* (L1), *Palomita Que Vienes Herida* (C14), *El Muchacho Alegre* (C48), and *El Celoso* (D37).

Intermixture of Song Texts. One of the surprises experienced by one who takes the trouble to read and compare the song texts is the unexpected reappearance of phrases or of whole verses already encountered in apparently unrelated songs. For example, the first verse of *La Playa Arenosa* (The Sandy Beach, A14a) is almost identical with the second verse of *Caballerito* (Little Gentleman, A14). Such a coincidence may denote a relationship of form or origin between the songs or merely that the singer knew both songs and got them mixed up. In this particular instance the songs contain other similarities and appear to be variants of the same *romance*. Again, *El Juramento* (R1746) in the second and third stanzas contains some twelve lines virtually identical with the first and second stanzas of *Cuando Escuches Este Vals* (When You Hear This Waltz, C83). *El Juramento* appears to be a more nearly complete version of the same song. On the other hand, the sixth and seventh verses of *La Inundación* (The Flood, R1999) appear to be irrelevant additions borrowed from some other song.

SUBJECTS, THEMES, AND VALUES

Nature and country life, scenery, behavior of animals, murders, floods, trips on a passenger train, love, marriage, card games, learning English, the crowing of the rooster, woman compared in an uncomplimentary way to a hen and in the opposite sense to a lily, money, liquor, saloons, sin and crime, war, incest, yearning, the loneliness of the shepherd, the suffering of Christ, miracles, praise of the Virgin, the nativity, the Mexican peso, the woman of many lovers, the faithful wife, an epidemic of malaria, death of a cowboy, the Ten Commandments, the absent-minded man, the vagabond—these and other themes tumble over one another in rich profusion making a many-colored tapestry of southwestern life. Nothing is too mundane to attract the attention of the village composer. The song *Mi Carro Ford* (My Ford Car), for instance, gives details of the mechanical malfunctions of a Model T Ford (Robb 13).

The music itself has an earthiness and accessibility that gives it universality. This is felt by virtually everyone who has had occasion to assist me over the years and thus has become somewhat familiar with the music. Gilbert K. Chesterton, in a book of essays which I devoured as a young man, made the observation that the truly important things are, first, those that all men share in common—birth, death, love, even common everyday adventures—and, second, by way of variation, the personal idiosyncrasies that make each person different from every other.

Great books have been written about the people of the Southwest—*Death Comes for the Archbishop*, *Red Sky at Morning*, and, in my opinion, the most intimate and revealing and understanding of all, *The Life and Death of Little Jo*, by Robert Bright. Yet these are not quite like letting the people speak for themselves. Their lives, their jokes, their adventures, their sins, their religious devotion are enshrined in their folk songs. Usually the words—plain, everyday speech full of colloquialisms—are not remarkable for their literary value, but they speak about the things that are important to the human race.

Attachment to Place. The folk songs of the Southwest are the songs of a settled people who love their native valleys and hills. The names of familiar places seem to provide the principal excuse for some songs of a type very popular in Central America and Mexico and imported into the Southwest. Two examples in this tradition are the songs *Albuquerque* (C89) and *Santa Fe* (C88), which glorify the streets, the beautiful women, the monuments, the scenery, and the history of these two cities. They were composed by Vicente Saucedo, who moved to New Mexico many years ago from his native Mexico. Long lists of place names known only to the local people are a feature of the *relación* type of song.

Hardship and Vice. Many songs deal with inebriety and other unattractive aspects of life. The subject is usually dealt with in a factual rather than a moralizing tone, and this tendency is not limited to the subject of drinking and drunkenness. Though the sympathies of the folk are occasionally apparent in these songs (for instance, some songs express hostility toward the rich and glorify bandits), the folk seem as a rule to take life as it is without glossing over its sordid or even agonizing aspects. Consider for instance the songs that deal with executions, *Carlos Saiz* (B10) and *Toribio Huertas* (B11). Such realism widens and enriches the tapestry.

The realistic portrayal of life does not preclude a vision of something better. Many songs describe the hardships of life, and there exists a vast body of religious songs in which the expectation of joy appears to be concentrated in the hope of a better life after death. Certain songs express mild protest, such as *Don Simón* (L1), or more violent reactions against human failings, such as *Jesucristo de la Luz* (B27).

Importance of Parents and Family. There is abundant evidence in the song texts of the respect and love felt for parents, brothers and sisters, sons and daughters, and other family members (see B26, C67, C75–C79). Southwestern folk music includes songs full of tenderness in which a son laments his separation from his beloved parents, grief-stricken songs memorializing the death of a child, and songs of orphans who have lost their parents.

Some of the songs, however, reveal not only this deep sense of family love but also an almost overpowering feeling of retribution for breach of duty within the family. The disobedient daughter is murdered at a dance, a recurrent theme (B17–B20a); the disobedient son dies after being cursed by his mother (B24); the disobedient son quarrels with and murders his parents and is swallowed up by the earth (B25); the incestuous father is tormented by devils (A2); the forbidden suitor is murdered (B30).

Wealth as a State of Mind. In southwestern folk songs one poor man's dreams may be centered on visions of wealth and power, whereas another, with relatively few worldly possessions, seems serene and contented. The former man's musings are represented by the song text *Una Bolsa sin Dinero* (Robb 13m). The latter point of view is expressed with invincible optimism in the song from Tomé, New Mexico, *Tengo, Tengo, Tengo* (C82), whose age I am unable to verify. I would hazard a guess that it is at least as old as the singer, Edwin Berry, fifty-four years. A wryly humorous attitude toward poverty is revealed in the charming *décima Un Testamento* (A Will, E28).

Children's Songs. I have omitted from this volume children's dance and game songs because there already exists a charmingly illustrated publication, *The Spanish American Song and Game Book*, by the Works Progress Administration, which for New Mexico at least covers the subject adequately. Spanish publications contain large numbers of *canciones infantiles* (children's songs) known in Spain (Matos 8a, Parte Literaria, pp. 74–99). Some of them are known as well in the Southwest (see, for example, *La Pulga y el Piojo* [The Nit and the Louse], Matos 8a, Parte Musical, p. 79). A number of children's songs are in fact included in this volume under different headings—*La Zagala* (A4); *Delgadina* (A2); *La Recién Casada* (A7), also known as *Las Señas del Esposo*; *Mambrú* (A1), or *Canción del Fraile*; *Don Gato* (A16); *Los Diez Perritos* (D28). Some of these are classified by Matos as both *romances* and *canciones infantiles*. For instance, he treats *Delgadina* as a *canción infantil* (Matos 8a, Parte Literaria, p. 99) and as a *romance* (Matos 8a, Parte Literaria, p. 37).

Los Pastores and Other Folk Plays. Richard Stark in his *Music of the Spanish Folk Plays of New Mexico* has published, with my permission, several of the versions of the Christmas play *Los Pastores* from my collection (namely, the versions from Valverde, Socorro, Tomé, Los Griegos, Corrales, and Bernalillo, New Mexico). For this and other reasons it would seem reasonable to "incorporate by reference," to use a legal term, his excellent discussion of the folk plays and avoid going over the same terrain. This will leave one rather substantial hiatus: Stark does not furnish English translations of the texts. Many of these, however, have already been made (a number can be found in the archives of the J. D. Robb Collection in the Fine Arts Library of the University of New Mexico).

Furthermore, there is probably no aspect of the Hispanic folk tradition of the Southwest about which so much has been written. In addition to Stark, Stanley Robe, Juan B. Rael, John Englekirk, T. M. Pearce, and others have covered the subject in some detail. Only Stark has given much attention to the music of the play. I have discussed and harmonized a number of melodies of the play in *Hispanic Folk Songs of New Mexico* (Robb 13, pp. 13–14, 24–41) and published an article, "The Music of *Los Pastores*," in *Western Folklore* (Robb 13d). In both places I included musical examples and directed my attention primarily to the music.

Los Pastores is not the only religious folk play known to have been performed in the Southwest. Nevertheless, it is the only one about whose music much is known, and that is largely because performances of *Los Pastores* have persisted into our own day, when sound recordings have become possible.

Arthur L. Campa in his *Spanish Religious Folktheatre in the Spanish Southwest* discussed two cycles of folk plays, dealing with subjects from the Old and New Testaments, respectively. My own collection contains some song texts from *Los Tres Reyes* (The Three Kings, R1478–85), *El Niño Perdido* (The Lost Child, RB100), and a fragment from *Herod and the Jews* (R2014). I have been able to record the melodies from only one of these, *Los Tres Reyes*, and, disappointingly, its texts were all sung to the same tune.

In some places only a few *letras* are sung during the course of a play. The text of the play itself may vary considerably and may even be drastically abbreviated. Some of the *letras* consist of only a verse or two, briefly interrupting the action of the play. These sometimes are repeated several times as a sort of refrain in response to intervening passages of spoken dialogue.

The musical material now available, with the exception of that relating to *El Niño Perdido*, does not promise results commensurate with the research necessary to uncover surviving melodies of the now apparently extinct or moribund plays. I gladly bequeath this task to younger men with more time to invest than I have.

Studies in Depth. Whereas this book is a panoramic study of a large number of forms and examples, various articles and even entire books have been devoted to the history and geographical dispersion of single songs or to the heroes of those songs. One of these books is *With a Pistol in His Hand*, by Américo Paredes, a study of the *corrido* of *Gregorio Cortés* (B49). A book relating to the hero of the *corrido Joaquín Murieta* (B35), although not to the *corrido* itself, is *The Life and Adventures of Joaquín Murieta*, by John Rollin Ridge. Another is Pablo Neruda's *Fulgor y Muerte de Joaquín Murieta*.

A book-length study, *Santa Bárbara*, was published by the late Virginia Rodríguez Rivera in Mexico City in 1967. Aided like this book by a grant from the Rockefeller Foundation, *Santa Bárbara* traces a prayer, or *oración*, to Saint Barbara for protection against storms from its roots in Spain to its hundreds of ramifications throughout Latin America, the Caribbean region, and, significantly for our purposes, the border states Texas, New Mexico, Arizona, and California, as well as Colorado. She found fifteen versions from New Mexico. Although the author generally limited herself to the literary aspects of the prayer, she included two versions with music from Bahia, Brazil.

Two of my own articles devoted to discussion of individual songs are "The Origins of a New Mexico Folksong" and "A Pocket Without Money" (see Bibliography).

THE SINGERS

The Mexican authority on folk music Vicente T. Mendoza spoke interestingly about the men who sang for him during his sojourn in New Mexico (November, 1945, to June, 1946). He stated that the European troubadours and jongleurs passed on their tradition to the Spanish minstrels, some of whom went to America during the years following the Conquest. He added that the tradition has never been so strongly manifested in the New World as in New Mexico. In that state, he said, are real troubadours, besides the almost legendary Viejo Vilmas and his other rivals (see Section G). A number of these *trovadores* lived in Spanish communities like Bernalillo, Chimayó, Pecos, Taos, La Jara, Cuba, Las Vegas, Sabinal, and Albuquerque itself. He named the following as having the silhouette of the old *copleros* of Andalucía or Castile: Amador Abeyta, the late Próspero S. Baca, the late Juan M. Sandoval, Juan Morales, Francisco Chávez, the late Antonio Medina, and Napoleón Trujillo (all but one of whom sang for me and are represented in this volume). These men, to use Mendoza's words, gave rebirth to the ancient lyric heritage of the *copla*. He went on to say that examination of the melodies

reveals ancient styles from the mountains of León, from the plains of La Mancha, from Extremadura, and also from Andalucía. He went so far as to remark that it is in fact New Mexico where the "traditional Hispanic culture maintains its lineaments most purely, and best conserved" (Mendoza 9d, p. 217, my translation).

The conclusion of this astute observer was that the *copla* in New Mexico is a magnificent example of transplantation of Hispanic culture into America, where it has flourished and spread its seeds and its roots through all the southwestern United States. One of the examples cited by Mendoza is the *Canción de Bodas* (Wedding Song), collected by Rubén Cobos in 1946 in Las Vegas, New Mexico, and sung by Louise Ulibarrí Nevárez, who at the time was fifty-five years old and, it seems, was feeling her age (Mendoza 9d, p. 222). Here is the opening verse:

> Me dicen que te casas,
> así lo dice la gente;
> pues todo será en un tiempo:
> tu casamiento y mi muerte.

> They tell me that you are about to marry,
> At least so it is said;
> Well, everything in its own time:
> Your wedding and my death.

As one by one the singers and musicians of a generation disappear, leaving behind them traces of the joys and desires, the cares and sorrows of their times, the uniqueness and irreplaceability of their art are gradually being realized and appreciated.

The charm of these songs and dances is addicting. Working with them is a pleasure, especially when they become so familiar that, out of hundreds, many songs can immediately be recognized, compared to similar ones, and placed in the appropriate category. Furthermore, virtually every melody or song text has some unusual features of rhythm, cadence, elision, mode, obsolescent or colloquial language, and the like that make it unique. Every example, if not beautiful, is at least interesting, and this explains my own long-sustained interest in this music.

Despite the size of this book, the examples included are the result of a rigorous process of selection, followed by an equally rigorous process of elimination prompted by the formidable costs of editing and printing and the sheer bulk of the work. For instance, only occasionally have I indulged in the luxury of publishing several examples of the same song for the purpose of side-by-side comparison. It can truly be said, and said regretfully, that only the tip of the iceberg is showing. Nevertheless, this book, pertaining to a relatively small segment of what was once the Spanish Empire in the New World, illustrates, more vividly perhaps than the historical accounts do, the ramifications of Spanish influence throughout the Western hemisphere during Spain's golden age, an influence that is still felt strongly in the American Southwest four hundred years later.

Part I: SECULAR SONG TEXTS AND MELODIES

CONTENTS

C34. *Cielito Lindo*
C34a. *Cielito Lindo*

Lovers' Farewell

C35. *Me Voy Muy Lejos*
C36. *Luisa*
C37. *La Mancornadora*
C38. *Me Voy Lejos*

Canciones in which Animals Personify Lovers

C39. *Cuatro Palomitas Blancas*
C40. *La Paloma y el Palomo*
C41. *Palomita Callejera*
C42. *El Pavo Real*
C43. *Pavo Real*
C44. *Pajarillo Barranqueño*
C45. *La Calandria*
C46. *No Llores Niña*

Love's Longing

C47. *La Noche Lóbrega*

Reckless or Carefree Love

C48. *El Muchacho Alegre*
C48a. *El Muchacho Alegre*
C49. *El Durazno*
C50. *Más Te Quisiera*
C51. *Juarecita*
C52. *Soy un Triste Venadito*
C53. *Los Barandales del Puente*
C54. *El Palo Verde*
C55. *El Quelite*
C55a. *El Quelite*
C56. *¿Paloma, de Dónde Vienes?*
C57. *Por Allí Viene Ya*

The Timid Lover

C58. *Eva*

Serenades

C59. *Waltz for the New Year*
C60. *Día de los Manueles*
C61. *Las Mañanitas*

The Musical Scale

C62. *Venid, Joven Bella*

The Rejected Lover's Reply

C63. *Tinaja de Agua*

Childhood and Homesickness

C64. *Los Chamacos*
C65. *Allá en Arizona*
C66. *Adiós Muchachos*
C67. *En el Mundo No Hay Tesoro*
C68. *La Golondrina*
C69. *Adiós a Guaymas*

Ranch Songs

C70. *Las Chaparreras*
C71. *El Sombrerito*
C72. *Carmelita*
C73. *El Toro*
C74. *El Jabalí*

Mourning

C75. *Aquí Madre*
C76. *Adiós de Fernández Gallegos*
C77. *Amor de Madre*
C78. *La Huerfanita*
C79. *El Golfo*

Happiness

C80. *Jazmín*

Boasting

C81. *Traigo Mi Cuarenta y Cinco*

Wealth as a State of Mind

C82. *Tengo, Tengo, Tengo*

Canción in the Form of a Waltz

C83. *Cuando Escuches Este Vals*
C84. *Valse*

Canción of Special Form

C85. *Rosita*

Localities

C86. *Cochití*
C87. *Los Chimayoses*
C88. *Santa Fe*
C89. *Albuquerque*
C90. *El Coyotito*

The Coming of Civilization

C91. *El Ferrocarril*
C91a. *El Ferrocarril*
C91b. *El Ferrocarril*

Song of an Immigrant

C92. *Cuando Salí de Mi País*

D. *RELACION* AND RELATED FORMS

Relación

D1. *La Semana*
D2. *Perfectita Estaba Enferma*
D3. *Yo No Me Quiero Casar*
D4. *La Severiana*
D5. *Canción Inglés*
D6. *Leonor*
D7. *La Enfermedad de los Fríos*
D7a. *La Enfermedad de los Fríos*
D8. *Las Lindas Mexicanas*

Disparate

D9. *Los Animales*

A. *Romance*

The *romance* was one of the earliest types of Hispanic folk songs to attract the attention of New Mexico folklorists, Aurelio M. Espinosa having published twenty-seven versions of ten traditional Spanish *romances* in an article entitled "Romancero Nuevo Mejicano" in the *Revue Hispanique* in 1915 with some of the melodies. In 1946 the late Arthur L. Campa published his *Spanish Folk Poetry in New Mexico*, in which he included ballads without music, classifying them as *romances*. The late Vicente T. Mendoza in his unpublished manuscript "Estudio y Clasificación de la Música Tradicional Español en Nuevo Mexico" includes a chapter on the *romance* (Mendoza 9d).

Briefly, the *romance* is a narrative ballad of Spanish origin, dealing generally with incidents in the lives of great or famous persons. It features a sixteen-syllable line that may be either rhymed or assonated. Occasionally, as in the *romance Delgadina* (A2–2j), there is an *estribillo*, or refrain. To make room for the English translations, I have divided the sixteen-syllable line into two lines of eight syllables each.

Of the forms included in this work, the song texts of the *romances* are the easiest to trace back to Spain, for the *cancioneros* published in that country contain many song texts of the same titles, subject matter, and even phraseology as some of those found in Mexico and the Southwest. For this reason I have included in this section a few song texts taken from Spanish *cancioneros*.

A1. *Canción del Fraile* (Song of the Friar)
R13, Francisco Chávez, age 43, and Juan Morales, age 40?, La Jara, N.Mex., 1944, Robb. See Appendix A.

1	1
Mambrú, señores míos,	Mambrú was pledged to marry
pues ya se va a casar	A lady fair and tall.
con una dama hermosa	The bride so young and lovely
nacida en Portugal,	Was born in Portugal,
nacida en Portugal,	Was born in Portugal,
nacida en Portugal.	Was born in Portugal.

2	2
Los condes y marqueses	A lot of counts and nobles,
En Dominus te ¡qué Sonceces!	Oh Lord, was that a show!
Los condes y marqueses	A lot of counts and nobles
lo van a apadrinar,	To honor the pair did go,
lo van a apadrinar,	To honor the pair did go,
lo van a apadrinar.	To honor the pair did go.

3	3
Los frailes manorrotas	And there were many friars,
En Dominus te ¡qué pelotas!	Good Lord, how fat they were!
Los frailes manorrotas	And there were many friars
rezándole van ya,	A-praying for him and her,
rezándole van ya,	A-praying for him and her,
rezándole van ya.	A-praying for him and her.

24

4

Al pie de un alto pino
En Dominus te ¡qué arrimo!
Al pie de un alto pino
lo van a apadrinar,
lo van a apadrinar,
lo van a apadrinar.

5

Me subí a una alta torre
En Dominus te ¡qué le corre!
Me subí a una alta torre
por ver si lo veía venir,
por ver si lo veía venir,
por ver si lo veía venir.

6

Ya veo venir un paje
En Dominus te ¡qué salvaje!
Ya veo venir un paje,
— ¿Qué noticias traerá?
— ¿Qué noticias traerá?
— ¿Qué noticias traerá?

7

La noticia que traigo—
En Dominus te ¡qué me caigo!
La noticia que traigo,
que Mambrú es muerto ya,
que Mambrú es muerto ya,
que Mambrú es muerto ya.

4

They gathered 'neath a pine tree,
Good Lord, 'twas a great affair!
They gathered 'neath a pine tree
With praise for the bridal pair,
With praise for the bridal pair,
With praise for the bridal pair.

5

I climbed a lofty tower,
Good Lord, a sight I see!
A man I saw come running
Across the distant lea,
Across the distant lea,
Across the distant lea.

6

It is a page that's coming,
Good Lord, a lad so rare!
It is a page that's coming,
What tidings do you bear?
What tidings do you bear?
What tidings do you bear?

7

The news I bear will shock you—
Good Lord, it's as I said!
The news I bear will shock you,
Mambrú, Mambrú is dead,
Mambrú, Mambrú is dead,
Mambrú, Mambrú is dead.

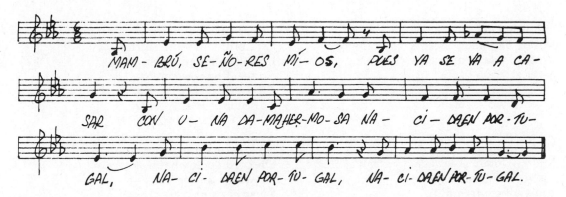

This is a version of the *romance Mambrú*, discussed by Campa in his *Spanish Folk Poetry in New Mexico* (Campa 2, pp. 85–87). Other variants are included below (A1a–1c), one of these being a version current in Spain. Matos describes this *romance* as a *coro de niñas* (little girls' dance). (Hereafter when I refer to Matos, I will be referring collectively not only to Matos the collector but also to the two joint authors of the Matos *Cancionero* [Matos 8a], namely Marius Schneider and José Romeu Figueras.)

Because tracing the evolution of folk melodies is, as I have said, extremely difficult, it is exciting when one finds clues or evidences of such evolution. This example furnishes such a clue. Campa cites as one of the sources of the example the well-known

French folk song about the Duke of Marlborough, victor in 1704 at the bloody battle at Blenheim, Mambrú here being a corruption of Marlborough.

As a youth around 1900 I learned this melody, as well as a parody known as *They Fed the Pig in the Parlor*, with words set to the same tune. The melody of *Canción del Fraile* recorded in New Mexico in 1944 bears a striking resemblance to the melody of the parody as I learned it in Minneapolis in the early 1900's, and the refrain turns out to be melodically identical (see A18). Because both are apparently descendants of an eighteenth-century melody, the comparison indicates that at least some tunes have come down to us little changed over centuries.

Francisco Chávez, singer of *Canción del Fraile* (A1), in La Jara, New Mexico, 1944.

A1a. *Membruz Se Fué a la Guerra* (Membruz Went Away to War)
R1418, Edwin Berry, age 38, Tomé, N.Mex., 1956, Robb.

1
Membruz se fué a la guerra
no sé cuando vendrá—
si vendrá por la Pascua
o por la Navidad,
o por la Navidad,
o por la Navidad.

1
Membruz went away to war
I don't know when he'll return—
Whether he will come back for Easter
Or for Christmas,
Or for Christmas,
Or for Christmas.

2
Yo subí a la alta torre.
Miren, Dominus Ustedes, como corre.
Yo subí a la alta torre
a ver si viene ya,
a ver si viene ya,
a ver si viene ya.

2
I climbed a high tower.
Oh Lord, look how he runs.
I climbed a high tower
To see if he was coming,
To see if he was coming,
To see if he was coming.

3
Ya veo venir un paje.
Miren, Dominus Ustedes ¡qué salvaje!
Ya veo venir un paje,
¿qué noticia traerá,
qué noticia traerá,
qué noticia traerá?

3
Now I see a page coming.
Oh Lord, look what a savage!
Now I see a page coming,
What news might he bring?
What news might he bring?
What news might he bring?

4
La noticia que traigo—
miren, Dominus Ustedes ¡qué me caigo!
La noticia que traigo
Membruz es muerto ya,
Membruz es muerto ya,
Membruz es muerto ya.

4
The news that I bring—
Oh Lord, look how I almost fall!—
The news that I bring
Is that Membruz is now dead,
Is that Membruz is now dead,
Is that Membruz is now dead.

26

5

Debajo de un sabino—
miren, Dominus Ustedes, que me empino—
debajo de un sabino
lo van a sepultar,
lo van a sepultar,
lo van a sepultar.

5

Underneath a cedar—
Oh Lord, see how drunk I am—
Underneath a cedar
They will bury him,
They will bury him,
They will bury him.

6

Los padres melancota—
miren, Dominus Ustedes ¡qué pelota!
Los padres melancota
lo van a sepultar,
lo van a sepultar,
lo van a sepultar.

6

The melancholy fathers—
Oh Lord, see how roly-poly—
The melancholy fathers
They will bury him,
They will bury him,
They will bury him.

Membruz is a corruption of Mambrú, which is itself a corruption of Marlborough. Edwin Berry, who sang this well-preserved version of the *romance*, has taken an active part in preserving the traditional Spanish culture of his native village, Tomé, New Mexico.

Edwin Berry, singer of *Membruz Se Fué a la Guerra* (A1a), atop the Calvario at Tomé, New Mexico.

A1b. *Mambrú Se Fué a la Guerra*
Matos 8a (Parte Musical, no. 187, p. 80), Gargantilla, Spain, 1951, Matos.

Mambrú se fué a la guerra.	Mambrú went away to war.
¡Viva el amor!	Long live love!
No sé cuando vendrá.	I don't know when he will return.
¡Viva la rosa en su rosal!	Long live the rose in its rosebush!

A1c. *Mambrú*
Campa 2 (p. 86), annotated by A. Armendáriz, Mesilla, N.Mex., 1946, Campa.

<table>
<tr><td>

1

Un niño nació en Francia,
do re mi.
Un niño nació en Francia,
muy bello y sin igual,
do re mi fa sol la,
muy bello y sin igual.

</td><td>

1

A boy was born in France,
Do re mi.
A boy was born in France,
Handsome and without an equal,
Do re mi fa sol la,
Handsome and without an equal.

</td></tr>
<tr><td>

2

Por falta de padrinos,
do re mi,
por falta de padrinos
Lauro se va a llamar,
do re mi fa sol la,
Lauro se va a llamar.

</td><td>

2

For lack of godparents,
Do re mi,
For lack of godparents
He was called Lauro,
Do re mi fa sol la,
He was called Lauro.

</td></tr>
</table>

A2. *Delgadina*
R2, Próspero S. Baca, Bernalillo, N.Mex., 1944, Robb.

<table>
<tr><td>

1

Delgadina se paseaba
en una sala cuadrada.
 Refrán:
Que din, que don, que don, don, don.

Con una mantona de oro
que la sala relumbraba.
 Refrán

</td><td>

1

Delgadina was walking
In the great hall.
 Refrain:
Que din, que don, que don, don, don.

Wearing a mantle of gold,
Which made the room shine.
 Refrain

</td></tr>
<tr><td>

2

Y le dice el rey su padre:
—¡Ay, qué linda Delgadina!
 Refrán
¡Ay, qué linda Delgadina!
puede ser mi hermosa dama.
 Refrán

</td><td>

2

And the king, her father, said to her:
"Ah, most beautiful Delgadina!
 Refrain
Ah, most beautiful Delgadina!
You will be my lovely mistress."
 Refrain

</td></tr>
</table>

3	3
—No lo permita mi Dios, ni la reina soberana. *Refrán* Ofensa para mi Dios, agravio para mi nana. *Refrán*	"May God not permit it, Nor the sovereign queen. *Refrain* It is an offense to God, And an affront to my mother." *Refrain*
4	4
—Apróntense aquí mis criados de la sala y la cocina, *Refrán* apróntense aquí mis criados, encierren a Delgadina.— *Refrán*	"Make haste my servants Of the hall and the kitchen, *Refrain* Make haste my servants And imprison Delgadina." *Refrain*
5	5
Si le dieren de comer, la comida muy salada; *Refrán* si le dieren de beber, la espuma de la retama. *Refrán*	If you give her food, Give her salty fare. *Refrain* If you give her drink, Give her foam of the broom weed. *Refrain*
6	6
A los tres días de encerrada se asomó en una ventana, *Refrán* en donde estaba su hermana cabello de oro peinaba. *Refrán*	After three days of imprisonment, She was seen at the window, *Refrain* Where her sister Was combing her hair of gold. *Refrain*
7	7
—Hermanita, si es mi hermana, socórrame un vaso de agua; *Refrán* que ya me abraso de sed y a mi Dios le entriego el alma. *Refrán*	"Little sister, if you are my sister, Bring me a glass of water; *Refrain* For I am burning with thirst And I deliver my soul to God." *Refrain*
8	8
—Delgadina, si es mi hermana, yo no te puedo dar agua; *Refrán* si lo sabe el rey mi padre, las dos somos castigadas.— *Refrán*	"Delgadina, if you are my sister, I cannot give you water. *Refrain* If it were known by the king my father, We would both be punished." *Refrain*
9	9
A los tres días de asomada, se asomó en otra ventana, *Refrán* en donde estaba su hermano bolitas de oro jugaba. *Refrán*	Three days after this appearance, She was seen at another window, *Refrain* Where her brother Was playing with marbles of gold. *Refrain*

10

—Hermanito, si es mi hermano,
socórrame un vaso de agua;
Refrán
que ya me abraso de sed
y a mi Dios le entriego el alma.
Refrán

11

—Delgadina, si es mi hermana,
yo no te puedo dar agua;
Refrán
si lo sabe el rey mi padre,
los dos somos castigados.—
Refrán

12

A los tres días de asomada,
se asomó en otra ventana,
Refrán
en donde estaba su madre
chapines de oro calzaba.
Refrán

13

—Madrecita, si es mi madre,
socórrame un vaso de agua;
Refrán
que ya me abraso de sed
y a mi Dios le entriego el alma.
Refrán

14

—Delgadina, si eres mi hija,
yo no te puedo dar agua;
Refrán
si lo sabe el rey tu padre,
las dos somos castigadas.—
Refrán

15

A los tres días de asomada,
se asomó en otra ventana,
Refrán
donde estaba el rey su padre
cojines de oro sentaba.
Refrán

16

—Padrecito, si es mi padre,
socórrame un vaso de agua;
Refrán
que ya me abraso de sed
y a mi Dios le entriego el alma.
Refrán

10

"My brother, if you are my brother,
Bring me a glass of water;
Refrain
For I am burning with thirst
And I deliver my soul to God."
Refrain

11

"Delgadina, if you are my sister,
I cannot give you water.
Refrain
If it were known by the king my father,
We would both be punished."
Refrain

12

Three days after this appearance,
She was seen at another window,
Refrain
Where her mother
Was wearing golden slippers.
Refrain

13

"My mother, if you are my mother,
Bring me a glass of water;
Refrain
For I am burning with thirst
And I deliver my soul to God."
Refrain

14

"Delgadina, if you are my daughter,
I cannot give you water.
Refrain
If it were known by the king, your father,
We would both be punished."
Refrain

15

Three days after this appearance,
She was seen at another window,
Refrain
Where the king her father
Was sitting on golden cushions.
Refrain

16

"Oh, father, if you are my father,
Bring me a glass of water;
Refrain
For I am burning with thirst
And I deliver my soul to God."
Refrain

<table>
<tr><td>

17

—Delgadina ¿no te acuerdas
lo que te dije en la mesa?
Refrán
—Padrecito, sí me acuerdo
y agacharé la cabeza.
Refrán

</td><td>

17

"Delgadina, don't you remember
What I told you at the table?"
Refrain
"Yes, Father, I remember
And I will humbly bow my head."
Refrain

</td></tr>
<tr><td>

18

—Delgadina ¿no te acuerdas
lo que te dije en la sala?
Refrán
—Sí me acuerdo, padrecito,
y haré lo que usted mandaba.
Refrán

</td><td>

18

"Delgadina, don't you remember
What I told you in the great hall?"
Refrain
"Yes, Father, I remember,
And I will do as you have commanded."
Refrain

</td></tr>
<tr><td>

19

—Apróntense aquí mis criados
de la sala y la cocina,
Refrán
apróntense aquí mis criados,
tráiganle agua a Delgadina.—
Refrán

</td><td>

19

"Make haste, my servants,
Of the hall and the kitchen.
Refrain
Make haste, my servants,
Bring water to Delgadina."
Refrain

</td></tr>
<tr><td>

20

Unos en vasos dorados
y otros en vasos de China,
Refrán
Cuando vinieron con l'agua
Delgadina estaba muerta.
Refrán

</td><td>

20

Some came with vessels of gold
And others with vessels of china,
Refrain
But when they came with the water,
Delgadina was dead.
Refrain

</td></tr>
<tr><td>

21
Moral:
La cama de Delgadina
de ángeles rodiada estaba.
Refrán
La cama del rey su padre
de diablos atormentada.

</td><td>

21
Moral:
The bed of Delgadina
Was surrounded by angels.
Refrain
The bed of the king her father
Was tormented by devils.

</td></tr>
</table>

DEL-GA-DI-NA SE PA-SEA-BA EN U-NA SA-LA CUA-DRA-DA, QUE DIN, QUE DON, DON, DON.

I have included a number of versions of the famous ballad *Delgadina* (A2a–2j), four of these being versions current in Spain. The refrain of A2 suggests the mournful tolling of bells. A2b is an interesting version because it comes from Santo Domingo, in the Caribbean, where the singer, Mrs. Boggs, was born.

Example A2e furnishes what seems to me to be rather persuasive evidence of the survival of medieval musical practices, which I discussed in *Hispanic Folk Songs of New Mexico* (Robb 13, pp. 6–8). The text deals with a climactic incident in the life of a king, a subject far removed from the preoccupations of the villagers of the American South-

west. It has the very narrow range of a perfect fifth, a narrow range being in the opinion
of scholars presumptive evidence of considerable age (see Bartók, p. 10; Sachs, p. 32).
Furthermore, example A2e is in one of the
medieval modes. It also employs one of the
typical melodic alterations of the medieval
musica ficta in the raising by a half step of

the last sixteenth note of the first measure.
Campa's discussion of this *romance* is
quite detailed (Campa 2, pp. 30–33). The
romance Un Rey Moro, published by Matos
seems to be a variant of *Delgadina*, but there
it is the king's son rather than the king who
has the incestuous desire (Matos 8a, Parte
Musical, pp. 43, 50, 51).

A2a. *Delgadina*
R148, Tomás Archuleta, Abiquiu, N.Mex., 1947, Robb. Cf. Schindler 14a (Parte
Musical no. 805, Parte Literaria p. 60).

1
Delgadina, hija mía,
ponte tu túnica de seda
para que vayas a misa
a la ciudad de Morela,
para que vayas a misa
a la ciudad de Morela.

1
Delgadina, my daughter,
Put on your silk gown
To go to mass
In the city of Morela,
To go to mass
In the city of Morela.

2
Delgadina, hija mía,
¿qué no quieres ser mi dama?
No lo permita el Señor,
ni la Virgen Soberana,
no lo permita el Señor,
ni la Virgen Soberana.

2
Delgadina, my daughter,
Don't you want to be my lady?
May neither God, nor the
Sovereign Virgin permit it.
May neither God, nor the
Sovereign Virgin permit it.

3
Vénganse los once criados,
encierren a Delgadina,
vénganse los once criados,
encierren a Delgadina,
remáchenle los candados
que no se oigan mandolinas.

3
Come, you eleven servants,
Lock up Delgadina,
Come, you eleven servants,
Lock up Delgadina,
Tighten the shackles, so one
Cannot hear them jingle.

4
Delgadina, si pide agua,
denle el agua salada,
y si pide de comer,
la comida enmezclada.

4
Delgadina, if she asks for water,
Give her salty water,
And if she asks for food,
Give her some swill.

5
Delgadina, sin francés,
se fué para una ventana,
adonde estaba su hermana,
cabello de oro peinaba.

5
Delgadina, without permission,
Went to a window,
Where her sister was
Combing her golden hair.

6
Hermancita, si es mi hermana,
socórrame un vaso de agua,
que ya me abrazo de sed,
a mi Dios le entrego el alma.

6
Little sister, if you are my sister,
Help me with a glass of water,
Lest in the grip of thirst,
I give up my soul to God.

7	7
Delgadina, sin francés, yo no te puedo dar agua, porque si mi padre sabe, las dos somos castigadas.	Delgadina, without permission, I cannot give you water, For if my father finds out, We'll both be punished.
8	8
Delgadina, sin francés, se fué para otra ventana, adonde estaba su madre, puros libros de oro hojeaba.	Delgadina, without permission, Went to another window, Where her mother was Leafing through some golden books.
9	9
Madrecita, si es mi madre, socórrame un vaso de agua, que ya me abrazo de sed, a mi Dios le entrego el alma.	Dear mother, if you are my mother, Help me with a glass of water, Lest in the grip of thirst, I give up my soul to God.
10	10
Delgadina, si eres mi hija, yo no te puedo dar agua, porque si tu padre sabe, las dos somos castigadas.	Delgadina, if you're my daughter, I cannot give you water, For if your father finds out, We'll both be punished.
11	11
Delgadina, sin francés, se fué para otra ventana, Adonde estaba su hermano, bolita de oro jugaba.	Delgadina, without permission, Went to another window, Where her brother was Playing with a golden ball.
12	12
Hermanito, si es mi hermano, socórrame un vaso de agua, que ya me abrazo de sed a mi Dios le entrego el alma.	Little brother, if you are my brother, Help me with a glass of water, Lest in the grip of thirst, I give up my soul to God.
13	13
Delgadina, si eres mi hermana, yo no te puedo dar agua, porque si mi padre sabe, los dos somos castigados.	Delgadina, if you're my sister, I cannot give you water, For if my father finds out, We'll both be punished.
14	14
Delgadina, sin francés, se fué para otra ventana, adonde estaba su padre, barajas de oro jugaba.	Delgadina, without permission, Went to another window, Where her father was Playing with golden cards.
15	15
Padrecito, si es mi padre, socórrame un vaso de agua, que ya me abrazo de sed, a mi Dios le entrego el alma.	Dear father, if you're my father, Help me with a glass of water, Lest in the grip of thirst, I give up my soul to God.

16

Delgadina, hija mía,
yo no te puedo dar agua,
¿no recuerdas aquel día,
lo que te dije en la mesa?

16

Delgadina, my daughter,
I cannot give you water,
Don't you remember that day
What I told you at the table?

17

Papacito, sí, me acuerdo,
agacharé la cabeza.
Papacito, sí, me acuerdo,
agacharé la cabeza.

17

Dear father, yes, I remember,
I'll bow my head.
Dear father, yes, I remember,
I'll bow my head.

18

Delgadina ya murió
y se fué para los cielos
y el cornudo de su padre
a los profundos infiernos.

18

Delgadina has died
And gone to heaven
And her lustful father
Has gone to the depths of hell.

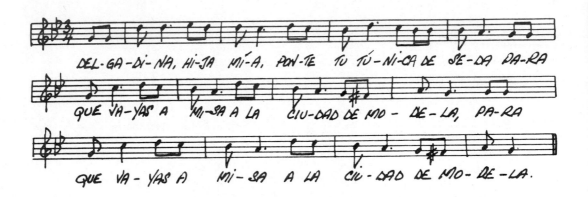

A2b. *Delgadina*
R1908, Edna Garrido de Boggs, recorded in Albuquerque, N.Mex., 1963, Robb.

1

Pues, señores, éste era un rey
que tenía tres hijitas.
La más chiquita y bonita
Delgadina se llamaba.

1

Well, gentlemen, there was a king
Who had three daughters.
The smallest and most beautiful
Was named Delgadina.

2

Cuando su madre iba a misa,
su padre la enamoraba,
y cuando ella no quería,
en un cuarto le encerraba.

2

When her mother went to mass,
Her father tried to make love to her,
And when she refused,
He locked her up in a room.

3

A la semana siguiente
Delgadina, en la ventana,
alcanzó a ver a su hermana
en silla de oro sentada.

3

The following week
Delgadina, at the window,
Saw her sister
Sitting in a golden chair.

<table>
<tr><td>

4
Hermana, por ser mi hermana,
me darás un vaso de agua,
que el alma la tengo seca
y la vida se me acaba.

</td><td>

4
Sister, since you're my sister,
You'll give me a glass of water,
For my soul is thirsty
And my life is ending.

</td></tr>
</table>

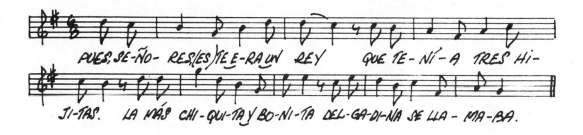

PUES, SE-ÑO- RES (ES) TE E-RA UN REY QUE TE-NÍ-A TRES HI-
JI-TAS. LA MÁS CHI-QUI-TA Y BO-NI-TA DEL-GA-DI-NA SE LLA-MA-BA.

A2c. *Delgadina*

Matos 8a (Parte Literaria, p. 37, Parte Musical, p. 54), Montejo de la Sierra, Spain,
Matos.

<table>
<tr><td>

1
Un rey tenía tres hijas
todas tres como la plata
y la más rechiquitita
Delgadina se llamaba.

</td><td>

1
A king had three daughters
All three of them like silver
And the most beautiful one
Was called Delgadina.

</td></tr>
<tr><td>

2
Un día estando a la mesa
su padre la remiraba.
—Mucho me mira usted, padre,
mucho me mira a la cara.

</td><td>

2
One day while at the table
Her father was looking at her.
"You are often looking at me, father,
You are often looking me in the eyes."

</td></tr>
<tr><td>

3
—Más te tengo que mirar
si has de ser mi enamorada.
—No lo quiera Dios del cielo
ni la Virgen soberana,
que el que usted sea mi padre
y yo sea su enamorada.

</td><td>

3
"I'll be looking all the more
Because you are going to be my mistress."
"The God of heaven does not wish,
Nor does the sovereign Virgin,
That, since you are my father,
I should become your mistress."

</td></tr>
<tr><td>

4
—Alto, alto, mis criados,
a Delgadina encerradla
en un cuarto muy oscuro
donde no se vea nada;
y si pide de comer,
dadle cocina salada;
y si pide de beber,
dadle agua de retama.—

</td><td>

4
"Up here, up here, my servants,
Lock up Delgadina
In a pitch black room
Where she can see nothing;
And if she asks to eat,
Give her salty food;
And if she asks to drink,
Give her juice of the broom."

</td></tr>
<tr><td>

5
Al cabo de siete años
el cuarto se hizo ventana.

</td><td>

5
At the end of seven years
A window was built in her room.

</td></tr>
</table>

Delgadina con gran sed
se ha asomado a la ventana
donde estaban sus hermanos
tirando al juego de barras.

Delgadina, being very thirsty,
Was sitting by the window
Where her brothers were playing
The game of bars.

6

—Hermanos, porque lo sois,
alcanzadme un jarro de agua.
Que con el alma lo pido
que la vida se me acaba.

6

"Brothers, because that's what you are,
Bring me a jug of water.
With all my soul I beg,
For I am dying."

7

—Hermanita Delgadina,
de buena gana lo alcanzara;
si el rey padre lo supiera
la cabeza nos cortara.—

7

"Sister Delgadina,
I would gladly help you;
But if the king our father knew it
He would behead us."

8

Delgadina se retira,
muy triste y desconsolada.
Delgadina con gran sed
se ha asomado en otra ventana
donde allí estaba su madre
en silla de oro.

8

Delgadina withdraws,
Very sad and disconsolate.
Delgadina, being very thirsty,
Seated herself at another window
Where her mother was
Sitting on a golden chair.

9

—Madre, porque lo es usted,
alcánceme un jarro de agua.
Que con el alma lo pido
que la vida se me acaba.

9

"Mother, because that's what you are,
Bring me a jug of water.
With all my soul I beg,
for I am dying."

10

—Quítate de ahí, Delgadina,
quítate de ahí, perra mala.
Siete años hace son hoy
que por ti estoy mal casada.

10

"Get away from here, Delgadina,
Get away from here, you wicked bitch.
It's seven years today
That you wrecked my marriage."

11

—Y otros tantos, madre mía,
hace que estoy yo encerrada.—
Delgadina se retira
muy triste y desconsolada.

11

"And it's much longer than that,
That I am imprisoned."
Delgadina withdraws,
Very sad and disconsolate.

12

Delgadina con gran sed
se ha asomado a otra ventana
donde allí estaba su padre
con los criados de caza.

12

Delgadina, being very thirsty,
Seated herself at another window
Where her father was
With his hunting servants.

13

—Padre, porque lo es usted,
alcánceme un jarro de agua.
Que con el alma la pido
que la vida se me acaba.

13

"Father, for that is what you are,
Grant me a jug of water,
With all my soul I beg,
For I am dying."

14	14
—Sí que te lo alcanzaré si has de ser mi enamorada. —Padre mío, lo seré, aunque sea de mala gana.	"Yes, I'll grant you that If you agree to be my mistress." "Father mine, I will do it, Even though unwillingly."
15	15
—Alto, alto, mis criados, a Delgadina dar agua.—	"Up here, up here, my servants, Give water to Delgadina."
16	16
Cuando llegaba el primero, Delgadina ya no hablaba; Cuando llegaba el segundo, Delgadina ya expiraba.	When the first one came, Delgadina already was speechless; When the second one came, Delgadina already was dying.
17	17
Cuando llegaba el tercero, Delgadina muerta estaba, no por la sed que tenía, ni por el hambre que pasaba, que en la cabecera tiene una fuente muy reclara.	When the third one came, Delgadina was dead, Not from the thirst which she felt, Nor from the hunger she suffered, But in her mind she had Good reason.
18	18
La cama de Delgadina de ángeles está rodeada; en la cama de su hermano una víbora enroscada; en la cama de su madre una serpiente alargada. Los demonios a su padre al infierno le llevaban.	The bed of Delgadina Is surrounded by angels; In the bed of her brother There is a viper curled up; In the bed of her mother A serpent is stretched out. The demons are carrying Her father to the inferno.

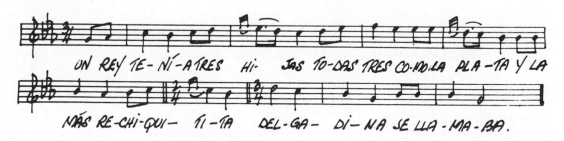

A2d. *Delgadina*
  RB534, Connie Domínguez, Arizona, 1947, V. Acosta.

1	1
Delgadina se paseaba en su sala muy cuadrada con su clavel en su pecho que la sala relumbraba.	Delgadina was passing by In the main salon hall With a pin at her breast Which lighted up the hall.

]
 ] *Bis*

2

—Delgadina, hija mía,
yo te quiero para dama.
—No lo permita mi Dios,
ni la reina soberana.
Es castigo de me Dios
un traición para mi mamá.

3

—Vénganse todos mis criados
encierren a Delgadina.
Si les pide de comer,
den comida muy salada;
Si les pide de beber,
espuma de la retama.—

4

Cuando llegaron con agua
Delgadina estaba muerta.
La cama de Delgadina
de ángeles está cubierta;
La cama del rey su padre
de diablos atormentada.

2

"Delgadina, my daughter,
I want you for my mistress."
"My God does not permit that,
Nor does the sovereign queen.
It is an affront to my God,
A betrayal of my mother."

3

"Come, all my servants,
Imprison Delgadina.
If she asks for food,
Give her very salty food;
If she wants to drink,
Foam of the broom weed."

4

When they came with water
Delgadina was dying.
The resting place of Delgadina
Is covered with angels;
The resting place of the king her father
Is tormented by devils.

A2e. *Delgadina*

Matos 8a (Parte Musical, p. 59), Navalagamella, Spain, 1951, Matos.

Un rey tenía tres hijas,
todas tres como la plata.
De las tres la más pequeña
Delgadina se llamaba.

A king had three daughters,
All three like silver.
Of the three the youngest
Was called Delgadina.

A2f. *Delgadina*

Matos 8a (Parte Musical, p. 53), Madrid, Spain, 1951, Matos.

1

Un rey tenía tres hijas
más hermosas que la plata,
y la más chiquirritita
Delgadina se llamaba.

2

Un día estando a la mesa,
su padre la remiraba.
—¿Qué me miras, padre mío,
qué me mira usted a la cara?

1

A king had three daughters
Lovelier than silver,
And the loveliest of all
Was named Delgadina.

2

One day while at the table,
Her father was gazing at her.
"Why are you looking at me, my father,
Why are you looking at me so intently?"

A2g. *Delgadina*

Matos 8a (Parte Musical, p. 47), Villavieja de Lozoya, Spain, 1951, Matos.

Un rey tenía tres hijas,
todas tres como la plata.
La más chica de las tres
Delgadina se llamaba.

A king had three daughters,
All three like silver.
The prettiest of the three
Was called Delgadina.

A2h. *Delgadina*
R2b, Mrs. C. T. Brown, Socorro, N.Mex., Robb.

Delgadina se paseaba
en una sala cuadrada
con su mantona de oro
que la sala relumbraba.

Delgadina was strolling
In a large square hall
With her cloak of gold
Which lighted up the hall.

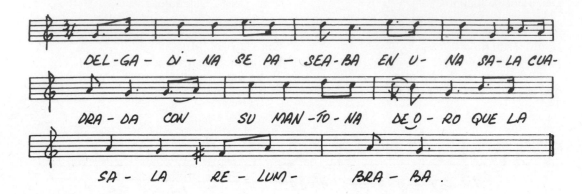

A2i. *Delgadina*
R537, Francisco S. Leyva, age 81, Leyva, N.Mex., 1951, Robb.

1
Delgadina se paseaba
en una sala cuadrada
con una túnica de oro
que hasta los pies le alcanzaba.

1
Delgadina was strolling
In a great square hall
With a golden tunic
That reached to her feet.

2
Y un día estando en la mesa
la solecitó su padre,
—Delgadina, Delgadina,
¿no pudieras ser mi dama?

2
One day while they were at the table
Her father wooed her,
"Delgadina, Delgadina,
Won't you be my mistress?"

3
—No lo permita mi Dios
ni la reina soberana.
No te alofes a mi Dios,
ni tal agravia a mi nana.

3
"God does not permit this
Nor does the sovereign queen.
Do not offend my God,
Nor thus aggravate my mother."

4
—Levántate, Delgadina,
ponte tu túnico blanco,
porque vamos ir a misa
al estado de Durango.—

4
"Get up, Delgadina,
Put on your white tunic,
Because we are going to mass
In the state of Durango."

5
Delgadina estaba hincada
rezando sus oraciones.

5
Delgadina was on her knees
Saying her prayers.

Su padre está en la puerta
con sus malas intenciones.

Her father was at the door
With his bad intentions.

6
Cuando se salieron de misa
su padre la preguntaba:
—Delgadina, Delgadina,
¿no pudieras ser mi dama?—

6
When they went out from mass
Her father asked her,
"Delgadina, Delgadina,
Won't you be my mistress?"

7
(Verso 3 se repite)

7
(Verse 3 repeated)

8
—Delgadina, Delgadina,
si no convienes conmigo
pronto te desengañarás
que te daré un buen castigo.

8
"Delgadina, Delgadina,
If you do not agree
You will soon realize
That you will be severely punished."

9
—Padrecito de mi vida,
eso no podré hacer
porque usted es mi papá
y mi mamá su mujer.

9
"Dearest father of my life,
That I will not do
Because you are my father
And my mother is your wife."

10
—Véngansen los once criados,
pongan presa a Delgadina,
remachen bien los candados
que no se oiga voz ladina.

10
"Come, my eleven servants,
Lock up Delgadina,
Check well the padlocks
So that her shrill cry cannot be heard."

11
—Padrecito de mi vida,
su castigo estoy sufriendo,
y aunque llene un vaso de agua
que de sed me estoy muriendo.—

11
"Dearest father of my life,
I am suffering your punishment,
And even with a glassful of water
I am still dying of thirst."

12
Cuando vinieron los criados
Delgadina estaba muerta
con sus bracitos cruzados,
su boquita bien abierta.

12
When the servants came
Delgadina was dead
With her arms crossed,
Her little mouth wide open.

13
La cama de Delgadina
de ángeles está rodeada.
Y la cama de su padre
de llamas atravesada.

13
The bed of Delgadina
Is surrounded by angels.
And the bed of her father
Is enveloped in flames.

14
Delgadina allí murió
y fué derecho a los cielos
y el cornudo de su padre
derechito a los infiernos.

14
Delgadina died there
And went straight to heaven
And the cuckold, her father,
Directly to the inferno.

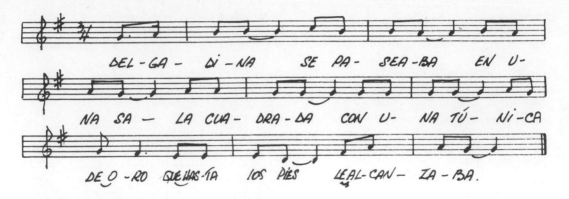

DEL-GA- DI -NA   SE PA- SEA-BA   EN U-

NA SA - LA CUA-DRA-DA   CON U- NA TÚ- NI-CA

DE O -RO QUE HAS-TA   IOS PIES   LE AL-CAN- ZA - BA.

Francisco S. Leyva, singer of *Delgadina* (A2i), in front of his ranch house at Leyva, New Mexico, 1951. With Próspero S. Baca, Leyva was one of the two outstanding Spanish folk singers of his era in New Mexico.

A2j. *Delgadina*
RB633, Grace Murrieta, Patagonia, Arizona, 1949, Doris Seibold.

1

Delgadina se paseaba
por su sala muy cuadrada
con su mantocino de oro
que no más le relumbraba.

2

—Delgadina, hija mía,
quiero que seas mi dama.
—No lo permita el Señor
ni la Virgen Soberana.

3

—'Próntense todos mis criados.
Enciérrenle a Delgadina.

1

Delgadina was strolling
Through her large square hall
In her golden shawl
Which no longer lighted her way.

2

"Delgadina, my daughter,
I want you to be my mistress."
"The Lord does not permit it
Nor does the sovereign Virgin."

3

"Come here, all my servants.
Lock Delgadina up.

Ciérrenle todas las puertas,
también la de la cocina.—

Lock all the doors,
Including the kitchen door."

4

Otro día su hermanito
otro día la fué a ver.
—Jesusito, hermano mío,
voy a perecer, merced.

4

The next day her brother
Came to see her.
"Jesusito, my brother,
I am going to perish. Have mercy."

5

—Delgadina, hermana mía,
yo no te puedo dar agua
porque no quisiste hacer
lo que mi papá mandaba.

5

"Delgadina, my sister,
I cannot give you water
Because you did not want to do
What my papa demanded."

6

—Mamacita de mi vida,
voy a perecer, merced.
Regálame un vaso de agua
que ya me muero de sed.

6

"Dearest mother of my life,
I am going to perish. Have mercy.
Give me a glass of water
For I am dying of thirst."

7

—Delgadina, hija mía,
yo no te puedo dar agua
porque desobedeciste
lo que tu papá mandaba.

7

"Delgadina, my daughter,
I cannot give you water
Because you refused to do
What your papa commanded."

8

—Papacito de mi vida,
voy a pedirte merced.
Regálame un vaso de agua
que ya me muero de sed.

8

"Dear father of my life,
I beg you—have mercy on me.
Bring me a glass of water
For I am dying of thirst."

9

—Júntense todos mis criados,
llévenle agua a Delgadina,
unos en copas de plata
y otros en tazas de China.—

9

"Come all my servants,
Bring water to Delgadina,
Some in vessels of silver
Others in cups of china."

10

Cuando le llevaron agua
Delgadina estaba muerta,
con sus ojitos cerrados
y con su boquita abierta.

10

When they arrived with the water
Delgadina was dead,
With her little eyes closed
And her little mouth open.

11

La cama de Delgadina
de ángeles está rodeada.
Y el cuarto de su papá
de diablos está apretado.

11

The bed of Delgadina
Is surrounded by angels.
The room of her father
Is besieged with devils.

12

Delgadina está en el cielo
dándole la cuenta al Creador.
Y el papá está en el infierno,
lo tiene el diablo mayor.

12

Delgadina is in heaven
Accounting to her Creator.
And her father is in hell,
In the claws of the chief devil.

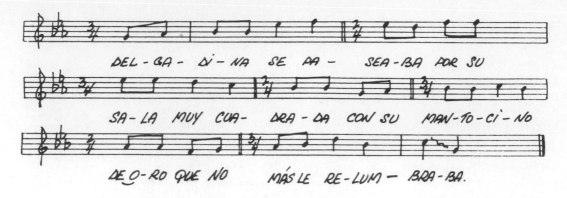

DEL-GA-DI-NA SE PA- SEA-BA POR SU

SA-LA MUY CUA-DRA-DA CON SU MAN-TO-CI-NO

DE O-RO QUE NO MÁS LE RE-LUM- BRA-BA.

A3. *La Zagala del Pastorcito* (The Maiden and the Shepherd)
R9, Próspero S. Baca, Bernalillo, N.Mex., 1945, Robb. Cf. RB731.

<table>
<tr>
<td>

1

Una niña en un balcón
le dice a un pastor: —espera,
que te llama una zagala
que de tu amor desespera.

</td>
<td>

1

A girl in a balcony
Calls to a shepherd, "Wait,
For there calls to you a maiden
Who is desperately in love with you."

</td>
</tr>
<tr>
<td>

2

—No soy tan enamorado—
respondió el niño David.
—Mi ganado está en la sierra;
con él me voy a dormir.

</td>
<td>

2

"I am not so in love,"
Replied the boy, David.
"My flock is on the mountain;
I am going to sleep with it."

</td>
</tr>
<tr>
<td>

3

—Oye, Pastor Amoroso,
lo que te habla una paloma.
Arrímate para acá,
no hayas miedo que te coma.

</td>
<td>

3

"Listen, amorous shepherd,
To what a dove tells you.
Come here close to me,
Don't be afraid that I'll eat you.

</td>
</tr>
<tr>
<td>

4

Mira que hermosos cabellos,
y llevarás que contar.
Cuando me siento a peinar,
el sol se enamora de ellos.

</td>
<td>

4

"Look at my lovely hair,
And you will be able to count it.
When I sit down to comb it,
The sun falls in love with it.

</td>
</tr>
<tr>
<td>

5

Mira que pie pulido
para un zapato bordado.
Mira, que estoy niña y tierna
y después a tu mandado.

</td>
<td>

5

"Look at what a nice foot I have
For an embroidered shoe.
Look, I am young and tender
And at your service.

</td>
</tr>
<tr>
<td>

6

Te pago tres pilas de oro
el hato y el almirez
tan sólo porque te quedes
esta noche y otras tres.

</td>
<td>

6

"I'll pay you three piles of gold
A shepherd's outfit and a brass bowl
If only you'll stay here
Tonight and three nights more.

</td>
</tr>
</table>

44

7

Te doy una pila de oro
y dos cañas de marfil
tan sólo porque te quedes
esta noche aquí a dormir.

7

"I'll give you a pile of gold
And two ivory canes
If only you'll stay
And sleep here tonight."

8

—Zagala, cuando me hablaste
tus palabras no entendí.
Perdóname, gran Señora,
si en algo ya os ofendí.

8

"Fair lady, when you spoke to me
I did not understand your words.
Pardon me, great lady,
If in any way I have offended you.

9

Cuando quise, no quisiste;
ahora que quieres, no quiero.
Llora tú, tu soledad
que yo la lloré primero.

9

"When I wanted you, you didn't want me;
Now that you want me, I don't want you.
Weep for your loneliness
For I wept for it first.

10

Haré de cuenta que tuve
una sortijita de oro.
En el mar se cayó.
Aquí la perdí del todo.

10

"I'll pretend that I had
A little ring of gold.
It fell into the sea.
Here I completely lost it."

This example was transcribed from my original recording by the late Vicente T. Mendoza when he was in residence at the University of New Mexico in 1946.

A4. *La Zagala* (The Maiden)
R37, Próspero S. Baca, age 67, Bernalillo, N.Mex., 1942, Robb. Cf. Schindler 14a (Parte Musical nos. 58, 595, Parte Literaria p. 111).

1

Orillas de una fuente de agua
una zagala vi,
y con el ruido del agua
me fuí acercando hacia ahí,
y me responde la joven:
—¡Ay de mí, ay de mí, ay de mí!—

1

At the edge of a fountain
I saw a maiden,
And with the murmur of the water
I silently approached her,
And she said to me:
"Alas, alas, alas!"

2

Me la encontré solita,
mi amor le declaré;
ella, todita turbada,
nada me respondió;
en donde dije yo entonces:
—¡Ya cayó, ya cayó, ya cayó!—

2

I found her so all alone,
That I declared my love;
She, in utter confusion,
Answered me not;
Then I spoke:
"She fell for it, fell for it, fell for it!"

3

La llevé junto de un árbol,
varias flores corté,
se las eché en el seno,
su blanco talle estreché,
y me responde la joven:
—¡Ay, Jesús, que grosero es usted!—

3

I took her to a tree,
I cut several flowers for her,
I tossed them on her bosom,
I clasped her gentle waist,
And the girl said to me:
"Heavens, how coarse you are."

4

Me la tomé del brazo,
me la llevé a un café.
En sus divinos labios
tres besitos le estampé,
y me responde la joven:
—¡Otros tres, otros tres, que sean seis!—

4

I took her by the arm
And led her to a café.
On her heavenly lips
I impressed three little kisses,
And she said to me:
"Three more to make it six."

5

Y al despedirme de ella,
un abrazo me dió,
y ella me dice llorando:
—¡Ay, no me olvide, por Dios;
porque mi amor cariñoso
solo a usted se rindió, se rindió!

5

As I took leave of her,
She embraced me,
And said to me, weeping:
"Alas, do not forget me;
For my love and affection
Were won only by you, only by you."

Mendoza identifies this as a Jewish *romance* (Mendoza 9d, p. 169), and Menéndez Pidal found a version of it in Bulgaria among Jews (Campa 2). Kurt Schindler also located this song in the spectacular walled city of Avila and published it in his famous *Cancionero* (Schindler 14a, melody no. 58, words p. 111).

Campa found versions in Bernalillo and

Avila, Spain, where Kurt Schindler found a Spanish version of *La Zagala* (A4).

in northern New Mexico. He included a text and an interesting discussion, but no music (Campa 2, p. 52). Campa's version was sung by Raphael Lucero, age 85, in El Pino in Mora County, New Mexico.

The melody of *La Zagala* has a rising inflection, the range is an octave, the meter 6/8, and the mode is major. The melody is asymmetrical, consisting of three periods.

This is a well-conserved text. The versification is irregular, some of the lines consisting of six syllables and others of ten.

Although examples A3 and A4 are different songs, the themes are similar.

A4a. *Al Pie del Arroyuelo* (At the Foot of the Brook), or *La Zagala*
Matos 8a (Parte Musical p. 84, Parte Literaria p. 98), Lozoya, Spain, 1951.

<table>
<tr><td>

1
Al pie del arroyuelo
una zagala vi;
como era tan bonita
para mí, para mí, para mí.

2
Me puse a obsequiarla
con flores a escoger;
las más encarnaditas
le parecieron bien.

3
He caído soldado
y me tengo que marchar;
a mi pobre zagala
la tengo que dejar.

</td><td>

1
At the foot of the brook
I saw a maiden;
And she looked so beautiful
For me, for me, for me.

2
I went to call upon her
With flowers I had chosen;
The reddest ones
She admired the most.

3
I have been called as a soldier
And I have to go away;
And my poor maiden
I have to leave behind.

</td></tr>
</table>

4

Adiós, zagala mía
de mi corazón;
he caído soldado
me marcho a la facción.

4

Farewell, my own dear maiden,
Love of my heart;
I've been called as a soldier
And must leave to join my troop.

A4b. *La Zagala*
R528, Francisco S. Leyva, age 81, Leyva, age 81, Leyva, N.Mex., 1951, Robb.

1

Salí una mañana al campo,
mi rebaño a apacentar,
y allí encontré una zagala
la que nunca he visto más.

1

I went out early one morning,
With my flock, my daily chore,
And there I met a young maiden
That I'd never seen before.

2

—Dame un besito, zagala,—
le dije y lleno de faz.
—Si con oro me lo pagas,
lo saldré pronto a buscar.

2

"Ah, give me a kiss, little maiden,"
I pleaded with joyous hope.
"If you pay me with gold I'll oblige you,
Otherwise, my friend, no soap."

3

—El oro que traigo, niña,
guardado en mi alforja está.
Mi alforja está en mi camello
y mi camello está en Fermal.—

3

"As far as my gold is concerned, lass,
My saddlebag holds it all.
My saddlebag's tied on my camel
And my camel's in Fermal."

4

Y me respondió con risa,
mirándome faz a faz:
—El beso está entre mis labios
mis dientes 'tan detrás.

4

And she replied, smiling sweetly,
All innocent, coy, and kind:
"I've kisses enough on my lips, dear,
But my teeth are there behind.

5

La boca con que los guardo
cerrada con llave está,
la llave la tiene mi madre
y mi madre está en Fermal.

5

"The mouth with which I will guard them
Is locked," said the winsome doll,
"The key is kept by my mother
And my mother is in Fermal."

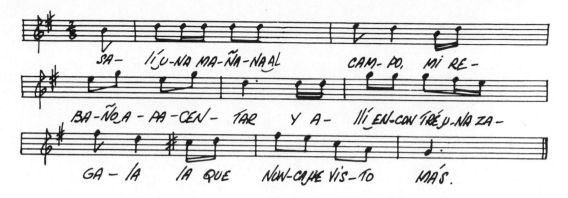

SA- LÍ U-NA MA-ÑA-NA AL CAM-PO, MI RE-
BA-ÑO A-AA-CEN- TAR Y A- LLÍ EN-CON-TRÉ U-NA ZA-
GA - LA LA QUE NUN-CA HE VIS-TO MÁS.

A5. *La Esposa Infiel* (The Unfaithful Wife)
R447, Arvino Martínez, Abiquiu, N.Mex., 1951, Robb. Cf. Robb 13 (pp. 15–16, 44–49);
R89; Cobos 4, RB729.

1	**1**
—Abreme la puerta, Elena,	"Open the door, Helen,
sin ninguna desconfianza,	Without any distrust,
que soy Fernando, el francés,	It is I, Ferdinand, the Frenchman,
que acabo de llegar de Francia.—	Just arrived from France."
2	**2**
Y al abrir la media puerta	When she partly opened the door
para dentro más metido	To get him inside, they began
dándose abrazos y besos	Embracing and kissing each other
como mujer y marido.	Just like man and wife.
3	**3**
Sería la medianoche	It might have been about midnight
cuando se estaban recreando,	They were having a good time,
cuando llegó don Benito	When Don Benito arrived
las puertas llegó tocando.	And knocked at the door.
4	**4**
Don Benito entra pa' dentro	Don Benito goes inside
lleno de la indignación	Full of indignation
con su pistola en la mano	With his gun in hand,
buscándolo pa' el rincón.	Looking for him in every corner.
5	**5**
—¿Pero, Benito, qué tienes	"But, Benito, what's the matter
que vienes tan enojado?	That you are so angry?
Mira no te andes creyendo	Look, don't you believe
de cuentos que te han contado.	The stories that you hear."
6	**6**
—Elena, no digas eso	"Helen, don't you say that
ni lo vuelvas a decir.	And don't say it again.
El día que encuentre a Fernando	The day that I find Ferdinand
los dos se van a morir.—	The two of you will die."

7

En ese Plan de Barrancas
sin saber como ni cuando,
allí fué donde se encontró
don Benito a don Fernando.

8

—Por el mérito que tiene,
por el mérito que goza,
mire, no se ande creyendo;
yo ni conozco a su esposa.

9

—Del más alto firmamento
vide solar una estrella,
nomás no se ande rajando
si yo no lo hallé con ella.—

10

Echó mano a su pistola
y a su rifle dieciseis
y tres balazos le dió,
Don Benito al francés.

11

Luego que ya lo mató
se puso la ropa de él
y se montó en su caballo
y fué a matar a la mujer.

12

—Abreme la puerta, Elena,
no me tengas desconfianza
que soy Fernando, el francés,
que acabo de llegar de Francia.—

13

Al abrir la media puerta
él mismo apagó el candil;
se agarraron de la mano
se fueron para el jardín.

14

Y en el jardín donde estaban
se agachaba y lo miraba
y don Benito tan serio
que ni la cabeza alzaba.

15

Le cambió de ropa blanca
como lo sabía vestir
le puso cama de flores
y se acuestan a dormir.

7

In that Plan de Barrancas
Not knowing how nor when,
That was where they met,
Don Benito and Don Ferdinand.

8

"Because of the goodwill you have,
Because of the worth that you enjoy,
Look here, don't you believe it;
I don't even know your wife."

9

"From the firmament most high
I saw a shooting star,
Don't you back down and deny
That I found you with her."

10

He reached for his pistol
And his sixteen-gauge gun
And he fired three shots at him—
Don Benito at the Frenchman.

11

When he had killed him
He put on the dead man's clothes
And got on his horse and
Went to kill the woman.

12

"Open the door, Helen,
Don't distrust me,
It is I, Ferdinand, the Frenchman,
Just arrived from France."

13

When she had barely opened the door,
He blew out the candle;
Hand in hand
They went into the garden.

14

In the garden where they were
She stooped and peered at him
And Don Benito, very sober-faced,
Didn't even raise his head.

15

She changed the white bed clothes
As she well knew how
And put on flowery sheets
And they went to bed.

16

—Media noche hemos dormido
media falta que dormir,
¿qué tiene mi rey francés
que no se ha llegado a mí?

16

"Half the night we've slept
Half the night is still left.
What's the matter, my French king
That you haven't come near me?"

17

¿Qué tiene amores en Francia
que los quiere más que a mí?
¿Por qué teme a mi marido
que está a cien leguas de aquí?

17

"Is it that you have someone in France
That you love more than me?
Why do you fear my husband
Who is one hundred leagues from here?"

18

—No tengo yo amor en Francia
ni quiero a otra más que a ti.
Solo témele a tu marido
que está a un lado de ti.

18

"I have no loves in France
Nor do I love another more than you.
Fear only your husband
Who is by your side."

19

—Perdóname, esposo mío,
perdona mi desventura;
mira, no lo hagas por mí,
hazlo por mis dos criaturas.

19

"Forgive me, my husband,
Forgive my misdeeds;
Look, don't do it for me,
Do it for my two young ones."

20

—No te puedo perdonar,
ni a ti ni a tus criaturas;
que te perdone el francés,
que gozó de tu hermosura.

20

"I cannot forgive you,
Neither you nor your young ones;
Let the Frenchman forgive you,
He who enjoyed your beauty."

21

—Agarra, criada, a esos niños,
llévaselos a mis padres,
si preguntan por Elena
les dices que tú no sabes.—

21

"Maid, take those children,
Take them to my parents,
If they ask for Helen
Tell them you know nothing."

22

Le quitó la crinolina
y la dejó en camisón,
Elena se arrodillaba
pero no alcanzó el perdón.

22

Taking off her robe
He left her in her nightgown.
Helen fell to her knees
But she was not forgiven.

23

Vuela, vuela, palomita,
no te vayas a parar;
que a Elena por traicionera
ya la llevan a enterrar.

23

Fly, fly, little dove,
Don't stop;
Helen for being unfaithful
Is being taken to her grave.

24

Les encargo, amigas mías,
no quieran vivir así;
les encargo a mis hermanas
que arrastren luto por mí.

24

I urge you, my friends,
Not to live that way;
I urge my sisters
To wear mourning for me.

25
Vuela, vuela, palomita,
párate en aquella higuera.
Aquí se acabó el corrido
de Elena, la traicionera.

25
Fly, fly, little dove,
Stop at that fig tree.
Here ends the corrido
Of Helen, the unfaithful.

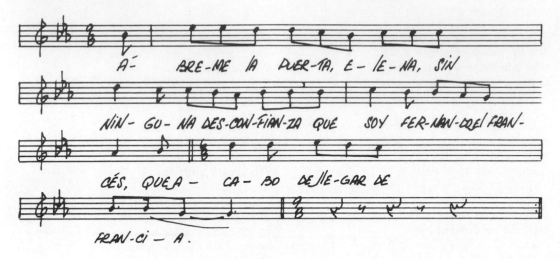

This is also known as the *Corrido de Elena* (although it is in origin a *romance*) and by other names. This version ends with the well-known *despedida* "*Vuela, vuela, palomita*" (Fly, fly, little dove) and is the first of many examples included in this volume to contain such a *despedida*, or farewell verse. *Doña Elena*, or *La Esposa Infiel* (A5a) is one of the California versions collected by Terrence Hansen.

A5a. *Doña Elena*, or *La Esposa Infiel*
Hansen 6a (p. 205), Rafael Salas, age 47, Corona, Calif., Hansen.

1
Fué don Fernando el Francés
un soldado muy valiente,
que combatió a los chinacos
de México independiente.

1
Fernando the Frenchman bold,
So valiant and brave was he,
Who fought against the champions
of Mexico's liberty.

2
Vió a doña Elena en su finca
y de ella se enamoró,
sabiendo que su marido
por un crimen se ausentó.

2
At the ranch of Doña Elena
He gave her his love sublime,
Knowing full well that her husband
Was gone because of a crime.

3
Doña Elena se hizo fuerte
pero al fin correspondió;
porque era un hombre temible
don Benito se perdió.

3
Doña Elena resisted
But then succumbed to his will;
Benito must be forsaken
Else Fernando would do her ill.

<table>
<tr><td>

4

Noche a noche tenían citas
donde gozaban su amor
y entonaban sus canciones
mancillando así su honor.

</td><td>

4

Night after night they would meet
To enjoy each other's love;
They raised their voices in song
But were scorned by heaven above.

</td></tr>
<tr><td>

5

Una tarde tempestuosa
don Benito fué a Jerez
y en el camino esperó
a don Fernando el Francés.

</td><td>

5

One tempestuous evening
Benito to Jerez did ride
And there by the roadside waited
Till Don Fernando he spied.

</td></tr>
<tr><td>

6

Benito, pistola en mano
y un rifle de dieciseis,
le acerta cuatro balazos
a don Fernando el Francés.

</td><td>

6

Benito, with his pistol
and sixteen-caliber gun,
Fires four shots at Fernando
As he turns and tries to run.

</td></tr>
<tr><td>

7

El Francés quedó tirado
muy cerca de la barranca,
y don Benito, iracundo,
montó en su briosa potranca.

</td><td>

7

The Frenchman, mortally wounded,
Fell in a nearby ravine,
And Benito, still enraged,
To mount his swift steed was seen.

</td></tr>
<tr><td>

8

Se fué todo enfurecido
para su pueblo natal
y allá en la puerta de hierro
se procuró serenar.

</td><td>

8

With his fury at its height
Toward his native town he stole
And there by the iron door
Tried to calm his troubled soul.

</td></tr>
<tr><td>

9

—Abreme la puerta, Elena,
sin ninguna desconfianza,
que soy Fernando el Francés
que vengo desde la Francia.

</td><td>

9

"Open the door, dear Elena,
Without any fret or fear
For I, Fernando the Frenchman
From faraway France, am here."

</td></tr>
<tr><td>

10

—¿Quién es ese caballero
que mis puertas manda abrir?
No es de Fernando el acento,
pues que se acaba de ir.

</td><td>

10

"Who is that strange gentleman
Who comes knocking at my door?
The accent can't be Fernando's
Since he's just been here before."

</td></tr>
<tr><td>

11

—Soy Fernando, no lo dudes,
dueña de mi corazón,
que regreso por decirte
que nos han hecho traición.

</td><td>

11

"It is I, your Don Fernando,
You must believe me, my dear.
I have come back to inform you
That we've been betrayed, it's clear."

</td></tr>
<tr><td>

12

—Oígame usted, don Fernando,
aunque no me importe a mí,
tiene usted amores en Francia
o quiere a otra más que a mí.

</td><td>

12

"Listen to me, Fernando,
Though it matters not to me,
You have a sweetheart in France
Or you love someone more than me."

</td></tr>
</table>

13

—No tengo amores en Francia
ni quiero a otra más que a ti.
Elena, soy tu marido,
que vengo en contra de ti.

13

"I have no sweetheart in France
Nor love I any but you.
Elena, I am your husband,
And I tell you now, we're through."

14

—Perdona, esposo querido,
perdona mis desventuras,
mira, no lo hagas por mí,
hazlo por mis dos criaturas.—

14

"Forgive, dear husband, I beg,
Forgive my thoughtless mistake,
If you won't do it for me,
Do it for our children's sake."

15

Al abrir la media puerta
se les apagó el candil
tomándola por las manos
la arrastró para el jardín.

15

When the door halfway opened
Out went the candle light,
And seizing her by the hands
He dragged her into the night.

16

—Toma, criada, estas criaturas,
llévaselas a mis padres;
y si preguntan de Elena,
les dices que tú no sabes.—

16

"Here, maid, you take these children;
To my parents they must go;
If they ask for Elena,
Just tell them you do not know."

17

Vestida estaba de blanco
que parecía un serafín,
que se cayó entre las flores
como se fuera a dormir.

17

She was dressed in a white robe,
An angel she seemed to be
That lay down among flowers
To sleep there eternally.

18

¡Ay! ¡Pobrecita de Elena!
¡Ay! ¡Qué suerte le tocó!
con tres tiros de pistola
que su marido le dió.

18

Oh! poor little Elena!
Alas! how cruel was her lot!
With three bullets from his pistol
His wife he cruelly shot.

19

Fué don Fernando el Francés
un soldado muy valiente,
que combatió a los chinacos
de México independiente.

19

Fernando the Frenchman bold,
So valiant and brave was he,
Who fought against the champions
of Mexico's liberty.

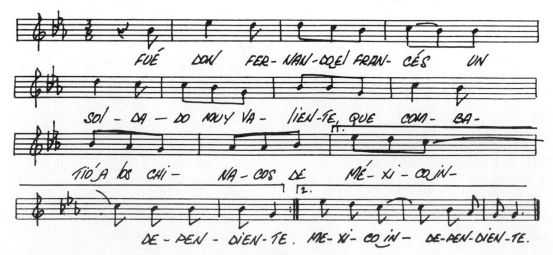

FUÉ DON FER-NAN-DOEL FRAN-CÉS UN
SOL-DA-DO MUY VA-LIEN-TE, QUE COM-BA-
TIÓ'A LOS CHI-NA-COS DE MÉ-XI-CO IN-
DE-PEN-DIEN-TE. ME-XI-CO IN-DE-PEN-DIEN-TE.

A5b. *Elena, la Traicionera* (Elena, the Traitress)
RB191, Chito Ochoa, Arizona, 1948, Frances Gillmor.

1

—Abreme la puerta, Elena,
sin ninguna desconfianza
que soy Fernando el francés
que vengo desde la Francia.

1

"Open the door, Elena,
Without any fear.
I am Fernando, the Frenchman
Who has come from France."

2

—¿Quién es ese caballero
que mis puertas manda abrir?
Mis puertas se hallan cerradas;
muchacha, prende el candil.—

2

"Who is that gentleman
Who asks me to open my doors?
My doors are locked;
Girl, light the candle."

3

Al abrir la media puerta
se les apagó el candil;
se tomaron de la mano,
y se fueron para el jardín.

3

On partly opening the door
The candle went out on them;
They joined hands,
And went into the garden.

4

En esta plaza de Barrancos
sin saber como ni cuando
se fué—don Benito,
Elena con don Fernando.

4

In this town of Barrancos
Without knowing how nor when
Don Benito went to find
Elena with Don Fernando.

5

Le echó mano a su pistola
y su rifle dieciseis
para darle de balazos
A don Fernando el francés.

5

He reached for his pistol
And his sixteen-gauge rifle
To fire shots
At Don Fernando, the Frenchman.

6

—No me tire, don Fernando (Benito),
por la verdad que usted goza.
Son falsos que me levantan,
yo ni conozco a su esposa.

6

"Don't shoot me, Don Fernando (Benito),
For the truth that you rejoice in.
What they say is false,
I don't even know your wife."

7

—No me diga, don Fernando,
ni diga que soy tirano.
¿Cómo que no la conoce?
¡Ahí! ¿No la trae de la mano?

7

"Don't tell me that, Don Fernando,
Nor say that I'm a tyrant.
What do you mean you don't know her?
There! Aren't you holding her hand?"

8

—Dispénsame, esposo mío,
dispensa mi desventura;
ya no lo hagas por mí,
hazlo por esta criatura.

8

"Forgive me, my husband,
Forgive my misfortune;
Spare me not for myself,
Spare me for this baby."

9

—De mí no alcanzas perdón,
De mí no alcanzas ni gloria.

9

"From me you get no pardon,
From me you get no glory.

Que te perdone el francés,
que gozó de tu hermosura.—

Let the Frenchman forgive you,
He who enjoyed your beauty."

10
Pobrecita de la Elena,
con que lástima murió,
con seis tiros de pistola
que su marido le dió.

10
Poor Elena,
In what grief she died,
With six pistol shots
That her husband gave her.

11
—Toma, lleva esta criatura,
llévasela a sus padres,
y si preguntan por mí,
Tú les dirás que no sabes.

11
"Here, take this baby,
Carry her to her parents,
And if they ask for me,
Tell them you know nothing."

The last two lines of verse 9 were missing.
Rather than leave it incomplete, I inserted
the corresponding lines from A5.

A6. *Firo Liro Li*
R337, H. Fountain, Mesilla Park, N.Mex., 1950, Robb. Cf. RB789; C70, verse 3; also
Van Stone 17 (p. 31).

1
Mi marido está en la cama,
y yo en la cabecera
con el rosario en la mano
rogando a Dios que se muera.

1
My husband is lying in bed,
And I am standing at the head
With a rosary in my hand,
Praying to God that he may die.

Coro
Firo liro li, firo liro li, firo liro lera,
firo liro li, firo liro li, firo liro lera;
ven aquí, firo liro li;
ven acá, firo liro li;
que tu amante esperándote está.

Chorus
Firo liro li, firo liro li, firo liro lera,
Firo liro li, firo liro li, firo liro lera;
Come here, firo liro li;
Go there, firo liro li;
For your lover is waiting for you.

2
La pobre viuda lloraba
la muerte de su marido.
Debajo de la camalta
ya tenía otro escondido.

2
The poor widow was weeping
The death of her husband.
Under the bed
She already had another man hidden.

Firo Liro Li (A6) is a cynical commentary on infidelity in marriage. *La Firolera* (RB789), collected by Cobos in 1950 from Felipe H. Martínez in Albuquerque, New Mexico, is textually identical with the version given here.

A6a. *La Firolera*
"Spanish Songs of New Mexico," by F. S. Curtis, Jr. in Dobie, Texas 18 (vol. 4, p. 22), Texas, 1925, F. S. Curtis, Jr.

1	**1**
Mi marido está en la cama	My husband in bed is lying
y yo en la cabecera	And I'm at the head of the bed
con el rosario en la mano	With the rosary in my hand
pidiéndole a Dios que muera.	Praying to God he'll soon be dead.
Coro	*Chorus*
Firoliroli, firoliroli, firolirolera,	Firoliroli, firoliroli, firolirolera,
firoliroli, firoliroli, firolirolera.	Firoliroli, firoliroli, firolirolera.
¡Ven acá, firoliroli!	Come here, firoliroli!
¡Ven acá, firoliroli!	Come here, firoliroli!
Tu marido esperándote está.	Your husband is waiting for you.
2	**2**
Mi marido ya se murió,	Now my husband is safely dead,
ya el diablo se lo llevó,	The devil has snatched him away,
y seguro que 'stará pagando	And surely he is now paying
las patadas que me dió.	For the kicks he gave me each day.

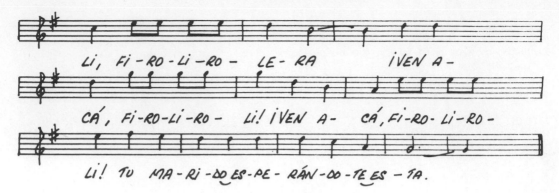

Li, FI-RO-LI-RO- LE-RA ¡VEN A-
CÁ, FI-RO-LI-RO- LI! ¡VEN A- CÁ, FI-RO-LI-RO-
LI! TU MA-RI-DO ES-PE-RÁN-DO-TE ES-TA.

La Firolera (A6a) is a Texas version. It was published in 1925 by the Texas Folklore Society, but the article was entitled "Spanish Songs of New Mexico." The texts of A6 and A6a are nearly identical.

A7. La Recién Casada (The Recent Bride)

R1489, S. Lavadie, age 86, Prado, N.Mex., 1957, Robb. Cf. RB732; RB733; Schindler 14a (Parte Literaria, pp. 57, 58).

<table>
<tr><td>

1
Yo soy la recién casada
y nadie me gozará;
mi marido me ha dejado
por amar la libertad.

</td><td>

1
I am the recent bride
And no one will enjoy my love.
My husband has left me
For the love of liberty.

</td></tr>
<tr><td>

2
—Caballero, por fortuna
¿no ha visto a mi marido?
—Señora, no lo conozco,
deme una seña y le digo.

</td><td>

2
"Sir, by chance
Have you seen my husband?"
"Lady, I don't know him,
Give me a sign and I'll tell you."

</td></tr>
<tr><td>

3
—Mi marido es artesano,
tiene el habla muy cortés,
en la copa del sombrero
trae un letrero en francés.

</td><td>

3
"My husband is an artisan
And speaks very courteously,
The crown of his hat
Carries a French label."

</td></tr>
<tr><td>

4
—Por las señas que usted ha dado
ya su marido muerto es;
en la guerra de Valverde
lo mató un traidor francés.

</td><td>

4
"By the signs that you have given
Your husband is now dead;
In the war at Valverde
A French traitor killed him."

</td></tr>
<tr><td>

5
—Mi marido fué a la guerra
y muy lejos se ha quedado,
yo me miro en el espejo
qué buena viuda he quedado.

</td><td>

5
"My husband went to war
And was left dead far away.
I see myself in the mirror
How good-looking a widow I still am."

</td></tr>
</table>

6	**6**
—Señora, si usted quisiera, por la voluntad de Dios, con los bienes del difunto, nos casaríamos los dos.	"Lady, if you would care to, By the will of God And with the property of the deceased, We two could get married."
7	**7**
—Yo sé que usted es hombre honesto y conoce la razón, pero la verdad le digo, no tengo disposición.	"I know that you are an honest man And can listen to reason, But I'll tell you the truth, I have no disposition to do so.
8	**8**
Diez años que lo he esperado y diez que lo esperaré, si a los veinte no viniera de monja me meteré.	"It's ten years that I have waited And ten more that I shall wait. If after twenty he should not come I shall become a nun.
9	**9**
Dos hijas que me han quedado; al pie me las llevaré a que rueguen por su madre y por su padre también.	"I've been left with two daughters; I shall take them with me That they may pray for their mother And for their father as well."

YO SOY LA RE-CIÉN CA-SA-DA Y NA-
DIE ME GO-ZA-RÁ; MI MA-RI-DO ME HA DE-
JA-DO POR A-MAR LA LI-BER-TAD.

La Recién Casada (A7) is also known as *Las Señas del Marido*. In contrast to some of the preceding songs, this *romance* extols the virtuous wife whose absent husband returns to test her fidelity. Campa discussed the diffusion of this ballad throughout Spanish America (Campa 2). The plot of this ballad reminds one of Darius Milhaud's opera *Le Pauvre Matelot* (The Poor Sailor).

A7a. *La Recién Casada*
   R1469, Esteban Torres, age 62, Tomé, N.Mex., 1957, Robb.

1	**1**
Yo soy la recién casada que no se me olvidará. Me abandonó mi marido por amar la libertad.	I am a recent bride A fact which I cannot forget. My husband abandoned me For the love of liberty.

2

—Caballero, por si acaso,
¿no conoce a mi marido?
—Señora, no lo conozco,
deme una seña,— le digo.

2

"Sir, by any chance
Do you know my husband?"
"Lady, I don't know him,
Give me a sign," he said.

3

—Mi marido es alto y rubio
y del habla muy cortés,
y en la copa del sombrero
trae un rótulo: marqués.

3

"My husband is tall and blonde
And speaks very courteously,
And in the crown of his hat
He carries a label: Marquis."

4

—Por las señas que usted ha dado
su marido muerto es.
En las guerras de Besquera
lo mató un traidor francés.

4

"By the signs which you have given
Your husband is dead.
In the wars of Besquera
A French traitor killed him.

5

Señora, que usted quisiera
nos casaríamos los dos,
siendo su gusto y el mío
y la voluntad de Dios.

5

"Lady, if you are willing
Let the two of us get married,
If it be your wish and mine
And the will of God, as well."

6

—Diez años que lo he esperado
y diez que lo esperaré.
Si a los veinte no viniera
de monja me meteré.

6

"It's ten years that I have waited
And ten more I will wait.
If after these twenty he does not come
I will become a nun.

7

Dos hijas que me ha dejado
conmigo las llevaré
a que rueguen por su padre
y por su madre también.

7

"Two daughters whom he has left me
I shall take with me
So that they may pray for their father
And for their mother also."

YO SOY LA RE-CIÉN CA-SA-DA QUE NO
SE ME OL-VI-DA-RÁ. ME A-BAN-DO-NÓ MI MA-
RI-DO POR A-MAR LA LI-BER-TAD.

A7b. *Las Señas del Esposo* (The Tokens of the Husband)
Matos 8a (Parte Literaria, p. 94), Robregordo, Spain, 1951, Matos. Cf. Campa 2, p. 42.

1	1
Un día, estando sentada al ladito de mi puerta, vi venir un caballero que venía de la guerra.	One day being seated At the side of my door I saw a man coming Who was coming from the war.

2	2
Yo le dije: —Caballero, ¿viene usted de hacer la guerra? —Sí, señora, de allí vengo. ¿Qué se le ha perdido en ella?	I said to him, "Sir, Do you come from making war?" "Yes, madam, I come from there. Have you lost someone in the war?"

3	3
—Se me perdió mi marido, que hace años anda en ella. —Por las señas que usted da, su marido muerto queda.	"Yes, I have lost my husband, Who several years ago went to war." "By the signs that you give me Your husband is dead."

4	4
—¡Válgame Dios, desgraciada! ¡Qué suerte será la nuestra! ¿Quién me calzará a mí el oro? ¿Quién me vestirá la seda?	"God help me this unfortunate one. What will be our fate? Who will earn money for me? Who will dress me in silk?

5	5
A mi hija la mayor, ¿quién la casará si es buena? Y a mis hijos los pequeños, ¿quién me los dará escuela?	"And my oldest daughter, Who will marry her if she is a good woman? And for my small children, Who will pay for their schooling?"

6	6
—Pues véngase usted conmigo, conmigo para mi tierra. Yo la calzaré a usté el oro, yo la vestiré de seda.	"Come with me, Come to my country. I will earn gold for you, I will dress you in silk.

7	7
A su hija la mayor yo la casaré, si es buena. Y a sus hijos los pequeños, yo se los daré escuela.	As for your oldest daughter, I'll see she is married, if she's a good woman. And as for your small children, I will send them to school."

8	8
—Váyase usted, caballero, váyase usted pa' su tierra, que mujer de buen marido no se va de esa manera.—	"Go away, sir, Go away to your country, For the wife of a good husband Does not act in that manner."

9	9
Al otro día de mañana a misa a todos los lleva,	The following day in the morning They all went to mass,

y a su hija la mayor,
delante con la candela.

And the oldest daughter went ahead
Carrying the candle.

10
Y al revolver de una esquina
con su marido se encuentra.
—¿Dónde va la mi mujer?
¿Dónde va la mía prenda?

10
And going around a corner
She met her husband.
"Where is my wife going?
Where is my beloved going?"

11
—Que un caballero ayer tarde . . .

¡Así a puñaladas muera!
—Calla tú la mi mujer,
que el caballero yo era,

11
"There was a gentleman yesterday
   afternoon . . .
Thus by knife wounds he died!"
"Be silent, my wife,
For that gentleman was I,

12
que lo hice por saber
si eras mala o eras buena.
Si tú hubiás venío conmigo
te habría cortado la cabeza,

12
And I did it in order to know
If you were good or bad.
If you had come with me
I would have cut off your head,

13
y como no te viniste,
por eso te quiero, prenda.

13
And because you did not come,
For this I love you, my dear."

Matos describes this version as a *corro de
niños* (children's song).

A7c. *Las Señas del Esposo*
    Mendoza 9d (p. 156), Josefa Atencio, Walsenburg, Colorado, 1870, Vicente T.
Mendoza.

1
Yo soy la recién casada
que lloraba sin cesar;
me abandonó mi marido
por amar la libertad.

1
I am the recent bride
Who weeps without ceasing;
My husband abandoned me
For the love of liberty.

2
. . . [undecipherable]
. . .
En la falda del sombrero
trae un letrero francés.

2
. . .
. . .
In the brim of his hat
He carries a French inscription.

3
—Por las señas que usted ha dado
tu marido muerto lo es;
en la ciudad de Varela
lo mató un traidor francés.

3
"By the signs you have given me
Your husband is dead;
In the city of Varela
A French traitor killed him."

<table>
<tr><td>

4

—Dos hijos que Dios me ha dado
de conmigo les llevaré,
para que rueguen por su padre
y por su madre también.

</td><td>

4

"Two children whom God has given me
I will take with me,
So that they may pray for their father
And for their mother as well.

</td></tr>
<tr><td>

5

Diez años que lo he aguardado,
veinte que lo aguardaré;
si a los treinta años no viene
de monja me meteré.

</td><td>

5

"I have waited ten years,
Twenty I will wait;
If at thirty he does not come
I will become a nun.

</td></tr>
<tr><td>

6

No más me pongo mi mantona negra
y mi listón colorado,
no más me arrimo al capejo:
¡Qué buena viuda he quedado!

</td><td>

6

"Whenever I put on my black cape,
And my red ribbon,
Whenever I look in the mirror, I'll think:
What a good-looking widow I still am!"

</td></tr>
</table>

YO SOY LA RE-CIÉN CA-SA-DA QUE LLO-RA-BA SIN CE-SAR, ME A-BAN-DO-NÓ MI MA-RI-DO POR A-MAR LA LI-BER-TAD.

A8. *Hilito de Oro* (Little Golden Thread)
R1912, Edna G. de Boggs, Albuquerque, 1963, Robb.

<table>
<tr><td>

1

Hilito, hilito de oro,
yo jugando al ajedrez.
En el camino me han dicho
¡qué lindas hijas tenéis!

</td><td>

1

Little thread, little golden thread,
I am here playing chess.
On the road they have told me
What pretty daughters you have.

</td></tr>
<tr><td>

2

Sí las tengo, no las tengo;
no las tengo para dar.
Que del pan que yo comiera
ellas también comerán,
y del agua que bebiera
ellas también beberán.

</td><td>

2

Yes, I have them and I don't have them;
I don't have them to give away.
Of the bread that I eat
They also will eat,
And of the water that I drink
They also will drink.

</td></tr>
<tr><td>

3

Yo me voy muy enojado
a los palacios del rey.
Que las hijas del rey moro
no me les dan por mujer.

</td><td>

3

I am going away very angry
To the palaces of the king.
Because the daughters of the Moorish king
Will not be married to me.

</td></tr>
</table>

4

Va, vuelva caballero,
no sea usted tan descortés.
Que de tres hijas que tengo,
la mejor será de usted.

5

Esta escojo por bonita,
por hermosa, y por mujer,
que me parece una rosa
acabada de nacer.

4

Come now, sir knight,
Don't be so discourteous.
Of the three daughters that I have
The best will be yours.

5

I choose this one as beautiful,
As lovely, and as a wife,
For to me she looks
Like a newborn rose.

Hilito de Oro (A8) comes from Santo Domingo. I have included it as a reminder that the Hispanic folk-song tradition, including many common examples, is in the patrimony of most of Central and South America, including the Caribbean countries.

A8a. *Hilitos de Oro* (Little Golden Threads)
WPA19 (p. 42), L. W. Brown, New Mexico, 1942.

1

Hilitos, hilitos de oro,
que se me vienen quebrando,
que dice el rey y la reina
¿qué tantas hijas tendrá?

1

Little threads, little threads of gold,
They're breaking in my hands,
For the king and queen say
I wonder how many daughters he has.

2

—Que tenga las que tuviere,
que nada importa al rey.
Yo ya me voy muy descontento
a darle cuenta al rey.

2

"The number of daughters I have,
Doesn't concern the king.
I'm going away dissatisfied
To tell this to him."

3

—Vuelva, vuelva, caballero.
No sea tan descortés,
que de las hijas que yo tengo
escoja la más mujer.

3

"Wait a minute, sir.
Don't be so rude,
For from all the daughters I have
You can choose the most womanly."

4

—No la escojo por bonita
ni tampoco por mujer.
Yo escojo una florecita
acabada de nacer.

4

"I do not choose her for beauty
Nor for womanliness.
I choose a tender,
newborn flower."

The above is a New Mexico version of A8.

A9. *Los Diez Mandamientos* (The Ten Commandments)
R2174, V. F. Gallegos, age 68, Albuquerque, N.Mex., 1966, Robb. Cf. Schindler 14a (Parte Literaria p. 69, Parte Musical nos. 452, 453, 841); García 5b (Parte Musical, pp. 103–104).

1

Con cuidado, vida mía,
La causa de mi tormento,
que yo por ti he quebrantado
de Dios los diez mandamientos.

1

Take care, love of my life,
And cause of my torment,
It is for you that I've broken
The ten commandments of God.

2

El primero: amar a Dios;
yo no lo amo como debo.
Sólo por pensar en ti,
hermosísimo lucero.

2

The first: To love God.
I don't love him as I should.
I can only think of you,
Most beautiful morning star.

3

El segundo: no jurar;
yo mil veces he jurado
ni comer ni bebir
hasta de estar a tu lado.

3

The second: Thou shall not swear.
A thousand times I've sworn
Neither to eat nor drink
Until I am at your side.

4

El tercero: que es la misa;
no la sigo con devoción
por estar pensando en ti,
prenda de mi corazón.

4

The third: To attend mass;
I never follow it with devotion
Because I'm thinking of you,
Beloved of my heart.

5

El cuarto: que a mis padres;
la obediencia les perdí;
en público y en secreto
sólo por pensar en ti.

5

The fourth: To honor my parents;
Obedience I've lost for them;
In public and in secret
For thinking only of you.

6

El quinto: no matarás;
yo éste lo he quebrantado,
porque mataré al traidor,
que yo encuentre a tu lado.

7

El sexto: ya no me acuso;
no tengo de que acusarme,
porque todas las muchachas
me gustan para casarme.

8

El séptimo: no levantar;
éste tú lo has quebrantado,
pues mi amor y voluntad
todo me la has ensultado.

9

El octavo: no levantar
testimonio no avertido;
yo jusgo que te enamoran
todos los que hablan contigo.

10

El noveno: no desear
la mujer de otro marido;
en este particular
vénganse todas conmigo.

11

El décimo: no codiciar
la mujer que tiene dueño;
cada vez que se me ofrece,
yo lo hago con mucho empeño.

12

En estos diez mandamientos
todos se encierran en dos:
en quererte y en amarte,
y en estar juntos los dos.

6

The fifth: You shall not kill;
This one, too, I have broken,
For I would murder the betrayer,
Whom I might find by your side.

7

The sixth: I do not accuse myself;
I don't have to accuse myself of that one,
Because all the young women
I see I would like to marry.

8

The seventh: Not to accuse falsely;
This one you surely have broken,
Because all my love and good will
You have repaid with insults.

9

The eighth: Not to bear false witness;
(This one I will not follow.)
I judge that all who talk to you
Are in love with you.

10

The ninth: Not to covet
Another man's wife;
In this particular
May all the ladies come to me.

11

The tenth: Not to lust after
A married woman;
Any time that I get a chance,
I do it with much ardor.

12

Of these ten commandments
All are contained in two:
To want you and to love you,
And the two of us to be united.

CON CUI-DA-DO, VI-DA MÍ-A, LA CAU-SA DE MI TOR-MEN-TO, QUE YO POR TI HE QUEBRAN-TA-DO DE DIOS LOS DIEZ MAN-DA-MIEN-TOS.

Los Diez Mandamientos (A9) is a New Mexican version of a *romance* that is well known in Spain. A9a–9c are three of the Spanish versions. The texts are clearly related. In the music there is no discernible relationship. A9b is a Phrygian melody. Two of the melodies observe one of the rules of *musica ficta*. (See Robb 13, pp. 7–8.)

The singer, Vicente F. Gallegos, is a nephew of the late Próspero S. Baca who passed on to him his devotion to the Spanish folk tradition of New Mexico.

A9a. *Mandamientos de Amor* (Commandments of Love)
Mingote (p. 140), Spain, Mingote.

1
Los mandamientos de amor
te voy a cantar, paloma,
para que me des el sí
y me lleves a la gloria.

1
I shall sing to you, my dove,
The commandments of love,
So that you will say yes
And lift me up to heaven.

2
El primero, amar a Dios:
nunca lo amo como debo,
sólo de pensar en ti,
hermosísimo lucero.

2
The first, to love God:
I have never loved him as I should
For thinking only of you,
Most beautiful star.

3
El segundo, no jurar:
toda mi vida he jurado
no separarme de ti,
permanecer a tu lado.

3
The second, not to swear:
All my life I have sworn
Never to part from you,
To stay at your side.

4
El tercero es ir a misa:
nunca voy con devoción
sólo de pensar en ti,
prenda de mi corazón.

4
The third is to go to mass:
I never go with devotion
Because I think only of you,
Darling of my heart.

5
El cuarto, honrar padre y madre:
el respeto les perdí;
el cariño y el respeto
sólo te los tengo a ti.

5
The fourth, honor your parents:
I have lost respect for them;
My affection and respect
I have only for you.

6
El quinto, no matarás:
yo nunca he matado a nadie;
el muerto yo soy, señores,
tú la culpa, bien lo sabes.

6
The fifth, thou shalt not kill:
I have never killed anyone;
The dead one is I, my lords,
You are to blame, as you know.

7
Mozas que estáis al balcón
sin meteros hacia adentro
hacéis pecar a los hombres
en el sexto mandamiento.

7
Girls who appear on the balcony
And don't go inside
Cause the men to sin
Against the sixth commandment.

8

El séptimo, no hurtar:
yo nunca he robado a nadie,
sólo robaré una niña,
si no me la dan sus padres.

8

The seventh, not to steal:
I have never robbed anybody,
I will only steal a girl
If her parents do not give her to me.

9

Octavo, no levantar
falso testimonio a nadie:
como a mí me lo levantan
los vecinos de mi calle.

9

The eighth, not to bear false witness:
I have never lied to anyone,
The way the people on my street
Lie about me.

10

Noveno, no desear
a la mujer de tu prójimo:
él que contigo ha de hablar
ha de vérselas conmigo.

10

The ninth, not to covet
Your neighbor's wife:
He who flirts with you
Will have to account to me.

11

Más estos dos mandamientos
sólo se encierran en
. . . [undecipherable]
que nos casemos los dos.

11

But these two commandments
Are both included in
. . .
That the two of us get married.

A9b. *Los Mandamientos de Amor* (The Commandments of Love)
García 5b (Parte Musical, p. 103), Dionisio Calera, Spain, 1956, García.

Los mandamientos de amor
vengo a explicarte, paloma,
para que me das el sí
y me lleves a la gloria.

I will explain to you,
My dove, the commandments of love,
So that you will say yes
And lift me up to heaven.

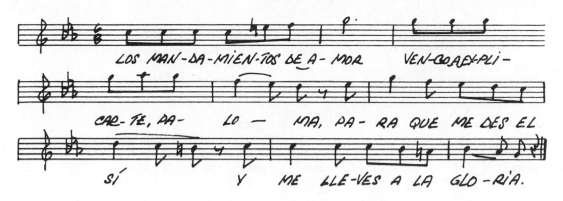

A9c. *Los Mandamientos de Amor* (The Commandments of Love)
García 5b (Parte Musical, p. 104), Rufino Toledo Gómez, Spain, 1956, García.

Los diez mandamientos santos
vengo a cantarte, paloma,
sólo porque me des gusto
y me tengas en memoria.

I shall sing for you, my dove,
The ten holy commandments
Solely for the pleasure
And so you will remember me.

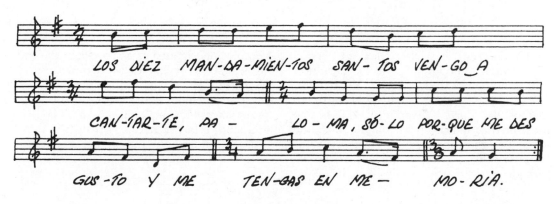

A10. *La Sirena* (The Mermaid)
R1751, Próspero S. Baca, age 70, Bernalillo, N.Mex., 1945, Robb.

1

El viernes por cierto fué
una niña salió a pasear
y de allá vino diciendo:
—Soy sirena del mar.—

1

It was on Friday, for sure,
That a girl went out for a stroll
And from there she returned, saying,
"I am a mermaid of the sea."

2

¡Ay! te vas, te vas;
¡ay! te vas al mar,
hija querida, bien de mi vida,
te vas al mar.

2

Oh, you are going, you are going;
Oh, you are going to the sea,
Dear daughter, love of my life,
You are going to the sea.

<table>
<tr>
<td>

3

Todo aquél que mataría pez
en lo más profundo del mar,
todas esas son congojas
pa' la sirena del mar.

</td>
<td>

3

All who would kill fish
In the deepest parts of the sea,
All these bring anguish
To the mermaid of the sea.

</td>
</tr>
</table>

<table>
<tr>
<td>

4

Dichoso aquel marinero
que murió el día de San Juan;
derechito subió al cielo
la sirena del mar.

</td>
<td>

4

Happy the sailor
Who died on Saint John's Day;
The mermaid of the sea
Took him straight to heaven.

</td>
</tr>
</table>

<table>
<tr>
<td>

5

En Belén se juntan todos
los moros para bailar,
y les toca la vihuela
la sirena del mar.

</td>
<td>

5

In Bethlehem all the Moors
Gather for their dance,
And the mermaid of the sea
Plays the guitar for them.

</td>
</tr>
</table>

<table>
<tr>
<td>

6

Adiós papá y mamá,
allá se va, la aborrecida;
hija querida, bien de mi vida,
te vas al mar.

</td>
<td>

6

Good-bye father and mother,
The hated one, she is going;
Dear daughter, love of my life
You are going to the sea.

</td>
</tr>
</table>

La Sirena (A10) is a New Mexican version of a *romance* known in Spain. By its subject matter it appears to be related to the remarkable Spanish Faustian *romance El Marinero* (Matos 8a, Parte Literaria, p. 47), not to mention the raucous English ballad *The Eddystone Light*. Because of its element of the supernatural, it seems to partake of the nature of a *disparate*. It employs the eight-syllable line, rhymed or assonated at the end of each sixteen syllables, with four lines to the verse.

Campa includes two versions of this song as *romances* (Campa 2, pp. 77–78). The first of Campa's two versions is from the same source as mine, but the second is a quite different version.

A11. *Bernardo*
  Curtin 4 (p. 18), Curtin 4a (p. 11), 1945, Campa and Armendáriz.

<table>
<tr>
<td>

1

Ayuda pido a Jesús
y a la reina soberana
para notar una carta
a una muy pulida dama.

</td>
<td>

1

I ask the help of Jesus
And the sovereign queen
In order to write a letter
To a very elegant lady.

</td>
</tr>
</table>

<table>
<tr>
<td>

2

¿Qué ha sucedido en el mundo
por el diluvio de agua?
Un niño de tierna edad
que ni a quince años llegaba,

</td>
<td>

2

What has happened in the world
Because of the Flood?
A boy of tender age
Who had not even reached the age of fifteen,

</td>
</tr>
</table>

3	**3**
Mató un alcalde en su tierra	He killed a mayor in his country
por una y bastante causa	For a good and sufficient cause
y al por evitar cuestión	And to avoid questioning
se fué a la villa de Francia.	He went to the town of France.
4	**4**
Donde allí se enamoró	While there he fell in love
donde allí se enamoraba	While there he was falling in love
de una muy pulida niña	With an exquisite girl
de una muy vizarra dama.	With a very high-spirited lady.
5	**5**
Bernarda tiene por nombre	Bernarda is her name
y él, Bernardo se llamaba;	and he is called Bernardo;
como eran de un propio nombre	Since they are of the same name
mucho se estiman y se aman.	They respect and love one another.
6	**6**
Ya los padres de esta niña	Now the parents of this girl
cuando la sienten liviana,	Suspecting her of unchaste conduct,
tratan de poner espillas,	Attempt to hire spies
espillas por sus pisadas.	To follow her footprints.
7	**7**
Ya proponen de casarla	They propose to marry her
con el más gran centurión,	To the chief centurion,
con el más gran centurión	To the chief centurion
de la ciudad de Gualana.	Of the city of Gualana.
8	**8**
Ya se declara y les dice	And she declares and says to them
—No se recintan en nada	"I agree to nothing
que estoy muy chica y muy tierna	For I am very small and tender
y no puedo ser casada.—	And cannot be married."
9	**9**
Tuvo lugar en la tarde	She took time one afternoon
para notar una carta	To write a letter
y con una criada de ella	And with a woman servant of hers
a Bernardo se la manda,	She sent it to Bernardo,
10	**10**
diciéndole, —Ay, Bernardito,	Saying to him: "Ah, dear Bernardo,
más ay Bernardo de mi alma,	Oh, Bernardo, my soul,
pues si me tienes amor	If you love me
sácame de hoy a mañana,	Take me away in twenty-four hours,
11	**11**
que ya me van a casar	"For they want me to marry
con el más gran centurión,	The chief centurion,
con el más gran centurión	The chief centurion
de la ciudad de Gualana.—	Of the city of Gualana."

12

Bernardo toma la carta
ni a lerla la comensaba
ni a lerla la comensaba
de pura cólera y rabia.

13

Ya se encasqueta el sombrero
y le da un tiemple a su espada;
dos amigos que él tenía
ya se iba y los convidaba;

14

Diciéndoles, —Amiguitos,
más ay amigos de mi alma,
traigo la vida vendida,
traigo la vida emprestada

15

por una pulida niña,
por una vizarra dama.—
Y el más chico le dicía:
—Como mi vida me dure
te acompañará mi espada.—

16

Luego que cierra la noche
se visten de ricas cotas,
se visten de ricas cotas,
de ricas cotas de malla,

17

y salen a caminar
por altas sierras marañas;
se vieron tan abatidos
sólo Bernardo quedaba.

18

Luego una bala velos
que del caballo le tiraba.
¡Ay, Bernardo de mi vida!
¡Más ay, Bernardo de mi alma!
¡Qué corta fué mi fortuna
y tan grande mi desgracia!

19

Otro día por la mañana
Bernardo se levantaba,
Curándose las heridas
a un punto que se alcansaba.

20

Luego que se vido bueno
ya se iba para la plaza

12

Bernardo taking the letter,
Had hardly started to read it
When he was filled
With anger and fury.

13

He has already put on his helmet
And tempered his sword;
As he left he invited two friends
To go along with him;

14

Saying to them: "Dear friends,
My beloved friends,
I have sold my life,
I'm living on borrowed time,

15

"All because of an exquisite girl,
Because of a high-spirited lady."
And the smallest one said to him:
"As long as my life shall last
My sword will accompany you."

16

When night had fallen
They dressed in rich coats,
They dressed in rich coats,
In rich coats of mail,

17

They took to the road
Through high impassable mountains;
They were so dejected that
Only Bernardo kept going.

18

A swift bullet came
And knocked him off of his horse.
Ah, Bernardo of my life!
Oh, Bernardo of my soul!
How short-lived was my good fortune!
How great is my misfortune!

19

The following morning
Bernardo arose,
Attending himself to as many
Of his wounds as he could.

20

When he had sufficiently recovered
He took off for the town

donde está un capitán
que "Brazo Fuerte" le llaman.

Where there lived a captain
Whose nickname was "Strong Arm."

21

—Dios guarde buen Capitán
que "Brazo Fuerte" le llaman,
hasta el tomar desengaño
de la reyerta.—

"God guard you, good Captain,
Whom they call 'Strong Arm,'
Will you help me to set right
This recent dispute?"

22

El hombre buen capitán
viendo lo bien que hablaba,
le emprestó un caballo blanco
que al par del viento volaba.

The captain, a good man,
Seeing how well spoken he was,
Loaned him a white horse
Which could run as fast as the wind.

23

Ya le hace la escaramusa,
la escaramusa le hacía;
ya alcanza la compañía
de la reyerta pasada.

Now the skirmish takes place,
There takes place the skirmish;
Now he overtakes the gang
Involved in the recent dispute.

24

A cual hiere ira, y a cual mata,
y a cual cuerpo destrozaba;
sólo uno que salió huyendo
en una yegua alazana.

This one he wounds, this one he kills,
This one he mangles;
Only one man escaped
Mounted on a sorrel horse.

25

Que si no se vale de eso
A los demás acompaña,
y lo que Dios determina
pues es muy justo que se haga.

If he had not escaped
He would have accompanied the rest,
For whatever God decides
It is only just that it be done.

A - YU - DA DI - DO A JE - SÚS   YA LA REI-

NA SO - BE - RA - NA   AA - RA NO - TAR U - NA

CAR - TA   A U - NA MUY PU - LI - DA

DA - MA   ¿ QUÉ HA SU - CE - DI - DO EN EL

MUN - DO   POR EL DI - LU - VIO DE

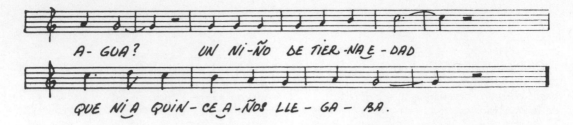

A- GUA? UN NI-ÑO DE TIER-NA E -DAD

QUE NI A QUIN-CE A-ÑOS LLE - GA - BA.

This *romance* reflects the habit of mind of a time when the preservation of the chastity of a daughter or the right of parents to choose a husband was taken seriously—when it was, in fact, a matter of life and death that could lead to the murder of an unwelcome suitor (cf. *Macario Romero*, B30).

Mendoza states that this song belongs to the class of *romances* that circulated in Spain and America in printed versions at the end of the eighteenth century; that the text maintains the assonance a–a, and that it conserves what he calls parallelistic verses. It relates occurrences in Spain in the city of Guadiana (Mendoza 9d, Parte Literaria, pp. 185–88).

A12. *Gerineldo*

Espinosa 5 (no. 8), New Mexico, 1915, A. M. Espinosa. Cf. Schindler 14a (Parte Musical, nos. 98, 264, 477, 594).

1

—Gerineldo, Gerineldo,
mi camarero aguerrido;
¡quién te pescara esta noche
tres horas en mi servisio!

1

"Gerineldo, Gerineldo,
My veteran steward;
If only I could trap you
For three hours tonight."

2

—Pues, ¿tres horas, mi señora?
¿como son tres jueran cinco?
que porque soy vuestro criado
quieri usted burlar conmigo.

2

"Well, only three hours my lady?
Why not make it five?
Just because I am your servant
Do you want to mock me?"

3

—No, Gerineldo de mi alma,
de deveras te lo digo.
— ¿A qué horas, mi señora,
compliréis lo prometido?

3

"No, Gerineldo, my love,
I tell you the truth."
"At what hour, my lady,
Will you redeem your promise?"

4

—A las doce de la nochi
cuando el rey esté dormido.—
Tuavia las dose nu han dado
ya Gerineldo había ido.

4

"At twelve o'clock at night
When the king is asleep."
Twelve o'clock had not yet struck
When Gerineldo was already on his way.

5

Huyo el castío serrado,
pego su vos y suspiro.
— ¿Quí alevoso, quí atrevido,
a me castiu ha venido?

5

From the locked castle
Came her voice and sigh.
"How cunning and how bold
You have come to my castle!"

<table>
<tr><td>

6

—Señora, soy Gerineldo,
que vengu a lo prometido.—
Ya lu agarra de la mano
para dentro lu ha metido.

7

A la ida de sus deleites
ya se han quedado dormidos,
dándose besos y abrasos
como mujer y marido.

8

A la una de la mañana
ya pide el rey sus vestidos;
ya va un page y se los da,
de Gerineldu es amigo.

9

—¿Dónde se haya Gerineldo,
mi camareru aguerridu?
—Señor, se hay' en la cama
con calenturas y frios.—

10

Ya tomaba el rey su espada,
para el castío si ha ido;
haya la puerta entri abierta,
para adentro se ha metido.

11

Los haya boca con boca,
como mujer y marido;
vuelve los ojos para atrás
y de esta manera ha dicho:

12

—Si matu a mi Gerineldo,
que es él que se crió conmigo,
si matu a mi hija la infanta,
queda mi reino perdido.

13

Pondré mi espada entre medio
para que sepan son sentidos.—
Cerca de la mañanita
ya pide el rey sus vestidos;

14

Ya Gerineldo yegó,
como siempri había ido.
—Gerineldo, Gerineldo,
mi camarero aguerrido,

</td><td>

6

"Lady, I am Gerineldo,
Who have come for what was promised."
She grasped him by the hand
And led him inside.

7

After enjoying their delights
They fell asleep,
After kissing and embracing
Like man and wife.

8

At one o'clock in the morning
The king called for his clothes;
A page who was a friend of Gerineldo
Brought them to him.

9

"Where is Gerineldo
My veteran steward?"
"My lord, he is sick in bed
With fever and chills."

10

Then the king took his sword
And went to the castle;
Finding the door half-opened
He went inside.

11

There he found them mouth to mouth,
Like a wife and husband;
The king looked away
And spoke in this manner:

12

"Do I kill Gerineldo,
Whom I have raised?
If I kill my daughter, the princess,
My kingdom will be lost.

13

"I will place my sword between them
So that they will know my feelings."
It was early morning
When the king asked for his clothes;

14

Now Gerineldo came
As he had always come.
"Gerineldo, Gerineldo,
My veteran steward,

</td></tr>
</table>

15
—¿Dónde la noche has pasado?
¿dónde la noche has dormido?
—Señor, jugando a los dados,
ni he ganado ni he perdido.

15
Where have you passed the night?
Where did you sleep last night?"
"My Lord, I was shooting dice,
I neither gained nor lost."

16
—Mucho disimulu es ese,
Gerineldu, a lo que he visto.—
Hinca la rodiy' en tierra
y de esta manera ha dicho:

16
"Gerineldo, you are lying,
I know everything."
He fell to his knees
And spoke in this manner:

17
—Señor, yo seré la carne,
vuestra mersed, el cuchio;
corte de donde quisiera,
de mí no quedo dolido.

17
"My Lord, I will be the flesh,
You, my lord, the knife;
Cut where you will,
I can no longer feel pain."

18
—Levántate, Gerineldo,
mi camareru aguerrido;
me dise mi hija la infanta
que te escoge por marido.—

18
"Arise, Gerineldo,
My veteran steward.
My daughter, the princess, tells me
She chooses you as her husband."

19
Se levanta Gerineldo
pegando saltos y brincos
de ver que se iba a casar
con la hija de Carlos Quinto.

19
Gerineldo arose
Leaping for joy
To see that he was going to marry
The daughter of Charles the Fifth.

GE-RI-NEL-DO, GE-RI-NEL-DO, MI CA-MA-RE-RQA-GUE-RRI-DO; ¡QUIÉN TE PES-CA-RA ES-TA NO-CHE TRES HO-RAS EN MI SER-VI-CIO!

This appears to be the oldest identifiable *romance* of the group. According to Mendoza, it is a Carolingian ballad (Mendoza 9d, pp. 125–27).

Examples A12a through A12g are Spanish versions, all of them fragmentary. Like other *romances*, *Gerineldo* is found better preserved in the American Southwest than in the mother country itself. I have included the Spanish versions of this seemingly very ancient *romance* because of my interest in tracing the melodies. The words are usually easy to trace; the melodies, almost impossible. There is very little resemblance between the several melodies of this *romance*. Example A12 is in the Aeolian mode, has the range of an octave, and has a rather regular period structure, whereas example A12a has a very narrow range of a major third and is in the Phrygian or Hypophrygian mode.

A12c has the range of an octave and a minor second and is in the Phrygian mode. It includes some neumatic ornamentation. A12b has a range of a minor sixth and is in the Aeolian mode. It has an irregular meter, and the double grace notes give it an ornamentation which suggests *flamenco* or Moorish influence. A12d has a range of an octave and a minor second and is in the Phrygian mode with triplet cadences like example A12c. Example A12e has a range of a minor seventh and employs similar triplet cadences.

A12a. *Gerineldo*
   Matos 8a (Parte Musical, p. 55), Spain, 1951, Matos.

Gerineldo, Gerineldo,
Gerineldito pulido,
¡Quién te pillara una noche
tres horas a mi albedrio!

Gerineldo, Gerineldo,
Beautiful dear Gerineldo,
Oh, to be able to steal you away
To do with you as I wish for three hours!

A12b. *Gerineldo*
   Matos 8a (Parte Musical, p. 48), La Acebeda, Spain, 1951, Matos.

Gerineldo, Gerineldo,
Gerineldito pulido,
¡Cuántas damas y doncellas
quisieran dormir contigo!

Gerineldo, Gerineldo,
Beautiful dear Gerineldo,
So many ladies and maidens
Would like to sleep with you!

A12c. *Gerineldo*
Matos 8a (Parte Musical, p. 49), Montejo de la Sierra, Spain, 1951, Matos.

Gerineldo, Gerineldo,
paje del rey muy querido,
¡Cuántas damas y doncellas
quisieran dormir contigo!

Gerineldo, Gerineldo,
Page of the most beloved king,
So many ladies and maidens
Would like to sleep with you!

A12d. *Gerineldo*
Matos 8a (Parte Musical, p. 49), Gargantilla del Lozoya, Spain, 1951, Matos.

Gerineldo, Gerineldo,
¡Ay, Gerineldo pulido!
¡Ay, Gerineldo pulido!

Gerineldo, Gerineldo
Ah, neat Gerineldo!
Ah, neat Gerineldo!

A12e. *Gerineldo*
Matos 8a (Parte Musical, p. 49), Chinchón, Spain, 1951, Matos.

Gerineldo, Gerineldo,
Gerineldo, Gerineldo,
Gerineldito pulido,
Gerineldito pulido.

Gerineldo, Gerineldo,
Gerineldo, Gerineldo,
Beautiful dear Gerineldo,
Beautiful dear Gerineldo.

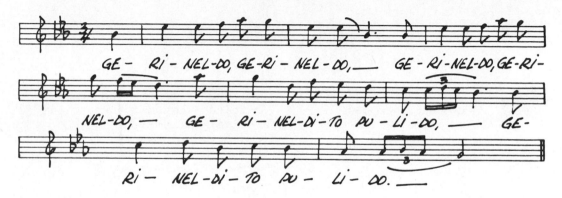

A12f. *Gerineldo*

Matos 8a (Parte Musical, p. 50), Corpa, Spain, 1951, Matos.

Gerineldo, Gerineldo,
Gerineldito pulido,
Gerineldito pulido.

Gerineldo, Gerineldo,
Beautiful dear Gerineldo,
Beautiful dear Gerineldo.

A12g. *Gerineldo*

Matos 8a (Parte Musical, p. 41), La Cabrera, Spain, 1951, Matos.

Gerineldo, Gerineldo,
Gerineldo, paje mío,
¡Quién te pudiera tener
dos horas al amor mío!

Gerineldo, Gerineldo,
Gerineldo, my page,
Oh, to be able to spend two hours
Making love to you!

A13. *El Gato Le Dice al Ratón* (The Cat Said to the Mouse)
R1471, Edwin Berry, age 39, Tomé, N.Mex., 1957, Robb.

1

El gato le dice al ratón, sin caridad.	The cat said to the mouse, without charity.
El gato le dice al ratón, sin caridad.	The cat said to the mouse, without charity.
Corre y diles a tus padres]	Go and tell your parents
que te echen la bendición,]	To give you their blessing;
te voy a quitar la vida.]	I am going to take your life.
¡Oyeme, linda de amor!] *Bis*	Hear me, my beautiful beloved!

2

El ratón le dice al gato, sin caridad.	The mouse said to the cat, without charity.
El ratón le dice al gato, sin caridad.	The mouse said to the cat, without charity.
No me mates todavía,]	Do not kill me yet,
déjame de hacer testamento]	Give me time to make my will
de toda mi lotería.]	And bequeath all my belongings.
¡Oyeme, linda de amor!] *Bis*	Hear me, my beautiful beloved!

3

El gato le dice al ratón, sin caridad.	The cat said to the mouse, without charity.
El gato le dice al ratón, sin caridad.	The cat said to the mouse, without charity.
Acusa y di tus pecados;]	Confess all of your sins;
porque tienes que morir]	For you're going to meet your death
en mis dientes apretados.]	In my clenched teeth.
¡Oyeme, linda de amor!] *Bis*	Hear me, my beautiful beloved!

4

Yo me acuso que robé, sin caridad.	I accuse myself of theft, without charity.
Yo me acuso que robé, sin caridad.	I accuse myself of theft, without charity.
De un cajón de marquesote[1]]	Of a cake from a bin
no esperando confesarme]	Not expecting to confess
con tan grande sacerdote.]	To such a great priest.
¡Oyeme, linda de amor!] *Bis*	Hear me, my beautiful beloved!

5

De esta sierra a la otra sierra, sin caridad.	From this mountain to the other, without charity.
De esta sierra a la otra sierra, sin caridad.	From this mountain to the other, without charity.
¡Mueran Márquez y Mejilla,]	Death to Márquez and Mejilla,
Mueran todos queretanos,]	Death to all the *Queretanos*,
Miramón y sus hermanos![2]]	Miramón and all his brothers!
¡Oyeme, linda de amor!] *Bis*	Hear me, beautiful beloved!

[1] In Mexico the *marquesote* is made usually from rice flour. The ingredients are flour, sugar, and egg. It is baked and turns out like a sponge cake.

[2] Márquez, Mejilla, and Miramón were generals in the service of the conservatives supporting Maximilian against Juárez. The *queretanos* were from Querétaro, where the generals and Maximilian were shot. (Rubén Cobos supplied these notes.)

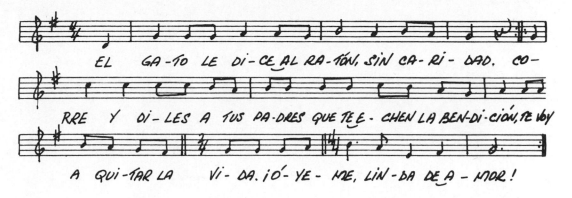

EL GA-TO LE DI-CE AL RA-TÓN, SIN CA-RI-DAD. CO-
RRE Y DI-LES A TUS PA-DRES QUE TE E-CHEN LA BEN-DI-CIÓN, TE VOY
A QUI-TAR LA VI-DA. ¡Ó-YE-ME, LIN-DA DE A-MOR!

A14. *El Caballerito* (The Little Lord)
R1735, Próspero S. Baca, age 70, Bernalillo, N.Mex., 1945, Robb. Cf. RB734, RB735.

1	1
Se acabó la flor de marzo,	The flower of March has died,
reventó la flor de abril,	The flower of April has bloomed,
se acabó la que reinaba	Dead is she who reigned
en la ciudad de Madrid.	In the city of Madrid.

1

Se acabó la flor de marzo,
reventó la flor de abril,
se acabó la que reinaba
en la ciudad de Madrid.

1

The flower of March has died,
The flower of April has bloomed,
Dead is she who reigned
In the city of Madrid.

2

—¿Dónde vas, caballerito,
dónde vas andando así?
—Voy en busca de mi esposa;
cuatro días no la ví.—

2

"Where are you going, dear sir,
Where are you going in such a hurry?"
"I am searching for my wife;
I haven't seen her for four days."

3

En una playa arenosa
una blanca sombra ví
que entre más me retiraba
más se acercaba de mí.

3

On a sandy beach
I saw a white ghost
And the more I moved away
The closer it came to me.

4

—Pues tu esposa es muerta ya,
es verdad que yo la ví,
cuatro duques la han paseado
por la ciudad de Madrid.

4

"Well, your wife is dead,
It's true for I saw her,
Four dukes have taken her
Through the city of Madrid."

5

—Cásate, caballerito,
cásate, no estés así.
El primer niño que tengas,
ponle el nombre como a mí.

5

"Get married, dear sir,
Get married, don't continue like this.
The first child that you have,
Name it after me."

SE_A-CA-BÓ LA FLOR DE MAR-ZO, RE-VEN-TÓ LA

FLOR DE_A-BRIL, SE_A-CA-BÓ LA QUE REI-NA-BA

EN LA CIU-DAD DE MA-DRID.

El *Caballerito* (A14) is also known as *La Playa Arenosa* and *La Aparición*. Mendoza, in commenting on this *romance*, says that it has to do with the death of the wife of King Alfonso XII but that it becomes mixed with another *romance*, *La Esposa Difunta*. Verse 3 of this song occurs in other songs (cf. A14a), sometimes as the first verse.

A14a. *La Playa Arenosa* (The Sandy Beach)
R2009, Clemente Chávez, age 68, Galisteo, N.Mex., 1943, Robb.

1
En una arenosa playa
una sombra blanca ví,
entre más me retiraba
más se acercaba de mí.

1
I saw a white ghost
On a sandy beach,
And the more I moved away
The closer it got to me.

2
En una playa arenosa
una sombra blanca ví.
¿qué camino agarraría?
ya de vista la perdí.

2
I saw a white ghost
On a sandy beach.
What road might it take?
Now I've lost it from sight.

3
—¿Adónde vas, caballerito?
alejándote de mí.
—Voy en busca de mi esposa
que hace tiempo que no la ví.

3
"Where are you going, dear sir,
Moving away from me?"
"I'm going in search of my wife
Whom I haven't seen for a long time."

4
—Ya tu esposa ya está muerta,
muy cierto, es que yo le ví.
Cuatro duques la llevaban
en la ciudad de Madrid.

4
"Your wife is dead now,
It's true, because I saw it.
Four dukes carried her
In the city of Madrid.

5
La tumba que ella llevaba
era de oro y de marfil,
el túnico que llevaba
era raso en carmesí.

5
The tomb that she had
Was of gold and ivory,
The tunic that she was wearing
Was of crimson satin."

6

—Los abrazos que le daba yo
a la tierra se los dí,
la boquita que besaba
un gusano en verde, sí.

6

"The embraces that I gave her
I gave to the earth,
The mouth that I kissed
Was turned green by a worm."

7

—Cásate, caballerito,
cásate, no estés así;
y el primer niño que tengas
ponle el nombre como a mí.—

7

"Get married, dear sir,
Get married, don't be that way;
And to the first child that you have
Give the same name as mine."

8

Reventó la flor de mayo,
se secó la flor de abril,
se acabó la que reinaba
en la ciudad de Madrid.

8

The May flower has bloomed,
The April flower has dried up,
Gone is she who reigned
In the city of Madrid.

A15. *La Manzana* (The Apple)
   R1753, Próspero S. Baca, age 70, Bernalillo, N.Mex., 1945, Robb.

1

Manzana, quien te comiera,
acabada de cortar,
con los colores por fuera
y tu aroma singular.

1

Apple, oh, to be able to eat you,
Just after you were picked,
With your color on the outside
And your singular aroma.

2

Linda de mi vida,
prendas de mi corazón,
lo que sufre la marina,
lo padezco por tu amor.

2

Pretty girl of my life,
Darling of my heart,
What the sailor's wife suffers,
I suffer for your love.

3

Mal haya el vestido negro
y el sastre que lo cortó;
mi negrita anda de luto
sin haberme muerto yo.

3

Woe to the black dress
And to the tailor who cut it out;
My little dark girl is in mourning
Without my having died.

4

Orillas de una laguna
hay barcos de Baltazar,
donde nació el niño hermoso,
nació para navegar.

4

At the shore of the lagoon
There are ships of Baltazar,
Where the beautiful child was born,
Born to travel.

A16. *Don Gato* (Mr. Cat)
   (transcribed and translated by J. D. Robb from memory). See Appendix A.

1

Estando el señor don Gato
sentadito en un tejado.

1

Sir Don Gato the cat
Was sitting on a roof.

2

Ha recibido una carta
que si quiere ser casado
con una gata montesa,
sobrina de un gato pardo.

Refrán

Aleyalapun, aleyalapun,
¡Sobrina de un gato pardo!

] Bis

2

He received a letter
Asking if he wished to marry
A lady cat of Montesa,
The cousin of a leopard.

Refrain

Aleyalapun, aleyalapun,
The cousin of a leopard!

Don Gato (A16) is well known in Spain as examples A16a and b and the cross references below indicate. There is a marked resemblance between the New Mexico melody given here and the Spanish version numbered A16b, one of the few such instances in which the melody can possibly be traced toward its Spanish origin. (Cf. also A17.)

Below is a rhymed English version of *Don Gato* based on A16 and the following examples. (See also Appendix A.)

1

Don Gato the cat, one sunny day,
Was seated upon the roof, they say,
When they handed him a letter,
When they handed him a letter.
The letter was from a lady cat and
Contained a proposal quite solemn.
In his surprise he fell off the roof
And fractured his vertebral column.

Refrain
Aleyalapun, aleyalapun,
A cat has nine lives and we but one.
Aleyalapun, aleyalapun,
A cat has nine lives and we but one.

2

The doctor he came and gave him pills
And told him to take them for his ills
But he didn't want to do it,
But he didn't want to do it.
At midnight he died. They took him out.
At Fishmarket Street, so it's stated,
So strong was the odor of the fish
Don Gato was resuscitated.

Refrain
Aleyalapun, aleyalapun,
A cat has nine lives and we but one.
Aleyalapun, aleyalapun,
A cat has nine lives and we but one.

A16a. *El Señor Don Gato* (The Lord Sir Cat)
Mendoza 9d (p. 184), *ca.* 1946, Cobos. Cf. Schindler 14a (Parte Musical no. 193).

1

Estaba el señor don Gato
en silla de oro sentado,
calzando media de seda
y zapatito bordado.

1

There was a lord, Sir Cat,
Seated in a gilded chair,
Wearing silk stockings
And little embroidered slippers.

2

Llegó su compadre un día
y le dijo si quería ser casado
con una gata morisca
que andaba por el tejado.

2

One day his friend dropped by
And asked if he'd like to marry
A Moorish lady cat
Who was walking by on the roof.

3

El gato por verla pronto
cayó del tejado abajo;
se ha rompido tres costillas,
se ha descoyuntado un brazo.

3

The cat on suddenly seeing her
Fell down off the roof;
He broke three ribs
And dislocated an arm.

4

Venga, venga pronto el médico,
sobador, y cirujano
que venga el doctor don Carlos.

4

Hurry and get the doctor,
The masseur, and the surgeon,
Get Dr. Don Carlos.

5

El doctor don Carlos manda
que maten una gallina
y le hagan sus buenos caldos.

5

Dr. Don Carlos orders
That they kill a hen
And make him some good broth.

6	6
Otra día por la mañana amaneció el gato muerto. Los ratones de alegría se visten de colorado.	The next day in the morning The cat woke up dead. The mice in their joy Dressed in their gayest clothes.
7	7
Las gatas se ponen luto, los gatos capotes largos, y los gatitos chiquitos dicen: —miau, miau, miau.	The she-cats put on mourning, The he-cats long cloaks, And the little cats Said: "meow, meow, meow."

A16b. *Don Gato*

    Matos 8a (Parte Literaria, p. 77), Algete, Spain, 1951, Matos. Cf. Matos 8a (Parte Musical, p. 78, 2 variants).

1	1
Estaba el señor don gato (¡Olé, pun, catapún!) sentadito en su tejado, (¡Olé, pun, catapún!)	There was a lord, Sir Cat, (¡Olé, pun, catapún!) Seated on his rooftop, (¡Olé, pun, catapún!)
2	2
y ha recibido una carta que si quiere ser casado con una gata montesa, sobrina de un gato pardo.	And he received a letter Which asked if he'd like to get married To a cat from Montesa, The cousin of a gray cat.
3	3
Al recibir esta carta se ha caído del tejado. Se ha roto siete costillas, el espinazo, y el rabo.	On receiving this letter He fell off the roof. He broke seven ribs, His spine, and his tail.
4	4
Ya lo llevan a enterrar por la calle del pescado, y el olor de la sardina el gato ha resucitado.	They took him out to bury him Through Fish Market Street, And with the odor of the sardines The cat was resuscitated.

E - STA - BA EL SE - ÑOR DON GA - TO IO - LÉ, PUN, CA - TA - PÚN! SEN - TA - DI - TO EN SU TE - JA - DO IO - LÉ, PUN, CA - TA - PÚN!

A17.   *A Comparison of Two Songs*

A1.   *Canción del Fraile*   *They Fed the Pig in the Parlor*

Mambrú, señores míos,	They fed the pig in the parlor,
pues ya se va a casar	They fed the pig in the parlor,
con una dama hermosa	They fed the pig in the parlor,
nacida en Portugal,	And that was Irish too,
nacida en Portugal,	And that was Irish too,
nacida en Portugal.	And that was Irish too.

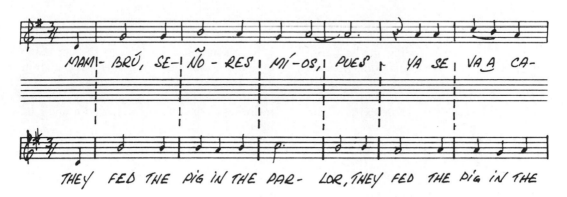

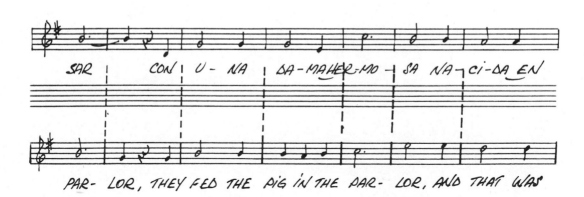

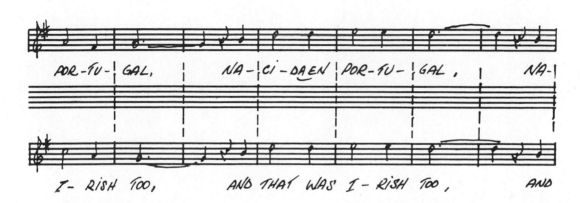

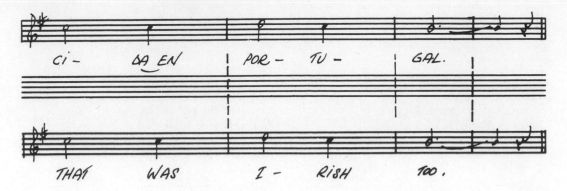

I learned "They Fed the Pig in the Parlor" in my early youth in Minneapolis, probably about 1904. That the melody of the two refrains is identical is curious and illustrates the common practice of borrowing a good tune and using it for a different and unrelated text.

Each song has four lines to the verse and a two-line refrain. Each melody has four measures to a line. The melodies of the two verses are recognizably similar, while the melodies of the refrains, as stated above, are identical.

B. *Corrido*

Like the *romance*, the *corrido* is a narrative ballad. Unlike the *romance*, it deals with ordinary people and their adventures or misadventures. It seems to have originated in Mexico, at least in the form in which it is encountered in the Southwest. Most of the *corridos* have been composed within the last century and a half, in contrast to the *romances*, many of which are centuries old.

Corridos have several peculiar distinguishing features. One is an emphasis on accuracy of detail. A *corrido* often begins with the exact date and year of the event commemorated in the song. These dates are often confirmed for us by references in the text to ox trains, political campaigns, even recently to automobiles and telephones, or more specifically to murders, which are a matter of record in the courts.

Another characteristic often found in the *corridos* is a final verse or verses in which the singer or composer will give his name, or a final verse beginning with the words *Vuela, vuela palomita* (Fly, fly little dove). This type of verse is known as a *despedida*, or farewell. Sometimes the *despedida* introduces a playful note at the end of a grimly tragic ballad, as in the following:

> Fly, fly, little dove
> Stop in that cypress tree.

> If you like, my friends,
> I will sing it again for you.

At other times the *despedida* includes a moral. The variety of imagination displayed in *despedidas* is in fact one of the most attractive features of the *corrido* (see Appendix C).

The *corrido* basically consists of a series of *coplas*, or four-line verses with eight syllables to the line; normally it rhymes. Often the last line or the last two lines are repeated. In some respects the *corrido* resembles the *indita* (see Section F). Terrence L. Hansen has provided an excellent brief description of the *corrido* in his article "Corridos of Southern California" (Hansen 6a and 6b).

A number of *corridos* are included in Section I under "Occupations" because of their subject matter (I6, I16, I17, I18, I18c, I23, I29). I have done this deliberately because it is well to remember that the minority groups, including the Mexican Americans or Spanish Americans or mestizos or chicanos, by whatever name they are called, were partners with the so-called Anglos in the adventurous nineteenth century in the Southwest.

The *corrido* and *canción* are the most numerous types of Hispanic music, and appropriately they deal largely with two great themes: the *corrido* with death, the *canción* with love.

B1. *Guadalupe Rayos*
R78, J. Gallegos, age 64, Abiquiu, N.Mex., 1946, Robb. Cf. R118, R1714, Mendoza 9e (p. 201).

1
Yo soy Guadalupe Rayos,
traigo en peligro mi vida;
ya escondido del Gobierno,
voy a ver a mi querida.

2
Su querida lo recibe
con un abrazo muy tierno,
—Guadalupe de mi vida,
te anda buscando el Gobierno.—

1
I am Guadalupe Rayos,
My life is in danger;
While hiding from the Government,
I am going to see my sweetheart.

2
His sweetheart greets him
With a tender embrace,
"Guadalupe, my life,
The Government is looking for you."

<table>
<tr>
<td>

3
Y Guadalupe le dice:
—Yo me defenderé con empeño,
yo no le temo a la muerte,
ni a las tropas del Gobierno.—

</td>
<td>

3
And Guadalupe says to her:
"I shall defend myself with boldness,
I am not afraid of death,
Nor of the government troops."

</td>
</tr>
</table>

4 Pablo dice a Guadalupe: —Ahora ¿qué es lo que hacemos? ya todititos corrieron, usted dirá si corremos.—	4 Pablo says to Guadalupe: "Now, what shall we do? Already they have all run away, You decide if we too should run away."
5 Y Guadalupe le dice: —No venimos a correr, hoy nos damos de balazos hasta morir o vencer.—	5 And Guadalupe tells him: "We didn't come to run away, Today we shall fight Until death or victory."
6 Llegan y tocan la puerta, sale Guadalupe a ver; le dieron las buenas noches y preguntaron por él.	6 (The troops) arrive and knock at the door, Guadalupe goes out to see; They said good evening And asked for him.
7 Y Guadalupe les dice, les responde en alta voz: —Yo soy Guadalupe Rayos, por la voluntad de Dios.—	7 And Guadalupe tells them, Answers them in a loud voice: "I am Guadalupe Rayos, By the will of God."
8 Volaron las palomitas de la casa a la morada, —No llores, madre querida, al cabo no me hacen nada.—	8 The little doves flew From the house to their own home, "Don't cry, mother dear, Anyway they will not harm me."
9 Su querida va y le dice: —Válgame la Virgen Santa, si no te matan aquí, te llevan para Solimanca.—	9 His sweetheart goes and tells him: "Blessed be the Sainted Virgin, If they do not kill you here, They'll take you to Solimanca."
10 Caballo prieto mentado, no se te olviden tus mañas, ahí te dejo ese hombrecito nacido de mis entrañas.	10 Renowned black horse, Do not forget your ways, There I leave you that little man Born of my own flesh and blood.
11 —No llores, madre querida, no llores, niña del cielo; va a morir tu hijo querido, al cabo no es el primero.—	11 "Do not cry, mother dear, Do not cry, child of heaven; Your beloved son is going to die, But he is not the first one."

12	12
Volaron las palomitas	The little doves flew away
con una voz muy sonora:	Saying, with a very harmonious voice,
—Ser valiente cuesta mucho,	"To be brave is very costly,
cuídense de malas horas.	Take care in your bad hours."

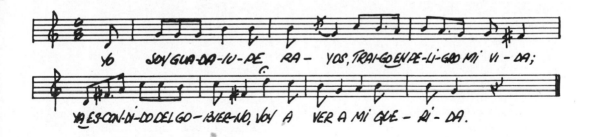

B1a. *Guadalupe Rallos*
R118, Próspero S. Baca, age 72, Bernalillo, N.Mex., 1947, Robb.

1	1
Adiós, Guadalupe Rallos,	Good-bye, Guadalupe Rallos,
traigo en peligro mi vida,	My life is in danger,
escondido del Gobierno,	A fugitive from the Government,
vengo a ver a mi querida.	I come to see my mistress.

2	2
Lo recibió su querida	His mistress received him
con un abrazo muy tierno:	With a tender embrace:
—Válgame Dios, Guadalupe,	"Dear Lord, Guadalupe,
te anda buscando el Gobierno.—	The Government is looking for you."

3	3
Su mamá se lo decía:	His mother said to him:
—Válgame la Virgen Santa,	"Help me, Holy Virgin,
y si ahora no te matan,	If they don't kill you now,
te llevan para Salamanca.—	They will take you to Salamanca."

4	4
Le responde Guadalupe:	Guadalupe answers her:
—No llores tú, mamacita,	"Don't cry, dear mother,
esta vida que yo tengo	This life that I have
sólo mi Dios me la quita.—	Only my God can take it from me."

5	5
Su mamá se lo decía:	His mother said to him:
—Válgame mi hijo querido,	"Help me, my dear son,
ya están cantando los gallos,	The roosters are already crowing,
nunca te quedes dormido.—	Don't be caught unprepared."

6

Le responde Guadalupe
con una voz muy sonora:
—El ser hombre cuesta mucho
con cuidado y malas horas.—

7

Le trajeron su caballo
ensillado y enfrenado,
su carabina de doce,
su sombrero galentado.

8

De allí se puso en camino
al lugar que había pensado,
donde había sido perseguido
por toditito el estado.

9

Entre las once y las doce
llegó a la casa mentada
hablándole a su querida
cuando ya estaba acostada.

10

Llegan y tocan la puerta,
sale Guadalupe a ver.
Le dieron las buenas noches
y preguntaron por él.

11

Guadalupe les responde
con valor y en alta voz:
—Yo soy Guadalupe Rallos
por la voluntad de Dios.—

12

Y le dice el comandante:
—Tienes que darte por reo.—
Le contestó Guadalupe:
—¿Desde cuándo andan con eso?—

13

Echaron mano a las armas
para quererle golpear;
les contestó Guadalupe:
—No se les vaya a voltear.—

14

Decía Guadalupe Rallos
a la hora de los balazos:
—Me he salido de aguaceros
cuanto más de nublinazos.—

6

Guadalupe answers her
With a sonorous voice:
"Being a man costs much
in caution and sleepless hours."

7

They brought him his horse
Saddled and bridled,
His twelve-shot carbine,
His lace-trimmed hat.

8

From there he headed
For the place he'd been thinking of,
Where he had been chased from
Over the entire state.

9

Between eleven to twelve
He arrived at the notorious house
Calling to his mistress
Who was already in bed.

10

They arrive and knock at the door,
Guadalupe goes out to see who it is.
They said good evening
And asked for him.

11

Guadalupe answers them
With courage and in a loud voice,
"I am Guadalupe Rallos
By the will of God."

12

And the commander tells him:
"You must give yourself up as a prisoner."
Guadalupe answered him:
"Since when do you tell me that?"

13

They put their hands to their guns
Because they wanted to beat him;
Guadalupe answered them:
"Don't try it."

14

Guadalupe Rallos said,
When the bullets began to fly,
"I have come out of thunderstorms
And plenty of dark clouds."

15	15
Vuela, vuela, palomita,	Fly, fly, little dove,
párate en esa barranca,	Stop in that gully,
todavía sobran casquillos	There are still too many
para esos de Salamanca.	For those from Salamanca.
16	16
Le decía su compadre:	His companion said to him:
—Compadre, ¿qué es lo que hacemos?	"Compadre, what shall we do?
Pues ya toditos se fueron,	Now they have all gone,
Usted dirá si corremos.—	You say whether or not we run."
17	17
Le contestó Guadalupe:	Guadalupe answered him:
—No venimos a correr,	"We didn't come here to run,
nos echaremos balazos	We will shoot
hasta morir o vencer.—	Until we die or conquer."
18	18
Corra, corra, caballito,	"Run, run, little horse,
no se te olviden tus maños,	Don't forget your nosebag."
que ahí les dijo un hombrecito	That is what a little man said to them,
nacido de mis entrañas.	The son born of my body.
19	19
Vuela, vuela, palomita,	Fly, fly, little dove,
nunca dejes de volar,	Never stop flying,
que el ser hombre cuesta mucho,	For being a man costs a lot,
despacito y sin menear.	Slowly and without making a noise.

A DIOS, GUA-DA-LU-PE RA-LLOS, TRAI-GO EN PE-LI-GRO MI VI-DA, ES-CON-DI-DO DEL GO-BIER-NO, VEN-GO A VER A MI QUE-RI-DA.

B2. *Teodoro Barajas*
  R1403, Juan Griego, age 46, Albuquerque, N.Mex., 1956, Robb.

1	1
Señores, tengan presente,	Gentlemen, take heed,
mucha atención y cuidado,	Pay attention and note that
murió Teodoro Barajas	Teodoro Barajas has died
en un día muy señalado.	On an appointed day.
2	2
Estos eran dos amigos,	There were two friends,
de mucha resignación;	Of strong wills;

donde querían robaban,
y sin mucha resolución.

Wherever they went they robbed
Without much concern.

3

Salieron de las Moritas
dirigidos a las laderas,
no más lo estaban cuidando
con una amostralladora.

3

They left Las Moritas
And took to the hills,
While someone was hunting them
With a machine gun.

4

Como a las ocho o las nueve
tocó Teodoro el clarín.
—Muchachos, yo no les corro,
aquí prefiero morir.—

4

Sometime around eight or nine
Teodoro blew the trumpet.
"Boys, I will not run from them,
I prefer to die here."

5

Como a las ocho o las nueve
oí un grito de repente,
—¡Arriba, arriba, muchachos,
Barajas viene con gente!—

5

Sometime around eight or nine
I heard a sudden shout.
"To arms! To arms, boys!
Barajas comes with his people."

6

El capitán de los mochos[1]
le dió vergüenza correr.
—¡Yo le hago frente a Barajas,
hasta morir o vencer!—

6

The captain of the soldiers
Was ashamed to run.
"I will face Barajas,
Until I die or prevail!"

7

Se agarraron tiro a tiro
como gallos con navajas.
Para hombrecitos de veras
allí está Teodoro Barajas.

7

They exchanged shots
Like fighting cocks armed with blades.
This Teodoro Barajas
Is a real man.

8

Se agarraron tiro a tiro
pero Dios le repartía
y a Barajas le tocó,
pues así le convenía.

8

They kept exchanging fire
But God had decided
That Barajas should die,
This was his fate.

9

Barajas fué muy temido
por donde quiera que andaba.
Barajas estaba muerto
todavía los asustaba.

9

Barajas was feared
Wherever he went.
Though Barajas was dead,
He still frightened them.

10

De México lo pidieron
vivo, muerto, o retratado,
porque conocer querían
ese valiente amado.

10

In Mexico City they wanted him
Alive, dead, or photographed,
Because they wanted to see
That brave and beloved man.

11

Adiós, mi cuate Barajas,
ya hiciste tu última hazaña.

11

Farewell, my buddy Barajas,
You have done your last feat.

[1] According to Rubén Cobos, Mexican soldiers were called *mochos* or *pelones* because of their crew cuts.

Ahora cuando me agarren,
quién sabe cómo me vaya.

Now when they catch me,
Who knows what will happen to me.

12
¡Ay, qué bonita es la plata!
pero más bonito el oro.
Aquí se acaba el corrido
del valiente hombre Teodoro.

12
Oh, how pretty is silver,
But gold is even prettier.
Here concludes this corrido
About the brave man, Teodoro.

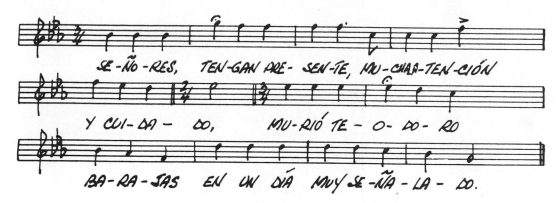

SE-ÑO-RES, TEN-GAN PRE- SEN-TE, MU-CHAA-TEN-CIÓN

Y CUI-DA - DO, MU-RIÓ TE - O- DO- RO

BA-RA-JAS EN UN DÍA MUY SE-ÑA-LA- DO.

In the recording the first verse was omitted.
The ballad is put into the mouth of Barajas'
partner in crime.

B3. *Jesús Leal*
R369, J. Gallegos, Abiquiu, N.Mex., 1947, Robb.

1
El día veinte y ocho de enero
no me quisiera acordar
cuando llegó Félix Alba
a prender a Jesús Leal.

1
The twenty-eighth day of January
I prefer not to recall
When Felix Alba came
To arrest Jesús Leal.

2
Preguntó quién era él,
que si cómo se llamaba,
que con tanta libertad
y moralidad se paseaba.

2
He asked who was he,
What was his name,
Who with such freedom
And confidence was strolling by.

3
—Yo soy un brasterito
que ha venido a comerciar.
Si quiere saber mi nombre,
yo me llamo Jesús Leal.

3
"I am a stranger
Who has come to do business.
If you want to know my name,
My name is Jesús Leal."

4
—Ello que se da por preso
porque lo vengo a llevar.
Pues me han dicho que aquí anda
el mentado Jesús Leal.

4
"Give yourself up
For I have come to take you.
They have told me that here is
The famous Jesús Leal."

5

—Pues usted me dice mucho,
pero no me ha de llevar.
Para que usted a mí me lleve
la vida le ha de costar.—

5

"Well, you talk a lot,
But you won't take me.
In order for you to take me
You must lose your life."

6

Al llegar a la garita,
su corazón le avisaba
por que don Félix Peña
ya toda su tropa armada.

6

Approaching the garrison,
His heart advised him
That Don Felix Peña
Had all his troops ready.

7

Lo pasaron por la plaza
para la cárcel nacional.
Y dice don Félix Alba, —Aquí
traigo a Jesús Leal.—

7

They marched him through the plaza
On the way to the national jail.
And says Don Felix Alba,
"Here I bring you Jesús Leal."

8

Al entrar a la capilla,
estaba un Cristo Divino,
y dice don Félix Alba,
—Este ha de ser tu padrino.—

8

At the entry to the chapel,
There was a divine Christ,
And Don Felix Alba says,
"He shall be your sponsor."

9

Cinco balazos le dieron
al lado del corazón,
y Jesús Leal les decía,
—Tírenmelos con valor.—

9

Five bullets they fired at him
On the side of his heart,
And Jesús Leal said to them,
"Shoot me bravely."

10

Adiós, Jesusito Leal,
amigo y fiel verdadero.
Estos versos te compuse
el veinte y ocho de enero.

10

Good-bye, dear Jesús Leal,
Good and loyal friend.
These verses I composed for you
On the twenty-eighth of January.

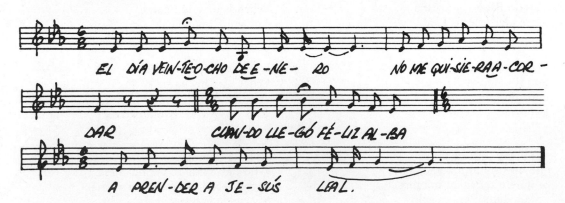

Examples B3 through B5 are ballads of death by execution. Death before a firing squad was fairly common during the Mexican Rev-olution, if one is to judge from the songs devoted to this subject. Mendoza, in his *Lírica Narrativa de México*, lists under the title *Fusilados* no less than eight *corridos* dealing with such executions for desertion, for what became known as "fragging" (the killing of one's commanding officers), and other offenses (Mendoza 9e, pp. 165–80). The word *brasterito* in verse 3 is a colloquialism derived from *forastero* (stranger) thus: *forasterito, frasterito, brasterito.*

B4. *Luis Arcos*
   R1402, Juan Griego, age 46, Albuquerque, N.Mex., 1956, Robb.

1

Luis Arcos fué ejecutado
según era su sentencia,
el día seis de noviembre
del mil novecientos treinta.

1

Luis Arcos was executed
In accordance with his sentence,
The sixth day of November
Of nineteen hundred thirty.

2

Lo ejecutaron las leyes
que gobiernan en el estado.
Pagó con su propia vida
tres vidas que había quitado.

2

The laws executed him
That govern in the state (Texas).
He paid with his own life for the
Three lives which he took.

3

Se fué por su carabina
y volvió inmediatamente.
Al primero que asegura
fué a don Luciano Valiente.

3

He went for his carbine
And immediately returned.
The first one he secured
Was Don Luciano Valiente.

4

Se viene José de allá,
—Y aquí sí serás valiente
y ahora cambiamos de vida
o no me llamo Valiente.—

4

Then José comes to him,
"Let's see how brave you are
And now we exchange lives
Or my name is not Valiente."

5

Se agarraron a balazos
y José fué más ligero.
Con una bala tercera
pues le agujeró el sombrero.

5

They exchanged bullets
And José was quicker.
With his third shot
He made a hole in his hat.

6

Se siguieron disparando
sobre los cuerpos tendidos.
Tuvo más suerte Luis Arcos,
cayó José mal herido.

6

They continued shooting
Over the dead bodies.
Luis Arcos had more luck,
José fell badly wounded.

7

Cayó José mal herido.
Le trajeron al doctor,
dice, —Me voy con mi padre,
no me curen, por favor.—

7

José fell badly wounded.
They brought him to the doctor,
He says, "I go with my father,
Don't cure me, please."

8

Dejando a los tres tendidos,
Arcos fué a presentar.
—Pues ya he matado tres hombres,
váyanlos a levantar.—

8

Leaving the three dead,
Arcos went to turn himself in.
"I have killed three men,
Go pick them up."

9

Allí pobrecitas familias
lloraban sin compasión [?]
de ver a los tres tendidos,
se estremecía el corazón.

9

Then the poor families
Cried without consolation
To see the three dead,
Their hearts saddened.

10

Después de mucho debate
y mucho de federal
lo sentenció el gran jurado
a la pena capital.

10

After much debating
And a lot of federal (courts)
The grand jury sentenced him
To capital punishment.

11

Arcos nunca mostró miedo
ni mostró arrepentimiento.
Se mantuvo muy sereno
hasta el último momento.

11

Arcos never showed fear
Nor did he show repentance.
He remained very serene
Until the last moment.

12

Le preguntan qué deseaba
en sus últimos momentos:
—Que me canten *La Paloma*
para morir más contento.

12

They asked what he wanted
In his last moments:
"Let them sing *La Paloma* for me
So that I can die happier."

LUS AR-COS FUÉ E-JE-CU-TA-DO SE-GÚN E-
RA SU SEN-TEN-CIA, EL DÍ-A SEIS DE NO-
VIEM-BRE DEL MIL NO-VE-CIEN-TOS TREIN-TA.

B5. *Valentín de la Sierra* (Valentín of the Mountain)
R1920, F. Espinosa et al., Chililí, N.Mex., 1963, Robb.

1

Voy a cantar un corrido
de un amigo de mi tierra
llamaba José Valentín,
que fué fusilado y colgado en la sierra.

1

I'm going to sing a ballad
About a friend from my country.
He was called José Valentin,
And was shot and hung in the mountains.

2 No me quisiera acordar y era una tarde de invierno, cuando por su mala suerte cayó Valentín en manos del gobierno.	**2** I don't want to remember. It was a winter afternoon When, by his bad luck, Valentín fell into the hands of the government.
3 Y el coronel le decía: —¿Cuál es la gente que manda? Son ochocientos soldados que tienen su tierra en la hacienda de Violanda.—	**3** And the colonel said to him: "Who is it that gives the orders? There are eight hundred soldiers Holding their ground on Violanda's hacienda."
4 El coronel le decía: —¿Cuál es la gente que guía? Son ochocientos soldados en la tierra de Mariano Violanda.—	**4** The colonel said to him: "Who is it that he commands? There are eight hundred soldiers On the land of Mariano Violanda."
5 Valentín como era hombre de coraje les dió nada: —Yo soy de los meros machos que han inventado la revolución.—	**5** Valentín, since he was a man Of courage, told them nothing: "I am one of those brave men Who have invented the revolution."
6 El coronel le decía: —Yo te concedo el indulto; pero me basta decir cual es el jurado y la causa que busco.—	**6** The colonel said to him: "I can grant you a pardon; I need only indicate The evidence and the verdict that I look for."
7 Antes de llegar al cerro Valentín quiso llorar. —Virgen mía de Guadalupe, por tu religión me van a matar.—	**7** Before going to the hill Valentín wanted to cry. "My Virgen of Guadalupe, For your religion they are going to kill me."
8 Vuela, vuela palomita, párate en aquel portil. Estas son las mañanitas de un hombre valiente que fué Valentín.	**8** Fly away, fly away little dove, Stop in at that passageway. These are the verses Of a brave man that was Valentín.

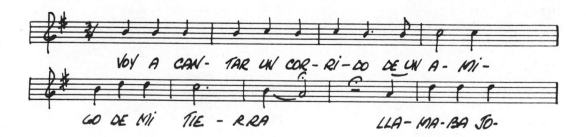

SÉ VAL-EN-TÍN, QUE FUÉ FU-SI-LA-DO Y COL-

GA-DO EN LA SIE - RRA.

This *corrido* is sung as a duet in thirds with
the second voice a third higher than the
melody as indicated.

B6. *Los Ortegas*
R2006, Clemente Chávez, age 88, Galisteo, N.Mex., 1963, Robb.

1	1
Año de 1802	Year of 1802
¿qué van a cantar?	What are you going to sing?
Mataron a los Ortegas,	They killed the Ortegas,
ya no los oirán mentar.	Now you won't hear of them anymore.
2	2
Eran cuatro compañeros	There were four companions
y tres eran hermanitos,	And three of them were brothers,
los que hicieron el asalto	Those who made the assault
en el rancho de Palmitos.	On the Palomitos ranch.
3	3
Llegaron como paisanos	They came as neighbors
tratándoles de comprar	Trying to buy from them
una cuartilla de azúcar	A quarter pound of sugar
para poderlos robar.	So that they could rob them.
4	4
Decía Gorgonio Navarros	Gorgonio Navarros said
—No vengan a molestar	"Don't come to bother me
por tres centavos de azúcar	For three cents worth of sugar
yo no me he de levantar.—	I'm not going to get up."
5	5
Respondieron los bandidos	The bandits replied
con muchísimo valor:	With a lot of courage:
—Véndenos, pues, una libra	"Sell us a pound, then
si usted nos hace el favor.—	If you will please."

6

Al abrir la media puerta
lo saludaron primero:
—Caíste a nuestras manos,
entréganos el dinero.—

6

When he opened the door halfway
They immediately greeted him:
"You have fallen into our hands,
Give us the money."

7

Decía Gorgonio Navarros
en una voz afligida:
—Llévense todo el dinero
y no me quiten la vida.—

7

Gorgonio Navarros said
In an anguished voice:
"Take all the money
But don't take my life."

8

Ya amarraron a Gorgonio
junto con la cocinera,
y el pobre de este Gorgonio
se salió por la tronera.

8

They tied up Gorgonio
Together with the cook,
And this poor old Gorgonio
Went out through an opening.

9

Al brincar por el potrero
con gusto y con alegría,
como llevaban dinero
tenían que *José, María.*

9

On jumping through the pasture land
With pleasure and happiness,
Because they had money
They thanked *Joseph* and *Mary.*

10

Llegó Martín a la casa
con el saco de dinero,
y el mismo día los prendió
el comandante Cordero.

10

Martín arrived home
With the bag of money,
And the same day
Comandante Cordero caught them.

11

El comandante Cordero,
hombre de capacidad,
—Entreguen todo el dinero,
yo les doy su libertad.—

11

Comandante Cordero,
A very capable man, said:
"Hand over all the money,
And I'll let you go."

12

Decía Concepción Delgado,
arrizcándose el sombrero,
—Al cabo siempre nos matan,
no entreguen todo el dinero.

12

Concepción Delgado said,
Raising up her hat,
"In the end they'll still kill us
Don't give them all the money."

13

—No llores, madre querida,
que me atormenta tu voz,
aquí terminan mis días,
sería voluntad de Dios.

13

"Don't cry, dear mother,
Your voice torments me,
My days end here,
It must be the will of God.

14

No llores, madre querida,
te lo digo con esmero
al cabo si a mí me matan
te quedas con el dinero.

14

"Don't cry, dear mother,
I'm telling you the truth,
In the end if they kill me
You'll be left with the money."

B7. *Luisito Núñez*
R2005, Clemente Chávez, Galisteo, N.Mex., 1942, Robb.

1 Año de 1895 infeliz me tomaron prisionero en México, Silver City.	**1** In the unlucky year of 1895 They took me prisoner In Mexico, Silver City.
2 Hombres de mucho valor allí me agarraron durmiendo, ya se tomaron mis armas y ahorita me fuí venciendo.	**2** Men of great courage Seized me there while I was sleeping, They took my weapons And now I was under their control.
3 Ya lo llevan a la cárcel con grillos y cadenas, Luisito se desespera de verse en tan crueles penas.	**3** Now they are taking him to jail With irons and chains, Luisito is despairing Seeing himself in such bad trouble.
4 Salió don Francisco Núñez a hablar con el general: —Te pagaremos en plata y dale su libertad.—	**4** Don Francisco Núñez went out To talk to the general: "We will pay you in silver To give him his freedom."
5 Ya lo meten a la cárcel a leerle su sentencia, que debe de ser ahorcado por esas leyes secretas.	**5** Now they put him in jail To read him his sentence, He is to be hanged By those secret laws.
6 Ya le dice el general: —Tu plata es en realidad, ya no veniste a tiempo, ya no es hora de arreglar.—	**6** The general now says: "Your silver is real But you didn't come in time. Now is no time to make such arrangements."
7 Salió don Francisco Núñez con un profundo dolor: —¡Ay! hijito de mi vida, ya no alcanzaste perdón.	**7** Don Francisco Núñez Left with profound sorrow: "Oh, dear son of my life, You didn't get your pardon."
8 —Padrecito de mi vida, no me acongoja el morir, déjeme morir ahorcado a pagar por lo que fuí.—	**8** "Dear Father of my life, Death does not vex me, Let me die hanged To pay for what I was."
9 Allí viene bramando el tren triste, dobla la campana; viene por Luisito Núñez a las diez de la mañana.	**9** Rumbling, there comes The sad train, the bell tolls; It comes for Luisito Núñez At ten in the morning.

<table>
<tr><td>

10

Ya lo embarcan en el tren,
lo sacan para el mesquital,
ya Luisito se despide
de todos en general.

</td><td>

10

They now put him on the train,
They take him out to the mesquite patch,
Now Luisito says good-bye
To everyone in general.

</td></tr>
<tr><td>

11

Ya lo suben al cadalso,
y ya le dejaron caer,
cuatro balazos le dieron
para acabarlo de matar.

</td><td>

11

They make him go up on the scaffold,
And they let him fall,
They shot him four times
To finish killing him.

</td></tr>
<tr><td>

12

Amigo Carlos Contreras
¿dónde te andas escondido?
Mira que tu amigo Luis
ahorita se va muriendo.

</td><td>

12

Friend Carlos Contreras
Where are you hiding?
Look, your friend Luis
Is this moment dying.

</td></tr>
<tr><td>

13

Amigo Carlos Contreras
¿dónde te vas a embarcar?
Mira que tu amigo Luis
ya lo van a embalsamar.

</td><td>

13

Friend Carlos Contreras
Where are you embarking?
Look, your friend Luis
Is going to be embalmed.

</td></tr>
</table>

Diciembre, el 28, día de los
inocentes, 1942
Clemente Chávez
Galisteo, New Mexico

This *corrido* comes from Silver City, New Mexico, despite the reference in verse 1 to "Mexico, Silver City." New Mexico was from 1821 to 1846 a part of Mexico, and after it became a territory of the United States, westerners continued to refer to it as Mexico. This confusion of terms is found in other songs, an example being the English language ballad *Murphy's Ranch in Mexico* (R397), the ranch in question being the ranch owned by Lawrence G. Murphy in Lincoln County, New Mexico. Murphy was one of the protagonists in the so-called Lincoln County War.

This text was copied from a notebook, and no recording was made. In lieu of the first eight-syllable lines of the first verse Clemente Chávez simply writes one line, "Año de 1895." It should be written out as follows:

Año de mil ochocientos
noventa y cinco infeliz.

B8. *Bonifacio Torres*
RB740, Alameda, N.Mex., 1950, Cobos.

<table>
<tr><td>

1

El día primero de marzo
sucedió en esta ocasión
en la plaza de Jarales
una gran revolución.

</td><td>

1

On the first day of March
There took place on this occasion,
In the plaza of Jarales,
A great disturbance.

</td></tr>
</table>

<table>
<tr><td>

2

Llegó el oficial mayor
que es don Ignacio Aragón
a tomarme prisionero
y me llamó la atención.

3

No me pude defender;
el sábado en todo el día;
al fin me dieron la muerte
porque así me convenía.

4

Uno grito muy valiente
presumió su valentía;
entró a arrestarme a la casa
y le puse balacería.

5

Otro de los oficiales
no hallaba donde escapar;
no hay arma como el talón
sabiéndolo manejar.

6

En sus clamores decía:
—Aunque me muera burlado,
valen más vivos barbones
que muertos ya rasurados.—

7

Se juntan los oficiales
de diferentes condados;
le prenden fuego a la casa
es un plan que me jugaron.

8

Les grito a los oficiales:
—Yo no ando de lava platos;
tengo mi par de pistolas
para divertirlos un rato.—

9

Cuando vide arder mi casa
yo no tuve precaución;
—Vas a vivir o morir—
le dije a mi corazón.

10

Me gritan que me rindiera
y yo no los atendí;
me tiraron muchos balazos
y yo les correspondí.

</td><td>

2

The official mayor came,
His name was Ignacio Aragón,
To take me prisoner
And called me to attention.

3

I could not defend myself;
All day Sunday passed;
Finally they killed me
Because that was my destiny.

4

He feigned courage by giving
A gallant shout
He came to arrest me at home
And I fired shots at him.

5

Another of the officers
Couldn't find a way to escape;
There is no weapon like the heel
For one who knows how to use it.

6

Among other things he said:
"Even though they get the best of me,
It's better to be alive with a beard
Than dead and clean shaven."

7

Officers of various counties
Came together;
They set fire to the house.
It was a trick they played on me.

8

I call out to the officers:
"I'll not go and wash your dishes;
I have my pair of pistols
To entertain you for a while."

9

When I saw my house burning
I threw caution to the winds.
"Either you live or you die,"
I said to my heart.

10

They yelled to me to surrender
And I paid no attention;
They fired many shots at me
And I replied in kind.

</td></tr>
</table>

11
Como a las seis de la tarde
mi muerte la conocí;
al oir yo los balazos
en vez de llorar, me reí.

11
At about six in the afternoon
I came face to face with death.
When I heard the bullets whistling by,
Instead of weeping, I laughed.

12
El mundo se oscureció
en la sangre de un valiente;
también el sol lo sintió
en la hora de la muerte.

12
The world grew dark
In the blood of a brave man;
The sun itself mourned
In the hour of death.

13
Vuela, vuela, palomita,
mira lo que aquí pasó;
anda dile a sus amigos
que Bone Torres murió.

13
Fly, fly, little dove,
See what happened here.
Go tell your friends
That Bone Torres is dead.

14
En memoria de Bone Torres
se compuso este corrido;
lo trovó Guillermo López
por su valor distinguido.

14
In memory of Bone Torres
This ballad was composed;
It was versified by Guillermo López,
A man distinguished for his bravery.

B9. *Lucrezia*
R2088, F. McCulloch, Jr., Albuquerque, N.Mex., 1965, Robb.

1
Ya son las once de la mañana
y el carcelero no viene a abrir
la pobre celda donde entre harapos
y desengaños, voy a morir.

1
It is now eleven in the morning
And the jailer doesn't come to open
The poor cell where among rags
And disappointments I'm going to die.

2
Eran las once de la mañana
del día veinte y ocho del mes de abril
cuando por celos y desengaños
en un momento yo me perdí.

2
It was eleven in the morning
of the twenty-eighth of April
When due to jealousy and disappointment
In a moment I was lost.

3
Serán las once de la mañana
cuando a mi celda vengan a abrir
los carceleros y la justicia
que certifiquen mi mal morir.

3
It will be eleven in the morning
When to open my cell come
The jailers and the justice
Who certify my evil death.

4
Ya son las once de la mañana,
se escucha sólo largo clarín
y en este toque quizás mañana
esté marcado mi triste fin.

4
It is now eleven in the morning,
Only the sound of the bugle is heard
And by this sound perhaps tomorrow
My sad end will be noted.

5

Hoy son las once de la mañana
sólo mi madre ya piensa en mí
serán las once de la mañana
cuando ya nada quede de mí.

5

Today it is eleven in the morning
Only my mother is thinking of me
It will be eleven in the morning
When nothing remains of me.

YA SON LAS ON-CE DE LA MA-ÑA-NA
YEL CAR-CE-LE-RO NO VIE-NE A AB-
RIR LA PO-BRE CEL-DA DON-
DE EN-TRE HA-RA-POS Y DES-EN-
GA-ÑOS, VOY A MO-RIR

B10. *Carlos Saiz*
RB741, M. A. Esquibel, Las Nutrias, N.Mex., 1950, Cobos.

1

En mil novecientos siete
y enero once señalado
en la cárcel del Socorro
Carlos Saiz fué muerto ahorcado.

1

In nineteen hundred and seven
On that famous January eleventh
In the jail at Socorro
Carlos Saiz was hanged.

2

Sin duda Carlos murió
porque sentencia fué dada
por dos hombres que mató
cerquita de La Salada,
y era deuda que él debía
y no la tenía pagada.

2

There's no doubt Carlos died
Because he was sentenced
For two men whom he killed
Near the town of La Salada,
And this was debt that he owed
And had not paid.

3

Lo sacaron de la cárcel
cuando vido la horca cerca,
y le dice al oficial:
—Déjame hablar con la gente,
que les quiero suplicar
que se duelan de mi muerte.

3

They took him from the jail
And when he saw the scaffold nearby,
He said to the official:
"Let me speak to the people,
For I want to beg them
To lament my death."

4

—Porque ya vas a morir,
voy a hacerte ese favor;
por último, sin decir   ]
no te quede ese dolor.—   ] *Bis*

5

Ya se paró Carlos Saiz
a todos pidió perdón:
—Jovencitos de mi vida,
no lleguen a esta ocasión;
ésto me sucedió a mí
por un amigo traidor.

6

Un dolor nomás me queda
y adentro de mi corazón:
que Eliseo Valles viva,   ]
siendo el principal autor.   ] *Bis*

7

Un favor nomás les pido
y aunque los tenga enfadados:
que me lleven a San Juan   ]
con los padres que me han criado.] *Bis*

8

Ellos que allí me reciban   ]
y allí sea sepultado.   ] *Bis*

4

"Because you are going to die,
I will grant you this favor;
You will not suffer the sorrow
Of being denied a final word."

5

Carlos Saiz came to his end
And begged everyone's pardon:
"Young people whom I have known,
Don't come to this fate;
This happened to me
Because a friend betrayed me.

6

"I have only one regret
Within my heart:
That Eliseo Valles lives on,
For he was the author of my misfortune.

7

"I ask only one favor of you
Even if I am annoying you:
That you carry me to San Juan
To be with the parents who raised me.

8

"May they receive me there
And may I be buried there."

This is a stark, powerful narrative of the 1907 hanging of Carlos Saiz in Socorro, New Mexico, for the murder of two men. There is no moral—only a grim recital of the condemned man's last speech.

B11. *Toribio Huertas*
RB755, José Faquis, Tijeras, N.Mex., 1950, Cobos.

1

En mil ochocientos uno
lo que les voy a decir,
ahorcaron al señor Huertas
día veintiseis de abril.

2

Lo trajeron a Las Cruces
y en el tren con mucho esmero;
en la vía de California
y ahí mató a su compañero.

1

In eighteen hundred and one
As I shall tell you,
They hanged Mr. Huertas
On the twenty-sixth of April.

2

They took him to Las Cruces
By train under heavy guard;
For on the way to California
He had killed his companion.

3

Del tren fué para la cárcel
ahí lo condució su suerte;
le leyeron su sentencia:
salió sentenciado a muerte.

4

Me leyeron mi sentencia
nada tuve que decir;
ahí me entregué culpable
y ahí es preciso morir.

5

Yo no culpo al alguacil
tampoco al juez de distrito;
lo que culpo es mala fortuna
que me hizo matar a Quico.

6

Me sacaron al cadalsio
donde pude hablar poquito;
ya me dice el padre Pero:
—Dime, Toribio, ¿estás listo?—

7

Ya le dije al padre Pero:
—Permítame un momento hablar,
que para decir las cosas
se necesita pensar.

8

Señor don José Lucero
y él que me quitó la mesa,
en esta vida o en la otra
y espera tu recompensa.—

9

El día veintiseis de abril
como a las once del día,
quedó la gente asombrada
por lo que Huertas decía.

10

—Mexicanos de Las Cruces,
extraños y conocidos,
pongan experiencia
por lo que me ha sucedido.

11

Adiós, todos mis amigos,
adiós, todos mis hermanos;
yo nací para ser ahorcado
y en países americanos.

3

From the train he went to the jail
Where they led him to his fate;
They read him his sentence:
He was sentenced to death.

4

They read me my sentence
And I had nothing to say;
There I pleaded guilty
And that means death.

5

I don't blame the constable
Nor the district judge;
That which I blame is my bad luck
That made me kill Quico.

6

They took me to the scaffold
Where I could speak a few words;
And Father Pero said to me:
"Tell me Toribio, are you ready?"

7

Then I said to Father Pero:
"Permit me to speak for a moment,
So that I can say a few things
Which it is necessary to think about.

8

"Mr. José Lucero
And the one who pulled the drop,
In this life or the other
You'll pay for what you've done."

9

The twenty-sixth day of April
At about eleven in the morning
The crowd was sobered
By what Huertas said.

10

"Mexicans of Las Cruces (New Mexico),
Acquaintances and others,
Take warning
From what has happened to me.

11

"Farewell, all my friends,
Good-bye, all my brothers;
I was born to be hanged
In American lands.

12

Y en la ciudad de Camargo
ahí está mi fe de bautismo;
Toribio Huertas me llamo,
y hasta aquí fué mi destino.—

12

"And in the city of Camargo
I was baptized in the faith;
Toribio Huertas is my name,
And now here I meet my fate."

13

Me pusieron mi corbata
nada fué, nada que hablamos;
son usos que traen las leyes
y no todos las usamos.

13

They put on my noose
And there was nothing to do or say;
There are things the law requires
That not everyone complies with.

This is the ballad of another New Mexico hanging. This one took place in Las Cruces. Like *Carlos Saiz* (B10), the condemned man expresses the hope of retribution for the person he holds responsible for his fate.

Despite the usual accuracy of the *corridos* in the matter of dates, the date of 1801 in verse 1 seems questionable for verse 2 states that they took him to Las Cruces by train and Las Cruces had no railroad until some eighty years later. Also in verse 11, Toribio is quoted as saying, "I was born to die in American lands," whereas Las Cruces in 1801 was still a part of Mexico. The true date is probably 1901.

B12. *Heraclio Bernal*
"Corridos of the Mexican Border," by Brownie McNeil, in Boatright, Texas 18 (vol. 21, pp. 7–8), Texas, Brownie McNeil.

1

Pueblo de Sinaloa,
Estado de Michoacán,
Donde sacaron el orden
Para aprender a Bernal.

1

Town of Sinaloa,
State of Michoacán,
Is where they took on the order
To arrest Bernal.

2

Salió el Escuadrón del Norte
del Colegio Militar
a remontarse en la sierra
para aprender a Bernal.

2

The Squadron of the North left
The Military College
To ride into the mountains
To arrest Bernal.

3

Heraclio Bernal decía
que era hombre y no se rajaba,
que él, montado en su caballo,
no más a Dios perdonaba.

3

Heraclio Bernal said
That he was a man and didn't back down,
That he, mounted on his horse,
Gave pardon only to God.

4

Decía Heraclio Bernal
en la Hacienda de los Pericos,
que él no robaba a los pobres
no más a los puros ricos.

4

Heraclio Bernal said
At the Pericos Hacienda,
That he did not rob the poor
Only the very rich.

5

Una familia en la sierra
se hallaba muy recortada,
les dió setecientos pesos
para que se remediaran.

5

A family in the mountains
Found itself in dire need,
He gave them seven hundred pesos
So they could redeem themselves.

6

¡Qué bonito era Bernal
en su caballito oscuro!,
en medio de la Acordada
con un elegante puro.

6

How handsome was Bernal
On his dark horse,
Amidst the mounted police troop
With a nice big cigar.

7

Bonito era Bernal
en su caballo retinto,
con su pistola en la mano
peleando con treinta y cinco.

7

Bernal was handsome
On his black horse,
With his pistol in his hand
Fighting with thirty-five.

8

Vuela, vuela, palomita,
párate en ese olivo,
porque don Porfirio Díaz
lo quiere conocer vivo.

8

Fly, fly, little dove,
Light on that olive tree,
Because Don Porfirio Díaz
Wants to meet him alive.

9

Bonito era Bernal
en su caballo overo,
él no robaba a los pobres,
antes les daba dinero.

9

Bernal was handsome
On his peach-colored horse,
He didn't rob the poor,
Instead he gave them money.

10

Decía don Crispín García
el jefe de Mazatlán:
—Vénganme dos acordadas
y la Guardia Nacional.

10

Don Crispín García,
The chief of Mazatlán, said:
"Bring me two police troops
And the National Guard.

11

Vénganme dos acordadas
y la Guardia Nacional
y vamos a Durango
a traer a Heraclio Bernal.—

11

"Bring me two police troops
And the National Guard
And let's go to Durango
And bring back Heraclio Bernal."

12

Y en Mazatlán lo mataron
por traición y por detrás,
porque ese don Crispín García
era bueno para entregar.

12

And in Mazatlán they killed him
By treachery and from behind,
Because that Don Crispín García
Was good at capturing outlaws.

13

¡Ay! ricos de la costa,
ya no morirán a susto,
ya mataron a Bernal
ahora dormirán con gusto.

13

Oh, you rich people of the coast,
You will no longer die of fright,
Now they have killed Bernal
You can sleep with ease.

14

Vuela, vuela, palomita,
párate en ese nogal,
ya están los caminos solos,
ya mataron a Bernal.

14

Fly, fly, little dove,
Light on that walnut tree,
Now the roads are empty,
Now they have killed Bernal.

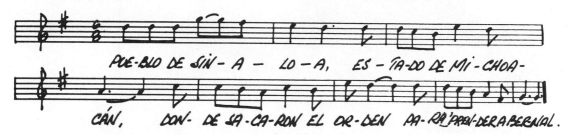

PUE-BLO DE SIN-A-LO-A, ES-TA-DO DE MI-CHOA-
CÁN, DON-DE SA-CA-RON EL OR-DEN PA-RA PREN-DER A BERNAL.

B12a. *Heraclio Bernal*
   "A Mexican Popular Ballad," by W. A. Whatley, in Dobie, Texas 18 (vol. 4, pp. 10–17), Texas, 1954, W. A. Whatley.

1

Año de noventa y cuatro
en la ciudad de Mazatlán
por primera vez se canta
la tragedia de Bernal.

1

In the year of ninety-four
In the city of Mazatlán
For the first time was sung
The tragedy of Bernal.

2

Heraclio Bernal decía
en su caballo alazán
que había de ser el jefe
de la ciudad de Mazatlán.

2

Astride his sorrel horse
Heraclio Bernal said
That he should be the mayor
Of the city of Mazatlán.

3

Heraclio Bernal decía
cuando iba para Saucillos
que en bolsa traía platas
y en la cintura casquillos.

3

When going to Saucillos
Heraclio Bernal said
That he was carrying silver in his purse
And cartridges in his belt.

4

Heraclio Bernal decía
cuando iba para Sonora,
—Este cuero que aquí traigo
lo traigo para tambora.—

4

When going to Sonora
Heraclio Bernal said,
"This hide that I carry,
I carry as a drum."

Coro
Vuela, vuela, palomita,
encarámate a aquel nopal:
di que diez mil pesos ofrecen
por la vida de Bernal.

Chorus
Fly, fly, little dove,
Perch on that cactus:
Proclaim that ten thousand pesos are offered
For the life of Bernal.

5

Una familia en la sierra
estaba muy arruinada;
y les dió quinientos pesos
para que se remediaran.

5

A family in the mountains
Was living in dire poverty;
And he gave them five hundred pesos
So they could redeem themselves.

6

Heraclio Bernal decía
cuando encontraba a un arriero
que él no robaba pobres,
antes les daba dinero.

6

Heraclio Bernal used to say
When he met a muleteer
That he didn't rob the poor,
But instead gave them money.

7

En la sierra de Durango
mató a diez gachupines
y mandó curtir los cueros
para lucirlos en botines.

7

In the mountains of Durango
He killed ten Spaniards
And had their skins tanned
To make them into boots.

8

Decía doña Bernardina,
la querida de Bernal:
—Más que la vida me cueste
yo lo mando a retratar.—

8

Said Doña Bernardina,
The sweetheart of Bernal:
"Even if it cost me my life
I shall order a portrait of him."

9

Y lo retrató entonces
en su caballo oscuro
que en medio de la acordada
se estaba fumando un puro.

9

And she had his picture taken
With him mounted on his dark horse
Surrounded by a mounted police troop
And smoking a cigar.

10

Desde Torreón de Coahuila
hasta las aguas del mar
todito aquello andaba
no lo osaban molestar.

10

From Torreón in Coahuila
To the waters of the sea
He wandered at will
And none dared to molest him.

11

En una vez en la sierra
de sorpresa lo tomaron;
a él y a Fabián el indio
en una playa los cercaron.

11

One time in the mountains
They took him by surprise;
He and Fabian the Indian
Were surrounded at a beach.

12

El indio Fabián le dijo:
—¡Pues esto no tiene fin!
Aquí nos formaron sitio
los Rochas del Copalquín.—

12

The Indian Fabian said to him:
"But this is endless!
The Rochas of Copalquín
Have us trapped!"

13

Y Heraclio Bernal decía,
en su caballo alazán:
—¡Pues ahora rompemos el sitio
y entramos a Mazatlán!—

13

And Heraclio Bernal said,
As he sat on his sorrel horse:
"Now we shall break the siege
And enter Mazatlán!"

14

Y de siete de los Rochas
que a prenderlos vinieron,
buenos y sanos a sus casas
solamente tres volvieron.

14

And of the seven Rochas
Who came to capture them
Only three returned safe and sound
To their homes again.

15

Y Heraclio Bernal decía,
ya camino de Mazatlán:

15

And Heraclio Bernal said,
As he rode toward Mazatlán:

—¡Ni un pelo nos han tumbado
y mira cómo se van!—

"They haven't touched a hair of our heads
And see what happened to them!"

16
Decía don Crispín García,
el jefe de Mazatlán:
—Vénganme dos acordadas
y la Guardia Nacional;

16
Said Don Crispin García,
The mayor of Mazatlán:
"Let me have two troops of mounted men
And the National Guard;

17
Vénganme dos acordadas
y la Guardia Nacional,
y vámonos a Durango
a traer a Heraclio Bernal.—

17
"Bring me two troops of mounted men
And the National Guard,
And let's go to Durango
And bring back Heraclio Bernal."

18
Y en Mazatlán lo mataron
por traición y por detrás,
porque ese don Crispín
era bueno para entregar.

18
And in Mazatlán they killed him
By treachery and from behind,
For this Don Crispin García
Was good at capturing people.

19
Todavía después de muerto
cuando en la caja lo tenían,
la acordada y los soldados
mucho miedo le tenían.

19
And even after he was dead
And lying in his coffin,
The troop and the soldiers
Were still afraid of him.

20
¡Ay, ricos de la costa!
¡ya no morirán de susto!
ya mataron a Bernal,
ahora dormirán a gusto.

20
Ah, you rich men of the coast!
No longer will you die of fear!
Now they have killed Bernal,
You may sleep in peace.

21
Y lloran todas las muchachas
del mineral de Mapimí:
—Ya mataron a Bernal,
ya no lo verán aquí.—

21
And all the young girls
Of the mining town of Mapimí
Weep, saying: "They killed Bernal.
He will never be seen here again."

22
Y aquí termino mi canto
pues así tuvieron final
la vida y los hechos
del gran Heraclio Bernal.

22
And here I end my song
For in this manner ended
The life and the deeds
Of the great Heraclio Bernal.

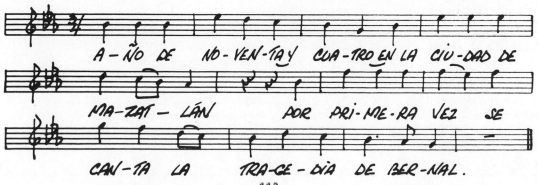

A-ÑO DE NO-VEN-TA Y CUA-TRO EN LA CIU-DAD DE MA-ZAT-LÁN POR PRI-ME-RA VEZ SE CAN-TA LA TRA-GE-DIA DE BER-NAL.

B13. *Rivera y Reyes García*
R67, Juan Sandoval, Chimayó, N.Mex., 1945, Robb.

1	**1**
En una sierra muy alta	On a lofty mountain
y al otro lado en Sonora	On the other side of Sonora
se mataron dos amigos	Two friends killed each other
por una mancornadora.	For a traitress.
2	**2**
Uno era Félix Rivera,	One was Félix Rivera,
y el otro Reyes García;	And the other was Reyes García;
¡quién había de suponer	Who, one would have supposed,
que por la patria morían!	Would have died for their country.
3	**3**
Se fueron para la cantina,	They went to the cantina,
se echaron buenos licores,	Drank some good liquor,
y se ponen a cantar	And began to sing
como buenos cantadores.	Like good singers.
4	**4**
Rivera le dijo a Reyes:	Rivera said to Reyes,
—Cántame una muy bonita,	"Sing me a pretty song,
que me quiero recordar	For I want to remember
de mi linda Ana Felita.	My pretty Ana Felita."
5	**5**
—Te cantaré la que gustes	"I'll sing what you want
y en ella te diré yo	And in it I'll tell you
que la linda Ana Felita	That pretty Ana Felita
nos ha mancornado a los dos.—	Has betrayed us both."
6	**6**
Salieron de la cantina,	They left the cantina,
se hallaron en el camino,	Found themselves in the road,
y se fueron a pelear	And they went to fight
y al otro lado del riyo.	On the other side of the river.
7	**7**
Como los dos eran hombres,	Since they were both brave men,
los dos traiban sus pistolas;	They both carried pistols;
cada uno saco la dél	Each one pulled out his own
y ahí se disparan a solas.	And both shot each other without witness.
8	**8**
Rivera cayó para atrás,	Rivera fell backwards,
con la sangre a borbollones,	With blood gushing forth,
diciéndole a su rival:	Saying to his rival:
—Y aquí se acabaron pasiones.—	"Here is the end of our passions."
9	**9**
Reyes cayó de rodillas,	Reyes fell to his knees,
como pidiendo perdón,	As if begging pardon,
—Adiós, madre de mi vida,	"Good-bye, mother of my life,
y échame tu bendición.—	Give me your blessing."

10

Decía la Ana Felita:
—¡Válgame Dios, qué hago yo,
se mataron dos amigos,
la culpa la tengo yo!

10

Ana Felita said:
"God save me, what have I done?
The two friends have killed each other,
And it is all my fault."

My recording of this song has been lost, but Vicente T. Mendoza transcribed the foregoing text from the recording. See Mendoza 9d, p. 422.

B14. *Roberto y Simón*
R1717, Próspero S. Baca, Bernalillo, N.Mex., 1945, Robb. Cf. Mendoza 9e (p. 200).

1

Andando tomando vino
José, Roberto, y Simón
pelearon en El Venado
para dar satisfacción.

1

Going around drinking wine
Joseph, Robert, and Simon
Fought to settle accounts
At the sign of The Deer.

2

Una mujer de allí vino;
ella trajo la razón
pelearon en El Venado—
José, Roberto, y Simón.

2

A woman came from there;
She was the reason
That they fought in The Deer—
Joseph, Robert, and Simon.

Coro

Pues sí, señores,
pues sí, será,
que así se mueren los hombres,
con mucha facilidad.

Chorus

Yes, gentlemen,
So it will be,
That thus men die,
With much ease.

3

Cuando llegó el comandante
Echándosele de lado
pregunta el Señor alcalde
—¿no esté aquí Simón Delgado?—

3

When the commander arrived
Taking him off to the side
The mayor asks
"Isn't Simon Delgado here?"

4

Simón como prisionero
le responde en alta voz,
—Aquí estoy a tu mandado
con la voluntad de Dios.—

4

Simon, a prisoner,
Answers him loudly,
"Here I am at your command
By the will of God."

5

Y le dice el comandante,
—Simón, dime la verdad:
¿quién eran tus compañeros?
y te doy la libertad.—

5

And the commander says to him,
"Simon, tell me the truth:
Who were your companions?
And I'll set you free."

6

Y le responde Simón,
como que le incomodaba,
— ¿Qué verdad quieres que diga
si yo solito robaba?—

6

And Simon answers him,
As if he were getting annoyed,
"What truth do you want me to tell
If I robbed all by myself?"

7

Y le dice el comandante,
—Simón, tú eres un cobarde,
no te perdona la muerte
porque has matado a mi padre.—

7

And the commander says to him,
"Simon, you're a coward,
Death doesn't pardon you
Because you killed my father."

8

Ay, le responde Simón,
haciendo muy feo modo,
—La tardanza no me gusta,
la delación me incomoda.—

8

"Aw," Simon answers him,
Making an ugly gesture,
"I don't like the delay,
The accusation bothers me."

9

Cuando salieron de allí,
dos canciones les cantó
y la mujer de Palomo
dos pesos le regaló.

9

When they left there,
He sang them two songs
And Palomo's wife
Gave him two pesos.

10

Entonces dice José,
—Pues hombre, yo no los quiero.
¿Si ya nos llevan a ahorcar
para que queremos dinero?—

10

Then José says,
"Say, man, I don't want them.
If they're taking us to hang
Why do we want money?"

11

Ya con ésta me despido
con las hojas del Simón
aquí se acaban cantando
los versitos de Simón.

11

Now with this I say good-bye
With the leaves of Simon
Here ends the singing
Of the verses of Simon.

Coro

Chorus

B15. *La Rafelita*
R2393, Juan Griego, age 61, Albuquerque, N.Mex., 1971, Robb.

1

Basilio estaba tomando
en casa de Juana García,
ya se estaba emborrachando,
ya por ser el último día.

1

Basilio was drinking
At Juana García's house,
He was getting drunk
On this, his last day.

<table>
<tr><td>

2

—Andele comadre Juana,
sírvame una botellita
para ir a ver a mis amores,
la mentada Rafelita.—

3

A mentar a Rafelita
don Reyes se encomodó;
—Basilio, no se equivoque.
Rafela la mando yo.—

4

Pues se salieron para fuera
con la intención de pelear.
Basilio pidió pistola
para poderlo encontrar.

5

Se dispararon los tiros
en aquella hora fatal.
Se han matado dos valientes
por no saberse tantear.

6

Sale Rafelita y dice:
—Válgame Dios, ¿qué haré yo?
Se han matado dos valientes
la culpa la tengo yo.

</td><td>

2

"Come on, *comadre* Juana,
Serve me a little bottle
So that I may go see my lover,
The famous Rafelita."

3

At the mention of Rafelita
Don Reyes was upset;
"Basilio, do not make that mistake.
Rafelita belongs to me."

4

Then they went outside
With the intention of fighting.
Basilio asked for a pistol
In order to meet him.

5

They discharged their shots
In that fatal hour.
Two brave men have killed each other
For not being careful.

6

Rafelita comes out and says:
"God help me, what will I do?
Two brave men have killed each other,
The blame falls on me."

</td></tr>
</table>

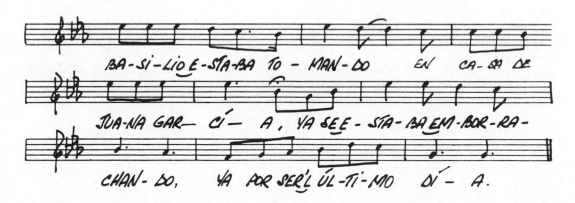

B16. *Canción del Minero* (Song of the Miner)
R2420, Juan Griego, age 61, Albuquerque, N.Mex., 1971, Robb.

<table>
<tr><td>

1

Qué cuadros compañeros
no quiero ni acordarme,
me lleno de vergüenza
de odio y de dolor.

</td><td>

1

Such square friends
I don't like to remember,
I am filled with shame,
Hate and pain.

</td></tr>
</table>

Nada vale ser bueno,
honrado buen marido.
Como hombre de trabajo
mi vida yo invertí.

Coro
En una tarde de Reyes
cuando a mi hogar regresaba
comprendo que me engañaba
con el amigo más fiel.
Yo rendido en amor propio,
quise vengar en el traje.
Lleno de odio y coraje,
sin compasión los maté.

2
La quise como un ángel,
tal vez la había querido
y la adoraba tanto
que hasta se lo sentí.
Por ella me hice bueno,
honrado buen marido.
Como hombre de trabajo
mi vida yo invertí.

Coro

3
(Verso 1 se repite)

It's no use being good,
Honorable and a good husband.
As a working man
I spent my life.

Chorus
One evening on the Day of the Kings
As I returned to my home
I found out that she was cheating
With my most faithful friend.
I was overcome by pride,
I wanted vengeance for this wrong.
Full of hate and anger,
Without compassion I killed them.

2
I loved her like an angel,
Perhaps I had loved her
And adored her so much
That I even felt it when she died.
For her I became a good man,
An honorable and good husband.
As a working man
I spent my life.

Chorus

3
(Verse 1 repeated)

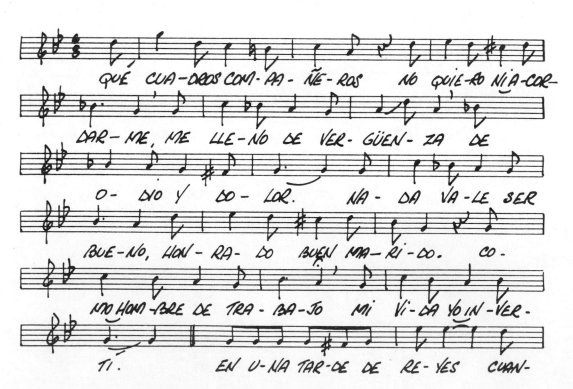

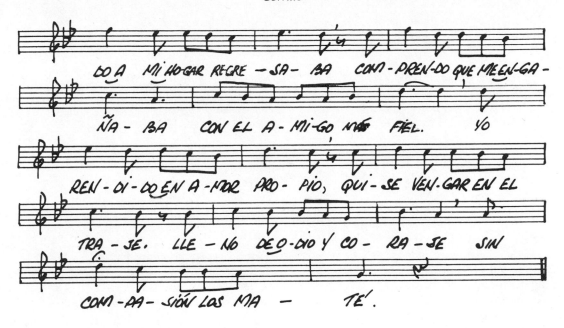

DO A MI HOGAR REGRE — SA — BA COM-PREN-DO QUE ME EN-GA-
ÑA — BA CON EL A-MI-GO MÁS FIEL. YO
REN-DI-DO EN A-MOR PRO-PIO, QUI-SE VEN-GAR EN EL
TRA-JE. LLE — NO DE O-DIO Y CO — RA-SE SIN
COM-PA-SIÓN LAS MA — TÉ.

B17. *Jesús Cadenas*
 R2400, Juan Griego, age 61, Albuquerque, N.Mex., 1971, Robb.

1	1
Y amigos, voy a cantarles	Friends, I am going to sing for you
de amores una detena	A story of love,
para cantarles los versos	By singing the verses
del joven Jesús Cadenas.	Of young Jesús Cadenas.

2	2
Un baile se celebraba	A dance was being celebrated
de mucha pompa y corrido,	With much pomp and song,
Chabela venía de brazos	Chabela was in the arms
de un hombre desconocido.	Of a man unknown there.

3	3
Estaba Jesús Cadenas	Jesús Cadenas was
desabrochando una espuela	Taking off his spurs
para comenzar el baile:	To begin the dance; he said:
—Voy a bailar con Chabela.—	"I am going to dance with Chabela."

4	4
Le dice María Antonia:	María Antonia said:
—Chabela, no andes bailando	"Chabela, do not be dancing
porque aquí pasó Jesús	For Jesús went by here
y por ti anda preguntando.—	And was asking about you."

5	5
Dice la güera Chabela	Blonde Chabela said
con una fuerte risada:	With a loud laugh:

—Muchachas, no tengan miedo,
yo conozco a mi bueyada.—

"Don't be afraid, girls,
I know my oxen."

6

Cuando Jesús entró al baile
Chabela andaba bailando
y les dice a sus amigos:
—Esa prenda yo la mando.—

6

When Jesús arrived at the dance
Chabela was dancing
And he said to his friends,
"I own that jewel."

7

Jesús sacó su pistola,
tres tiros le dirigió.
Dos se fueron por el viento
y uno fué él que le pegó.

7

Jesús took out his pistol,
Three shots he aimed at her.
Two went into the air
And one hit her.

8

—Adiós mi comadre Juana,
también mi comadre Antonia,
tengan cuidado muchachas,
que la vida no retoña.

8

"Good-bye my *comadre* Juana,
And good-bye my *comadre* Antonia,
Be careful girls,
For life does not bloom twice."

B17a. *Jesús Cadenas*

Hansen 6a (p. 221), R. Salas, age 47, Corona, Calif., 1959, Hansen. See also Hansen 6a (p. 222); R52.

1

Ranchito de San Antonio
estado de Nuevo León,
murió la güera Chabela
por jugar una traición.

1

On the ranch of San Antonio
Nuevo León, name of the state,
Fair Chabela had to die
By treason, this was her fate.

2

Jesús le decía a José:
—Vamos a bailar las parras,
entonar una canción
a compás de una guitarra.—

2

Jesús was telling José:
"Let us go dance down the street
And strike up a merry song
The guitar to give the beat."

3

José le decía a Jesús:
—La verdad, yo aquí me quedo
son las once de la noche
la verdad, yo tengo miedo.—

4

Y sale Jesús Cadenas
abrochándose una espuela,
que no más llegando al baile
fué a bailar con Chabela.

5

Cuando Jesús llegó al baile
Chabela andaba bailando,
y dice Jesús: —Compañeros,
desprenda yo la mano.—

6

Comadrita de Chabela,
comadrita anda bailando:
—Por aquí pasó Jesús
dice que la anda buscando.—

7

Dice la güera Chabela
con una fuerte risada:
—No se asuste comadrita,
que al cabo no me hace nada.—

8

Y dice Jesús Cadenas:
—Fíjate bien lo que dices,
no pienses que estás tratando
con chamaquitos de escuela.—

9

Luego sacó su pistola,
tres tiros le disparó.
Dos fueron para el viento,
el otro él que le pegó.

10

Decía la güera Chabela,
cuando estaba mal herida:
—De eso de querer a dos,
comadre, cuesta la vida.—

11

Decía la güera Chabela,
cuando estaba agonizando:
—Mucho cuidado, muchachas,
con andarlos mancornando.—

3

José then answered Jesús:
"Truly, I think I'll stay here,
Since it's eleven at night
I really have cause to fear."

4

And Jesús Cadenas leaves,
Pausing to fasten his spur,
For as soon as he arrives,
Chabela, he'll dance with her.

5

When Jesús got to the ball
Chabela was out there dancing,
And Jesús says: "My good friends,
I'll have to stop this romancing."

6

Chabela's most faithful friend
Is dancing on the floor too:
"Jesús has been all around here
And says he's looking for you."

7

Then fair Chabela replies
With a burst of laughter bold:
"Don't become frightened, my dear,
He'll only do what he's told."

8

And Jesús Cadenas says:
"Careful what you say and how,
Remember you are not dealing
With little schoolboys now."

9

With that he drew his pistol,
Three shots rang out in the dark.
Two were aimed into the wind,
The third squarely hit its mark.

10

Fair Chabela had to die;
When she knew her death was near:
"This business of loving two
Has cost me my life, my dear."

11

Fair Chabela tried to say
As she lay there on the ground:
"Be careful, all you young girls,
Don't give men the run around."

12
Aquí me siento a cantar
para disipar mis penas,
y aquí me siento a cantar
versos de Jesús Cadenas.

12
Here I sit to sing my song,
To drive away life's reverses,
Here I am to sing about
Jesús Cadenas, some verses.

13
(Verso 1 se repite)

13
(Verse 1 repeated)

RAN-CHI-TO DE SAN AN-TO-NIO, ES-TA-DO DE NUE-VO LEÓN, MU-RIÓ LA GÜE-RA CHA-BE-LA POR JU-GAR U-NA TRAI-CIÓN.

B17b. *Jesús Cadenas*
R30, Chimayó, N.Mex., 1945, Robb.

1
Estaba Jesús Cadenas
abrochándose una espuela:
—Y esta noche voy al baile,
voy a bailar con Chabela.—

1
Jesús Cadenas
Was buckling on his spurs:
"Tonight I'm going to the dance,
I'm going to dance with Chabela."

2
Cuando Jesús llegó al baile
ya el baile estaba prendido,
Chabela andaba bailando
con uno desconocido.

2
When Jesús came to the ball
The dance was already in full swing.
Chabela was dancing
With an unknown man.

3
Decía Jesús Cadenas
en su caballo tomando,
diciéndole a sus amigos:
—A esa güera yo la mando.—

3
Said Jesús Cadenas
As they were going on horseback,
Speaking to his friends:
"This blonde belongs to me."

4
Decía la güera Chabela,
dando una juerte risada:
—Yo no dejo de bailar,
yo conozco a mi quevada.—

4
But the blonde Chabela said,
Giving a derisive laugh:
"I will not stop dancing,
I know whom I like."

5

Decía Jesús Cadenas,
en su caballo montó
tres tiros le ha disparado
a Chabela le pegó.

6

Decía a la comadre Antonia,
decía a la comadre Juana:
—Mucho cuidado, muchachas,
que la vida no retoña.—

5

Jesús Cadenas
Mounted his horse
And fired three times
Hitting Chabela.

6

He said to her friend Antonia,
He said to her friend Juana:
"Take care, girls,
For life does not bloom twice."

E-STA-BA JE-SÚS CA-DE-NAS A-BRO-CHÁN-DO-SE U-NA E-SCUE-LA: YES-TA NO-CHE VOY AL BAI-LE, VOY A BAI-LAR CON CHA-BE-LA.

B18. *Rubén Leyva*
R161, R. Maés, Cebolla, N.Mex., 1949, Robb.

1

Para comenzar a cantar
licencia pido primero—
y este caso sucedió
sábado, seis de febrero.

2

Fueron a un baile a Rivera,
Rubén y Delia Maés,
sin saber lo que esperaba—
este Crespín traicionero.

3

Cuando llegaron al baile
Rubén se para a bailar.
No baila más de tres piezas
con la Julia Sandoval.

4

Crespín se para en la puerta
y les dice ¿cuántos son?
—Semos tres—le dicen ellos,
pues sin ninguna cuestión.

] *Bis*

] *Bis*

] *Bis*

] *Bis*

1

In order to begin singing
I ask permission first—
And this event occurred
Saturday, February sixth.

2

They went to a dance at Rivera,
Rubén and Delia Maés,
Without knowing what was waiting—
This treacherous Crespín.

3

When they arrived at the dance
Rubén stands up to dance.
He dances no more than three pieces
With Julia Sandoval.

4

Crespín stands in the doorway
And asks how many they are.
"We are three," they tell him,
Then, without further ado.

5

Allí se toman de brazo
y caminan poco allá
y a los cuarenta segundos
se oyó ese tiro fatal.　　　　　] *Bis*

6

Cuando Amadeo llegó
a rumbo donde él estaba,
Cuando Amadeo llegó
ya Rubén no se quejaba.　　　　] *Bis*

7

Amadeo, vete para atrás
a decirle al bastonero
que termine su baile—
este Crespín traicionero.　　　　] *Bis*

8

Crespín fué para su casa
y le dice a su mujer:
—¿Conoces a Rubén Leyva?
ese es él que yo maté.—　　　　] *Bis*

9

Ya su mujer le responde:
—Muy presto van a ver.
Ya Rubén está en el cielo;
tú te irás a padecer.—　　　　] *Bis*

10

El Bill le telefoneó
al oficial de Las Vegas
que a Rubén lo habían matado
en esa plaza de Rivera.　　　　] *Bis*

11

Su madre está en el pueblo
soñando un sueño profundo
sin saber que su hijo Rubén
se encontraba en otro mundo.　　] *Bis*

12

Entra su mamá al cuarto
y se dirige al cajón.
—Adiós Rubén de mi vida,
prenda de mi corazón.　　　　　] *Bis*

13

—Adiós, hermano Miguel,
que es hermano muy querido.
Mira a tu hermano Rubén
como se encuentra de herido.　　] *Bis*

5

There they take each other's arm
And go a little distance
And after forty seconds
That fatal shot was heard.

6

When Amadeo arrived
At the place where he was,
When Amadeo arrived
Rubén no longer complained.

7

Amadeo, go back
To tell the man in charge
To end his dance—
This treacherous Crespín.

8

Crespín went to his home
And he says to his wife:
"Do you know Rubén Leyva?
He is the one I killed."

9

And his wife answers him:
"Very soon everyone will see.
Rubén is already in heaven;
You will suffer for this."

10

Bill telephoned
The official at Las Vegas
That Rubén had been killed
In this town of Rivera.

11

His mother is in the village
Dreaming a profound dream
Without knowing that her son Rubén
Was already in another world.

12

His mother enters the room
And directs herself to the coffin.
"Good-bye, dear Rubén,
Jewel of my heart.

13

"Good-bye, brother Miguel,
You are a dear brother.
Look at your brother Rubén
How he is wounded.

14 Adiós, hermana Lucinda, que es hermana muy querida. ¡Cuánto es que yo voy a esperar esta traición en mi vida!] *Bis*	**14** "Good-bye, sister Lucinda, You are a dear sister. How can I endure This treachery in my life!
15 (Verso 13 se repite)	**15** (Verse 13 repeated)
16 Pues oigan, amigos míos, ésta es la declamación. Con una cuarenta y cinco le traspasó el corazón. —] *Bis*	**16** "Well then, listen my friends, This is my declaration. With a forty-five He pierced the heart."
17 Ya con ésta me despido por las hojas de una hierba, y aquí se acaban cantando los versos de Rubén Leyva.] *Bis*	**17** With this I am leaving Through the leaves of a plant, And here we finish singing The verses of Rubén Leyva.

PA' CO-MEN-ZAR A CAN-TAR LI-CEN-CIA PI-DO PRI-ME-RO Y E-SE CA-SO SU-CE-DIÓ SÁ-BA-DO, SEIS DE FEB-RE-RO, SÁ-BA-DO, SEIS DE FEB-RE-RO.

My notes indicate that the events narrated took place in San Miguel County, New Mexico.

B19. *Rosita Alvírez*

R240, Cecilia Gallegos, age 15?, Cienega, N.Mex., 1950, Robb. Cf. R788, R1693, R1695, R2087, RB499 (Texas), RB543 (Arizona), Hansen 6a (no. 3, p. 224 [California]), Mendoza 9d (p. 424).

1 Año de mil novecientos presente lo tengo yo en un barrio de Castillo Rosita Alvírez murió.] *Bis*	**1** In the year nineteen hundred I well recall, In a barrio of Castillo Rosita Alvírez died.

2

Su mamá se lo decía:
—Esta noche no me sales.—] *Bis*

2

Her mama said to her:
"Don't go out tonight."

3

Entró Pólito a la sala
y a Rosa se dirigió
como era la más bonita;
Rosita lo desairó.] *Bis*

3

Pólito entered the hall
And went up to Rosita
Because she was the prettiest;
Rosita slighted him.

4

—Rosita no me desaires,
la gente lo va a notar.—
—Que digan lo que queran,
contigo no he de bailar.—] *Bis*

4

"Rosita, don't you slight me.
The people will notice it."
"Let them say what they please,
I don't have to dance with you."

5

Metió mano a la cintura
y una pistola sacó;
y a la pobre de Rosita
nomás tres tiros le dió.] *Bis*

5

He put his hand to his belt
And drew a pistol;
And at poor Rosita
He fired three shots.

6

Rosita le dijo a Irene:
—No te olvides de mi nombre;
cuando vayas a un baile
no desaires a los hombres.—] *Bis*

6

Rosita said to Irene:
"Do not forget my name;
When you go to a dance
Do not rebuff the men."

7

Rosita estará en el cielo
dándole cuenta al Creador
y Pólito está en la cárcel
dando su declaración.] *Bis*

7

Rosita is in heaven
Accounting to the Creator;
And Pólito is in the jail
Making his statement.

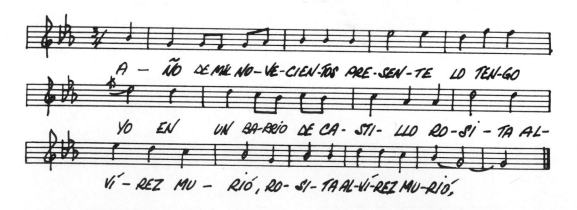

It is difficult, if not impossible, to decide why certain folk songs become very popular while others do not enjoy wide circulation. *Rosita Alvírez* is one of the former. The stern fate of the disobedient son or daughter is emphasized in a number of the *corridos* and is presumably one of the reasons for the popularity of this particular one.

The popularity and wide diffusion of *Rosita Alvírez* enables us to print several versions and compare them.

B19a. *Rosita Alvírez*
R2087, Frank McCulloch, Jr., Albuquerque, N.Mex., 1965, Robb.

1 En año mil novecientos muy presente tengo yo en un barrio de mi pueblo Rosita Alvírez murió.] *Bis*	**1** In the year nineteen hundred I can still remember In a district of my town Rosita Alvírez died.
2 Su mamá se lo decía: —Rosita, esta noche no bailes. —Mamá, yo no tengo la culpa que a mí me gustan los bailes.—] *Bis*	**2** Her mother said to her "Rosita, do not dance tonight." "Mother, it is not my fault That I like dances so much."
3 Llegó Hipólito a la fiesta y a Rosita se dirigió como era la más bonita. Rosita lo despreció.] *Bis*	**3** Hipólito arrived at the party And went up to Rosita Because she was the prettiest. Rosita turned him down.
4 —Rosita, no me desprecies, la gente lo va a notar. —Pos que digan lo que digan, contigo no he de bailar.—] *Bis*	**4** "Rosita, don't turn me down, People will notice." "Let them say what they will say, I will not dance with you."
5 Echó mano a la cintura y una pistola sacó, a la pobre de Rosita no más tres tiros le dió.] *Bis*	**5** He reached for his belt And drew out a pistol, And shot poor Rosita Three times.
6 Rosita está en el cielo dándole cuenta al Creador, Hipólito está en la cárcel dando su declaración.] *Bis*	**6** Rosita is in heaven Accounting to her Creator, Hipólito is in jail Giving his statement.

B19b. *Rosita Alvírez*
Hansen 6a (no. 3, p. 224), Cosme Chávez, age 33, Los Angeles, Calif., 1959, Hansen.

1

Año de mil novecientos,
muy presente tengo yo,
en un barrio de Saltillo
Rosita Alvírez murió.   ] *Bis*

1

In the year nineteen hundred,
This event I cannot hide,
In a district in Saltillo
Rosita Alvírez died.

2

Su mamá se lo decía:
—Hija, esta noche no sales.
—Mamá no tengo la culpa,
que a mí me gusten los bailes.—   ] *Bis*

2

Her mother was heard to say:
"My child, don't go out tonight."
"Mother dear, I'm not to blame
If dancing gives me delight."

3

Hipólito llegó al baile
y a Rosa se dirigió.
Como era la más bonita,
Rosita lo desairó.   ] *Bis*

3

To this dance came Hipólito
And to Rosa went direct.
As she was the most beautiful,
She eyed him with disrespect.

4

—Rosita, no me desaires,
la gente lo va a notar.
—Pues, que digan lo que queran,
contigo no he de bailar.—   ] *Bis*

4

"Slight me not, Rosita dear,
People will be quick to see."
"Let them say all that they wish,
You won't ever dance with me."

5

Echó mano a la cintura,
y una pistola sacó,
y a la pobre de Rosita,
no más tres tiros le dió.   ] *Bis*

5

To his belt he reached his hand
And then his pistol withdrew,
And at poor helpless Rosita
Three fatal bullets soon flew.

6

Su mamá se lo decía:
—Ya vistes, hija querida,
por andar de pizpireta,
te había de llegar el día.—   ] *Bis*

6

Her mother was heard to say:
"Now you see my daughter dear,
Since you were so smart and brisk,
What I had feared is now here."

7

Rosita ya está en el cielo
dándole cuenta al Creador;
Hipólito está en la cárcel
dando su declaración.   ] *Bis*

7

Rosita's now in heaven,
Account to the Lord she gives;
Hipólito is in jail,
With his statement he still lives.

B20. *El Día de San Juan* (The Day of Saint John)
R1219, Tom Dickerson, Albuquerque, N.Mex., 1954, Robb.

1

El veinte cuatro de junio
el mero día de San Juan,
un baile se celebraba
en el pueblo de Aztlán.

1

The twenty-fourth of June,
The very day of Saint John,
A dance was being held
In the town at Aztlán.

2

Micaela desde temprano
sonriendo le dijo a Juan:
—Por ser el día de tu santo
al baile me has de llevar.

2

Micaela since early morning
Had happily been telling Juan:
"Since it is your saint's day
You should take me to the dance."

3

—Oye, Micaela, ¿qué traes el diablo?
No vayas a esa función.
Está tentándome el diablo
de echarle un plato a Simón.

3

"Listen, Micaela, you just
Better not go to that party.
The devil has been tempting me
To pick a fight with Simón!

4

Oye, Micaela, que cuando te vayas
a esa función
que no permito que bailes
ni hagas mucho jalón.—

4

"Listen, Micaela, when you go
To that celebration
I don't want you to dance
Or to flirt."

5

Se fué Micaela primero
y ahí mero se puso a bailar;
encontró de compañero
al mero rival de Juan.

5

Micaela went first to the dance
And by and by she started dancing;
She met as a partner
The very rival of Juan.

6

Alegres pasan las horas,
las doce marca el reloj
cuando un tiro de pistola
dos cuerpos atravesó.

6

Happily the hours went by,
The clock struck twelve
When one pistol shot
Pierced their two bodies.

7

Vuela, vuela, palomita,
pasa por ese panteón
donde ha de estar Micaelita
con su querido Simón.

7

Fly, fly away, little dove,
Go by the graveyard
Where little Micaela and
Her lover Simón must be.

EL VEIN-TE CUA-TRO DE JU-NIO EL ME-RO DÍA DE SAN JUAN, UN BAI-LE SE CE-LE-BRA-BA EN EL PUE-BLO DE AZT-LÁN. MI-CAE-LA DES-DE TEM-PRA-NO SON—

RIEN-DO DI-JO A JUAN: POR SER EL DÍA DE TU

SAN-TO AL BAI-LE ME HAS DE LLE— VAR.

This *corrido* text, based on the familiar theme death at a dance, is remarkable for the epic brevity and lack of sentimentality of its conclusion. At twelve o'clock a pistol shot pierced two bodies. Little dove fly to the cemetery where the two must be. There is no moralizing, though morals could be drawn. It is stark narration.

B20a. *El Día de San Juan*
RB140, Arvino Martínez, Abiquiu, N.Mex., 1950, Robb.

<table>
<tr><td>

1
El veinte y cuatro de junio,
el mismo día de San Juan,
un baile se celebraba
en ese pueblo de Exeltán.

</td><td>

1
The twenty-fourth of June,
The day of Saint John,
A dance was being held
In that town of Exeltán.

</td></tr>
<tr><td>

2
Micaila desde temprano,
sonriendo le dijo a Juan:
—Por ser día de tu santo
al baile me has de llevar.

</td><td>

2
Micaila early in the morning
Smiling, said to Juan:
"Since it is the day of your saint,
You must take me to the dance."

</td></tr>
<tr><td>

3
—No quiero hacerte el desaire
pero algo presiento yo;
que esta noche en el baile
se te amargue la función.

</td><td>

3
"I do not want to rebuff you
But I have a presentiment
That tonight at the dance
You will regret that you went."

</td></tr>
<tr><td>

4
—Te lo diré por lo claro
que le recalo a Simón
y no permite que bailes
ni le hagas mucho jalón.

</td><td>

4
"I will tell you straight out
That Simón will get drunk
And won't let you dance
Or have much fun."

</td></tr>
<tr><td>

5
—Adiós Castita, yo vuelvo—
le dijo ya para salir.
—Me voy con unos amigos
ya que tú no quieres ir.

</td><td>

5
"Good-bye, chaste girl, I will return,"
He said as he left.
"I shall go with some friends
Since you don't want to go."

</td></tr>
<tr><td>

6
—Oye, Micaila, que te hablo,
no vayas a esa reunión,
que está tentándome el diablo
de echarme al rastro al Simón.—

</td><td>

6
"Listen, Micaila, to what I say,
Don't go to this party,
For the devil is tempting me
To get on the trail of Simón."

</td></tr>
</table>

7

Se fué Micaila primero,
se puso luego a bailar
y encontró de compañero
al mismo rival de Juan.

7

Micaila went first
And started to dance
And found herself dancing
With the very rival of Juan.

8

Alegres pasan las horas,
Los doce marca el reloj,
cuando un tiro de pistola
dos cuerpos atravesó.

8

The hours pass happily,
The clock strikes twelve
When a pistol shot
Struck two bodies.

9

¡Vuela, vuela, palomita!
Pasa por ese panteón
donde ha de estar Micailita
con su querido Simón.

9

Fly, fly, little dove!
Pass by this cemetery
Where little Micaila
Must be with her beloved Simón.

B21. *Reyes Ruiz*
   R151, Tomás Archuleta, Abiquiu, N.Mex., 1949, Robb. Cf. Mendoza 9e (p. 262).

1

Adiós, Guajuquía del alto,
año de noventa y seis
mataron a Reyes Ruiz
víspera de un diez y seis.

1

Good-bye, high Guajuquía,
It was the year of ninety-six
When they killed Reyes Ruiz
On the eve of the Sixteenth (a party).

2

Salió Reyes del trabajo
en compañía de otros tres
y le dice a su mamá:
—Yo me voy al diez y seis.—

2

Reyes left work
Along with three others,
and he said to his mother:
"I am going to the Sixteenth."

3

Y le respondió su madre:
—Hijo de mi corazón,
a ese diez y seis no vas,
ahí irás en otra ocasión.—

3

And his mother answered him:
"My dear son,
Do not go to that Sixteenth,
You shall go there some other time."

4

Y le respondió este Reyes:
—Madre de mi corazón,
con su voluntad o sin ella
yo me voy a esa función.—

4

And Reyes answered her:
"My dearest Mother,
With or without your permission,
I shall attend that function."

5

Y le dicen sus amigos:
—Reyes, es mejor no ir,
si tu mamá no te deja.
No sabes el porvenir.—

5

And his friends tell him:
"Reyes, it's better not to go,
If your mother doesn't permit you.
You don't know about the future."

<table>
<tr><td>

6

Salieron de San Antonio,
agarraron el camino,
llegaron a Guajuquía
brindando copas de vino.

7

Reyes se puso borracho,
por las calles muy trompeto
se encontró con dos muchachos
luego les trató de pleito.

8

Y le dicen que es muy terco.
—Hombre, no quiero pelear
y viendo que eres mi amigo
te quiero considerar.—

9

Y le respondió este Reyes:
—Yo no peleo en el centro,
pasaremos a la orilla
y a ver si no hay cumplimiento.—

10

Se fueron a un callejón,
se agarraron a pedradas,
y a poco que se acercaron
echándose puñaladas.

11

Cuando Reyes escupió
en los hilos del acero,
ahí con ansia de la muerte
fué a morir a un basurero.

12

Reyes cumple con la muerte
y trató con arrancar
diciendo que en Guajuquía
no me volveré a pasear.

13

Ensíllenme mi caballo,
ya me tenderé en la silla,
me he paseado en otras sierras
cuanto más en Guajuquía.

14

Vuela, vuela, palomita,
párate en aquel reliz,
y aquí se acaban cantando
los versos de Reyes Ruiz.

</td><td>

6

They left San Antonio,
Taking the road,
They arrived at Guajuquía
Toasting with cups of wine.

7

Reyes became drunk,
Going noisily through the streets
He met two boys
And soon provoked a fight.

8

And they tell him he is foolish.
"Man, I do not wish to fight
And being that you're my friend
I want to be considerate of you."

9

And Reyes answered him:
"I do not fight in the plaza,
We shall go aside
To see whether there is satisfaction."

10

They went to an alley
And started throwing stones,
And as they neared one another
They began stabbing at each other.

11

When Reyes felt
The edge of the steel,
With a longing for death
He went to die in a garbage dump.

12

Reyes complies with death
And tries to get away,
Saying that in Guajuquía
He won't be seen again.

13

Saddle my horse,
I shall stretch myself across the saddle,
I have been to other mountains
Let alone in Guajuquía.

14

Fly, fly, little dove,
Stop upon that bluff,
And here we finish singing
The verses of Reyes Ruiz.

</td></tr>
</table>

15
Vuela, vuela, palomita,
A llevarte a las regiones,
Anda y dile a mi mamá
que quiero sus bendiciones.

15
Fly, fly, little dove,
Go to other regions,
Go and tell my mother
That I want her blessings.

The last verse is certainly heartrending, a
powerful ending to this ballad of useless
slaughter.

B21a. *Reyes Ruiz*
R302, Jacobo Maestas, age 67, Llano de San Juan, 1950, Robb.

1
Adiós Guajuquía del alto.
Fecha de noventa y seis
mataron a Reyes Ruiz
víspera de un Diez y Seis.

1
Farewell Guajuquía in the heights.
In the year of ninety-six
They killed Reyes Ruiz
On the eve of a Sixteenth.

2
Salió Reyes del trabajo
en compañía de otros tres,
y le dice a su mamá:
—Yo me voy al Diez y Seis.—

2
Reyes came from work
With three others,
And said to his mother:
"I'm going to the Sixteenth."

3
Su mamá le contestó:
—Hijo de mi corazón,
ese Diez y Seis no vayas,
ahí irás otra ocasión.—

3
His mother replied to him:
"Son of my heart,
Do not go to this Sixteenth,
You'll go some other time."

4
Sus amigos le decían:
—Tu mamá no te deja ir,
lo mejor es que no fueras,
no sabes el porvenir.

4
His friends said to him:
"Your mother won't allow you to go,
It's better not to go,
You can't tell what might happen."

5

—Ensíllenme mi caballo,
apriétenle bien la silla.
Me he paseado en otras tierras,
contimás en Guajuquía.—

6

Pasaron por San Antonio,
agarraron el camino,
llegaron a Guajuquía
tomando copas de vino.

7

Otra día por la mañana
anda Reyes muy trompeto,
se encontró con dos muchachos
luego les trató de pleito.

8

Plutarco le respondió:
—Hombre, no quiero pelear.
Hemos sido muy amigos,
te quiero considerar.—

9

Y Reyes le contestó,
diciéndole estas razones:
—Y yo sé tener amigos,
menos consideraciones.—

10

Plutarco le contestó:
—Yo no peleyo en el centro,
nos saldremos a la orilla
a ver si no hay cumplimiento.—

11

Se salieron a la orilla,
se agarran a las pedradas,
poco a poco se acercaron
dándose de puñaladas.

12

Cuando ya Reyes sintió
los filos del acero
con las ansias de la muerte
fué a morir a un basurero.

13

Reyes cumplió con moriri,
Plutarco con arrancari,
diciendo que en Guajuquía
no se volvería a paseari.

5

"Saddle my horse,
Fasten the saddle well.
I have traveled in other lands,
Let alone in Guajuquía."

6

They passed through San Antonio,
And took to the road,
They came to Guajuquía
Drinking a lot of wine.

7

The next day in the morning
Reyes got very drunk,
He met two lads
And got into a quarrel.

8

Plutarco answered him:
"Man, I don't want to fight.
We have been good friends,
I want to treat you with consideration."

9

And Reyes answered him,
Telling him this:
"I know how to keep my friends,
Let alone being considerate."

10

Plutarco answered him:
"I won't fight you in the plaza,
Let's go to the outskirts
And see if satisfaction will be given."

11

They went to the outskirts,
And started throwing rocks,
Then slowly drew closer
And started stabbing at each other.

12

When Reyes felt
The sharpness of the blade,
With the anxiety of death
He went to die at a garbage dump.

13

Reyes answered the call of death
And Plutarco took to his heels,
Saying that in Guajuquía
He would never step again.

14 Vuela, vuela, palomita, párate en aquel alambre, anda dícele a mi madre que estoy y en un charco de sangre.	**14** Fly, fly, little dove, Perch on yonder wire, Go tell my mother That I am in a puddle of blood.
15 Vuela, vuela, palomita, párate en aquel picacho, anda dícele a mi madre que me mataron borracho.	**15** Fly, fly, little dove, Perch in yonder peak, Go tell my mother That they killed me when I was drunk.
16 Vuela, vuela, palomita, párate en aquella higuera, los consejos de la madre no se toman como quiera.	**16** Fly, fly, little dove, Perch in yonder fig tree, One does not disregard a Mother's advice just like that.
17 Vuela, vuela, palomita, párate en aquel relís, aquí se acaban cantando los versos de Reyes Ruiz.	**17** Fly, fly, little dove, Perch in yonder cliff, Here ends the singing Of the verses of Reyes Ruiz.

B22. *Bill Mentado* (Famous Bill)
R210, Tomás Archuleta, Abiquiu, N.Mex., 1949, Robb.

1 El catorce de septiembre era un tiempo de rodeo.	]] *Bis*	**1** On the fourteenth of September It was rodeo time.
2 Bajaron allá a Antón Chico una hatajo de vaqueros.	]] *Bis*	**2** And there came down to Antón Chico A group of cowboys.
3 Llegaron a la cantina se ponen a echar los vasos.	]] *Bis*	**3** They went to the saloon They drank cup after cup.

4

Y allí montan a caballo]
salen tirando balazos.] *Bis*

4

Then they mount their horses
And go away firing their guns.

5

Donde llegan a una casa
donde estaban unas mujeres solas.
Las mujeres eran solas
las querían atropellar.

5

From there they came to a house
Where there were some women alone.
The women were alone whom
They wanted to outrage.

6

De allí salieron huyendo]
para casa de don Bonifacio García.] *Bis*

6

Getting tired of this they went
To the house of Don Bonifacio García.

7

A poco que la llegaron]
Se aproxima una gavilla.] *Bis*

7

They arrived and
Were acting like a gang.

8

Don Bonifacio García]
era un hombre muy honesto.] *Bis*

8

Don Bonifacio García
Was a very honest man.

9

Don Bonifacio García]
era un hombre nada escaso.] *Bis*

9

Don Bonifacio García
Was always ready.

10

Echó mano a su pistola]
le dió un tiro a Bill Mentado.] *Bis*

10

He drew his pistol
And shot Bill Mentado.

11

Aquí se acaba el corrido]
del valiente Bill Mentado.] *Bis*

11

Here ends the ballad
Of brave Bill Mentado.

12

Con una bala de plomo,]
le han quitado lo valiente.] *Bis*

12

With a bullet of lead
They killed the brave man.

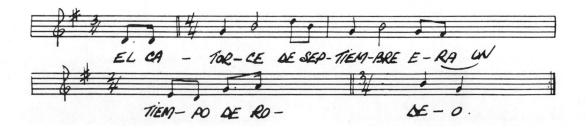

EL CA - TOR-CE DE SEP-TIEM-BRE E - RA UN
TIEM- PO DE RO - DE - O.

Although Billy the Kid was well known to the Spanish-speaking people as Bill Mentado or El Bilito, this song is apparently about another famous Bill.

Cobos advises me that there are those who do not accept the historical account of Billy's death but whisper conspiratorially that he was killed by someone else, usually an uncle.

B23. *Leandro*
R2402, Juan Griego, Albuquerque, N.Mex., 1971, Robb.

<table>
<tr><td>

1

Al pasar el Río Pecos
se sentaron platicar:
—Vamos a invitar a Leandro
porque vamos dos no más.—

</td><td>

1

As they crossed the Río Pecos
They sat down to talk:
"Let's invite Leandro
Because we are only two."

</td></tr>
<tr><td>

2

Le echaron el envite a Leandro,
Leandro les dijo que no;
—Miren que yo estoy enfermo
y no quisiera ir yo.—

</td><td>

2

They made the offer to Leandro,
Leandro answered no;
"Note that I am ill
And I wouldn't want to go."

</td></tr>
<tr><td>

3

Al fin de tanto rogarle,
Leandro los acompañó,
y en la sala del gordito,
un tumulto se prendió.

</td><td>

3

After much pleading,
Leandro accompanied them,
And at the little fat man's saloon
A fight began.

</td></tr>
<tr><td>

4

Entre dagas y pistolas,
se completaron dieciocho.
Leandro sacó su pistola,
calibre de treintaiocho.

</td><td>

4

Amidst knives and pistols,
There were eighteen men there.
Leandro took out his pistol,
Thirty-eight caliber.

</td></tr>
<tr><td>

5

Se siguieron disparando
sobre los cuerpos tendidos,
y tuvo más suerte Leandro,
cayó Nestor mal herido.

</td><td>

5

They continued shooting
Over the dead bodies,
And Leandro was luckier,
Nestor fell badly wounded.

</td></tr>
<tr><td>

6

Salió Nestor mal herido,
le trajeron el dotor,
Dice: —Me voy con mi padre,
no me curen por favor.—

</td><td>

6

Nestor left badly wounded,
They brought him the doctor,
He said: "I go with my father,
Don't cure me please."

</td></tr>
<tr><td>

7

Al fin de tanto pelearse,
también el Leandro cayó.
En la sala del gordito,
allí fué donde Leandro murió.

</td><td>

7

After so much fighting,
Leandro also fell.
At the fat man's saloon,
That was where Leandro died.

</td></tr>
</table>

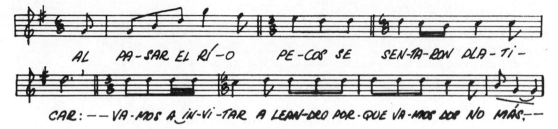

The singer Juan Griego omitted the final verse.

B24. *José Lisorio*
R370, José Gallegos, Abiquiu, N.Mex., 1947, Robb. Cf. Mendoza 9e (p. 257).

1

El lunes por cierto fué
cuando el caso sucedió;
que el pobre José Lisorio
a su madre le faltó.

1

For sure it was a Monday
When this took place;
That poor José Lisorio
Failed his mother.

2

Su madre como enojada
una maldición le echó,
pues al pie de un Santo Cristo
que hasta la tierra tembló.

2

His mother, as if angry,
Laid a curse upon him,
There at the foot of a Holy Christ
So that the earth shook.

3

—Permita Dios, hijo mío,
permitan todos los santos,
que allá al llegar a la mina
te hagas doscientos pedazos.

3

"God grant, my son,
May all the saints also grant,
That when you approach the mine
You are blown into two hundred pieces."

4

—¡Madrecita de mi vida,
retira tu maldición!
Soy hijo de tus entrañas;
nacido del corazón.—

4

"Mother dear of my life!
Lift your spoken curse!
I am son from your womb;
I was born of your heart."

5

Otro día en la mañana
a la mina se aprontó.
Les dice a sus compañeros,
—No quisiera bajar yo.—

5

Early the next day
He went to the mine.
He tells his companions,
"I don't want to go down."

6

Ya se volvió José
a buscar a quien dejar.
Sus amigos se han negado
se devolvió a su lugar.

6

José went back to find
Someone to take his place.
His friends having refused,
He returned to his place.

7

Bajó el primer escalón,
y luego se encomendó:
—Jesucristo, me acompañe
y a la cruz en que murió.—

7

He descended the first step,
And then he prayed:
"Jesus Christ, be with me
And the cross on which you died."

8

Bajó el segundo escalón,
y luego se desprendió.
La compañía que llevaba
y en un paño lo sacó.

8

He descended the second step,
And there it was that he fell.
His companions who carried him
Brought him out in a cloth.

9

Sus sesos le pepenaron
en la copa del sombrero.
Esto es para enternecer
los corazones de acero.

9

They gathered his brains
In the crown of his hat.
This is enough to move to pity
Hearts of steel.

10 —No llores, madre querida. No llores, tu disconsuelo, que ya tu hijo está tendido y en la casa del minero.	**10** "Don't cry, dear mother. Do not weep, disconsolate, Though your son lies dying In the mine office.
11 Adiós, todos mis amigos, mis hermanos y parientes. Que éste es el fin que tenemos los hijos desobedientes.—	**11** "Good-bye, all my friends, My brothers and relatives. This is the end that we Disobedient sons have."
12 Una despedida nota. En el viento se contiene. Que en esta vida y en la otra lo que uno granjea tiene.	**12** Take note of a farewell. It is contained in the wind. In this life and the other One gets what he earns.

EL LU-NES POR CIER-TO FUÉ CUAN-DOEL CA-SO SU-CE-DIÓ, QUE EL PO-BRE JO-SÉ LI-SO-RIO A SU MA-DRE LE FAL-TÓ.

B24a. *José Leonardo*
R2008, C. Chávez, Galisteo, N.Mex., 1943, Robb.

1 Jueves santo, viernes santo, miren lo que sucedió, que al joven José Leonardo con su mamá se peleó.	**1** Holy Thursday, Good Friday, Look what happened To the youth José Leonardo Who fought with his mother.
2 Su mamá como enojada, una maldición le echó que en los pies de un santo Cristo hasta la tierra tembló.	**2** His mother, since she was mad, Threw a curse at him At the feet of a Holy Christ So even the earth trembled.
3 —Anda, bien, hijo mío, y allá en la mina te caigas y a la puerta de tu casa en cuatro cuartos te traigan.—	**3** "Go on, my son, And there in the mine may you fall, May they bring you in four pieces To the door of your house."

4

Ya se fué para la mina
muy triste y desconsolado,
pensando en la maldición
que su mamá le había echado.

5

Allá al llegar a la mina
cuatro suspiros pagó;
les dice a sus compañeros:
—No quisiera bajar yo.—

6

Le responden los mineros:
—Si tú no quieres bajar
pues, búscate otro de pronto
que se baja a tu lugar.—

7

Ya salió José Leonardo
a ver si podía hallar;
anduvo calle por calle,
nadie quiso trabajar.

8

Pues ya encendieron las velas
para comenzar a bajar;
¿quién te dijera, Leonardo,
tu muerte vas a buscar?

9

Bajó el primer escalón
y a Dios se encomendó,
y del segundo escalón
y ahí mero se deslizó.

10

Los sesos los pepenaron
en la copa de un sombrero;
esto era para ablandar
los corazones de acero.

11

Toda la gente lloraba
de verlo de compasión,
sus amigos le decían:
—Le traeremos su cajón.—

12

Y su mamá les decía:
—No le tengan compasión,
la compañía de la mina
le mandará su cajón.—

4

He went to the mine
Very sad and disconsolate,
Thinking about the curse
That his mother had put on him.

5

There, on arriving at the mine
He sighed four times;
He says to his companions:
"I don't want to go down."

6

The miners answer him:
"If you don't want to go down,
Then find someone quick
Who will go in your place."

7

José Leonardo left
To see if he could find someone;
He walked street by street,
No one wanted to work.

8

Now they lit the candles
To begin to descend;
Who is there to tell you, Leonardo,
That you are seeking your death?

9

He went down the first step
And commended himself to God,
And on the second step
Right there he slipped.

10

His brains they gathered
In the cup of a hat;
This was enough to soften
Any heart of steel.

11

Everyone cried,
It was pitiful to see him,
His friends said:
"We'll bring him his coffin."

12

And his mother said to them:
"Don't have pity on him,
The mining company
Will send his coffin."

13

Allí viene saliendo la estrella
del oriente así al poniente,
con eso viene a parar
un chico desobediente.

13

The star is now coming
From the east to the west,
To this end comes
A disobedient child.

B25. *El Hijo Desobediente* (The Disobedient Son)
Hansen 6a (no. 3, p. 225), N. Ruiz, Colton, Calif., 1959, Hansen.

1

Un domingo estando errando
se encontraron dos mancebos
echando mano a sus fierros
como queriendo pelear.

1

On a Sunday afternoon
two young men by chance did meet,
each quickly reached for his gun,
one the other to defeat.

2

Cuando se estaban peleando
llegó su padre de uno.
—Hijo de mi corazón,
ya no pelées con ninguno.

2

When the fight had just begun
The father of one came by.
"Please listen to me, my son,
Do not fight with any guy."

3

—Quítese de aquí mi padre,
que ando más bravo que un león.
No vaya a sacar la espada
y le traspase el corazón.

3

"Father, you must go away,
I feel like a lion fierce,
If his sword he should unsheath,
With it his heart I will pierce."

4

—Válgame Dios, hijo mío,
por lo que acabas de hablar,
antes de que raye el sol,
la vida te han de quitar.

4

"May God defend me, my son,
For what you have just now said,
Before the sun rises
I am sure that you will be dead."

5

—Lo que le encargo a mi padre,
que no me entierre en sagrado,
que me entierre en tierra rasa
donde me trille el ganado.—

5

"In any holy place, father,
Me you should not ever bury,
Rather, the wide open country
Where the cattle roam the prairie."

6

Con una mano de fuera,
y un papel sobre dorado,
con un letrero que diga,
Felipe fué desgraciado.

6

Written in a style so free
And printed on paper gold,
May the message clearly state,
Luckless was Felipe bold.

7

Bajaron el toro prieto,
que nunca lo habían bajado,
pero ahora sí ya bajó,
revuelto con el ganado.

7

They brought down the old black bull,
Something not done heretofore,
But this time he did come down
Among the cattle galore.

8

Y a ese mentado Felipe
la maldición le alcanzó,
y en las trancas del corral
el toro se lo llevó.

8

And to the man named Felipe
Came the curse that he well knew,
On the fence of the corral
By the bull he was gored through.

9

Ya con ésta me despido,
con la estrella del oriente.
Esto le puede pasar
a un hijo desobediente.

9

Now with this I bid adieu,
And the star shines far away.
This can happen to a son
Who does not want to obey.

El Hijo Desobediente (B25–25b): the third of these is a different song but due to their identical title and theme I have made an exception to my usual practice and grouped them all under number B25.

B25a.   *El Mal Hijo* (The Bad Son)
RB752, Ezequiel Candelaria, Santa Barbara, N.Mex., 1950, Cobos.

1

El día dieciseis de octubre
de este año noventa y nueve,
fué un día de gran pesadumbre
porque un hijo ingrato, aleve,
dió a su padre muerte fiera,
y como ejemplar castigo,
abrió la boca la tierra
para tragarse al mal hijo.

1

The sixteenth of October
Of this year of ninety-nine
Was a day of great sorrow
Because an ungrateful, treacherous son
Killed his father savagely,
And as an exemplary punishment,
The earth opened its mouth
To swallow up the wicked son.

2

Román Guzmán, que tenía
de beber la fiera costumbre,

2

Román Guzmán, who
Drank to excess,

142

dió fin a su vida impía el día dieciseis de octubre.	Put an end to his impious life On the sixteenth of October.

3	3
Porque su padre ordenó que más licor no bebiera con una hacha lo mató este año de noventa y nueve.	Because his father ordered That he should drink no more liquor, He killed him with an axe In this year of ninety-nine.

4	4
La pobre madre angustiada derrama llanto salubre y loca y desesperada tuvo horrible pesadumbre. Tres golpes sin compasión le dió cerca de la sien y uno sobre el corazón, este hijo traidor y cruel.	The poor mother in anguish Wept profusely And crazed and desperate Felt horrible grief. He struck him three times In the temple, without pity, And once over the heart, This traitorous and cruel son.

5	5
Sin oír su consejo sano y con furia de pantera, el mal hijo tirano dió a su padre muerte fiera.	Without listening to his wise counsel And with the fury of a panther, This wicked tyrannical son Dealt his father a savage death.

6	6
Pensó huir el desdichado, pensó que no había testigo; pero aquel hijo malvado le espera ejemplar castigo.	The wretch thought he could escape, He thought there was no witness; But this vicious son Was destined for exemplary punishment.

7	7
Pensó poder ocultarse de la justicia severa; y cuando iba a escaparse abrió su boca la tierra.	He thought that he could hide From the severity of justice; But when he was trying to escape The earth opened up its mouth.

8	8
Pues muerte tan alevosa merece un castigo fijo, y hasta con furia espantosa la tierra tragó al mal hijo.	For such a treacherous murder Deserves a severe punishment, And with frightful fury The earth swallowed the evil son.

B25b. *El Hijo Desobediente*
RB751, Elisa Castillo, Belén, N.Mex., 1950, Cobos.

1	1
El Santo Niño de Atocha, el glorioso San Gabriel, me ha de dar entendimiento para lo que pienso hacer.	The Holy Child of Atocha, The glorious Saint Gabriel, Must give me the understanding For that which I plan to do.

2

Escuchen bien, mis amigos,
todo aquél que esté presente,
de lo que aquí sucedió
a un hijo desobediente.

3

A la edad de dieciocho años,
asegún entiendo yo,
por seguir a sus amigos
sus padres abandonó.

4

El día que se ausentó
su madre lo acariciaba;
le daba sus bendiciones
y él su espalda le volteaba.

5

La agarró de los cabellos,
con palabras desgraciadas;
la levantó en el aire,
por el suelo la arrastraba.

6

Cuando su padre vió esto
le dijo una maldición:
—Se te ha de pintar el diablo
al lado del corazón.—

7

La pobrecita de su madre
por su nombre le gritaba;
con palabras lastimosas
su padre lo aconsejaba.

8

La pobre madre decía:
—El diablo se te ha metido;
hijito de mis entrañas,
¿por qué haces esto conmigo?—

9

Cuando salió de su casa
se metió de bandolero;
su carrera no duró;
lo tomaron prisionero.

10

Cuando en la prisión estaba,
le preguntaron lo cierto
que si vivían sus padres
o que si se habían muerto.

2

Listen well, my friends,
All of you who are present,
To what happened here
To a disobedient son.

3

At the age of eighteen years,
As I understand it,
He abandoned his parents
To go with his friends.

4

The day that he left
His mother was caressing him;
She was giving him her blessing
When he turned his shoulder.

5

He seized her by the hair,
With shameful words;
He lifted her into the air,
And dragged her along the ground.

6

When his father saw this
He pronounced a curse on him:
"You will have the devil
Painted on the side of your heart."

7

His poor little mother
Was calling him by name.
With painful words
His father was advising him.

8

The poor mother was saying:
"The devil has possessed you;
Dear son of my body,
Why are you doing this to me?"

9

When he left his home
He became a robber;
His career did not last long;
They took him prisoner.

10

When he was in prison,
They asked him to certify
Whether his parents were living
Or whether they had died.

11

Con el sombrero en los ojos
él les contestó que no,
que los había abandonado
y la historia les contó.

11

With his hat over his eyes
He replied with a no,
That he had abandoned them
And told them the story.

12

De penitencia le dieron,
cuando de allí lo soltaron,
que se fuera a la cabaña
donde sus padres lo criaron.

12

This penance they gave him,
When he was released from there:
That he should go to the cabin
Where his parents raised him.

13

Cuando se paró en la puerta
los perros lo arrebataron,
y al asomarse para adentro
los ojos se le secaron.

13

When he stopped in the doorway
The dogs bit at him,
And as he peeked inside
His eyes dried up.

14

Después que esto sucedió,
asegún la historia decía,
para su mayor desgracia
puro zacate comía.

14

After this happened,
As the story goes,
For his greater misfortune
He was eating forage.

15

Cuando este ingrato murió
su cuerpo quedó tirado,
y al lado del corazón
tenía el diablo pintado.

15

When this ingrate died
His body was thrown out,
And on the side of his heart
The devil was painted.

16

Reflejen, pongan cuidado,
miren lo que sucedió
a este hijo desobediente
que a sus padres les faltó.

16

Reflect and pay attention,
See what happened
To this disobedient son
Who failed his parents.

17

Jóvenes, a todititos
les encargo demasiado,
no abandonen a sus padres,
pues ya ven lo que ha pasado.

17

Young people, all of you,
I cannot charge you too much,
Do not abandon your parents,
For you see what has happened.

18

Obedezcan a sus padres
les encargo en alta voz,
que un hijo desobediente
no le ve la cara a Dios.

18

Obey your parents
I charge you emphatically,
For a disobedient son
Will not see the face of God.

19

Ya con esto me despido
encargando lo presente,
llamándole a este corrido
El hijo desobediente.

19

Now with this I say good-bye,
Charging all those present,
Naming this ballad
The disobedient son.

<table>
<tr><td>

20

Con J.B.H. me firmo
por dar la conclusión;
despúes que leí la historia
hice la composición.

</td><td>

20

I sign myself J.B.H.
To bring it to conclusion.
After I read the story
I composed this poem.

</td></tr>
</table>

B26. *Carlos Briley*
R1393, Boleslo Gallegos, Albuquerque, N.Mex., 1956, Robb.

1	1
Año del cincuenta y cinco esta desgracia pasó que el día catorce de julio Carlitos Briley se ahogó.	In the year of fifty-five This misfortune occurred. On the fourteenth day of July Little Carlos Briley was drowned.
2	2
A que joyo tan ingrato que desdichado lugar que allí su vida perdió Cuando allí se fué a bañar.	In that most unhappy swimming hole, That unfortunate locality, There he lost his life When he went there to swim.
3	3
Como a las ocho de la noche esta desgracia pasó que en ese malvado joyo Carlitos Briley se ahogó.	At about eight o'clock at night This disaster took place, At that wicked swimming hole Carlos Briley was drowned.
4	4
Lo convidan sus compañeros, él no se quiso salir; Dios lo tenía decretado que allí tenía que morir.	His companions invited him, He did not want to go out; But God had decreed That there he had to die.
5	5
Lumbreros y policías mucho trabajaron en él, pero ya era muy tarde, no lo pudieron volver.	The firemen and policemen Worked hard to save him, But it was already too late, And they couldn't bring him back.
6	6
Recuerda, Joe Mirabal, no se te vaya a olvidar, que la culpa tú tuviste que allí lo dejaste bañar.	Remember, Joe Mirabal, Don't try to forget, It was your fault That you left him there swimming.
7	7
Recuerda, Joe Mirabal, no se te vaya a olvidar, que a Dios tendrás que dar cuenta de ese malvado lugar.	Remember, Joe Mirabal, Don't try to forget, That you'll have to account to God Concerning that wicked place.

Corrido

8

Avisarle a sus abuelos
fué el padre y la policía;
¡cómo lo lloraban triste!
el corazón se partía.

9

Pobre de esos abuelitos
la companía que tenían,
mucho lo van a sentir
porque mucho lo querían.

10

Desde que él era un baybito
sus abuelitos lo criaron,
y con amor y cariño
muy bien siempre lo cuidaron.

11

Le dicen sus abuelitos:
—Carlos de nuestro querer,
Adiós hijito querido,
no te volveremos a ver.—

12

Al Fred y a su mamá Inga
les avisó el policía;
pobrecita de esa madre
ella mucho lo quería.

13

Su mamá Inga le dice:
—Carlos de mi corazón,
te fuiste y nos dejaste
en esta terrible aflicción.—

14

Pobrecito de Carlitos,
un joven tan buen queriente,
respectaba a sus mayores,
y amaba a toda la gente.

15

Sus compañeros y amiguitos
todos mucho lo querían;
por eso han echado menos
su amable y fiel companía.

16

Aquí se acaba cantando
la tragedia de Carlitos
que Dios lo tenga en el cielo
junto con sus angelitos.

8

The priest and the police
Went to notify his grandparents;
How sadly they wept for him,
Their hearts broken.

9

Those poor, dear grandparents
With whom he had lived
Will grieve for him very much
Because they loved him very much.

10

Since he had been a little baby
His grandparents had raised him,
And with love and tenderness
Had always taken good care of him.

11

His grandparents said:
"Carlos whom we loved,
Beloved little son, good-bye,
We shall never see you again."

12

The police notified
Fred and his mother Inga;
That poor mother
Loved him dearly.

13

His mother Inga said:
"Carlos of my heart,
You went away and left us
In this terrible affliction."

14

Poor little Carlos,
A very loving youth,
He was respectful of his elders,
And loved everyone.

15

His companions and friends
All loved him very much;
And so his loving and faithful friends
Miss him.

16

Here ends the singing
Of the tragedy of little Carlos
Whom God now has in heaven
Together with his little angels.

17	17
Carlitos tuvo una dicha	Little Carlos had a blessing
en esos tristes momentos—	In those sad moments—
de recebir de su Iglesia	To receive the last sacraments
los últimos Sacramentos.	Of his Church.

18	18
Adiós, Carlitos querido,	Good-bye, dear little Carlos,
no te volveremos a ver.	We shall not see you again.
Que Dios te tenga en su Reino,	May God keep you in his kingdom,
lugar que debes tener.	A place which you deserve.

19	19
Un favor voy a pedir—	I am going to ask a favor—
no se les vaya a olvidar,	Do not forget,
por el descanso de su alma	Everyone ought to pray
todos deben de rogar.	For the peace of his soul.

As stated in verse 1, the death of Carlos Briley occurred in 1955. The poem was composed by Boleslo Gallegos, who gave me a copy on March 26, 1956. This known fact furnishes some evidence that the date of occurrences mentioned in the *corridos* is usually correct as such poems ordinarily appear to have been composed while the emotional impact of the events is still strong.

B27. *Jesucristo de la Luz* (Jesus Christ of the Light)
R1382, Juan Griego, age 46, Albuquerque, N.Mex., 1956, Robb.

1		1
Jesucristo de la Luz,		Jesus Christ of the Light,
alivia mi lengua mía		Help my speech
para poder explicar	]	So that I may explain
lo que pasó en siete días.	] *Bis*	What happened in seven days.

2		2
Había una buena mujer,		There was a good woman,
la cual dos hijas tenía.		Who had two daughters.
Se casan con dos hermanos,	]	They married two brothers,
que en nada se parecían.	] *Bis*	One so different from the other.

3		3
El chiquito era variz,		The younger was shiftless,
cuanto tenía vendía;		Everything he had he sold;
y el grande trabajador	]	And the older was a worker
que del arado vivía.	] *Bis*	Who lived by his plowing.

4	4
Llegan los años fatales	Then came the fateful years
y el chiquito se muría	And the younger one died,
y queda la pobre viuda	Leaving a poor widow
muy triste y muy afligida,	Very sad and afflicted,
y queda la pobre viuda	Leaving a poor widow
con dos niños que tenía.	With two children.

5	**5**
Allí se va para casa su hermana	Thereupon she goes to her sister's
con dos niños que tenía.	With the two children.
—Concédeme una limosna]	"Grant me alms
que Dios te lo pagaría.] *Bis*	That God may repay your kindness."
6	**6**
—Y enséñate a trabajar.—	"Learn to work!"
Esto le decía María.	This, María told her.
Y sale la pobre viuda,	Out goes the poor widow,
muy triste y muy afligida.	Very sad and afflicted.
Y sale la pobre viuda	Out goes the poor widow
con dos niños que tenía.	With the two children.
7	**7**
Ya allí se va para su casa	Then she returns to her house
con dos niños que tenía	With the two children
y pronto atranca sus puertas]	And quickly locks her doors
ventanas ensolesidas.] *Bis*	And draws the shades.
8	**8**
Seis días le duró el hambre.	She suffered hunger six days.
Y a los siete se muría,	On the seventh day she died,
sufriendo calamidades]	Suffering calamities
con dos niños que tenía.] *Bis*	With her two children.
9	**9**
Llega el hombre del trabajo.	María's husband comes home.
Dice que comer quería.	He says he would like to eat.
Agarra un pan y lo parte,]	He takes some bread and breaks it,
vido que sangre vertía.] *Bis*	He saw that blood flowed from it.
10	**10**
—¿Qué es esto, esposa de mi alma?	"What is this, wife of my soul?
¿Qué es esto, esposa querida?	What is this, beloved wife?
Tal vez alguna limosna]	Perhaps it is alms
que yo se los negaría.—] *Bis*	Which I have denied someone."
11	**11**
Y agarra tres panes el hombre	The man takes three loaves of bread
para casa su cuñada se iba;	And goes to his sister-in-law's;
Halla puertas atrancadas,]	He finds doors locked
ventanas ensolesidas.] *Bis*	And the shades drawn.
12	**12**
Por los resquesitos vido	Through a crack he saw
tres luces vido encendidas.	Three lighted candles.
Vido a su cuñada muerta]	He saw his sister-in-law dead
y a dos niños que tenía.] *Bis*	And the two children she had.
13	**13**
Allí con sus ojos llorosos	There with his eyes weeping,
sus ojos en lagrimías:	His eyes in tears, he cried out:
—Adiós, cuñada de mi alma,]	"Farewell, sister-in-law of my heart,
sobrinitos de mi vida.—] *Bis*	And nephews of my life."

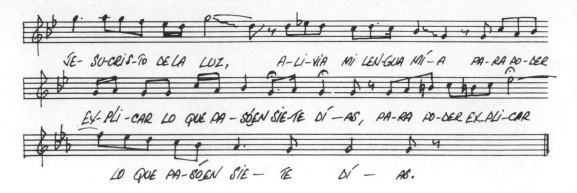

JE-SU-CRIS-TO DE LA LUZ, A-LI-VIA MI LEN-GUA MÍ-A PA-RA PO-DER

EX-PLI-CAR LO QUE PA-SÓ EN SIE-TE DÍ-AS, PA-RA PO-DER EX-PLI-CAR

LO QUE PA-SÓ EN SIE — TE DÍ — AS.

The melody of this *corrido* resembles the familiar *décima* melody. The text, however, is not couched in ten-line *décimas* but in four-line *coplas*, assonated throughout the thirteen verses on the vowels *i* and *a*.

B28. *Jesús y Nestor*
R129, Vidal Valdez et al., Albuquerque, N.Mex., 1947, Robb.

1
Jesús y Nestor se encuentran
y se trataron de amigos;
se fueron a una cantina,
se fueron a tomar vino.

1
Jesús and Nestor met
And became friends;
They went to a bar
To drink some wine.

2
Salieron de la cantina
por en medio de la gente;
se fueron a echar Albures
a la casa de Vicente.

2
They went out of the bar
Through the crowd;
They went to play cards
At the house of Vicente.

3
En el camino donde iban
encuentran a una mujer.
Jesús le dice a Nestor:
—¿qué nos podrá suceder?—

3
On the way
They met a woman.
Jesús said to Nestor:
"I wonder what will happen to us."

4
Cuando llega don Vicente
—Muchachos, ¿qué están haciendo?—
Le respondieron los dos:
—Nos estamos divirtiendo.—

4
When Don Vicente came, he said:
"Boys, what are you doing?"
They both replied:
"We are entertaining ourselves."

5
Una sota para un dos,
la sota vino a la puerta.
Jesús le dice a Nestor:
—¡Ay! te ganas la peseta.—

5
A jack came before a deuce,
The jack came in the door.
Jesús said to Nestor:
"Ah! You win a dollar."

150

6

Nestor le dice a Jesús:
—Yo no te estoy jugando.
Yo te aposté cuatro reales,
a mí me pagas parejo.—

6

Nestor said to Jesús:
"I am not playing for fun.
I bet you two dollars,
You pay me properly."

7

Sacan los dos las pistolas
y se quedaron mirando;
Jesús le dice a Nestor:
—Suéltale. ¿Qué estás temblando?—

7

They both drew their guns
And looked at one another;
Jesús said to Nestor:
"Go on. Why are you trembling?"

8

Les sueltan a las pistolas
y dieron fuego los dos.
Jesús murió renegando;
Nestor aclamando a Dios.

8

They both fired their pistols
And both were hit.
Jesús died cursing;
Nestor died praising God.

B29. *Lucila Ramírez*
R330, S. Ruiz, H. Little, Tijeras, N.Mex., 1950, Robb.

1

Año de mil novecientos
cuarenta y ocho el presente,
ha pasado una tragedia
que se horrorizó la gente.

1

In the year of nineteen hundred
And forty-eight,
A tragedy took place
Which filled people with horror.

2

El día diez y seis de agosto
un cadáver se encontraron;
lo llevaron al mortorio,
pronto lo identificaron.

2

The sixteenth day of August
They found a corpse;
They took it to the mortuary,
Quickly they identified it.

Refrán

¡Ay, qué dolor!
lo siente la sangre nuestra;
ya a ver si el procurador
pone a la raza una muestra.

Refrain

Oh, what sorrow
Is that which our blood feels;
Now we'll see if the prosecutor
Sets an example for our people.

3

Cuando hallaron el cadáver
era cosa muy terrible;
no se sabía quién era,
porque estaba inconocible.

3

When the corpse was found
It was a terrible thing;
You couldn't tell who it was,
Because it was unrecognizable.

4

Pero así tocó la suerte
despúes que ya investigaron;
pronto supieron quien era
por dos prendas que le hallaron.

Refrán

5

Pronto corrió la noticia
y a la ley comunicaron,
que era Lucila Ramírez
el cadáver que encontraron.

6

De Modesto, California,
volando por aeroplano,
salió Lucila Ramírez
para ayudarle a su hermano.

Refrán

7

Cuando ya llegó a Albuquerque
su suerte allí le falló;
y a la orilla de un drenaje,
un criminal la mató.

8

De Modesto, California,
por aeroplano voló;
y una amiga muy querida
y ella la identificó.

Refrán

9

Lester Hay y el Orebeck,
jefes de la policía,
para desolver el crimen
trabajaron noche y día.

10

Después que ya se informaron
según la prensa lo enseña,
fueron por el criminal
al estado de Pennsylvania.

Refrán

11

Ya Lucila está en el cielo,
ya de Dios tiene clemencia;
y el malechor en la cárcel
esperando su sentencia.

4

But that's the way it was
When they investigated;
Soon they knew who it was
By two articles found on the body.

Refrain

5

Soon came the news
And the authorities were informed,
That it was Lucila Ramírez
Whose corpse had been found.

6

From Modesto, California,
Lucila Ramírez
Came by airplane
To help her brother.

Refrain

7

When she came to Albuquerque
Her luck ran out;
On the banks of a drainage ditch
A criminal killed her.

8

From Modesto, California,
A very dear girl friend of hers
Came by plane
And identified the corpse.

Refrain

9

Lester Hay and Orebeck,
The sheriff and chief of police,
In order to solve the crime
Worked night and day.

10

Once they were informed,
As the press told it,
They went to Pennsylvania
To get the criminal.

Refrain

11

Now Lucila is in heaven,
Now she has the pardon of God;
And the evil doer is in jail
Waiting to be sentenced.

A- ÑO DE MIL NO-VE- CIEN-TOS CUA-REN-TAY O-CHOEL PRE-
SEN-TE, HA PA-SA-DO U-NA TRA-GE-DIA QUE SE HO-
RRO RI-ZÓ LA GEN-TE. ¡AY! ¡QUÉ DO-LOR! LO SIEN-
TE LA SAN-GRE NUES-TRA; VAA VER SI EL PRO-CU-RA-
DOR PO-NE A LA RA-ZAU-NA NUES-TRA.

Note that instead of inserting the refrain after each verse, the singer employs it after each pair of verses.

Lucila Ramírez was a nurse who was slain in July, 1947, by Franklin Lester Lindemuth. He was tried and sentenced to life imprisonment, having been found guilty of murder in the first degree for shooting Lucila Ramírez in the head on the banks of the Río Grande.

Lindemuth roomed with Miss Ramírez' brother in Albuquerque and met her when she came to Albuquerque from Modesto, California, to see her brother, who had telephoned her that he was in trouble. Lindemuth had a previous criminal record, begin-

ning when he was fifteen years old. In prison he forged another man's name, and he stabbed another inmate, for which he was locked in solitary confinement.

For further details see the *Albuquerque Journal* of March 27, 1952, and May 8, 1954. I talked to Lester Hay, former sheriff of Bernalillo County, New Mexico, about this case. He gave me the following additional details. The Orebeck referred to in verse 13 must be his deputy, a man named Slaughterback, who worked with him on the case. Lindemuth was convicted only of murder, although there was also evidence of rape.

B30. *Macario Romero*
R2396, Juan Griego, age 61, Albuquerque, N.Mex., 1971, Robb.

1

Dice la niña Rosita:
—Papá, ahí viene Macario.
—Pues hija, ¿en qué lo conoces?
—En el andar de caballo.—

2

Dice la niña Rosita:
—Papá, ahí viene Romero.
—Pues hija, ¿en qué lo conoces?
—Lo conozco en el sombrero.—

1

The child Rosita says:
"Father, there comes Macario."
"Daughter, how do you recognize him?"
"Because he rides a horse."

2

The child Rosita says:
"Father, there comes Romero."
"Daughter, how do you recognize him?"
"I recognize him by his hat."

3

Dice la niña Rosita:
—Papá, ¿pues cómo le haremos?
—Le formaremos un baile,
y asina lo mataremos.—

4

Ahí le formaron un baile
como su padre planeó.
En la entrada de la puerta
Allí fué donde él murió.

5

Dice la niña Rosita:
—Válgame Dios, ¿qué haré yo?
El consuelo que me queda
que un hombre por mi murió.—

6

Dice Macario Romero
cuando sintió los balazos:
—¡Ay! Rosita de mi vida,
quiero morir en tus brazos.

3

The child Rosita says:
"Father, what shall we do?"
"We will arrange a dance,
And then we will kill him."

4

Then they arranged a dance
As her father planned.
As he entered the hall
That is where he died.

5

The child Rosita says:
"God help me, what will I do?
The only consolation I have
Is that a man died for me."

6

Macario Romero says
As he felt the shots:
"Oh, Rosita of my heart,
I want to die in your arms."

This is one of the most popular and widely diffused of the *corridos*. The present version is clearly related to the two versions published by Campa (Campa 2, p. 94). Mendoza published in 1939 no less than six versions in one book from different regions of Mexico (Mendoza 9f, pp. 436, 437, 439, 440, 441, 535). The subject matter of the various versions differs considerably.

I have commented elsewhere (see *Bernardo*, A11) on the theme present here: the authority of the father over his daughter, to defy which is a matter of life and death.

B30a. *Macario Romero*
RB637, Juan Urías, Patagonia, Arizona, 1949, Doris Seibold.

1

Dice Macario Romero:
—Oiga, mi General Plata,
permítame una licencia
para ir a ver a mi chata.—

1

Macario Romero says:
"Listen, General Plata,
Grant me a leave
To go and see my kitten."

<table>
<tr><td>

2

General Plata le dice:
—Macario ¿qué vas a hacer?
Te van a quitar la vida
por esa ingrata mujer.—

</td><td>

2

General Plata says to him:
"Macario, what are you going to do?
They will kill you and all
Because of that ungrateful woman."

</td></tr>
</table>

(Remainder of fifteen verses undecipherable)

DI-CE MA-CA-RIO RO-ME-RO: —OI-GA, MI

GE-NE-RAL PLA-TA, PER-MI-TA-ME-U-NA LI-
(GUITAR INTERLUDE)

CEN-CIA-PA-RA IR A VER A MI CHA-TA.—

B31. *Andrés Mora y Lola Chávez*
R1907, A. Mendonca, Moriarty, N.Mex., Robb.

<table>
<tr><td>

1

Año de mil novecientos
diecisiete al terminar,
miren lo que ha sucedido,
y ahora lo voy a cantar.

</td><td>

1

In the year of nineteen hundred
And seventeen, to be brief,
Look at what happened,
And now I'm going to sing it for you.

</td></tr>
<tr><td>

2

El veintitrés de noviembre,
presente lo tengo yo,
murió Lolita Chávez,
Andrés Mora la mató.

</td><td>

2

The twenty-third of November,
I remember well,
Lolita Chávez died,
Andrés Mora killed her.

</td></tr>
<tr><td>

3

Lola estaba muy contenta
cuando se sentó a almorzar
sin pensar un momento
lo que le iba a pasar.

</td><td>

3

Lola was very contented
When she sat down to lunch
Without thinking for a moment
Of what was to come.

</td></tr>
<tr><td>

4

Lola iba para la escuela
con mucho ánimo y valor;
como no tenía nada de culpa
no tuvo ningún temor.

</td><td>

4

Lola went to school
With much spirit and courage;
Since she had nothing to be ashamed of
She felt no fear.

</td></tr>
<tr><td>

5

Doña Juanita Padilla
es la que la acompañó
hasta al puente donde estaba
Andrés, él que la mató.

</td><td>

5

Doña Juanita Padilla
Is the one who went with her
As far as the bridge where
Andrés, who killed her, was waiting.

</td></tr>
</table>

<table>
<tr><td>

6

A las ocho de la mañana
en el puente la encontró
con su pistola en la mano
dos balazos le pegó.

7

Antes que llegase alguno
cuando estaba caída Lola
Andrés se pegó otro tiro
y allí soltó su pistola.

8

Don Gumesindo García
fué el primero que llegó
y la levanta del suelo
y en sus brazos la llevó.

9

Se vino toda la gente
junto del puente se juntó;
toditos muy asustados
de ver lo que sucedió.

10

Cuando Lola fué llevada
para su hogar paternal
le pide su bendición
que ya se va a descansar.

11

Su madre cuando la vió
sorprendida de dolor;
abrazó y besó a su hija
y le echó su bendición.

12

Su padre de igual manera
de ver a su hija querida
le echó su bendición
por última despedida.

13

—Adiós, hija de mi vida,
prenda de mi corazón,
por última despidida
recibe mi bendición.

14

—No esté triste, madre mía,
no llore, tenga consuelo,
que yo me voy a gozar
la gloria y reina del cielo.—

</td><td>

6

At eight in the morning
He met her at the bridge
With his pistol in his hand
And fired two shots at her.

7

Before anyone came
While she was lying there
Andrés wounded himself
And his pistol fell there.

8

Don Gumesindo García
Was the first one who came
And picked her up from the ground
And carried her in his arms.

9

All the people came
And gathered at the bridge;
Everyone was very agitated
When they saw what had happened.

10

When Lola was carried
To her father's home
She asked his blessing
Before going to rest.

11

When her mother saw her
She was overcome with anguish;
She embraced and kissed her daughter
And gave her her blessing.

12

Her father likewise
On seeing his beloved daughter
Gave her his blessing
For her last farewell.

13

"Farewell, daughter of my life,
Darling of my heart,
For a last farewell
Receive my blessing."

14

"Don't be sad, dear mother,
Don't weep, take comfort,
For I am going to enjoy
The glory and queen of heaven."

</td></tr>
</table>

15

Andrés se fué por la calle,
caminando adolorido,
hasta la casa del juez
donde fué bien recibido.

16

Sin saber lo que pasaba
y lleno de compasión,
don Rómulo lo llevaba
y lo acuesta en el colchón.

17

Cuando llegó al aguacil
él informa al juez de una vez:
—Señor, yo he venido aquí
por el arresto de Andrés.—

18

El juez pregunta por qué
lo vinieran a arrestar.
—Señora Lolita Chávez
la acaba de matar.—

19

El juez se asustaba mucho
de oír lo que se decía.
—Señora (sic), ahí lo tiene usted,
yo nada de esto sabía.—

20

Llaman pronto al sacerdote,
al alguacil, y al doctor,
junto con ellos vino
también el procurador.

21

Hicieron su confesión ante
su adminestron reciben
los sacramentos
para ir ante su Creador.

22

Los llevan a Santa Fe
después de su confesión.
Lola llega al sanitorio
y Andrés llega a la prisión.

23

Pero ninguno de ellos fué
posible que vivieran;
a entregaron su alma a Diós
antes de que amaneciera.

15

Andrés went down the street,
Wandering, beset with sorrow,
To the house of the judge
Where he was welcomed in.

16

Without knowing what had happened
And full of compassion,
Don Rómulo took him
And laid him to rest on the couch.

17

When the constable came
He told the judge at once:
"Sir, I have come here
To arrest Andrés."

18

The judge asks why
They should come to arrest him.
"He has just killed
Señora Lolita Chávez."

19

The judge was very upset
To hear what was said.
"Señora, you have him there,
I knew nothing of this."

20

They promptly called the priest,
The constable, and the doctor,
And along with them came
The prosecutor, too.

21

They heard his confession
Before administering
The last sacrament
So she could go before her Creator.

22

They took them to Santa Fe
After the confession.
They took Lola to the hospital
And they took Andrés to prison.

23

But for neither of them was it possible
That they should live;
They delivered their souls to God
Before daybreak.

24

Dos noches fueron velados
en el modo más decente;
también a los dos les dieron
misa de cuerpo presente.

24

For two nights wakes were held
In the most decent manner;
Likewise masses for the dead
Were held for both of them.

25

Iguales son sepultados
con mucho lujo y aseo,
Andrés en la capital
y Lolita en Galisteo.

25

Likewise they were buried
With much luxury and neatness,
Andrés in the capital
And Lolita in Galisteo.

26

Les mencionaré el lugar
por que dirán donde fué en
la plaza de Galisteo,
condado de Santa Fe.

26

I will mention the place,
It was in
The town of Galisteo
In the county of Santa Fe.

27

Adiós padres de Lolita,
con gran pesar y dolor
pedimos que Dios le dé
resignación y valor.

27

Farewell, parents of Lolita,
With great heaviness and sorrow
We pray that God will give you
Resignation and courage.

28

Señor Apolonio Chávez,
hombre de honor y sentido,
reciba usted estos versos,
perdone lo mal servido.

28

Señor Apolonio Chávez,
Man of honor and sentiment,
Receive these verses,
Pardon their shortcomings.

29

Luisito Antonio Sánchez,
para expresarme mejor,
es el joven que se ofrece
de usted su servidor.

29

Luisito Antonio Sánchez,
To be more specific,
Is the young man who offers
Them to you as your servant.

B32. *Federico Chávez*
RB748, 1950, Cobos.

1

A Dios le pido licencia
y que me preste sentido
para que todos se informen
lo que en Cuba ha sucedido.

1

I ask God's permission
And that he lend me the fervor
So that everyone may learn
What has happened in Cuba (New Mexico).

2

Pues en la plaza de Cuba,
Condado de Sandoval,
donde ha pasado este caso
por una mano fatal.

2

Well, in the town of Cuba,
In Sandoval County,
It was there that this happened
By a fatal hand.

3

Vuela, vuela, palomita,
a la gloria con las aves
y busquen un buen asiento
para Federico Chávez.

4

Año de mil novecientos
y treinta y cinco al saber
por manos de un huero ingrato
deja viuda a una mujer.

5

Dejó a su esposa querida
y también a dos hijitas;
por medio de trampe hambriado
se quedaron huerfanitas.

6

El diecinueve de agosto
el lunes en la mañana
sería a la una y treinta
que llegó la hora tirana.

7

Treinta y seis años de edad
es lo que Chávez contaba;
de aquella edad tan temprana
él la muerte no esperaba.

8

Esa noche el pobrecito
nunca podía esperar
que un trampe como era Shorty
a él venía a matar.

9

Yo quisiera que el gobierno
se informará de estos casos
porque aquí a sus ciudadanos
los trampes les dan balazos.

10

Cualesquier trampe maldito
que cae de país lejano
viene a quitarle la vida
a todo buen ciudadano.

11

¿Qué corazón tan maldito
con confianza y sin pesar;
de lo que había pasado
agarró sueño normal?

3

Fly, fly, little dove,
To heaven with the birds
To seek a good seat
For Federico Chávez.

4

In the year of nineteen hundred
And thirty-five as is known
By the hand of a rotten ingrate
A woman was made a widow.

5

He left his beloved wife
And also two little daughters;
By the act of a hungry tramp
They became orphans.

6

The nineteenth of August,
Monday, in the morning,
At about one thirty
The fatal hour arrived.

7

Thirty-six years of age
Was what Chávez had attained;
At such an early age
He was not expecting to die.

8

That night the poor man
Could never have expected
That a tramp like Shorty
Would come to kill him.

9

I should like that the government
Be informed of these cases
Because here the tramps
Shoot the citizens.

10

Any cursed old tramp
Who comes from some faraway land
Comes to take away the life
Of a perfectly good citizen.

11

What heart is so cursed
That confidently and without sorrow
Could sleep normally
In view of what has happened?

12

Llegó derecho a su casa
y en su cama se acostó;
bien dormido en sus cabales
la policía lo halló.

13

Lo trajeron a la cárcel
del condado de Sandoval,
y todavía el maldito
acusa que no hizo mal.

14

Federico Chávez pide
desde su sueño profundo
que castiguen con lo mismo
al que lo quitó del mundo.

15

Un tal de nombre James Shorter
fué el asesino fatal;
que de Dios espere el pago
en el alto tribunal.

16

Pues Federico fué muerto
y de Dios fué decretado;
de un balazo en un sentido,
pasándole al otro lado.

17

Fred Chávez perdió su vida
con un balazo fatal,
afuera de la cantina
de Fernando Sandoval.

18

De la cantina salió
y con Shorter platicaba,
sin saber el pobrecito
que su muerte lo rodeaba.

19

Platicando allí los dos
el diablo a Shorter tentó
y sacando su pistola
a Federico mató.

20

Pues Fernando Sandoval,
el dueño de la cantina,
tan luego que oyó un balazo
salió a asomarse a la esquina.

12

He went straight to his house
And in his bed he went to sleep;
He was actually sleeping soundly
When the police found him.

13

They took him to the jail
Of the county of Sandoval,
And still the cursed man
Claimed that he had not done wrong.

14

Federico Chávez pleads
From his profound sleep
That they punish with death
The man who killed him.

15

A fellow named James Shorter
Was the fatal assassin,
Who awaits his sentence from God
In the high tribunal.

16

Well, Federico was dead
And it was decreed by God;
With a bullet in one temple,
Passing to the other side.

17

Fred Chávez lost his life
With a fatal bullet,
Outside the cantina
Of Fernando Sandoval.

18

He came out of the cantina
And was chatting with Shorter,
Without knowing, poor man,
That death hovered over him.

19

While the two were talking there
The devil tempted Shorter
And drawing his pistol
He killed Federico.

20

Then Fernando Sandoval,
The proprietor of the cantina,
As soon as he heard a shot
Came out and looked around the corner.

21

Lo primero que encontró
fué a Federico tirado
y a Shorter le preguntaba
que es lo que había pasado.

21

The first thing he saw
Was Federico shot
And he asked Shorter
What had happened.

22

Shorter le contestó
con la pistola en la mano:
—Déme ese frasco de whiskey
o despacho otro chicano.

22

Shorter replied
With his pistol in his hand:
"Give me that flask of whiskey
Or I'll dispatch another chicano."

23

Vete a tu casa—le dijo,
—sin moverte ni el sombrero,
sí no lo haces yo a tu cuerpo
lo vuelvo un puro agujero.—

23

"Get back in your house," he said,
"Without even touching your hat,
Or if you don't
I'll put a hole through you."

24

Pues el matador maldito
se retira de la cantina;
se subió a una troquita
y se fué para Regina.

24

Then the cursed killer
Left the cantina;
He took a few more drinks
And went to the town of Regina.

25

Sofía Chávez, su esposa,
abranzaba a sus hijitas;
lloraba por su marido
y de ver sus huerfanitas.

25

Sofía Chávez, his wife,
Embraced her two little daughters;
She wept for her husband
And at the sight of her little orphans.

26

A Delurdes y a Corina
Sofía así les decía:
—Mataron a Federico,
se fué de nuestra compañía.—

26

To Delurdes and to Corina
Sofía spoke in this manner:
"They killed Federico,
He has gone from our company."

27

El que lea este corrido
por favor yo le suplico:
que rece tres padre nuestros
por el alma de Federico.

27

He who reads this ballad
I beg to do me this favor:
Say three Our Fathers
For the soul of Federico.

28

Con los parientes de Chávez
me uno con ellos en duelo
pidiendo que Federico
mi Dios lo tenga en el cielo.

28

I join in sorrow
With the relatives of Chávez,
Praying that God
Will keep Federico in heaven.

This *corrido* comes from Cuba, New Mexico. The date is given as August 19, 1935. It is interesting to observe in verse 22 the use of the word *chicano*, which has more recently come into common use. It is used here in a derisive sense and reveals the racial antagonism felt by and for the murderer, James Shorter, known as Shorty, who is described as a hungry tramp.

B33. *Juan Charrasqueado*
Hansen 6a (no. 4, p. 299), G. Villagrano, age 52, Corona, Calif., Hansen.

1

Voy a cantarles un corrido muy
  mentado
lo que ha pasado allá en la Hacienda
  de la Flor,
la triste historia de un ranchero
  enamorado,
que fué borracho, parrandero, y
  jugador.

2

Juan se llamaba y lo apodaban
  Charrasqueado,
era valiente y arriesgado en el amor,

y a las mujeres más bonitas se
  llevaba
y en esos campos no dejaba ni una flor.

3

Un día domingo que se andaba
  emborrachando
a la cantina le corrieron a avisar:

—Cuídate, Juan, que ya por ahí te
  andan buscando,
son muchos hombres, no te vayan a
  matar.—

4

No tuvo tiempo de montar en su
  caballo,
toda la gente se le echaron de a montón.

—Que estoy borracho—les gritaba—y
  soy buen gallo,—
cuando una bala atravesó su corazón.

5

Ya las campanas del santuario están
  doblando,
todos los fieles se dirigen a rezar,

y por los Cerros los rancheros van
  bajando
un hombre muerto que lo llevan a enterrar.

1

A well-known *corrido* I will now sing
  for you,
What happened there at the Ranch of
  the Flowers,
The sad story of a rancher whose love
  was true,
Who drank, caroused, and even gambled
  at all hours.

2

Charrasqueado he was called but Juan
  was his name,
In matters of love he was both valiant and
  bold,
And the most beautiful girls all loved him
  the same,
And in every place his promise to all was
  told.

3

One Sunday morning after beginning to
  drink,
His friends ran to the canteen to try and
  advise:
"Be careful, Juan, they will find you here,
  so they think,
They are many and want to kill you by
  surprise."

4

There was not even time to climb upon his
  horse,
All the men who were there rushed from
  every side.
"Well, I'm drunk," he shouted, "but I'm not
  quite so coarse."
And then a bullet pierced his heart and there
  he died.

5

And now the bells of the sanctuary are
  ringing,
All of the faithful ones are going there to
  pray,
And down from the mountainside the
  ranchers are bringing
The body of a dead man to bury this day.

6

Ya creció la milpa con la lluvia del potrero,

ya las palomas van volando al palomar,

bonitos toros llevan ahora al matadero,

que buen caballo va montando el caporal.

6

The corn land in the pasture is covered with rain,

And to the dovecote all the pigeons are now flying,

Handsome bulls to be killed are taken once again,

And a beautiful horse the foreman is now riding.

7

Y en una choza muy humilde llora un niño
y las mujeres se aconsejan y se van,

mientras su madre lo consuela con cariño

mirando al cielo, llora, y reza por su Juan.

7

In a humble cabin a little child is crying,
All the women come to council and then they leave,

While the mother to console her poor child is trying,

She prays for her Juan, and sobs and now she must grieve.

8

Aquí termino de cantar este corrido
de Juan, ranchero, charrasqueado, y burlador,

que se creyó de las mujeres consentido,

que fué borracho, parrandero, y jugador.

8

And now I must bring this *corrido* to an end,
Of Juan, a rancher, deceiver, and jester bold,

Who thought himself of every woman a good friend,

But who drank, caroused, and even gambled, I'm told.

MOR, YA LAS MU-JE-RES MÁS BO-NI-TAS SE LLE-VA-BA Y EN E-SOS CAMPOS NO DE-JA-BA NI U-NA FLOR.

B34. *Pedro Sandoval*
RB747, Carmelita Trujillo, Truchas, N.Mex., 1950, Cobos.

1

El día veintiuno de junio,
presente lo tengo yo,
que Pedro Sandoval mi primo
con un rifle se mató.

1

On the twenty-first day of June,
The date is always present to me,
My cousin Pedro Sandoval
Killed himself with a rifle.

2

El estaba travesiando,
según lo entiendo yo,
con un rifle treinta treinta
y solito se mató.

2

He was playing around,
As I understand it,
And with a thirty-thirty
All alone he killed himself.

3

Delfino y Victoriano
estaban en su compañía
cuando Pedro se mató
y sólo trece años tenía.

3

Delfino and Victoriano
Were in his company
When Pedro killed himself
And he was only thirteen years old.

4

Los tres solitos estaban
divirtiéndose con juguetes
porque sus padres y hermanos
todos estaban ausentes.

4

The three of them were alone
Amusing themselves with games
Because their parents and brothers
All were absent.

5

En la casa de don Gregorio
allí fué donde murió;
también ellos estaban ausentes
cuando el caso sucedió.

5

In the house of Don Gregory
It was that he died;
They also were absent
When the thing happened.

6

Cuando Delfino entró
él un fósforo prendió
y allí lo vido tirado
nomás los ojos abrió.

6

When Delfino entered
He lighted a match
And saw him there, wounded,
Briefly open his eyes.

7

Pobrecito de Pedrito,
ya él no pudo hablar,
y en eso entró Marcial
como queriendo llorar.

7

Poor little Pedro,
He could not speak,
And just then Marcial came in
As if wanting to weep.

8

El le preguntó a Delfino
que si qué había pasado;
y Delfino respondió
que Pedro se había matado.

8

He asked Delfino
What had happened;
And Delfino replied
That Pedro had killed himself.

9

Cuando la noticia llegó
que Pedro se había matado
su padre con sus hermanos
se quedó muy asustado.

9

When the news came
That Pedro had killed himself
His father and his brothers
Were very agitated.

10

Ya con ésta me despido
como flor de amapolita;
mi apelativo es Trujillo
y mi nombre Carmelita.

10

Now with this I conclude
Like the flower of the little poppy;
My last name is Trujillo
And my first name is Carmelita.

As the final verse reveals, this *corrido* was
composed by the singer, Carmelita Trujillo,
of Truchas, New Mexico.

B35. *Joaquin Murieta*
R2423, Juan Griego, age 61, Albuquerque, N.Mex., 1971, Robb. Cf. RB555 (Arizona).
Also see Introduction above, "Studies in Depth," pp. 14–15.

1

Me pasié por California
en el año del cincuenta
con mi sillita plateada
y mi pistola repleta.
Si quieren saber mi nombre
me llamo Joaquín Murieta.

1

I rode through California
The year of eighteen fifty
With my silver saddle
And my loaded pistol.
If you want to know my name
My name is Joaquín Murieta.

2

Me signa Joaquín Murieta,
desgraciado Americano.
Tú serás el capitán
que matates a mi hermano;
lo matates sin defensa,
desgraciado Americano.

2

I sign myself Joaquín Murieta,
Wretched American.
You must be the captain
Who killed my brother;
You killed him in cold blood,
Wretched American.

3

Me signa Joaquín Murieta,
desgraciado Americano.
Asina yo lo esperaba
que ya no había esperanza.
Procurando la venganza,
desgraciado Americano.

3

I sign myself Joaquín Murieta,
Wretched American.
This is how I expected it
That there was no longer any hope.
Now I seek vengeance,
Wretched American.

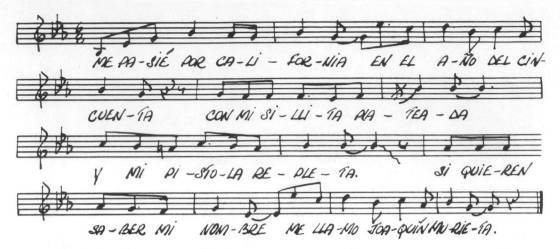

ME PA-SIÉ POR CA-LI-FOR-NIA EN EL A-ÑO DEL CIN-
CUEN-TA CON MI SI-LLI-TA PLA-TEA-DA
Y MI PI-STO-LA RE-DLE-TA. SI QUIE-REN
SA-BER MI NOM-BRE ME LLA-MO JOA-QUÍN MU-RIE-TA.

As Ridge's *The Life and Adventures of Joaquín Murieta* makes clear, this account is fictional, and there is much doubt concerning the identity of the "real" Joaquín Murieta. However, Joaquín Murieta does exist as a mythical, bloodthirsty California outlaw rivaling in fame New Mexico's Billy the Kid.

B36. *El Merino*
R27, Juan Morales, Cuba, N.Mex., 1944, Robb.

1
Y oyes, "Merino" mentado
¿qué siente tu corazón?
¿Por qué estás tan apasionado
siendo que tú en el Tucsón
y eras el caballo acreditado,
dueño de tu situación?

1
Hear ye, "Merino" of great fame,
What does your heart feel?
Why are you so passionate
Seeing that you in Tucson
Were the favorite horse,
Master of any situation?

2
No eras aquel fanfarrón
que llegas haciendo ruido
y en la plaza de Tucsón
puro un discracha has tenido.

2
You were not that great blow hard
That came in making a great noise
And in the plaza of Tucson
You only got a lucky break.

3
De la carrera pasada
no mereciste el nido,
ni llegaste a la jugada.
¿Qué es lo que tienes perdido?
Ganaste de chiripada.

3
In the past race
You did not deserve the prize,
Nor did you carry it off.
How much did you lose?
You won only by lucky accident.

4
No vuelvas a prospectar
sin conocer los metales,
que no hay mina más formal
que la de Tomás González.
Tiene puestos animales
dispuestos para el combate
y en el asilo de la mina
toneladas de zacate.

4
Never again go prospecting
With no knowledge of metals,
For there's no mine more sure
Than that of Tomás González.
He keeps animals ready
Well disposed for combat
And in the "asylum of the mine"
Many tons of hay.

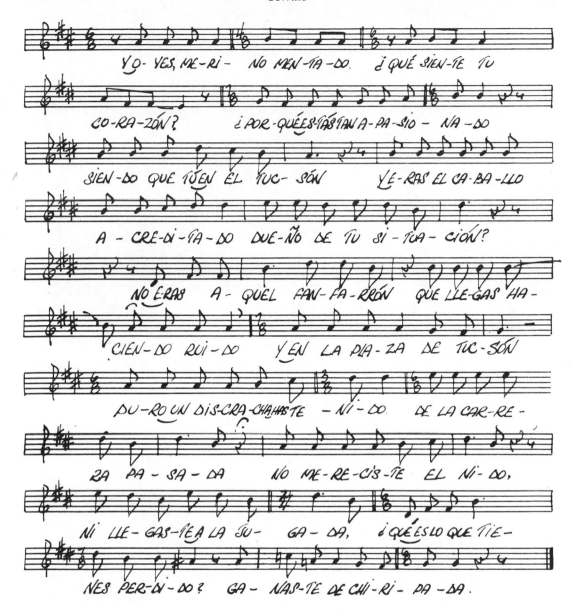

YO-YES, ME-RI-NO MEN-TA-DO. ¿ QUÉ SIEN-TE TU
CO-RA-ZÓN? ¿ POR-QUÉ ES-TÁS TAN A-PA-SIO-NA-DO
SIEN-DO QUE TIEN EL TUC-SÓN YE-RAS EL CA-BA-LLO
A-CRE-DI-TA-DO DUE-ÑO DE TU SI-TUA-CIÓN?
NO ERAS A-QUEL FAN-FA-RRÓN QUE LLE-GAS HA-
CIEN-DO RUI-DO Y EN LA PLA-ZA DE TUC-SÓN
DU-RO UN DIS-CRA-CHAHSTE - NI-DO. DE LA CAR-RE-
ZA PA-SA-DA NO ME-RE-CIS-TE EL NI-DO,
NI LLE-GAS-TEA LA JU-GA-DA, ¿QUÉ ES LO QUE TIE-
NES PER-DI-DO? GA-NAS-TE DE CHI-RI-PA-DA.

B37. *Valentín Manceras*
R1417, Edwin Berry, Tomé, N.Mex., 1956, Robb. Cf. Mendoza 9e (pp. 183–88).

1

Año de mil ochocientos
ochenta y cuatro en que estamos
murió Valentín Manceras;
¡ahora sí nos atrasamos!

Refrán

¡Ay, qué dolor!
para su madre querida
que por querer tía Juana
le hayan quitado la vida.

1

In the year of eighteen hundred
And eighty-four in which we now are,
Valentín Manceras died;
How well we remember!

Refrain

Oh, what sorrow!
For his beloved mother,
That because he loved Aunt Juana
They have taken away his life.

167

2

En San Juan de Dios nació
y en San Juan de Dios murió,
y Sanjuana se llamaba
la ingrata que lo entregó.

Refrán

3

Juana le dice a su hermana:
—¿Qué dices, lo entregaremos?
Tres cientos pesos nos dan
con eso nos mantendremos.—

Refrán

2

In San Juan de Dios he was born
And in San Juan de Dios he died,
And Sanjuana was the name
Of the traitoress who betrayed him.

Refrain

3

Juana says to her sister:
"What do you say? Let's turn him in.
They'll give us three hundred pesos,
We can live on that."

Refrain

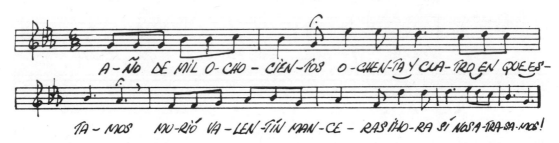

B38. *María*
R220, C. Segura, Canjilón, N.Mex., 1949, Robb.

1

María se levantó
una noche desperada
apreviniendo su ropa
para irse a la madrugada.

2

—¡Ay!— su madre pregunta:
—¿María, qué andas haciendo?
¿Qué tráfico traes ahí dentro,
que parece que es de día?

3

—Mamacita de mi vida,
al fin que se hace tarde,
ando buscando un remedio
que está enferma mi comadre.—

4

Otro día por la mañana
María amaneció en la loma
devisando para su tierra
un sospiro a su paloma.

1

María got up
One night in desperation,
Getting her clothes ready
To go away at daybreak.

2

"Ah!" her mother asked her:
"María, what are you doing?
What's going on in here?
You act as if it were daylight."

3

"Dear mama of my life,
It may soon be too late,
I am looking for medicine
For my friend is sick."

4

The next day in the morning
María arrived at the hilltop
Looking down at her country
And sighing to her dove.

5

—Jesusito, Jesusito,
este corazón es tuyo,
pero antes que nos alcancen
échale cuarta seguro.—

6

México en una laguna,
Guadalajara en un llano.
Esta canción fué compuesta
por un fino Mexicano.

7

Dos por siete son catorce,
tres por siete veintiuno.
Si habrá cantadas bonitas,
pero como ésta ninguna.

5

"Jesusito, Jesusito,
This heart is yours,
But before they catch us
Whip the horse fiercely."

6

Mexico is in a lake,
Guadalajara is in a plain.
This song was composed
By a fine Mexican.

7

Two times seven make fourteen,
Three times seven, twenty-one.
There may be beautiful songs,
But none equal to this one.

The first and second lines of verse 6 are borrowed from a well-known Mexican folk song, *El Pavorial* (see *El Pavo Real*, C42).

B39. *Nestorita*
R2399, Juan Griego, age 61, Albuquerque, N.Mex., 1971, Robb. Cf. C36.

1

Tortolitas, tortolitas,
no lloren con aflicción,
dejen que duerma y descanse
este herido corazón.

2

Iba Víctor Archuleta
trote y trote en su burrita,
chiflando para la estafeta
y trateando a Nestorita.

3

Cuando a la estafeta llega
y por sus cartas preguntó
las gracias de Nestorita
fueron las que recibió.

1

Doves, singing doves,
Don't cry with such affliction,
Let this wounded heart
Sleep and rest.

2

Víctor Archuleta was going
On his little burro trotting and
Whistling towards the post office
And thinking about Nestorita.

3

When he arrived at the post office
And asked for his letters
Nestorita's thanks (a dear John letter)
Is what he received.

4

Luego que tomó la carta
con asunto la leyí.
Le dió un atarantamiento
que no supo ni hayí.

4

As soon as he got his letter
With interest he read it.
He felt so faint
He did not know what to do.

5

—Pues ¿qué te mandó a decir?—
le dice don Ginio Ortega.
—Las gracias de Nestorita
acabo de recibir.—

5

"Well, what is her message?"
Asked Don Ginio Ortega.
"I have just received
Nestorita's rejection."

6

¡Arbolito de manzanas!
¿Qué es el fruto que das más?
Ahora sí estoy satisfecho
con conocerte no más.

6

Little apple tree!
Which is the fruit you bear most?
Now I am satisfied
With only knowing you.

7

La Conferinas Domingues
fué la de la perdición,
el teléfono sin alambre,
hija de don Concensión.

7

Conferinas Domingues,
Daughter of Don Concensión,
Is to blame for our failure.
She's a wireless telephone.

B40. *La Cantada de Guerra* (The Song of War)
R627, Nicolás Martínez, age 75, Chimayó, N.Mex., 1951, Robb.

1

Año de 1941 esa parte.
La guerra se puso dura, señores, por muchas
partes.
Señores, por muchas partes, yo les digo la
verdad,
que la guerra estalló dura, en realidad.

1

In the year 1941 this begins.
The war was very difficult, sirs, in many
places.
Sirs, in many places, I'm telling you the
truth,
The war broke out in reality.

2

El día siete de diciembre, pero con mala
intención,
quiso tener conferencia, ese maldito
Japón.   ] *Bis*

2

On the seventh of December, but with evil
intentions,
That cursed Japan wanted to have a
conference.

3

Ese Saburo Kurusu, no debemos de olvidar,
fué él que vino a Estados Unidos con mente
de traicionar.   ] *Bis*

3

That Saburo Kurusu, we mustn't forget,
Was the one who came to the United States
with a mind set on treachery.

4

Ya de mañana fué mandado, ese maldito
Japón,
Tiene que ser redactado y acaba con su
nación.   ] *Bis*

5

Ya de mañana se creó, ese maldito Japón,

Por eso quiso acabar con parte de nuestra
nación.   \

6

Presidente Roosevelt no sabía su intención,

por ese le recibió, y él con su buen corazón.

7

Como a las once del día ya estaban
conferenciando,
Japón y Estados Unidos ya estaban
acabando.   ] *Bis*

8

Entre las cinco y las nueve de la mañana una
cosa sucedía
cuando Japón le pagó esta noble
compañía.   ] *Bis*

9

Pobrecitos de estos jefes de los Estados
Unidos,
Llegaron de la parranda, Japón les pegó
dormidos.   ] *Bis*

10

Pobrecitos de estos jefes, dando su
reclamación,
la reclamación de Dios palpite en el corazón.

11

Les encargó a los soldados de los Estados
Unidos
no se crean de Japón y no vuelvan ya
dormidos.   ] *Bis*

12

Pobrecita de esa gente del estado de Pearl
Harbor,
¡cómo no se encontrarían por los suelos bien
tirados!   .   ] *Bis*

13

Pobrecita de esa gente de la ciudad de
Bataan,

4

It was already ordered in the morning, that
cursed Japan,
That relations must be broken off with their
nation.

5

It was already begun in the morning, that
cursed Japan,
That's why they wanted to break with our
country.

6

President Roosevelt didn't know his
intentions,
That's why he, with his good heart, received
him.

7

Around eleven in the morning they were
already in conference,
Japan and the United States were already
breaking off relations.

8

Between five and nine in the morning
something happened
When Japan attacked that noble company.

9

The poor leaders of the United States,

The party was over, Japan had attacked
while they slept.

10

These poor leaders, issuing their protest,

May the protest of God throb from their
hearts.

11

They ordered the soldiers of the United
States
Not to believe Japan and not to fall asleep
again.

12

The poor people of the state of Pearl Harbor,

How they found themselves well thrown to
the ground!

13

Those poor people of the city of Bataan,

en los tiempos de saberla, ¿cómo no se acordarán? 　　　] *Bis*	At the time of learning of it, how can they ever forget it?

14	**14**
Eran mil o dos mil soldados los que estaban en Bataan, pobrecitos prisioneros, Dios sabe si volverán. 　　　] *Bis*	There were one or two thousand soldiers on Bataan, Poor prisoners, God knows if they'll return.

15	**15**
Seguía Corregidor, no debemos de olvidar, pobrecitos prisioneros, Dios sabe si ellos vendrán. 　　　] *Bis*	Corregidor followed, we shouldn't forget, Poor prisoners, God knows if they'll come back.

16	**16**
Todos los soldados de los Estados Unidos, Dios que vaya con ustedes y los traiga si han servido.	To all the soldiers of the United States, May God go with you and bring you back if you have served well.

17	**17**
El poder de Dios valga y la fuerza de la reina que si Dios nos da licencia, nos volveremos a ver. 　　　] *Bis*	May the power of God and the strength of the Virgin prevail, That if God permit, we will see one another again.

18	**18**
Señor Presidente Truman, escuche con atención, que si ha poco hace descuido, pues le pega otra nación. 　　　] *Bis*	President Truman, listen carefully, If you are careless, then another nation will attack you.

19	**19**
Adiós, Estados Unidos, lo digo de corazón. Y así se acaban cantando, los versos de esta traición.	Good-bye, United States, I say it from my heart. And thus ends the singing of the verses of this treachery.

Both this *corrido* and *Las Islas Hawaiianas* (B41) could equally well have been classified under Section J "Patriotism, History, Politics."

B41. *Las Islas Hawaiianas* (The Hawaiian Islands)
R2172, Vincent F. Gallegos, age 68, Albuquerque, N.Mex., 1966, Robb. Cf. RB970 (a different song with the same title).

1	1
El día siete de diciembre	The seventh of December
lo vamos a mencionar	As we shall mention
llegaron los japoneses	The Japanese arrived
las Islas a bombardear.	To bomb the Isles.

2	2
El día siete de diciembre	The seventh of December
eran las dos de la tarde	It was two in the afternoon
cuando oyimos en el radio	When we heard over the radio
el reporte del alarme.	The alarming report.

3	3
Llegaron los japoneses	The Japanese arrived
el día siete de diciembre	On the seventh of December
a las Islas Hawaiianas	In the Hawaiian Islands
tratando matar la gente.	Threatening to kill the people.

4	4
Como tres mil fueron muertos	About three thousand were killed
y seiscientos los heridos.	And six hundred wounded.
No es nada matar la gente	It is nothing to kill the people
cuando los hallan dormidos.	When you find them asleep.

5	5
Los pobrecitos soldados	The poor soldiers
no tenían ningún recelo	Had no suspicion
que vieron lloviendo bombas	When they saw the bombs flying
cuales venían del cielo.	Down from the sky.

6	6
Se levantan asustados	They arise, frightened,
despertados derrepente	As suddenly awakened,
y vieron en los aviones	They saw on the airplanes
la emblema del sol saliente.	The emblem of the rising sun.

7	7
Llegaron los japoneses	The Japanese arrived
a darnos una invasión.	To invade us.
Los pobrecitos civiles	The poor civilians—
los siento de corazón.	I feel for them in my heart.

8	8
Hermanos, novias, y padres,	Our brothers, sweethearts, and fathers,
también cuñados tenemos	Also our brother-in-laws are
peleando por nuestra patria,	Fighting for our country,
pronto nos encontraremos.	We soon shall meet.

9

Las madres que tienen hijos
que en la otra guerra pelearon,
así como ellos volvieron
a estos los esperamos.

10

Los Nuevo Mexicanitos
peleando por la nación
con nuestras madres queridas,
rezando de corazón.

11

Del hospital del estado
fueron los compositores.
Que son Melecio Perea,
Marcos Ortega, y Juan Flores.

12

No somos compositores
ni nos vamos al poetismo.
Estos versos compusimos
para enseñar el patriotismo.

13

Con ésta nos despedimos
nuestra palabra formal,
diciendo buena fortuna
a MacArthur General.

14

Con ésta nos despedimos
al sonido de metralla.
Y allá nos veremos juntos
en el campo de batalla.

9

The mothers who have sons
That fought in the other war,
Just as they returned,
So for these we are waiting too.

10

For the New Mexicans
Fighting for their country,
With our dear mothers,
We pray with our hearts.

11

The composers are from
The New Mexico state hospital.
They are Melecio Perea,
Marcos Ortega, and Juan Flores.

12

We are not composers
Or inclined to being poets.
We composed these verses
To teach patriotism.

13

With this we say
Our formal word of farewell,
Saying good luck
To General MacArthur.

14

With this we bid farewell
To the sound of the machine gun.
There we shall see each other
On the field of battle.

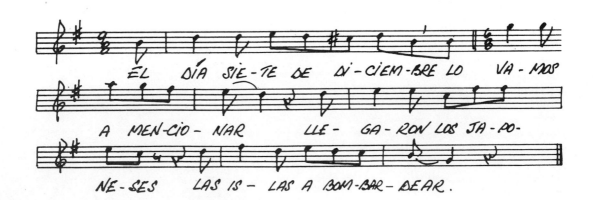

EL DÍA SIE-TE DE DI-CIEM-BRE LO VA-MOS A MEN-CIO-NAR LLE-GA-RON LOS JA-PO-NE-SES LAS IS-LAS A BOM-BAR-DEAR.

B42. *Douglas MacArthur*

Hansen 6a (no. 4, p. 314), Rafael Salas, age 47, Corona, Calif., 1959, Hansen. Cf. Mendoza 9e (p. 399).

1

Ya no llores madrecita,
ya me llevan a la guerra,
échame tu bendición,
solo sé que ya no vuelva.

2

Ya Japón se declaró,
vamos a poner las minas,
porque ya nos capturó
esas islas filipinas.

3

Y también los alemanes
nos han querido invadir;
puede que seamos esclavos,
vale más mejor morir.

4

General Douglas MacArthur
que en Australia se sostiene
con sus tropas allá al frente
no le ha temido a la muerte.

5

Las Américas no han perdido
ni tampoco perderán
porque toditas unidas
algún día triunfarán.

6

Si dicen que estoy alegre
es porque yo me hago fuerte,
que no hay corazón valiente
que no tiene a mal la muerte.

7

(Verso 1 se repite)

1

Please don't cry now, mother dear,
To fight I will have to learn,
Grant me a mother's blessing,
Chances are I'll not return.

2

Japan now has declared war,
So some mines we'll have to lay,
Since from us they now have taken
The Philippine Islands away.

3

And even the Germans, too,
To invade our land will try;
If it means we'll all be slaves,
It seems much better to die.

4

General Douglas MacArthur
Defends from Australia near
With his troops there at the front
Of death he has shown no fear.

5

The Americas have not lost
Nor will they lose any fight
Because all of them united
Some day will triumph in might.

6

If they say I am happy
It's because I must be strong,
Since there is no valiant heart
Who with death finds nothing wrong.

7

(Verse 1 repeated)

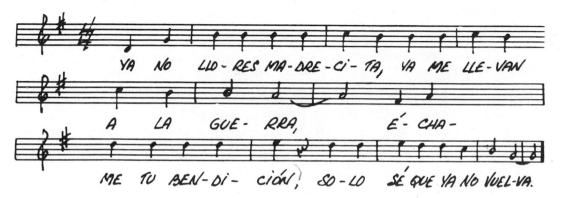

YA NO LLO-RES MA-DRE-CI'-TA, YA ME LLE-VAN A LA GUE-RRA, É'-CHA-ME TU BEN-DI-CIÓN, SO-LO SÉ QUE YA NO VUEL-VA.

Another song, *La Traición Japonesa* (RB971), is worthy of comment if not inclusion. It was recorded in Mexico City in 1943 and represents the generally friendly attitude of Mexico toward the United States in World War II. While of Mexican origin, it might, because it is so much a part of the same tradition, pass for a patriotic song like some of those included in Section J "Patriotism, History, Politics."

B43. *Corrido de Cananea*
R176, Peter Hurd, San Patricio, N.Mex., 1949, Robb. Cf. RB659 (Arizona).

1
Voy a hacer un pormenor
de lo que a mí me ha pasado.]] *Bis*

1
I am going to give an account
Of what has happened to me.

2
Como me han agarrado preso
siendo un gallo tan jugado.]] *Bis*

2
Of how I have been made prisoner
Being such a free cock.

3
Me fuí para el Agua Prieta
para ver si me conocía.]] *Bis*

3
I went to Agua Prieta
To see if they knew me.

4
Y a los once de la noche
me agarró la policía.]] *Bis*

4
At eleven at night
The police got me.

5
La cárcel de Cananea
está situada en una mesa.]] *Bis*

5
The jail of Cananea
Is situated on a plateau.

6
Y en ella fuí procesado
por causa de mi torpeza.]] *Bis*

6
And there I was processed
Because of my dullness.

7
Me agarraron los gendarmes
al estilo americano.]] *Bis*

7
The gendarmes took me
In the American style.

8
Como a un hombre de delito
todos con pistola en mano.]] *Bis*

8
As if I were a man of crime
They all had pistol in hand.

9
Ya con esto me despido
por las hojas de un granado.]] *Bis*

9
Now with this I leave you
Through the leaves of a pomegranate tree.

10
Y aquí da fin el corrido
de este gallo tan jugado.]] *Bis*

10
And here the ballad is finished
Of this cock so free.

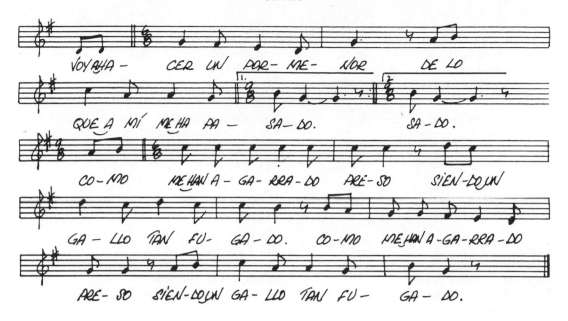

B43a. *Corrido de Cananea*
R325, R. and T. Gonzales, Tijeras, N.Mex., 1950, Robb.

1

Voy a dar un pormenor
de lo que a mí me ha pasado;
que me han tomado preso
siendo un gallo tan paseado.

1

I am going to give the details
Of what has happened to me;
That they've taken me prisoner
For being such a cocky fellow.

2

Que me han tomado preso
siendo un gallo tan paseado,
y a pasar para Cananea
y atravesando la sierra.

2

That they've taken me prisoner
For being such a cocky fellow,
As I was going to Cananea
And crossing the mountains.

3

Y a pasar para Cananea,
me prendió la policía;
me prendió la policía
al estilo americano.

3

And as I was going to Cananea,
The police arrested me;
The police arrested me
In the American way.

4

Me prendió la policía
al estilo americano.   ]
                                    ] Bis

4

The police arrested me
In the American way.

5

Como era hombre de delito
llevaba pistola en mano.   ]
                                    ] Bis

5

Since I was an outlaw,
I was carrying a gun.

177

6

Y a pasar para Cananea
y atravesando la sierra;
no me les pude pintar
por no conocer la tierra.

7

No me les pude jugar
por no conocer la tierra.
La cárcel de Cananea
cárcel de cuatro paredes.

8

Donde yo fuí procesado
a causa de las mujeres.

]] *Bis*

9

La cárcel de Cananea
está sentada en una mesa,
donde me tuvieron preso
a causa de mi cabeza.

10

Donde me tuvieron preso
a causa de mi cabeza.
Y en la cárcel donde estaba
sólo yo me divertía.

11

Contando los eslabones
que mi cadena tenía.

]] *Bis*

12

De los amigos que traiba
y aquí los voy a nombrar:
comenzando con la Changa,
el Osito, y el Caimán.

]] *Bis*

6

And as I was going to Cananea
And crossing the mountains;
I couldn't avoid them
For I didn't know the area.

7

I couldn't escape them
For I didn't know the area.
The Cananea jail had nothing
But four walls.

8

Where I was tried
Because of women.

9

The Cananea jail sits
On top of a mesa,
Where I was held prisoner
Because of my stupidity.

10

Where I was held prisoner
Because of my stupidity.
And in the jail where I was
Alone I amused myself.

11

Counting the links
Of my chains.

12

Here I am going to name
The friends I had with me:
Beginning with the Monkey,
Little Bear, and the Crocodile.

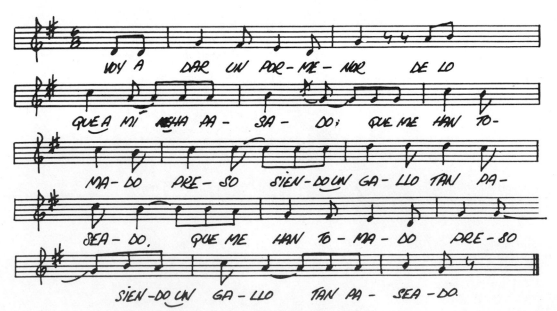

B44. *El Gavilancillo* (The Little Hawk)
R119, Próspero S. Baca, age 72, Bernalillo, N.Mex., 1947, Robb.

1	**1**
Yo soy el gavilancillo que era	I am the little hawk who has
salido de la prisión,	Just escaped from prison,
y en busca de una paloma	And in search of a dove
que ha logrado mi corazón.	Who has won my heart.
2	**2**
Dices que me quieres mucho,	You say that you love me dearly,
me quieres mucho, di la verdad;	You love me dearly, tell the truth;
no quiero otro amor a fuerza	I want no other love that is forced,
ni yo te mando tu voluntad.	Nor do I demand your submission.
3	**3**
Quise en quien la acordava	I wanted someone to warn you
con una ventura de capitán,	When the captain was coming,
dondequiera que me encuentren	For wherever they find me
y en de matar y en de matar.	It will be kill and be killed.

YO SOY EL GA-VI-LAN-CI-LLO QUE ERA SA-LI-DO DE LA PRI-SIÓN, Y EN BUS-CA DI U-NA PA-LO-MA QUE HA LO-GRA-DO MI CO-RA-ZÓN.

B45. *Preso en la Cárcel Estoy* (I Am a Prisoner in Jail)
R163, Adolfo Maés, Canjilón, N.Mex., 1949, Robb.

1	**1**
Preso en la cárcel estoy	I am a prisoner in jail
mis delirios en quererte;	Deliriously in love with you;
ya me van a dar la muerte	Now they're going to execute me
por el amor, por el amor,	For the love, for the love,
por el amor de una mujer.	For the love of a woman.
2	**2**
Ya me voy para la cueva nevada	I am going to the snowy cave
donde está pintado un león.	Where there is painted a lion.
Soy hombre, no soy cobarde,	I am a man, I am no coward,
ni me tiem—, ni me tiem—,	I don't trem—, I don't trem—,
ni me tiembla el corazón.	I don't tremble in my heart.

<table>
<tr><td>

3

Debajo de un fuente de agua
todo el agua resistí.
Es cierto es agua, es amarga,
pero si, pero si,
pero si yo no la bebí.

</td><td>

3

Beneath a fountain of water
I resisted all the water.
Surely it's water, it's bitter,
But only, but only,
But only, I did not drink it.

</td></tr>
<tr><td>

4

Una madeja de seda
enredada entre bellos ramos.
Yo solo no la enredé,
si entre ci—, si entre ci—,
si entre cinco la enredamos.

</td><td>

4

There was a skein of silk
Tangled among beautiful branches.
I alone did not tangle it,
There were fi—, there were fi—,
There were five who tangled it.

</td></tr>
<tr><td>

5

Yo, yo, usted, y mi valet,
y otro dos que convidamos;
yo, yo, usted, y mi valet,
y otros dos, y otros dos
y otros dos que convidamos.

</td><td>

5

I, myself, you, and my valet,
And two others that we asked;
I, myself, you, and my valet,
And two others, and two others,
And two others that we asked.

</td></tr>
</table>

PRE-SO EN LA CÁR-CEL E- STOY MIS DE-LI-RIOS EN QUE-RER-TE Y ME VAN A DAR LA MUER-TE POR'LA-MOR, POR'LA-MOR, POR'LA-MOR DE U-NA MU-JER.

B45a. *Preso en la Cárcel Estoy*
    R1452, Señora Adolfo Maés, Canjilón, N.Mex., 1957, Robb. Cf. García 5b (Parte
Musical, no. 400, p. 202, Castilblanco, Spain).

<table>
<tr><td>

1

Preso en la cárcel estoy.
Mi delirio es el quererte.
Ya me van a dar la muerte
por la amor de una mujer.

</td><td>

1

I am arrested and in jail.
My foolishness is to love you.
Now they are going to execute me
For the love of a woman.

</td></tr>
<tr><td>

2

Debajo de un fuente de agua
toda el agua resistí.
Dicen que esa agua es amarga
pero sí me la bebí.

</td><td>

2

Beneath a fountain of water
I resisted all the water.
They say that this water is bitter
But I drank it.

</td></tr>
</table>

3

Una madeja de seda,
enredada en bellos ramos.
No solo le enredé
si entre cinco les enredamos.

4

Entre yo y mi vale
y otros tres que convidamos.

3

A skein of silk was
Entangled in beautiful branches.
I did not tangle it alone,
There were five who tangled it.

4

There were myself and my pal
And three others whom we invited.

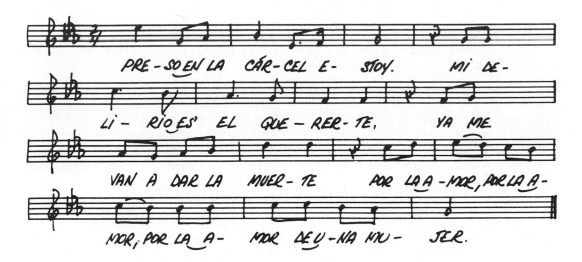

PRE-SO EN LA CÁR-CEL E-STOY. MI DE-
LI-RIO ES EL QUE-RER-TE, YA ME
VAN A DAR LA MUER-TE POR LA A-MOR, POR LA A-
MOR; POR LA A-MOR DE U-NA MU-JER.

Of this song García remarks that "its use is
quite common in the jails" (my translation).

B45b. *Preso Me Tienen en una Cárcel* (They Hold Me Prisoner in a Jail)
R2001, Clemente Chávez, Galisteo, N.Mex., 1963, Robb.

1

Preso me tienen en una cárcel,
de alto preso me tienen.
¿Será porque habré robado?
Soy pajarito que del campo me han tomado.

Soy pajarito,
soy pajarillo encantador.

2

Preso me tienen porque me robé una flor

y la llevé a lo verde de una encina.
Soy pajarito,
que ése ha sido mi destino.
Soy pajarito,
soy pajarillo encantador.

1

They hold me prisoner in a jail,
From above they hold me prisoner.
Could it be because I have robbed?
I am a bird whom they have taken from
    the fields.
I am a bird,
I am an enchanting little bird.

2

They hold me prisoner because I stole a
    flower
And carried it to the shade of a live oak.
I am a bird,
For that has been my destiny.
I am a bird,
I am an enchanting little bird.

3

Preso me tienen en una jaula de oro.
Preso me tienen encerrado en la prisión.
Soy pajarito que fuí criado en la región.
Soy pajarito,
soy pajarillo encantador.

3

They hold me prisoner in a golden cage.
They have me locked up in the prison.
I am a bird that was raised in this region.
I am a bird,
I am an enchanting little bird.

B46. *Sierra Nevada*
    R22, Frank Chávez et al., La Jara, N.Mex., 1944, Robb. Cf. Robb 13 (pp. 18, 61, for discussion and a piano-vocal setting of this song).

1

A orillas de una laguna
se quejaba un triste león,
y en el quejido decía:
—¡ay, mujeres, ay, mujeres cómo son!

1

By the margin of a lake
A lonely lion sat and said,
In his sadness: "Oh, women!
Oh, women! I could wish that I were dead.

2

No se duelen de los hombres,
no les tienen compasión;
no se duelen de los hombres,
no les tienen, no les tienen compasión.

2

"They've no mercy on a fellow,
They've no love for humankind,
They've no mercy on a fellow,
They've no love, they've no love for
    humankind.

3

Traigo grillos y cadenas,
óyelos, van a sonar;
tengo grillos y cadenas,
óyelos, óyelos, van a sonar.

3

"Here am I in chains and fetters,
You can hear them as I move;
Here am I in chains and fetters,
You can hear, you can hear them as I move.

4

Si me echaran a la cárcel,
no me vayas a llorar;
ya que penas no me quitas,
no me las, no me las vayas a dar.

4

"Though they've thrown me in jail, please
Don't come weeping to the door;
If you can't remove my troubles,
Please don't bring, please don't bring me
    any more.

5

Tengo un nicho de cristal
hecho con mis bellas manos,
para colocarte en él
si seguimos, si seguimos como vamos.

5

"I've a niche of purest crystal
Which I've made with loving care,
And in it, dear, I'll place you
If we stay, if we remain as we are.

6

Pero si tú quedas mal,
te juro que lo quebramos;
pero si tú quedas mal,
te juro, te juro que lo quebramos.

6

"But if you don't keep your promise
To be true to me, I swear
That I'll break it into pieces,
And my life, and my life no more you'll
    share.

<table>
<tr><td>

7

¡Qué bonito es el verano
cuando están sus hojas verdes!
¡Qué bonita es mi chinita
cuando viene a mis brazos y se duerme!

</td><td>

7

"Oh, how lovely is the summer
When it shows its verdant charms!
Oh, how lovely is my sweetheart
When I hold, when I hold her in my arms!

</td></tr>
</table>

8	8
¡Qué bonito es el verano cuando están las gotas de rocío! ¡Qué bonita es mi chinita imitada, imitada de rocío!	"Oh, how lovely is the summer When the grass is wet with dew! Oh, how lovely are the teardrops Of the lady I love—and that is you!
9	9
Soy de la sierra nevada donde está pintado un león; yo soy hombre, no cobarde; no me tiembla, no me tiembla el corazón.	"I am from the snowy mountain Where the mountain lion dwells; I'm a man, not a coward; My heart all thought of fear and pain expels."

O - RI - LLAS DE U - NA LA - GU - NA SE QUE-
JA - BA UN TRIS - TE LEÓN, Y EN EL QUE - JI - DO DE-
CÍ - A ¡AY MU- JE- RES, AY MU - JE - RES, CÓ - MO SON!

In this song, the mood is one of triumph over adversity and specifically over confinement in jail. An animal, this time the mountain lion, symbolizes the courage of the man who refuses to be daunted by his misfortunes. Verses 5 and 6 are found in other songs. The melody is in the Dorian mode (the mode of D).

B47. *El Contrabando de El Paso* (The Bootlegger of El Paso)
   R177, Peter Hurd, San Patricio, N.Mex., 1949, Robb. Cf. Campa 2 (pp. 103–104), RB754, Texas 18 (vol. 21, pp. 30–37).

1	1
En el día siete de agosto estábamos desesperados que nos sacaron de El Paso para Kansas mancornados.	The seventh day of August We were desperate For they took us from El Paso To Kansas, handcuffed.
2	2
Nos sacaron de la corte a las doce de la noche; nos llevaron para el dipo, nos montaron en un coche.	They took us from the courthouse At twelve at night; They took us to the depot, They put us in a day coach.

3

Mis amigos me miraban
por todita la estación,
a mi madre idolatrada
que me dé su bendición.

3

My friends were looking at me
From the whole station,
And at my mother whom I idolized
Who gave me her blessing.

4

Ni mi madre me esperaba
ni siquiera mi mujer.
Adiós todos mis amigos
¿Cuándo los volveré a ver?

4

Neither my mother was waiting
Nor even my wife.
Farewell all my friends
When shall I see them again?

5

Ya viene silbando el tren,
ya no tardará en llegar,
y les dije a mis compañeros
que me fueran a llorar.

5

Already the train comes whistling,
It will not delay in arriving,
And I speak to my friends
Who were weeping for me.

6

Ya voy a tomar el tren
me encomiendo a un santo fuerte.
Yo no vuelvo al contrabando
porque tengo mala suerte.

6

I am going to take the train
Entrusting myself to a strong saint.
I shall not return to bootlegging
Because I have bad luck.

7

Ya comienza andar el tren,
a repicar la campana.
Le pregunto a Mister Hill
que se vamos a Louisiana.

7

Already the train is beginning to move,
And the bell to ring.
I ask Mr. Hill
If we are going to Louisiana.

8

Mister Hill con su risita
me contesta —No, señor,
pasaremos de Louisiana
derechito a Leavenworth.—

8

Mr. Hill with a little smile
Replies, "No sir,
We shall bypass Louisiana
And go directly to Leavenworth."

9

¡Corre, corre, maquinista!
¡Suéltale todo el vapor!
¡Anda déjanos jaulitos
hasta el plan de Leavenworth!

9

Drive, drive, engineer!
Open the throttle!
Take us jailbirds
To the plain of Leavenworth!

10

Yo les digo a mis amigos,
por amor de su buenestar
que si creen de contrabando
a ver donde van a dar.

10

I say to my friends,
For love of your well-being,
If you think of bootlegging,
See where it gets you.

11

Les encargo a mis paisanos
los que charco y carco
no se crean de los amigos
que son cabezas de puerco.

11

I charge my countrymen
Who are far or near,
Don't believe in those friends
Who are pigheads.

12 Que por cumplir la palabra amigos en la realidad, cuando uno esté en la corte se olvidan de amistad.	**12** Who by their words are Friends in reality but When one is in the court Forget friendship.
13 Y lo digo con razón porque algunos compañeros en la calle son amigos porque son conbenencieros.	**13** And I say it with reason Because some companions On the street are friends only When it is convenient.
14 Pero de esto no hay cuidado, ya lo que pasó voló. Algún día se han de encontrar donde me he encontrado yo.	**14** But I don't care about this, I've already given my opinion of what is past. Some day they will experience What has happened to me.
15 Es bonito el contrabando, se gana mucho dinero. Pero lo que más me puede es andarme prisionero.	**15** Bootlegging is delightful, It gets you much money. But what it can also do to me Is to make me a prisoner.
16 Víspera de San Lorenzo como a las once del día que pasamos los umbrales de la penitenciaría.	**16** On the eve of Saint Lawrence At about eleven in the day We pass the threshold Of the penitentiary.
17 El que hizo estas mañanitas, ya te tolera el perdón, Si no está bien corregido queda nuestra opinión.	**17** He who made these morning songs, I ask your pardon, If it is not well corrected, Still it remains my opinion.
18 Unos vienen con dos años, otros con un año y un día, otros con diez y ocho meses a la penitenciaría.	**18** Some come with two years, Some with a year and a day, Others with eighteen months To the penitentiary.
19 ¡Ay! le mando, mamacita, un suspiro y un abrazo. Aquí dan fin las mañanas del contrabando de El Paso.	**19** Ah! my dear mother, I send you A sigh and an embrace. Here end the tomorrows Of the bootlegger of El Paso.

EN EL DÍA SIE-TE DE A-GO-STO E-STA-BA-MOS

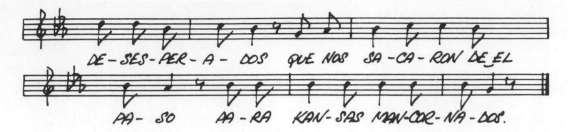

This song reveals a point of view that, despite the evident unhappiness of the prisoner, has a wryly comic aspect. The prisoner is full of remorse not for having broken the law but for the unprofitability of the experiment and having been caught (see verses 6 and 10).

B47a. *El Contrabando de El Paso*
"Verses of the Texas Vaqueros," by J. Frank Dobie, in Dobie, Texas 18 (vol. 4, pp. 30–37), Texas, 1954.

1	1
El diecisiete de agosto	The seventeenth of August
estábamos desesperados,	We were in despair,
y nos sacaron del Paso	And they took us from El Paso
para Kansas mancornados.	Handcuffed on the way to Kansas.

2	2
Nos sacaron de la cárcel	They took us from the jail
a las ocho de la noche,	At eight at night,
nos llevaron por el dipo,	They took us through the depot,
nos montaron en un coche.	They put us aboard a coach.

3	3
Yo dirijo mi mirada	I direct my glances
por todita la estación,	All around the station,
a ver mi madre idolatrada	To look for my beloved mother
que me dé su bendición.	So that she might give me her blessing.

4	4
Ni mi madre me esperaba,	Neither my mother was waiting for me
ni mi señora, mi mujer,	Nor my lady, my wife,
Adiós, todos mis amigos,	Good-bye, all my friends,
¿cuándo les volveré a ver?	When shall I see you again?

5	5
Allí viene silbando el tren,	There comes the train whistling,
y no tardará en llegar,	It won't be long in arriving,
Yo les digo a mis amigos	I tell all my friends
que no se vayan a llorar.	Not to cry.

6	6
Ya voy a tomar el tren,	I'm going to take the train,
me encomiendo al santo fuerte,	I commit myself to the strong saint,

ya no vuelvo al contrabando
porque tengo mala suerte.

7
El contrabando es muy bueno,
se gana muy buen dinero
pero lo que no me gusta
es que me lleven prisionero.

8
Ya comienza a andar el tren,
y a repicar las campanas,
yo le digo a mister Gil
que si vamos a Louisiana.

9
Mister Gil con su risita
me contesta: —No, señor,
pasaremos la Louisiana
derechito a Livenvor.—

10
Corre, corre, maquinita,
suéltale todo el vapor,
Anda a llevar esta gaviota
hasta el plan de Livenvor.

11
Les encargo a mis amigos
que salgan a experimentar,
que le entren al contrabando
a ver donde van a dar.

12
Les encargo a mis paisanos
que brinquen el charco seco,
no se crean a los amigos,
esos cabezas de puerco.

13
Que, por cumplir la palabra,
amigos, es la verdad,
cuando uno se halla en la corte
se olvidan la amistad.

14
Pero de eso no hay cuidado,
ya, lo que pasó, voló,
algún día se han de encontrar
como me encontraba yo.

15
Expresos de San Lorenzo
eran las once del día,

I shall never go back to smuggling
Because I have bad luck.

7
Smuggling is very good,
One makes good money,
But what I don't like
Is that they take me prisoner.

8
Now the train begins to move,
And the bells to ring,
I ask Mister Hill
If we are going to Louisiana.

9
Mister Hill with his little laugh
Answers me: "No, sir,
We'll pass through Louisiana
Right straight to Leavenworth."

10
Run, run, little machine,
Turn loose all the steam,
Hurry and take this seagull
To the plain of Leavenworth.

11
I recommend to my friends
That they go give it a try,
That they get into smuggling
And see where they will land.

12
I recommend to my countrymen
That they avoid the dry marsh,
Don't believe those friends,
Those pigheads.

13
Who, as for sticking by their word,
Friends, it's the truth,
When one finds himself in court
They forget friendship.

14
But as for that there's no remedy,
Now, what's happened is past,
Some day they're bound to find themselves
In the same situation as I.

15
Right straight from Saint Lawrence
It was eleven in the morning,

que pisamos los umbrales
de la penitenciaría.

That we stepped on the threshold
Of the penitentiary.

16

El que cuenta estos versos
le ha pedido el perdón,
si no están incorregibles
pues, estando tu opinión.

16

He who recites these verses
Has asked your pardon,
If they are not incorrigible
Well, that being your opinion.

17

Allí te mando, mamacita,
un suspiro y un abrazo.
Aquí dan fin las mañanitas
del contrabando del Paso.

17

I send you there, dear mother,
A sigh and an embrace.
Here end the verses
About the smuggler of El Paso.

EL DÍ — A SIE —TE DE A— GOS —TO 'STÁ—BA—
NOS DES— ES— PER—A— DOS, Y NOS SA— CA—
RON DEL PA— SO PA— RA KAN— SAS MAN— COR —NA —DOS.

B48. *El Hijo Pródigo* (The Prodigal Son)
Hansen 6a (no. 3, p. 227), Rafael Salas, age 47, Corona, Calif., Hansen. Cf. Mendoza
9f (no. 200, p. 640).

1

Yo soy como el hijo pródigo
nacido de la inocencia,
que abandoné yo a mis padres
por falta de la experiencia.

1

I'm like the prodigal son,
In innocence I was born,
I left home to gain experience
But now I'm back, tired and torn.

2

Yo le dije a mi mamá:
—Ya no quiero estar contigo,
dame mi parte de herencia
para tomar mi camino.—

2

To my mother dear I said:
"I no longer want to stay,
So give me my inheritance
That I can be on my way."

3

A los quince años me fuí,
a los veinte años volví.
No encontré padre ni madre
¡Ay! desgraciado de mí.

3

I left home when just fifteen,
I came back when I was twenty,
And both my parents were gone.
Woe is me, things have changed plenty!

4

Cuando yo tenía mis padres
toda la gente me hablaba

4

When I was with my parents
To me everybody spoke,

y ahora que no tengo nada
ni quien me dé un trago de agua.

But now that I have nothing,
Even for water I choke.

5

Para mi mayor desgracia
quise meterme a robar.
Me agarraron prisionero
para la ley nacional.

5

Then came my greatest misfortune,
At stealing I tried my hand.
I was seized and promptly sentenced
To serve the law of the land.

6

Yo les dije a mis amigos:
—Todos los que están presentes,
no abandonen a sus padres
ni les pase lo que a mí.—

6

So now I say to my friends:
"All of you present today,
Don't ever leave your parents,
And you'll not end up this way."

7

(Verso 1 se repite)

7

(Verse 1 repeated)

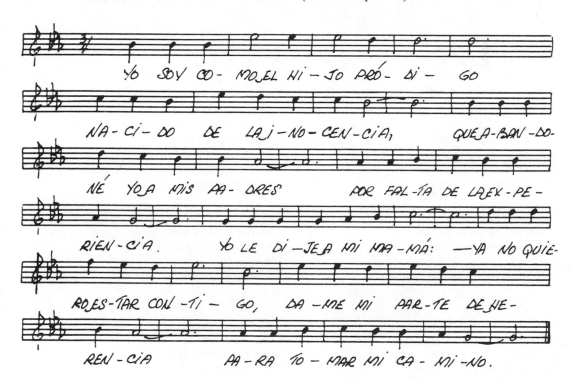

B49. *Gregorio Cortés*

R2412, Juan Griego, age 61, Albuquerque, N.Mex., 1971, Robb. Cf. Hansen 6a (p. 297 [California]); Mendoza 9e (p. 204); Mendoza 9b (p. 788); RB496–497, Paredes 10 (p. 5), the last two being Texas versions. See also Introduction above, "Studies in Depth."

1

Aquí me siento a cantar
en la sombra de un safrás
a ver si puedo cantar
la tragedia de Cortés.

1

Here I seat myself to sing
In the shade of a sassafras,
To see if I can sing
The tragedy of Cortés.

2

Dice Gregorio Cortés,
con su pistola en la mano,
—Maté al cherife mayor
por defender a mi hermano.—

3

Dice Gregorio Cortés,
con su rifle y decidido,
—Maté al cherife mayor
cayendo Román herido.—

4

Iban los americanos
que parecía que volaban,
de ver que iban a ganar
tres mil pesos que les daban.

5

Persiguieron a Cortés
por toditita la huella,
pero alcanzar a Cortés
era alcanzar una estrella.

6

Para ya por el encinal
lo alcanzaron a rodear.
Y a pocos más de trecientos
allí les brincó el corral.

7

Andaron los americanos
por entre los noguerales
buscando huella de Cortés
para echarle los perros "gaunes."

8

Se agarraron tiro a tiro
como dos gallos conqueados,
luego que cayeron tres.
Los demás se arrancaron.

9

En la orilla del encinal
varios bolíos lo vieron
pero no le quisieron entrar
porque le tuvieron miedo.

10

Dice Gregorio Cortés,
con su pistola en la mano,
—Entrenle rinches cobardes
si al cabo no soy su hermano.—

2

Gregorio Cortés says,
With his pistol in his hand,
"I killed the head sheriff
In order to defend my brother."

3

Gregorio Cortés says,
With his rifle, determined,
"I killed the head sheriff,
Román having fallen wounded."

4

The Americans were going,
They seemed to fly,
At the thought of gaining
Three thousand pesos offered them.

5

They pursued Cortés
Along his trail,
But to catch Cortés
Was to catch a star.

6

Down by the brush
They managed to surround him.
There were over three hundred men
Yet he escaped.

7

The Americans were going
Through the walnut groves
Looking for Cortés
To set the hounds on his trail.

8

There was an exchange of shots
Like two fighting cocks,
Then three men fell.
The rest retreated.

9

At the edge of the brush
Several gringos (?) saw him
But they didn't want to enter
Because they were afraid of him.

10

Gregorio Cortés says,
With his pistol in his hand,
"Come on, cowardly rangers,
Anyway I am not your brother."

11

Al llegar al Temilboq
un mexicano encontró,
—Platíqueme que hay de nuevo
y le diré quien soy yo.—

11

Upon arriving at Temilboq
He met a Mexican,
"Tell me what is the news
And I will tell you who I am."

12

Se sientan a platicar
con bastante rapidez,
—Pues por la gracia de Dios
yo soy Gregorio Cortés.—

12

They sat down to converse
With a great deal of haste,
"Well, by the grace of God
I am Gregorio Cortés."

13

Decían los americanos,
—Y ahora, ¿cómo le haremos?
Si le entramos por derecho
muy poquitos volveremos.—

13

The Americans said,
"Now, what shall we do?
If we tackle him head on
Very few of us will return."

14

Y aquí termina el corrido
debajo de este safrás,
aquí se acaban cantando
la tragedia de Cortés.

14

Here ends the ballad
Under this sassafras,
Here ends the singing
Of the tragedy of Cortés.

(Additional verses follow)

15

Siguió con rumbo a Laredo
sin ninguna timidez.
—Síganme, rinches cobardes,
yo soy Gregorio Cortés.—

15

He fled toward Laredo
Without any timidity.
"Follow me, cowardly rangers,
I am Gregorio Cortés."

16

Decía Gregorio Cortés,
con su pistola en la mano,
—No siento haberlo matado.
La defensa es permitida.—

16

Gregorio Cortés said,
With his pistol in his hand,
"I am not sorry I killed him.
Personal defense is permitted."

17

Buscaban a Cortés
por toditito el estado.
—¡Vivo o muerto que se aprenda!
porque a un cherife ha matado.—

17

They searched for Cortés
Throughout the state.
"Dead or alive, get him
Because he has killed a sheriff."

18

Decía Gregorio Cortés,
con su pistola en la mano,
—No corran, rinches cobardes,
ante un sólo mexicano!—

18

Gregorio Cortés said,
With his pistol in his hand,
"Don't run, cowardly rangers,
Before just one Mexican."

19

Decía Gregorio Cortés,
—Los gringos no me llevan vivo
porque en Tejas no hay justicia
para un pobre mexicano.—

19

Gregorio Cortés said,
"The gringos won't take me alive
Because in Texas there's no justice
For a poor Mexican."

A - QUÍ ME SIEN-TRA CAN-TAR EN LA SOM-
BRA DE UN SA-FRÁS A VER SI PUE-DO CAN-TAR LA
TRA-GE- DIA DE COR - TÉS.

Américo Paredes has devoted an entire book to this one *corrido*, which portrays an outlaw as a hero and the Texas Rangers and Anglos in general as cowards (Paredes 10).

Gregorio Cortés belongs in the distinguished company of the California outlaw hero Joaquín Murieta (B35) and his New Mexico counterpart, Billy the Kid (R774).

B50. *En la Laguna del Moro* (At Lake Moro)
R1399, Nick Griego, Albuquerque, N.Mex., 1956, Robb.

1

En la laguna del Moro
yo vi pelear dos osos.
Uno era medio platiado,
el otro medio barroso.

2

Los vi tan enojados
me llamaron la atención
de ver a esos animales
ser de tan mal corazón.

3

Yo traiba mi rifle treinta
y mi pistola de estrella,
moreal lleno de parque,
y también mi cartuchera.

4

Me dirigí a donde estaban ellos
y me dirigí como amigo.
Luego me sintió el platiado
y ése me pegó un bramido.

5

Lo vi tan enojado
no me pude sujetar
agarré mi rifle treinta
y me puse en mi lugar.

1

At Lake Moro
I saw two bears fighting.
One had a silvery coat,
The other brown.

2

I saw them so mad
They caught my attention
Seeing those animals
To be of such bad heart.

3

I had my thirty caliber rifle
And my hand pistol,
My pouch full of ammunition,
And also a full magazine.

4

I headed toward them
And I went as a friend.
Then the silver one sensed me
And he bellowed at me.

5

I saw him so mad
I could not keep myself from
Grabbing my thirty caliber rifle
And I found a position.

6	**6**
Cuando llegó a donde estaba yo	When he arrived where I was
venía cosido de balazos,	He was wounded with bullets,
no traiba ni una onza de fuerza	He had not an ounce of strength
ni en sus piernas ni en sus brazos.	In his legs or in his arms.
7	**7**
El oso medio barroso	The brown bear
agarró el cañón para arriba.	Ran up the canyon.
Yo no lo quise seguir	I don't want to follow him
por no ir a perder mi vida.	For I might lose my life.

This melody is a variant of that of *Indita de Cochití* (F10). Such use of the same tune for different texts is an international phenomenon in the domain of folk music.

B51. *Guanajuato*
R1516, Esteban Torres, Tomé, N.Mex., 1957, Robb. Cf. RB788 (Cobos).

1	**1**
Año de mil ochocientos	In the year of eighteen hundred
noventa y dos en que estamos	Ninety-two in which we are
salimos de Guanajuato]	We left Guanajuato
para Sonora mentado.] *Bis*	For that noted state, Sonora.
2	**2**
Cuando salí de me tierra	When I left my country
me decía mi señora:	My wife said to me:
—Se me hace que usted no vuelve]	"It seems to me that you won't return
del estado de Sonora.—] *Bis*	From the state of Sonora."
3	**3**
Adiós, mis queridos padres	Farewell, my dear parents,
los que me quisieron bien.	Those who loved me well.
Ya me voy a Estados Unidos,]	I am going to the United States,
ya me voy a tomar el tren.] *Bis*	I am going to take the train.

4	4
Cuando llegamos a Yuma	When we came to Yuma
¡Ay! Nos apeamos un rato.	Ah! We got off for a while.
Uno al otro se decía:]	We said to each other:
—¡Qué lejos se queda el justo!—] *Bis*	"How far away justice remains!"

5	5
Válgame la Santa Cruz	Bless me, Holy Cross
de los padres misioneros,	Of the missionary fathers,
ya me voy a Estados Unidos.]	I'm going to the United States.
Vamos a ganar dinero.] *Bis*	We are going to earn money.

6	6
Vieron el puente de Yuma,	They saw the bridge of Yuma,
¡Ay, qué bonito quedó!	Oh, how beautiful it was!
En semblado de madera]	It is made of wood
porque el fierro no alcanzó.] *Bis*	Because iron would not reach.

7	7
Al pasar por San Francisco	On going through San Francisco
hay muchas cosas que ver;	There are many things to see;
muchas muchachas bonitas]	Many pretty girls
y un viejito sin comer.] *Bis*	And an old man without food.

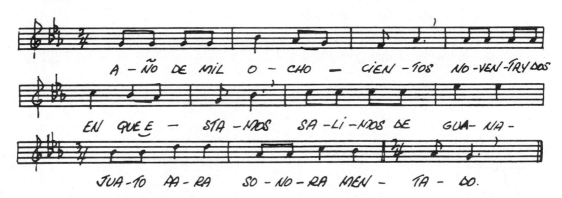

The title of this *corrido* is a misnomer, for it is not a song in praise of Guanajuato.

There are, however, many songs in praise of localities; see C88–89 for examples.

B52. *San Marcial*
R243, Juan Luján, Riverside, N.Mex., 1950, Robb. Cf. R924, R1629, R1999, RB739. RB749 is a corrido about a flood in Tecolote, New Mexico.

1	1
El día veinte de agosto,	The twentieth day of August,
no me quisiera acordar,	I do not wish to remember,
que se llegó el Río Grande	For on that day the Río Grande
la plaza de San Marcial.	Flooded the town of San Marcial.

2	2
Era una tarde muy triste,	It was a very sad afternoon,
pues yo la tengo presente.	How well I remember it.
Trenes llegaron de El Paso	Trains came from El Paso
para auxiliar a la gente.	To help the people.
3	3
La gente andaba excitada	The people walked about excitedly
pues no hallaba qué pensar	Unable to decide
si marcharse para El Paso	Whether to go to El Paso
o quedarse en San Marcial.	Or to remain in San Marcial.
4	4
Pues no era tan poca el agua,	The water was pretty high,
casas andaban nadando,	Houses were floating around,
y por arriba de las lomas	And the people went weeping
la gente andaba llorando.	To the top of the hills.
5	5
Pobrecita de mi gente,	My poor people,
¡ah, qué suerte les tocó!	Oh, what luck befell them!
Todos sus casas perdieron	They all lost their houses,
no más el Harvey quedó.	Only the Harvey house remained.
6	6
¡Ah, qué lástima de pueblo	Oh, how sad that the town
como quedó destrozado!	Remains so destroyed!
Por en medio de las calles	In the middle of the streets
lomas de arena quedaron.	Mounds of mud remained.
7	7
Adiós, mi pueblo querido,	Farewell, my beloved town,
¡Cuándo te volveré a ver!	When shall I see you again?
Aunque esté todo arruinado	Though everything is ruined
no te digo de querer.	I do not tell you to weep.
8	8
Les compuse este corrido	I composed this ballad
a los paisanos de aquí.	For the country people from here.
Voy a decirles mi nombre	I am going to tell them my name
para que se acuerden de mí.	So that they may remember me.
9	9
Pues mi nombre es Ramón Luna,	Well, my name is Ramón Luna,
yo soy nacido de aquí,	I was born here,
pues por cierto me duele	And certainly I am sorry
la plaza donde nací.	For the town where I was born.

EL DÍ-A VEIN-TE DEA-GO-STO NO ME QUI-SIE-RA' COR-

DAR QUE SE LLE-GÓ EL RÍO GRAN-DE

LA PLA-ZA DE SAN MAR - CIAL.

This is a song with well-known antecedents. The flood occurred on August 20, 1929. Ramón Luna, the author of the words, was a native of San Marcial, and was well known to the singer Eduardo Gallegos, also a native of that town. Gallegos frequently sang this *corrido* in public and informed me that he composed this tune among others, including *Corrido of the Big Five* (J8).

Juan Luján (center), singer of *San Marcial* (B52), in Santo Niño, New Mexico, 1949.

B53. *En la Cantina de Denver* (In the Denver Saloon)
R24, Frank Chávez, La Jara, N.Mex., 1944, Robb. See Appendix A.

1		1
En la cantina de Denver		In the Denver saloon
fué donde yo comencé		I learned a lesson one night.
a tomar tragos de whiskey	]	I took my first drink of whiskey
hasta que me emborraché.	] *Bis*	And kept on till I was tight.

2		2
Y le dije a mi chinita:		And I said to my sweetheart:
—'Ora sí me voy pa' casa		"I think I'd best hit the trail
porque si sigo el "batito"		For if I drink one more whiskey
en esta noche me atrasan.—		Tonight I'll end up in jail."

3

Me decía mi chinita:
—No se vaya tan temprano;
no se vaya tan temprano,
todavía no son las siete.

3

But this was not what she wanted.
"It's far too early," said she,
"It's not yet seven o'clock,
It's such a wonderful spree.

4

Y verá llegar los novios
a ese salón de "skating."—] *Bis*

4

"Some newlyweds are coming,
Coming to skate in the rink."

5

Yo le dije a mi chinita:
—Es nada verlos llegar,
si yo no sirvo pa' nada,
si al cabo no sé bailar.—

5

So I said to my sweetheart:
"I'm not for taking a chance;
I'm really good for nothing,
I don't even know how to dance."

6

Me decía mi chinita:
—No le hace que no sepa bailar,
pero a la marcha sí puede
si al cabo no es más que andar.—

6

She said it didn't matter,
In the grand march we could go;
It's only walking and talking
As she could easily show.

7

Esta de andar yo si puede
y con bastante grandeza;
a lo que sí no me atrevo
si me nombran otra pieza.

7

Well, there's no problem with walking,
I can do that with a flair;
But if they change to some dance tune
I'd have to quit then and there.

8

Y con ésta me despido
porque yo traigo las llaves.
Si quieren saber mi nombre
me llamo Francisco Chávez.

8

And with this I will be going,
There's really no one to blame.
If you would know who is singing,
Frank Chávez, that is my name.

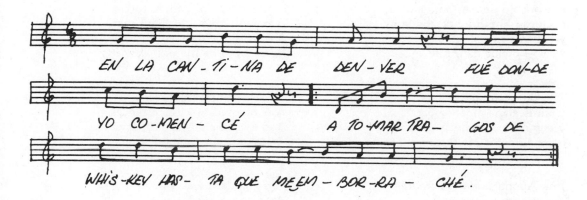

EN LA CAN-TI-NA DE DEN-VER FUÉ DON-DE
YO CO-MEN-CÉ A TO-MAR TRA-GOS DE
WHIS-KEY HAS-TA QUE ME EM-BOR-RA-CHÉ.

I used this melody as an aria in the prologue
to my opera *Little Jo*. Santiago sings it as he
reels home half drunk from the cantina.

B54. *El Borracho* (The Drunkard)

R426, Nicolás Martínez, age 74, Chimayó, N.Mex., 1951, Robb. Cf. D31 (same title but a different song).

Lunes Santo en la mañana	On Monday morning of Holy Week
cuando me salí a pasear,	When I went out for a walk,
me fuí para una cantina	I went to a bar
y se — emborrachar.	And proceeded to get drunk.

(The two remaining verses are undecipherable.)

B55. *Corrido de José Apodaca*

R333, Salomón Ruiz, Tijeras, N.Mex., 1950, Robb.

1	1
Señores, voy a cantar	Gentlemen, I am going to sing
lo que traigo en mi memoria	That which I carry in my memory
de un hombre que fué notable.	About a man who was notable.
Voy a cantarles la historia.	I am going to sing you the story.

2	2
Del pueblo de San Antonio	In the village of San Antonio
nació un hombre muy brillante,	Was born a very brilliant man,
y con el tiempo llegó	And with the passage of time
a ser el mejor danzante.	He came to be the best dancer.

3	3
Esta dichosa carrera	This distinguished career
circunstancia mucho abarca,	Was favored by circumstances,
y con el tiempo llegó	And with the passage of time
a ser el mejor Monarca.	He came to be the best Monarca.[2]

4	4
José Apodaca era el hombre	José Apodaca was a man
de tan grande corazón.	With a very great heart.
Siempre lleva en su mente	Always he carried in his mind
de servirle a su patrón.	The thought of serving his Lord.

[2] The Monarca is the leader of the *matachines* dancers.

5

Con su guajito y su palma
y aquel cupil de diamantes
se enfrentaba de San Antonio
con un grupo de danzantes.

6

Con aquel cupil dorado
le nació del corazón
y la Malinche a su lado
bailándole a su patrón.

7

Vestido de mil colores
en nuestra iglesia se alegraba,
y el pueblo lleno de gusto
cuando Apodaca bailaba.

8

Quedó triste San Antonio
con grande luto se vía;
tan pálido y tan sereno
como un aurora del día.

9

En su tumba está grabado
con letras interesantes
con un letrero que dice:
—viva el rey de los danzantes.

10

Nos despedimos, señores.
Aquí termina la historia.
Y Apodaca está en el cielo
gozando de Dios y gloria.

5

With his *guajito* and his *palma*[3]
And his headdress of diamonds
He presented himself before San Antonio
With a group of dancers.

6

With this gilded headdress
He touched his heart
And the Malinche[4] at his side,
He danced before his patron.

7

Dressed in a thousand colors
In our church he danced,
And the entire village rejoiced
When Apodaca danced.

8

San Antonio was left sad
And appeared in deep mourning;
As pale and serene
As the dawn of the day.

9

On his tomb is engraved
In interesting letters
An inscription which says:
"Long live the king of the dancers."

10

Now farewell, gentlemen.
This is the end of the story.
And Apodaca is in heaven
Rejoicing with God in his glory.

This *corrido*, composed as a poem without music, is a tribute to José Apodaca, *Monarca* (leader) of the *matachines* dancers of San Antonio, Bernalillo County, New Mexico. I published the complete text of this *corrido*, together with a translation and a brief discussion of the place of the *matachines* dance in the life pattern of this particular village, in an article on the *matachines* dance in *Western Folklore* (Robb 13e).

See Section W, numbers W1–17, for the dance tunes from the village of San Antonio, Bernalillo County, New Mexico, where Apodaca lived and danced.

[3] The *guajito* is a rattle, and the *palma* is a three-forked stick often carved and colored.
[4] The Malinche is a little girl in white who dances with the *matachines* dancers.

A number of *corridos* of Mexican provenance and dealing with the Mexican revolutions of 1864–67 and 1910–20 have been omitted with regret, for, while they show the keen interest of the people of the border states in the events transpiring in Mexico and their sympathy with what some appear to regard as their motherland, some of the *corridos* (for instance, *La Cucaracha*) are so well known as hardly to need further exposure to United States readers. For the benefit of anyone interested in becoming familiar with particular versions of such *corridos*, the following list is appended:

The Mexican Revolution of 1864–67

Hidalgo (R523)
El Dieciseis de Septiembre (Hansen 6a, no. 3, pp. 207–209)
Al Pasar por las Calles (R59)
Las Diez y Seis (R1474)

The Revolution of 1910–20

Obregón y Villa (Hansen 6a, no. 3, p. 209)
Corrido del Norte (R171)
Corrido del Norte (Hansen 6a, no. 4, pp. 311–13)
Corrido del Norte (R1223)
La Cucaracha (R2520)
La Cucaracha (Texas 18, vol. 4, p. 25)
Valentina (Hansen 6a, no. 3, pp. 215–16)
Valentina (R2043)

Execution of a General

Felipe Angeles (R1396)
Felipe Angeles (Hansen 6a, pp. 211–12)
El General Condenado (R448)

The Soldier's Sweetheart

Adelita (Hansen 6a, no. 3, pp. 214–15)
Adelita (R481)
Adelita (Texas 18, vol. 4, p. 28)

Pancho Villa

Las Dijo General Villa (R1705)
Pancho Villa (Hansen 6a, no. 3, pp. 210–11)
Pancho Villa (R1191)
Siete Leguas (R1355)
Siete Leguas (R1257)

C. Canción

In contrast to the *romance* and the *corrido*, which are basically narrative ballads, the *canción* is usually introspective in mood. Normally it is found in the form of *coplas*, or four-line verses. Whereas the largest group of *corridos* deals with death, as I have said, the *canción* concentrates on love in its many forms.

The *canciones* of my collection appear to outnumber any of the other forms of folk songs, and I have selected for inclusion in this volume only a few of the best ones or those that are the most widely diffused. Campa (Campa 2, p. 181ff.) devoted a chapter to the *canción* with many examples of song texts (without music), including some from Spain and Latin America, as well as a few that he identified as of New Mexican origin.

In *Hispanic Folk Songs of New Mexico* (Robb 13) I have discussed the *canción* briefly, along with other representative types. In that volume I also included the texts and a simple musical setting for voice and piano of three songs that I classified at the time as *canciones: Muchacho Alegre, Palomita Que Vienes Herida*, and *Sierra Nevada*. In retrospect, none of these can be regarded as entirely typical, and this illustrates the difficulty of classification. Perhaps *Muchacho Alegre* (C48 below) is most typical in its observance of the octosyllabic lines arranged in *coplas*, or four-line verses, its introspective rather than narrative character, and its preoccupation with the subject dealt with most frequently in the *canciones*, love. It is exceptional in its lighthearted treatment of the subject. *Palomita Que Vienes Herida* (C14 below) may also be regarded as fairly typical, despite its unusual departure from the octosyllabic line. *Sierra Nevada* (B46 above) is a prisoner's song and might be classified as a *corrido* except that the introspective elements of the text outweigh the narrative. I incorporated all three of these melodies in my opera *Little Jo*.

Mendoza's exhaustive volume *La Canción Mexicana* (Mendoza 9g) is recommended for those who wish to pursue the subject further. Mendoza spent several months during the academic year 1945–46 as guest lecturer at the University of New Mexico. During that time he made a study of the traditional Spanish folk music of New Mexico which culminated in his "Estudio y Clasificación de la Música Tradicional Hispánica de Nuevo México" (Mendoza 9d).

C1. *Lupita*
R164, Mrs. Adolfo Maes, Canjilón, N.Mex., 1949, Robb.

1	1
Tan bonita mi Lupita	My Lupita is so lovely
cuando se sale a pasear;	When she goes out for a walk;
parece una amapolita	She resembles a poppy
al acabar de arrancar.	Freshly cut from the stalk.

2	2
Ya amanece, que amanece,	Does she waken? Yes she wakens!
ya amanece, pero no.	No! She doesn't! Ah, despair!
Yo me quiero ir otro rato,	I must come a little later.
pero sí, ya amaneció.	Ah! What joy! Now she is there.

3

De tu ventana a la mía
me dirás y te diré,
franqueame un vaso de agua
que ya me abrazo de sed.

4

No tengo vaso ni copa
ni en que darte de beber,
pero tengo mi boquita
que es más dulce que la miel.

5

Por la luna doy un peso,
por un lucero un tostón;
por la atención de Lupita
la vida y el corazón.

3

From your window to my own,
I can say to you alone,
Things like, "Give me some water
For I'm as dry as a bone."

4

"I don't have a glass of water.
Indeed I have not any.
But I have two rosy lips
That taste sweeter than honey."

5

For the moon I'd give a peso,
For a star I'd give four bits;
For the favors of Lupita
All my life and heart and wits.

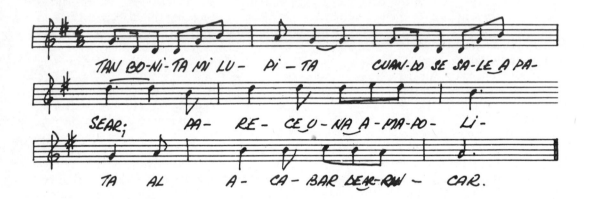

The man declares his love in poetic terms to the four winds when he is alone. When he actually has a chance to talk to Lupita in verse 3, all he can think of—or dares—to say is, "Give me a glass of water." Lupita, however, is not so timid and in verse 4 has the nerve to encourage him, so that we may surmise that everything probably turns out all right. The man in this song acts like many another lover, whose love, when still in the domain of dreams, is charming but, when confronted by reality, becomes terrifying.

C2. *Juanita*
R121, Próspero S. Baca, age 72, Bernalillo, N.Mex., 1947, Robb.

1

¡Cuánto me duele
verte llorando, Juanita!
¡Cuánto me duele
verte pasando trabajos!

1

How much it hurts me
To see you weeping, Juanita!
How much it hurts me
To see you suffering!

2
Cierres tus ojos.
Ven a mis brazos.
Cierres tus ojos.
Ya basta de llorar.

Coro
Oye a él que te ama
cantándote una canción
que no recuerdas
que un tiempo fuí tu dueño.

3
Trigueña mía,
anoche te ví en el sueño.
Cierres tus ojos.
Ya basta de llorar.

4
Nos pasearemos
por este jardín de flores.
Cierres tus ojos,
chinita encantadora.

5
Cierres tus ojos.
Ya basta de llorar.

2
Close your eyes.
Come to my arms.
Close your eyes.
That's enough weeping.

Chorus
Listen to him who loves you
Singing you a song
So that you may remember
That at one time I was your love.

3
My dark one,
Last night I saw you in my dreams.
Close your eyes.
That's enough weeping.

4
We will stroll through
This flower garden.
Close your eyes,
My enchanting darling.

5
Close your eyes.
That's enough weeping.

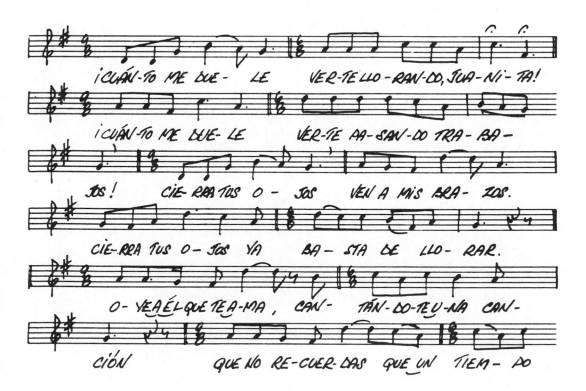

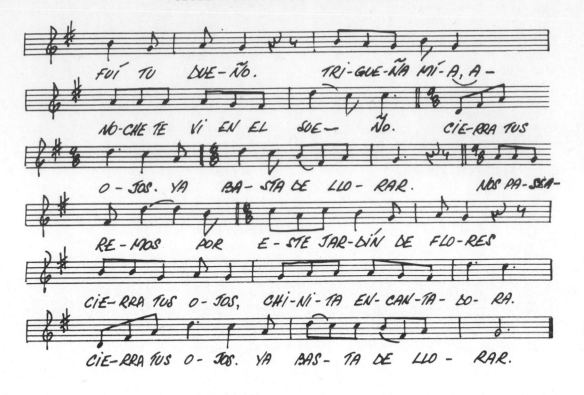

FUÍ TU DUE-ÑO. TRI-GUE-ÑA MÍ-A, A-NO-CHE TE VÍ EN EL SUE-ÑO. CIE-RRA TUS O-JOS. YA BAS-TA DE LLO-RAR. NOS PA-SEA-RE-MOS POR E-STE JAR-DÍN DE FLO-RES CIE-RRA TUS O-JOS, CHI-NI-TA EN-CAN-TA-DO-RA. CIE-RRA TUS O-JOS. YA BAS-TA DE LLO-RAR.

C3. *Al Pie de la Ladera* (At the Foot of the Slope)
R175, Peter Hurd, San Patricio, N.Mex., 1949, Robb. Cf. Campa 2 (pp. 210–11).

1 Al pie de la ladera está una casita azulita. Al pie de la ladera está una muchacha bonita.	**1** At the foot of the slope Is a little blue house. At the foot of the slope Is a pretty girl.
2 Con jardín y enredadera que se llama la Rosita que en la tarde allá me espera para decirle una cosita.	**2** With garden and twining plants She, whose name is Rosita, In the afternoon awaits me So that I can tell her something.
3 Vuela, vuela, pajarito.] Vuela donde está Rosita.] *Bis*	**3** Fly, fly, little bird. Fly to where Rosita is.
4 Si tu mamá me prohibe y me manda que me retire logrará que no te mire pero que te olvide, ¿cuándo?	**4** If your mother prohibits me And tells me to go away She will keep me from seeing you But from forgetting you, never.

This *canción* was composed by Solomón García, of Arroyo Hondo, New Mexico (Campa 2, p. 210).

C4. *Huapango*
R267, Garcilán Pacheco, Córdova, N.Mex., 1950, Robb.

1	1
Debajo del brazo	Under my arm
voy con mi guitarra	I carry my guitar
que me ha acordado	Which I have tuned up
para echar un cantar,	To make a song,
a ver si consigo	To see if I get
que vuele conmigo	A little dove
una palomita	From this place
de aquí del lugar.	To run away with me.

2	2
Ya varias noches	It's already several nights
que le hablo de amores,	That I have spoken to her of love,
pero como nadie	But as nobody
me quiere entender,	Wants to understand me,
aunque yo le cante	Even if I sing her
los versos mejor,	The verses better and better,
esa ingrata no quiere	That ungrateful one does not want
darme su querer.	To give me her love.

(Versos 1 y 2 se repiten)

(Verses 1 and 2 repeated)

Refrán

¡Su querer
y su amor!
¡eso pido!
¡nada más!
¡dulce bien!
¡mi ilusión!
ya no me hagas padecer.

3

La luz de la luna llena
corre por todo el potrero,   ] Bis
la van siguiendo las nubes   ]
con gotitas de aguacero.   ] Bis

4

Me acuesto pensando en ti   ]
que en mi sueño estás conmigo,   ] Bis
y me siento muy feliz   ]
con soñar que estoy contigo.   ] Bis

5

Hubo noches que soñé
que tu boquita besaba,
y cuando yo desperté
fuí viendo que era la almohada
la que de besos llenaba.

(Verso 1 se repite)

Refrain

Her affection
And her love!
That I ask!
Nothing more!
My sweetheart!
My illusion!
Don't make me suffer any more.

3

The light of the full moon
Floods the entire pasture,
And the clouds follow it
With droplets of rain.

4

I go to bed thinking of you,
In my dreams you are with me,
And I feel very happy
In dreaming that I am with you.

5

There were nights when I dreamed
I was kissing your little mouth,
And when I woke up
I saw it was the pillow
I was showering with kisses.

(Verse 1 repeated)

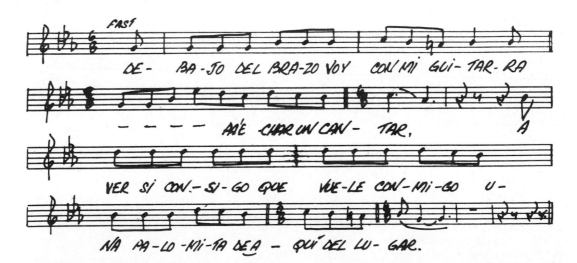

Garcilán Pacheco is a villager who has traveled more widely than most of his fellow villagers. He learned this *huapango* in 1945 from some Texans he met in Slater, Wyoming, where he had gone to herd sheep.

Garcilán is a composer in his own right. Among the songs he has composed is the *Corrido of the Death of Pete Domínguez* (R255). Domínguez was a friend of Garcilán's who was killed in a knife fight at a dance in Truchas, New Mexico, in December, 1949. I heard the song for the first time two months later. Garcilán also composed a love song, *¿Dónde Se Halla Rafaelita?* (Where Are You, Rafaelita?, R264) and a song that he calls simply *Cowboy Song* (I19).

Huapango (C4) is a Mexican dance from the region of Veracruz. It is apparently used nowadays as a song more often than as a dance. The *huapango*, like the *corrido*, sometimes tells a story, although this example is a love song more like the introspective *canción*. The *huapango* melody is sometimes used as the basis for improvised verses made up by two singers as they go along, some-what in the manner of the *trovos* (see Section G). A young Mexican musician told me that he learned the rhythm of the *huapango* to the words "tomá tu muñeca" (take your doll), with a strong accent on the second syllable at the word *tomá*.

The *huapango* given above is in 6/8 time. It illustrates the constant infiltration of Mexican tunes among the Spanish people of the Southwest, who pass on the songs from one to another. In this manner Garcilán has picked up songs in such scattered places as Juárez, Mexico, and Bingham Canyon, Utah, where he worked for a time in the copper mines.

C5. *Las Estrellas* (The Stars)
R120, Próspero S. Baca, age 72, Bernalillo, N.Mex., 1947, Robb.

1
Pregúntales a las estrellas
si por la noche me ven llorar.
Pregúntales que si es bueno
para quererte la soledad.

1
Ask the stars
If they see me weep at night.
Ask them if solitude
Is good for loving you.

Coro
No dudes nunca
que yo te quiero,
que por ti muero
loco de amor.

Chorus
Never doubt
That I love you,
That for you I am dying
Crazed with love.

2
Pregúntale al manso río
si el llanto mío se va en querer.
Pregúntale a todo el mundo
que si es eterno mi padecer.

2
Ask the gentle river
If my weeping is because I'm in love.
Ask all the world
If my suffering is eternal.

Coro

Chorus

3
Pregúntales a las flores
si mis amores son por querer.
Pregúntales a las aves
que si es eterno mi padecer.

3
Ask the flowers
If my loves are to be desired.
Ask the birds
If my suffering is eternal.

Coro

Chorus

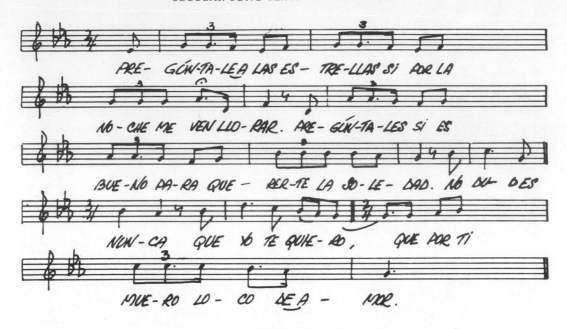

PRE- GÚN-TA-LE A LAS ES- TRE-LLAS SI POR LA
NO-CHE ME VEN LLO-RAR. PRE-GÚN-TA-LES SI ES
BUE-NO PA-RA QUE- RER-TE LA SO-LE-DAD. NO OL DES
NUN-CA QUE YO TE QUIE-RO, QUE POR TI
MUE-RO LO-CO DE A- MOR.

C6. *Peña*

R417, J. Kearns Plauche and Manuel Chávez, Albuquerque, N.Mex., 1950, Robb.
(Recorded at the home of Erna Fergusson.) Cf. Curtin 4a (p. 1).

1	1
Peña del cerro alto,	Peña of the high mountain,
Peña la consentida,	Peña my sweetheart,
Peña la vida mía,	Peña my life,
morena hermosa,	Lovely brunette,
no me vayas a olvidar.	Don't go and forget me.

2	2
Si estoy despierto,	If I am awake,
si estoy morando,	If I am alive,
Si estoy durmiendo,	If I am sleeping,
te estoy soñando.	I am dreaming of you.
Siempre te estoy amando,	Always I am loving you,
morena hermosa,	Lovely brunette,
no me vayas a olvidar.	Don't go and forget me.

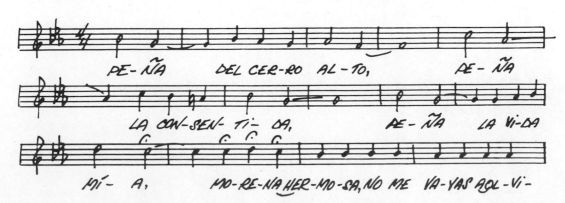

PE-ÑA DEL CER-RO AL-TO, PE-ÑA
LA CON-SEN-TI- DA, PE-ÑA LA VI-DA
MÍ- A, MO-RE-NA HER-MO-SA, NO ME VA-YAS A OL-VI-

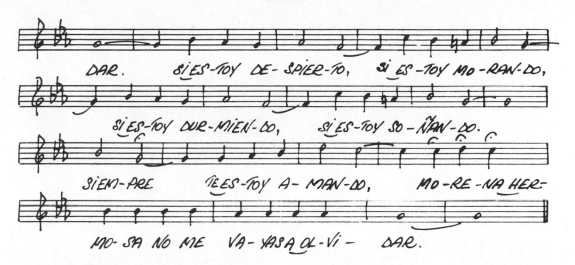

The text of this *canción* is in lines of seven or five syllables, like those of the *seguidilla*, but without the latter's regular alternation of the two-line lengths.

C7. *El Sombrero de Jipijapa* (The Panama Hat)

R725, Francisco S. Leyva, age 81, Leyva, N.Mex., 1951, Robb. Cf. RB213 (Lummis, California).

1	1
Con mi sombrero de jipijapa,	With my Panama hat,
¡ay! marchando a nuevo Madrid.	Ah! I'm leaving for new Madrid.
¡Ay! marchando a nuevos amores	Ah! I'm leaving to find new loves
que no me gustan los que hay aquí.	For I don't like those that are here.
2	2
Chinita hermosa, te doy un premio	Beautiful girl, I'll give you a prize
si des tus labios, recibo el sí,	If you give me your lips, if you say yes,
te doy la plata que hay en Chihuahua,	I will give you silver from Chihuahua,
en Zacatecas, y en Potosí.	From Zacatecas, and from Potosí.

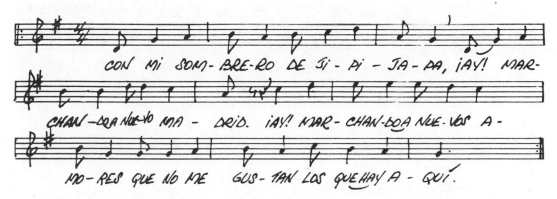

Jipijapa is a coastal town in Ecuador. Fine straw hats are woven there and then are shipped to Panama, where they are sold as Panama hats.

C8. *En la Calle del Hospital* (In the Street of the Hospital)
R728, Francisco S. Leyva, age 81, Leyva, N.Mex., 1951, Robb.

1

A mi amigo, te contaré lo que ayer.
Allá en la calle del hospital,
una muchacha tan bonita como un real,
¡qué muchacha tan bonita que me he de
casar!

1

My friend, I will tell you about yesterday.
There in the street of the hospital,
I met a girl as pretty as a dollar,
A girl so pretty that I just had to marry
her!

2

Y ella me dice que me quiere mucho.
Me ve en su casa donde me hace buen
placer.
Por esto digo que se hace mi mujer,
y ella conmigo en mi casa aunque no me
puedan ver.

2

And she says that she loves me a lot.
She sees me in her house where she gives
me great pleasure.
For this I say that she must be my wife,
And be with me in my house, even though
they (her folks?) cannot stand me.

C9. *Morena* (Brunette)
R1422, Myrtle Bernal, Taos, N.Mex., 1956, Robb.

1

Morena, graciosa, del rostro encendido,
dime si has amado alguna vez en realidad.
Si porque tienes el alma tranquila,
ámame, morena, un poquitito y nada más.

1

Graceful brunette, of glowing countenance,
Tell me if you have ever really been in love.
Because you have a tranquil soul,
Love me, brunette, a little bit and no more.

2

Tienes una enredadera en tu ventana,
cada vez que paso y miro se enreda mi alma.
Tienes una enredadera en tu balcón,
cada vez que paso y miro, digo
ahí está la dueña de mi corazón.

2

You have a vine in your window,
Every time I pass, it entangles my soul.
You have a vine in your balcony,
Every time I pass and look, I say
There is the mistress of my heart.

211

C10. *La Facundita*
   RB771, Mrs. C. M. Jaramillo, Santa Fe, N.Mex., 1950, Cobos.

1	1
Al pasar por Alamogordo	Passing through Alamogordo (New Mexico),
yo compuse esta canción	I composed this song
a mi amada Facundita,	To my beloved Facundita,
prenda de mi corazón.	Darling of my heart.

Coro	*Chorus*
Enséñame a amar.	Teach me to love.
Enséñame a querer,	Teach me to desire,
pero menos a olvidar	But not to forget
que eso no quiero aprender.	For that I don't want to learn.

2	2
Entré a un jardín de flores	I entered a flower garden
y corté una amapolita;	And picked a little poppy;
y entre sus hojas hallé	And among its leaves I found
el amor de Facundita.	The love of Facundita.

Coro	*Chorus*

3	3
Entré a un jardín de flores	I entered a flower garden
y corté una rosa morada;	And plucked a red rose;
y entre sus hojas hallé	And among its leaves I found
a Facundita enojada.	An angry Facundita.

Coro	*Chorus*

C11. *¿Qué Voy a Hacer?* (What Shall I Do?)
   R11, Juan Morales, La Jara, N.Mex., 1944, Robb.

1	1
¿Qué voy a hacer,	What shall I do,
si ya te fuiste de mi lado?	If you have fled from my side?
¿Qué voy a hacer,	What shall I do
si ya engañaste a mi amor?	If you have betrayed my love?
Yo pasaré	I shall pass
toda la vida apasionado,	My entire life impassioned,
porque yo sé	Because I know
lo que es sufrir este dolor.	What it is to suffer this sorrow.

2	2
Fuiste tan cruel	You were so cruel
que una traición tú me jugaste,	That you betrayed me,
pero algún día	But some day
tú de mí te acordarás;	You will remember me;

212

era tan fino	It was so fine,
el amor que me engañaste,	The love that you betrayed,
mujer ingrata,	Ungrateful woman,
tú algún día la pagarás.	Some day you will pay for it.

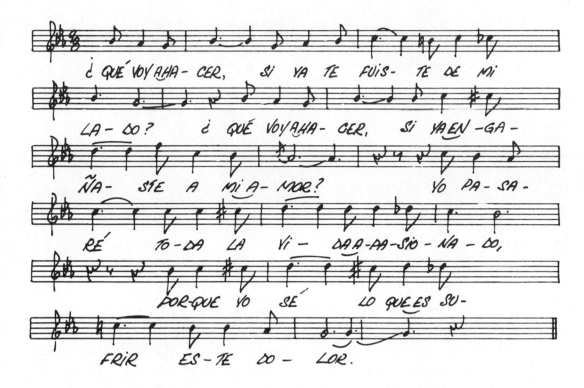

¿QUÉ VOY A HA-CER, SI YA TE FUIS-TE DE MI LA-OO? ¿QUÉ VOY A HA-CER, SI YA EN-GA-ÑA-STE A MI A-MOR? YO PA-SA-RÉ TO-DA LA VI-DA A-PA-SIO-NA-OO, POR-QUE YO SÉ LO QUE ES SU-FRIR ES-TE DO-LOR.

This *canción* is sung in thirds. Note the alternation of four- and nine-syllable lines, the eight-line verses, and the interesting rhyme scheme.

C12. *Las Fuentes* (The Fountains)
R14, Mr. and Mrs. Aaron Durand, Cuba, N.Mex., 1944, Robb.

1		1
¡Ah, qué las fuentes!	]	Ah! What fountains!
¡Cómo se fueron,	]	How they went away,
y me dejaron	]	And left me
aquí a padecer!	] *Bis*	Here to suffer!
Si porque te amo,		If only because I love you,
joven querida,		Beloved girl,
dueña de mis amores, ven . . .		Mistress of my love, come . . .

Estribillo	*Refrain*
¡En el jardín de las flores, ven,	Into the garden of flowers, come,
ven a hacerme feliz!	Come and make me happy!

2

En esa escuela]
donde tú estás,]
pasé una tarde]
y te oí cantar] *Bis*
unos versitos
tan singulares
que en mi memoria grabado están. . . .

2

In that school
Where you are,
I passed by one afternoon
And heard you singing
Some little verses
So singular
That they are engraved in my memory. . . .

Estribillo

Refrain

3

Si te preguntan
si te amo yo,
contesta pronto,
diles que no;
si te preguntan
si te amo a ti,
contesta pronto y
diles que sí,
unos versitos
tan singulares
que en mi memoria grabado están. . . .

3

If they ask you
Whether *I* love you,
Answer quickly,
Tell them no;
If they ask you
Whether I love *you*,
Answer quickly and
Tell them yes,
Some little verses,
So singular
That they are engraved in my memory. . . .

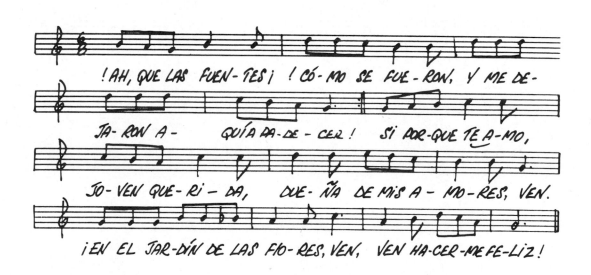

Las Fuentes is sung in sixths like the medieval fauxbourdon (see Robb 13, p. 8). A man sings a sixth below a woman.

C13. *Consolación* (Consolation)
R17, Rose Gutiérrez, La Jara, N.Mex., 1944, Robb.

1

Llevo mi siembra dolorosa
aquel recuerdo que no morirá.
Llevo en mi pecho sangrando una herida
y cruel fatiga que me matará.

2

Tratas de amarme y quizás quererme
y yo te he amado con adoración.
Un día te fuiste y dejé de verte,
dejándome penas y desolación.

3

Llorando solo en mis noches
cuando sueño con tu amor,
y veo tu imagen traidora
y me dispierta el dolor.

4

Mas si algún día te ves abatida
del desengaño que me hace llorar,
ven a curar y sangrar la herida
que tu presencia sabrá consolar.

1

I carry with me a sad thing
That memory that will not die.
I carry in my bleeding heart a wound
And cruel exhaustion that will kill me.

2

You try to love me and perhaps desire me,
And I have loved you with adoration.
One day you left and I stopped seeing you,
Leaving me troubles and desolation.

3

Weeping alone in the night
When I dream of your love,
I see your traitorous image
And sorrow awakens me.

4

But if some day you are dejected
By the realization of my sorrow,
Come to clean and cure the wound
Which your presence knows how to heal.

C14. *Palomita Que Vienes Herida* (Little Dove That Comes to Me Wounded)
R18, Celao Trujillo and Fidel Romero, La Jara, N.Mex., 1944, Robb. Cf. Robb 13 (pp. 18, 58–60); R1267, a version from Saltillo, Mexico.

<table>
<tr><td>

1

Palomita que vienes herida
de las manos de un buen tirador,
anda y dile que rinda sus armas,   ]
mientras duerme y descansa mi amor.   ] *Bis*

2

Allá duras y tristes montañas
son testigos del mal que padezco
y me dicen y me responden tristes   ]
ya tu amada no existe aquí.   ] *Bis*

3

¿Dónde se halla mi amada querida?   ]
Pero tú ni siquiera un instante   ]
ni un momento recuerdas de mí.   ] *Bis*

</td><td>

1

Little dove that comes to me wounded
By the hands of a hunter today,
Go and tell him to lay down his weapons,
While my love lies asleep far away.

2

Those forbidding and stern rocky mountains
Give sad witness of all that I bear
And they tell me in melancholy accents
"Now your beloved one does not dwell here."

3

Ah, where are you my joy and my treasure?
That you think not of me for an instant
Nor remember the days of our love.

</td></tr>
</table>

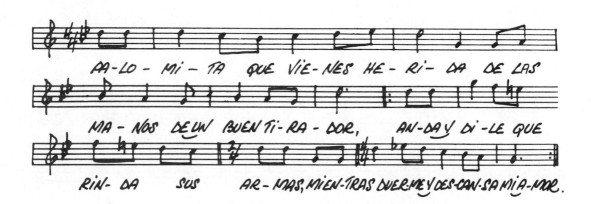

This *canción*, or introspective song, deals with love and longing. The dove is a very frequent messenger of love in the folk songs of the people of New Mexico. The wounded dove symbolizes the wounded heart of the singer.

Musically this example is exceptionally interesting. The melody is of such beauty as to rival the greatest of folk songs. Moreover, it is an example of a modal melody couched in scales of the type that prevailed in Europe before the end of the sixteenth century, and it also illustrates the obsolete practice of modal modulation. Starting in the Aeolian mode on D, it modulates in the twelfth full measure to the Dorian mode on D, modulating back to the Aeolian mode in the fifteenth full measure, and closes in the original mode. This gives it a melodic originality quite foreign to the familiar inflexions of the major- and minor-key system.

Rhythmically it is equally interesting. Whereas almost invariably the melodies of English-language ballads of the Southwest consist of four phrases of four measures each, this song is asymmetrical, due to the insertion of a measure in 2/4 time (the third from the end). This gives the melody a haunting, elusive, off balance feeling of rhythmic freedom that is one of the characteristics of the Spanish folk song in the Southwest.

The syllabic structure is unusual, consisting of alternate lines of ten and nine and eleven syllables.

This melody appears as an aria in Act II, Scene 1, of my opera *Little Jo*. I published a choral arrangement of this song in 1946 (Broadcast Music, Inc., New York), which is now out of print.

C15. *Una Noche Serena y Oscura* (One Serene and Dark Night)
R42, Juan Sandoval, Chimayó, N.Mex., 1945, Robb. Cf. Mendoza 9g (p. 296).

<table>
<tr><td>

1

—Una noche serena y oscura
en silencio juramos los dos,
en silencio me diste tu mano,
y de testigo pusimos a Dios.

</td><td>

1

"One serene and dark night
In silence we two swore our love,
In silence you gave me your hand,
And we bore witness before God.

</td></tr>
<tr><td>

2

Las estrellas, el sol, y la luna
son testigos que fuiste mi amada,
y hoy que vuelvo te encuentro casada.
¡Ay, qué suerte infeliz me tocó!

</td><td>

2

"The stars, the sun, and the moon
Are witnesses that you were my lover,
And today I return and find you married.
Oh, what an unhappy lot is mine!"

</td></tr>
<tr><td>

3

—Soy casada y amarte no puedo
porque así lo dispuso la ley;
quiero serle constante a mi esposo
y en silencio por ti lloraré.

</td><td>

3

"I am married and cannot love you
For thus the law commands;
I wish to be true to my husband
And in silence I shall weep for you."

</td></tr>
<tr><td>

4

—Cuando estés en los brazos de otro hombre
que te sepa amar con ternura,
quiera Dios y te maten dormida

por ingrata y traidora a mi amor.

</td><td>

4

"When you are in the arms of another man
Who knows how to love you tenderly,
May God grant that they kill you in your
 sleep
As an ingrate and traitor to my love."

</td></tr>
</table>

This *canción* is also known as *La Casada*.

C16. *Me Dices Que Tú Ya No Me Quieres* (You Tell Me That You Don't Love Me Anymore)
R263, Garcilán Pacheco, Córdova, N.Mex., 1950, Robb.

1

Me dices que tú ya no me quieres—no.
Piensas separarte de mí.
Me tratas con tan crueles desvelos
porque te quise en lo pobre que fuí.

Coro
Adiós, adiós, ilusión de ayer,
no me vuelvas a hablar ya no
ni me vuelvas a ver jamás.
Recordarás al hombre que te amó,

y en tu pecho guardarás
un suspiro de amor.

2

Cuando ya yo no te mire, amor,
o cuando ya esté lejos de ti,
Recuérdate de aquél que te amó tanto,
Yo de un amor puro, que ya perdí.

1

You tell me that you don't love me anymore.
You are thinking of leaving me.
You make me suffer such cruel anxiety
Because I loved you, poor as I was.

Chorus
Good-bye, illusion of yesterday,
You will speak no more to me
Nor will you ever see me again.
But you will remember the man who
loved you,
And in your heart you will keep
A sigh of love.

2

When I see you no more, love,
Or when I am far from you,
Think of him who loved you so much,
And I'll think of a pure love, which I
have lost.

218

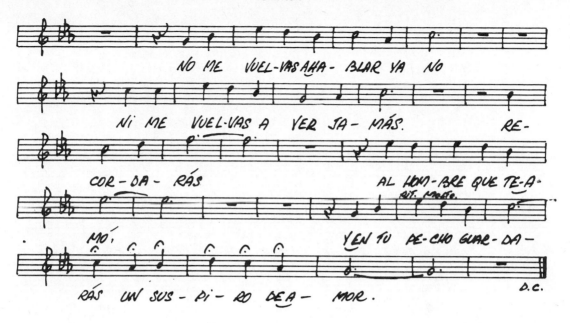

NO ME VUEL-VAS A HA-BLAR YA NO

NI ME VUEL-VAS A VER JA-MÁS. RE-

COR-DA-RÁS AL HOM-BRE QUE TE-A-

MÓ, Y EN TU PE-CHO GUAR-DA-

RÁS UN SUS-PI-RO DE A-MOR. *D.C.*

C17. *Mariana*

R342, Vidal Valdez, Albuquerque, N.Mex., 1946, Robb. Cf. RB222 (Lummis, 1904).

1 Voy a cantar un corrido, señores pongan cuidado, que el ángel de mis amores es un ángel adorado de mí. No tengan cuidado.	**1** I'm going to sing a ballad, Gentlemen pay attention, For the angel of my loves Is an angel adored By me. But don't weep for me.
2 Mariana ¿porqué no me amas? ¿Qué hay de mi amor disconfianza? No hay de su amor disconfianza. Les temo a los de mi casa. De mí no tenga esperanza.	**2** Mariana, why don't you love me? Don't you trust in my love? I don't mistrust yours, But I fear my own folks. Do not hope for me.
3 ¡Ay! Chatita de mi vida, mi amor no te compitió. Tus espertos fueron muchos por interés de otro amor. Lo que le falta es valor.	**3** Oh! Doll that I love, My love did not compete for you. You have had many lovers, You were interested in others. What you lack is courage.
4 A mí valor no me falta ni mi cariño lo niego. Quise mucho a mi mamá. Corresponderle no puedo. Paciencia pídale al cielo.	**4** I do not lack courage, Nor do I deny my love. I dearly loved my mother. But I cannot argue. I beg heaven for patience.

<table>
<tr><td>

5

Paciencia le pido al cielo
que hoy de mi suerte no ayuda.
Es en vano enamorar
donde la suerte no ayuda.
Me quejo mi desventura.

</td><td>

5

I beg heaven for patience
For my luck has been bad.
It's useless to fall in love
When fate does not aid you.
So I lament my misfortune.

</td></tr>
</table>

VOY A CAN-TAR UN COR-RI-DO, SE-ÑO-RES PON-GAN CUI-DA-DO, QUE EL ÁN-GEL DE MIS A-MO-RES ES UN ÁN-GEL A-DO-RA-DO DE MÍ. NO TEN-GAN CUI-DA-DO.

C18. *El Trovador* (The Troubadour)
R522, Francisco S. Leyva, age 81, Leyva, N.Mex., 1951, Robb.

<table>
<tr><td>

1

A pie de la alta ventana
de tu gótico palacio,
recruzo la noche despacio,
adorando tu beldad.
Y vide volar la aurora
con nítidos resplandores
sin que tú de mis amores,
tengas, Elvira, piedad.

</td><td>

1

Beneath the high window
Of your Gothic palace,
Slowly I paced in the night,
Adoring your loveliness.
And I saw the dawn come
With its glowing splendors
But you did not heed, my love.
Elvira, have pity.

</td></tr>
<tr><td>

2

Por ti pregunté a las flores
que te pintan tus jardines
y del bosque a los confines
interrogo al ruiseñor
y me respondió la hermosa
cuando calladas las miró
que ni escuchas un suspiro
de este infeliz trovador.

</td><td>

2

For you I asked the flowers
To paint your gardens
And wandering from the woods to the walls
I interrogated the nightingale
And the lovely bird answered me
When it saw everything was quiet
That you don't even hear a sigh
Of this unhappy troubadour.

</td></tr>
<tr><td>

3

Y en fin, mi querida Elvira,
tienes una alma de acero.
Tú bien sabes que te quiero
pero me negaste amor.

</td><td>

3

And finally, my dear Elvira,
You have a soul of steel.
You know very well that I love you
But you denied me your love.

</td></tr>
</table>

Sólo me queda el consuelo	My only consolation is
que conserves la memoria	That you retain the memory
y que no olvides la historia	And that you don't forget the story
de este infeliz trovador.	Of this unhappy troubadour.

A PIE DE LA AL-TA VEN-TA-NA DE TU GÓ-TI-CO PA-
LA-CIO, RE-CRU-ZO LA NO-CHE'E-SPA-CIO A-DO-
RAN-DO TU BEL-DAD. Y VI-DE VO-LAR LA AU-RO-RA
CON NÍ-TI-DOS RE-SPLAN-DO-RES SIN QUE TÚ DE MIS A-
MO-RES, TEN-GAS, EL-VI-RA, PIE-DAD.

C19. *Mi Unico Bien* (My Only Good)
R542, Francisco S. Leyva, age 81. Leyva, N.Mex., 1951, Robb.

1	1
Tardé en amarte meses	I loved you for months
y entre la risa de	And between the laughter of
espuma quedó el sol	foam the sun remained
y en tanto yo quedo solo	And meanwhile I am alone
sin luz, sin fe,	without light, without faith,
por ser luz tu esperanza,	because your hope was light,
tú mi consuelo y mi único bien.	You were my comfort and my only good.

2	2
Ya no veré tu sonrisa	Now I won't see your smile
tan pura	as pure
como el incienso	as the incense
que da el jazmín.	that jasmine gives off.
Veré al amanecer del día	I will see the day dawn
sin poderme dormir	without being able to sleep
pensando en ti.	thinking about you.

3	3
No olvides que dejaste	Don't forget that you left
mi corazón,	my heart
que así yo me siento oprimido	In a state of depression
desde que nos estuvimos juntos,	Since we were together,
tú y yo.	you and I.

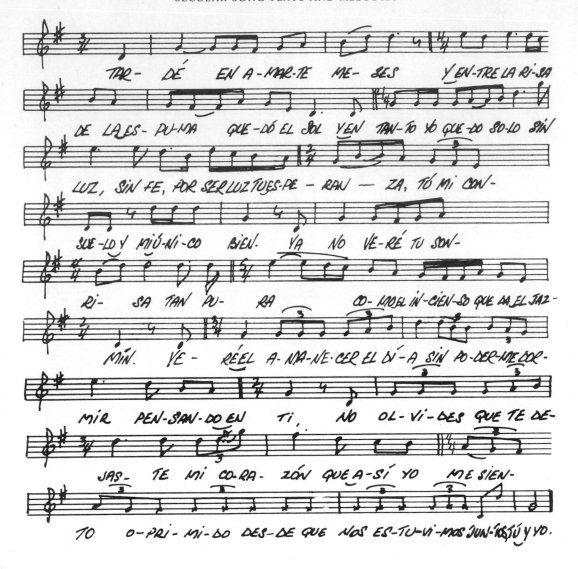

TAR - DÉ EN A-MAR-TE ME-SES Y EN-TRE LA RI-SA
DE LA ES-PU-MA QUE-DÓ EL SOL Y EN TAN-TO YO QUE-DO SO-LO SIN
LUZ, SIN FE, POR SER LUZ TU ES-PE - RAN - ZA, TÓ MI CON-
SUE-LO Y MI Ú-NI-CO BIEN. YA NO VE-RÉ TU SON-
RI- SA TAN PU- RA CO- MO EL IN-CIEN-SO QUE DA EL JAZ-
MÍN. VE - RÉ EL A-MA-NE-CER EL DÍ-A SIN PO-DER-ME DOR-
MIR PEN-SAN-DO EN TI, NO OL-VI-DES QUE TE DE-
JAS- TE MI CO-RA- ZÓN QUE A-SÍ YO ME SIEN-
TO O-PRI- MI-DO DES-DE QUE NOS ES-TU-VI-MOS JUN-TOS TÚ Y YO.

C20. *Subí al Cielo* (I Ascended to Heaven)
R727, Francisco S. Leyva, age 81, Leyva, N.Mex., 1951, Robb.

1	1
Subí al cielo, toqué y no me oyeron,	I ascended to heaven, I knocked and they didn't hear me,
pues hay un Dios, que usted ya menciera.	For there is a God, whom you already mentioned.
¿Y lo que hoy hay aquí en esta tierra?	And what is there here today in this land?
Que responda el Señor y no llores.	Let the Lord answer and don't cry.

2	2
Ya subí silenciosa a la tumba, a los caminos perdidos sosiego. De rodillas, ingrata, te ruego que en la ausencia te acuerdas de mí.	I ascended silently to the tomb, On the lost roads quietly. On my knees, ungrateful one, I pray you That in my absence you remember me.

3	3
Descendió de los cielos un ángel y voló con sus alas doradas, y esas son de delicias pasadas que le nombran delicias de amor.	From the heavens descended an angel And flew with gilded wings, And reminded me of past delights, The delights of love.

C21. *Ya Tú No Soplas* (You No Longer Thrill Me)
R734, Francisco S. Leyva, age 81, Leyva, N.Mex., 1951, Robb.

1	1

No me impresionas, ni me vengas con tus
  cosas,
ni te molestes en pensar en mi querer.
	Don't pressure me, nor come to me with
	  your things,
	Nor bother yourself in thinking of my love.

Refrán	*Refrain*

Quiero que tú sepas cuando oigas estas
  coplas
que ya tú no soplas como mujer.
	I want you to know when you hear these
	  couplets
	That, as a woman, you no longer thrill me.

2	2
Cuando te quise, te pusiste muy fachosa, y por el mundo tú me echaste a correr.	When I loved you, you became very boastful, And through the world you ran away from me.

Refrán	*Refrain*

3

Pues con espejo te verás que estás muy chocha.
No me cuajas como me cuajaste ayer.

Refrán

4

De estos días felices no me importan,
no están de moda, hoy no es ayer.

Refrán

5

De estos días felices no me importan,
no están de moda, hoy no es ayer.

¿Para qué me sigues y me dices que no me ahorcas?

Refrán

3

Well with the mirror you'll see you are now doddering.
You do not suit me as you suited me yesterday.

Refrain

4

Those happy days are not important to me,
They are not in fashion, today is not yesterday.

Refrain

5

Those happy days are not important to me,
They are not in fashion, today is not yesterday.
Why do you follow me and tell me you won't hang me?

Refrain

Verse 3 is repeated. The recording ends after verse 4, but verse 5 was furnished by the singer. This song is unique in that the refrain is not melodically separate from the verse but is incorporated in the verse itself as the second period of a double period consisting of four phrases.

C22. *El Abandonado* (The Abandoned Man)
    R2091, Frank McCulloch, Jr., 1965, Robb. Cf. R614, R614a, R828; also Mendoza 9g
(p. 412, 1913); Dobie, Texas 18 (vol. 4, pp. 41–43).

1	**1**
Me abandonaste, mujer, porque soy muy pobre	You abandoned me, woman, because I'm very poor
y la desgracia es ser hombre apasionado.	And my misfortune is being a passionate man.
Refrán	*Refrain*
Pues ¿qué he de hacer si yo soy el abandonado?	Well, what shall I do if I am the abandoned one?
pues ¿qué he de hacer? será por el amor de Dios.	Well, whatever I do will be for the love of God.
2	**2**
Tres vicios tengo, los tres tengo muy adoptados,	Three vices I have, the three I have adopted,
el ser borracho, jugador, y enamorado.	Being a drunk, a gambler, and a lover.
Refrán	*Refrain*
3	**3**
Pero ando ingrato si con mi amor no quedo,	But I'd be ungrateful if I don't stay with my love,
tal vez otro hombre con su amor se habrá jugado.	Perhaps another man with his love would have gambled.
Refrán	*Refrain*

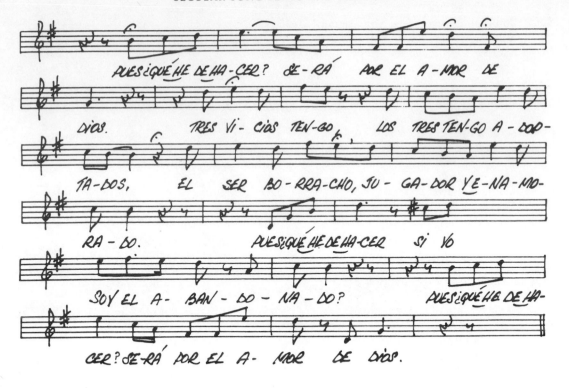

C22a. *El Abandonado*
Dobie, Texas 18 (vol. 4, pp. 41–43), Texas, 1925, J. Frank Dobie.

The text is similar to the above version but sung to a variant of the same melody.

C23. *La Tumba* (The Tomb)
R1419, Myrtle Bernal, Taos, N.Mex., 1956, Robb.

<table>
<tr><td>

1

¡Cuántas veces pensando en que te adoro,

te he soñado mi bien con embeleso!

¡Cuántas veces, mi dicha y mi tesoro,
te he entregado mi amor en cada beso!

Coro
Quiero estar a tu lado y contemplarte
y sentir de tu pecho los latidos.
Quiero vivir, quiero morir y siempre
  amarte,
y bajar hasta la tumba, siempre unidos.

2
Contemplando que si mi vida acaba,
y aumentan en mi pecho los rigores,
me hacen falta los besos que me dabas,
me hace falta el calor de tus amores.

Coro

</td><td>

1

How many times, thinking of how I adore
  you,
I have dreamed of you my darling with
  delight!
How many times, my joy and my treasure,
I have given you my love in every kiss!

Chorus
I want to be at your side and look at you
And feel the beating of your heart.
I want to live, I want to die and always
  love you,
And descend to the tomb, always united.

2
Considering that if my life ends,
And the pains in my breast increase,
I miss the kisses you used to give me,
I miss the warmth of your love.

Chorus

</td></tr>
</table>

227

C24. *Hay Recuerdos* (There are Memories)
R1420, Myrtle Bernal, Taos, N.Mex., 1956, Robb.

1	1
Hay recuerdos que el tiempo no ha borrado.	There are memories that time has not erased.
Hay recuerdos que me quitan la calma,	There are memories that rob me of calm,
pero, mujer, tú me has robado el alma,	But, woman, you have robbed me of my soul,
y la paz y la quietud del corazón.	And of peace and serenity of heart.

2	2
Me es imposible amar otra mujer,	It is impossible for me to love another woman,
vivir sin ella sin estar llorando,	Or to live without her without weeping,
la copa del placer siempre apurando,	The cup of pleasure completely exhausted,
cual la punzante espina de una flor.	And my heart pierced by the thorn of a flower.

3	3
Para el hombre se hicieron las penas.	For man pains were made.
Para el hombre se hizo el padecer.	For man suffering was made.
Para el hombre se hicieron cadenas.	For man chains were made.
Para amar a una ingrata mujer.	All for love of an ungrateful woman.

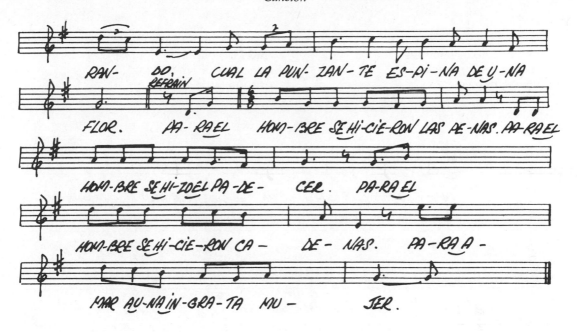

RAN- DO, *REFRAIN* CUAL LA PUN- ZAN- TE ES-PI-NA DE U-NA FLOR. PA- RA EL HOM-BRE SE HI-CIE-RON LAS PE-NAS. PA-RA EL HOM-BRE SE HI-ZO EL PA-DE- CER. PA-RA EL HOM-BRE SE HI-CIE-RON CA- DE-NAS. PA-RA A-MAR AU-NA IN-GRA-TA MU- JER.

C25. *Ojitos Verdes* (Little Green Eyes)

R1919, Melesio García, Fidencio Espinosa, and Vincent Jaramillo, Chililí, N.Mex., 1963, Robb.

1	1
Aquellos ojitos verdes,	Those little green eyes,
¿con quién se andarán paseando?	With whom are they strolling?
Ojalá que me recuerden	God grant that they remember me
aunque sea de vez en cuando.	If only from time to time.

1

Aquellos ojitos verdes,
¿con quién se andarán paseando?
Ojalá que me recuerden
aunque sea de vez en cuando.

2

Dicen que cuando sospiran
aquellos ojitos verdes,
me sospiran con la vida
porque todavía me quieren.

Refrán

¡Ay, ay, ay, ay!
¿Dónde andarán?
esos ojitos
que me hicieron sospirar.
¡Ay, ay, ay, ay!
¿Dónde andarán?
esos ojitos
que no los puedo olvidar.

3

(Verso 2 se repite)

1

Those little green eyes,
With whom are they strolling?
God grant that they remember me
If only from time to time.

2

They say that when
Those little green eyes sigh,
They sigh for me with their life
Because they love me still.

Refrain

Ay, ay, ay, ay!
Where can they be?
Those little eyes
That made me sigh.
Ay, ay, ay, ay!
Where can they be?
Those little eyes
That I can't forget.

3

(Verse 2 repeated)

4

Cuando paso por los campos
y me afijo en los laureles,
parece que estoy mirando
aquellos ojitos verdes.

4

When I walk through the country
And I look upon the laurels,
It seems as if I'm looking
At those little green eyes.

Refrán

Refrain

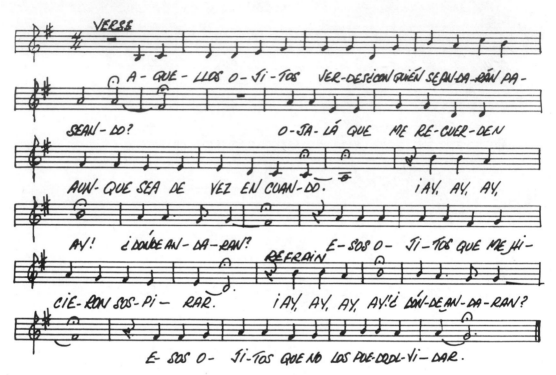

C26. *Hoy si Albierte*
R1996, Clemente Chávez, Galisteo, N.Mex., 1963, Robb.

1

El:
Hoy si albierte mucha indiferencia.[1]
Yo te adoro mujer celestial,
aunque venga mano sumergida
a clabarle a mi pecho un puñal.

1

He:
Today you were very indifferent.
I adore you celestial woman,
Although a hidden hand comes
To plunge a dagger in my breast.

2

Ella:
No te puedo querer. Soy casada.
Otras leyes me siguen el querer,
por amor y constancia a mi esposo
que ante Dios y los hombres juré.

2

She:
I can't love you. I am married.
Other laws come before desire, I owe
Love and faithfulness to my husband
Which I swore before God and man.

[1]Possibly *Hoy se advertió. Albierte* is one of a number of New Mexican colloquialisms found in the manuscript from which this text was copied.

3

El:

Yo comprendo, mujer de mi vida.
¿Quién pudiere ocultar mi dolor?
Pero veo tu imagen querida.
No puedo vivir sin tu amor.

3

He:

I understand, woman of my life.
Who could hide my sorrow?
But I see your beloved image.
I cannot live without your love.

4

Ella:

Si tú quieres, seremos hermanos.
Juraremos amarnos los dos
y tal vez ganaremos el premio
en el trono sagrado de Dios.

4

She:

If you like, we will be brother and sister.
We will swear to love one another
And perhaps we shall win the prize
Before the sacred throne of God.

5

El:

Hoja bella del árbol ya caída
que el impulso a los vientos voló,
nube rota en el mar del olvido
navegando sin rumbo voy yo.

5

He:

Lovely leaf now fallen from the tree
That impulse blew away to the winds,
Broken cloud over the sea of forgetfulness,
I go on sailing without a course.

C27. *Cuando Vayas para la Iglesia* (When You Go to Church)
R2007, Clemente Chávez, Galisteo, N.Mex., 1943, Robb.

1

Cuando vayas para la iglesia
con tu novio y tu madrina,
con la punta del zapato
me echarás la tierra encima.

1

When you go to church
With your boyfriend and your godmother,
You will kick dust on me
With the tip of your shoe.

2

Allí, cuando en la iglesia estés
en la presencia del cura,
voltearás la cara atrás
y verás mi sepultura.

2

There, when you're in the church
In the presence of the priest,
You will turn your face around
And you will see my grave.

3

Cuando de la iglesia salgan,
la gente los ha de ver,
que van a salir de brazo
como marido y mujer.

3

When they leave the church,
The people will see them,
Since they're leaving arm in arm
Like husband and wife.

4

Cuando llegues a tu casa,
no te vayas a acordar
que veías recuerdos míos,
no vayas a ir a llorar.

4

When you get home,
You won't remember
That you were reminded of me,
You won't go and cry.

5

¡Ay! cuando en tu casa estés
con los músicos tocando,
¡ay! a mí los de mi casa
todos me estarán llorando.

5

Ah, when you are at home
With the musicians playing,
Ah, those of my house
Will all be mourning me.

6

Cuando en el baile te veyas,
rodeada de mucha gente,
ya a mí me estarán diciendo
misa de cuerpo presente.

6

When you go to a dance,
Surrounded by a lot of people,
They will already be saying
Mass for my body.

7

Si su nombre no les digo
por no correr mala fama,
la que yo estimo y adoro
ya saben como se llama.

7

If I don't tell you her name
So as not to give a bad reputation
To the one I esteem and adore—
You already know her name.

C28. *Medio Abril* (Mid-April)
R2402, Juan Griego, Albuquerque, N.Mex., 1971, Robb.

1

Anteayer tarde la ví,
cortando flores,
y cortó una flor
nacida en el mes de abril
que en sus manos se abotona,
y en la mía se ha de abrir.

1

Two days ago in the evening
I saw her cutting flowers,
And she cut a flower
Born in the month of April;
In her hands it buds
And in mine it is to bloom.

2

Yo la lloraba,
con lágrimas de mis ojos.
Yo la adoraba,
con todo mi corazón.
¡Ay! la joven que yo amaba
se secó hasta el corazón.

] *Bis*

2

I cried for her,
With tears in my eyes.
I adored her,
With all my heart.
Oh! The girl I loved,
Her heart has dried up.

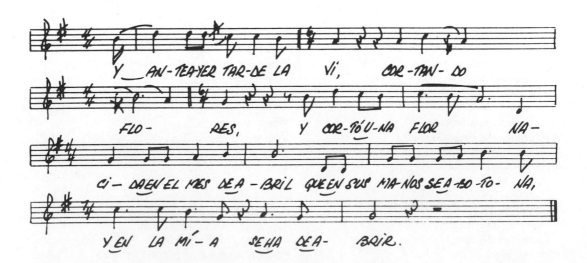

C29. *El Profundo Tormento* (The Profound Torment)
R544, Francisco S. Leyva, Leyva, N.Mex., 1951, Robb.

1

Déjame, ingrata, por Dios.
Déjame sufrir
el profundo tormento
que padezco por ti.

2

Ya que te amo con tanto
me niegas este amor,
y marchito le das
su infeliz corazón.

3

¡Piedad, piedad!
¡Piedad de mí!
que sin tu amor
voy a morir.

4

¡Amame pues!
Veme conpasión.
Si no, déjame, ingrata,
tu cruel deshonor.

1

Let me be, ungrateful woman.
Let me suffer
The profound torment
Which I feel because of you.

2

Although I love you so,
You deny my love,
And your unhappy heart
Withers away.

3

Pity, pity!
Have pity on me!
For without your love
I am going to die.

4

Then love me!
Look at me with passion.
If not, leave me, ungrateful woman,
Your cruel dishonor.

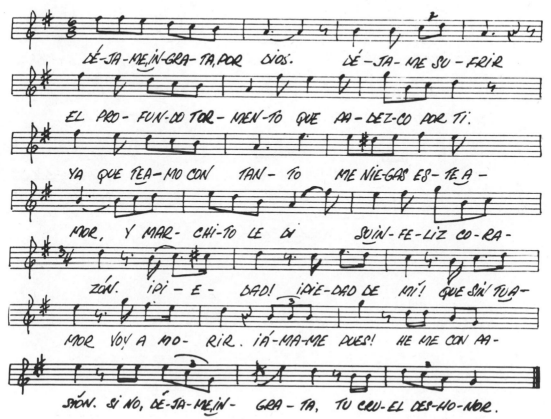

C30. *Canción del Casado* (Song of the Husband)
R3, Próspero S. Baca, age 69, Bernalillo, N.Mex., 1944, Robb. Cf. R123, R1723.

1

No hay como Dios, amigos, en este mundo;

después de Dios, como sus padres de uno;
después de sus padres, como el estado
  ninguno;
y el hombre casado ni es pobre, ni es
  infeliz.

1

There is no one like God, friends, in this
  world;
After God, none like ones parents;
After ones parents, none like the state;

And the married man is neither poor nor
  unhappy.

2

Sólo la mujer es para cuidar al hombre,
cuando le tiene su casa separada;
mientras un soltero en la vida tiene nada,
el hombre casado ni es pobre, ni es
  infeliz.

2

The wife is only to look after her man,
When he has his own house;
While a bachelor in this life has nothing,
The married man is neither poor nor
  unhappy.

3

Sólo la mujer es compañía del hombre,
sabiéndola el hombre bien sobrellevar;
es la compañera con que se ha de acariñar,
el hombre casado ni es pobre, ni es
  infeliz.

3

The wife is only company for her man,
Knowing how to ease a man's burdens;
She is the companion whom he must cherish,
The married man is neither poor nor
  unhappy

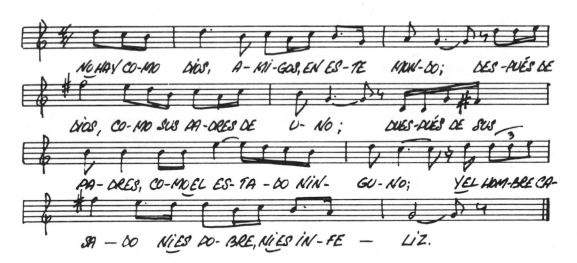

NO HAY CO-MO DIOS, A-MI-GOS, EN ES-TE MUN-DO; DES-PUÉS DE DIOS, CO-MO SUS PA-DRES DE U-NO; DUES-PUÉS DE SUS PA-DRES, CO-MO EL ES-TA-DO NIN-GU-NO; Y EL HOM-BRE CA-SA-DO NI ES PO-BRE, NI ES IN-FE-LIZ.

C31. *Blanca*
R262, Garcilán Pacheco, Córdova, N.Mex., 1950, Robb.

1

Mujer tan sin igual,
tan blanca y tan sutil,
eres conmigo leal.
Soy tuyo hasta el morir.

1

Woman so without equal,
So fair and so subtle,
You are loyal to me.
I am yours till death.

2
Te tuve junto a mí
y en sueños te besé;
y loco desperté
cuando sin ti me ví.

2
I held you close to me
And in my dreams I kissed you;
And I woke up insane
When I saw I was alone.

Coro
Eres toda mi alma
y mi pasión.
Eres tú mi ensueño,
encantador.

Chorus
You are all my soul
And my passion.
You are my dream,
My enchantment.

3
Mi vida te confié
y el corazón te dí;
no sé cómo te amo,
que vivo para ti.

3
I entrusted my life to you
And I gave you my heart;
I don't know how much I love you,
But I do live for you.

C32. *Senaida*

R449, Arvino Martínez, Tierra Azul, N.Mex., 1951, Robb. Cf. Mendoza 9f (no. 145, p. 576); Mendoza 9d (pp. 581–84); R1266 (Mexico).

1
Cuatrocientos kilómetros tiene
la ciudad donde vive Senaida.
Voy a ver si la puedo encontrar
para ver si me da su palabra.

1
It is four hundred kilometers
To the town where Senaida lives.
I'm going to see if I can find her
To see if she'll give me her word.

2
Al momento en que ví yo a la joven
al momento yo la saludé;
al momento me dijo la niña,
—oiga, joven, ¿de dónde es usted?

2
The moment I saw the young lady
I greeted her at that moment;
Just then the girl said to me,
"Listen, where are you from?"

3

Oiga, joven, yo vengo de lejos,
me he venido en un tren pasajero,
sólo vengo a pedirle un favor
que acompañe a este pobre soltero.

3

"Listen, young lady, I come from afar,
I have come in a passenger train,
I only come to ask you a favor
That you join this poor bachelor."

4

Joven, si usted es soltero
y si usted me quisiera también,
a pasear con usted yo me fuera
si me diera el transporte para el tren.

4

"Young man, if you're a bachelor
and if you love me, too,
I'd come traveling with you
If you'd provide the train fare."

5

Hoy viene ese tren pasajero
que sin duda lo estoy esperando.
Ya se vienen quedando los pueblos,
ya parece que voy caminando.

5

Today arrives the train
That I'm waiting for without doubt.
Now the towns are left behind,
It seems that I am moving.

6

Con el deseo que traía de verla
estrecharla en mis brazos quería
aguardé a que fuera de noche
para verla mejor que de día.

6

How much I wanted to see her
And hold her in my arms,
I waited until night came
To see her better than in the daytime.

7

Cinco meses duré sin mirarla,
trabajé con afán, con esmero,
esperando encontrar a Senaida
para ofrecerle todo mi dinero.

7

Five months since I've seen her,
I've worked long and hard,
Waiting to meet Senaida
To offer her my fortune.

8

Cuando al fin yo tuve mucho dinero,
otra vez en el tren me volví
al pueblo donde vive Senaida
y corriendo de a dos por la vía.

8

When at last I had lots of money,
I returned again on the train
To the town where Senaida lives
Running upon the tracks.

9

Me bajé en la estación presuroso
y a su casa corrí a saludarla,
muy envuelta en su lindo rebozo
encontré a mi Senaida de mi alma.

9

I quickly jumped off at the station
And to her house I ran to greet her,
All wrapped in her beautiful shawl
I found my Senaida, my soul.

10

Yo no quiero, me dice Senaida,
el dinero que usted me propone.
Si le dije yo a usted en otro tiempo
se lo dije por ver si era hombre.

10

"I don't want," said Senaida,
"The money that you proposed.
If I told you that the last time
It was but to see if you were a man."

11

Ahora miro que usted si me quiere
y si son sus amores legales,
deberá de pasar a mi casa
a pedirlo el permiso a mis padres.

11

"And now if you really love me
And if your love is honorable,
"You'll come with me to my home
And ask my parents for my hand."

236

12
Yo me vuelvo en un tren pasajero
al servicio que sus padres mandaron.
Para nada sirvió mi dinero,
yo me llevo a Senaida a mi lado.

12
Again I return to the train,
Her parents are satisfied.
My money is good for nothing,
For I have Senaida at my side.

CUA-TRO — CIEN-TOS KI-LÓ-ME-TROS TIE-NE LA CIU-DAD DON-DE VI-VE SE-NAI-DA. VOY A VER SI LA PUE-DO-EN-CON-TRAR PA-RA VER SI ME DA SU PA-LA-BRA.

Note the unusual ten-syllable lines. I used
a version of this melody in my opera *Little Jo*.

C32a. *La Zenaida*
Hansen 6b (no. 4, p. 302), Lupe Flores, age 48, Riverside, Calif., 1959, Hansen.

1
Cuatrocientos kilómetros tiene
la ciudad donde vive Zenaida;
voy a ver si la puedo encontrar,
para ver si me da su palabra.

1
Four hundred kilometers it measures,
The city in which Zenaida lives;
I'm going to see if I can find her
And hope that to me her love she gives.

2
Al momento que la ví venir,
al momento yo le saludé;
al momento me dijo la joven:
—Oiga, joven, ¿de dónde es usted?

2
At the moment I saw her coming
To say hello seemed the thing to do,
But quickly the young girl answered back:
"Listen here, young man, from where are
      you?"

3
—Oiga, joven, yo vengo de lejos
y me vine en un tren pasajero;
no más vengo a decirle a Zenaida
que acompañe a este pobre soltero.

3
"Well, young lady, I come from afar
And I came on a passenger train;
I've come only to ask Zenaida
To go with this bachelor again."

4
Con las ganas que traía de verla,
estrecharla en mis brazos quería,
esperé que se hiciera de noche
para verla mejor que de día.

4
I was ever so anxious to see her,
I wanted to hold her in my arms,
And I was hoping it would be night
So I could see better all her charms.

5

Allá viene ese tren pasajero
que sin duda lo estoy esperando,
ya se vienen quedando los pueblos,
ya parece que voy caminando.

6

Cuatro meses duré sin mirarla,
trabajé con afán y esmero,

esperando volver a encontrarla
y ofrecerle todo mi dinero.

7

(Verso 1 se repite)

5

There comes the passenger train again,
I am here waiting for it no doubt,
Now all the towns are passing from view,
That I'm returning I'll soon find out.

6

I endured four months without seeing her,
Working all the time with heartfelt
   yearnings,
Hoping to go back and find her there
So I could offer her all my earnings.

7

(Verse 1 repeated)

CUA-TRO-CIEN-TOS KI- LÓ-ME-TROS TIE-NE LA CIU-DAD CON-DE VI-VE ZE-NAI-DA; VOY A VER SI LA PUE-DEN-CON-TRAR, PA-RA VER SI ME DA SU PA-LA-BRA.

C33. *China de los Ojos Negros* (Girl with Black Eyes)
R134, Daniel López, Lupe Rodríguez, Albuquerque, N.Mex., 1947, Robb.

1

China de los ojos negros,
¿por qué me miras así?
Chaparrita de mi vida,
mañana de voy de aquí.

2

Si quieres platicar conmigo
asómate de tu balcón,
para mi alma no hay consuelo.
¡Qué haré yo sin este amor!

3

Ella se puso muy triste
cuando le dije me voy;
para mi alma no hay consuelo.
¡Qué haré yo sin este amor!

1

Girl with black eyes,
Why do you look at me so?
Beloved little one,
Tomorrow I am going away.

2

If you want to talk to me
Look out from your balcony,
For my soul there's no consolation.
What shall I do without this love?

3

She became very sad
When I told her I was going;
For my soul there's no consolation.
What shall I do without this love?

4	4
Ella me dice llorando,	She said to me, weeping,
—Si tú de veras te vas,	"If you are really going,
si tú te embarcas mañana,	If you are embarking tomorrow,
sin duda no volverás.—	No doubt you will not return."

5	5
(Verso 1 se repite)	(Verse 1 repeated)

C34. *Cielito Lindo* (Beautiful Cielito)
R2533, J. D. Robb, age 80, Albuquerque, N.Mex., 1972, Robb.

1	1
De la Sierra Morena,	From the dark mountain you come,
Cielito lindo,	Beautiful Cielito,
vienes bajando	Lowering a pair of
un par de ojitos negros,	Black eyes,
Cielito lindo,	Beautiful Cielito,
de contrabando.	Like contraband.

Coro	*Chorus*
¡Ay! ¡Ay, ay, ay!	Ay! Ay, ay, ay!
Canta y no llores	Sing and don't weep
porque cantando se alegren,	Because singing brings happiness,
Cielito lindo,	Beautiful Cielito,
los corazones.	Into our hearts.

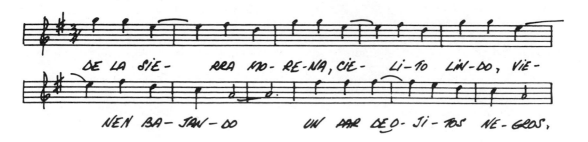

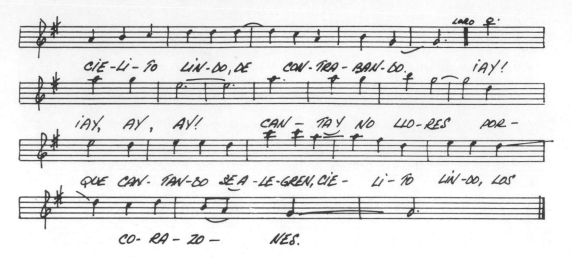

CIE-LI-TO LIN-DO, DE CON-TRA-BAN-DO. ¡AY!

¡AY, AY, AY! CAN-TA Y NO LLO-RES POR—

QUE CAN-TAN-DO SE A-LE-GREN, CIE-LI-TO LIN-DO, LOS

CO-RA-ZO— NES.

C34a. *Cielito Lindo*
"Spanish Songs of New Mexico," by F. S. Curtis, Jr., in Dobie, Texas 18 (vol. 4, p. 28), Texas, 1925, F. S. Curtis, Jr.

1	1
¡Ay! De la Sierra Morena,	Ay! From the Sierra Morena,
Cielito Lindo, vienen bajando,	Cielito Lindo, they are coming down,
un par de ojitos negros,	A pair of black eyes,
Cielito Lindo, de contrabando.	Cielito Lindo—forbidden fruit.
¡Ay, ay, ay, ay! Vienen bajando,	Ay, ay, ay, ay! They are coming down,
un par de ojitos negros,	A pair of black eyes,
Cielito Lindo, de contrabando.	Cielito Lindo—forbidden fruit.

2	2
Una flecha en el aire	Cupid shot, Cupid shot,
botó Cupido, botó Cupido,	An arrow into the air,
y andando en el aire,	And coming through the air, Cielito Lindo,
Cielito Lindo, bien me ha herido.	It has wounded me grievously.
¡Ay, ay, ay, ay! botó Cupido,	Ay, ay, ay, ay! Cupid shot it,
y andando en el aire	And coming through the air, Cielito Lindo,
Cielito Lindo, bien me ha herido.	It has wounded me grievously.

3	3
Si porque nos amamos,	If because we are in love,
Cielito Lindo, tienen envidia,	Cielito Lindo, they envy us,
mueran los envidiosos,	Let the envious die,
Cielito Lindo, nuestro amor viva.	Cielito Lindo, our love lives.
¡Ay, ay, ay, ay! tienen envidia.	Ay, ay, ay, ay! They envy us.
Mueran los envidiosos, Cielito Lindo,	Let the envious die, Cielito Lindo,
nuestro amor viva.	Our love lives.

4	4
Pájaro que abandona	The bird who abandons
su primer nido, su primer nido,	His first nest, his first nest,
si lo encuentre ocupado,	If he finds it occupied,
Cielito Lindo, bien merecido.	Cielito Lindo, it's his own fault.

¡Ay, ay, ay, ay! su primer nido,	Ay, ay, ay, ay! His first nest,
si lo encuentre ocupado, Cielito Lindo,	If he finds if occupied, Cielito Lindo,
bien merecido.	It's his own fault.

5

Ese lunar que tienes,	This mole that you have,
Cielito Lindo, junto a mi boca,	Cielito Lindo, that I'm kissing,
no se lo des a nadie,	Don't let anyone touch it,
Cielito Lindo, que a mí me toca.	Cielito Lindo, except me.
¡Ay, ay, ay, ay! junto a mi boca,	Ay, ay, ay, ay! This that I kiss,
no se lo des a nadie,	Don't let anyone touch it,
Cielito Lindo, que a mí me toca.	Cielito Lindo, except me.

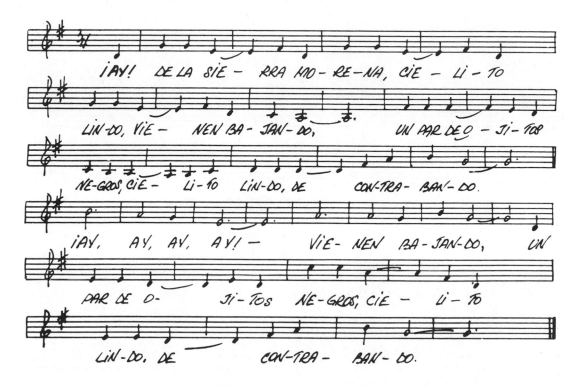

C35. *Me Voy Muy Lejos* (I Am Going Very Far Away)
R2415, Juan Griego, age 61, Albuquerque, N.Mex., 1971, Robb.

1

Voy a poner mis ojos	I am going to set my eyes
en más adelante	On the future
porque sin duda	Because without doubt
ya me voy a separar.	I am going to leave here.

2

Pues yo le dije	Well, I told her
que no le había de rogar.	That I would not beg her.
Me voy muy lejos	I am going very far away
donde no me oigan mentar.	Where they haven't heard about me.

3

Que creías que tratabas
con un gringo.
Y es que dijiste,
—como quiera lo hago bola.—

4

Te quedarás
como él que chifló en la loma.
Yo de aquí
quince días más allá.

5

Las caricias que me hiciste
Aquí las traigo
y aquel tiempo tan feliz
que ya pasó.

3

You thought that you were dealing
With a gringo.
I heard you say,
"In any case I will fool him."

4

You will be left
Like one whistling in the wind.
For I will not be here
Fifteen days hence.

5

These caresses you gave me
I carry here
Along with those happy times
Which now are gone.

C36. *Luisa*
R2407, Juan Griego, age 61, Albuquerque, N.Mex., 1971, Robb.

1

Y mira, Luisa, tan sólo hace falta
que decidas seguir o dejarme
que mañana yo voy a ausentarme,
pero quiero saber tu decisión.

2

Y anteayer tarde te hallé platicando
con un tipo vestido a la moda.
Ya arreglada tenías la boda,
yo no tengo ni tiempo que perder.

3

Mira, Luisa, decídete pronto,
Piensa pronto y después no te amargues
que mañana será ya muy tarde
para que no puedas después repentir.

1

Look, Luisa, the only thing that's left
Is for you to decide to follow or to leave me
For tomorrow I am going away,
But I want to know your decision.

2

The evening before last I found you talking
With a dude dressed in style.
You had the wedding already arranged,
Now I don't have any time to lose.

3

Look, Luisa, decide soon,
Think fast and later don't regret
For tomorrow will be too late
For later you cannot change your mind.

4

Y ayer tarde pasé por tu casa,
pregunté que si qué estabas haciendo,
y me dijeron que estabas escribiendo
una carta que me ibas a mandar.

4

Last evening I passed by your house,
I asked what you were doing,
And they told me you were writing
A letter which you were sending me.

Y MI-RA, LUI-SA, TAN SÓ-LO HA-CE FAL-TA QUE DE-
CI-DAS SE-GUIR O DE-JAR-ME QUE MA-ÑA-NA YO
VOY A AU-SEN-TAR-ME PE-RO QUIE-RO SA-
BER TU DE-CI-SIÓN.

C37. *La Mancornadora* (The Traitress)
R28, Mr. and Mrs. Aaron Durand, Cuba, N.Mex., 1944, Robb.

1

Ando ausente del bien que adoré,
apasionado por una mujer,
mientras yo vivo en el mundo y no muero
yo nunca en la vida la vuelvo a querer.

1

I went away from the sweetheart I loved,
Full of passion for a woman,
While I live in the world and do not die
Never in my life will I love her again.

2

Y si lo hiciste de mala intención
y con el fin de hacerme padecer,
tú bien lo sabes que vivo entre flores
y nuevos amores me pueden querer.

2

If you did it with bad intentions
And with the purpose of making me suffer,
You well know that I live among flowers
And other sweethearts can love me.

3

Si tú fueras legal con mi amor,
tú gozarías de mi protección;
pero en el mundo tú fuiste traidora:
la mancornadora de mi corazón.

3

If you were faithful to me,
You would enjoy my protection;
But in the world you were a betrayer:
The one who threw my heart to the ground.

4

La despedida yo no sé las doy,
la despedida será esta canción,
la despedida yo sé las daré
cuando yo me vaya de esta población.

4

I do not know how to say good-bye,
My farewell will be this song,
The farewell I know, I'll give
When I leave this town.

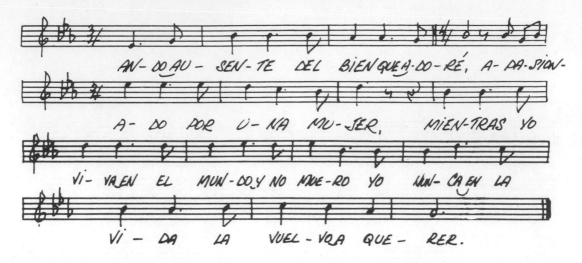

AN-DO AU-SEN-TE DEL BIEN QUE A-DO-RÉ, A-PA-SION-
A-DO POR U-NA MU-JER. MIEN-TRAS YO
VI-VA EN EL MUN-DO Y NO MUE-RO YO NUN-CA EN LA
VI-DA LA VUEL-VO A QUE-RER.

C38. *Me Voy Lejos* (I Go Far Away)
R40, Francisco Chávez, La Jara, N.Mex., 1944, Robb. Cf. RB505 (Texas); C35.

1	1
Me voy lejos, me voy con la esperanza	I go far away, I go with the hope
de volver a tu lado, mi vida.	Of returning to your side, my life.
Aunque llevo mi alma entristecida,	Even though my soul is sad,
yo juro el quererte, aunque lejos me voy.	I swear to love you, even though I go far away.
2	2
Me voy lejos, me voy con la esperanza	I go far away, I go with the hope
de volver a tu lado, mi vida,	Of returning to you side, my life,
no me dejes el alma partida,	Do not leave my soul broken,
yo juro el quererte, aunque lejos me voy.	I swear to love you, even though I go far away.
3	3
Tú, que has sido la que he querido tanto,	You, whom I have loved so much,
no me impongas tan duro castigo.	Do not impose so hard a punishment.
Ya no seas ingrata conmigo.	Be not ungrateful to me.
Acuérdate un poco de mi corazón.	Think a bit about my heart.
4	4
Tu retrato lo tengo aquí guardado.	Your picture I carefully keep here.
Cada vez que lo miro me acuerdo	Each time I see it, I remember
de tu amor, que al marcharme yo pierdo,	Your love, which on going away I lose,
tus dignas memorias que no olvidaré.	And your fine memories, which I will not forget.
5	5
Me voy lejos, para nunca recordar	I go far away, never to recall
ese amor que yo amé tan profundo,	That love which I loved so profoundly,
que era mi único aliento en el mundo,	Which was my only encouragement in the world,
y que yo adoraba con loca pasión.	And which I adored with insane passion.

ME VOY LE - JOS, ME VOY CON LA E -SPE- RAN- ZA

DE VOL- VER A TU LA - DO, MI VI - DA.

AUN-QUE LLE - VO MI AL-MA EN-TRIS - TE - CI -DA, YO

JU - RO EL QUE - RER-TE AUN-QUE LE - JOS ME VOY.

C39. *Cuatro Palomitas Blancas* (Four White Little Doves)
R10, Próspero S. Baca, age 70, Bernalillo, N.Mex., 1945, Robb. Cf. R545, R1752, RB785. See also Appendix A.

<table>
<tr><td>

1

Cuatro palomitas blancas
que vienen de Santa Fe
una a la otra se decía,
no hay amor como él de usted.

2

Cuatro palomitas blancas
que vienen de Cochití
una a la otra se decía,
no hay amor como él de aquí.

3

Cuatro palomitas blancas
que vienen de Ochipá
una a la otra se decía,
no hay amor como él de allá.

4

Cuatro palomitas blancas
que vienen de un romero
una a la otra se decía,
no hay amor como el primero.

Estribillo

Haciendo curru cucú, curru cucú,
me voy quedando.
Alma mía de mis amores,
¿dónde se andarán paseando?

</td><td>

1

Four white little doves
That come from Santa Fe
Said, one to the other,
There is no love like yours.

2

Four white little doves
That came from Cochití
Said, one to the other,
There is no love like the one here.

3

Four white little doves
That came from Ochipá
Said, one to the other,
There is no love like the one there.

4

Four white little doves
That came from a journey
Said, one to the other,
There is no love like the first.

Refrain

Singing curru cucu, curru cucu,
I shall stay here.
My soul of my loves,
Where are they going?

</td></tr>
</table>

CUA - TRO PA-LO-MI-TAS BLAN-CAS QUE VIE-NEN DE SAN-TA FE U - NA A LA OTRA SE DE - CÍ - A, NO HAY A-MOR CO-MO EL DE U-STED. HA - CIEN-DO CUR-RU CU- CÚ, CUR-RU CU-CÚ, ME VOY QUE-DAN-DO. AL-MA MÍA DE MIS A-MO-RES, ¿DÓN- DE SE AN-DA-RÁN PA-SEAN-DO?

Note the formal structure, the gently humorous mood, the narrow range of a perfect fifth, and the employment of the Mixolydian mode (the mode of G). This is not only a *canción* but also a perfect example of the *relación*. See Section D.

References to animals and birds are frequent in Hispanic folk music of the Southwest and Mexico. These animals and birds usually represent a veiled allusion to a beloved person or the personification of some human quality, be it a vice or a virtue. C39 to C45 are examples of such songs.

C40. *La Paloma y el Palomo* (The Lady Dove and the Man Dove)
R84, Adela Romero, San Antonio, Socorro County, N.Mex. (recorded in Albuquerque, N.Mex.), 1946, Robb.

1		1
La paloma y el palomo	] *Bis*	The lady dove and the man dove
se fueron a confesar.	] *Bis*	Went to confession.

2		2
La paloma se arrendó	] *Bis*	The lady dove held back
porque no sabía rezar.	] *Bis*	Because she didn't know how to pray.

Refrán		*Refrain*
¡Qué bonito fuera	]	How nice it would be
que mi amor me amanaciera!	]	If my love would wake me!
¡Ay, chinita, no más,	]	Oh, darling, no more,
no más, no más!	] *Bis*	No more, no more!

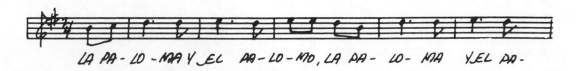

LA PA-LO-MA Y EL PA-LO-MO, LA PA- LO- MA Y EL PA-

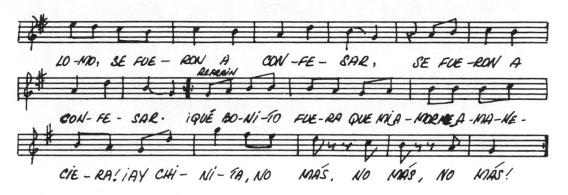

LO-MO, SE FUE-RON A CON-FE-SAR, SE FUE-RON A
CON-FE-SAR. ¡QUÉ BO-NI-TO FUE-RA QUE M'A-MOR ME A-MA-NE-
CIE-RA! ¡AY CHI-NI-TA, NO MÁS. NO MÁS, NO MÁS!

C41. *Palomita Callejera* (Little Dove of the Streets)
R1356, Peter Hurd, San Patricio, N.Mex. (recorded in Albuquerque, N.Mex.), 1955,
Robb. Cf. R168; also Folkways Album FA2204.

1 Palomita callejera que comes trigo en mi mano.	]] *Bis*

1
Palomita callejera
que comes trigo en mi mano.   ] *Bis*

1
Little dove of the streets
That eats grain in my hand.

2
Hoy no viniste a la cita,
por tu culpa estoy penando,
palomita callejera,
Sabes que te quiero tanto.

2
Today you didn't come to our date,
Because of you I am worried,
Little dove of the streets,
You know I love you so.

Coro 1
¡Ay! palomita,
muero por ti.   ] *Bis*

Chorus 1
Oh! Little dove,
I die for you.

3
Palomita arrulladora,
sabes que te quiero tanto.   ] *Bis*

3
My little cooing dove,
You know I love you so.

4
¿Para qué me haces sufrir
y me dejas esperando?
Palomita arrulladora,
sabes que te quiero tanto.

4
Why do you make me suffer
And leave me waiting?
My little cooing dove,
You know I love you so.

Coro 2
¡Ay! palomita,
muero por ti.
No me abandones,
no me abandones,
no seas así.

Chorus 2
Oh! Little dove,
I die for you.
Do not abandon me,
Do not abandon me,
Do not be so.

5
Si por otro me dejaste,
paloma, paloma ingrata.   ] *Bis*

5
If you left me for another,
Dove, ungrateful dove.

6

Es mejor que me lo digas
porque la duda me mata.
Si por otro me dejaste,
paloma, paloma ingrata.

Coro 2

7

(Verso 1 se repite)

6

It is better that you tell me
Because doubt kills me.
If you left me for another,
Dove, ungrateful dove.

Chorus 2

7

(Verse 1 repeated)

C42. *El Pavo Real* (The Peacock)
R343, Vidal Valdez, Albuquerque, N.Mex., 1946, Robb.

1

Ya se secó el arbolito
donde duerme el pavo real.
Ahora dormirá en el suelo,
y ahora dormirá en el suelo,
y ahora dormirá en el suelo
como cualquier animal.

1

Now the little tree
Where the peacock sleeps has dried up.
Now he will sleep on the ground,
Now he will sleep on the ground,
Now he will sleep on the ground
Like any animal.

2

Guadalajara en un llano,   ]
México en una laguna.   ] *Bis*
Aunque me espine la mano   ]
me he de comer esta tuna.   ] *Bis*

2

Guadalajara is in a plain,
Mexico is in a lake.
Even though I prick my hand
I must eat this prickly pear.

3

La águila, siendo animal,
trae su retrato en el dinero.] *Bis*
Para subir al nopal,
para subir al nopal,
para subir al nopal
pidió permiso primero.

3

The eagle, being an animal,
Has his portrait on money.
To ascend the prickly pear,
To ascend the prickly pear,
To ascend the prickly pear
He first asked permission.

4

(Verso 2 se repite)

4

(Verse 2 repeated)

5

Dicen que soy hombre malo,]
malo y mal averiguado,] *Bis*
porque me comí un durazno]
de corazón colorado.] *Bis*

5

They say that I'm a bad man,
Bad and proved to be bad,
Because I ate a peach
With a red heart.

6

Bonitas las tapatías]
cuando se van a bañar.] *Bis*
Lo primero que se lavan]
son los pies para bailar.] *Bis*

6

The girls of Guadalajara are lovely
When they go to bathe.
The first things they wash
Are their feet, in order to dance.

7

Ya se secó el arbolito]
donde duerme el pavo real.] *Bis*
Ahora dormirá en el suelo
como cualquier animal.
Ahora dormirá en el suelo
porque no hay otro lugar.

7

Now the little tree
Where the peacock sleeps has dried up.
Now he will sleep on the ground
Like any animal.
Now he will sleep on the ground
Because there's no other place.

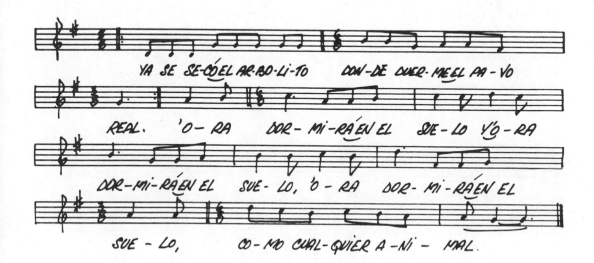

The *tapatías*, mentioned in verse 6, are the girls of Guadalajara, Mexico. *Pavo Real* has, in verse 5, two lines starting with "Dicen que soy hombre malo," almost identical with two lines from another song in my collection. The reason for this coincidence is obscure.

C43. *Pavo Real*
R178, Peter Hurd, San Patricio, N.Mex., 1949, Robb. Cf. Folkways Album FA2204, R1353.

1

Me parezco al pavo real	]
si encuentra una pava sola.	] Bis
La acaricia con el pico,	
la acaricia con la cola,	
y si se pone rejaga	
le digo que siga sola.	
¡Pavito Real, Pavito Real!	

1

I am like a peacock
If he meets a lady peacock.
He caresses her with his beak,
He caresses her with his tail,
And if she objects
I tell her to live alone.
O little peacock! O little peacock!

2

Muchas veces te dí pruebas	]
de lo mucho que te quiero.	] Bis
Anteanoche fuí a tu casa	
y me agarró un aguacero;	
tanto me mojé, mi vida,	
que por poquito me muero.	
¡Pavito Real, Pavito Real!	

2

Many times I've given proof
Of how much I love you.
The other night I went to your house
And I ran into a shower of rain;
The rain so wet me, my love,
That for a little bit I was extinguished.
O little peacock! O little peacock!

3

Para que cante el jilguero	]
se le da fruta morada.	] Bis
Y para que yo te cante	
tú me pones enojado	
como si fuera posible	
beber en agua salada.	
¡Pavito Real, Pavito Real!	

3

To make a linnet sing
You give it purple fruit.
And to make me sing to you
You must make me angry,
Mad enough to drink
A drink of salty brine.
O little peacock! O little peacock!

4

Yo le dije a un pavo real,	]
extiende tu cola, pavo.	] Bis
Para que mire mi amada,	
que ayer aposté un centavo	
y un besito de su boca,	
a que era cola y no rabo.	
¡Pavito Real, Pavito Real!	

4

I said to a peacock,
O peacock, spread your tail.
So that my love can see,
For yesterday I bet a penny
And a little kiss from her mouth,
That it was a tail and not a stub.
O little peacock! O little peacock!

RI - CIA CON EL PI - CO, LA A-CA - RI-CIA CON LA

CO - LA, Y SI SE PO - NE RE - JA-GA LE DI-

GO QUE SI - GA SO - LA. ¡PA-

VI - TO REAL, PA - VI - TO REAL!

C44. *Pajarillo Barranqueño* (Little Bird of the Valley)

R826, Peter Hurd, San Patricio, N.Mex., 1949, Robb. Cf. R252 (Garcilán Pacheco singing the same song).

1	**1**
¡Pajarillo, pajarillo!	Little bird, little bird!
¡Pajarillo barranqueño!	Little bird of the valley!
¡Qué bonitos ojos tienes!	What beautiful eyes you have!
¡Lástima que tengan dueño!	Too bad that they have an owner!
2	**2**
¿Qué pajarillo es aquél	What bird is that one
que canta en aquella lima?	Who sings in that lime tree?
Anda dile que no cante	Go and tell him not to sing
que el corazón me lástima.	Because my heart aches.
3	**3**
¿Qué pajarillo es aquél	What bird is that one
que canta en aquella higuera?	Who sings in that fig tree?
Anda dile que no cante,	Go and tell him not to sing,
que aguarde a que yo me muera.	To wait until I die.

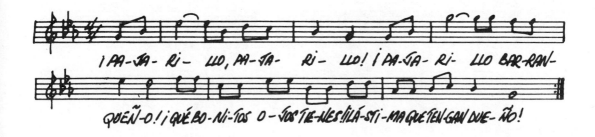

¡PA-JA-RI- LLO, PA-JA- RI - LLO! ¡PA-JA-RI- LLO BAR-RAN-

QUEÑ-O! ¡QUÉ BO-NI-TOS O - JOS TIE-NES! ¡LÁ-STI-MA QUE TEN-GAN DUE- ÑO!

C45. *La Calandria* (The Lark)

R1354, Peter Hurd, San Patricio, N.Mex., 1955, Robb. Cf. Folkways Album FA2204; also R1254, R1339, R2002; Lummis (pp. 186–88, 1893).

1

En una jaula de oro
pendiente de un balcón
se hallaba una calandria
cantando su dolor.
Hasta que un gorrioncillo
a su jaula llegó.
—Si usted puede sacarme
con usted yo me voy.—
Y el pobre gorrioncillo
que ya se enamoró
y el pobre como pudo
los alambres rompió.

1

Once in a golden cage
Hanging from a balcony
There lived a little lark
Singing of her sadness.
Until one day a sparrow
Came up to her cage.
"If you could set me free
I'd gladly go with you."
Right then the poor sparrow
Fell in love with her
And, working as best he could,
He tore the wires apart.

2

Y la ingrata calandria,
después que la sacó,
tan luego se vió libre,
voló, voló, y voló.
El pobre gorrioncillo
todavía la siguió
para ver si le cumplía
lo que le prometió.

2

And the ungrateful lark,
After he got her out,
As soon as she saw freedom,
She flew, she flew, and flew.
The poor little sparrow
Flew off to follow her
To see if she would keep
The promises she had made.

3

La malvada calandria
así le contestó,
—A usted no lo conozco
ni presa he sido yo.—

3

The wicked little lark
Answered him thus,
"I do not know you
Nor was I ever prisoner."

4

Y triste el gorrioncillo
luego se regresó.
Se paró en un manzano
lloró, lloró, lloró.
Y ahora en esa jaula
pendiente del balcón
se encuentra el gorrioncillo
cantando su pasión.

4

Sadly the little sparrow
Went back to where they were.
He perched in an apple tree
And wept, and wept, and wept.
And now in that cage
Hanging from the balcony
You'll find the little sparrow
Singing of his love.

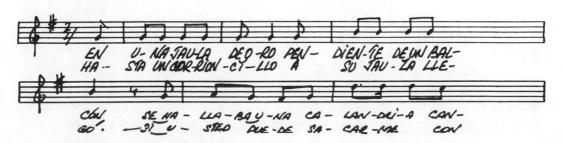

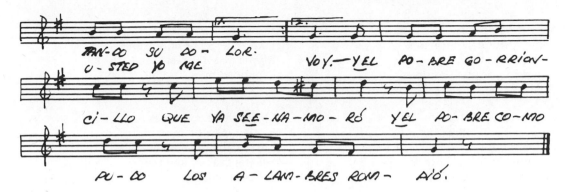

Here birds are used in an allegorical sense, the unhappy sparrow representing the singer and the lark his faithless sweetheart. (See note to C39 above.)

C46. *No Llores, Niña* (Don't Cry, Child)
R44, Antonio Medina, Chimayó, N.Mex., 1945, Robb.

1	1
No llores, niña linda,	Don't cry, beautiful child,
pálida flor que el viento mece,	Pale flower stirring in the wind,
¿no ves que se entristece	Can you not see that your
de pesar mi corazón?	Weeping saddens my heart?

2	2
Yo ví en un jardín una flor	I saw in a garden a flower
como de violeta	Like a violet
y después la ví	And as I watched I saw it
moverse pálida, inquieta.	Move, pale and restless.

3	3
Sus ojos entreabrío,	It opened its eyes a bit
las gotas de rocio	And the dewdrops
caían en abundancia;	Fell in abundance;
lágrimas corren de amor.	Streaming tears of love.

4	4
¡Ay, quiéreme, ay, quiéreme,	Oh, love me, oh, love me,
hermosa flor del campo!	Beautiful flower of the fields!
Ni pálida, ni tímida,	Neither pale, nor timid,
derrama vuestro llanto.	Shed your tears.

5	5
Por ti me vivo llorando,	I weep my life away for you,
sígueme lamentando,	Continue lamenting,
y herido por una pasión.	Wounded by passion.

6

Mi alma te encuentra constante,
como ángel de adoración;
mi pecho palpitante
y herido por una pasión.

6

My soul is unceasingly fixed on you
Like an angel of adoration;
My heart beats fast,
Wounded by passion.

7

Abre, pues, tus ojos
para que con ellos
calme mi dolor.
Mira que es muy triste
ver un llanto en una flor.

7

Open, then, your eyes
So that with them
I may calm my sorrow.
See how sad it is to see
A flower crying.

No llores, niña linda, pálida flor queel viento mece, ¿ no
ves que se entristece de pesar mi corazón? Yo vi en un jardín una flor como de violeta y después la vi mo-
verse pálida inquieta. Sus ojos entrea brío, las gotas de ro-
cío caían en abundancia; lágrimas corren de amor, ¡ ay,
quiéreme, ay, quiéreme, hermosa flor del campo! Ni pálida, ni
tímida, derrama vuestro llanto. Por ti me vivo llorando, sí-
gueme lamentando y herido por una pasión. Mi alma te encuentra constante, como ángel de adoración; mi pecho pal-pi-
tante y herido por una pasión. A bre, pues, tus

C47. *La Noche Lóbrega* (The Sad Night)
R543, Francisco S. Leyva, age 81, Leyva, N.Mex., 1951, Robb.

<table>
<tr><td>

1

O mal silencio de la noche lóbrega,
mi pensamiento vuela hacia ti;
tú lo miras tranquila en mi alma,
ni un suspiro, ni un suspiro,
ni un suspiro consagras para mí.

2

Mi pensamiento todo lleno de imposible
y un grande celo
que separa mi alma,
diciendo así:
no cese, hora de la calma.

3

Gozar no puedo,
gozar no puedo,
gozar no puedo de tu tranquilidad.

</td><td>

1

O evil silence of the sad night,
My thoughts fly toward you;
You calmly see it in my soul,
Not even a sigh, not even a sigh,
Not even a sigh do you consecrate to me.

2

My thoughts are filled with the impossible
And a great jealousy
That tears my soul apart,
Saying thus:
Do not end, calm hour.

3

I cannot enjoy,
I cannot enjoy,
I cannot enjoy your tranquility.

</td></tr>
</table>

255

CE-LO QUE SE — PA-RA MI AL-MA, DI-CIEN-DO A-
SÍ: NO CE-SE, HO-RA DE LA CAL — MA. GO-ZAR NO PUE-
DO, GO-ZAR NO PUE — DO, GO-ZAR NO PUE-
DO DE TU TRAN-QUI-LI — DAD.

C48. *El Muchacho Alegre* (The Happy Lad)

R20, Rosanna Gutiérrez and others, Cuba, N.Mex., 1944, Robb. Cf. Robb 13 (pp. 19, 66); R1451; Hansen 6b (no. 4, p. 301 [California]).

1 Yo soy el muchacho alegre que me divierto cantando, con mi botella de vino y mi baraja jugando.	**1** I am the happy lad Who finds contentment in singing, In playing cards, my *compadre*, And in the good wine I'm drinking.
2 Si quieren saber quien soy, vengan les daré la prueba; jugaremos un conquián con esta baraja nueva.	**2** If you would know more about me, Let's play a few hands of poker; I have a new deck of cards here And we can throw out the joker.
3 No tengo padre ni madre ni quen se duela de mí. Sólo la joven que yo amo se compadece de mí.	**3** I have no father or mother To make a fuss over me. Only the girl that I love Has any pity for me.
4 No tengo padre ni madre ni quien se duela de mí. Sólo la cama en que duermo se compadece de mí.	**4** I have no father or mother To make a fuss over me. Only the bed that I sleep in Has any pity for me.
5 Las madres que tengan hijas ténganse mucho cuidado. Yo soy el muchacho alegre y soy muy enamorado.	**5** Oh, let the mothers with daughters Watch over them with devotion, For I'm a happy young fellow Enthralled by love's sweet emotion.

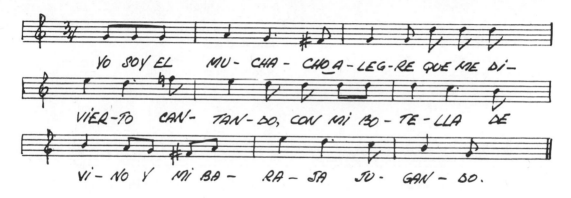

YO SOY EL MU-CHA-CHO A-LEG-RE QUE ME DI-VIER-TO CAN-TAN-DO, CON MI BO-TE-LLA DE VI-NO Y MI BA-RA-JA JU-GAN-DO.

C48a. *El Muchacho Alegre*
Hansen 6b (no. 4, p. 301), José García, age 42, Perris, Calif., 1959, Hansen.

YO SOY EL MU-CHA-CHO A-LE-GRE QUE ME A-MA-NEZ-CO CAN-TAN-DO, CON MI BO-TE-LLA DE VI-NO Y MI BA-RA-JA JU-GAN-DO.

From California, this is a slightly longer and somewhat varied version of C48.

C49. *El Durazno* (The Peach)
R65, Juan Sandoval, Chimayó, N.Mex., 1945, Robb. Cf. Mendoza 9d (p. 530).

1 Me iba a comer un durazno, porque lo ví colorado, pensando que estaba dulce y era que estaba dañado.	**1** I was going to eat a peach, Because I saw it was red, I thought it was sweet But it was wormy and bad.
Coro Dile que sí, dile que no, dile porque se baña; y eso de querer a tres no se me quita la maña.	*Chorus* Say yes! Say no! Say why you are bathing; This habit of loving three Is part of my nature.

2

Me he de comer un durazno
desde la raíz hasta el hueso,
que le hace que sea trigueña
será mi gusto y por eso.

Coro

2

I shall eat a peach
Seed and all,
No matter what her color,
In love I'm color blind.

Chorus

ME I-BAA CO-MER UN DU-RAZ-NO, POR-QUE LO VÍ CO-LO-RA-DO, PEN-SAN-DO QUE E-STA-BA DUL-CE Y E-RA QUE E-STA-BA DA-ÑA-DO. DI-LE QUE SÍ, DI-LE QUE NO, POR-QUE SE BA-ÑA; Y E-SO DE QUE-RER A TRES NO SE ME QUI-TA LA MA-ÑA.

The *durazno* (peach) seems to be associated with the idea of a pretty woman who is bad inside.

La voy a ver, le voy a hablar,
para un asunto particular.
La he de seguir,
la he de encontrar,
y hasta la muerte,
yo la he de amar.

Another informant, Edwin Berry, tells me that there is a third verse:

I will see her, I will speak to her,
For a very special reason.
I am to follow her,
I am to meet her,
And until death,
I am to love her.

C50. *Más Te Quisiera* (I Would Love You More)
R2090, Frank McCulloch, Jr., Albuquerque, N.Mex., 1965, Robb.

1

Yo vendo unos ojos negros.]
¿Quién me los quiere comprar?]
Los vendo por hechiceros,]
porque me han pagado mal.] *Bis*

1

I'm selling some black eyes.
Who wants to buy them from me?
I'm selling them because they're bewitched,
Because they've paid me poorly.

Canción

Coro	**Chorus**
Más te quisiera,	I would love you more,
más te amo yo,	I love you more,
y todas las noches las paso	And I spend every night
suspirando por tu amor.] *Bis*	Pining for your love.

2	**2**
Cada vez que siento las penas	Every time I feel the pains
me voy a la orilla del mar	I go to the edge of the sea
y pregúntales a las olas	And ask the waves
si han visto mi amor pasar.] *Bis*	If they've seen my love go by.

Coro	**Chorus**

3	**3**
Ojitos aceitunados,	Little olive eyes,
¿por qué me miráis así?	Why do you look at me that way?
¡tan alegres para otro,	So happy for somebody else,
y tan tristes para mí!	And so sad when looking at me.

The singer Frank McCulloch, like Peter Hurd, is an Anglo. Like me, he has been captivated by the Hispanic folk music of the Southwest, and he sings the songs with great gusto.

C51. *Juarecita* (Little Girl of Juárez)
R1972, Vicente Saucedo, Albuquerque, N.Mex., 1964, Robb. Cf. R234.

1

Juarecita de me tierra
en el pueblo de la sierra,
viviendo tan triste estás,
olvida ya tus quereres.
Alcabo ¿para qué los queres?
Han de volver jamás.

1

Juarecita of my country
In the city of the mountain,
You are living in such sadness,
Forget your lovers.
Why not finish with those loves?
They'll never return again.

2

Me da besos de amontones,
algunos dos mordilones
que a veces me hacen llorar.
Ella de a veces llora
y al llorar se descolora
pero se vuelve a pintar.

2

She gives me passionate kisses,
Sometimes biting me
Until I cry.
Sometimes she cries
And when crying turns pale
But then makes up her face again.

3

Me da besos de amontones,
ardorosos mordilones,
y a veces por el calor
tiene las cejas pintadas,
y su pelo colorado,
y sus uñas de color.

3

She gives me passionate kisses,
And bites me fiercely,
And at times to heat things up
She has her eyebrows made up,
Her hair dyed,
And her fingernails painted.

4

(Verso 1 se repite)

4

(Verse 1 repeated)

C52. *Soy un Triste Venadito* (I Am a Sad Little Deer)

Hansen 6b (no. 4, p. 307), José García, age 42, Perris, Calif., 1959, Hansen. Cf. R432, R923, R1918.

1

Soy un triste venadito
que habito en la serranía,
como no soy tan mansito
no bajo al agua de día,
de noche, poco a poquito,
y a tus brazos, vida mía.

1

I'm like a deer, sad but sleek,
Who lives in the mountains near,
Since I'm not so very meek
To come down by day I fear,
But at night I try to seek
Tender arms like yours, my dear.

2

Caballo que es tan visible
nunca come pasto vano,
me admiro, que siendo liebre
no sepas correr en llano.
No hay canilla que se quiebre
apretando bien la mano.

2

A horse that's seen everywhere
Never eats in pasture vain,
I'm surprised that being a hare
You can't run on open plain.
No armbone is broken where
You have clenched your fist again.

3

Quisiera ser perla fina
de tus lúcidos aretes,
para besarte esa boquita
y morderte los cachetes.
¿Quién te manda ser bonita?
que hasta a mí me comprometes.

3

A pearl fine I'd like to be
Of one of your earrings bright,
Then I'd give a kiss to thee
And those little cheeks I'd bite.
Who makes you pretty to see?
For you even bind me tight.

4

Ya tengo listo el nopal
donde he de arrancar la tuna.
Como soy hombre formal
no me gusta tener una;
me gusta tener de a dos
para si se me enoja alguna.

4

The place is ready and new
where I'll be idle and glad.
And I'm a formal man who
with but one would be quite sad;
I want to have at least two
Just in case one may get mad.

5

Yo soy como el gavilán
que en el aire ando volando,
la polla que no me llevo
la dejo cacareando,
la polla que no me llevo
la dejo cacareando.

5

I am like the sparrow hawk
Who flies in the sky all day,
The chick I leave in the flock
Really chatters, so they say,
The chick I leave in the flock
really chatters, so they say.

6

Voy a hacer una barata
y una gran realización:
las viejitas a centavo,
las muchachas a tostón,
los yernos a dos centavos,
y las suegras de pilón.

6

I'm going to offer a sale
And this is what there will be:
One cent for old ladies pale,
Young girls for a four-bit fee,
Sons-in-law, two cents, all hail,
And mothers-in-law for free.

7

Ya con ésta me despido,
pero pronto doy la vuelta.
No más que nos libre Dios
de una niña mosca muerta,
de esas que iay, mamá, por Dios!
pero salen a la puerta.

7

Now with this I bid adieu,
But I'll soon be back again.
May the good Lord spare us too
From all girls who meekness feign,
Who say they'll have naught to do
But who at the door remain.

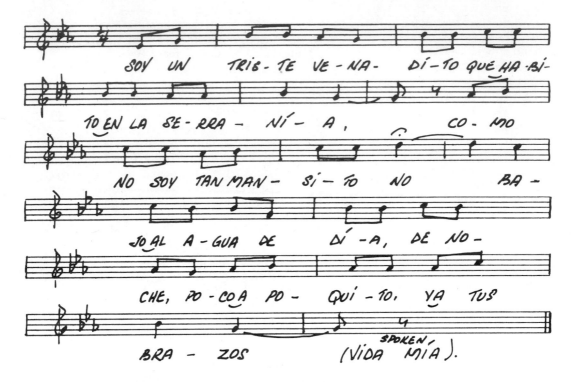

Because it was impossible, in making the transcription of this and other melodies from Hansen's otherwise excellent collection, to synchronize the syllables with the notes, I felt obliged to space the syllables under the notes where they must belong in accordance with the practice of elision. In some cases there are more notes than syllables. For an intelligible version they must be combined by ties or slurs with other notes. I have taken the liberty of doing this since I did not have access to the recordings.

C53. *Los Barandales del Puente* (The Railings of the Bridge)
  R170, Peter Hurd, San Patricio, N.Mex., 1949, Robb. Cf. R1360, Folkways Album FA2204.

1

Los barandales del puente
se estremecen cuando paso,
chinita mía, dame un abrazo.

1

The railings of the bridge
Shake when I pass,
Embrace me, my darling.

2

Dame tu mano, morena,
para subir al tranvía
que está cayendo la nieve fría.

2

Give me your hand, my dark one,
To climb on the tramway
For the cold snow is falling.

3

Si está cayendo, que caiga,
y asómate a tu ventana,
morena mía de mi alma.

3

If it is falling, let it fall,
And come to your window,
Dark one of my heart.

4

Si está cayendo, que caiga,
y asómate a tu balcón.
Dame un besito de corazón.

4

If it is falling, let it fall,
And come to your balcony.
Give me a kiss from your heart.

5

De todas a ti te quiero,
de las demás no hago caso,
chinita mía, dame un abrazo.

5

Of all, I love you,
Of the rest I take no notice,
Embrace me, my darling.

6

De todas a ti te quiero,
de las demás a ninguna,
chinita mía, luz de la luna.

6

Of all, I love you,
Of all the rest no one,
My darling, light of the moon.

7

Por debajo de aquel puente
corre el agua y nacen flores,
chinita mía de mis amores.

7

Underneath that bridge
The water runs and flowers are born,
My darling, my love.

8

Las blancas son muy bonitas
y las morenas hermosas;
guardan sus amores entre sus flores.

8

The fair ones are very pretty
And the dark ones beautiful;
They keep their love among their flowers.

9

De todas a ti te quiero,
y por eso yo lo repito,
morena mía, dame un abrazo.

9

Of all, I love you,
And that is why I repeat it,
Embrace me, my dark one.

10

Y estos son los barandales
conmigo no más tres piedras
y más arriba otros pedernales.

10

And these are the railings
With me only three stones
And higher up other flint rocks.

11

Dame la mano, morena,
para subir a tu nido,
no duermas sola, duerme conmigo.

11

Give me your hand, my dark one,
To climb to your nest,
Do not sleep alone, sleep with me.

12

Yo con ésta me despido
entre perfume de azahares,
aquí se acaban los barandales.

12

Now with this I take my leave
Among perfume of orange blossoms,
Here end the railings.

13

¡Ay, mamacita!
Ya con ésta me despido
entre perfume y azahares,
aquí se acaban los barandales,
aquí se acaban los barandales.

14

Y por ésta me despido
entre perfume y las flores,
aquí se acaban los barandales.

13

Ah, dear mother!
Now with this I take my leave
Among perfume and orange blossoms,
Here end the railings,
Here end the railings.

14

And with this I take my leave
Among perfume and flowers,
Here end the railings.

LOS BA-RAN-DA-LES DEL PUEN-TE SE ES-TRE-ME-CEN CUAN-DO PA-SO, CHI-NI-TA MÍ-A, DA-ME UNA-BRA-ZO.

The recording ends with verse 12, but Peter
wrote out the two remaining verses for me.

C54. *El Palo Verde* (The Green Stalk)
   R173, Peter Hurd, San Patricio, N.Mex., 1949, Robb. Cf. R1358 (another version of
the same song by the same singer).

1

Señora, su palo verde
se le estaba secando,
y anoche se lo r-r-r-regué
y ahora se le amaneció floreando.
La, la, la, la, *etc.*

1

Lady, your green stalk
Was drying up,
Last night I watered it
And now it awoke blooming.
La, la, la, la, *etc.*

2

Una guacamaya pinta
esperaba que amaneciera
para dar un agarrón
a un pájaro cualquiera.
La, la, la, la, *etc.*, —a—huy!

2

A spotted macaw
Was waiting for morning
To catch
Any bird whatsoever.
La, la, la, la, *etc.*, —a—huy!

3

Ya se cayeron las peras
del árbol que las tenía,
y así te caiste tú
en mis brazos, vida mía—a—huy!　] *Bis*
La, la, la, la, *etc.*

3

The pears have fallen
From the tree which had them,
And thus you fell
Into my arms, my life—a—huy!　] *Bis*
La, la, la, la, *etc.*

4

Una guacamaya pinta
le dijo a una colorada,
—A las bonitas un beso,　]
y a las feas una patada.　] *Bis*
La, la, la, la, *etc.*

4

A spotted macaw
Said to a red one,
"Give the pretty ones a kiss,
And the ugly ones a kick."
La, la, la, la, *etc.*

C55.　*El Quelite*

R415, Manuel Chávez, Albuquerque, N.Mex., 1950, Robb. Cf. RB233 (Lummis, Calif., 1904).

1

¡Qué bonito es El Quelite!
bien haya quien lo formó,
que por sus orillas tiene
de quien acordarme yo.

1

How pretty El Quelite is!
Bless its creator,
For along its borders
There's someone I'll always remember.

2

Debajo de un arbolito
me dió sueño y me dormí
y me desperté un gallito
cantando "quiquiriquí."

2

Beneath a tiny tree
I got drowsy and fell asleep
And a little rooster awoke me
Crowing "cocka-doodle-doo."

3

Mañana me voy, mañana,
mañana me voy de aquí,
el consuelo que me queda
que se han de acordar de mí.

3

Tomorrow I'm going, tomorrow,
Tomorrow I'm going from here,
The only thought that comforts me is
That they'll remember me.

4

(Verso 1 se repite)

4

(Verse 1 repeated)

¡QUÉ BO - NI - TO ES EL QUE - LI - TE! —
BIEN HAI- GA QUIEN LO FOR - MÓ,
QUE POR SUS O - RI - LLAS TIE - NE
DE QUIEN A - COR - DAR - ME YO.

"El Quelite" in this song may refer to the
village of this name near Mazatlán, Mexico.

C55a. *El Quelite*
Hansen 6b (no. 4, p. 303), Pancho Gonzales, age 30, Los Angeles, Calif., 1959, Hansen.

1

¡Qué bonito es el quelite!
Bien haya quien lo sembró,
que por sus orillas tiene
de quien acordarme yo.

1

How beautiful is the garden!
To him who planted it, thanks,
Because I'll always remember
The girl I found on its banks.

2

Camino de San Ignacio,
me dió sueño y me dormí,
y me despertó un gallito
cantando ki-ri-ki-ki.

2

On the way to San Ignacio,
I was tired, asleep I fell,
A young cock awakened me
Singing cocka-doodle-doo so well.

3

Yo no canto porque sé,
ni porque mi voz sea buena;
canto porque tengo gusto
en mi tierra y en la ajena.

3

I don't sing because I can,
Nor because my voice is good;
I sing because I'm so happy
Here, abroad, and know I should.

4
Mañana me voy, mañana,
mañana me voy de aquí,
y el consuelo que me queda,
que te has de acordar de mí.

4
Tomorrow, I'll go, tomorrow,
Tomorrow I'll go from here,
And it will give joy to me
If you keep my memory near.

C56. *¿Paloma, de Dónde Vienes?* (Dove, Where Do You Come From?)
R21, Rosanna Gutiérrez and others, La Jara, N.Mex., 1944, Robb.

1
¿Paloma, de dónde vienes?
Vengo de San Juan del Río.
Cúbreme con tus alas
que ya me muero de frío.

1
Dove, where do you come from?
I come from San Juan del Río.
Cover me with your wings
For I am dying of cold.

2
Conchas se me hacen las manos
y caracoles los dedos
por esa prieta orgullosa
que me anda cobrando celos.

2
My hands become like seashells
And my fingers look like snails
Because of that proud dark woman
Who makes jealous demands on me.

3
Si fuera papel, volara,
si fuera tinta, corriera.
Quisiera ser estampilla,
y en ese sobre me fuera.

3
If I were paper, I would fly,
If I were ink, I would run.
I'd like to be a postage stamp,
And on that envelope I'd go.

4
De la pila nace el agua,
del agua los pez.
Dime ¿qué te ha sucedido?
que no aguantamos tus gritos.

4
From the fountain, water is born,
From water, the fish.
Tell me, what has happened to you?
For we can't stand your shouts.

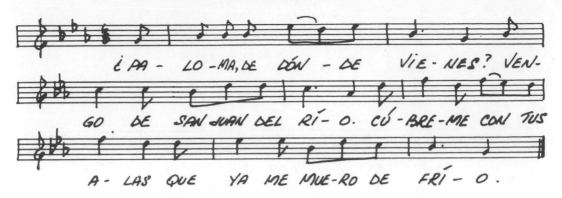

¿*Paloma, de Dónde Vienes*? could also be
classified as a *disparate*.

C57. *Por Allí Viene Ya* (There She Comes)
R2395, Juan Griego, age 61, Albuquerque, N.Mex., 1971, Robb.

Por allí viene ya
la joven a quien yo adoro
y en la mano trae
una bella copa de oro
y en la copa trae
el veneno de mi amor.
Y viene a dar la muerte
a este pobre corazón.

There she comes,
The young girl I love
And in hand she carries
A beautiful goblet of gold
And in the goblet she brings
The poison of my love.
And she comes to give death
To this poor heart.

C58. *Eva*
R2398, Juan Griego, age 61, Albuquerque, N.Mex., 1971, Cipriano Griego.

1

Mi Eva, tú tienes el nombre
de cuando el mundo empezó.
Y quisiera llamarme Adán,
y que nos juntara Dios.

1

My Eve, you have a name
From when the world began.
I wish my name was Adam,
And that God would unite us.

2

Y tú tienes una hermosura
que todos los hombres suspiran
al verte pasar.
Yo, como soy tan callado,
todo se me va en pensar.

2

You have such beauty
That all the men sigh
When they see you go by.
But since I am so shy,
All I do is think.

3

Hace cinco años, mi vida,
y se llegaron los diez.
Yo, con la flor en la mano,
soñando me quedaré.

3

Five years have passed, my love,
And ten years will soon pass.
I, with a flower in my hand,
Will keep on dreaming.

C59. *Waltz for the New Year*
R486, Jacobo Maestas and V. Frescas, Llano de San Juan, N.Mex., 1951, Robb.

1

Hoy es día de año nuevo,
nadie lo puede negar.
Venemos a dar los días
A todos en general.

1

This is New Year's Day,
No one can deny it.
We come to bring the day's greetings
To all in general.

2

A la entrada de esta casa
el pie derecho pondré.
Si me permiten la venia
también para adentro entraré.

2

At the entrance of this house
I present myself.
I trust that I may be
Permitted to enter.

3

Hoy es día de año nuevo,
es el día de los Manueles,
porque el Señor se llamaba
Manuelito de los reyes.

3

This is New Year's Day,
It is the day of the Manuels,
For the Lord was called
Manuel of the kings.

270

C60. *Día de los Manueles* (Day of the Manuels)
R1924, Rubén Cobos, Albuquerque, N.Mex., 1963, Robb.

Desde mi casa he venido
con la nieve a la rodilla
a darle los buenos días
a esta rosa de Castilla.

From my house I've come,
Walking in the knee-high snow,
To bid good day
To this rose of Castile.

C61. *Las Mañanitas* (The Little Mornings)
R1397, Juan Griegos, age 46, Albuquerque, N.Mex., 1956, Robb.

1

En el marco de esta puerta
el pie derecho pondré,
y a los señores caseros
los buenos días les daré.

1

On the threshold of this door
I will place my right foot,
And to the hosts
I bid them good morning.

Coro
Despierta, mi amor, despierta.
Mira que ya amaneció.
Ya los pajarillos cantan,
la luna ya se metió.

Chorus
Awake, my love, awake.
Look, it's dawning.
The birds are now singing,
The moon has disappeared.

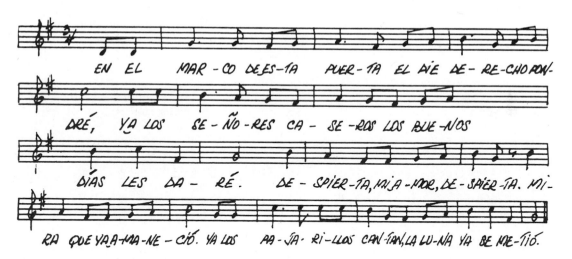

C62. *Venid, Joven Bella* (Come, Pretty Girl)
R1720, Próspero S. Baca, age 70, Bernalillo, N.Mex., 1945, Robb.

1

Venid, joven bella,
venid al balcón,
oír mis canciones —
do, re, mi, fa, si, la, sol.

1

Come, pretty girl,
Come to the balcony,
To hear my songs —
do, re, mi, fa, si, la, sol.

2
Adorada prenda mía,
denotada por su hermosura—
re: do, re, mi, fa, si, la, sol.

2
My adorable sweetheart,
Outstanding for your beauty—
re: do, re, mi, fa, si, la, sol.

3
Venid, joven bella,
venid a escuchar,
oír mis canciones
de la escala musical.

3
Come, pretty girl,
Come to listen,
To hear my songs
Of the musical scale.

This is one of a number of songs that incorporate references to the solfège syllables describing the musical scale—do, re, mi, fa, sol, la. Compare the *romance Mambrú*, A1c (Campa 2, p. 86).

C63.   *Tinaja de Agua* (Water Jar)
       R2394, Juan Griego, age 61, Albuquerque, N.Mex., 1971, Cipriano Griego.

1
Al otro lado del río
te chiflaba sin consuelo,
tú acostadita en tu cama
y yo rendido de sueño.

1
On the other side of the river
I whistled to you inconsolably,
You lying comfortably in your bed
And I worn out without sleep.

2
Dime si no has de salir
para no estarte aguardando,
si no soy tinaja de agua,
para estarme serenado.

2
Tell me if you are not coming out
So that I may not be waiting for you,
For I am not a water jar
To serenade myself.

3
Te ladeates tu rebozo
para no volverme a hablar,
pero a mí ni fuerza me hace
ya yo tengo a quien amar.

3
You have turned your shawl
So as not to speak to me,
But this does not bother me
For now I have someone else to love.

4
Dices que ya no me quieres
y que ya tienes nuevo dueño,
pero a mí ni falta me haces
que ya tengo otra vieja.

4
You say that now you don't love me
And that you have a new man,
But I won't ever miss you
For now I have another old woman.

AL O- TRO LA- DO DEL   RÍ -O TE CHI— FLA-BA SIN

con - SUE - LO, TÚ A - COS - TA - DI - TA EN TU CA - MA

Y YO REN - DI - DO DE SUE - ÑO.

C64. *Los Chamacos* (The Kids)
R430, Félix Ortega, Chimayó, N.Mex., 1951, Robb. Cf. R72.

1	1
En mi infancia fuí dichoso y muy feliz.	In infancy I was fortunate and very happy.
Y ay, de mi madre al fin yo era su ilusión.	And oh, I was my mother's illusion.
Recuerdo que me dió su santa bendición	I remember her giving me her holy blessing
el día fatal en que murió.	On the fatal day on which she died.
2	2
Madre querida, madre del alma,	Mother dear, mother of my soul,
tu hijo se encuentra hoy en horrible orfandad,	Your son today met the horrible fate of an orphan,
recuerdo siempre la dulce calma,	I always recall the sweet calm,
y las caricias con que junto a ti en la niñez gocé.	And the caresses I enjoyed as a child by your side.
3	3
Son los chamacos el placer,	Kids are the pleasure,
la inmensa dicha del hogar,	The immense good fortune of a home,
¡cómo se goza al ver	How enjoyable it is to see
cuando comienzan a jugar!	When they begin to play!
4	4
Con su inocencia sin igual,	With their unequaled innocence,
forman un grupo seductor;	They form an enchanting group;
edad feliz, edad de amor,	Happy age, age of love,
pronto nos deja para nunca más volver.	Quickly it leaves us never to return.
5	5
Y después allá en la vida	And later in life we enter
un mar de dudas y de engaños,	A sea of doubt and deceit,
y ¡ay! sin sentir pasan los años	And Oh! the years pass by without feeling
y con tristeza recordamos nuestra niñez.	And with sadness we remember our childhood.
6	6
(Verso 3 se repite)	(Verse 3 repeated)
7	7
(Verso 4 se repite)	(Verse 4 repeated)

EN MI IN-FAN-CIA FUÍ DI-CHO-SO Y MUY FE-LIZ.

Y AУ, DE MI MA-DRE AL FIN YO E-RA SU I-LU-SIÓN.

RE-CUER-DO QUE ME DIÓ SU SAN-TA BEN-DI-CIÓN

EL DÍA FA-TAL EN QUE MU-RIÓ.

MA-DRE QUE-RI-DA, MA-DRE DEL AL-MA, TU HI-

JO SE EN-CUEN-TRA HOY EN HO-RRI-BLE OR-FAN-DAD,

RE-CUER-DO SIEM-PRE LA DUL-CE CAL-MA,

Y LAS CA-RI-CIAS CON QUE JUN-TO A -TIEN LA NI-ÑEZ GO-CÉ.

C65. *Allá en Arizona* (There in Arizona)
R256, Encarnación Trujillo, Chimayó, N.Mex., 1950, Robb.

1	1
Allá en Arizona	Out in Arizona
y allá en sus cabañas	In its cabins
mis tiempos pasé,	I spent my time
y entre montañas.]] *Bis*	In the mountains.

2	2
Y este país si es rico	And since this land is rich
no me han de negar;	No one can deny me;
se ve por los suelos	All over the ground
y el oro brillar.	The gold shines.

3	3
Y en cualquier peñasco	On every cliff
me siento a llorar,	I sit and cry,
creyendo que allí encuentro	Believing that there I'll find
mi felicidad.	My happiness.

274

4

Pobres de mis padres,
¡cómo no estarán!
de verme yo ausente
y de mí no sabrán.

4

Oh! My poor parents,
How troubled they must be!
Feeling my absence,
And not knowing what has become of me.

5

Quisiera de un vuelo
cruzar esa sierra
y llegar a mi tierra
de mi país natal.

5

I would like to fly
Over that mountain,
And land on the soil
Of my native country.

Although a recording exists of this song, I have not included the music because the singer, an old man, sings in such a quivering voice that the pitches are indistinguishable.

The scheme of syllabification is basically that of the *seguidilla* (7, 5, 7, 5), though irregular after the first verse.

C66. *Adiós, Muchachos* (Good-bye, Boys)
R276, Bruce Griffith, Greentree, N.Mex., 1950, Robb.

1

Adiós, muchachos,
compañeros de mi vida.
Barra querida
de aquellos tiempos.

1

Good-bye, boys,
Companions of my life.
Beloved bar
Of those good old days.

2

Me toca a mí ahora
emprender la retirada.
Debo alejarme
de mi buena muchachada.

2

The time has come
When I must go away.
I must separate
From my good comrades.

3

Adiós, muchachos,
ya me voy y me resigno
contra el destino
nadie delata.

3

Good-bye, boys,
I'm leaving and
Against destiny
There is no delay.

4

Se terminaron
para mí todas las penas.
Mi cuerpo enfermo
no les dice más.

4

For me all those hardships
Are over.
My sickly body
Can say no more.

5

Acuden en mi mente
recuerdos de otros tiempos,
de los bellos momentos
que ante años disfruté.

5

There come to my mind
Memories of other times,
Of the beautiful moments
Which former years provided.

6

Cerquita de mi madre,
santa viejita,
y de mi noviecita
que tanto idolatré.

6

Near my mother,
Saintly old lady,
And my girlfriend
Whom I so greatly idolized.

7

Se acuerdan tierra hermosa,
más bella que una diosa,
que ebrio yo de amor, le dí
mi corazón.

7

They recall the beautiful land,
More beautiful than a goddess,
To which burning with love,
I gave my heart.

8

Mas el Señor, celoso de sus encantos,
hundiéndome de llanto,
me la llevó,
me la llevó.

8

But the Lord, jealous of her enchantments,
Drowning me with tears,
Took her from me,
Took her from me.

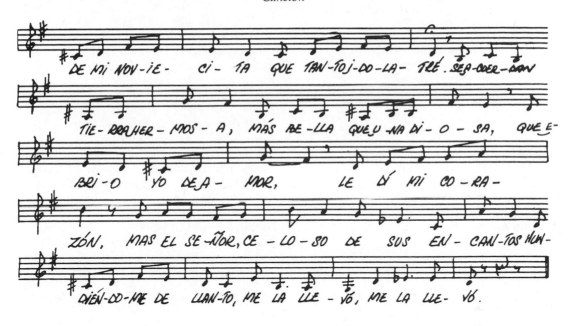

C67. *En el Mundo No Hay Tesoro* (In the World There's No Treasure)
R58, Jacinto Ortiz, Chimayó, N.Mex., 1945, Robb.

Planta
En el mundo no hay tesoro
más rico que el tener madre;
que si ¡ay! si viera mi padre
estas lágrimas que lloro.

1
Es el mayor amor,
que una madre con su hijo,
pues no hay contento más fijo
que el gozar de su calor.
Ni es desventura, ni es favor,
es verdad lo que le imploro;
luego con razón la lloro,
pues me ha llegado a faltar,
con esto puedo probar
que en el mundo no hay tesoro.

2
En verdad, pues, considero,
que entre tanto padecer,
que aunque uno tenga mujer,
no es amor tan verdadero.
Este resulta primero,
es mucho amor el de padre;

Planta
In the world there's no treasure
Richer than having a mother;
Ah! if only my father
Could see these tears that I weep.

1
It is the greatest love,
That of a mother for her son,
And there's no contentment more secure
Than to enjoy its warmth.
It is neither good fortune nor bad,
It is the truth which I employ;
And now I weep with good reason,
For I have lost her,
And so indeed I can prove that
In the world there's no treasure.

2
Truly, then, I consider
That amid so much sorrow
Even the love of a wife
Is not so true a love.
First I will say
That the father's love is great;

aunque mi pecho se alargue
y se rompa al padecer
(no hay en el mundo otro ser)
en el mundo no hay tesoro
más rico que el tener madre.

My bosom swells
And breaks with suffering
(There is no other being on earth)
In the world there's no treasure
Richer than having a mother.

3

¡Qué no sentirán mis ojos!
las desdichas en corriente,
que no hay tíos, no hay parientes
que me cumplan mis antojos;
antes me ven con enojos
por la falta de mis padres,
no hay uno solo que calle;
la grandeza en balde espera,
eso sí que es cosa seria.
¡O, si vivieran mis padres!

3

What things must not my eyes feel!
Misfortunes, one after another,
For there are no uncles nor kinfolk
To indulge my whims;
Instead they look at me with disgust
Because I have no parents,
Not a single one keeps quiet;
Greatness waits in vain,
That is really a serious thing.
Oh, if only my parents were alive!

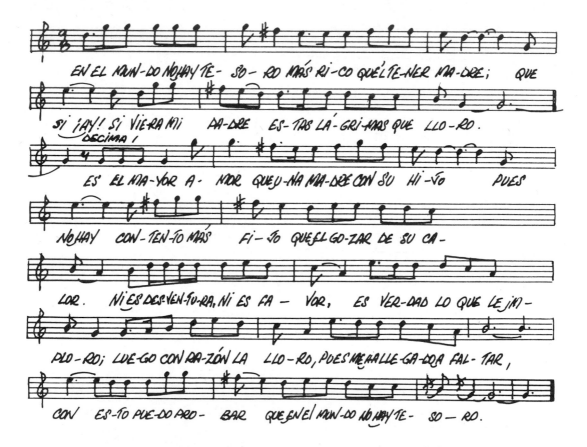

This *canción*, also known as *La Madre*, is a true *canción* in its subject matter, a true *décima* in its literary and musical form. The recording was made in 1945 when the singer and his wife (both now deceased) were el- derly people and the spiritual mentors of their family. I can only describe them as superior persons. In fact, Jacinto Ortiz on his death was honored by being buried in the corner of the churchyard of the famous

Jacinto Ortiz, singer of *En el Mundo No Hay Tesoro* (C67), and his wife, in Chimayó, New Mexico, 1945.

Grave of Jacinto Ortiz in the churchyard of the Sanctuary, Chimayó, New Mexico.

Sanctuary in his native village of Chimayó. This is true also of his wife. One of their grandsons, Orlando Ortiz, has had a distinguished career as superintendent of schools in Taos, New Mexico.

The original recording of this *canción* was lost, but fortunately both the Spanish text and the melody were transcribed by Vicente T. Mendoza, and it is these that are reproduced above.

C68. *La Golondrina* (The Swallow)
R949, E. Gonzáles, Jacobo Maestas, age 69, Llano de San Juan, N.Mex., 1952, Robb. Cf. Mendoza 9g (p. 618); R540, R541, R1713, R1998; RB225 (Lummis, Calif., 1904).

1

¿A dónde irá veloz y fatigada
la golondrina que de aquí se va?
O, si en el aire gemirá estraviada,

buscando abrigo y no lo encontrará,
junto a mi lecho le pondré su nido
en donde pueda la estación pasar:
también yo estoy en la región perdida,
¡o, cielo santo! sin poder volar a ti.

1

Where will the swallow fly swift and weary
When she leaves here?
Oh, if in the air she weeps for having lost
    her way,
Searching for shelter and finding none,
Next to my bed I'll place her nest
Where she may spend the season:
I too, am lost in this region,
Oh, heavens! and am unable to fly to you.

2

Dejé también mi patria idolatrada,
esa mansión que me miró nacer;
mi vida es hoy errante y angustiada,
y ya no puedo a mi mansión volver.

2

I, too, left my beloved land,
And the house that witnessed my birth;
Today I roam, living in misery,
And now I cannot return to my home.

¡Ay! ven, querida, amable peregrina,	Oh, come, darling, lovable pilgrim,
mi corazón al tuyo estrecharé,	I shall join my heart with yours,
oiré tu canto, tierna golondrina,	I shall hear your song, sweet swallow,
Recordaré mi patria, y lloraré.	I shall remember my land, and weep.

¿A-DÓN-DE I-RÁ VE-LOZ Y FA-TI-GA-DA LA GO-LON-DRI-NA QUE DE AQUÍ SE VA? O, SI EN EL AI-RE GE-MI-RÁ ES-TRA-VIA-DA, BU-SCAN-DO A-BRI-GO Y NO LO EN-CON-TRA-RÁ, JUN-TO A MI LE-CHO LE PON-DRÉ SU NI-DO EN DON-DE PUE-DA LA E-STA-CIÓN PA-SAR: TAM-BIÉN YO E-STOY DE LA RE-GIÓN PER-DI-DA IO CIE-LO SAN-TO! SIN PO-DER VO-LAR JUN-TO A TI. -LAR.

C69. *Adiós a Guaymas* (Farewell to Guaymas)
R539, Francisco S. Leyva, Leyva, N.Mex., 1951, Robb.

1	1
Adiós, adiós,	Good-bye, good-bye,
yo salgo en la vida.	I set forth in this life.
Nunca más de verte volveré.	Nevermore shall I return to see you.
En ir tú al cielo	On going to heaven
mi pasión olvidas,	You will forget my passion,
yo por tu ausencia,	But I, for your absence,
siempre lloraré.	Will always weep.

2	2
Pero si me amas, esa dicha	But if you love me,
que no se olvide	May that happiness not be forgotten
y en el inmenso	And in the world beyond
al saber de nuestra historia.	Remember our story.
Nos diremos adiós	We will say good-bye
en esta vida,	In this life,
nos citaremos para vernos	We will arrange to see one another
en la gloria.	In heaven.

A - DIÓS, A - DIÓS, DIOS SA-BE SIEN LA VI - DA. NUN CA MÁS A

VER-TE VOL-VE - RÉ. EN IR TÚ AL CIE - LO

MI PA - SIÓN OL - VI - DAS, YO POR TU AU-

SEN - CIA, SIEM-PRE LLO - RA-

RÉ. A - DIÓS, A - RÉ. PE-RO SI ME A-MAS,

E - SA DI-CHA QUE NO SE OL-VI - DE Y EN EL IN-

MEN-SO AL SA-BER DE NUES-TRA HI-STO-RIA. NOS DI-

RE - MOS A - DIÓS EN ES -TA VI - DA. NOS CI -TA-

RE - MOS PA-RA VER-NOS EN LA GLO-RI-A. GLO - RIA.

Each verse is repeated. The melody is, like *Susanita* (M1), a curious example of a borrowed melody altered to suit the style of the Mexican *canción*. In this case the borrowed melody is *Home, Sweet Home*. In both cases the meter is transformed from a regular duple to an irregular and somewhat more languid compound triple meter. The opening, however, bears a strange resemblance to that of the preceding *canción*, *La Golondrina*.

C70. *Las Chaparreras* (The Chaps)
R1352, Peter Hurd, Albuquerque, N.Mex., 1955, Robb. Cf. Folkways Album FA2204.

1		1
Cuando vine a la ciudad	]	When I came to the city
me compré mis chaparreras	]	I bought myself some chaps
y regresé por el rancho	]	And then I returned to the ranch
para enamorar rancheras.	] *Bis*	To make love to the ranch girls.

Coro

¡Chaparreras, Chaparreras!
¡Chaparreritas de cuero!
Váyanse lejos las güeras
que yo a las morenas quiero.

Chorus

Chaparreras, chaparreras!
Little chaparreras of leather
Away with the fair ones
For I like the brunettes.

2

Las muchachas de mi rancho]
éstas sí saben querer]
y cuando muerden rebozo]
es para corresponder.] *Bis*

2

The girls on my ranch
They really know how to love
And when they coyly bite their shawls
They are actually ready to go.

Coro

Chorus

3

Tu marido está en la cama
vente para la cabecera
con el rosario en la mano
ruega a Dios que pronto muera.

3

Your husband is sick in bed
Come and stand by the bedside
With a rosary in your hand
Pray to God he dies soon.

Coro

Chorus

CUAN-DO VI-NE A LA CIU-DAD ME COM-PRÉ MIS CHA-PA-RRE-RAS Y RE-GRE-SÉ POR EL RAN-CHO PA-RA E-NA-MO-RAR RAN-CHE-RAS. ¡CHA-PA-RRE-RRAS! ¡CHA-PA-RRE-RAS! ¡CHA-PA-RRE-RI-TAS DE CUE-RO! VÁ-YAN-SE LE-JOS LAS GÜE-RAS QUE YO A LAS MO-RE-NAS QUIE-RO.

The pride of the cowboy in his rugged, masculine, outdoor life, and big hats is not unmixed with a certain vanity and a consciousness of the attractiveness of his personality and clothes to the fair sex, as this song and *El Sombrerito* (C71) clearly reveal. *Chaparreras*, or chaps, are, of course, the leather protectors worn by cowboys over their trousers when riding after cattle through heavy brush. They are belted around the waist and cover both legs and fasten in back of the legs. For the cowboy of this song, the *chaparreras* are important more because they give him a gallant appearance than for their utility. Verse 3 about the spouse in bed is borrowed from *Firo Liro Li* (A6).

C71. *El Sombrerito* (The Little Hat)
R600, Peter Hurd, Albuquerque, N.Mex., 1951, Robb. Cf. R1359.

1
Este sombrero que traigo
me lo traje de Chicón,
me lo traje de Chicón ¡ay!
este sombrero que traigo.

1
This hat that I'm wearing
I have brought from Chicón,
I have brought from Chicón—oh!
This hat that I'm wearing.

2
Cuando el sombrero me pongo
me lo pongo de ladito,
me lo pongo de ladito ¡ay!
cuando el sombrero me pongo.

2
When I put on the hat
I put it on slantwise,
I put it on slantwise—oh!
When I put on the hat.

3
Cuando el sombrero me pongo
se le da la piedradita,
se le da la piedradita ¡ay!
cuando el sombrero me pongo.

3
When I put on the hat
It charms all who see it,
It charms all who see it—oh!
When I put on the hat.

4
Yo le dije a mi chinita
échame el jorongo al hombro,
échame el jorongo al hombro ¡ay!
porque voy de pasadita.

4
I said to my sweetheart
Throw my serape over my shoulder,
Throw my serape over my shoulder—oh!
Because I'm just passing through.

5
Allá tras de la montaña,
donde temprano se oculta el sol,
quedó mi pueblito triste
y abandonada ya mi labor.

5
On the other side of the mountain,
Where the sun sets early,
There lay my sad little village
And my abandoned fields.

6
Allí me pasé los años
y allí encontré mi primer amor;
y fueron les desengaños
los que mataron a mi ilusión.

6
There I passed the years
And there I met my first love;
It was the cheating that
Killed my illusion.

7
¡Ay! corazón que vas
para nunca volver.
No me digas adiós,
No te despidas jamás,
si no quieres saber
de la ausencia el dolor.

7
Oh! Heart, you are going
Never to return.
Don't say good-bye,
Never say farewell,
If you don't want to know
The sorrow of absence.

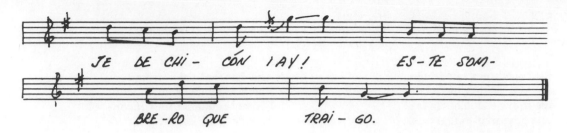

The recording ends with verse 6, but the singer wrote out the remainder of the words for me. The rather attractive formal construction of the first three verses (an *abba* formation) is varied in verse 4 and thereafter abandoned by the singer.

Las Chaparreras (C70) and *El Sombrerito* are both included in the album *Peter Hurd Sings Ranchera Songs*, Folkways Album FA2204, for which I wrote album notes.

C72. *Carmelita*
R1728, Próspero S. Baca, age 70, Bernalillo, N.Mex., 1945, Robb.

1
Carmelita, te soñé
la primera noche de abril,
donde entonces juré amarte
con ardiente frenesí.

Coro
Pero te lo juro
que algún día yo he de ser
tu adorador.

2
En el mar está una palma verde,
verde hasta la planta.
Si tú te llamas que no,
yo me llamo más que nunca.

3
En la sombra de un laurel
me dió sueño y me dormí.
Si estás durmiendo con otro
y no te acuerdas de mí.

4
Las naranjas y limones
en el árbol se maduran;
los ojitos que se quieren
desde lejos se saludan.

5
Tengo un nicho de cristal,
hecho de tus bellas manos,
para colocarte en él
si seguimos como vamos;

1
Carmelita, I dreamed of you
The first night of April,
Since then I've sworn to love you
With burning frenzy.

Chorus
But I swear to you
That one day I will be
Your admirer.

2
In the sea is a green palm tree,
Green to the very bottom.
If your name is "no,"
My name is "more than ever."

3
In the shade of a laurel
I got sleepy and fell asleep.
Perhaps you are sleeping with another
And don't remember me.

4
The oranges and the lemons
Ripen on the tree;
Eyes that love one another
Gaze from afar.

5
I have a crystal niche,
Made by your beautiful hands,
In which to place you
If we continue as we are going;

pero si me pagas mal,	But if you repay me ill,
entre los dos lo quebramos.	Between us we will break it.

6	6
Entre la escarcha y la nieve	Amid the frost and the snow
me puse a torear el frío;	I began to fight the cold;
mal haya quien se atraviesa	Woe to him who would trespass
si este ranchito era mío.	If this ranch were mine.

Verse 5 occurs in almost the same form in
Sierra Nevada (B46), verses 5 and 6.

C73. *El Toro* (The Bull)
  R169, Peter Hurd, San Patricio, N.Mex., 1949, Robb. Cf. Folkways Album FA2204,
R1357; Mendoza 9d (p. 386).

1		1
Por ahí viene el caporal	]	There goes the foreman
cayéndose de borracho.	] *Bis*	So drunk he is falling.

2		2
Gritándole a los vaqueros,	]	Shouting to the cowboys,
Echenme ese toro gacho.	] *Bis*	Turn loose the bull with the bent horns.

Coro	*Chorus*
Heya, heya, heya.	Heya, heya, heya.

Hablando:	*Speaking:*
Allá va el toro.	There goes the bull.
¡Lázalo!	Rope him.
Ya lo lacé.	I've roped him.
¡Túmbalo!	Throw him.
Ya lo tumbé.	I've thrown him.
Ponle el cabestro.	Tie him.

Cantando:	*Singing:*
De esto no sé.	This I do not know how.
Si lo sabes, enséñame.	If you know, show me.
Heya, heya, heya.	Heya, heya, heya.

3		3
Echenme ese toro pinto,	]	Turn loose that spotted bull,
hijo de la vaca mora.	] *Bis*	Son of the roan cow.
¡Ey-he, he, huey!		Ey-he, he, huey!

4		4
Que lo quiero capotear	]	For I want to use the cape on him
delante de las señoras.	] *Bis*	Before the ladies.

Coro	*Chorus*
Heya, heya, heya.	Heya, heya, heya.
Allá va el toro.	There goes the bull.
Lázalo.	Rope him.
Ya lo lacé.	I've roped him.
Túmbalo.	Throw him.
Ya lo tumbé.	I've thrown him.
Ponle el cabestro.	Tie him.
De esto no sé.	This I do not know how.
Si lo sabes, enséñame.	If you know how, show me.
Heya, heya, heya, heya.	Heya, heya, heya, heya.

Hablando:	*Speaking:*
Allá va el otro versito,	Here comes the next little verse,
Ya éntrese, chico.	Go to it, boy.

5

Cantando:	*Singing:*
La vaca era pinta	The cow was spotted
y el becerro era moro.] *Bis*	And the calf was roan.

6

Y los vaqueros decían	And the cowboys said
que era hijo de otro toro.] *Bis*	That he was the son of another bull.
Heya, heya, heya, heya, heya, heya.	Heya, heya, heya, heya, heya, heya.

Hablando:	*Speaking:*
¡Allá va el toro!	There goes the bull!

C74. *El Jabalí* (The Wild Boar)

R167, Peter Hurd, San Patricio, N.Mex., 1949, Robb. Cf. Folkways Album FA2204; also R1362.

<table>
<tr><td>

1

Andando yo trabajando
en la hacienda del jazmín
que por estar almorzando
se me fué mi jabalí.　　　　] *Bis*

</td><td>

1

While I was working
On the jasmine ranch,
Because I was eating lunch
My wild boar got away from me.

</td></tr>
<tr><td>

2

Andando yo traficando
por toda la serranía
buscando a mi jabalí
sin haberlo visto todavía.　　] *Bis*

</td><td>

2

I was walking up and down
All the ridges
Looking for my wild boar
Without having seen it so far.

</td></tr>
<tr><td>

3

Andándolo yo buscando
por las orillas del cerro;
ayer no lo agarré
porque me hizo falta el perro.　] *Bis*

</td><td>

3

I was looking for him
Along the edges of the mountain;
Yesterday I did not get him
For I didn't have a dog.

</td></tr>
</table>

C75. *Aquí, Madre* (Here, Mother)
R247, Garcilán Pacheco, Córdova, N.Mex., 1950, Robb.

1
Aquí, madre, yo te canto
y me duele el corazón.
Espero que allá en el cielo
me mandes tu bendición.

Refrán
¡Ay, madrecita!
¡Madrecita consentida!
Veniste a dejarme solo
a sufrir en esta vida.

2
Tú me cuidabas de noche,
tú me cuidabas de día,
y cuando estaba en peligro
cerca de ti me tenías.

Refrán

3
¡Adiós, madre encantadora!
Triste te alejas de mí.
Nunca borres de tu mente
que mi corazón te dí.

Refrán

4
Estaba yo en mi trabajo
con mi guitarra cantando
sin saber que en ese instante
tú estarías agonizando.

Refrán

5
También mi padre y hermanos
tristes quedan por tu ausencia.
Hemos perdido toditos,
el tesoro y la riquesa.

Refrán

1
Here, mother, I sing to you
And my heart aches.
I hope that from heaven
You will send me your blessing.

Refrain
Oh, dear mother!
Beloved, dear mother!
You came and left me alone
To suffer in this life.

2
You cared for me at night,
You cared for me in the daytime,
And when I was in danger
You kept me near you.

Refrain

3
Farewell, charming mother!
Sadly you leave me.
Never erase from your mind
That I gave my heart to you.

Refrain

4
I was working at my trade
Singing with my guitar
Without knowing that in that moment
You were dying.

Refrain

5
Also my father and brothers
Grieve for your absence.
We have lost everything,
Our treasure and our riches.

Refrain

288

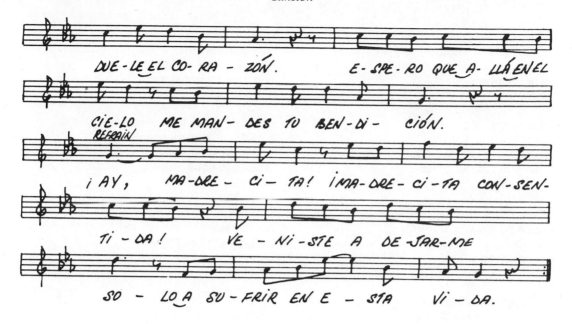

DUE-LE EL CO-RA - ZÓN. E-SPE-RO QUE A-LLÁ EN EL

CIE-LO ME MAN-DES TU BEN-DI - CIÓN.

REFRAIN
¡AY, MA-DRE-CI-TA! ¡MA-DRE-CI-TA CON-SEN-

TI - DA! VE - NI-STE A DE-JAR-ME

SO - LO A SU-FRIR EN E - STA VI - DA.

For other songs expressing love for a mother, see *En el Mundo No Hay Tesoro* (C67), *Murió Mi Madre* (E14), and *Amor de Madre* (C77).

C76. *Adiós de Fernández Gallegos* (Farewell of Fernández Gallegos)
R1392, Mary Inez Jaramillo, Albuquerque, N.Mex., 1956, Robb.

<table>
<tr><td>

1
Voy a cantar esto
con mi corazón partido.
Es el último adiós
de nuestro hijo querido.

</td><td>

1
I am going to sing this
With my heart broken.
It is the last farewell
Of our beloved son.

</td></tr>
<tr><td>

2
Adiós, mi Dessie querida,
amante y fiel compañera.
Ya se te va tu Fernández.
En la otra vida te espera.

</td><td>

2
Farewell, my beloved Dessie,
Beloved and faithful companion.
Know your Fernández is leaving you.
In the other life he waits for you.

</td></tr>
<tr><td>

3
Adiós, mi Nita querida,
prenda de mi corazón.
Ya se va el Daddy querido.
Recibe mi bendición.

</td><td>

3
Farewell, my beloved Nita,
Cherished one of my heart.
Now the Daddy you love is going.
Receive my blessing.

</td></tr>
<tr><td>

4
Adiós, mamacita mía,
vieja de mi corazón.
Ya se va su hijo querido.
Echeme su bendición.

</td><td>

4
Farewell, my dear mother,
Sweet lady of my heart.
Now your beloved son is going away.
Give me your benediction.

</td></tr>
</table>

5

Adiós, hermanas queridas.
No me vayan olvidar.
Y también a mis hermanos,
por mí tendrán que rogar.

6

Adiós, Sister Rose Anita.
Ya no te volveré a ver.
Presente en tus oraciones
tú me tendrás que tener.

7

Adiós, mis suegros queridos,
que ya yo me voy de aquí.
Les pido que me perdonen
si en algo los ofendí.

8

Adiós, todos mis cuñados.
De ustedes yo me despido.
Por mí tendrán que rogar
y nunca echarme en olvido.

9

Adiós, parientes y amigos
y a todos en general.
Por el descanso de mi alma
todos deben de rogar.

10

Adiós para siempre, adiós,
que aquí nunca nos veremos.
Pero en aquella otra vida,
allí nos encontraremos.

11

¿Qué año, qué mes, qué mañana?
Presente lo tengo yo
que en esa triste cruzada
su día se le llegó.

12

A su trabajo salió
de su casa muy contento
sin pensar que lo esperaba
ese terrible momento.

13

¡Ah, qué arriador tan ingrato,
qué fuerte golpe le dió
que allí en ese pavimento,
allí sin vida quedó!

5

Farewell, beloved sisters.
Do not forget me.
And also my brothers,
You must pray for me.

6

Farewell, Sister Rose Anita.
I shall not see you again.
You must keep me
Present in your prayers.

7

Farewell, my beloved parents-in-law,
For I am going away from here.
I beg you to forgive me
If in any way I offended you.

8

Farewell, all my brothers-in-law.
I take my leave of you.
You must pray for me
And never consign me to forgetfulness.

9

Farewell, relatives and friends
And everyone in general.
All of you ought to pray
That my soul may rest in peace.

10

Farewell forever, farewell,
For we'll never see each other here.
But in that other life,
There we shall meet again.

11

What year, what month, what morning?
I am thinking
Of that sad crossing
When his day came.

12

He left for work
From his house very contented
Without realizing what awaited him
In that terrible moment.

13

Ah, what a harsh stroke,
What a strong blow he was dealt
That there on the pavement,
There without life he lay!

<table>
<tr><td>

14
¡Pobrecita de su esposa!
¡Cómo tendrá que sufrir!
que Dios no le concedió
de que lo viera morir.

</td><td>

14
Poor wife of his!
How she will have to suffer!
Since God did not grant
That she should see him die.

</td></tr>
<tr><td>

15
Pobrecitos de esos padres,
esos padres muy queridos.
Hoy se encontrarán llorando
y muy malamente heridos.

</td><td>

15
Those poor parents,
Those beloved parents.
Today they are weeping
And very badly wounded.

</td></tr>
<tr><td>

16
Cuando su esposa lo vió,
con su corazón partido
y con gran dolor le dice:
—¡Ay, compañero querido!—

</td><td>

16
When his wife saw him,
With her heart broken
And with great sorrow she said:
"Oh! beloved companion!"

</td></tr>
<tr><td>

17
Cuando sus hermanos llegaron,
traspasados de dolor,
amargamente lo lloran,
lo lloran con gran dolor.

</td><td>

17
When his brothers came,
Overcome with sorrow,
They wept bitterly for him,
They wept for him with great sorrow.

</td></tr>
<tr><td>

18
Y con gran dolor le dicen:
—¡Ay! hermanito querido,
qué cosa tan terrible,
¡Ah! esto que te ha sucedido.

</td><td>

18
And with great sorrow they said:
"Ah! Beloved little brother,
What a terrible thing this is
That has happened to you."

</td></tr>
</table>

This song has a special interest for me, for the grief-stricken father who composed it was a friend of mine. In his home in 1956 he furnished me with the text of this song, along with other material (R1384–1393). Although it does not meet the criterion of having circulated long enough to have acquired a cultural rather than a personal quality, it is one of those strange examples in which a man steeped in the style of his own place and time is able to turn out songs indistinguishable from examples of earlier origin.

The text includes the following inscription:

Ultimo adiós de
Fernández Gallegos que fué
atropellado a muerte por un
automóbil. El día dos de julio, 1954.
Compuesto por su querido padre,
el Sr. Boleslo Gallegos.

Last farewell of
Fernández Gallegos who was
Rushed to death by an
Automobile the second day of July, 1954.
Composed by his loving father,
Mr. Boleslo Gallegos.

C77. *Amor de Madre* (Mother's Love)
R1973, Vicente Saucedo, Albuquerque, N.Mex., 1964, Robb. Cf. E14 on the same theme.

1

Dame por Dios tu bendición
¡o madre mía adorada!
que yo a tus pies pido perdón
por lo que tanto has sufrido.
De la mansión donde tú estás
una mirada te pido.
Madre querida, ruega por mí
ante el Creador.

1

Give me your blessing, for God's sake,
O my adored Mother!
Because I beg forgiveness at your feet
For all that I have made you suffer.
From the mansion where you are
I beg you to look down.
Beloved mother, pray for me
Before the Creator.

2

Tú que estás en la mansión
de ese trono celestial.
Mándale a mi corazón
un saludo maternal,
un saludo maternal
que me llene el corazón,
que me llene y que me abrace el corazón.

2

You who are in the mansion
Of that celestial throne.
Send to my heart
A maternal blessing,
A maternal blessing
That will fill my heart,
That will fill and embrace my heart.

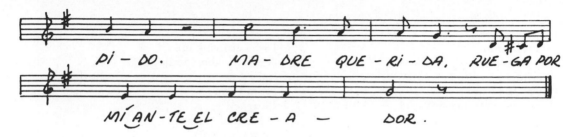

C78. *La Huerfanita* (The Orphan Girl)

R92, Félix Ortega, Chimayó, N.Mex., 1946, Robb. Cf. R1759, the virtually identical version of Frank Chávez; R308; R491.

1

Allá en la cima
de una montaña,
allá en la choza
donde vivía,
andando un día
en la pasada,
joven tan bella
yo conocí.

2

Luego que vide
la bella joven,
me acerqué a ella y
la saludé.
Ella con gusto
su vista baja.
Me dió su mano,
se la estreché.

3

Yo le hice varias
observaciones.
Ella contenta
las escuchó.
Le pregunté si
tenía padres.
Ella llorando
me dijo—No.

4

Si por desgracia
soy huerfanita;
me abandonaron
en mi niñez.
Yo no recuerdo,
estaría chiquita,
tendría apenas
la edad de un mes.

1

There on the ridge
Of a mountain,
There near the hut
Where I was living,
One day out walking
Some time ago,
I met
A beautiful girl.

2

As soon as I saw
The beautiful girl,
I drew near her
And greeted her.
She was pleased
But lowered her gaze.
She gave me her hand,
And I grasped it.

3

I said
A few words to her.
She listened
Quite contentedly.
I asked her if
She had parents.
Weepingly
She told me, "No.

4

"To my sorrow
I am an orphan;
They abandoned me
In my infancy.
I don't remember it,
As I was very small,
I was hardly
One month old.

5

Pasaron años
fuí creciendo.
Una familia
honrada me crió.
Por ellos mismos
estoy comprendiendo
lo que a mis padres
les sucedió.—

5

"Years passed.
I was growing up.
An honorable family
Raised me.
From them
I learned
What had happened
To my parents."

6

—. . . niña,
venir conmigo
y a aquí a la choza
donde nací.
Allí estaremos
. . . amor dos almas;
alegres canas
verán morir.—

6

". . . child,
To come with me
To the hut
Where I was born.
There we will be
. . . two souls in love;
We will be happy
Until we die."

7

Y aquí se acaban,
amigos míos,
mis tristes versos
en que fuí hacedor,
porque estos versos
fueron compuestos
por él que sufre
ante el amor.

7

This is the end,
My friends,
Of my sad verses
Which I composed,
Because these verses
Were composed
By him who suffers
Because of love.

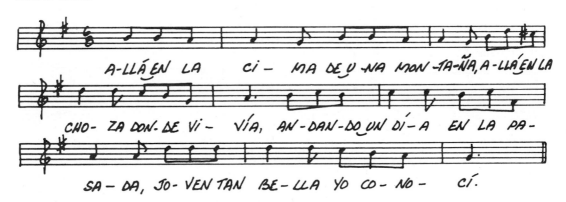

A-LLÁ EN LA CI-MA DE U-NA MON-TA-ÑA, A-LLÁ EN LA CHO-ZA DON-DE VI-VÍA, AN-DAN-DO UN DÍ-A EN LA PA-SA-DA, JO-VEN TAN BE-LLA YO CO-NO-CÍ.

La Huerfanita is popular in New Mexico, as evidenced by the four versions in my collection emanating from the following locations: Llano (near Peñasco), Chimayó, Córdova, and La Jara, New Mexico.

C79. *El Golfo* (The Ragamuffin)
   R2419, Juan Griego, Albuquerque, N.Mex., 1971, Cipriano Griego.

Coro
Pues hay un golfo
me dicen por la calle.

Chorus
There is a ragamuffin
They tell me in the streets.

Canción

Hay un golfo me dicen al pasar. Y si canto me obligan a que calle, a que calle, y si lloro no me dejan llorar.	There is a ragamuffin They tell me as I pass. If I sing They oblige me to be silent, To be silent, And if I cry They don't let me cry.

1	1
Pues he rodeado perdido en el arroyo según la escuela que educa el malechar. Mas nunca más supe quien fué mi padre ni reconozco del beso su calor.	I have wandered lost in the gutter, Living according to the school of wrong. I never knew who my father was Nor knew the warmth of a kiss.

Coro — *Chorus*

2	2
Mas nunca más supe quien fué mi madre, pero sí supe que yo era hijo del amor. Pues también supe que al morir dijo mi 　madre que yo era su vergüenza y su dolor.	I never knew who my mother was, But I do know that I was a child of love. I also know that as my mother died she 　said That I was her shame and her sorrow.

Coro — *Chorus*

3	3
Pues yo soñaba que unos labios me besaban, y mas no supe lo que siento pasar por mí. También soñaba que unos ojos me 　miraban, y en sus negras pupilas me perdí.	I dreamed that some lips were kissing me, But I didn't know what I felt pass over me. I also dreamed a pair of eyes were looking 　at me, And in their black pupils I became lost.

Coro — *Chorus*

NO ME DE-JAN LLO- RAR.

The melody starts in the Ionian, or major, mode on G and at the eighth measure modulates to the Aeolian mode, also on G. Both the method of modulation and the use of the lowered seventh in the Aeolian section resemble medieval practices and appear here to be survivals of ancient musical practices (see Robb 13, pp. 6–8).

The verses are sung to the same tune as that of the chorus.

C80. *Jazmín* (Jasmine)
R340, Henry Fountain et al., Mesilla Park, N.Mex., 1950, Robb.

1
Y estaba una niña hermosa
en un jardín
viendo una mariposa
en un jazmín.
Y ella la contemplaba,
y le decía así:
—Pobre flor que le roban su miel
que le roban su bien.—

2
También las mujeres tienen
cual la flor
quien le robe de su alma
la dulce miel.
Y el hombre cual mariposa,
y a la mujer le roba la paz,

1
And there was a beautiful girl
In a garden
Looking at a butterfly
In a jasmine flower.
And she was watching it
And saying to it:
"Poor little flower, how she has
To give and give of her nectar."

2
Women, too, are like the flower
In that they give their souls
To those who rob them
Of their nectar.
And man, like the butterfly,
Doesn't give woman any peace,

The remainder is undecipherable.

Y E- STA-BA U -NA NI-ÑA HER-MO-SA, EN UN JAR-

DÍN VIEN-DO U -NA MA-RI- PO-SA, EN UN JAZ-

MÍN. Y E-LLA LA CON -TEM- PLA-BA Y LE DE-CÍA A-

SÍ:—PO-BRE FLOR QUE LE RO-BAN SU

MIEL QUE LE RO-BAN SU BIEN:—

C81. *Traigo Mi Cuarenta y Cinco* (I'm Wearing My Forty-five)
R1365, Peter Hurd, Albuquerque, N.Mex., 1955, Robb.

1	1
Traigo mi cuarenta y cinco	I'm wearing my forty-five
con sus cuatro cargadores	With its four magazines
y traigo cincuenta balas.	And I carry fifty bullets.
Las traigo para los traidores.	I carry them for traitors.

Coro	*Chorus*
¿Quién dijo miedo, muchachos,	Who said fear, boys,
si para morir nacimos?	If we are born to die?
Traigo mi cuarenta y cinco	I carry my forty-five
con sus cuatro cargadores.	With its four magazines.

2	2
En el llano de Socorro	In the plain of Socorro
dicen que no hay hombre macho,	They say there are no he-men,
pero si esos quieren ver,	But if they want to see some,
a San Patricio los despacho.	Send them to San Patricio.

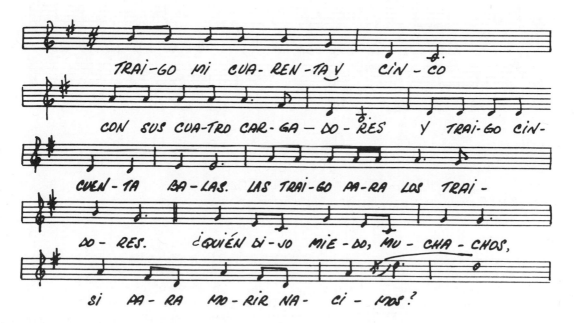

TRAI-GO MI CUA-REN-TA Y CIN-CO

CON SUS CUA-TRO CAR-GA-DO-RES Y TRAI-GO CIN-

CUEN-TA BA-LAS. LAS TRAI-GO PA-RA LOS TRAI-

DO-RES. ¿QUIÉN DI-JO MIE-DO, MU-CHA-CHOS,

SI PA-RA MO-RIR NA-CI-MOS?

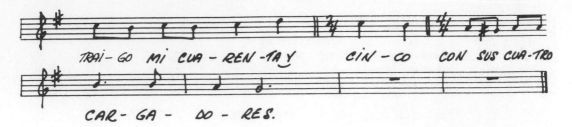

TRAI-GO MI CUA-REN-TA Y CIN-CO CON SUS CUA-TRO
CAR-GA-DO-RES.

The singer, Peter Hurd, true to the boasting spirit of the song, inserts the New Mexican place names of Socorro and San Patricio (where he lives) in a song of Mexican origin.

C82. *Tengo, Tengo, Tengo* (I Have, I Have, I Have)
R2507, Edwin Berry, Tomé, N.Mex., 1972, Robb.

<table>
<tr><td>

1
Tengo, tengo, tengo
y tú no tienes nada;
tengo tres ovejas
allá en la cañada.

</td><td>

]
]
]
] *Bis*

</td><td>

1
I have, I have, I have plenty
And you have nothing;
I have three ewes
There in the valley.

</td></tr>
<tr><td>

2
Una me da leche,
y otra me da lana,
y otra mantequilla
para la semana.

</td><td></td><td>

2
One gives me milk,
And another gives me wool,
And another gives butter
That lasts for a week.

</td></tr>
</table>

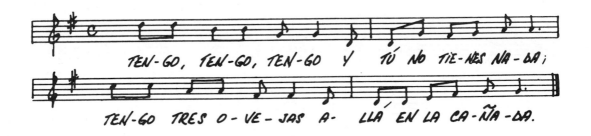

TEN-GO, TEN-GO, TEN-GO Y TÚ NO TIE-NES NA-DA;
TEN-GO TRES O-VE-JAS A- LLÁ EN LA CA-ÑA-DA.

C83. *Cuando Escuches Este Vals* (When You Hear This Waltz)
R26, C. Velarde, Cuba, N.Mex., 1944, Robb.

<table>
<tr><td>

1
Cuando escuches este vals
haz un recuerdo de mí,
piensa en los besos de amor
que me diste y que te dí.

</td><td>

1
When you hear this waltz
Have a memory of me,
Think of the kisses of love
Which you gave me and I gave you.

</td></tr>
</table>

2
Si alguien quisiera robar
tu divino corazón,
dile que mi alma te dí
y la tuya tengo yo.

3
¿Cómo quieres, ángel mío,
que te olvide si eres mi ilusión?
En el cielo, en la tierra,
en el mar, en el sol,
estaremos los dos.

4
¿Cómo quieres, ángel mío,
que te olvide si eres mi ilusión?
Si mi alma toda es tuya
y la tuya tengo yo.

2
If anyone should seek to steal
Your divine heart,
Tell him I gave you my soul
And that I have yours.

3
How could you wish, my angel,
That I forget you, if you are my illusion?
In the sky, in the earth,
In the sea, in the sun,
We shall be together.

4
How could you wish, my angel,
That I forget you, if you are my illusion?
If my soul belongs to you
And I have yours.

CIE- LOES- TA - RE - MOS LOS DOS. ¿CÓ- MO

QUIE - RES, AN- GEL MI - O, QUE TE OL-VI -DE SIE-

RES MI I - LU - SIÓN? SI MI AL - MA TO -DA ES

TU - YA Y LA TU - YA TEN - GO YO.

C84. *Valse* (Waltz)
R1721, Próspero S. Baca, age 70, Bernalillo, N.Mex., 1945, Robb.

1	**1**
A la una te empecé a amar,	At one I began to love you,
vida mía, con alegría	My love, with happiness
acompañando tu amor	Accompanying your love
a las dos mil maravillas.	With two thousand marvels.
2	**2**
¿Qué será posible,	Would it be possible,
mujer adorada,	Adored woman,
qué será posible	Would it be possible
que muera de amor?	That I die of love?
¿Qué será posible	Would it be possible
que ya tú no me amas	That you don't love me anymore
con todito el corazón.	With all your heart?
3	**3**
A las dos me recordé,	At two I was reminded,
vida mía, de tu amor;	My love, of your love;
si me quieres, vida mía,	If you love me, my love,
dímelo por compasión.	For pity's sake tell me.
4	**4**
A las tres me levanté,	At three I got up,
vida mía, pensando en ti,	My love, thinking of you,
aguardando una respuesta,	Awaiting a reply,
si tu amor es para mí.	Whether your love is for me.
5	**5**
A las cuatro, vida mía,	At four, my love,
me acosté pensando en ti;	I lay down thinking of you;
si me quieres, vida mía,	If you love me, my love,
da un suspiro por mí.	Sigh for me.

6

A las cinco, vida mía,
me senté pensando en ti;
si me quieren tus ojitos
sin poderlos ver aquí.

6

At five, my love,
I sat up thinking of you—
If your little eyes love me
Without being able to see me here.

7

A las seis yo me ausenté,
vida mía, con dolor;
no te olvides, vida mía,
te quiero de corazón.

7

At six I went away,
My love, with sorrow;
Don't forget, my love,
I love you with my heart.

The theme of the passage of the hours resembles that of the *décima Qué Largas las
Horas Son* (E1).

C85. *Rosita*
R570, Alfred Campos, age 21, and Edwin Lobato, age 20, Albuquerque, N.Mex., 1951,
Robb.

1

Rosita, tú eres mi encanto.
Eres mi única ilusión;
eres mi única ilusión,
Rosita, tú eres mi encanto.
Tú sabes que te amo tanto.
Es tuyo mi corazón.
Rosita, no siempre tanto
corresponde a mi amor.

1

Rosita, you are my enchantment.
You are my only illusion;
You are my only illusion,
Rosita, you are my enchantment.
You know how much I love you.
My heart is yours.
Rosita, don't always respond
So coldly to my love.

2

Cuando el sol está ya entre la nube   ]
no quema su resplendor.   ] *Bis*
¡Ay! Rosita, no dudes que
yo he de cortar la flor;
que yo he de cortar la flor
del jardín de tus verduras.

2

When the sun is under a cloud
This love does not burn.
Ah, Rosita, don't doubt that
I shall cut this flower;
That I shall cut this flower
From your green garden.

3

Cuando esa rosa te pones
haces mi amor delirar;
haces mi amor delirar
cuando esa rosa te pones.
Quisiera con mis canciones
poderte acá encerrar;
poderte acá encerrar
horita que te pones.

3

When you wear that rose
You make my love delirious;
You make my love delirious
When you wear that rose.
I would like with my songs
To be able to keep you here;
To be able to keep you here
Now that you wear it.

4

Una mariposa humilde   ]
hasta tus labios voló.   ] *Bis*

4

A humble butterfly
Flew to your lips.

5

Una mariposa humilde
hasta tus labios voló,
hasta tus labios voló.

5

A humble butterfly
Flew to your lips,
To your lips flew.

6

Una mariposa humilde.
La pobrecita creía que
la rosa allí se engañó;
que la rosa se engañó,
por eso te perseguía.

6

A humble butterfly.
The poor thing was deceived
By the rose there;
The rose deceived it
And so it pursued you.

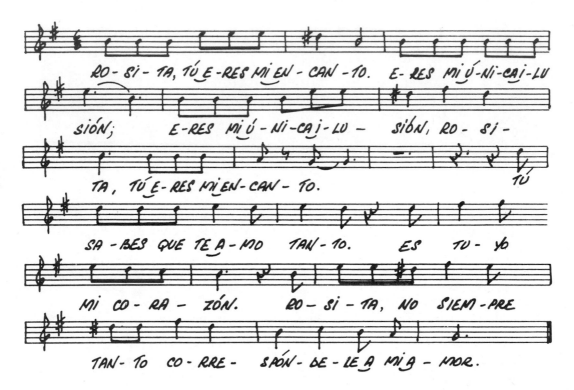

Verses 1 and 3 of C85 exhibit an *abba* type
of formal construction similar to that of C71,
above.

C86. *Cochití*
RB769, Abrahán Sánchez, Las Lagunitas, N.Mex., 1950, Cobos.

1

Al pasar por Cochití
me dijo una prenda amada:
—Las fiestas no son aquí,
pásese para La Cañada.—

1

While visiting Cochití
A girl that I loved said to me:
"The fiestas aren't here
Go to La Cañada."

302

2 En Sile están las iglesias, en Peña Blanca las flores, en Santa Fe las aromas y en Cochití mis amores.	**2** In Sile are the churches, In Peña Blanca the flowers, In Santa Fe the aromas And in Cochití my loves.
3 Esta sala está medida con cien yardas de listón; en cada esquina una rosa y en medio mi corazón.	**3** This room is measured With a hundred yards of ribbon; In each corner is a rose And in the center is my heart.
4 Estimo como agradezco, agradezco lo servido; de sus gracias y favores quedo muy agradecido.	**4** It is a pleasure To be of service; I am very pleased With your graces and favors.
5 Al pasar el Río Grande, al pasarlo poco a poco, no creas que estoy sentido porque tu amor fué muy poco; antes vivo agradecido, ahí está tu arpa, iya no toco!	**5** On crossing the Río Grande, On crossing it very slowly, Don't think that I am crushed Because your love was so puny; Rather I'm grateful it's over, There's your harp, I'll play it no more.

This song is named after Cochití, an Indian pueblo west of the Río Grande between Albuquerque and Santa Fe. Peña Blanca is a Spanish-speaking village near Cochití. During the fiestas at the New Mexico Indian pueblos, one room in the village is decorated with shawls, ribbons, photographs—almost every inch of the walls and ceilings covered with ornament—and an Indian couple hold open house for visitors. In an adjoining room the women of the village serve food to all comers.

C87. *Los Chimayoses* (The People of Chimayó)
RB770, Napoleón Trujillo, Bernalillo, N.Mex., 1950, Cobos.

1 Los Chimayoses son dones de los que el chango precura van a hablarle como al cura matándose a trompezones, a gritos, y a fanfarrones; ahí naiden se muestra escaso por ver si tocan un vaso, se apeñuscan de a montones.	**1** The people of Chimayó act like lords Of those from down the river. They talk as if to the priest, Killing themselves with trumpeting, Shouts, and boasting; There no one is niggardly With the bottle. They embarrass everyone.
2 Van a andar el mundo entero para jallar una zaleya, el diablo que se los creya ya tanto pelagartero.	**2** They travel over the whole world To find a sheepskin, The devil himself Made thieves out of them.

Como hombre de varillero
sin aprivinir vitualla,
y lo que buscan primero
es corretear la gandalla.

Like peddlers
Who earn no bread,
And that which first of all they seek
Is to go about stealing food.

3

Los que vienen desde el río
son los que han de aprovechar;
son de tan buen natural
que a naiden le dan cormío;
los changos son de tildio,
naiden me lo ha de negar,
que salen con el costal
y aunque lo traigan vacío!

Those who come from the river
Are the thrifty ones;
They are so good by nature
They give no one a break;
Those from down river are like waterbirds,
No one can deny this,
Who come from the coast
And carry nothing with them.

4

¡Ay! cantada rabajeña
ya sabes quien te escribió
pero no digas que yo,
aunque te hagan una seña
ahí solamente a tu dueña
le has de decir pero no,
porque también compran leña
y algunos de Chimayó.

Ah, song of down river,
You know who writes to you
But you don't tell that it is I,
Even if they try to find out
There even to your nurse
You would have to say no,
Because others can't keep a secret
Including some folks from Chimayó.

There is a certain rivalry, mostly good-natured, between the people of the *río abajo* (downriver), the towns along the Río Grande south of *la bajada*, and those of the *río arriba* (upriver). Chimayó is a fascinating upriver Spanish village famous for its lovely *santuario* and the weaving of Chimayó rugs, the latter an art borrowed from the Navajo Indians.

C88. *Santa Fe*
R2428, Vicente Saucedo, Albuquerque, N.Mex., 1971, Robb.

1

Santa Fe, ciudad bonita
con su estilo colonial,
en los Estados Unidos
no hay otra ciudad igual;

Santa Fe, beautiful city
With its colonial style,
There is not its equal
In the United States;

2

con sus muchachas bonitas,[2]
bonitas como un clavel,
españolas y mexicanas
y americanas también.

With its pretty girls,
As pretty as a carnation,
Spanish and Mexican
And American girls as well.

[2] At this point the singer gets a laugh by imitating a "wolf whistle," sliding his finger up and down the guitar string.

3

En mil seis cientos ochenta	In sixteen hundred and eighty
Diego de Vargas perdió,	Diego de Vargas was lost,
derrotado por los indios	Vanquished by the Indians
a Santa Fe abandonó.	And he abandoned Santa Fe.

4

Pero doce años más tarde	But twelve years later
Diego de Vargas volvió	Diego de Vargas returned
con su escolta de soldados	With his escort of soldiers
Santa Fe reconquistó.	And reconquered Santa Fe.

Coro 1 / *Chorus 1*

¡Nuevo México! ¡Nuevo México!	New Mexico! New Mexico!
Santa Fe es su capital.	Santa Fe is your capital.
Es mi orgullo haber nacido	It is my pride to be born
en esta gran ciudad sin igual.	In this great city without an equal.

5

En mil setecientos doce	In seventeen hundred twelve
fué cuando se aprobó;	It was approved;
se celebra la gran fiesta	They held a great fiesta
honrando al conquistador.	Honoring the conqueror.

6

La Virgen Conquistadora	The Virgin Conquistadora
la sacan en procesión	They carry in the procession
porque ya es la patrona	Because she is now the patron
de esta bonita función.	Of this beautiful function.

7

Cado año el día de trabajo	Each year on Labor Day
celebramos con honor	We celebrate with honor
los cuatro días de tu fiesta	The four days of your fiesta
y tu linda procesión.	And your handsome parade.

8

Tus calles tan angostitas	Your streets so narrow,
y tu plaza principal,	And your central plaza,
tu Palacio de Gobierno	Your Palace of the Governors,
y tu antigua catedral.	And your ancient cathedral.

Coro 2 / *Chorus 2*

Cuando queman al Zozobra	When they burn Zozobra
es para empezar la función,	It is the beginning of the function,
es cuarenta pies de alto	He is forty feet in height
causa mucha, mucha admiración.	And the object of much admiration.

9

Tu desfile es muy bonito	Your parade is very pretty
y también tu procesión	And also your procession
que va a la cruz de los mártires	Which goes to the Cross of the Martyrs
y adoran con devoción.	In adoration and devotion.

10

Los caballeros de Vargas
marchan triumfantes también;
entran a la plaza vieja
y lo reciben muy bien.

Coro 3

¡Nuevo México! ¡Nuevo México!
Santa Fe es su capital,
por muy lejos que yo vaya
yo de ti siempre me he de acordar.

10

The Caballeros de Vargas
Also march in triumph;
They enter the old plaza
Where they are well received.

Chorus 3

New Mexico! New Mexico!
Santa Fe is your capital,
No matter how far away I go
I will always remember you.

An amusing feature of *Santa Fe* (C88) and *Albuquerque* (C89) is that they are composed according to a pattern prevalent south of the border, where the composer-singer of the songs about localities for some reason—perhaps to lend an air of sincerity or just because it is the style of such songs—is usually represented as a loyal son separated by fate from the place where he was born, to which he sends back his undying love. As a matter of fact, the composer, Vicente Saucedo, was born in Mexico, has never lived in Santa Fe, and has been living happily with his charming wife and daughter in Albuquerque.

C89. *Albuquerque*
   R1957, Vicente Saucedo, Albuquerque, N.Mex., 1964, Robb.

1
Albuquerque, ciudad tan bonita,
con tu nombre que tienes del rey,
tus mujeres, preciosas y hermosas
y tus parques, que son un placer.

1
Albuquerque, a most beautiful city,
With your name that of a king,
Your women, precious and lovely
And your parks, which are a delight.

2
De la sierra se ve el panorama
muy bonito al anochecer,
Nuevo México tierra de encanto,
tierra linda que me vió nacer.

2
From the mountains is seen a panorama
Very lovely at nightfall,
New Mexico land of enchantment,
Beautiful land of my birth.

3
Tu bonito Cañon de Tijeras,
tus paseos, que no hay cosa igual,
Albuquerque, la ciudad del Duque,
nunca, nunca te voy a olvidar.

3
Your beautiful Tijeras Canyon,
Your drives, which have no equal,
Albuquerque, the Duke City,
I will never, never forget you.

4
Tus montañas, tus valles dorados,
tus volcanes que muertos están,
y tu Río Grande tan famoso
que es orgullo de esta gran ciudad.

4
Your mountains, your golden valleys,
Your now inactive volcanoes,
And your famous Río Grande
That is the pride of this great city.

5
Muy bonita es tu Plaza Vieja
muy antigua es por tradición
y la iglesia es de San Felipe
de Albuquerque el santo patrón.

5
Your Old Town is very lovely
By tradition very old
And the Church is San Felipe's,
Albuquerque's patron saint.

6
Albuquerque, de ti me despido,
Me voy lejos muy lejos de aquí.
Por muy lejos que de ti me encuentre
nunca, nunca me olvido de ti.

6
Albuquerque, I bid you farewell,
I am going very far from here.
But however far from you I wander
Never, never will I forget you.

AL- BU - QUER-QUE, CIU- DAD TAN BO-
NI - TA, CON TU NOM-BRE QUE
TIE - NES DEL REY, TUS MU - JE-RES, PRE-
CIO - SAS Y HER - MO - SAS Y TUS
PAR - QUES, QUE SON UN PLA - CER. *FIN*
DE LA SIE - RRA SE VE EL PA-NO-
RA - MA MUY BO - NI - TO AL
A - NO - CHE - CER, NUE - VO MÉ - XI - CO
TIE - RRA DE EN - CAN - TO, TIE - RRA
LIN - DA QUE ME VIÓ NA - CER. *D.C. al FIN.*

C90. *El Coyotito* (The Little Coyote)
Lummis (p. 178), Charles F. Lummis, California, 1904, Lummis. Cf. RB232.

<table>
<tr><td>1</td><td>1</td></tr>
</table>

1	1
Cuando salí de Hermosillo,	When I parted from my city,
lágrimas vine llorando,	Tears and tears I came a-crying,
y con la flor del trompillo	And with trumpet-flower pretty
me venía consolando.	To comfort myself was trying.

2	2
Yo soy como el coyotito	I am like the *coyotito*
que los revuelco y los dejo,	That rolls them over and leaves them,

y me voy al trotecito
mirando por debajejo.

And I go trotting so neat, oh,
My downcast glance deceives them.

3

Ya se cayó el pino verde
donde habitan los pichones;
y cayó él que andaba ausente,
ahora verán pelones.

Already is fallen the stately
Pine where doves perched by the air-full;
He who was gone returned lately,
Now the short-haired must be careful.

4

Ya se cayó el jacalito
donde colgaba mi espada.
¿Para qué es tanto laberinto
si alcabo todo se acaba?

Already fallen is the humble
Hut where my sword was suspended.
What is the use of fuss and grumble,
If all things at last are ended?

5

Ya se cayó el jacalito
donde colgaba mi espejo.
Debajo del roble encinito
tendió su cama un conejo.

Already is fallen the lonely
Hut where my mirror was peeping.
And in the oak-thickets only
The rabbit has stretched for sleeping.

6

Ya se secó el nopalito
donde íbamos a las tunas.
Ya no me andarás celando
con tus celos en ayunas.

Dried is now the prickly-pear cooling
That we both hunted when younger;
Now me no more will you go fooling
With your jealous tricks in my hunger.

7

Les encargo a mis amigos
que si ven a mi querida,
no le digan que estoy preso,
porque es el bien de mi vida.

Friends, I charge you all unshaken,
If my sweetheart you'll be seeing,
Tell her not that I've been taken,
For she is the good of my being.

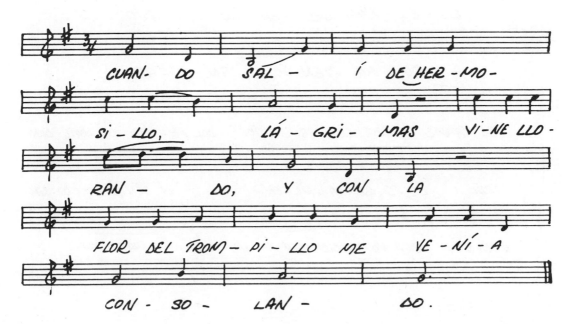

CUAN-DO SAL - Í DE HER-MO-SI - LLO, LÁ - GRI - MAS VI-NE LLO-RAN - DO, Y CON LA FLOR DEL TRON - DI - LLO ME VE - NÍ - A CON - SO - LAN - DO.

I transcribed the recording of this song, as sung by the legendary Charles F. Lummis himself, onto tape from an old Ediphone cylinder in the archives of the Southwest Museum, in Los Angeles. The words are largely indistinguishable, but fortunately Lummis published both the Spanish text and his own rhymed English translation in *Land of Poco Tiempo* (Lummis, pp. 178–80). The above is his text and translation.

El Coyotito is a song about Hermosillo, Mexico. The melody alone, because of its asymmetrical construction, consisting of three phrases with the third interestingly extended, would justify including the song here. But the age of the recording, now over seventy years old, and its collector-singer, the author of *The Land of Poco Tiempo*, makes its inclusion imperative.

C91. *El Ferrocarril* (The Railroad)

Mendoza 9d (p. 433), Próspero S. Baca, age 71, Bernalillo, N.Mex., 1946, Cobos. Cf. I14–15.

1	1
En el nombre sea de Dios	In the name of God
aquí me siento a cantar,	I sit down here to sing,
que ya me sé otros versitos	For I know some verses
del Ferrocarril Central.	About the Central Railroad.
2	2
El Ferrocarril Central,	The Central Railroad—
dicen que no es cosa buena;	They say it's a bad thing;
que anocheciendo en su tierra	You go to sleep in your own country
va a amanecer a la ajena.	And wake up in another.

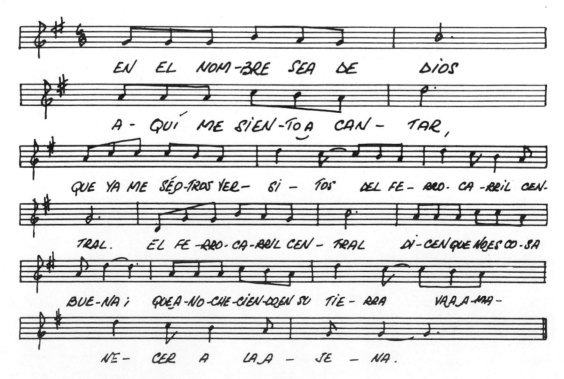

Mendoza comments that this song emanates from the state of Zacatecas, Mexico, and that it refers to the railroad constructed from that place to the border city of Juárez (Mendoza 9d, p. 433).

C91a. *El Ferrocarril*
Mendoza 9d (p. 433), Mrs. Cleofas E. R. Larranaga, Hot Springs, N.Mex., 1945, Cobos.

1
Ahí viene el ferrocarril,
vamos a ver donde está;
¡ah! ¡qué gusto nos dará
cuando lo veamos venir!

Coro
Llegando a la emigración
—Good morning— repetiré;
—camín, camín— les diré,
—vengan a oír mi canción.—

2
Digo a las americanas
—hoy las vengo a vesitar,
ahora que son mis paisanas
ahora les vengo a cantar.

1
There comes the train,
Let's go and see it;
Ah, what fun it will be
To see it arrive.

Chorus
Coming to the emigration office
I'll say, "Good morning";
"Come in, come in," I'll tell them,
"Come listen to my song."

2
I say to the American girls,
"Today I've come to visit you.
Now that you are my compatriots
I'll come and sing for you."

This is another *canción* that mentions the coming of the railroad. *Senaida* (C32) also refers to the coming of the railroad. Other songs relating to railroads are included in Section I: *Yo Soy Rielera* (I14), *La Rialera* (I14a), and *El Pasajero* (I15). Further comments on the coming of industrial society are found in such songs as *Luz Electrica* (R533, R534).

C91b. *El Ferrocarril*
Lummis (p. 180), California, 1893, Lummis.

1
Allí viene el ferrocarril.
Vamos a ver donde está.
¡A, qué gusto nos dará
cuando lo veamos venir!

Coro
Llegando la emigración,
—*Good morning*,— repetiré;
—*Come in! Come in!*— les diré,
—vengan oír mi canción.—

1
The railroad is coming this way.
Let us go look at it near.
When we shall see it appear,
Ah, what a joy it will be!

Chorus
And then the tourists shall throng,
"Good morning!" I will repeat;
"Come in! Come in!" I'll entreat,
"Come in and hear my song!"

2

De Chihuahua Franquilín
corren los americanos,
ganándoles el dinero
a todos los mexicanos.

Coro

3

Si fueras al campamiento
donde vienen trabajando,
yo así me vivo cantando
para ganar el sostento.

Coro

4

Ni el sol ni el viento podrá
hacerme retroceder;
millas y millas correr,
para ganar nuestro bien.

Coro

5

La máquina va partir,
estén toditos alerta.
Vayan sacando el dinero
que ya vamos a partir.

Coro

2

Up from the town on the line
Come running the *Americanos*,
Taking our money away,
Money from all us *paisanos*.

Chorus

3

Were you at camp where they're giving
Work and the laborers bringing—
That's just the way I live singing
Only to earn me a living.

Chorus

4

Neither the sun, nor the wind could
Make me turn back till I've done;
Mile after mile I'll run
That I may win us some good.

Chorus

5

The engine is going to start.
Lively! Be all of you ready!
Come pull your money out—steady,
For now we are going to start.

Chorus

The rhymed translation is by Charles F. Lummis. Franklin, according to Lummis (see verse 2), was a former name for El Paso, Texas (Lummis, p. 180).

C92. *Cuando Salí de Mi País* (When I Left My Country)
R2534, Josefina Flores, age 54, Albuquerque, N.Mex., 1962, Robb.

1

Cuando salí de mi país
con mi corazón entristecido
y mi cara debanecida
dejando a mis hijos   ]
que son todo mi amor.   ] *Bis*

2

Algunas golondrinas
volaron y volaron

1

When I left my country
It was with sadness in my heart
And my face downcast
Leaving my children
Who are all my love.

2

Some swallows
Kept on flying

312

en frente mi camino,	Ahead of me on the road,
pero era mi destino	But it was my destiny
y no pude parar.	And I could not stay.

3	3
Ahora siento emoción	Now I feel emotion
viviendo en gran nación,	Living in a great nation,
algunas veces lloro, lloro,	Sometimes I weep,
lloro con esperanza	I weep with hope
que tarde algún día	That some day later
estarán cerca de mí.	They will be with me again.

This touching *canción* was composed and sung by Josefina Flores, a native of Huemango, a tiny village in El Salvador distinguished for its delicious mangoes. My wife and I employed Josefina as cook and housekeeper in San Salvador (the capital of El Salvador) in 1962 when I was visiting professor of composition at the National Conservatory of Music there under a State Department grant.

At the end of that year Josefina wished to accompany us to the United States, and we were able, under the more lenient laws then prevailing, to arrange for a permanent immigration visa for her and her son Oscar Flores. We returned by automobile, and as we approached the border of Guatemala, some larks *(golondrinas)* for a time flew ahead of the car. Josefina, as she later explained, experienced mixed emotions—sadness at leaving behind several other children (one of them a crippled lad to whom ever since she has sent a monthly check) and happy expectation of coming to the United States, that *gran nación* to which the song refers. In 1973, after a heroic struggle with the English language, she was sworn in as a citizen of the United States. Only then did she shyly reveal that she had just composed this song and, at my request, sang it for me and permitted me to make a recording.

Josefina's song meets few of the usual definitions of a folk song, such as venerable age, widespread usage, and the like. Yet I have included it because it is a completely authentic example of how songs arise out of a human need to give vent to deeply felt emotions. It is also an example of songs that from their inception bear the imprint of the Hispanic folk song tradition. Josefina is of mixed Spanish and Pepiles Indian ancestry, but I find no trace of the latter in her song.

D. *Relación* AND RELATED FORMS

Mendoza states that the *relación*, having the same form as the *romance*, differs from it only in its fluent narrative and in its light tone and occasional humor (Mendoza 9d, p. 194). He groups the *relación* together with children's games under the heading *La Relación y los Juegos Infantiles*. Under this heading he includes also what he calls *corridos de disparates, relaciones aglutinantes, romancillos, corridos de exageraciones, mentiras*, and others he calls simply *enumerativos*. This is all very confusing, since the *romance* and the *corrido* are distinct though related forms, the former with a sixteen-syllable line, the latter with an eight-syllable line. Both are narrative, but the *romance* is about remote events and deals with more or less important people, whereas the *corrido* is earthy in tone and deals with the extraordinary things that happen to plain everyday people.

According to Mendoza, the *relaciones* have persisted until our own time more than four centuries after the time of Juan de la Encina, who was one of the most fortunate creators of the type.

Actually, *El Borrego*, one of the New Mexican examples that Mendoza cites, does preserve the sixteen-syllable line of the *romance*:

Yo tenía un borrego gordo que de gordo lo maté,
me puse a vender la carne treinta pesos le saqué.
Los sebitos del borrego los hicimos chicharrones
del tamaño de esta casa salieron treinta montones.

But while some of the Spanish-American *relaciones* show traces of the form of the *romance*, most of them appear to have evolved away from it.

It is not surprising that, in view of the continuous process of change inherent in the aural tradition, the folk singer should not adhere to any hard-and-fast definition and yet should sense certain simple basic elements that characterize a type of song. I think that therefore it is not oversimplifying to say that the *relación* is the name given in Old Mexico to a type of humorous folk songs characterized by lists of things, people, or places. Those given to exaggeration or nonsense are sometimes called *disparates*, and those relating a tall story are sometimes known as *mentiras*. When they consist of many verses with an additional item added to the list in each verse, they are said to be *relaciones aglutinantes*. All these types may be found in the Spanish-speaking areas of the United States, and examples of each of them are included in the following pages.

The *disparate* I believe requires special consideration. The word *disparate* is defined in one Spanish-English dictionary as "nonsense, blunder, absurdity, extravagance." Mankind finds humor in the absurd. It is an appreciation shared by people of all levels — by the simplest country folk at one extreme and by the most highly sophisticated cosmopolitan creative artists at the other. I need only to mention Mozart's *A Musical Joke* (Köchel no. 522), the ridiculous creations of the Dadaists in art and music, or the plays of Ionesco to establish the fact that all manner of men have learned not only to laugh at the absurd but to use it purposefully to evoke laughter. This is found in abundance in the *disparates* below.

RELACIÓN

D1. *La Semana* (The Week)
Mendoza 9d (p. 209), Amador Abeyta, Sabinal, N.Mex., 1945, Cobos.

1
El domingo la conocí,
el lunes le dí un recado.

1
On Sunday I met her,
On Monday I gave her a message.

El martes le pedí
y el miércoles nos casamos.

On Tuesday I proposed
And on Wednesday we were married.

Coro
¡Ay! pero toma y toma, toma,
toma tu pico, paloma.

Chorus
Ah! but kiss me, kiss me,
Give me a kiss, my dove.

2

El jueves le dí de palos,
el viernes la administraron;
el sábado se murió
y el domingo la enterraron.

2

On Thursday I beat her up,
On Friday they treated her;
On Saturday she died
And on Sunday they buried her.

Coro

Chorus

3

Del gusto que se murió
yo gané para la casa
para matar a mi suegra
para que se acabe esa raza.

3

I was so glad she was dead
That I returned to the house
To kill my mother-in-law
And put an end to all her kind.

315

This song exhibits the characteristics of the *relación*. Although the humor is grim, it is there, as is the list of names, in this instance of the days of the week. This example also conserves the sixteen-syllable line of the *romance*. Mendoza remarks that, while this *relación* is found throughout the central region of Mexico, the United States version given above is in a better state of preservation than the Mexican versions (Mendoza 9d, p. 209).

D1a. *La Semana*
RB227, Mrs. D. Abadie, California, 1904, Charles F. Lummis.

<table>
<tr><td>

1
El domingo la conocía,
el lunes le dí un recado,
el martes la he yo pedí,
el miércoles nos casamos.

Coro
¡Ay! Toma, toma,
toma tú, tu paloma.
Toma, toma, toma,
toma, toma, toma,
toma, toma tu pico paloma.

2
El jueves le dí de palos,
el viernes la administraron,
el sábado se murió,
el domingo la enterraron.

Coro

</td><td>

1
On Sunday it was I met her,
On Monday I gave her a gift,
On Tuesday I proposed to her,
On Wednesday we got married.

Chorus
Ah! Kiss her, kiss her,
Kiss your dove.
Kiss her, kiss her, kiss her,
Kiss her, kiss her, kiss her,
Kiss your dove.

2
On Thursday I beat her up,
On Friday they treated her,
On Saturday she died,
On Sunday they buried her.

Chorus

</td></tr>
</table>

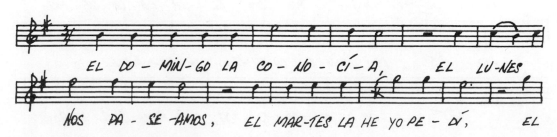

MIÉR-CO-LES NOS CA — SA-NOS ¡AY! TO-MA, TO-MA,

TO-MA TÚ, TU PA-LO-MA. TO-MA, TO-MA, TO-MA,

TO-MA, TO-MA, TO-MA, TO-MA, TO-MA TU

PI — CO PA — LO-MA.

This text is reproduced by permission from the collection of the Southwest Museum, Highland Park, Los Angeles, California. Having been recorded on old Edison cylinders in 1904, it was difficult to decipher.

D2. *Perfectita Estaba Enferma* (Perfectita Was Sick)
RB774, María Teresa Gallegos, Santa Fe, N.Mex., Cobos.

1
Perfectita estaba enferma,
le dolía la cabeza
y de remedio le dieron
que bebiera la cerveza.

1
Perfectita was sick,
With a headache
And for a remedy they gave her
Beer to drink.

2
Perfectita estaba enferma,
le dolía la garganta
y de remedio le dieron
que bebiera mula blanca.

2
Perfectita was sick,
With a sore throat
And for a remedy they gave her
"White mule" to drink.[1]

3
Perfectita estaba enferma,
le dolía el corazón
y de remedio le dieron
que se fuera al vacilón.

3
Perfectita was sick,
With a pain in her heart
And for a remedy they told her
To go on a spree.

4
Perfectita estaba buena,
se paseaba en la alameda,
y de mal nombre le dieron,
Perfectita parrandera.

4
Perfectita was well,
She went walking in the grove,
And they gave her a bad name,
Perfectita the wild woman.

[1]"White mule" was the illegal or bootleg whiskey of the Prohibition era.

D3. *Yo No Me Quiero Casar* (I Don't Want to Get Married)
R146, Rafaelita and Leonardo Salazar, El Rito, N.Mex., 1949, Robb.

Coro
Yo no me quiero casar.
Yo no me quiero casar,
porque mujer a mi gusto
no la he podido encontrar.

Chorus
I don't want to get married.
I don't want to get married,
Because a woman to my taste
Cannot be found.

1

Las altas parecen flautas.
Las gordas parecen costal.
Las chaparras son juguetes
que se pierden donde están.

1

The tall ones resemble flutes.
The fat ones resemble a sack.
The short ones are toys that
Get lost where they are.

Coro

Chorus

2

Si son las descoloridas
que parecen un alambre;
se dan una retorcida
porque ya les anda de hambre.

2

If they are pale
They resemble a wire;
They give themselves a twist
Because already they're dying of hunger.

Coro

Chorus

3

Si son las coloradas
que parecen un payaso;
se dan una repintada
y se pegan un brochazo.

3

If they are redheaded
They resemble a clown;
They make themselves up so
With a paint brush.

Coro

Chorus

4

Las blancas son muy celosas
ni el diablo las puede aguantar;
las trigueñas solo piensan
con el hombre coquetear.

4

The white ones are very jealous,
Not even the devil can get used to them;
The brunettes think only
Of flirting with a man.

Coro

Chorus

5

Y si es también las viejitas
que parecen orejones;
de que arrugan su boquita
que parecen chicharrones.

5

The old ones
Play dumb;
They purse up their little mouths
Which look like fritters.

Coro

Chorus

6

Ya yo me voy de este mundo
que me ha pagado tan mal;
voy a ver si en el infierno
allá me puedo casar.

6

Well, I'm going from this world
Which has paid me so badly;
I'm going to see if in hell
I can get married.

7

Y si en caso en el infierno
no me incuentro una bonita
de ahí me paso al purgatorio
con las ánimas benditas.

7

And if in hell
I don't meet a charmer
From there I'll go to purgatory
With the blessed souls.

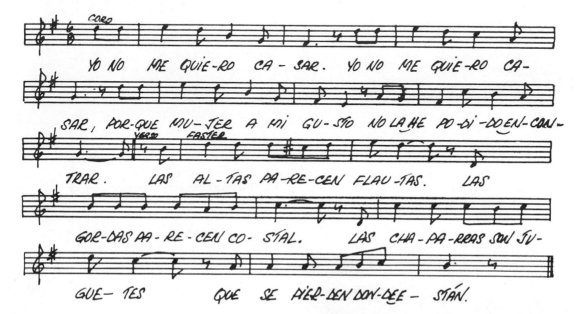

YO NO ME QUIE-RO CA-SAR. YO NO ME QUIE-RO CA-SAR, POR-QUE MU-JER A MI GU-STO NO LA HE PO-DI-DO EN-CON-TRAR. LAS AL-TAS PA-RE-CEN FLAU-TAS. LAS GOR-DAS PA-RE-CEN CO-STAL. LAS CHA-PA-RRAS SON JU-GUE-TES QUE SE PIER-DEN DON-DE E-STÁN.

Rafaelita and Leonardo Salazar, singers of *Yo No Me Quiero Casar* (D3), outside their home in El Rito, New Mexico, 1949. The Salazars were both blind.

D4. *La Severiana*

R613, Napoleón Trujillo, age 63, Bernalillo, N.Mex., 1951, Robb. Cf. R332; also Mendoza 9d (p. 532).

Señores, vamos cantando	Gentlemen, let's sing
una canción mexicana,	A Mexican song,
ahora que me ando paseando,	Now that I'm passing by
buscando a mi Severiana.	Looking for my Severiana.

1	1
Como he sido aventurero	As I have been an adventurer
y en mí se ha visto el primor	And I have seen the beauty
y en Durango, Nuevo León,	Of Durango, Nuevo León,
Valverde y su contadero,	Valverde and its shipping point,
y México todo entero.	And all of Mexico.
Disfruté de mi alegría.	I have enjoyed myself.
¡Cuántas tierras no andaría	How many lands would I not visit
buscando a mi Severiana!	Looking for my Severiana!

2	2
En un vapor de Jalisco	On a Jalisco steamship
mi salí a pasear un día,	I went out to take a stroll and
de allí me pasé a Sevilla	From there I went to Seville,
llegué a los Ranchos de Atrisco,	Passing through Ranchos de Atrisco,
comprando durazno prisco,]	Buying a Prisco peach,
llegué al pueblo de Santa Ana] *Bis*	I went to the Pueblo of Santa Ana
y allí entre la raza indiana,	And there among the Indian race,
me entretuve platicando;	I entertained myself talking;
de allí me volví llorando,	From there I returned weeping,
buscando a mi Severiana.	Looking for my Severiana.

3	3
Bajé a Peña Blanca un día	I came down to Peña Blanca one day
y en La Bajada paré,	And at La Bajada I stopped
y al llegar a Santa Fe	And en route to Santa Fe
pasé por La Cieneguía;	I passed La Cienega;
en Los Cerillos tenía]	In Cerrillos I had to
que me embarcar para Doña Ana.] *Bis*	Embark for Doña Ana.
y a las tres de la mañana	And at three in the morning
pasé por los Algodones	I passed through Algodones
para pararme en los Rincones	In order to stay a while in Rincones
buscando a mi Severiana.	Looking for my Severiana.

4	4
Llegué todo desvanecido	I arrived all tired out
y en Fernández me paré	And stopped in Fernández
y al Colorado llegué	And came to Colorado
con mi corazón partido	With a broken heart
de ver que había tenido]	To see that there was no news,
razón mayor o mediana.] *Bis*	Neither good nor bad.
Y bailando varseliana	And dancing the Varsoviana[2]
en los Córdovas me ví	I came into the Cordovas

[2]See examples of the Varsoviana in Section X (X22, X29, X34, X39–40).

pero prontito partí
buscando a mi Severiana.

But very soon left
Looking for my Severiana.

5

Ya tarde bajé al Embudo
cansado de caminar,
de allí pasé a Lemitar
a donde llegué ya oscuro.
Y en San Miguel, de seguro,   ]
me embarqué para Doña Ana.   ] *Bis*
Y al toque de una campana
gritó el conductor: —¡A bordo!—
Pero yo me hacía sordo
buscando a mi Severiana.

5

It was late when I went down to Embudo,
Tired of traveling,
From there I came to Lemitar
Where it was already dark.
And in San Miguel, for sure,
I embarked for Doña Ana.
When the bell rang
The conductor shouted, "All aboard."
But I pretended to be deaf,
Looking for my Severiana.

6

Llegué a Los Lunas de vuelta
con mi jornada rendida;
allí tomé la comida
pasando por lo de Isleta.
Recordé de la Glorieta   ]
otro día por la mañana.   ] *Bis*
Se cumplía una semana
que andaba rodeando el mundo
y andando de vagamundo
buscando a mi Severiana.

6

I came back to Los Lunas
With my journey ended;
There I ate a little food
On the way to Isleta.
I woke up in Glorieta
The other day in the morning.
A week passed
While I was roaming the world
And traveling like a tramp
Looking for my Severiana.

7

De Las Vegas fuí a La Junta
pasando por Loma Parda,
llego y me visto una albarda
y una mujer me pregunta:]
—Señor ¿qué usted no se apunta?] *Bis*
En este juego se gana
oro y plata mexicana.—
Respondile con anhelo:
—Yo no ando buscando juego,
yo busco a mi Severiana.—

7

From Las Vegas I went to La Junta
Passing through Loma Parda,
I came and put on a pack saddle
And a woman asked me:
"Sir, would you like to gamble?
In this game one wins
Gold and Mexican silver."
I responded firmly:
"I'm not looking for gambling,
I'm looking for my Severiana."

8

En fin, para no cansarme
me bajé al Río Bonito,
pasando por Antoñito
y a Las Vegas vine a dar;
y en San Miguel, al parar   ]
me encontré una americana   ] *Bis*
y me hizo una caravana,
me dijo: —Like you me?—
—Si yo no te busco a ti,
yo busco a mi Severiana.—

8

In short, in order not to get tired
I went down to Río Bonito
Passing by Antoñito
And I came to Las Vegas;
In passing through San Miguel
I met an American girl
And I bowed to her.
She said, "Like you me?"
"I'm not looking for you,
I'm looking for my Severiana."

9

Llegué a la plaza de abajo
a Mora, verán ustedes,
y enfinidad de mujeres.

9

I went to the plaza
Below Mora, you'll see,
There is an infinity of women.

Pero yo me fuí de atajo,
deseando mal y malajo   ]
y ¡ay, qué suerte tan tirana!   ] Bis
Cuando me encontró una Juana
que me saludó cortés,
pero yo le hablé en inglés;
—Me looking for Severiana.—

But I kept on going
To see what would happen.
And, oh, what a sad fate!
When I met a girl from San Juan
And she greeted me with courtesy.
I spoke to her in English:
"Me looking for Severiana."

10

Donde me dieron posada
dí el caballo por un burro,
pues ahora voy de seguro
y hasta donde me dé la gana.
En este burro mañana
camino con elegancia,
y ¡ay, Dios! que me muero de ansia
buscando a mi Severiana.

Where they gave me lodging
I gave a horse for a burro,
So now I am going safely
Wherever I want to go.
On this burro tomorrow
I'll travel in style,
But—oh, Lord!—I'm dying of anxiety
Looking for my Severiana.

11

(Verso 9 se repite)

(Verse 9 repeated)

12

(Verso 8 se repite)

(Verse 8 repeated)

This is a *relación* in the form of a *décima*, sung not to the traditional *décima* melody but rather to another interesting melody that sounds like that of an *indita* with medieval-style modulations (Aeolian—Ionian—Aeolian) and *musica ficta* alterations (see Robb 13, pp. 6–8). Elfego Gonzáles of San Ildefonso, New Mexico, told me, during a field trip, that this song was composed by his father, Higinio V. Gonzáles, a famed composer of the turn of the century who died about 1915. My records include a copy of a notebook of Gonzáles and a considerable amount of information about his interesting life. The many village names mentioned in *La Severiana* are familiar to New Mexico residents.

D5. *Canción Inglés* (English Song)
R8, Próspero S. Baca, Bernalillo, N.Mex., 1945, Robb. Cf. Folkways Album P4426, R492, R1725.

1

Desde que llegué a este punto
ya voy aprendiendo inglés,
y estoy tan aventajado
que ya aprendí a decir, *"yes."*

1

Since I came to this place
I have begun to learn English,
And I am already so advanced
That I have learned to say, "yes."

2

Sé contar perfectamente
del número *one* al *ten;*
saludar con el *good morning,*
good morning, how are you, my friend.

2

I can count perfectly
From the number one to ten;
Greet a person with good morning,
Good morning, how are you, my friend.

3

Oyeme, americana.
No desprecies nuestra lengua;
que sería derrota y mengua
el ser americano.

3

Listen to me, American girl.
Don't despise our language;
That would be to lessen our pride
In being American.

4

Yo soy un mexicanito
de la lengua verdadera.
Ya no quiero una morenita;
no quiero más que a mi güera.

4

I am a little Mexican
Of the true language.
I do not want a little brunette;
I only want my blonde.

5

Si no quieras que esté mudo
pregunte: ¿Cómo estás tu?
salude con el *good morning,*
good morning, how are you?

5

Unless you want me to be silent,
Ask me, "cómo estás?"
Greet me with a good morning,
Good morning, how are you?

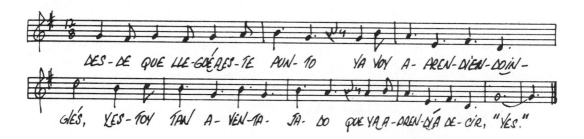

DES-DE QUE LLE-GÉ A ES-TE PUN-TO YA VOY A-PREN-DIEN-DO IN-GLÉS, YES-TOY TAN A-VEN-TA-JA-DO QUE YA A-PREN-DÍ A DE-CIR, "YES."

The comedians who frequent the fiestas in New Mexican villages find the interpolation of English words a never-failing source of amusement for their audiences. This device is employed in the *Canción Inglés.* A percussive sound is made by the singer as he keeps time with his foot. This is one of a number of versions (all different) of the song collected in New Mexico (cf. Campa 2, p. 214). In one of these (R1725) the lively interest of the people in new developments, such as the railroad train, is revealed. Other songs displaying a like interest are *El Ferrocarril* (C91–91b) and *Luz Eléctrica* (R533).

D6. *Leonor*
R304, Jacabo Maestas, age 67, Llano de San Juan, N.Mex., 1950, Robb. Cf. R2410. See also Appendix A.

1
En un llano muy la-la-la-la-la-la-la-la-la-la-largo
se paseaba un cantador,
cantando las mañani-ti-ti-ti-ti-ti-ti-ti-ti-ti-ti-tas
de mi querida Leonor.

Estribillo
Despierta, Leonor,
despierta, Leonor,
despierta, Leonor,
adiós, adiós, Leonor.

2
En un bosque muy la-la-la-la-la-la-la-la-la-la-largo
se paseaba un cazador,
buscando los venaditi-ti-ti-ti-ti-ti-ti-ti-ti-tos
de mi querida Leonor.

Estribillo

3
En un río muy la-la-la-la-la-la-la-la-la-la-largo
se paseaba un pescador,
pescando los pescariti-ti-ti-ti-ti-ti-ti-ti-ti-tos
de mi querida Leonor.

Estribillo

1
In a plain very la-la-la-la-la-la-la-la-la-la-large-o
There passed by a troubadour,
And he sang a song of da-da-da-da-da-da-da-da-da-da-dawning
Of my dearest love, Leonore.

Refrain
Awaken, Leonore,
Awaken, Leonore,
Awaken, Leonore,
Farewell, farewell, Leonore.

2
In a wood very la-la-la-la-la-la-la-la-la-la-large-o
There passed by a hunter,
Hunting for the de-de-de-de-de-de-de-de-de-de-deer-o
Of my dearest love, Leonore.

Refrain

3
In a river very la-la-la-la-la-la-la-la-la-la-large-o
There passed by a fisherman,
Fishing for the ti-ti-ti-ti-ti-ti-ti-ti-ti-ti-ti-tiny fish
Of my dearest love, Leonore.

Refrain

EN UN LLA-NO MU-Y LA-LA-LA-LA-LA-LA-LA-LA-LA-LA-LAR — GO SE AA-
SEA-BAUN CAN-TA-DOR, CAN-TAN-DO LAS MA-ÑA-NI-TI-TI-TI-TI-TI-TI-TI-TI-TI-

TI- TAS DE MI QUE-RI-DA LEO-NOR . DE-SPIER-TA, LEO-NOR, DE-SPIER-TA LEO-NOR, DE-SPIER-TA, LEO-NOR , A- DIÓS, A- DIÓS, LEO- NOR .

D7. *La Enfermedad de los Fríos* (The Sickness of the Chills)
R225, Juan Luján, age 66, Riverside, N.Mex., 1949, Robb. Cf. R160, R429, R622.

Planta

La enfermedad de los fríos
no hallo como puedan ser.
Estos traen mil disvaríos,
son de quitar y poner.

Planta

The sickness of the chills
I find hard to understand.
The chills give you hallucinations
And they come and go.

1

De repente están temblando,
de repente abochornados,
a ratos andan andando
doliéndoles los costados
y allí caen rematados
que no pueden ni comer,
sólo pura agua beber
sin cortarse la sequía
y si pienso todo un día
no hallo como puedan ser.

1

Suddenly you are shivering,
Suddenly sweltering,
They come and go,
Leaving you ruined
With your insides aching so
That you cannot even eat,
Only drink pure water
Without assuaging your thirst,
And if I think all day,
I can't understand it.

2

Tengan presente, señores,
él que sea de más valor:
le han de pegar los temblores
en la fuerza de la calor;
también un fuerte dolor
que traspasa los vacíos;
les pega a hermanos y tíos
en la fuerza de la calor.

2

Pay attention, gentlemen,
He who is really brave
Will still get the chills
Even in the hottest weather;
Also a sharp pain
Which pierces your entrails;
It strikes family and relatives
Even in the hottest weather.

3

Llegaron a Santa Cruz,
pasaron por Los Ranchitos,
los dejaron afirús,
pegándoles a toditos,
lo mismo a grandes que a chicos
que aquél que mira a doctor,
éstos le hacen el favor;
aunque los vean borrachos,
les da a viejos y a muchachos,
en la fuerza de la calor.

3

They came to Santa Cruz,
Then passed on to Los Ranchitos,
It left them dizzy,
Sparing no one,
Big and little alike,
Even those who had the good fortune
To see a doctor.
They didn't overlook the drunks,
The old men and boys,
Even in the hottest weather.

4

Dicen que la quina es buena,
el doctor la recetó,
pero yo les digo asina
que unos sanan, y otros no,
y esta enfermedad corrió
por todos los pobladores,
y hasta los más habladores
los hace comer molido
y no lo echen en olvido,
tengan presente, señores.

5

El juisque es otro remedio
que llevándole interés,
mézclendo con enjengibre
y échenle tantita nuez;
pues yo me curé una vez
se me fueron los dolores
y hasta los más habladores
han de nadar con disvaríos
porque éstos sí les echan grillos
que no los dejan ni andar
y a nadien han de agraviar,
les pega a hermanos y tíos.

6

Los viejos quiero decir
de la enfermedad tan fea,
que quedan a no servir
si no estacan la zalea,
porque éstos no pintan huella
pero caminan mejor,
y éstos le hacen el favor
aunque los vean borrachos,
les da a viejos y a muchachos
en la fuerza de la calor.

7

Les pegó a los naturales
en el pueblo de San Juan,
y en la plaza del Alcalde,
y aquí estos mismos dirán
porque esto es como un refrán
que en toditos permanece
cada día que amanece,
según yo voy conociendo,
y a una voz todos diciendo
pues, señor, ¿de qué padece?

8

Llegaron al Bosque Grande
y en La Joya los dejó
ves, para éstos no hay alcalde
ni alguacil que los citó,

4

They say that quinine is good
And the doctor prescribed it.
But I say this:
It cures some and others no,
And this sickness spread
Through all the towns.
It even makes the gossips
Eat their words.
And don't forget it,
Remember this, gentlemen.

5

Whiskey is another remedy
And those who try it
Mix it with ginger
And a little nutmeg;
Well, I cured myself once
And my pains went away,
But even the most talkative ones
Suffer from hallucinations
Because they have them in chains
So that they cannot even walk
And they don't have to overlook anyone,
The disease strikes brothers and uncles.

6

I want to ask the old folks
About this bad sickness,
Whether it does any good
To stay in bed.
The chills leave no trail
And they travel like the wind,
And they are kind enough
To visit even the drunks.
It hits both old men and boys
In the hottest weather.

7

It also hits the natives
In the Indian pueblo of San Juan,
And in the town of Alcalde,
And here they say the same thing
For it is like a refrain
That it stays with everyone
Every day that dawns,
As I understand it.
And everyone exclaims with one voice,
Well, sir, from what do you suffer?

8

The chills came to Bosque Grande
And stayed in La Joya awhile,
For there was no mayor
Or constable to arrest them,

y esta enfermedad corrió
por todos los pobladores,
y no lo echen en olvido,
tengan presente, señores.

And this sickness spread
Throughout all the towns,
And don't forget it,
Remember this, gentlemen.

9

Llegaron a La Villita
y a la plaza de Los Luceros,
se pasaron para Chamita
por casados y solteros;
porque hasta los más guerreros
han de andar con desvaríos,
porque éstos sí les echan grillos
que no los dejan ni andar
y a nadien han de agraviar,
les pega a hermanos y tíos.

They came to La Villita
And to the town of Los Luceros,
Passed on to Chamita
Attacking married and single alike;
Because even the bravest ones
Suffer from hallucinations
Because they have them in chains
So that they cannot even walk
And they don't have to overlook anyone,
The disease even hit brothers and uncles.

10

Se pasaron para el Tizón,
y la placita del Guache;
no reservan ni al apache
ni a cualquiera otra nación.
Ha aceptado a religión
ésto se le da a entender,
que no hay más que padecer
hasta que Dios determine,
y cuando bien se examine
son de quitar y poner.

They passed through Tizón,
And the town of Guache;
They didn't even spare the Apache
Or any other nation.
Religion has accepted this
As understandable,
For there is nothing to do but suffer
Until God determines otherwise.
And however you look at it, well,
They come and go.

11

Llegan a la Plaza Larga,
pasaron por la Angostura,
porque éstes nunca se atrasan,
siempre la llevan segura
y al corral de Piedra Pura
haremos unos avíos
que pasen a Los Cerrillos
y vuelvan a Santa Fe.
Yo en Pojoaque comencé
a padecer estos fríos.

They come to Plaza Larga,
Then pass on to Angostura,
Because they would never delay.
Always they come, you can be sure,
And at the corral of Piedra Pura
We'll try and get them
To go to Los Cerrillos
And return to Santa Fe.
In Pojoaque I began
To suffer from these chills.

12

Soy más fino que un reloj
que nadien me da doctrina.
Digan todos de una voz,
que al que no le guste asina,
que la voluntad de Dios
es la mejor medecina.

I am finer than a watch
And no one can teach me doctrine.
Everyone says with one voice,
Whether you like it or not,
To accept the will of God
Is the best medicine.

LA EN-FER- ME-DAD DE LOS FRÍ-OS NO HA-LLO   CÓ -MO PUE-DAN SER. ES-TOS TRAEN MIL DIS-VA-

RÍ-OS, SON DE QUI-TAR Y DO-NER. DE RE-PEN-TE ES-TÁN TEM-BLAN-DO, DE RE-
PEN-TE A-BO-CHOR-NA-DOS, A RA-TOS AN-DAN AN-DAN-DO DO-LIÉN-DO-LE LOS CO-
STA-DOS Y A-LLÍ CA-EN RE-MA-TA-DOS QUE NO PUE-DEN NI CO-MER, SÓ-LO
PU-RA-GUA BE-BER SIN COR-TAR-SE LA SE-QUÍ-A Y SI PIEN-SO TO-DO UN DÍ-A NO HA-LLO
CÓ - MO PUE-DAN SER.

Like *La Severiana* (D4), this *relación* was composed by the late Higinio V. Gonzales, whose songs sometimes betray a lively sense of humor. It resembles a very irregular, perhaps degenerated or garbled, *décima*.

D7a. *La Enfermedad de los Fríos*
R160, Pedro Trujillo y Chacón, Cebolla, N.Mex., 1949, Robb.

La enfermedad de los fríos
no hallo como puedan ser.
Estos tremeldiarillos
Son de quitar y poner.

The sickness of the chills
I cannot understand it.
The shivering
Comes and goes.

1
De repente están temblando
de repente abochornados
a ratos andan andando
doliéndoles los costados.
Y allí caen rematados
que no pueden ni comer.
Solo pura agua beber
sin cortarle la sequía
y si pienso todo un día
no hallo como puedan ser.

1
Suddenly they're trembling,
Suddenly sweltering,
At times they walk
With pains in their sides.
And they fall like dead
For they cannot even eat.
They can only drink water
Without quenching their dryness
And if I think a whole day
I cannot understand it.

2
Y llegaron al Tizón
y a la placita del Guache;
no reservan al Apache
pero a ninguna nación

2
They arrived at Tizón
And at the little town of Guache;
They don't spare the Apaches,
But also no other people

a cualquiera religión.
esto se le da a entender
que no hay más que padecer
hasta que Dios determine
que cuando bien se examine
son de quitar y poner.

3

El ajo dicen que es bueno
y yerba buena del campo,
pues en esto no hay rebajo
para aquél que padece tanto.
Por eso caigo y levanto
porque yo he hecho poderillos.
He bebido tacarillos
por no beber el agua pura,
pero con la calentura
tenemos mil desvaríos.

4

El whiskey dicen que es bueno
y el doctor lo recetó,
pero yo le digo a Dina
unos sanan y otros no.
Y esta enfermedad corrió
por todos los pobladadores
y hasta a los más habladores
los echó a comer molido.
No tengan en olvido.
Tengan presente, Señores!

5

El chamizo hediondo
dicen que hace operación.
Dios ha de poner un fondo
para todita la nación
y a cualquiera religión.
Esto se le da a entender
que no hay más que padecer
hasta que Dios determine
que cuando bien se examine
son de quitar y poner.

6

A la plaza larga llegan
pasando por Angostura
porque ésta nunca se atrasa.
Siempre la llevan segura
y al corral de piedra pura
pondremos unos ladrillos.
Que pasen a Santa Fe
y lleguen a Los Cerrilos
y en Pojoaque comencé
a componer estos fríos.

Of any religion.
This can be understood
That one must suffer
Till God decrees otherwise
For when you look at it calmly
The chills come and go.

3

They say garlic is good
And herbs from the country,
Well, in this there is no improvement
For him who suffers so much.
That is why I fall and rise
Because I have made efforts.
I have drunk tacarillos
So as not to drink pure water,
But with fever
We have a thousand deliriums.

4

They say whiskey is good
And the doctor prescribed it,
But I say to Dina
Some get well and some do not.
And this sickness spread
Through all the villages
And even those who talked most
Were made to eat flour.
Do not forget!
Always remember, gentlemen!

5

The smelly chamiza
Works, they say.
God will set a limit
For the whole nation
And of any religion.
This must be understood,
That one must suffer
Until God decrees otherwise
For when you look at it calmly
The chills just come and go.

6

They reach the long plaza
Passing by way of Angostura
For they are never late.
They are inevitable
And to the stone corral
We shall add a few bricks.
Next they come to Santa Fe
And then to Cerrillos
And in Pojoaque I began
To compose these chills.

7

Les pegó a los naturales
del Pueblo de San Juan
y en la plaza de Alcalde
pues esto mismo dirán
porque esto es como un refrán.
Han de quedar amarillos
y de diferentes colores
y aunque quieran detenerse
les han de pegar los temblores.

7

They attack the natives
Of the San Juan pueblo
And in the town of Alcalde
It's the same story
For it's like a refrain.
People turn yellow
And different colors
And although they want to hold them back
Still the chills will get them.

8

Llegan al orilla
de la plaza de los Luceros
y allí les pegó a todos
por casados y solteros.
Ya . . .

8

They come to the edge
Of the town of the Luceros
And there they hit everyone
Both married and single.
Already . . .

D8. *Las Lindas Mexicanas* (The Pretty Mexican Girls)
R278, Macario Leyva, Leyva, N.Mex., 1950, Robb.

1	1
¡Ay! Mexicanas ingratas	Ah, ungrateful Mexican girls
que no comprenden lo que es.	Who don't understand how it is!
Desprecian a un mexicano	They look down on a Mexican man
porque les hablan inglés.	Because he speaks to them in English.

2	2
Estando un tiempo en Italia,	Being at one time in Italy,
conocí las italianas,	I got to know the Italian girls,
y en Inglaterra unas inglesas,	And in England some English girls,
pero esas hablan mexicana.	But they speak Mexican.

3	3
(Verse 1 se repite)	(Verse 1 repeated)

4	4
Distintas tierras he andado	I have visited various countries
reconociendo las damas.	Getting acquainted with the ladies.
De cual te doy las inglesas	Of them all I give you the English
porque odian las mexicanas.	Because they hate the Mexican women.

5	5
(Verse 1 se repite)	(Verse 1 repeated)

DISPARATE

D9. *Los Animales* (The Animals)
R206, Patricio Pacheco, Chimayó, N.Mex., 1949, Robb.

1

Es cuestión de ver al juez
lo que hacen los animales.
Yo los ví cocer tamales
y sacarlos a vender.

2

Esto pasó por mi vista.
Escúcheme por favor.
Yo vide de motorista
un conejo y un ratón—
y un sapo de conductor.
(Risita)

3

Cuando se casó la rata
Hubo música especial
le tocaron clarinete
tres burros y un pavo real.

4

Este baile continuó
poco después de las siete,
un sapo tocaba el piano
y una liebre el clarinete.
(Risita)

5

Cuando ya se emborracharon
la culpa tuvo un conejo
a trompadas se agarraron
tres caimanes y un cangrejo.

6

Los charifes celosos
a la cárcel los llevaron
y en diez pesos los multaron
por ebrios y escandalosos.

1

What the animals did
Is a question for the judge.
I myself saw them cooking tamales
And taking them out to sell.

2

This passed before my eyes.
Kindly listen.
I saw a train go by
With a rabbit and a mouse for engineers—
And a large toad for conductor.
(Giggles)

3

When the lady rat got married
Three burros and a peacock
Played special music
On the clarinet.

4

This dance continued
Until a little after seven,
A large toad played the piano
And a hare the clarinet.
(Giggles)

5

When they all got drunk—
It was all the fault of a rabbit—
They all started fighting,
Three alligators and a crab.

6

The zealous sheriffs
Took them all to jail
And fined them ten pesos
For drunken and scandalous conduct.

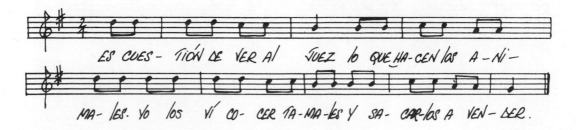

After the second and fourth verses the singer giggles, and after a struggle to recover control of himself, he continues. The same charming and amusing thing occurs and is recorded at the conclusion of two other songs, *Arroz con Leche* (D15) and *Tango, Tarango, Tango* (D36).

D10. *Arre, Arre, Mi Burrito* (Git up, Git up, My Little Burro)
R991, Carolyn Waring, San Miguel Regla, Mexico, 1952, Robb. Cf. WPA 19 (p. 22).

<table>
<tr><td>

1
¡Arre que llegando al caminito!
Aquí me chu', aquí me chu',
Aquí me chubo a mi burrito
aunque vaya enojadito
porque no le dí su alfalfa,
porque no le dí su maíz.

</td><td>

1
Git up! We're heading for the road!
I'm getting on, I'm getting on,
I'm getting on my little burro
Even though he is a little angry
Because I didn't give him his alfalfa,
Because I didn't give him his corn.

</td></tr>
<tr><td>

2
Pobrecito mi burrito
ya no quiere caminar.
Da unos pasos para adelante
y otros pasos para atrás.

</td><td>

2
My poor little burro
He doesn't want to go.
He takes a few steps forward,
Then he takes a few steps back.

</td></tr>
<tr><td>

3
Arre, arre, mi burrito,
ya no me hagas enojar.
Que ya pronto llegaremos
y te voy a dar tu maíz.

</td><td>

3
Git up, git up, my little burro,
Don't get mad at me.
Soon we'll get there
And I'll give you your corn.

</td></tr>
</table>

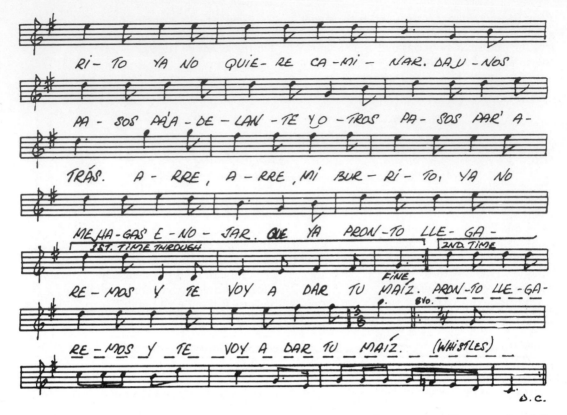

RI-TO YA NO QUIE-RE CA-MI-NAR. DAJU-NOS

PA-SOS AĄÁ-DE-LAN-TE Y O-TROS PA-SOS PAR' A-

TRÁS. A-RRE, A-RRE, MI BUR-RI-TO, YA NO

ME HA-GAS E-NO-JAR. QUE YA PRON-TO LLE-GA-

RE-MOS Y TE VOY A DAR TU MAÍZ. PRON-TO LLE-GA-

RE-MOS Y TE VOY A DAR TU MAÍZ. (WHISTLES)

This is probably of Mexican origin, because few burros are used in the Southwest as beasts of burden, whereas in Mexico they have been common. However, this is a Texas version sung by a young Texan in San Miguel Regla, Mexico. A different tune and words are to be found in the *Spanish American Song and Game Book* (WPA 19, p. 22).

D11. *Los Animalitos* (The Little Animals)
R152, Tomás Archuleta, Abiquiu, N.Mex., 1949, Robb.

<table>
<tr><td>

1
Unos animalitos (3 times)
se mueren de hambre. (2 times)

</td><td>

1
Some animals
Are dying of hunger.

</td></tr>
<tr><td>

2
Y porque son huerfanitos (3 times)
de padre y madre. (2 times)

</td><td>

2
Because they are orphans,
No father or mother.

</td></tr>
<tr><td>

3
Yo soy como la hiedra (3 times)
que me mantengo
por las paredes.

</td><td>

3
I am like the ivy
For I hang
On the walls.

</td></tr>
<tr><td>

4
De tu cama a la mía (3 times)
no hay más de un paso. (2 times)

</td><td>

4
From your bed to mine
Is not more than a step.

</td></tr>
</table>

5

De las aves del viento (3 times)
me gusta el cuervo. (2 times)

5

Of the birds of the wind
I like the crow.

6

Y porque mi amor se viste (3 times)
de puro negro. (2 times)

6

Because my love dresses
In pure black.

7

De tres camisas que tengo (3 times)
dos no me vienen. (2 times)

7

Of three shirts that I have
Two don't fit me.

8

Y porque están en la tienda (3 times)
donde las venden
las rete venden.

8

Because they are in the shop
Where they sell them,
Sell them—but not cheap.

Tomás Archuleta, the singer, was blind but was gifted with perfect pitch. He was in demand as a piano tuner and also as a fiddler at country dances in his area of New Mexico.

Tomás Archuleta, singer of *Los Animalitos* (D11), and his wife, outside their adobe home in Tierra Azul, New Mexico, 1949.

D12. *Una Gorra Galonada* (A Precious Cap)
R2397, Juan Griego, age 61, Albuquerque, N.Mex., 1971, Cipriano Griego. Cf. R536.

1	1
Una gorra galonada se ha perdido,	A precious cap has been lost,
Tula, Amada, y Adelaida sí la hallaron,	Tula, Amada, and Adelaida found it,
y la jugaron, la empañaron, la jugaron,	They played with it, hocked it, played with it,
en la tienda del Rey sabio Solomón.	In wise King Solomon's store.

2	2
Solomón de ver tanta porfía	When Solomon saw so much excitement
les dió vino hasta que se emborracharon,	He gave them wine until they were drunk,
y la jugaron, la empañaron, la jugaron,	They played with it, hocked it, played with it,
en la tienda del Rey sabio Solomón.	In wise King Solomon's store.

3	3
Tula dice: —¡Qué bonita gorra!—	Tula said: "What a pretty cap."
Adelaida: —¡Qué bonito está el comal!	Adelaida: "What a pretty skillet.
Tomaremos, fumaremos marijuana,	We will drink and smoke marijuana,
y dejaremos de moler el nistamal.	And forget about grinding nistamal."

D13. *Doña Clara*
R424, Manuel Chávez, Albuquerque, N.Mex., 1950, Robb.

1		1
La vecina de aquí enfrente,	] *Bis*	The neighbor woman across the street,
se llamaba Doña Clara,		Was named Doña Clara.
y ay, ay, ay, ay.		Ay, ay, ay, ay,
Y si no se hubiera muerto,	] *Bis*	And if she hadn't died yet,
todavía se llamara,		Then she'd still be called Clara,
ay, ay, ay, ay.		Ay, ay, ay, ay.

<table>
<tr><td>

2

La vecina de aquí enfrente,
tenía un gato barato,
y ay, ay, ay, ay.
Y le dice a su marido,
—Mira, mi alma, tu retrato.—
Ay, ay, ay, ay.

</td><td>

] *Bis*

] *Bis*

</td><td>

2

The neighbor woman across the street,
Had a cheap cat,
Ay, ay, ay, ay.
And she says to her husband,
"Look, my soul, at your picture."
Ay, ay, ay, ay.

</td></tr>
<tr><td>

3

Su mamá le dice a Julia,
—¿Qué te dice ese señor?—
Ay, ay, ay, ay.
—Mamá, no me dice nada,
sólo me trataba de amores.—
Ay, ay, ay, ay.

</td><td>

] *Bis*

] *Bis*

</td><td>

3

Her mama says to Julia,
"What does that man say to you?"
Ay, ay, ay, ay.
"Mama, he doesn't say anything to me,
He only makes love."
Ay, ay, ay, ay.

</td></tr>
</table>

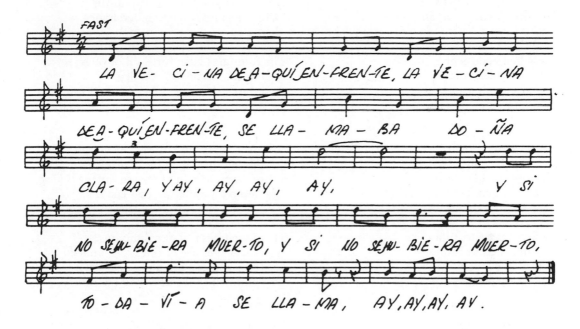

D14. *La Ciudad de Juaja* (The City of Juaja)
R1715, Próspero S. Baca, age 70, Bernalillo, N.Mex., 1945, Robb.

<table>
<tr><td>

1

Desde la ciudad de Juaja
me mandan solicitar,
que me vaya, que me vaya,
de un tesoro a disfrutar.

</td><td>

1

From the far city of Juaja
They sent a card to invite me
To come and partake of a treasure
That they were sure would delight me.

</td></tr>
<tr><td>

2

¿Qué dices, amigo, vamos
a ver si dicen verdad?
Si es verdad de lo que dicen
nos quedamos por allá.

</td><td>

2

What do you say, shall we go, pal?
Let's go and see what we learn.
If it's the truth that they tell us,
We'll probably never return.

</td></tr>
</table>

<table>
<tr><td>

3

Los cerros son de tortillas,
las quebradas de buñuelos,
las piedras, frutas cubiertas,
pinos con los caramelos.

</td><td>

3

The hills are made of tortillas
The valleys of fritters are made,
The stones are fruit, and the pine cones
Are with caramel overlaid.

</td></tr>
</table>

3

Los cerros son de tortillas,
las quebradas de buñuelos,
las piedras, frutas cubiertas,
pinos con los caramelos.

3

The hills are made of tortillas
The valleys of fritters are made,
The stones are fruit, and the pine cones
Are with caramel overlaid.

4

Para toditos los flojos
es un punto regular,
porque allí le dan de palos
al que quiere trabajar.

4

Everyone sits in the sunlight,
And that is the daily routine.
If you're caught working they beat you,
Unless you can do it unseen.

5

Con cinco mercas chaqueta,
con cuartía, pantalón;
con un real mercas el terno,
sombrero, leva, y bastón.

5

Five cents will buy you a jacket,
A quarter will buy you some pants.
For a buck you can buy an outfit,
With cane and sombrero perchance.

6

Pilares llenos de aceite,
llenos y sin derramar;
por allá vuelan los patos
con su pimienta y su sal.

6

The fountains gush forth oil of olives,
And never, no never, run dry.
And the ducks come seasoned and salted,
As they fly on their way through the sky.

7

Hay un arroyo de leche,
un arroyo de café,
una montaña de queso
y una montaña de té.

7

A brook full of milk flows through it,
There's another of coffee nearby.
There's a mountain of cheese for the taking,
And a mountain of tea you can try.

8

Hay árboles de tortillas,
hay gumatitos de atole,
con tatitas de menudo
y patitas de posole.

8

There are trees full of sopaipillas,
And the leaves are of finest corn meal.
For tripe you can dig up the rootlets,
Or hominy if that's how you feel.

9

De todo les doy razón
de todo lo que yo ví,
traiban el talón rajado
como las de por aquí.

9

Now in spite of all that I tell you,
And all of the things I have seen,
I still walk around here barefooted,
Like the rest of you people, I mean.

D15. *Arroz con Leche* (Rice with Milk)
R1913, Edna Garrido de Boggs, Albuquerque, N.Mex., 1963, Robb.

1

Arroz con leche,
se quiere casar
con una viudita
de la capital.

1

Rice pudding,
He wants to marry
A little widow
From the capital.

2	**2**
Que sepa tejer,	Who knows how to knit,
que sepa bordar,	And how to embroider,
que ponga la mesa	Who sets the table
en su mismo lugar.	In its proper place.
Coro	*Chorus*
Ding, dong,	Ding, dong,
sopita de pan,	A sop of bread.
¡si no me la dan!	If they'd only give me some!
(Risa)	(Laughter)
3	**3**
Yo soy la viudita	I am the little widow
del Conde Laurel;	Of Count Laurel;
quisiera casarme,	I want to get married
y no encuentro con quien.	But I can't find the right one.
4	**4**
Por ser tú tan bella	Since you are so beautiful
y no encuentras con quien,	And can't find anyone,
elige a tu gusto,	Choose at your pleasure
que aquí tienes cien.	For here you have a hundred.
5	**5**
Contigo sí,	With you, yes;
contigo no,	With you, no;
contigo, mi vida,	With you, my life,
me casaré yo.	I will be married.

D16. *En Capricho*
R55, Juan Sandoval, Chimayó, N.Mex., 1945, Robb.

1	**1**
En capricho y en muy mala ropa ¡ay, ay, ay!	Whimsically—and in bad attire, ay, ay, ay!
mi muchacha conmigo riñó;	My girl started quarreling with me;
se pasaron seis días sin verla]	For six days I didn't see her
y mi amor olvidarla intentó.] *Bis*	With intent to forget her.

2

A las cinco paseaba la joven, ¡ay, ay, ay!
Bajo un verde naranjo me halló.
Bajo un verde y pulido naranjo   ]
una tarde a la puesta del sol.   ] Bis

3

Hablado:
Cuando la ví venir me puse a persignar.
sacudiendo mi levita nada más, preguntando:

Estribillo
—¿Cómo va? ¿Cómo ha ido?
Me habían dicho que ibas a casar.—   ] Bis

4

Y apenas me oyó la maldita, ¡ay, ay, ay!
luego al pelo la mano me echó;
me tiraba confusa y decía:
—Perro, pícaro, infame, traidor.—   ] Bis

5

Hablado:
—Suelte, suelte, señorita, ¿que está usted
    loca?—

—Ande, perro, infame, traidor;
que usted ama a otra más que a mí.—
—¿Cómo he de amar otra más que a usted?
    Siendo así.

Estribillo
Se acabaron las delicias,
se acabaron los enojos
y otras cosas que suelen pasar.   ] Bis

2

At five she came walking, ay, ay, ay!
She found me in the shade of an orange tree.
Under this green and clean tree
One afternoon at sunset.

3

Spoken:
When I saw her coming, I crossed myself.
I shook my coat and asked:

Refrain
"Howdy do?
I hear you're getting married."

4

The minute the shrew heard me, ay, ay, ay!
She pulled my hair, then and there;
And she called me:
"You dog! You ill-bred, infamous traitor!"

5

Spoken:
"Let go, let go, Miss, are you crazy?"

"You dog, ill-bred, infamous traitor!
Do you love another more than me?"
"How could I love another?
    Being as it is."

Refrain
So ended all delight,
So ended all discord
And so end cases like this.

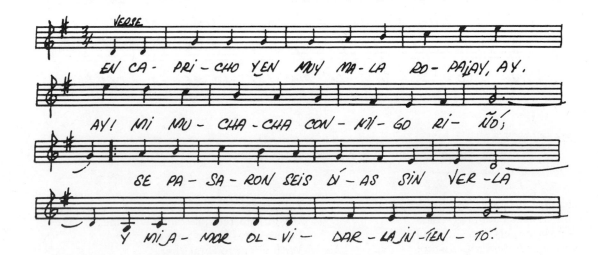

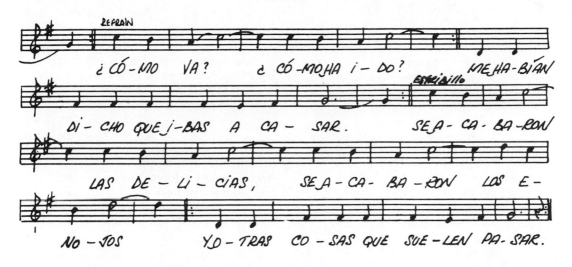

D17. *La Vaca del Condado* (The County Cow)
R538, Francisco S. Leyva, age 81, Leyva, N.Mex., 1951, Robb.

1		1
Les cantaré unos versitos	]	I am going to sing some verses
de una vaquita afamada,	] *Bis*	About a famous little cow,
que es la vaca del condado		The cow of the county
numerosa de pesada,		She is very heavy and nervous,
y él que pesca descuidado		And he whom she catches off guard
lo vuelva de una patada.		She overturns with one kick.

Refrán	*Refrain*
Ta-da-dum-ta-dum-ta-da y	Ta-da-dum-ta-dum-ta-da y
li-lai-la-la-la-li	li-lai-la-la-la-li
di-di-la-la-ta-ta	di-di-la-la-ta-ta
di-di-di-la.	di-di-di-la.

2		2
Cuando esta vaca se para	]	When this cow stops
dos partidos la rodean,	] *Bis*	Two calves surround her,
le ven las chiches		They see her udder full
todos quieren mamar de ella,		All of them want to nurse from it
tratan de sus convenciones		They attend to their business
y salen a la carrera.		And then start racing around.

Refrán	*Refrain*

3		3
Esta vaca en los condados	]	This cow is not to be found
no la encuentran donde quiera,	] *Bis*	Just anywhere in the counties,
le hace formar un tesoro		She is a treasure
donde en ella se halla,		Wherever she is found,
y es causar que los empleados		And this is why the employees
de ambiciones se desesperan.		Are desperate with ambition.

4

Muy gorda está la vaca,   ]
Fina aumentada de leche   ] *Bis*
para ordeñarla los empleados
aguardan que sola se eche
para ordeñarla sin apuro
como dueños de la leche.

4

The cow is very fat,
Full of fine milk
In order for the employees to milk her
They wait for her to lie down
In order to milk her without anxiety
As owners of the milk.

5

Diferente está la vaca   ]
aunque esté de leche aumentada   ] *Bis*
y al que pierde la carrera
le amarga la saboriada
dice que la leche es fea
porque la vaca está echada.

5

This cow is different
Although she is full of milk
And to him who loses the race
It is bitter to the taste
And he says that the milk is terrible
Because the cow is lying down.

6

Vean en la casa de corte,   ]
las aguilitas pintadas,   ] *Bis*
dentro de las oficinas
están con la vaca echada,
el pueblo les dió el derecho
que las uñas le enterrarán.

6

See in the courthouse
The little painted eagles
And inside in the offices
They are with the cow lying down,
The people gave them the right
To sink their nails in the cow.

7

Arrímense a una roleta   ]
y verán voltear la rueda;   ] *Bis*
pobres los perdedores
no más el ardor les queda
para agarrar el pago doble,
con la bolsa seca quedan.

7

Draw near a roulette table
And you will see the wheel turn;
The poor losers
Only their bitterness is left,
They try double or nothing
And end up with an empty purse.

8

Amigos me quedé tonto   ]
yo no me pude educar,   ] *Bis*
tengan paciencia a los tontos
que no pudimos mamar,
pero aquél que lo merece
lo debemos de botar.

8

Friends, I have remained ignorant
I could not educate myself,
Have patience with the ignorant
For we were not able to nurse,
But we know one thing: There are those
Who deserve to be thrown out.

9

Si la vaca nueva viene   ]
con la vieja se va a amar   ] *Bis*
y en poder de americanos
sólo que sabe añudar;
novillos los mexicanos
no los saben fabricar.

9

If the new cow arrives
She gets ready to fight with the old,
And only by the power of the Americans
Do they know how to unite;
The Mexicans are amateurs,
They don't know how to do it.

10

Dicen venía la vaca   ]
del patente mantequilla   ] *Bis*
era delgada la leche
se detuvo todavía
esperar que más engruesa
que sea Inglés la mantequilla.

10

They say the cow was coming
But the milk was too thin
To make good butter,
But still she held it back
Waiting for it to thicken
And make English butter.

342

11

Un Indio me dió un consejo   ]
en un idioma *graseja:*   ] *Bis*
cuando Indio sea Español
entonces la cabra—oveja
mexicano-americano,
pero la sangre no deja.

11

An Indian gave me some advice
In a *graseja* (?) language:
When an Indian becomes a Spaniard,
Then the she-goat becomes a
Mexican-American ewe,
But the blood does not cease to run.

12

Llegamos al año nuevo   ]
saludando el nuevo estado,   ] *Bis*
trabajan con honradez
todos los nuevos empleados.
No les vayan a suceder
lo que a los malos casados.

12

We come to the new year
Saluting the new state,
May all the new employees
Work with honesty.
Don't let happen to you
What happens to the badly married.

La Vaca del Condado, a satire on the seekers
of jobs and other forms of political spoil, is
from Valencia County, New Mexico.

D18. *Frijolitos Pintos* (Little Pinto Beans)
R2479, Edwin Berry, Tomé, N.Mex., 1972, Robb.

1

Frijolitos pintos,
blancos y morados.
¡Ay, cómo sufren
los enamorados!

1

Little pinto beans,
White and purple.
Oh! How they suffer
Who are in love!

Refrán

Le pegó virhuela,
le dió el zarampión;
le quedó la cara
como un chicharrón.

2

¡Ay! viene mi suegra
bajando la loma,
brinco la leña
y hecha la maroma.

Refrán

3

Andale muchacha,
ahí viene Vicente.
Sácale un banquito
para que se siente.

Refrán

4

Una perra pinta,
pinta y orejona,
le buscaban cola
y la tenía rabona.

5

Ahí viene el borracho
empinando la botella,
corre muchacha,
sube a la azotea.

Refrán

(Verso 1 se repite)

Refrán

Refrain

He was struck by smallpox,
He also caught the measles;
It left his face
Like a pigskin.

2

Oh! Here comes my mother-in-law
Descending the hill.
She jumps over the wood pile
Turning somersaults.

Refrain

3

Run along little girl,
Here comes Vicente.
Bring him a little bench
So that he can sit down.

Refrain

4

A spotted bitch,
Spotted and dried up,
They looked for her tail
But her tail was bobbed.

5

Here comes the drunkard
Drinking out of the bottle.
Run along, little girl,
Climb up on the roof.

Refrain

(Verse 1 repeated)

Refrain

D19. *San Fernándico* (Saint Ferdinand)
R306, Jacobo Maestas, age 67, Llano de San Juan, N.Mex., 1950, Robb.

1
Padre mío San Fernándico
solíviame estas cadénicas
que me están atormentándico
por las mujeres ajénicas.

Refrán
Por lo que sítico,
por lo que nótico,
por lo denótico,
tengo de práctico.

2
Una mujer muy chatónica
y encontraré su hermosúrica
me dice señor figúrica
—compóngame alguna cósica.—

Refrán

3
Dicen que soy hombre málico
malo y mal averiguádico
porque me comí un duráznico
de corazón colorádico.

Refrán

4
Ya yo vide un carromático
y ahorita andar la sílvica
y adentro vide otro diáblico
y su reyeonítico.

Refrán

(Verso 2 se repite)

1
My father, Saint Ferdinand,
Lift up these my chains,
They give me torment
Because of other men's women.

Refrain
Yes it is so,
Yes it is no,
Yes it is doubtful,
I'll have to find out.

2
I met a lovely woman
And enchanted by her beauty,
She speaks to me,
"Compose some little thing for me."

Refrain

3
They say I am a bad man,
Bad and disorderly,
Because I ate a peach,
With a red heart.

Refrain

4
I saw a float
Coming from the woods,
Inside I saw another devil
And his little king.

Refrain

(Verse 2 repeated)

PA - DRE MÍ-O SAN FER-NAN-DI-CO SO-LÍ-VIA-ME ES-TAS CA-
DÉ-NI-CAS QUE ME E-STÁN A-TOR-MEN-TÁN-DI-CO
POR LAS MU-JE-RES A - JÉ-NI-CAS. POR LO QUE
SÍ - TI - CO, POR LO QUE NÓ-TI-CO, POR LO DE-
NÓ - TI - CO, TEN-GO DE PRÁC-TI - CO.

D19 displays an artificial rhyme produced by the addition of *ico* or *ica* to the last word of each line.

Verse 4 is almost identical with verse 5 of *El Pavo Real* (C42).

D20. *El Pez Espada* (The Swordfish)
R1750, Próspero S. Baca, age 70, Bernalillo, N.Mex., 1945, Robb.

1
Allá en el mar
donde yo me estuve
dentro del agua
cerca de un mes,
ví unos pescaditos
tan chiquititos
como la punta
de un alfiler.

1
Down there in the sea
Where I was
In the water
For about a month,
I saw some little fish
As small
As the point
Of a needle.

2
¡Ay! ¡Cómo me quemaba!
—Agua por Dios,— pedía.
Un camarón decía,
—Eso no hallará usted aquí.—

2
Oh! How I was burning with thirst!
I begged, "Water, for God's sake."
A shrimp said to me,
"You won't find any around here."

3
Estando durmiendo
en una cama
de pura esponja
y caracolitos

3
Being asleep
On a bed
Of pure sponge
And little snails,

346

yo ví una paraja
de pescaditos.

I saw a pair
Of little fish.

4

La sardinita y
el salmoncito
se divertían
en platicar;
ellos me consolaban
cuando yo iba
en el ancho mar.

4

The sardine
And the salmon
Were amusing themselves
With conversation;
They consoled me
When I was going
Out into the open sea.

5

En conclusión
de esta cantada,
de la sardina
y el salmoncito,
cuatro parejas eran,
el pez espada
y el pescadito.

5

In conclusion
Of this song
Of the lady sardine
And the gentleman salmon,
There were four couples,
The swordfish
And the little fish.

D21. *El Borrego Pelón* (The Bald Sheep)
R1454, Onofre Maés Canijilón, N.Mex., 1957, Robb.

1

Comadre, vamos al huerto
a cortar alfalfa de roda.

1

Friend, let us go to the field
To cut alfalfa *de roda*.

2

Me puse a lavar un negro
para ver si se desteñía.

2

I tried to wash a black
To see if he would get whiter.

3

Entre más jabon le hechaba
más negro se me ponía.

3

The more soap I used
The blacker he got.

4

Me casé con un viejito
malhaya la chuchería.

4

I married an old man,
Cursed be the gossip.

5

En el día me regañaba
ya en la noche me tosía.

5

In the daytime he scolded me,
And at night he coughed at me.

6

Me casé con un ranchero
con interés del colchón.

6

I married a rancher
Being interested in a mattress.

7

Ahora me cayo el ranchero
que el borrego está pelón.

7

Now he tells me
The sheep is bald.

CO - MA - DRE, VA - MOS AL HUER - TO A COR -

TAR AL - FAL - FA DE RO - SA.

The little girl who sang this song learned it from a record titled "Besos Jocosos." It was an old, worn Okeh record (#16717 w402681). This is only one of a number of songs learned not by listening to the old bards at *tertulias* but by hearing them on the radio, phonograph, or television. This manner of transmission, whatever its other effects, diminishes the uniqueness of the traditional song literature of a particular village or region by letting in extraneous ideas, such as, for instance, jazz, an element foreign to the Hispanic folk tradition. That tradition so long conserved by reason of the isolation of the villages is being rapidly eroded by the development of rapid communication and replaced by something, to my mind, very much less unique and noteworthy.

D22. *El Pescado Nadador* (The Swimming Fish)
R1921, G. Mora and F. Espinosa, Chililí, N.Mex., 1963, Robb.

1
Señores, pido licencia
para cantarle a mi amor,
y a decirle lo que siente
el pescado nadador.

1
Gentlemen, I ask your permission
To sing to my love
And to tell her what
The swimming fish feels.

2
Yo andando en la mar pescando
pescando en la mar pesqué
una niña de quince años
que de ella me enamoré.

2
I was fishing in the ocean and
In the ocean, fishing, I caught
A young girl of fifteen years
With whom I fell in love.

3
Soy como el agua del río
que no consiente basura.
Tengo un amorcito nuevo
que huele a piña madura.

3
I am like the water of a river
That carries away the trash.
I have a little new love
Who smells of ripe pineapple.

4
Ya mi prieta anda de luto
sin haberme muerto yo.
¡Malhaya el vestido negro,
malhaya quien se murió!

4
Now my love is in mourning,
Without my having died.
Cursed be the black dress,
And whoever he was who died!

5
Soy como la agua del río
que corre hacia esos arenales.
Contigo nomás si quieres
y también tres pedernales.

5
I am like the water of the river
That runs toward the sandbank.
I'll be yours only, if you want it
And that will be all right with me.

348

6

Ya con ésta me despido,
ya de este infortuno amor.
Aquí se acaban los versos
del pescado nadador.

6

Now with this I take my leave
Of this unfortunate love.
Here end the verses
Of the swimming fish.

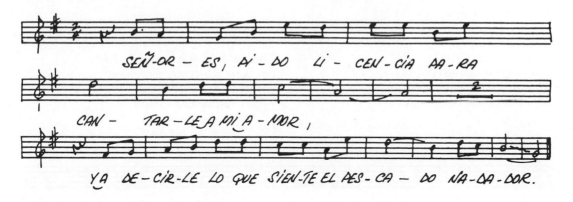

D23. *Cuatro Reales Pongo Yo* (Fifty Cents I Will Pitch In)
R2389, Juan Griego, age 61, Albuquerque, N.Mex., 1971, Robb.

Coro
Cuatro reales pongo yo,
cuatro el hijo del pelón,
compramos una anforita
y ahí andamos de un jalón.

Chorus
Fifty cents I will pitch in,
Fifty, the son of the bald one,
We will buy an amphora
And we'll all pull together.

1

Cuatro reales pongo yo,
cuatro el hijo del pelón,
compramos una anforita
y ahí andamos de un jalón.
Vuelta, vuelta los muchachos
en redondo de Sención.

1

Fifty cents I will pitch in,
Fifty, the son of the bald one,
We will buy an amphora
And we will all pull together.
In circles, in circles boys,
Around Sención.

2

Allí viene don José Reyes
también viene chapaliando,
viene a decirle a Susano
ya el manil se está acabando.

2

There comes Don José Reyes
He also is splashing about,
He comes to tell Susano
We are running out of money.

Coro

Chorus

3

En las salas de Rincón
ya no hallamos a cual,
en las dos se cuecen habas
y se muele nistamal.

3

In the dance halls of Rincón
We cannot decide which one,
They cook beans in both
And they also grind nistamal.

Coro

Chorus

4

Ya no mueven bailadoras
pero aclaran todavía
en redondo de Sención
vueltos una maravilla.

Coro

5

Chávez no tenía canas
pero ya ahora tiene compasión
por andar atrás de esos tontos
que andan atrás de Sención.

Coro

4

They no longer draw dancing girls,
But they still brighten things up.
Around Sención
We do wonderfully well.

Chorus

5

Chávez did not have white hair
But now he is compassionate
Because he followed those fools
Who chase after Sención.

Chorus

CUA-TRO REA-LES PON-GO YO. CUA-TRO EL HI-JO DEL PE-
LÓN, COM-PRA-MOS U-NA JAN-FOR-I-TA Y AHÍ AN-
DA-MOS DE UN JA-LÓN. VUEL-TA, VUEL-TA LOS MU-
CHA-CHOS EN RE-DON-DO DE SEN-CIÓN.

Note the fascinating change from major to minor in the last three notes of the melody, which for me has an Indian sound. According to the singer, Juan Griego, this song was composed by Victor Chaves in Los Ranchos in del Picacho, near Santa Rosa, New Mexico.

D24. *Tilinigo Matinigo*
   R2408, Juan Griego, age 61, Albuquerque, N.Mex., 1971, Cipriano Griego.

Tilinigo Matinigo
mató a su mujerí,
con un garrotito
del tamaño delí.
Y la hizo cecinitas
y la fué a venderí
al Puerto de Luna   ]
que no hay que comeri.   ] *Bis*

Tilinigo Matinigo
Killed his wife
With a little club
About as big as himself.
Then he made jerky of her
And went to sell her
At Puerto de Luna
Where there's nothing to eat.

The letter "*i*" at the end of *mujerí, venderí,* and *comerí* are playful additions. Compare Reyes Ruiz (B21a), verse 13, where the same practice is followed. This is a typical *disparate* featuring grim humor.

D25. *Los Cinco Poetas* (The Five Poets)
R2425, Juan Griego, age 61, Albuquerque, N.Mex., 1971, Cipriano Griego.

Cuando vengan los cinco poetas,
viejos desaparecidos;
para que sirvan de testigos
y que puedan dibujar.

When the five poets came,
Old men who had disappeared;
They came to serve as witnesses
And to draw pictures.

Refrán
Tai-da, rai-da,
rai-da di-da
lai-ra li-ra la.
tai-da lai-da li-ra la.

Refrain
Tai-da, rai-da,
Rai-da di-da
Lai-ra li-ra la.
Tai-da lai-da li-ra la.

MENTIRA

D26. *El Piojo* (The Louse)

R135, Tomás Archuleta, age 55, Abiquiu, N.Mex., 1949, Robb. Cf. R450 (a décima), R1755, RB154; Garcia 5b (Parte Musical, p. 75); Matos 8a (Parte Literaria, p. 74); Matos 8c (Parte Musical, p. 41).

1	**1**
Ahora que quieren que cante	Now that you want me to sing
les cantaré una mentira.] *Bis*	I'll sing a lie.
2	**2**
Yo vide venir un piojo	I saw a louse coming
de banda a banda del río,	Down the river,
cuando en el medio venía	And I noticed that one of his
ví que le faltaba un ojo.	Eyes was missing.
3	**3**
Al pobrecito del piojo	Poor louse
le cortaron la cabeza	They cut off his head,
ahí se la llevan para Francia	They took it to France
de presente a la princesa.	To present it to the princess.
4	**4**
De las patitas del piojo	From the louse's legs
me puse a hacer arquibeches;	I fashioned hunting bows;
por uno de ellos me dieron	For one of these I got
treinte vacas dando leche.	Thirty milk cows.
5	**5**
Ahí del cuerito del piojo	And with the hide
puse una corticería;	I opened a leather factory;
al cabo de tres semanas	Three weeks later
puse una zapatería.	I opened a shoe store.
6	**6**
De la manteca del piojo	From the louse's lard
puse una fritandería;	I opened a fry shop;
tuve para toda la gente,	I fed all the people,
toda la gente de Turquía.	All the people of Turkey.
7	**7**
Y la poca que quedó	And what little was left over
se acabó casi en tortillas.] *Bis*	We ate with tortillas.
8	**8**
De las costillas del piojo	From the louse's ribs
hemos de formar un puente;	We shall build a bridge;
por el piquito del gallo	Over the rooster's beak
pasaba toda la gente.	All the people traveled.

9

Y la colita del piojo
y es un puro movimiento;
ahora diré la verdad:
que si no he dicho ésta reviento.

9

Now the louse's tail
It just keeps on wiggling;
And now I will tell the truth:
If I hadn't told this, I'd have burst.

'O-RA QUE QUIE-REN QUE CAN-TE LES CAN-TA-RÉ U-NA MEN-

TI-RA. 'O-RA QUE QUIE-REN QUE CAN-TE LES CAN-TA-RÉ U-NA MEN-TI-RA.

According to Mendoza, this is a children's game song, a New Mexico version "of un-doubted Spanish origin" from the colonial period, that is, the sixteenth and seventeenth centuries, better preserved here than in the countries on the south (Mendoza 9d, p. 204). It is sometimes known as *La Boda* (The Wedding). Like *Los Diez Perritos* (D28), *El Piojo* is known and sung in Spain.

AGLUTINANTE

D27. *Dos Reales* (Two Dollars), or *La Polla* (The Hen)
R338, Henry Fountain et al., Mesilla Park, N.Mex., 1950, Robb. Cf. R1122.

1

Por unos dos reales que tenga
compro una polla:] *Bis*
y tengo mi polla
que pone su huevo,
y siempre me queda
mi mismo dinero.

1

If I have a couple of dollars
I'm buying a hen:
Then I have my hen
Who lays her egg,
And I still have
The same money.

2

Con otros dos reales que tenga
compro una vaca,   ] *Bis*
y tengo mi vaca
que tiene becerra,
y tengo mi polla
que pone su huevo,
y siempre me queda
mi mismo dinero.

2

If I have another couple of dollars
I'm buying a cow:
Then I have my cow
Who has a calf,
And I have my hen
Who lays her egg,
And I still have
The same money.

3

Con otros dos reales que tenga
compro una casa,   ] *Bis*

3

If I have another couple of dollars
I'm buying a house:

y tengo mi casa,
y tengo casero,
y tengo mi vaca
que tiene becerra,
y tengo mi polla
que pone su huevo,
y siempre me queda
mi mismo dinero.

Then I have my house,
And I have a butler,
And I have my cow
Who has a calf,
And I have my hen
Who lays her egg,
And I still have
The same money.

4

Con otros dos reales que tenga
compro una huerta,   ] Bis
y tengo mi huerta,
y tengo huertero,
y tengo mi casa,
que tiene casero,
y tengo mi vaca
que tiene becerra,
y tengo mi polla
que pone su huevo,
y siempre me queda
mi mismo dinero.

4

If I have another couple of dollars
I'm buying a garden:
Then I have my garden,
And I have my gardener,
And I have my house,
And I have my butler,
And I have my cow
Who has a calf,
And I have my hen
Who lays her egg,
And I still have
The same money.

5

Con otro dos reales que tenga
compro una mina,   ] Bis
y tengo mi mina,
y tengo minero,
y tengo mi huerta,
y tengo huertero,
y tengo mi casa,
y tengo casero,
y tengo mi vaca
que tiene becerra,
y tengo mi polla
que pone su huevo,
y siempre me queda
mi mismo dinero.

5

If I have another couple of dollars
I'm buying a mine:
Then I have my mine,
And I have a miner,
And I have my garden,
And I have my gardener,
And I have my house,
And I have my butler,
And I have my cow
Who has a calf,
And I have my hen
Who lays her egg,
And I still have
The same money.

D28. *Los Diez Perritos* (The Ten Puppies)
    R946, J. Romero, Córdova, N.Mex., 1952, Robb. Cf. Schindler 14a (Parte Musical, no. 729, Parte Literaria, p. 107); Garcia 5b (Parte Literaria, p. 175, Parte Musical, p. 196).

1	1
Yo tenía diez perritos	I had ten puppies
y uno se enterró en la nieve.	And one was buried in the snow.
No me quedan más que nueve,	Then I had only nine,
nueve, nueve, nueve, nueve.	Nine, nine, nine, nine.

2	2
Y de nueve que tenía	And of the nine I had left
uno se tragó un biscocho.	One swallowed a biscuit.
No me quedan más que ocho,	Then I had only eight,
ocho, ocho, ocho, ocho.	Eight, eight, eight, eight.

3	3
Y de ocho que tenía	And of the eight I had left
uno se tragó un tranchete.	One swallowed a knife.
No me quedan más que siete	Then I had only seven,
siete, siete, siete, siete.	Seven, seven, seven, seven.

4	4
Y de siete que tenía	And of the seven I had left
uno se lo llevó el Rey.	One was taken away by the King.
No me quedan más que seis, y	Then I had only six,
seis, y seis, y seis, y seis.	Six, six, six, six.

5	5
Y de seis que tenía	And of the six I had left
uno se murió de un brinco.	One died in a fall.
No me quedan más que cinco,	Then I had only five,
cinco, cinco, cinco, cinco.	Five, five, five, five.

6	6
Y de cinco que tenía	And of the five I had left
uno se llevó el teatro.	One was carried away by the theater.
No me quedan más que cuatro,	Then I had only four,
cuatro, cuatro, cuatro, cuatro.	Four, four, four, four.

7	7
Y de cuatro que tenía	And of the four I had left,
uno se voltió al revés.	One was turned inside out.
No me quedan más que tres y	Then I had only three,
tres, y tres, y tres, y tres.	Three, three, three, three.

8	8
Y de tres que tenía	And of the three I had left
uno se murió de tos.	One died of the whooping cough.
No me quedan más que dos, y	Then I had only two,
dos, y dos, y dos, y dos.	Two, two, two, two.

9	9
Y de dos que tenía	And of the two I had left
uno se murió de ayuno.	One died of starvation.

No me quedan más que uno,
y uno, y uno, y uno, y uno.

10
Y de uno que tenía
me lo mató una pedrada.
No me queda más que nada,
nada, nada, nada, nada.

11
Y de nada que tenía
se lo lleva un embustero.
No me quedan más que cero,
cero, cero, cero, cero.

Then I had only one,
One, one, one, one.

10
And the one I had left
Was stoned to death.
Then I had nothing,
Nothing, nothing, nothing, nothing.

11
And of nothing I had left
A liar took it away.
Then I had only zero,
Zero, zero, zero, zero.

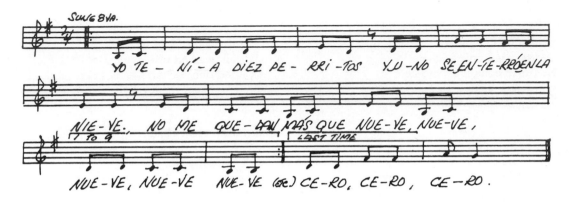

D29. *La Rana* (The Frog)
R2401, Juan Griego, age 61, Albuquerque, N.Mex., 1971, Cipriano Griego.

1
Sale a pasearse la rana.
Viene la araña y la hace llorar.
La araña a la rana,
la rana del agua se sienta a llorar.

2
Sale a pasearse la araña.
Viene el ratón y la hace llorar.
El ratón a la araña,
la araña a la rana,
la rana del agua se sienta a llorar.

3
Sale a pasearse el ratón.
Viene el gato y lo hace llorar.
El gato al ratón,
el ratón a la araña,
la araña a la rana,
la rana del agua se sienta a llorar.

1
The frog went out for a walk.
The spider came along and made her weep.
The spider to the frog
The frog in the water sat down to cry.

2
The spider went out for a walk.
The mouse came along and made her weep.
The mouse to the spider,
The spider to the frog,
The frog in the water sat down to cry.

3
The mouse went out for a walk.
The cat came along and made him weep.
The cat to the mouse,
The mouse to the spider,
The spider to the frog,
The frog in the water sat down to cry.

4

Sale a pasearse el gato
viene el perro y lo hace llorar.
El perro al gato,
el gato el ratón,
el ratón a la araña,
la araña a la rana,
la rana del agua se sienta a llorar.

4

The cat went out for a walk
The dog came along and made him weep.
The dog to the cat,
The cat to the mouse,
The mouse to the spider,
The spider to the frog,
The frog in the water sat down to cry.

5

Sale a pasearse el perro.
Viene el palo y lo hace llorar.
El palo al perro,
el perro al gato,
el gato al ratón,
el ratón a la araña,
la araña a la rana,
la rana del agua se sienta a llorar.

5

The dog went out for a walk.
The stick came along and made him weep.
The stick to the dog,
The dog to the cat,
The cat to the mouse,
The mouse to the spider,
The spider to the frog,
The frog in the water sat down to cry.

6

Sale a pasearse el palo.
Viene la lumbre y lo hace llorar.
La lumbre al palo,
el palo al perro,
el perro al gato,
el gato al ratón,
el ratón a la araña,
la araña a la rana,
la rana del agua se sienta a llorar.

6

The stick went out for a walk.
The fire came along and made him weep.
The fire to the stick,
The stick to the dog,
The dog to the cat,
The cat to the mouse,
The mouse to the spider,
The spider to the frog,
The frog in the water sat down to cry.

7

Sale a pasearse la lumbre.
Viene el agua y la hace llorar.
El agua a la lumbre,
le lumbre al palo,
el palo al perro,
el perro al gato,
el gato al ratón,
el ratón a la araña,
la araña a la rana,
la rana del agua se sienta a llorar.

7

The fire went out for a walk.
Water came along and made him weep.
The water to the fire,
The fire to the stick,
The stick to the dog,
The dog to the cat,
The cat to the mouse,
The mouse to the spider,
The spider to the frog,
The frog in the water sat down to cry.

8

Sale a pasearse el agua.
Viene el buey y lo hace llorar.
El buey al agua,
el agua a la lumbre,
la lumbre al palo,
el palo al perro,
el perro al gato,
el gato al ratón,
el ratón a la araña,
la araña a la rana,
la rana del agua se sienta a llorar.

8

Water went out for a walk.
The ox came along and made him weep.
The ox to the water,
The water to the fire,
The fire to the stick,
The stick to the dog,
The dog to the cat,
The cat to the mouse,
The mouse to the spider,
The spider to the frog,
The frog in the water sat down to cry.

9

Sale a pasearse el buey.
Viene el cuchillo y lo hace llorar.
El cuchillo al buey,
el buey al agua,
el agua a la lumbre,
la lumbre al palo,
el palo al perro,
el perro al gato,
el gato al ratón,
el ratón a la araña,
la araña a la rana,
la rana del agua se sienta a llorar.

9

The ox went out for a walk.
The knife came along and made him weep.
The knife to the ox,
The ox to the water,
The water to the fire,
The fire to the stick,
The stick to the dog,
The dog to the cat,
The cat to the mouse,
The mouse to the spider,
The spider to the frog,
The frog in the water sat down to cry.

10

Sale a pasearse el cuchillo.
Viene el herrero y lo hace llorar.
El herrero al cuchillo,
el cuchillo al buey,
el buey al agua,
el agua a la lumbre,
la lumbre al palo,
el palo al perro,
el perro al gato,
el gato al ratón,
el ratón a la araña,
la araña a la rana,
la rana del agua se sienta a llorar.

10

The knife went out for a walk.
Along came blacksmith and made him weep.
The smith to the knife,
The knife to the ox,
The ox to the water,
The water to the fire,
The fire to the stick,
The stick to the dog,
The dog to the cat,
The cat to the mouse,
The mouse to the spider,
The spider to the frog,
The frog in the water sat down to cry.

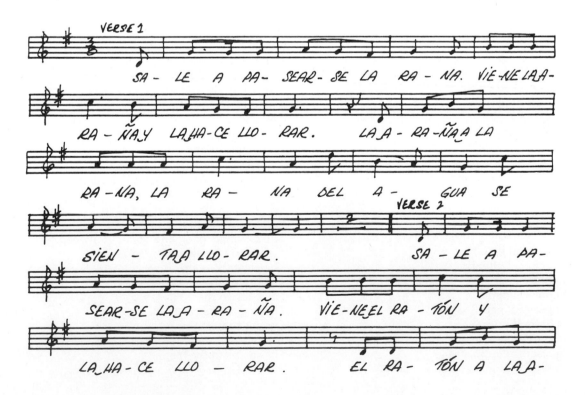

RA-ÑA, LA A- RA-ÑA A LA RA-NA, LA RA-

NA DEL A— GUA SE SIEN- TA A LLO-

VERSE 3

RAR. SA- LE A PA-SEAR-SE EL RA-TÓN.

VIE-NE EL GA-TO Y LO HA-CE LLO-RAR. EL

GA-TO AL RA-TÓN, Y EL RA- TÓN A LA A-

RA-ÑA, LA A- RA-ÑA A LA RA- NA, LA RA-

NA DEL A — GUA SE SIEN —

TA A LLO- RAR. ETC.

D30. *La Misa* (The Mass)
Mendoza 9d (p. 377), Amador Abeyta, Albuquerque, N.Mex., 1893, Cobos.

1
El cura no va a la iglesia,
la niña sabe por qué;
porque no tiene zapatos.
—Zapatos yo le daré
y zapatos con tacón.—
Kyrie Eleison.

1
The priest does not go to the church,
The little girl knows why;
Because he has no shoes.
"I will give him shoes,
Shoes with heels."
Kyrie Eleison.

2
El cura no va a la iglesia
la niña sabe por qué;
porque no tiene calzones.
—Calzones yo le daré,
Los calzones con botones
y zapatos con tacón.—
Kyrie Eleison.

2
The priest does not go to the church
The little girl knows why,
Because he has no pants.
"I will give him pants,
Pants with buttons
And shoes with heels."
Kyrie Eleison.

3

El cura no va a la iglesia,
la niña sabe por qué;
porque no tiene camisa.
—Camisa yo le daré,
la camisa con su cinta,
los calzones con botones,
los zapatos con tacón.—
Kyrie Eleison.

3

The priest does not go to the church
The little girl knows why;
Because he has no shirt.
"I will give him a shirt,
A shirt with its belt,
Pants with buttons,
Shoes with heels."
Kyrie Eleison.

4

El cura no va a la iglesia
la niña sabe por qué;
porque no tiene chaleco.
—Chaleco yo le daré,
el chaleco con su fleco,
la camisa con su cinta,
los calzones con botones,
y zapatos con tacón.—
Kyrie Eleison.

4

The priest does not go to the church
The little girl knows why;
Because he has no vest.
"I will give him a vest,
A vest with its fringe,
A shirt with a belt,
Pants with buttons,
And shoes with heels."
Kyrie Eleison.

5

El cura no va a la iglesia
la niña sabe por qué;
porque no tiene chaqueta.
—Chaqueta yo le daré,
la chaqueta con sus güeltas,
el chaleco con su fleco,
la camisa con su cinta,
los calzones con botones,
y zapatos con tacón.—
Kyrie Eleison.

5

The priest does not go to the church
The little girl knows why;
Because he has no jacket.
"I will give him a jacket,
A jacket with vents,
A vest with its fringe,
A shirt with its belt,
Pants with buttons,
And shoes with heels."
Kyrie Eleison.

6

El cura no va a la iglesia
la niña sabe por qué;
porque no tiene sotana.
—Sotana yo le daré,
la sotana de badana,
la chaqueta con sus güeltas,
el chaleco con su fleco,
la camisa con su cinta,
los calzones con botones,
y zapatos con tacón.—
Kyrie Eleison.

6

The priest does not go to the church
The little girl knows why;
Because he has no cassock.
"I will give him a cassock,
A cassock of sheepskin,
A jacket with its vents,
A vest with its fringe,
A shirt with its belt,
Pants with buttons,
And shoes with heels."
Kyrie Eleison.

7

El cura no va a la iglesia
la niña sabe por qué;
porque no tiene bonete.
—Bonete yo le daré,
el bonete de soquete,
la sotana de badana,
la chaqueta con sus güeltas,

7

The priest does not go to the church
The little girl knows why;
Because he has no bonnet.
"I will give him a bonnet,
A bonnet of mud,
A cassock of sheepskin,
A jacket with its vents,

el chaleco con su fleco,
la camisa con su cinta,
los calzones con botones,
y zapatos de tacón.—
Kyrie Eleison.

A vest with its fringe,
A shirt with its belt,
Pants with buttons,
And shoes with heels."
Kyrie Eleison.

EL CU-RA NO VA A LA I-GLE-SIA, LA NI-ÑA SA-BE POR QUÉ, POR-QUE NO TIE-NE ZA-PA-TOS.—ZA-PA-TOS YO LE DA-RÉ Y ZA-PA-TOS CON TA-CÓN.— KY-RIE E-LEI-SON.

OTHER HUMOROUS SONGS

D31. *El Borracho* (The Drunkard)
R221, Tomás Archuleta, age 55, Abiquiu, N.Mex., 1949, Robb. Cf. R297.

All couplets are repeated

1
Yupalá, yupalá, yupalá yi,
las culebras están nudas.

1
Yupala, yupala, yupala yi,
All snakes are naked.

2
Vámonos emborrachando
hasta que nos lleve Judas.

2
Let us get drunk
Till Judas takes us.

3
Dicen que yo ando borracho,
Por Dios, y no traigo nada.

3
They say I'm drunk,
By God, there's nothing wrong with me.

4
Si borrachito viniera
siquiera me bambaleara.

4
If I were even a little drunk
I would at least rock and roll.

5
—Vente, borracho, conmigo
yo te llevaré a tu casa.—

5
"Come, you drunk, come with me
And I'll take you home."

6

Estimo más mi botella
que ir a dormir con mi dama.

7

¡Qué bonito es un borracho
cuando está en la cantina!

8

Con la botella en la mano,
su mujer sin harina.

9

Lo que le pasa a un borracho
por entrar a la cocina.

10

Lo peló la cocinera
pensando que era gallina.

11

Lo que parece un borracho
cuando ya se anda cayendo.

12

Se parece al vivo Judas
cuando sale del infierno.

13

Dicen que yo ando borracho,
por Dios, si no traigo nada.

14

Si borrachito viniera
siquiera me bambaleara.

15

El domingo ya no bebo
voy a hacer un buen vivir.

16

Cada día una botella,
cada semana un barril.

17

El lunes en la mañana
me salí a trabajar.

18

Me encontré un amigo mío,
ese me hizo emborrachar.

19

Cuando me parió mi madre
me parió en una zalea.

6

I esteem my bottle more
Than to sleep with my woman.

7

What a fine sight is a drunkard
When he is in the saloon.

8

With a bottle in his hand,
His wife without flour.

9

But think what befalls a drunkard
Who enters the kitchen.

10

The cook plucked him
Because she took him for a chicken.

11

Know what a drunk looks like
When he is falling all over himself?

12

He looks just like Judas himself
Walking out of hell.

13

They say I'm drunk,
By God, there's nothing wrong with me.

14

If I were even a little drunk
I would at least rock and roll.

15

On Sunday I do not drink
I will live the good life.

16

Each day one bottle,
Each week one vat.

17

On Monday morning
I went out to work.

18

And I met a friend of mine,
He made me get drunk.

19

When my mother gave me birth
I was born on a pelt.

20

Cuando la partera vino
yo andaba con la botella.

21

Cuando me parió mi madre
me parió en un serapito.

22

Cuando la partera vino
ya yo andaba borrachito.

20

When the midwife arrived
I had a bottle in my hand.

21

When my mother bore me
I was born on a blanket.

22

When the midwife arrived
Already I was a bit drunk.

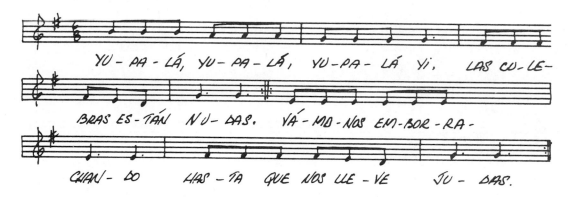

". . . Everyone in Abiquiu knew the old standard, *El Borracho*" (Cordova, p. 59).

Verses 7 and 8 are a classic example of irony in the true sense of sarcasm couched in a statement that implies its very opposite.

D32. *La Havana Se Va a Perder* (Havana Is Going to Be Lost)
R1421, Myrtle Bernal, Taos, N.Mex., 1956, Robb.

1

La Havana se va a perder,
la culpa tiene el dinero.
Los negros quieren ser blancos,
los mulatos caballeros.

1

Havana is going to be lost,
It's all the fault of money.
The Negroes want to be white,
And the mulattos gentlemen.

2

A la jo, a la jo,
¿qué dice María, a la jo?
¡qué es más bonita que yo!
Más bonita si será
pero más graciosa ¡no!

2

A la ho, a la ho,
What say María, a la ho?
That you are prettier than I!
Well perhaps you are prettier
But are you more graceful? No!

3

A mí no me quema ma,
a mí no me quema ma,
a mí no me quema, a mí no me quema,
ni la candela, ni el aguarras.

3

I'm not burning mama,
I'm not burning mama,
I'm not burning, I'm not burning,
Neither is the candle, nor the oil.

4

¡Ay! Chiquitita mía.
Si tú me dieras
una canita dulce
me la comiera.

5

Que chupa, que chupa, que chupa,
que chupa, que chupa, que chu, papá.

6

Manitos, con el mulato yo no me quiero
  casar.
Yo quiero que sea un blanco
con quien yo me he da esposar.

(Versos 2–6 se repiten)

4

Ah! My little girl.
If you would give me
A piece of sugar cane
I would eat it.

5

Go eat it, go eat it, go eat it,
Go eat it, go eat it, papa.

6

Manitos, I don't want to marry a mulatto.

I want it to be a white man
To whom I shall get married.

(Verses 2–6 repeated)

This song is distinguished by the puns on the words *mamá* and *papá*.

D33. *Veinte y Tres* (Twenty-three)
R1473, Edwin Berry, age 39, Tomé, N.Mex., 1957, Robb.

Una y una y una y una
y una y dos son tres.
Contaban y contaban y contaban
al revés. Contaban y contaban
y contaban veinte y tres.

One and one and one and one
And one and two are three.
They counted and counted and counted
In reverse. They counted and counted
And counted twenty-three.

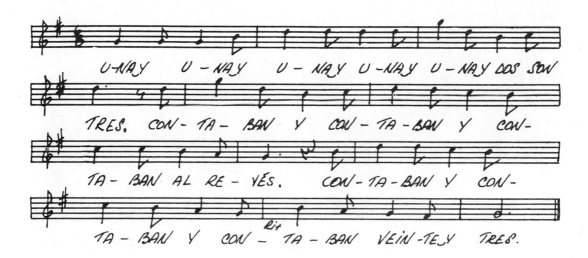

D34. *Jesusita*
R130, Vidal Valdez, age 27, and L. Rodríguez, Albuquerque, N.Mex., 1947, Robb.

1

Cuando salí de mi tierra
me fuí a una tienda a tomar.
Me encontré con Jesusita y
me empecé a enamorar.

2

Le pregunté a su mamá
cuál es la edad que ella tiene.
—Quince años cumple Jesús
para el dieciseis de septiembre.—

3

Es una edad muy completa
para que sepa de amores.
No dejes pasar el tiempo.
Vamos cortando esas flores.

4

Dos imposibles me puso
para podernos casar:
que le cuente las estrellas
y le enladrille la mar.

5

—No le cuento las estrellas,
ni le enladrillo la mar.
Que se las cuente su mamá
porque yo no sé contar.—

6

Su madre será la arena,
su padre será la cal,
y sus hermanos los ladrillos
para enladrillar la mar.

7

Ya con ésta me despido,
blanca flor de amapolita.
Aquí se acaban cantando
los versos de Jesusita.

1

When I left my country
I went to a bar to drink.
I met Jesusita and
Began to fall in love.

2

I asked her mother
How old she was.
"She will be fifteen years old
The sixteenth of September."

3

It is a very suitable age
So she may know about love.
Do not let the time pass.
Let us go cut those flowers.

4

Two impossibilities she gave me
Before we could get married:
That I count the stars and
Pave the sea with bricks.

5

"I can't count the stars,
And I cannot pave the sea.
Let your mother count them herself
Because I don't know how to count."

6

Her mother will be the sand,
Her father will be the lime,
And her brothers, the bricks
With which to pave the sea.

7

With this I say good-bye
White poppy flower.
Here ends the singing of
The verses of Jesusita.

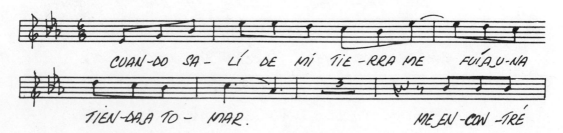

366

CON JE-SU-SI-TA Y ME EM-PE-CÉ A E-NA-MO-

RAR.

D35. *La Suegra* (The Mother-in-Law)
R2411, Juan Griego, Albuquerque, N.Mex., 1971, Cipriano Griego.

Coro	*Chorus*
¡Ay! ¡ay! ¡ay!	Alas, alas, alas,
déjen me llorar	Let me bewail
los tristes tormentos	The sad torments
que voy a pasar.	Which I must endure.
1	1
Suegra:	*Mother-in-law:*
Mi hijo casó,	My son got married,
ya tiene mujer,	Now he has a wife,
manaña sabremos	Tomorrow we will know
lo que sabe hacer.	What she can do.
Coro	*Chorus*
2	2
Levántate mujer	Get up woman
como es por costumbre.	As is the custom.
Barre tu cocina	Sweep your kitchen
y sóplale a tu lumbre.	And blow on your fire.
Coro	*Chorus*
3	3
Nuera:	*Daughter-in-law:*
Levántese usted	You get up,
que será soplona	You old gossip,
que yo me casé	For I got married
para siñorona.	To be a lady.
Coro	*Chorus*
4	4
Suegra:	*Mother-in-law:*
Hijo de mi vida	Son of my heart
mira a tu mujer,	Look at your wife,
llévala al infierno;	Take her to hell;
no la puedo ver.	I cannot stand her.
Coro	*Chorus*

5

Nuera:
Pues váyase usted
que conoce el lugar
que las malas suegras
allá van a dar.

Coro

5

Daughter-in-law:
Well, you can go
You know where
For the evil mothers-in-law
End up in that place.

Chorus

MI HI-JO CA-SÓ, YA TIE-NE MU-JER, MA-
ÑA-NA SA-BRE-MOS LO QUE SA-BE HA-CER.
¡AY! ¡AY! ¡AY! DÉ-JEN ME LLO-RAR LOS
TRIS-TES TOR-MEN-TOS QUE VOY A PA-SAR.

D36. *Tango, Tarango, Tango*
R305, Jacobo Maestas, age 67, Llano de San Juan, N.Mex., 1950, Robb.

Coro
Y al tango, tarango, tango,
y al tango, tarango té,
y arrime su cafetera,
su cafetera con su café.

Chorus
The tango, tarango, tango,
The tango, tarango te,
Bring your coffee pot,
Your coffee pot with its coffee.

1

Los toros son los que braman
debajo de los palos gachos.
Las mujeres son las que aman
a aquellos más reborrachos.

1

It's the bulls who bellow
Under the crooked trees.
The women fall in love with
Those who are the biggest drunks.

Coro

Chorus

2

Los toros son los que braman
debajo de los chamisitos.
Las mujeres son las que aman
a aquellos más chaparritos.

2

It's the bulls who bellow
Beneath the sage.
The women fall in love with
Those who are the shortest.

Coro

Chorus

<table>
<tr><td>

3

Los toros son los que braman
debajo de los ocotes.
Las mujeres son las que aman
a aquellos más grandotototes.

Coro

4

Los toros son los que braman
debajo de los carrizos.
Las mujeres son las que aman
a aquellos más socarrizos.

Coro

5

(Verso 3 se repite)

Coro

</td><td>

3

It's the bulls who bellow
Under the pitch-bearing trees.
The women fall in love with
Those who are biggest of the big.

Chorus

4

It's the bulls who bellow
Beneath the reed grass.
The women fall in love with
The slyest and the craftiest.

Chorus

5

(Verse 3 repeated)

Chorus

</td></tr>
</table>

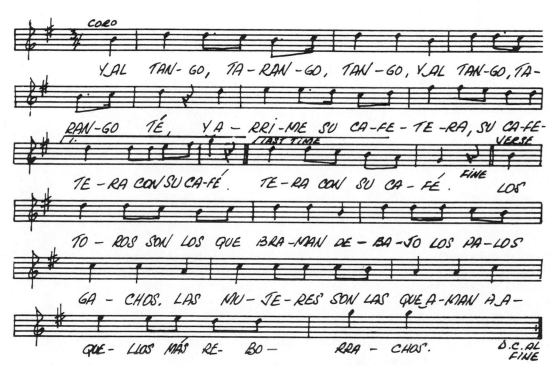

D37. *El Celoso* (The Jealous Man)
R2391, Juan Griego, age 61, Albuquerque, N.Mex., 1971, Cipriano Griego.

<table>
<tr><td>

1

Celoso y muy celoso,
celoso siempre lo he sido
desde que yo me casé.
Ese ha sido mi martirio.

</td><td>

1

Jealous, in fact, very jealous,
Jealous I always have been
Since I married.
That has been my martyrdom.

</td></tr>
</table>

2

A los tres días de casado
yo le dije a mi mujer
no platiques con los hombres.
Mira que no me caí bien.

2

After three days of marriage
I told my wife
Don't converse with the men.
See that I don't approve.

3

Temiendo estoy que te enfermes
y te quieras confesar,
porque el curita es un hombre
no te vaya a enamorar.

3

I am dreading that you may fall ill
And will want to go to confession,
Because the priest is a man
Don't let him inspire your love.

4

Temiendo estoy que te mueras
te he de llevar al pantión.
No sea que ahí los difuntos
se valgan de la ocasión.

4

I am dreading that you die
I would take you to the cemetery.
It may be that the dead men
Take advantage of the occasion.

5

Te voy a poner tu casa
en el centro de la tierra
donde el aire no te dé,
y la gente no te vea.

5

I will place your house
In the center of the earth
Where the breeze won't blow on you
And the people won't see you.

6

Te voy a poner un criado
para que te haga el mandado
pero ha de ser chiquito
no me vaya hacer un lado.

6

I will get you a servant
So he may do your bidding
But he must be little
Lest he put me to one side.

7

Me puse a hacer un cajón
no sé ni como ni de donde,
me puse a considerar
que también el pino era hombre.

7

I began to make a box
How or where is not important,
I began to consider
That the pine tree was also a man.

8

Ya mi marido murió
el diablo se lo llevó;
allá está ya desquitando
los palos que a mí me dió.

8

Now my husband is dead
The devil took him away;
There he is paying for
The beatings he gave me.

The verses are actually sung in this order:
2, 6, 3, 4, 5, 7, 8.

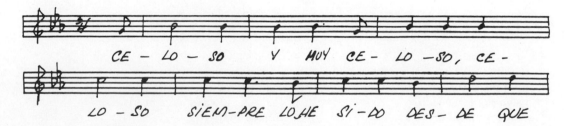

YO ME CA - SÉ. E - SE HA SI - DO MI MAR-TI - RIO.

D38. *Ya Me Voy para California* (Now I'm Going to California)
    Mendoza 9d (notebook 4, p. 74), 1909, Cobos. Cf. RB788 (different song with the same title).

1
Ya me voy para California,
y al estado de Nevada,
donde se habla sólo inglés
entre la americanada.

1
Now I'm going to California,
By way of Nevada,
Among the Americans,
Where they speak only English.

2
Las muchachas de California,
gastadoras de dinero,
para salir a pasear
usan guantes y sombrero.

2
The girls of California
Are big spenders,
When they go out for a walk
They take gloves and a parasol.

3
Las muchachas de California,
y les *laike* la cerveza,
y luego me van saliendo,
que les duele la cabeza.

3
The girls of California
Like their beer,
And then they leave me,
For they get headaches.

4
Las muchachas de California,
no les *laike* la tortilla,
pero lo que si les *laike*,
es el *bread* con mantequilla.

4
The girls of California
Don't like tortillas
But what they like
Is bread with butter.

5
Las muchachas de California,
no saben ganar un peso;
lavaditas de la cara
y roñositas del pescuezo.

5
The girls of California
Don't know how to earn a dollar;
They have clean faces
But grubby necks.

6
Las muchachas de California,
son altas y delgaditas,
pero son más pedigüeñas
que las ánimas benditas.

6
The girls of California
Are tall and slender,
But they are more demanding
Than the blessed spirits.

7
Me enredé con una pocha,[3]
para que me enseñara inglés,
cuando la traté de amores
ella me respondió: *yes.*

7
I got mixed up with a chicana
In order to learn English,
When I spoke to her of making love
She answered with a "yes."

[3] *Pocha* is a colloquialism for a Mexican-American girl.

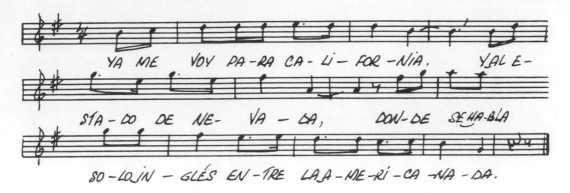

YA ME VOY PA-RA CA-LI-FOR-NIA. YAL E-

STA-DO DE NE-VA-DA, DON-DE SE HA-BLA

SO-LO IN-GLÉS EN-TRE LA A-ME-RÍ-CA-NA-DA.

D39. *La Llorona* (The Weeping Woman)

Cancionero Occidental (No. 119, ed. by Bruno Carrillo, Angulo 137, Guadalajara, Mexico), which describes the song as a "porro de José Barros." Cf. Toor (p. 443).

1		1
En una calle de Tamalamengue	]	In a street in Tamalamengue
dicen que sale	]	They say there roams
una llorona loca,	] *Bis*	A crazy weeping woman,
Que baila para allá,	]	Who dances there,
que baila para acá	]	Who dances here
con un tabaco	]	With a cigar
prendido en la boca.	] *Bis*	Held in her mouth.

2	2
A mí me salió una noche,	She came up to me one night,
una noche en carnaval,	One night during the carnival,
que meneaba la cintura	And she was wriggling her belt
como iguana en matorra!	Like an iguana in a thicket!
Le dije: —Pare un momento, héi,	I said, "Wait a moment! Hey,
no mueva tanto el motor.—	Don't start your motor so fast!"
Y al que ver era un gran espanto,	Believe me, that was frightening.
ay, compadre, ¡qué zofocón!	Ah, my friend, what a man eater!

3		3
Que me coje, no te coje,	]	Will she catch me? No, she won't.
que me agarra, no te agarra,	]	Will she seize me? No, she won't.
que me coje, que me agarra,	]	Will she catch me? Will she seize me?
la llorona por detrás.	] *Bis*	Leave that weeping woman behind.

Although it is of Mexican origin, *La Llorona* is well known in the Southwest, and the superstitious fear of the mystic weeping woman is apparently widespread. There are several legends about la Llorona.

In his recently published novel *Heart of Aztlán*, Rudolfo A. Anaya refers to her sev-eral times. The novel deals with the people of Barelas, a suburb of Albuquerque:

The night air was full of strange sounds. Some-where a siren wailed and for a moment they thought they heard the cry of la Llorona as she ran along the dark river valley, crying for her demon-lover, mourning the death of her sons. But no, this was a new Llorona! It was the siren of the police car. . . . (Anaya, p. 18).

Mothers hushed their children and told them to be good or else la Llorona would come and take them away. . . . (p. 33).

"It's getting dark and I was thinking about the old witch who lives near la Golondrinas—" He shivered.

"What about her?"

Willie shrugged. "Some say she is la Llorona—" (pp. 48–49).

Again, in *Abiquiu and Don Cacahuate*, Benito Córdova has this to say: "In New Mexico there are a number of famous bogie men and women who, during dark nights, emerge to frighten people of all ages. One of the best known is la Llorona, who reputedly threw her own son to death from atop a balcony. Even today she is often heard throughout the countryside screaming her endless, sorrowful cry" (Córdova, p. 68).

The present version of *La Llorona* is about a crazy woman (a witch) who, during the fiesta, is smoking a lighted cigar and accosts a man. It may be an example from one of the Latin-American countries where the voodoo cults flourish. I have seen witches, at a *macumba* (Brazilian voodoo) celebration south of Río de Janeiro, with a wild and weird look in their eyes, hair standing straight out from their heads, and smoking cigars until they glowed red as they insisted on touching their right and left shoulders alternately with the left and right shoulders, in that order, of the spectators. At midnight a ceremonial meal was offered to el Diablo (the Devil) before his altar in the garden. The propitiation of the devil followed hours of dancing before a Christian altar to responsorial singing and the hypnotic rhythms of drums played by two black youths with the bare hands.

La Llorona is well known in the Southwest as a result of frequent broadcasts of a recording made by the Hermanos Mendoza over KABQ in Albuquerque and other Spanish-language radio stations.

D39a. *La Llorona*
RB980, cassette furnished by León J. Márquez of the University of New Mexico, June, 1977.

1

La pena y la que no es pena, Llorona,
todo es pena para mí:
ayer lloraba por verte, Llorona,

y hoy lloro porque te ví.

1

Pain and what is not pain, Llorona,
All is pain for me:
Yesterday I wept wanting to see you, Llorona,
And today I cry because I saw you.

2

¡Ay de mí!, Llorona,
Llorona de azul turquí,
aunque la vida me cuesta, Llorona,
no dejaré de quererte.

2

Oh, my Llorona,
Sky-blue Llorona,
Even if it cost me my life, Llorona,
I will not stop loving you.

3

Salías del templo un día, Llorona,
cuando al pasar yo te ví;
hermosa huipil que llevabas, Llorona,

que la Virgen te creí.

3

You left the church one day, Llorona,
As I was passing by;
Such a beautiful blouse you were wearing, Llorona,
I thought you must be the Virgin.

4

¡Ay de mí!, Llorona,
Llorona de ayer y hoy;
aunque la vida me cueste, Llorona,
no dejaré de quererte.

4

Alas, my Llorona!
Llorona of yesterday and today
Even if it cost me my life, Llorona,
I will not stop loving you.

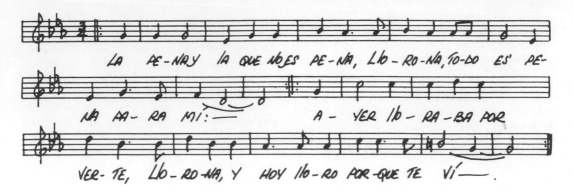

La pe-nay la que no es pe-na, Llo-ro-na, to-do es' pe-na aa-ra mi: A - ver llo-ra-ba por ver-te, Llo-ro-na, y hoy llo-ro por-que te ví.

This song has little to do with the many legends that circulate today in the Southwest about la Llorona, the weeping woman. It is, in fact, a love song, but the temptation to include a melody that could just as well have been composed about the weeping woman was irresistible. Márquez tells me that this song is of mid-nineteenth-century Mexican origin.

D40. *Señor don Juan de Pancho*
R320, Helen Little, Tijeras, N.Mex., 1950, Robb.

1	1
Señor don Juan de Pancho,	Señor don Juan de Pancho,
Señor don Juan de Dios,	Señor don Juan de Dios,
mañana se va para el rancho;	Goes off to the ranch tomorrow;
quién sabe si volverá.	Who knows if he'll return.

Estribillo	*Refrain*
Shoo fly, don't bother me.	Shoo fly, don't bother me.
Shoo fly, don't bother me.	Shoo fly, don't bother me.

2	2
El gato con su pantalón	The cat with his pants
se mira muy bien plantado	Looks real good all dressed up
con su leva de cola,	With his coat tails,
y su sombrero riscado.	And his high hat.

Shoo fly, don't bother me.	Shoo fly, don't bother me.
Shoo fly, don't bother me.	Shoo fly, don't bother me.
I belong to Company D.	I belong to Company D.

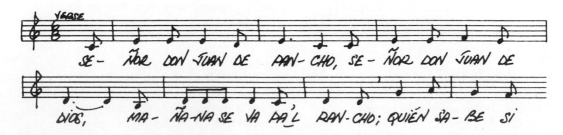

Se- ñor don Juan de Pan-cho, se-ñor don Juan de Dios, ma-ña-na se va pa'l ran-cho; quién sa-be si

For additional examples of the *relación* see the following:

Ford Paseado (R208) (cf. also Robb 13, pp. 21, 78–83)
El Zapatero (I25)

Mujer de Cien Maridos (E29)
La Indita Vagabunda (F14)
El Piojo (R450)
Amigos Yo Me Casé (R1836)
Una Bolsa sin Dinero (R1847)
Salvador Se Enamoró (R1864)

E. *Décima*

One type of folk song that formerly flourished in New Mexico and other parts of the Southwest is the *décima*. Although now moribund in New Mexico, it is remembered in other areas in the New World. It is known in Chile, for example, as the *verso* and in Panama as the *mejorana* (see Schaeffer 14, pp. 10–11). The form is apparently very old. Campa in his *Spanish Folk Poetry in New Mexico* said that it originated in Spain and flourished in the fifteenth century (Campa 2, pp. 127–30). Mendoza has devoted an entire seven hundred-page volume to the *décima* in Mexico (Mendoza 9c).

Briefly, the *décima* takes its name from its ten-line verses or stanzas. When it consists of four such verses preceded by a four-line stanza, each line of which in its turn becomes the last line of one of the ten-line stanzas, it is known as a *décima glosada*. The four-line stanza is known in Mexico as the *planta* and in Chile as the *cuarteto*. When the ten-line verses follow the rhyme scheme *abbaaccddc*, the *décima* is called an *espinela*, after the sixteenth-century poet Vincent Espinel, who introduced it. The term *valona* is sometimes used to include (1) an entire poem that includes *décimas* or (2) all the various types of *décimas*, which beside the *décima glosada* and the *espinela* include such forms as the *quintilla*, in which a five-line *planta* is followed by five ten-line stanzas; long strings of ten-line verses with or more usually without a *planta*; and poems featuring verses of twelve lines, for which I employ the term *duodécima*. In subject matter the *décimas* tend to be philosophical or to consist of reflections on the state of the world.

The most common form of the *décima* in New Mexico is the *décima glosada*, with a *planta* and four *décimas*, following the rhyme scheme of the *espinela* as defined above. Other forms may be regarded as exceptions. In the foreword to Próspero S. Baca's "One Hundred Twenty-one Décimas and Other Folk Songs" (Baca 1, Robb 13j), I have commented on the variants of the *décima* form included in this unpublished notebook. A number of the *décimas* in the following pages are taken from Baca's manuscript.

A unique and rather surprising New Mexico tradition required that the singer sing all *décimas* to a standard tune. All but one or two of the twelve or more singers who sang *décimas* for me, although living in widely separated parts of the state, employed the same recognizable tune. It started high, like many Indian melodies, and gradually sank

Próspero S. Baca, one of the great folk singers of his time and place, in Bernalillo, New Mexico, about 1942. Several of the *décimas* in Section E are taken from Baca's "One Hundred Twenty-One Décimas and Other Folk Songs."

to end an octave lower. Naturally, since the tunes were apparently never written down and the singers were unfamiliar with musical notation anyway, there were variations; and, too, the tune had to be modified to fit the words of each song, but this was accomplished by the singers with amazing naturalness and facility. In the *décima* tune a major seventh is almost immediately followed by the minor-seventh tone of the scale, giving it a sort of modal ambiguity. One of my informants, Elfego Sánchez, of Tijeras, New Mexico, added that in singing *décimas* "you start out loud and get softer." A good example of the New Mexico *décima* melody is *Qué Largas las Horas Son* (E1).

Many of the *décimas* in my collection exist only as song texts, without music, copied from the notebooks of the singers. This is largely due to the custom of using the same melody for all the *décimas* known to the singer. Baca, for instance, made no recordings to accompany the *décimas* from his notebook because, as he explained, he

sang them all to the same basic melody, adapted freely in each case to the words of the particular text, and he was embarrassed to sing virtually the same melody over and over again. A sufficient number of the variants of the melody exist to give a good idea of the traditional melody, which, once heard, is easy to recognize, even when encountered in an altered form. For these reasons I have included a number of *décima* texts without corresponding melodies. The name of the singer suffices to identify the melody (see Table E1).

A number of other *décimas*, sometimes sung to one of the many free variants of the traditional New Mexico *décima* melody, are classified in this volume under other headings. Among these is *Indita de Celestino Segura* (I2), an *indita* and also a sort of pseudo-*décima* that uses the *décima* melody. Another amusing *décima*, *Una Bolsa sin Dinero* (R1847), is the subject of an article of mine that appeared in *Western Folklore* (Robb 13m).

Table E1

Singers Using the Traditional New Mexico *Décima* Melody

Singer	Village	Example
Próspero S. Baca	Bernalillo	E1, E2, E11, E16, E18–22, E24–27
Antonio Medina	Chimayó	E3, E6, E14, E29
Juan Griego	Albuquerque	E4
Julianita Trujillo	Chimayó	E5
Elfego and F. Sánchez	Tijeras	E10, E13
Juan Luján	Santo Niño	E17
Francisco S. Leyva	Leyva	R505
Juan Morales	La Jara	R12
José M. Gallegos	Abiquiu	Q1

E1. *Qué Largas las Horas Son* (How Long the Hours Are)
R1, Próspero S. Baca, age 70, Bernalillo, N.Mex., 1945, Robb. Cf. Mendoza 9d (pp. 314–15).

Planta	*Planta*
Qué largas las horas son	How long the hours are
en el reloj de mi afán	By the clock of my anxiety,
y que poco a poco dan	Which little by little give
alivio a mi corazón.	Relief to my heart.

1

Para mí no hay sol ni luna,
no hay tarde, noche, no hay día.
Tan solo estoy vida mía,
pensando en ti desde la una;
ha quedado mi fortuna.
A las dos con atención
se aflije mi corazón.
A las tres diciendo suerte,
y así mi alma para verte
¡qué largas las horas son!

2

De buena fe te idolatro
y con buenas excelencias,
pues mi alma las tres potencias[1]
en pie me tienen a las cuatro.
Y a las cinco con recato
mis sentidos en ti están,
pensando siempre que dan
las seis sin ver tu hermosura;
y así no hay hora segura
en el reloj de mi afán.

3

No hay hora que me sujete,
vida mía, de ti el desvelo
porque la luz de tu cielo
en pie me tiene a las siete.
Y a las ocho me promete
que mis penas cesarán
y que a las nueve serán
mis caricias bien pagadas.
¡A qué horas tan dilatadas
y qué a poco a poco, dan!

4

En fin, cuantas horas veo
que el día y la noche tienen,
otras tantas me aprevienen;
mi bien, te ofrezco a las diez,
a las once pienso que es
bien pagada mi afición,
y cuando a las doce son
te deseo con más anhelo
porque la luz de tu cielo
dió alivio a mi corazón.

1

For me there is neither sun nor moon,
There is no evening, night, or day.
Alone I have been thinking of you
My love, since one o'clock;
That is my good fortune.
At two I am alert and
My heart is afflicted.
At three it says good luck,
And so, my soul, until I see you
How long the hours are!

2

In good faith I idolize you
And your surpassing goodness.
Well, my darling, the three powers
Have me on my feet at four.
And at five, full of care,
My feelings reach out to you,
Always I'm thinking the clock will strike
Six without my having seen your beauty;
And so there is no safe hour
By the clock of my anxiety.

3

There is no hour, my love,
That will let me sleep
Because the light of your heaven
Keeps me on my feet until seven.
And by eight it gives me the promise
That my sorrows will cease
And that by nine my acts of love
Will be well rewarded.
But, how long these hours are
And how slowly they strike!

4

Finally, despite the many hours which I see
That the day and night have,
As many more await me;
My dear, I offer you my love at ten,
At eleven I think that
My fondness will be well paid,
And when it is twelve
I desire you with more longing
Because the light from your heaven
Has given relief to my heart.

---

[1] See *potencias* in Velázquez 17a, where *potencias del alma* are defined as memory, understanding, and will.

QUÉ LAR-GAS LAS HO-RAS SON EN EL RE-LOJ DE MI A-
FÁN, Y, QUE PO-CO A PO-CO DAN A-LI-VIO A MI CO-RA-
ZÓN. PA-RA MÍ NO HAY SOL NI LU-NA,
NO HAY TAR-DE, NO-CHE, NO HAY DÍ-A. TAN SO-LO ES-TOY VI-DA
MÍ-A, PEN-SAN-DO EN TI DES-DE LA U-NA HA QUE-
DA-DO MI FOR-TU-NA. A LAS DOS CON A-TEN-
CIÓN SE A-FLI-JE MI CO-RA-ZÓN. A LAS TRES
DI-CIEN-DO SUER-TE, YA-SÍ MI AL-MA PA-RA VER-TE
¡QUÉ LAR-GAS LAS HO-RAS SON!

This is a good example of the *décima glo-sada* with the rhyme scheme of the *espinela* rigorously observed, sung to the traditional New Mexican *décima* melody. The text and consequently the translation leave something to be desired.

E2. *Tristes los Dos Estaremos* (We Will Both Be Sad)
R4, Próspero S. Baca, age 70, Bernalillo, N.Mex., 1945, Robb. Cf. Mendoza 9c (p. 473).

Planta	*Planta*
Tristes los dos estaremos	We will both be sad
y que, pene solo yo,	And I shall suffer alone,
Dejaré de verte, sí;	I will forbear seeing you, yes;
pero de quererte, no.	But forbear loving you, no.

1

Bello clavel que venero,
astro bello, reluciente,
clara estrella del oriente,
hermosísimo lucero;
con toda mi alma te quiero,
mas como lejos nos vemos,
que un momento no tenemos
a solos para mirarnos,
si no podemos hablarnos,
tristes los dos estaremos.

1

Beautiful carnation whom I worship,
Fair and brilliant star,
Bright star of the east,
My most beautiful Venus;
With all my soul I love you,
But we see each other only from afar,
And have not a moment
Alone together,
If we cannot speak,
We will both be sad.

2

Bellísimo serafín,
florida y fragante palma,
querida prenda del alma,
rosa del mejor jardín;
oye, fragante jazmín,
lo que te suplico yo:
si a tus sentidos llegó
esta creída dolencia,
al cielo pido licencia
y que pene solo yo.

2

Most beautiful angel,
Lovely and fragrant palm,
Sweetheart of my soul,
Rose of the finest garden;
Listen, fragrant jasmine,
To what I ask:
If to your senses has come
This grave disease,
I beg permission of heaven
That I alone shall suffer.

3

¡Escucha, prenda preciosa!
Oyeme, bien de mi vida,
que mi amor por ti sospira
de esa prisión cautelosa
y verás cual lastimosa
se halla mi vida por ti,
mi alma, desde que te ví
te aseguré mi firmeza,
de esta crecida tristeza
dejaré de verte, sí.

3

Listen, precious love!
Hear me, darling of my life,
My love for you sighs
From this closely guarded prison
That you may see how sad
My life is made for want of you,
My soul, since first I saw you.
I will promise you my devotion
To this growing sadness,
I will forbear seeing you, yes.

4

Ya te he dicho mi intención,
ya sabes que a ti te quiero,
ya sabes que por ti muero,
prenda de mi corazón;
ya se llegó la ocasión
que mi amor se declaró
ya todo se me acabó,
ya no tengo más que darte,
pues ya dejo de mirarte,
pero de quererte, ¡no!

4

Now I have told you of my feelings,
Now you know that I love you,
Now you know that I am dying for you,
Beloved of my heart;
The occasion has arrived,
And my love is declared.
Everything is ended for me,
I have no more to offer you,
So I will forbear seeing you,
But forbear loving you, no!

SO-LO YO, DÉ-JA-RÉ DE VER-TE,

SÍ; PE-RO DE QUE-RER-TE, NO. BE-LLO

CLA-VEL QUE VE-NE-RO, A-STRO BE-LLO, RE-LU-CIEN-TE,

CLA-RA E-STRE-LLA DEL O -RIEN-TE HER-MO- SÍ-SSI-MO LU-

CE-RO; CON TO - DA MI AL-MA TE QUIE-RO, MAS CO-

MO LE-JOS NOS VE-MOS, QUE UN MO -MEN-TO NO

TE - NE - MOS A SO - LOS DA-RA MI - RAR-NOS,

SI NO PO - DE-MOS HAB-LAR-NOS, TRIS-TES LOS DOS ES -TA-RE - MOS.

E3. *Yo Me Voy Contigo* (I Shall Go with You)
R48, Antonio Medina, Chimayó, N.Mex., 1945, Robb. Cf. R12.

Planta	*Planta*
—Yo me voy contigo que	"I shall go with you
yo no me quedo solita.	That no more I may be alone."
—Ya voy sintiendo el dejarte,	"I am sorry to leave you,
pero adiós chiquitita. —	But farewell little girl."

1	1
. . . [undecipherable]	. . .
De ahí agarré mi camino	From there I took off
para recortar mi jornada	To shorten my journey
y ahí la vide sentada	And I saw her sitting here
capeando con su manita	Waving her little hand
y que me estaba diciendo:	And saying to me:
—Yo me voy contigo que	"I will go with you
yo no me quedo solita.	That no more I may be alone."

2

—En un coche de vidriera,
mi alma, te quisiera traer
pero el no tener dinero
haré el hombre renegar.
Ahí te volveré a mirar
si Dios vida no nos quite;
. . . [undecipherable]
Dame un abrazo de amor
porque, adiós chiquitita.—

2

"My dear, I'd like to carry you off
In a coach of glass
But not having money
Makes a man give up such dreams.
I shall return to see you
If God lets us live;
. . .
Give me a loving embrace
Because it's good-bye, little girl."

The foregoing fragment of a *décima* is included because of the version of the *décima* melody that accompanies it. A more nearly complete text, divided improperly by the singer into *coplas* and set improperly to an interesting but different melody, is *Yo Me Voy Contigo* (R12).

E4. *Rosa de Castilla Fresca* (Fresh Rose of Castile)
    R2424, Juan Griego, age 61, Albuquerque, N.Mex., 1971, Cipriano Griego.

Planta
Rosa de Castilla fresca,
prende y se vuelve a secar.
Desde aquí te estoy mirando
y no te puedo olvidar.

Planta
Fresh rose of Castile,
It blooms and it withers again.
From here I'm looking at you
And I can't forget you.

1

Son las ocho que me acuesto.
No me puedo estar un rato
porque me levanta el acto
de la obligación que resto.
Yo vivo pensando en esto
y el reloj es mi cordel
como hago memorias de él
de mi vista tan crecida.
Yo por ti he de dar la vida,
Rosa de Castilla fresca.

1

It is eight when I go to bed.
I can't stay there
Because the fact of the
Obligation that I owe makes me move.
I live thinking about this
And the watch is my reminder
Since my memories
Loom large before me.
I would give my life for you,
Fresh climbing rose of Castile.

2

Son las nueve y ando andando
que se me hace que la veo
y en la sombra del deseo
que a mí me procede tanto.
A las once agonizando
¿Qué dices, bien de mi vida?
Por ti yo vivo penando.

2

It is nine and I am out walking
And I imagine I see her
And in the shadow of desire
That follows me so much of the way.
At eleven I'm in agony.
What do you say, my dear?
For you I live in a state of pain.

3

A las doce es mi agonía
y a la una y media dobla,
y a las tres son penas doble
sin estar sin tu compañía.
Y a las cuatro viene el día
y no ni he encontrado a quien
preguntarle por mi bien.
Que siempre mi dolor crece
ya de ver que amanece
y mis ojos no la ven.

3

At twelve I am in agony
And at one-thirty it doubles,
And at three my pains are redoubled
Being without your company.
And at four the day arrives
And I haven't found anyone to
Ask about my loved one.
My pain keeps on growing
When I see that dawn comes
And yet my eyes do not see her.

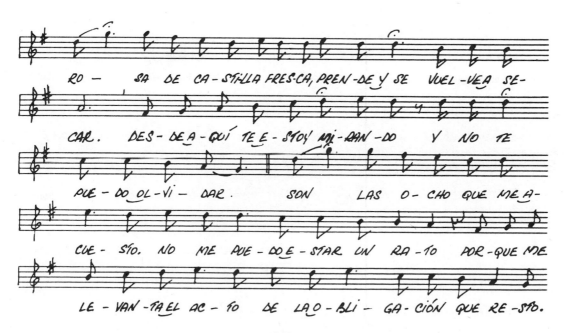

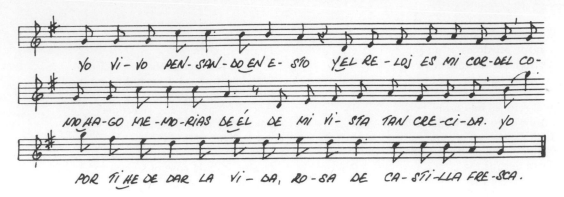

yo vi-vo pen-san-do en e-sto y el re-loj es mi cor-del co-

mo ha-go me-mo-rias de él de mi vi-sta tan cre-ci-da. yo

por ti he de dar la vi-da, ro-sa de ca-sti-lla fre-sca.

This is an imperfect *décima* with the rhyming
pattern of the *espinela*.

E5. *María Teresa*
R74, Julianita Trujillo, Chimayó, N.Mex., 1946, Robb. Cf. R204 by same singer.

Cuando me salí a pasear	When I went out to walk
a casa María Teresa	To the house of María Teresa
hecho mano con Francesa	I grasped Francesa's hand
y en lo que pude agarrar.	And whatever else I could.
No digas que fuí a robar	Don't say that I went to rob
que no estoy creado con gatos	For I was not raised with cats,
ni tampoco con ingratos,	Nor with ingrates,
sólo con gente decente,	Only with decent people,
y agarrando de repente,	And suddenly seizing her, I said,
—Ahí te traigo unos zapatos.	"Here I bring you some shoes."

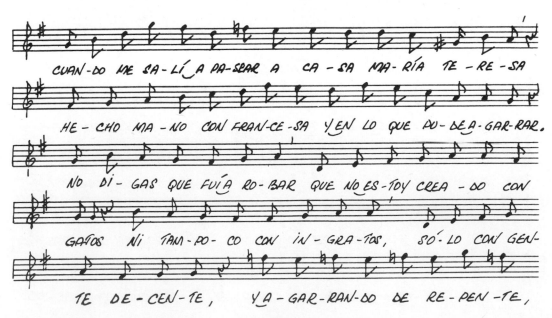

CUAN-DO ME SA-LÍ A PA-SEAR A CA-SA MA-RÍA TE-RE-SA

HE-CHO MA-NO CON FRAN-CE-SA Y EN LO QUE PU-DE A-GAR-RAR.

NO DI-GAS QUE FUÍ A RO-BAR QUE NO ES-TOY CREA-DO CON

GATOS NI TAN-PO-CO CON IN-GRA-TOS, SÓ-LO CON GEN-

TE DE-CEN-TE, Y A-GAR-RAN-DO DE RE-PEN-TE,

--AHÍ, TE TRAI- GO U -NOS ZA - PA - TOS.--

This is a fragment of a *disparate* in the form
of a *décima glosada*.

E6. *Cuando Ya Mi Amor* (When My Love)
R50, Antonio Medina, Chimayó, N.Mex., 1945, Robb.

1	1
Cuando ya mi amor sintió	When my love heard
de su marido los pasos,	Her husband's footsteps,
me fué quitando los brazos	She left my arms
más de fuerza que de gana.	More from compulsion than desire.
Yo me rodé de su cama,	I fell from her bed,
sin saber cómo ni cuándo.	I know not how or when.
Cien azotes me fué dando	He lashed me one hundred times
con un demonio de lazo,	With a devilish whip,
y no me dió un testarazo	And he did not beat me more
porque me vido estar miando.	Only because he saw I was voiding.

2	2
Pronto me fuí levantando	Quickly I got up
mirándome mil visiones;	Amid a thousand hallucinations;
me fuí para un arroyuelo	I went to a brook
para lavar mis calzones,	I washed my pants,
me vide los verdugones	I saw my scars and blue spots
de la cabeza a los pies.	From head to foot.
. . . [undecipherable]	. . .
. . .	. . .
y no me quedaron ganas	And I was left with no desire
de ir a su casa otra vez.	To go near her house again.

This is a deteriorated fragment of a *décima*.
It was recited and not sung.

E7. *En Una Ocasión* (On One Occasion)
R1600, Frank García, age 53, Tierra Amarilla, N.Mex., 1957, Robb. Cf. E6, E8.

1	1
Estando en cierta ocasión	Being on one occasion
con mi dueña muy gustoso	With my mistress and very happy,
vide venir a su esposo	I saw her husband coming
y me tembló el corazón.	And my heart trembled.
Yo me metí en un cajón	I hid in a box,
del susto que me cernía.	Frightened to death.
Cerca de las tres sería	It was about three
cuando el esposo llegó.	When her husband came.

385

2

Se pusieron a cenar
en amable y dulce unión.
Pero yo en aquel cajón
las agonías me tocaron.
Más luegito se acostaron
y se ponen en porfía
—Quita ese cajón, María,
que no está bien en la entrada.—
Me servirá de experiencia.
¡Madre de Dios consagrada!

2

They got ready to dine
In sweet and friendly union.
But in that box
I went through agonies.
A little later they went to bed
And began to wrangle.
"Get rid of that box, María.
It's no good there in the entry."
That will be a lesson to me.
Holy Mother of God!

3

Otro día por la mañana
el esposo se levantó,
enojado y reguroso.
Sobre el cajón se sentó.
El corazón me tiembló.
Los fríos me querían dar.
No les quisiera contar
lo que a mí me sucedió.

3

The next day in the morning
The husband got up,
Angry and demanding.
He sat down on the box.
My heart trembled.
I got the chills.
I wouldn't want to tell
All that happened to me.

4

El esposo se salió.
Más como un ligero viento,
más en mi pensamiento,
a un cerro me remonté.
A verla yo arrendé.
Ella me habla con compás:
—Toma tu chichita más.—
Yo, como libre mesteño,
—No quiero chiches con dueño
ni las apedesco más.

4

The husband went out.
Like a swift breeze,
And more swift in my thoughts,
I ran up a mountain.
I came back to see her.
She spoke to me with pity:
"Come fondle my breast again."
But I, like a free rabbit, said,
"I don't want breasts owned by a husband,
Nor do I desire them any longer."

E8. *Dime, Alma ¿Qué Has Pensado?* (Tell Me, My Soul, What Have You Thought?)
RB135, Abiquiu, N.Mex., 1950, from a notebook of Arvino Martínez.

Dime, alma ¿qué has pensado:
dónde estará su marido—
él en los campos tirado
y yo durmiendo contigo?

Tell me, my soul, what have you thought:
Where is your husband—
Stretched out in the fields
And I, sleeping with you?

1

El:
Quisiera mudar de traje
para no ser conocido
para llegar al paraje
en donde está tu marido.
Es el pobre tan perdido.
Que hasta lástima le tengo
por eso de noche vengo
hacia su propiedad.

1

He:
I'd like to change clothes
In order not to be recognized
When I go to the place
Where your husband is.
The poor guy is so bad off.
Even I pity him,
That's why I come at night
To his property.

Yo pagaré cuanto tenga por saber cuando vendrá.	I would pay whatever I had To know when he was coming.

2

Ella:

Deja, no te acuerdes de él
que lo tengo aborrecido.
La fuerza que es mi marido
le sirvo como mujer,
y así le hago buen placer
cuando lo veo presente,
pero cuando él se halla ausente
de sus huesos digo y hablo.
Duerme tú a gusto conmigo
y a él que se lo lleve el diablo.

2

She:

Don't talk about him
For I abhor him.
By force is he my husband
I serve as his wife,
And so I please him
When I see him here,
But when he is absent
I say what I please about him.
Sleep with me to your heart's content
And let him go to the devil.

3

El:

Mira no hables mucho de él.
Conduélete de sus males.
Que él trabaja y se desvela
para que tú te regales.
Yo paso dos mil afanes
porque de mí no se cele
ni de mí tiene malicias.
El pagará las albricias
por saber de esta cautela.

3

He:

Look, don't talk so much about him.
You should feel sorry for him.
He works and worries
So you'll enjoy yourself.
I undergo a thousand worries
So he won't get jealous of me,
Nor does he have any malice toward me.
He would give a lot
To know about this affair.

4

Ella:

Te lo digo y es así
que si él lo llega a saber,
él no se duele de ti
ni de la pobre de mí,
pero para que no se cele
yo te daré este consejo
que lo dejes que se muela
quien le manda ser pendejo.

4

She:

I'll tell you this straight,
That if he finds out
He'll not weep any tears
For you or for poor me,
But so that he won't be jealous
I will give you this advice—
That you let him do the worrying.
That's what he gets for being a fool.

E9. *Nada en Esta Vida Dura* (Nothing in This Life Lasts)
R1983, Clemente Chávez, Galisteo, N.Mex., 1963, Robb.

Planta

Nada en esta vida dura,
fenecen bienes y males;
a todos nos hace iguales
una triste sepultura.

Planta

Nothing in this life lasts,
Good men and evil perish;
A sad tomb
Makes us all equal.

1

Se acaba la vanidad,
la avaricia y la largueza,
la soberbia y la riqueza,
la pompa y autoridad;

1

Vanity ends,
Avarice and generosity,
Arrogance and wealth,
Pomp and authority;

se acaba la falsedad,
el garbo y la compostura,
la permanente hermosura
que tanto el mundo alaba;
todo en el mundo acaba,
nada en esta vida dura.

Falsehood ends,
Grace and circumspection,
Permanent beauty
That the world lauds so much;
Everything in the world ends,
Nothing in this life lasts.

2

Muere el justo, el pecador,
muere el grande, muere el chico,
muere el pobre, muere el rico,
el esclavo y el señor.
Se acaba el mundano amor,
puestos, honores, caudales,
mueren traidores y leales;
y claro el discurso advierte
que llegándose la muerte
fenecen bienes y males.

The just man dies, and the sinner,
The great man dies, and the little man,
The poor man dies, and the rich man,
The slave and the master.
Worldly love ends, likewise
Positions, honors, fortune.
Traitors die, and faithful men;
And the message comes clearly
That when death arrives,
Good men and evil perish.

3

Mueren subditos, prelados,
mueren virreyes, oidores,
alcaldes, gobernadores,
obispos, curas, vasallos;
mueren solteros, casados,
arzobispos, generales,
papas, reyes, cardenales;
pues en siete pies de tierra
toda medida se encierra
y a todos nos hace iguales.

Inferiors die and prelates,
Viceroys die and judges,
Mayors and governors,
Bishops, priests, and vassals;
Bachelors die and married men,
Archbishops and generals,
Popes, kings, and cardinals;
All sizes will fit
In seven feet of earth
And it makes us all equal.

4

En fin mueren escribanos,
alguaciles y soplones,
comisarios y ladrones,
médicos y cirujanos;
abran los ojos mundanos,
ya no pequen, que es locura;
hagan clara conjetura
que nos hemos de morir,
y a todos ha de cubrir
una triste sepultura.

Finally, scribes die,
Constables and cheaters,
Deputies and thieves,
Doctors and surgeons;
Open your mundane eyes,
Don't sin any more, it is folly;
Make clear the realization
That we must die
And all of us will be buried
In a sad tomb.

This is a *décima glosada—espinela.*

E10. *Estando de Ocioso un Día* (Having Nothing To Do One Day)
R321, E. and F. Sánchez, Tijeras, N.Mex., 1950, Robb. Cf. R2011.

Planta
Estando de ocioso un día,
esto me quedé pensando:
mientras que el tiempo se pasa
también yo me voy pasando.

Planta
Having nothing to do one day,
This is what I started to think:
While time is passing by,
So am I passing by.

1

¡Qué largo es un año entero!
digo para mí solito;
un mes poco más cortito, y
más corta una semana.
Un día es cosa nada,
una hora cosa de menos,
y un minuto ya sabemos
cuan pronto se pasaría.
Esto me puse a pensar
estando ocioso un día.

2

Enero y febrero pasan;
sigue marzo y abril.
Mayo tiene que seguir
como junio su carrera;
julio y agosto no esperan
como septiembre y octubre.
Noviembre como es costumbre,
ya diciembre va llamando;
un día por pasar tiempo,
esto me quedé pensando.

3

Era un domingo en la tarde
cuando me puse a pensar:
tendría que pasar
lunes y martes llorando.
Y el miércoles preparando
para el jueves diversión,
y el viernes con precaución
de estar el sábado en casa.
Porque algo tendré que hacer
mientras el tiempo se pasa.

4

Cuando acabé de pensar,
un sobresalto sentí,
y luego me decidí
a buscar quien me quisiera;
sea linda o sea fiera
el cuento es hallar alguna.
Aunque es poca mi fortuna,
no debo de estar esperando,
porque si el tiempo se pasa,
también yo me voy pasando.

1

How long a whole year is!
I say, all to myself;
A month is a little shorter,
And a week is still shorter.
A day is nothing,
An hour hardly anything,
And we already know how
Fast a minute would go by.
This is what I started to think
One day at my leisure.

2

January and February pass;
And March and April follow.
May like June
Has to follow its path;
July and August don't wait
And neither do September and October.
November, as usual, is already
Announcing December.
One day, to while the time away,
This is what I was thinking.

3

It was a Sunday afternoon
When I started to wonder
If I would have to spend
Monday and Tuesday crying.
And I'd spend Wednesday
Preparing something to do Thursday,
And Friday I'd make sure that
I'd be home Saturday.
Because I'll have to do
Something to pass the time.

4

When I came to my senses,
A sudden dread came over me,
And then and there I decided
To look for someone to love;
No matter is she is pretty or ugly,
What matters is to find someone.
Even though I am unlucky,
I mustn't wait,
Because if time goes by,
So do I.

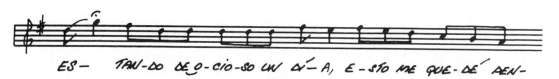

ES— TAN-DO DE O-CIO-SO UN DÍ-A, E-STO ME QUE-DÉ PEN-

SAN - DO: MIEN - TRAS QUE EL TIEM - PO SE PA - SA
TAM - BIÉN YO ME VOY PA - SAN - DO.
décima 1
¡QUÉ LAR - GO ES UN A - ÑO EN - TE - RO! DI - GO PA - RA
MÍ SO - LI - TO; UN MES PO - CO MÁS COR - TI - TO, Y MÁS
COR - TA U - NA SE - MA - NA. UN DÍ - A ES CO - SA NA - DA,
U - NA HO - RA CO - SA DE ME - NOS, Y UN MI - NU - TO
YA SA - BE - MOS CUAN PRON - TO SE PA - SA -
RÍ - A. ES - TO ME PU - SE A PEN - SAR
E - STAN - DO O - CIO - SO UN DÍ - A.

Estando de Ocioso un Día is an imperfect
version of *décima glosada—espinela*.

E11. *Yo en lu Vida Solicito* (I Seek in Life)
R1779, Próspero S. Baca, age 70, Bernalillo, N.Mex., 1945, Robb.

Planta	*Planta*
Yo (nunca?) en la vida solicito	I never court in life
a quien de mí se retira,	Anyone who turns away from me,
porque tengo por venganza	Because I take vengeance
de olvidar a quien me olvida.	By forgetting the person who forgets me.

1	1
Yo nunca he querido bien	I have never liked anyone
a quien corresponde mal;	Who repays good with evil;

yo en todo soy general
y de nada hago un nivel;
y si me olvidan, también
a olvidarlas precipito,
pues que soy tan exquisito
que hoy puedo decirlo así
que a quien no me quiere a mí
yo en la vida solicito.

I treat everyone alike
And in no way do I establish levels;
If they forget me
I quickly forget them,
For I am so excellent
That today I can say
That those who don't like me
I seek in life.

2

Si me tratan con amor
yo con amor correspondo;
si me hablan bien, bien respondo,
si con amor, con amor;
yo conozco a superior,
bien miro a quien bien me mira,
si alguna por mí suspira,
con un suspiro le pago;
y jamás cariños le hago,
a quien de mí se retira.

2

If they treat me with love
I return their love;
If they speak well to me, I answer well,
If with love, with love;
I know my superior,
I look well on anyone who looks well on me,
If someone sighs for me
I repay them with a sigh;
And I'm never tender
With anyone who turns away from me.

3

Yo soy de tal condición
que como me dicen, digo,
y a la que me obliga, la obligo
con todo mi corazón;
pero no en toda ocasión
viviré en esta confianza;
si me preguntan por qué
yo entonces responderé
porque tengo por venganza.

3

I am in such a position
That as they speak to me, so I reply,
And the woman who obliges me, I oblige
With all my heart;
But not on all occasions
Will I live with such trust;
If they ask me why
I will then respond
Because I take vengeance.

4

La venganza que yo tengo
es que mi amor jamás temí,
y a la que amor me apreviene
amor también le aprevengo;
pues nunca jamás me atengo
yo a vivir en mala vida,
si acaso es muy advertida,
ya mi lealtad está propuesta;
de dar siempre por respuesta
de olvidar a quien me olvida.

4

The vengeance that I have
Is that I never feared love,
And to her who arranges love for me,
I also arrange it for her;
I never in my life
Have led an evil life, even
If perchance it is very entertaining.
My loyalty is fixed;
I shall always give tit for tat,
Forgetting the person who forgets me.

E12. *El Cantor Que Se Ejercita* (The Singer Who Tries Too Hard)
R2136, Chile, 1965, Ester Grebe.

El cantor que se ejercita
queriendo sobresalir
conmigo no va a cundir
porque lo tengo en mis listas.

The singer who tries too hard
Trying to be the winner
Will get nowhere with me
For I have his number.

Vengan a mi propia vista
los ilustrados de letras,
los que quieran a mi cuenta.
Los recibo muy contento
y prevéngase con el tiempo
todo fantástico poeta.

Let the well educated ones
Come before my eyes,
Those who want to. For my part
I'll take them on with pleasure,
But let all who fancy themselves poets
Be forewarned in time.

This ten-line fragment of a *décima* from Chile, apparently part of a prelude to a song contest, is included here for purposes of comparison with the *décimas* of the American Southwest. It sounds strangely like the challenge to rival singers found in the opening verse of some of the New Mexican *trovos* (cf. verses 1–13 of *Trovo del Viejo Vilmas*, G1) and is possibly part of a *trovo* in the form of a *décima*.

Gilbert Chase advised me that the *trovos* are known in various Latin American countries, as this example would indicate. Their wide diffusion indicates a common Spanish origin.

The eight Chilean *décimas* in the J. D. Robb Collection (R2129–36), of which this is one, are remarkable for their parallel descending harmonies at the final cadence and other features that give them a strange and fascinating beauty.

E13. *Y Anoche Estando Acostado* (Last Night Lying in Bed)
R317, Elfego Sánchez, Tijeras, N.Mex., 1950, Robb.

Planta
Y anoche estando acostado,
negrita, estaba soñando
que al pie de un álamo verde
el pecho me estabas dando.

Planta
Last night lying in bed,
Little love, I was dreaming
That you were giving me your breast
Under a green cottonwood.

1
Me acosté pensando en ti
y en el Señor, prenda amada;
también te vide acostada
de un ladito y junto a mí;
me echaste el brazo, sí,
desperté muy halagüeño,
buscándote con empeño y
luego que no te hallé:
solo a llorar me senté,
y anoche en el primer sueño.

1
I went to bed thinking about you
And the Lord, my dearest.
I also saw you lying down on
One side next to me;
You put your arm around me;
Of course I woke up wanting
To hug and fondle you
And when I didn't find you, I
Sat down to weep by myself,
Last night in my first sleep.

2
Como el sueño es tan atroz,
me levanté desvariando;
solo me senté pensando:
¡conciencia! ¡válgame Dios!
oí tocar el reloj,
las horas que estaba dando
y nos queríamos los dos—
iba! qué sueño tan atroz—
negrita, estaba soñando.

2
Since sleep was so difficult
I awoke talking in my sleep;
I got up and sat down
By myself, thinking: Good God!
I heard the clock strike the hours
The hours that were ticking away,
The hours of our lovemaking.
Bah! What a terrible dream
Little love, I was dreaming.

3
Y alto quede la campana,
si mi amor te solicita,
y óyeme esta palabrita,
chatita, no seas tirana.
Cierto mi amor te proclama,
no estrañe tus cariñitos:
¡Qué halagüeños! ¡Qué bonitos!
pues que me vivo pensando:
pues que soñó tu negrito
que el pecho le estabas dando.

3
Let the bell ring loud.
If my love entreats you,
Listen to this little word,
Darling, don't be a tyrant.
I declare my love for you,
Don't deny me your charms,
So alluring, so beautiful are they
That I spend all my time thinking
That your lover dreamed
That you are giving him your breast.

E14. *Murió Mi Madre* (My Mother Died)
R47, Antonio Medina, Chimayó, N.Mex., 1945, Robb.

1

Murió mi madre y fué cierto
y yo nací desgraciado;
para mis mayores penas
ya mi padre está finado,
y en un abrir me he quedado
con el corazón partido;
pero de todos querido
de mí no hay separación.
Sientan conmigo a mi madre
los que hagan estimación.

1

My mother died and it is surely truc
That I was born unfortunate.
And to make my sorrows greater
Now my father is dead,
And I am left behind
With a broken heart;
But from all those whom I have loved
There is no separation.
Mourn with me for my mother,
Those who esteem me.

<table>
<tr><td>

2

De que veo esa parroquia,
de ese pueblo de San Juan
comience mi corazón
gotas de sangre de llorar.
¿Cuándo se me ha de olvidar
el tesoro que perdí?
Dios mío, confío en ti
la suerte que me tocó.
Si es tu voluntad acordarte
de un huérfano, aquí estoy yo.

</td><td>

2

As I look at that parish,
Of that town of San Juan
My heart commences to weep
Tears of blood.
When shall I ever forget
The treasure that I have lost?
My God, to thee do I entrust
The fate that has befallen me.
If it is thy will to remember
An orphan, here I am.

</td></tr>
<tr><td>

3

Por fin, tengo una hermanita
que el corazón me traspasa,
pues ella es la idolatría
y es la alegría de mi casa.
Lo digo sin ignorancia,
porque me sustancie el sueño;
sólo en sentir hago empeño
supuesto que me tocó.
Bien haría en dejarme Dios
la madre que me parió.

</td><td>

3

Finally, I have a little sister
Who fills my heart with compassion,
For she is the idol
And the happiness of my house.
I speak with knowledge
And my dreams sustain me;
Only in kindly sentiment do I find courage
Provided that I have it.
Ah, if only God had left me
The mother who bore me.

</td></tr>
</table>

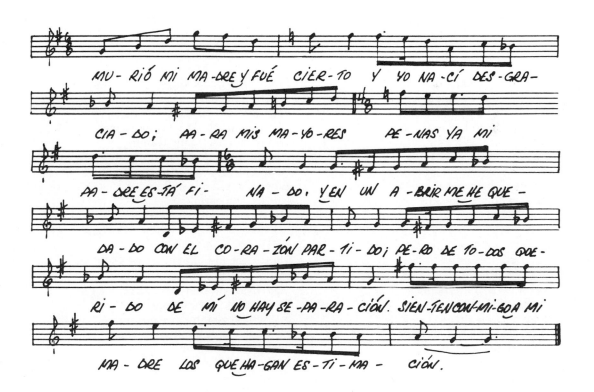

Murió Mi Madre is a *décima* without a *planta*.

E15. *El Huérfano* (The Orphan Boy)
R1994, Clemente Chávez, Galisteo, N.Mex., 1963, Robb. Cf. R1848.

1

Pensando esto me confundo,
es muy triste y notable,
gran desdicha en el mundo
no tener uno a sus padres;
como la pluma en el aire
anda el hijo ya perdido.
El huérfano desvalido
pierde el honor y el decoro.
Escuchen, amigos míos,
estas lágrimas que lloro.

1

Thinking of this confounds me,
It is very sad and noteworthy,
A great misfortune in the world
Not having one's parents;
The lost child fares
As a feather in the wind.
The destitute orphan
Loses honor and dignity.
Hear, my friends,
These tears that I weep.

2

El que es huérfano, señores,
todos le corren desaires
y sufre crueles rigores
porque le faltan sus padres;
no hay un solo que calle
la gran orfandad que espera,
esto es triste y cosa seria.
¡Ay! si vivieran mis padres
o sus palabras oyera hoy,
que reflejo ya es tarde.
¡Ay! si vivieran mis padres.

2

Gentlemen, he who is an orphan
Is slighted by everyone
And suffers cruel hardships
Because he has no parents;
There is not one who fails to speak
Of the great sadness of being an orphan,
It is a sad and serious thing.
Oh! If only my parents were alive
Or I could hear their voices today,
But it is too late to think of this.
Oh! If my parents were still alive!

3

Recuerdo de aquellos días
de cuando yo me paseaba,
mi madre me bendecía,
mi madre por mí lloraba;
¡ay! que desgracia la mía,
todo acabó en un momento,
no tengo hora de contento,
Dios mío, tú bien lo sabes.
Causa mucho sentimiento
no tener uno a sus padres.

3

I remember those days
When I enjoyed myself,
My mother would bless me,
My mother would weep over me;
Oh! what misfortune is mine,
Everything ended in a moment,
I don't have an hour of contentment,
As you, my God, well know.
Not having parents
Causes much sorrow.

4

Cantaba un preso una tarde
en un triste prisión,
—¡Ay! si viviera mi madre
viéndome en esta prisión,
me echera su bendición
o por mí ya hubiera hablado.—
Hoy me encuentro aquí,
encerrado sólo su premio imploro.
Dice el preso desgraciado:
—Después de Dios, no hay tesoro.—

4

One afternoon a prisoner was singing
In a dreary prison,
"Oh! if my mother were alive,
Seeing me in this prison,
She would give me her blessing
Or would have spoken for me."
Today I find myself here, locked up,
I ask only for her love.
The unfortunate prisoner says:
"After God, there is no treasure."

El Huérfano is a *décima* without a *planta*.

E16. *Ni a Tu Más Intimo Amigo* (Not Even to Your Closest Friend)
R1770, Próspero S. Baca, Bernalillo, N.Mex., 1945, Robb.

Planta

Ni a tu más íntimo amigo
le descubras tu secreto;
te puedes ver algún día
arrepentido y sujeto.

1

Mientras vivas en el mundo,
sujeta y rige tu lengua
porque la cara se mengua
puede darte un mal profundo;
sin consejo y sin segundo
hay en tu pecho metido
y escarmentado te digo;
para tu mayor provecho
que no descubras tu pecho,
ni a tu más íntimo amigo.

2

No con todos seas afable
ni tengas mucha estrechez
solamente con él que es
en sus acciones estable
y si él es inconversable,
cosa que muchos lo son.
Callarás con precaución
y a todos guarda respeto
y sólo a tu confesor
le descubras tu secreto.

3

No seas liviano en decir
todo aquello que sintieres
ni publiques lo que vieres
porque te has de arrepentir.
Callando podrás vivir,
que el mucho hablar es defecto
y si quieres ser discreto,
huye de lisonjerías
porque esquivo y afrentado
te puedes ver algún día.

4

No procures de valiente
ni de chartador falaz.
Procura con todos paz,
y con Dios principalmente;
no le digas facilmente
a ninguno su defecto

Planta

Not even to your closest friend
Should you divulge your secret;
For some day you may be
Sorry, and it will be too late.

1

As long as you live in the world,
Guard and control your tongue,
Because one loses face
And it can cause you profound sorrow;
Without advice and without help
There are worry and pain
In your breast, I tell you;
For your own good,
Don't open your heart,
Not even to your closest friend.

2

Don't be affable with everyone,
Nor get too close to them, but
Only with him who is
Stable in his actions
And if he is able to keep a secret,
As many are.
You should cautiously keep quiet
And have respect for everyone,
And only to your confessor
Should you tell your secret.

3

Don't be imprudent in saying
All that you may feel,
Nor publish that which you see
Because you will have to repent.
You can live, keeping silent,
For talking a lot is a defect
And if you wish to be discreet,
Avoid gossip
Because you may see yourself
Scorned and offended some day.

4

Don't try to be brave
Nor a chattering gossip.
Seek peace with everyone
And principally with God;
Don't be quick to tell
Anyone his faults

y con precaución te advierto
que algún día podrás hallarte
arrepentido y sujeto.

And with care, I warn you,
That some day you may find yourself
Sorry and it will be too late.

E16 is a *décima glosada*, assonated rather
than rhymed and following, with some variations, the pattern of the *espinela*.

E17. *Margarita*
R224a, Juan Luján, age 66, Santo Niño (near Riverside), N.Mex., 1949, Robb.

Planta
El día dieciocho de octubre,
el mil novecientos once
sólo un corazón de bronce
no oye mi llanto lugubre.

Planta
On the eighteenth day of October
In nineteen hundred eleven
Only a heart of bronze
Would fail to hear my sad complaint.

1
¡Ay! Dios de mi corazón,
¿qué es lo que me sucedió?
que mi hijita se murió
muy lejos de Canjilón,
donde está mi habitación,
mi hogar, mi casa, y morada.
Antes de ser avisada
buena y sana se creía
llegando el infausto día
de su última retirada.

1
Oh! God of my heart,
What is this that has happened to me,
That my little daughter should die
Very far away from Canjilón,
Where my habitation is,
My home, my house, and my hearth?
Before receiving the news
She was thought to be well and happy,
Approaching the unhappy day
Of her last withdrawal from life.

2
La carta de precisión
me llegó el día veintiuno
en tiempo tan inportuno.
¡Ay! Dios de mi corazón.
Tú ——— mi dolor
con tu poder soberano,
pues murió el ser más lozano
que jamás tuvo mi amor.

2
The letter bearing the news
Came to me on the twenty-first
At such an inopportune time.
Oh! God of my heart,
You (can assuage?) my sorrow
With your sovereign power,
Dead now is the dearest being
Who ever held my love.

3
Ausente y lejos de mí
murió mis ojitos divinos (?),
espero los juicios divinos
se han de condoler de ti.
¿Jesús, qué será de mí?
No ver a mi luz hermosa
de mi amada mariposa;
murió mi hija Margarita
y a mí me dejó solita
como tortola llorosa.

3
Absent, and far from me
My divine eyes died,
I hope that the divine judges
Will have pity upon you.
Jesus, what will happen to me
Without the lovely light
Of my beloved butterfly?
My daughter Margarita has died
And I have been left alone
Like the mourning dove.

4	**4**
No tuve el gusto de verte	I missed the joy of seeing you
para echarte la bendición,	In order to give you my blessing,
lejos en Canjilón;	Far away in Canjilón;
me toco la mala suerte,	My bad fortune struck me
en instinta y en tu muerte,	In my instincts and in your death,
por lo que lloro y lamento,	Wherefore I weep and lament
que ni por el pensamiento	For never in my thoughts
me imaginé tal fortuna;	Did I imagine such bad fortune;
hoy se han eclipso la luna	Today the moon has been eclipsed
de dolor y sentimiento.	By sorrow and sentiment.
5	**5**
Lloro y siento a tu chiquito	I weep for you, my little one,
como barbano hablillo	Like a *barbano hablillo*
del mundo desconocido,	Of the unknown world,
por estar tan chiquitito,	Because being so small, so tender
tan tierno y ya huerfanito	And already a little orphan boy
tu amor se fué y lo dejó;	Your love has gone and left you;
por lo tanto lloro yo	And for this reason I weep
la suerte del angelito.	For the fate of this little angel.
6	**6**
Al pie de tu sepultura	At the foot of your grave
me verás arrodellada	You see me on my knees
de mis lágrimas bañada,	Bathed in my own tears,
y con amor y ternura	And with love and tenderness
llorando al ver tu criatura	Weeping to see your baby
y mi desdichada suerte;	And my unfortunate fate;
de mí si quieren la muerte	When the time comes for me to die
tuve el consuelo de verte.	I'll have the consolation of seeing you.

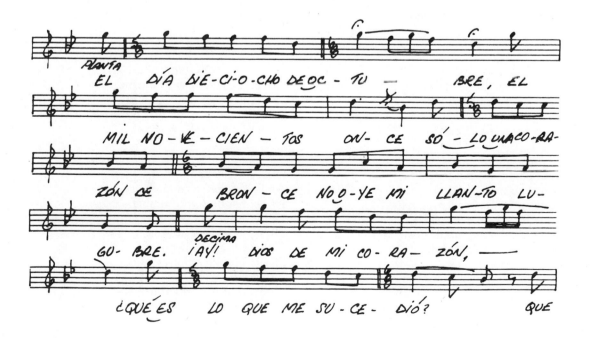

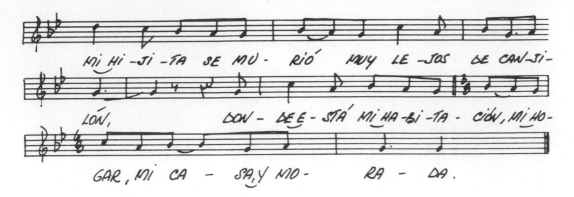

This is a *despedimento* of New Mexican origin in the form of a *décima* with a *planta* and six *décimas*. It is a lament composed by the noted folk poet Higinio V. Gonzales on the occasion of the death of Higinio's stepdaughter, who died at Ranchitos, near Riverside, New Mexico. The song dates from 1911 (FTR, 6/7/49). The singer has a habit of dropping the final vowel. When this happens, it is indicated by an apostrophe.

This song indicates to me that the *Corrido de la Muerte de Antonio Maestas* (I17), as sung by José Gallegos, was originally written as a *décima*. Juan Luján sings *Margarita* to virtually the same tune as I17. The melody in fact appears to be a simplification of the familiar *décima* melody. It starts high like the *décima* melody and ends low. In this respect it resembles many Indian melodies and leads to the conjecture that the New Mexico *décima* melody may have evolved as a result of the familiarity of the singers with Indian melodies.

The text seems to be a degeneration of the literary form as a result of aural transmission.

E18. *A Que No Me Lleva el Río* (I'll Bet the River Can't Take Me)
R7, Próspero S. Baca, age 70, Bernalillo, N.Mex., 1945, Robb (transcribed by Vicente T. Mendoza). Cf. Mendoza 9d (p. 337–38).

Planta	*Planta*
A que no me lleva el río,	I'll bet the river can't take me,
a que me voy de pasada,	I'll bet I can go through with it,
a que la dejo tusada,	I'll bet I can trim her down to size,
a que con agua la enfrío.	I'll bet I can cool her with water.

1	1
Aquí paran sus paseadas	Here end her ramblings
y aquí no tiene defensa	And here she has no defense,
a que le tumbo la trenza,	I'll bet her hair will tumble,
a que le doy de trompadas,	I'll bet I slap her around,
a que la canso a patadas,	I'll bet I kick her around,
a que lleva un susto mío,	I'll bet I frighten her,
a que de todo me río,	I'll bet I laugh at everything,
a que la hago disvariar,	I'll bet I make her delirious,
a que si la voy ahogar,	I'll bet that if I drown her—well,
a que no me lleva el río.	I'll bet the river can't take me.

2

A que la pongo de chico,
a que le corto su luburia
a que la meto de luria,
a que le corto el hocico,
a que si la trata un rico,
a que la ve moretiada,
a que le doy su trillada,
a que le hago atachones,
a que le doy de trompadas,
a que la dejo tusada.

3

A que queda para los flojos,
a que le tumbo una ceja,
a que le corto una oreja,
a que vengo mis enojos,
a que le escarbo los ojos,
a que de todo me río,
a que corto lo que es mío,
a que la mitad le prendo,
a que si la dejo ardiendo
a que con agua la enfrío.

4

A que la dejo burlada,
a que la dejo borracha,
a que la dejo tancuacha,
a que como por mi achada,
a que queda desmuelada,
a que queda manca y chueca,
a que la dejo perpleja,
a que si la veo hacer señas,
a que le tumbo las greñas,
a que me voy de pasada.

2

I'll bet I can bring her down to size,
I'll bet I can break her pride,
I'll bet I can make her look silly,
I'll bet I can cut off her snout,
I'll bet that if a rich man comes to see her,
I'll bet he will see her black and blue;
I'll bet I can thrash her,
I'll bet I can bend her badly,
I'll bet I can slap and smack her,
I'll bet I can cut her down to size.

3

I'll bet she is left for the worthless,
I'll bet I can knock off one eyebrow,
I'll bet I can cut off one ear,
I'll bet I can avenge all my anger,
I'll bet I can pluck out her eyes.
I'll bet I can laugh at everything,
I'll bet I can cut what belongs to me,
I'll bet I can take my half,
I'll bet that if I leave her raving,
I'll bet I can cool her with water.

4

I'll bet I can make a fool of her,
I'll bet I can get her drunk,
I'll bet I can make her money crazy,
I'll bet I can eat my spoils,
I'll bet she will remain toothless,
I'll bet she will be lame and bowlegged,
I'll bet I can leave her perplexed,
I'll bet that if I see her making gestures,
I'll bet I can knock off her hairdo,
I'll bet I can go through with it.

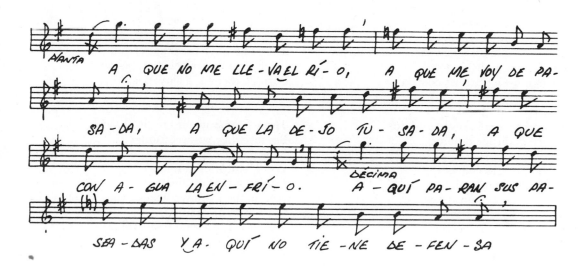

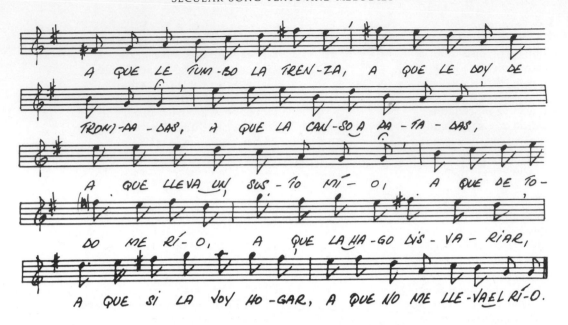

A QUE LE TUM-BO LA TREN-ZA, A QUE LE DOY DE
TRON-AA-DAS, A QUE LA CAN-SO A AA-TA-DAS,
A QUE LLEVA UN SUS-TO MI-O, A QUE DE TO-
DO ME RÍ-O, A QUE LA HA-GO DIS-VA-RIAR,
A QUE SI LA VOY HO-GAR, A QUE NO ME LLE-VAEL RÍ-O.

Though the text resembles the raving of a madman, it is included because of its unusual formal structure (each line throughout beginning with the words *A que*) and because it incorporates another variant of the dé-cima melody as sung by Próspero S. Baca, permitting comparison with other examples (see E1 and E2). *A Que No Me Lleva el Río* is a *décima glosada—espinela*.

E19. *Vale Más Volverse Loco* (It Would Be Better to Go Crazy)
R1761, Próspero S. Baca, age 70, Bernalillo, N.Mex., 1945, Robb.

Planta
Vale más volverse loco,
no ver lo que está pasando.
Lucifer anda alistando,
quemándose poco a poco.

Planta
It's better to go crazy
Than to see what is happening.
Lucifer continues enlisting people,
Burning them in a slow fire.

1
Ya no hay quien respete a Dios
por respetar los dineros,
las ovejas, los carneros,
la lana, el trigo, el arroz;
la injuria, la infamia atroz,
y en la fe creyemos poco;
por una vara de coco
piden bien lleno el costal;
ponerse esto a imaginar,
vale más volverse loco.

1
There is no one who respects God,
Because they respect money,
Sheep, mutton,
Wool, wheat, and rice;
Insults, atrocious dishonor,
And in the Faith we believe very little;
For a vara of coco
They ask for a whole sackfull;
Just think of it!
It's better to go crazy.

2
Si un pobre sale debiendo
de este año para él que viene,
el rico que cobrar tiene
o le dobla su dinero;
si queda debiendo un medio
luego lo van demandando,
y el juez, la va sentenciando
que satisfaga a su vista;
vale más sordo y sin vista,
no ver lo que está pasando.

2
If a poor man winds up owing money
From this year to the next,
The rich man charges him so much
So that he doubles the debt;
If he ends up owing a half
They foreclose on him,
And the judge sentences him
According to his fancy;
It's better to go deaf and sightless
Than to see what is happening.

3
Si un rico roba, no peca,
porque eso es multiplicar
y está en el saber contar
número dos a la diestra,
y cuando el juez observa ésta
le calla, al rico adulando;
le manda le baja trayendo
sean deudores y embusteros
a los jueces y usureros.
Lucifer anda alistando.

3
If a rich man robs, he does not sin,
For this is just multiplication,
And he knows how to count two
With his right hand,
And when the judge observes this
He keeps quiet, flattering the rich man,
Who keeps on bringing men,
Be they debtors and liars, to the
Judges and usurers.
Lucifer continues enlisting people.

4
Un rico todo su fin es
el hacer su diligencia,
y la misa, en contingencia,
dejan por ir a cobrar.
Piensan se lo han de llevar,
no quiere dejárselo a otro;
muy pronto se harán al trono.
¿Dónde está aquel rico avaro?
en los infiernos sentado
quemándose poco a poco.

4
The whole purpose of a rich man
Is tending to business,
And they quit going to Mass
For that costs money.
They think they can take it with them,
And don't want to leave it to another;
Soon they will go to judgment.
Where is that avaricious rich man?
Seated in Hell,
Burning in a slow fire.

This happens to be a very good example of the *espinela* complete with *planta*, four *décimas*, and the correct rhyming scheme *abbaaccddc*.

E20. *Guerras, Pleitos Sucediendo* (Wars, Battles Are Happening)
R1771, Próspero S. Baca, age 70, Bernalillo, N.Mex., 1945, Robb.

Planta
Guerras, pleitos sucediendo,
muerte y hambre amenazando,
todos los vicios creciendo,
y las virtudes menguando,
sin pedir misericordia,
el mundo está falleciendo.

Planta
Wars, battles are happening,
Death and hunger threatening,
Vices are growing
And virtues waning.
Without even asking for mercy,
The world is dying.

1

Ya no hay quien trate verdad
ya no hay palabra en la gente,
en estos tiempos presente
ninguna formalidad;
no hay quien tenga caridad;
según lo estoy advirtiendo,
la malicia está rigiendo,
y la venganza privando;
por eso estamos mirando
guerras, pleitos sucediendo.

1

There is no longer anyone who deals fairly,
There is no word of honor among the people,
In these times
There is no formality;
There is no one who has charity;
Accordingly, I am giving warning,
Malice is reigning,
And vengeance despoiling;
And this is why we are seeing
Wars and battles happening.

2

No hay ninguna educación
en niños, mozos, ni ancianos;
no hay unión en los cristianos,
ni en pícaros reprensión,
priva la mala intención.
La fe de Dios quebrantando,
la de María abandonando,
la usura en el mercader;
por eso se llega a ver
muerte y hambre amenazando.

2

There are no manners
Among children, young people, or adults.
There is no unity among Christians,
No censure of evil doers,
No punishment of bad intention.
Faith in God is waning,
Faith in Mary is being abandoned,
There is usury in the merchant;
That is why one sees
Death and hunger threatening.

3

Ya no hay reverencia al templo,
ni a los retratos sagrados;
no hay respeto a los prelados,
ni en ellos hay buen ejemplo;
según lo que yo contemplo
el antecristo reinando,
y sus hijos gobernando
en esta historia divina;
por eso se ven las ruinas
y las virtudes menguando.

3

There is no longer reverence for the church,
Nor for the holy pictures;
There is no respect for the prelates,
Nor in them does one find a good example;
According to what I see
The anti-Christ is reigning
And his sons governing
In this divine history;
That is why one sees ruins
And virtue on the wane.

4

No hay prudencia en la justicia,
ni urbanidad en los parientes,
no hay unión entre las gentes,
sólo la pura codicia;
resplandece la malicia,
la sodomía está creciendo,
y la herejía está rigiendo,
y la venganza privando;
por eso estamos mirando
todos los vicios creciendo.

4

There is no prudence in justice,
Nor urbanity in parents,
No union between the people,
Only pure covetousness;
Malice is resplendent,
Sodomy is growing,
And heresy is in force,
Vengeance is on the rampage;
That is why we are seeing
All the vices growing.

5

No hay para que preguntar
el origen de todo esto,
habiéndolo Dios dispuesto
por nuestro modo de obrar;

5

There is no need to ask
The origin of all this,
God ordered it so
Because of our manner of working;

ahora no se ve guardar	Now one doesn't see
de Dios ningún mandamiento,	Any commandment of God kept,
según lo que yo comprendo,	As I see it,
por la desgracia y discordia,	Because of misfortune and disharmony,
sin pedir misericordia	Without even asking for mercy,
el mundo está falleciendo.	The world is dying.

Guerras, Pleitos Sucediendo (E20) is pessimistic social commentary in an unusual form. It has a six-line *planta* but only five *décimas*.

E21. *Ya el Mundo Está Caducante* (The World Is Already in Its Dotage)
R1775, Próspero S. Baca, age 70, Bernalillo, N.Mex., 1945, Robb.

Planta	*Planta*
Ya el mundo está caducante,	The world is already in its dotage,
prevaleciente la gente,	Prevalent among the people,
los vicios van en creciente,	Vice is growing,
las virtudes en menguante.	Virtue is waning.

1	1
Cesó la crianza en los niños	Children are not maturing
y en los padres el gobierno	And parents are not controlling them,
ya se hospedó, Padre eterno,	And, Eternal Father, evil has now
la maldad dentro de casa;	Invaded the home;
ya salió ya asentó plaza	Now malice spreads among the people
la malicia en un instante,	In an instant,
como lo diré, constante,	How shall I say it, it is constant
a todo ya es de criatura;	In the whole creation;
es decir la verdad pura	The pure truth is
ya el mundo está caducante.	The world is already in its dotage.

2	2
Ya cesó el recojimiento	Self-discipline has ceased
entre las niñas doncellas,	Amongst young maidens,
solo el refrán vive en ellas,	Only the appeal of music lives in them,
el encanto, y lucimiento,	The charm and brilliance of things,
la elección del casamiento,	The election of marriage,
el murmuro del ausente.	Sighs for the absent one.
De ahí aprende el inocente	From these the innocent learns
la lección que se le da,	The lesson that is given him,
y así de este modo está	And thus these things become
prevaleciente la gente.	Prevalent among the people.

3	3
Ya no hay mayor ni menor,	There are no adults or minors,
ni el anciano ni el mancebo;	Nor old men, nor young, any more;
en la taberna y el juego	In the tavern and in gambling
compiten con tal primor;	Everyone competes with great vigor;

éste es el hijo mejor	The most highly regarded son
que a su padre es impaciente,	Is he who is impatient with his father,
gravedoso e insolente.	Vain and insolent.
Entre los grandes y chicos	Among the great and small,
en los pobres y en los ricos,	In the poor and rich,
los vicios van en creciente.	Vice is growing.

4	4
En fin ya no hay jubileo,	Finally, there is no public celebration,
ni quien contemple ayuno;	Nor anyone who contemplates fasting;
ya no hay cilicio ninguno,	There is now no sackcloth,
ni el rezo ni otros empleos;	Nor prayer, or other holy offices;
sólo privan los paseos	They only prohibit the excesses
de la botita el amante;	Of the lover.
la vanagloria constante	Constant vaingloriousness
que a todos causa alegría;	Makes everyone happy;
por eso van cada día	Because of that every day
las virtudes en menguante.	Virtue is waning.

E22. *Los Padres Consentidores* (The Permissive Parents)
RB767, Justiniano Atencio, Cebolla, N.Mex., 1950, Cobos.

Planta	*Planta*
Los padres consentidores,	You permissive parents,
escuchen, pongan cuidado;	Listen and pay attention;
oigan los tristes clamores	Listen to the sad complaints
de un hijo mal educado.	Of a badly educated son.

1	1
¿Adónde estás, padre mío?	Where are you, my father?
mírame triste y penoso;	Behold me sad and full of suffering;
entre este abismo espantoso	In this frightening abyss
que ya me tiene abrasado	Into which I have fallen,
entre el fuego devorado	Within the fire devoured
hoy que he sido tan atroz;	Today because I have been so awful;
la sentencia de mi Dios	The sentence of my God
avilenta mis clamores;	Makes my complaint more intense;
oigan mi afligida voz,	Hear my afflicted voice,
los padres consentidores.	You permissive parents.

2	2
Estar conmigo debías	You ought to be with me
para así tomar venganza,	In order thus to be punished
porque no me disteis crianza	Because you didn't raise me properly
y en todo me consentías;	And in everything you let me have my way;
tú de mí el cargo tenías;	You had charge of me
como fuiste no alvertido;	But you were not prepared;
oye de tu hijo querido,	Hear your beloved son,
las quejas que ha dedicado	The complaint that he has voiced,
de este ejemplo sucedido;	About the example that you have given;
escuchen, pongan cuidado.	Listen, pay attention.

3	3
Cuando yo en tu compañía me oías con inclemencia, blasfemiar en tu presencia y a ti gracia os parecía; ¡qué conciencia tan impía de un padre que así se atreve, el consentir cual no debe, a un hijo con tanto amor! válgame la Virgen pura, ante el Supremo Creador.	When I was in your company You heard me, without rebuking me, Blaspheming in your presence, And you thought it was cute; What a wicked conscience Is that of a parent who so dares To spoil, when he shouldn't, A son with so much love! May the pure Virgin help me, Before the Supreme Creator.

4	4
En fin, mis quejas relato y al mundo las patentizo, dándote el postrer aviso, a ti, padre, por ingrato; mira mi infeliz retrato que al tuyo ha de ser igual; me perdiste de un total, mira bien lo que has causado; qué clamor tan general de un hijo mal educado.	In short, I am telling my complaints And I advertise them to the world, Giving this last advice, To you, father, as an ingrate; Look at my unhappy portrait Which should resemble yours; You lost me entirely— Look well at your handwork; What a general complaint Of a badly brought-up son.

5	5
Mira, padre, te voy guiando por eterna perdición; mira esta sierpe o dragón que me está despedazando, y a ti está amenazando con esa cizaña fiera; mira bien y considera entre este abismo de error; nadien este cargo quiera ante el Supremo Creador.	Look, father, I am guiding you To eternal perdition; Look at this serpent or dragon Which is tearing me to pieces, And which is menacing you With this fierce discord; Look well and consider me In this abyss of error; No one wants to be charged with this Before the Supreme Creator.

6	6
Por ley y justa razón castigado debo ser; quien con el justo deber no cumple su obligación; tú, padre, tú en la ocasión tú que no me corregiste, para pagar como deudor; mira bien lo que has causado entre este abismo de error.	By law and just reason I ought to be punished; One who does not comply With his just duty; You, father, when the occasion arose, You did not correct me, So I should pay for misdeeds; Look well at what you have caused In this abyss of error.

7	7
Oígame, todo, viviente, escúchame, mi infeliz retrato, aqueste infeliz moderno que a su padre llama ingrato en la puerta del infierno.	Listen to me, all living things, Hear me, my unhappy portrait, To this unhappy modern man Who calls his father ingrate In the gate of hell.

<table>
<tr><td>

8

Se acabó la educación
que padre daba frecuente;
se acabó el hijo obediente;
se acabó la estimación;
mala crianza, religión
es la que hoy viene reinando;
ya Dios quiere ir descargando
el brazo de su justicia
ya el mundo se está acabando.

</td><td>

8

The training that parents
Used to give their children is gone;
The obedient son is gone;
Respect is gone;
Today bad upbringing and bad religion
Are all that prevail;
Already God feels like exercising
The arm of his justice,
The world is now coming to an end.

</td></tr>
</table>

E23. *Año de 1837* (In the Year of 1837)
R1763, Próspero S. Baca, age 70, Bernalillo, N.Mex., 1945, Robb.

<table>
<tr><td>

Planta
Año de mil ochocientos
treinta y siete desgraciado,
Nuevo México infeliz,
¿qué es lo que nos ha pasado?

</td><td>

Planta
In the ill-fated year of
Eighteen hundred thirty-seven,
Unlucky New Mexico,
What has happened to us?

</td></tr>
<tr><td>

1

Ya murió el juez de distrito,
murió el prefecto y el jefe,
y así ninguno se queje
cuando pague su delito.
Estaba desvelocito
cuando pagó el inocente,
y que padezca la gente
estos crecidos tormentos;
siempre te tendrán presente,
año de mil ochocientos.

</td><td>

1

The district judge has died,
The prefect, and the sheriff also,
And thus no one complains
When a crime is committed.
I have observed
When the innocent man paid,
And how the people suffer
These great torments;
They will always remember you,
Year of eighteen hundred.

</td></tr>
<tr><td>

2

Junta de departamento
constituída por la fuerza
quien ha de tener a bien
la inicua desobediencia;
¿quién se pondrá en la presencia
de aquella Corte Suprema?
¿quién será aquel que no tema
hablar por su territorio
viendo la venganza, el odio,
de lo que nos ha pasado?
No quisiera haberte visto,
treinta y siete desgraciado.

</td><td>

2

The state's committee
Convened by necessity
And had to consider
The wicked violations of law;
Who will stand in the presence
Of that Supreme Court?
Who will be the one without fear,
To speak for their territory
Seeing the vengeance, the hate,
Of that which has happened to us?
I wish that I had not seen you,
Ill-fated thirty-seven.

</td></tr>
<tr><td>

3

Desgraciado territorio,
¿qué hiciste con la obediencia,
con la cordura, y paciencia
que era para ti un tesoro?

</td><td>

3

Unfortunate land,
What have you done with obedience,
With prudence, and patience,
That used to be a treasure for you?

</td></tr>
</table>

Es lo que siento y lloro,
verte desacreditado;
de la fuerza cautivado,
sin defensa ¿no advertís?
Llora tu desdicha, llora,
Nuevo México infeliz.

This is what I regret and I weep for —
Seeing you discredited;
Captured by force,
Without defense, unwarned.
Weep for your misfortune, weep,
Unhappy New Mexico.

4

Conquistadora feliz,
si no pones tú el remedio
se perderá nuestra vida
y no lo permita el cielo.
Madre mía, seas tú mi empeño,
para sembrar paz y unión
y evitar toda ocasión
de discordia entre los hombres
y amparar a los moradores
de tu reino conquistado;
yo estoy confuso y no sé
que es lo que nos ha pasado.

4

Happy Conquistadora,
If you don't grant the remedy
Our life will be lost
And may heaven not permit this.
Mother of mine, be my protection,
To sow peace and unity
And avoid all occasions
Of discord among men
And help the inhabitants
Of your conquered land;
I am confused and don't know
What has happened to us.

This is an interesting *décima* of social protest dating from the period when New Mexico was under the domination of Old Mexico after the Mexican revolt from Spain and before the coming of the North Americans. The incident that gave rise to this *décima* is obscure, although historians might pinpoint it. Mexican rule continued in New Mexico from 1825 to 1845.

This *décima*, if the date is correct, furnishes evidence, along with other *décimas* relating to events taking place in Mexico or the Southwest, that *décimas* were composed in this area in the early nineteenth century. They were still being composed there at least until the early years of the twentieth century; Higinio V. Gonzales, who died about 1915, is known to have been a composer of *décimas*.

The quaint notation "Fin y Comienzo" appears in the original notebook of Próspero Baca.

In verse 4 reference is made to La Conquistadora (The Conquering Lady), a venerated statue of the Virgin as the patron of New Mexico.

E24. *Comienzo* (Beginning)
R1796, Próspero S. Baca, age 70, Bernalillo, N.Mex., 1945, Robb.

Planta
Un mudo estaba cantando,
un sordo lo estaba oyendo
un ciego estaba mirando
un muerto salió huyendo.

Planta
A mute was singing,
A deaf man was listening,
A blind man was watching,
A dead man ran away.

1

Con una guitarra un gallo
y un gato con un violón
le tocaban a un ratón
para que bailara un payo;

1

A rooster with a guitar
And a cat with a double bass
Were playing for a mouse
So that a clown would dance;

un guajolote a caballo
a un toro estaba toreando,
dos chapulines bailando
al son de aquel bandejón;
y al eco de su violón
un mudo estaba cantando.

A turkey on horseback
Was fighting a bull,
Two grasshoppers were dancing
To the music of the dishpan;
And to the echo of his double bass
A mute was singing.

2

En la puerta de una chinche
ví una liendre aparejada,
ví una rana colgada
de la cola en una viga;
y también ví una hormiga
estar echando un remiendo
y un tecolote escribiendo;
lo ví echar un pregón
un sordo lo estaba oyendo.

2

At the door of a bedbug
I saw a nit saddling a horse,
I saw a frog hanging
By his tail from a beam;
And I also saw an ant
Doing some mending
And an owl writing;
I saw him give out a cry
And a deaf man was listening.

3

Un tejón con gran pachorra
lo ví estar unciendo un buey
porque iba a sembrar maguey
a los campos de una zorra;
un sapo en una mazmorra
a un toro estaba toreando,
dos jicalotes guerreando
con piezas de artillería;
y el sangrío que corría
un ciego estaba mirando.

3

I saw a badger
Slowly yoking an ox
Because he was going to plant maguey
In the fields of a fox;
A frog in a dungeon
Was fighting a bull,
Two snakes were warring
With artillery pieces;
And a blind man was watching
The blood that was flowing.

4

A los tiros de fusiles,
y a los ruidos de cuchillos,
salieron los alguaciles
de conejos y zorrillos;
prendieron los armeríos
por las calles van reuniendo,
las espadas van hiriendo
a las voces y a los gritos;
al ruido de dos mosquitos
un muerto salió huyendo.

4

At the shots of the rifles
And the sounds of the knives,
The skunks and rabbits
Came out as constables;
They grabbed their guns
And are meeting in the streets,
The swords are stabbing
At the voices and the shouts;
At the sound of two mosquitoes
A dead man ran away.

This is a good example of a *disparate* (featuring the ridiculous) in the form of a *décima* *glosada*. See other examples of the *disparate* in Section D (D9–25).

E25. *Hombre No Lo Hay Como Yo* (There Is No Man Like Me)
R1798, Próspero S. Baca, age 70, Bernalillo, N.Mex., 1945, Robb.

Planta
Hombre no lo hay como yo,
ni mujer como la mía,
ni ruin como mi cuñado,
ni bola como mi tía.

Planta
There is no man like me,
No woman like mine,
Nor any trouble like my brother-in-law,
Nor any liar like my aunt.

1

Hoy soy jugador eterno
que tal aprendí el oficio,
que todo mi ramo es vicio
en particular juego;
menos él que me amanervo
porque eso no lo uso yo,
bien haya quien me parió
tan campirano el sin segundo;
que en la redondez del mundo
hombre no lo hay como yo.

2

Tengo una buena mujer
que en todo gusto me da
porque ella gana y se va
y viene al amanecer;
que comer y que beber
yo tengo en su compañía;
me para en una pulquería
y seis me para de pronto;
hombre no lo habrá mas tonto,
ni mujer como la mía.

3

Tengo un cuñado pulquero
que cuando voy a su puesto
me dice muy indispuesto:
—Beberás si traes dinero.—
Yo le digo: —Majadero,
yo nunca bebo de fiado.—
Mi tía me muestra agrado
cuando está junto a la tina;
no habrá vieja más mezquina,
ni ruin como mi cuñado.

4

Tengo una tía que canta
que a beber le echo una apuesta
porque borracha se acuesta
y borracha se levanta;
mi tío todo le aguanta,
con los borrachos la envía
y le dice: —esposa mía,
si has de traer dinero, vete.—
No hay viejo mas pirnete,
ni bola como mi tía.

1

I'm a gambler forever,
I have learned my task so well
That I lead the field in vice
Especially gambling;
Except for him who ——— (?)
Because I don't use that,
Blessed be the one who bore me
So unmannerly and without equal;
For in the whole round world
There is no man like me.

2

I have a good woman
Who pleases me in every way
Because she earns money and she goes
And comes again at dawn;
I have her company
For eating and drinking;
I stop at a bar
And six drinks stop me;
There is no man more foolish,
Nor any woman like mine.

3

I have a brother-in-law, a barkeeper
Who, when I go to his place,
Tells me very annoyed:
"You can drink if you have money."
I call him a louse,
I never drink for free.
My aunt shows me her gratitude
When she's near the vat;
There is no old woman more sneaky,
Nor any trouble like my brother-in-law.

4

I have an aunt who sings
And when she drinks I bet with her,
Because she goes to bed drunk
And gets up drunk;
My uncle endures it all,
He sends her out with the drunks,
And says, "My wife,
If you must bring money, get out."
There is no old man more contemptible,
Nor any liar like my aunt.

This is a *décima glosada* with the *espinela*
rhyming pattern.

411

E26. *Mi Confesor Me Ha Mandado* (My Confessor Has Ordered Me)
R1792, Próspero S. Baca, age 70, Bernalillo, N.Mex., 1945, Robb.

Planta
Mi confesor me ha mandado
que olvide a mi señorita,
lástima, si es tan bonita,
pajarito colorado.

Planta
My confessor has ordered me
To forget my girl,
It's too bad, she is so pretty,
Little red bird.

1

Estando en su casa un día,
solitos los dos, yo y ella,
quise despedirme de ella,
me dijo que no podía;
ni tampoco convenía
apartarnos del pecado
que mi Dios tendría el cuidado
de apartarnos al morir;
y yo le quería decir
mi confesor me ha mandado.

1

One day while I was at her house,
The two of us alone, she and I,
I tried to say good-bye to her,
She told me that I couldn't;
Nor did she wish
To give up our sin
For God would take the precaution
Of separating us on death;
And I wanted to tell her
That my confessor had instructed me.

2

Dicen los diez mandamientos
que al prójimo como a ti
y el padre me dice a mí
que no le vaya con cuentos;
ni me agarre de pretextos
al decirle que es bonita,
ni tampoco que es gordita,
porque no me he de salvar;
pero padre hay que dudar,
que olvide a mi señorita.

2

The Ten Commandments say
Do unto others as unto yourself,
And the priest says to me
Not to come to him with stories;
Nor did I come up with excuses
Telling him she was pretty,
Nor that she is a little plump,
Because I'll not save myself that way;
But father, don't deceive yourself
That I'll forget my girl.

3

Te prometo, vida mía,
con todo mi corazón
un acto de contrición
el día del impedimento;
yo te prometo mi afecto,
mi idolatrada negrita,
que aunque el padre me lo quita
él que yo te venga a ver;
pero esto no ha de poder,
lástima, si es tan bonita.

3

I promise you, my love,
With all my heart,
An act of contrition
On the day of the request;
I promise you my affection,
My idolized little dark one,
For even though the priest forbids me
I will come to see you;
For this he'll not be able to do,
It's too bad, she is so pretty.

4

—Hombre, deja esa mujer,
piensa en que te has de morir
y que por ella te has de ir
al infierno a padecer.—
—Padre, eso no podrá ser,
me tiene tan obligado
y para mi mayor cuidado
¿se la dejaré a otro necio?

4

"Man, leave that woman,
Consider that you must die
And that because of her
You'll go to hell to suffer."
"Father, that cannot be,
She has me so obligated to her
And for my greater worry,
Should I leave her to another fool?

siendo mujer de mi aprecio,
pajarito colorado.

Seeing that she is the woman I esteem,
Little red bird."

The reference in verse 3 to "el día de impedimento" refers to the days when the boy's
parents would call on the girl's parents to
ask their consent to a marriage. The word
"impedimento," I am advised, is a New Mexico colloquialism for "pedimento." The word
"colorado" repeatedly appears in the song
texts with reference to a woman who is no
better than she should be (see *El Durazno*,
C49). The word "palomita" not infrequently
appears with a similar connotation (see *Palomita Callejera*, C41).

This is a *décima glosada* with the rhyming
pattern of an *espinela*.

E27. *Yo Digo Que No Hay Infierno* (I Say That There Is No Hell)
R1801, Próspero S. Baca, age 70, Bernalillo, N.Mex., 1945, Robb.

Planta
Yo digo que no hay infierno
ni misericordia en Dios,
también digo que no hay cielo
tan fino como un reloj.

Planta
I say there is no hell
Nor mercy in God,
I also say there is no heaven
As fine as a watch.

1
Virgen sagrada, María,
madre de mi buen Jesús,
dame un rayo de tu luz
pues eres alba del día;
madre y abogada mía
líbrame del fuego eterno,
pues mi alma con llanto tierno
te ha de buscar vigilante;
para él que tema constante
yo digo que no hay infierno.

1
Mary, sacred Virgin,
Mother of my good Jesus,
Give me a ray of your light
For you are the dawn of day;
My mother and my intercessor,
Free me from the eternal fire,
For my soul, with tender sobs,
Will seek you vigilantly;
For him who constantly worries,
I say there is no hell.

2
Y tú, pecador, advierte
que aquél que vive pecando
morirá desesperando,
como es la vida, es la muerte;
y con desastrada suerte
arderá en fuego veloz,
Virgen, ten piedad de nos,
que él que peca y no se enmienda,
no hallará quien lo defienda
ni misericordia en Dios.

2
And you, sinner, take notice
That he who lives in sin
Will die despairing.
As is life, so is death;
And with disastrous fate
He will burn in a raging fire;
Virgin, have pity on us,
For he who sins and doesn't repent,
Will find no one to defend him,
Nor mercy in God.

3
Todo el mundo te venerá
como reina celestial,
con Dios en su tribunal,
Virgen, sé mi medianera;

3
The whole world venerates you
As the queen of heaven,
With God in his tribunal,
Virgin, be my mediator;

mi alma en tus manos espera	In your hands my soul
el alivio y el consuelo;	Awaits relief and consolation;
yo te adoro con anhelo,	I adore you ardently,
de los ángeles princesa;	Princess of the angels;
para alabar tu belleza	To praise your beauty
también digo que no hay cielo.	I also say there is no heaven.

4	4
Eres reina poderosa	You are the powerful queen
de Dios, espíritu amado,	Spirit, beloved of God,
de su reino sagrado,	And the most beautiful princess
la princesa más hermosa;	In your sacred kingdom;
Dios te hizo madre y esposa	God made you mother and wife
del mismo que nos hizo; a vos	Of the very one who made us; you
Virgen, ten piedad de nos,	Virgin, have pity on us,
Virgen santa esclarecida;	Holy, enlightened Virgin,
digo que sois consolida	I say that you are a comforter
tan fina como un reloj.	As fine as a watch.

This, again, is a *décima glosada* with the rhyming pattern of an *espinela*. In this song the apparently irreligious sentiments of the four lines of the *planta* are explained away in the successive *décimas*, except for the third, which departs from the logic of the other three.

It is said that the padres would use these *décimas* to good effect from the pulpit during their sermons.

E28. *Un Testamento* (A Will)
Schaeffer 14 (p. 23), Panama, 1944, Schaeffer.

Planta	*Planta*
Voy a hacer un testamento	I am going to make my will
de todos los bienes míos,	Of all my worldly goods,
por si acaso me muriese	So that if I should die
que nada quede perdido.	Nothing will be lost.

1	1
Te dejo una hermosa casa	I leave you a beautiful house
que nada más le falta el techo,	Which lacks only a roof,
las paredes, y los cimientos	Walls, and foundations,
y también labrar las bases;	And the lot on which to stand it;
y también dejo una hamaca	I also leave you a hammock
que ya no resiste el viento,	Which does not resist the wind,
que en ella no me acuesto	In which I don't sleep
por no perder las costillas;	So as not to lose my ribs;
y de estas grandes maravillas	And with these marvellous things
voy a hacer un testamento.	I am going to make my will.

2	2
Dejo un caballo de paso	I bequeath my horse,
propio para correr,	Suitable for racing,
pero creo que en este mes	But I think that this month
se lo comió un gallinazo,	A vulture ate him,

pero tiene el espinazo	But he still has a backbone
como la quilla una nave	Like the keel of a ship
siempre vive con frío,	As it lies there in the cold,
es de tanto que lo cuido	Because of all the care I give it
y quien cogerá el residuo	And someone will seize the residue
de todos los bienes míos.	Of all my worldly goods.

3

Dejo un baulito nuevo	I leave a new little trunk
lleno de tentaciones,	Full of tempting things,
de cucurachas y ratones	Cockroaches and mice
y pedazos de pellejo	And pieces of hide
y las patas de un conejo,	And a rabbit's feet,
dejo para las mujeres;	I leave this for the ladies;
también los dientes de un peine,	Also the teeth of a comb,
también dejo un mecedor;	Also I leave a rocking chair;
y esto he dejado yo	And these things I have left
por si acaso me muero.	In case of my death.

4

Tengo una esterita vieja,	I have an old mattress,
que era donde reposaba	On which I have rested
con una funda de almohada	With a slip cover for a pillow
puede dormir cualquiera;	In which anyone else can sleep;
la falda de unas polleras	Also an old skirt
con que me arropó mi amigo	With which my boyfriend covered me
donde me quedé dormido,	When I lay asleep,
pensando en tantas riquezas	I am thinking of all these riches
y trayendo en mi cabeza	And bearing in mind that
que nada quede perdido.	Nothing will be lost.

Un Testamento is a *décima glosada* with the *espinela* rhyme scheme.

I have included this text because of its interesting subject matter. I have not included the music to which the present text is sung because the original recording was not available and because it might have been one of some eight traditional *mejorana* tunes from which, in the Panamanian tradition, the singer was free to choose (Schaeffer 14, p. 2). None of the eight, however, resembles the traditional New Mexico *décima* melody.

E29. *Mujer de Cien Maridos* (Woman of a Hundred Husbands)
RB697, Antonio Medina, Chimayó, N.Mex., 1945, Robb. Cf. L5, R795, R798, R1472.

Planta	*Planta*
Décima de una mujer	*Décima* of a woman
que quiso hacer experencia	Who wanted to have the experience
de querer y aborrecer	Of loving and deserting
y tener para su existencia.	And having men to take care of her.

1

El primer amor que tuvo	The first love that she had
fué firme, constante, y fiel,	Was firm, constant, and proud
y se llamaba Miguel,	And his name was Miguel,
el simple que la mantuvo;	The simpleton, he took care of her;

con él unos días anduvo
mientras nuevo amor halló,
a Bernardo lo engañó
andando con Bonifacio
por andar queriendo a Ignacio,
Salvador la enamoró.

She stayed a few days with him
Until she found a new love,
And cheated Bernardo by
Going away with Bonifacio
Only to go on to Ignacio,
Then Salvador fell in love with her.

2
Agustín se la llevó
con un amor permamente,
ella quería a Vicente
cuando éste la idolatriaba;
Felipe la recuestaba
sólo de verla tan bella
y le dice: —soy doncella
y he de querer a uno solo.—
Esto le decía a Bartolo,
andando Lucas con ella.

2
Agustín brought her
A permanent love,
But she yearned for Vicente
Who idolized her;
Felipe begged her
Only to be beautiful
And she replied: "I am a virgin
And can only love one."
This she also told to Bartolo,
While Lucas was going with her.

3
Y de Teodoro salió
y entró con Jesús María,
dejó a Navarro García
para ensillar su caballo,
a Cayetano, de gallo
lo lleva para su defensa;
pues con Mariano comienza
a tener nuevo sembiante,
a Luis lleva por detente
la lleva para su asistente,
pronto entre con Clemente,
porque quería a Donaciano,
a Félix le dió la mano
y a nadie le dió la prenda.

3
And she left Teodoro
And went to live with Jesús María,
She left Navarro García
Saddling his horse,
For Cayetano to whom
She turned to protect her;
Then she started with Mariano
To have a new affair,
She made a conquest of Luis
To have his assistance,
Soon she moved in with Clemente,
For she wanted Donaciano,
To Felix she gave her hand
But gave her pledge to no one.

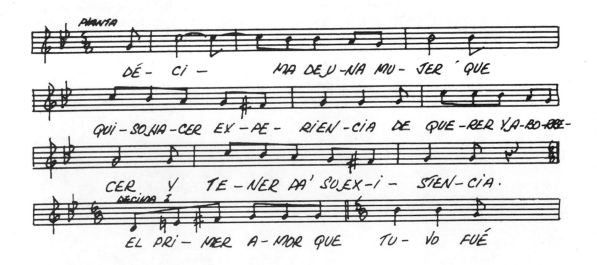

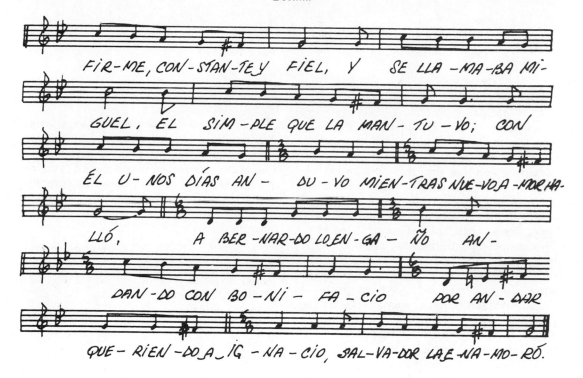

FIR-ME, CON-STAN-TE Y FIEL, Y SE LLA-MA-BA MI-

GUEL, EL SIM-PLE QUE LA MAN-TU-VO; CON

ÉL U-NOS DÍAS AN- DU-VO MIEN-TRAS NUE-VO A-MOR HA-

LLÓ, A BER-NAR-DO LO EN-GA-ÑO AN-

DAN-DO CON BO-NI-FA-CIO POR AN-DAR

QUE-RIEN-DO A IG-NA-CIO, SAL-VA-DOR LA E-NA-MO-RÓ.

Mujer de Cien Maridos is a *relación* in the form of a *décima* (see Section D on the *relación*). The original recording (R45), which I made in 1945, was lost, but in 1969 numbers R44–49 were copied on tape from a scratchy old disc given in 1945 to the singer's family (RB697). The transcription, which is incomplete (only three instead of the usual four *décimas*) and irregular (the third *décima* has fourteen instead of the usual ten lines), was made, as I recall, by Vicente T. Mendoza in 1945 when he was in residence at the University of New Mexico.

F. *Indita*

There seems to be a good deal of confusion over the nature and origins of the *indita*. Campa in his *Spanish Folk Poetry in New Mexico* stated that the term *canción* has always been used in New Mexico to include *décimas*, *corridos*, *cuandos*, and *inditas* and that in actual metrical form the last three types are exactly alike (Campa 2, p. 181). This statement ignores what appears to me to have been the one most characteristic feature of the *indita:* its melody. Furthermore, since many more forms have been identified than those mentioned, it seems necessary for precision of thought to isolate and classify all the forms that actually exist, even if appropriate terminology has not been heretofore employed. Let us then review the various descriptions of the *indita* offered by scholars and singers and try to identify the distinguishing characteristics of this form.

Mendoza, who has identified many forms for us, says that musically the *indita* has a *local* form consisting of a *copla* followed by a refrain, or *estribillo*, in which the word "indita" always appears (Mendoza, 9d). While this is certainly true of some examples, such as *Indita de Amarante Martínez* (F2), other so-called *inditas* do not have the *estribillo* of which Mendoza speaks. And the mere occurrence of the word "indita"— while as important perhaps as the word "cuando" in the *cuando* form—unless used consistently in the same manner as the word "cuando," is hardly sufficient to serve as the basis of the definition of a separate form. Either word might, for instance, occur accidentally in a different type of song.

Two of my informants, commenting on *inditas* sung by them (R218 and F2), have said that they were called *inditas* "because of the tune." Celestín Segura said, "You sing an *indita* softly, with feeling. A *corrido* you can sing loud." But that does not correspond with my own experience, for I find in my notes the comment that "the *indita* seems to have more gusto and vitality than many of the other forms. The singers sing faster with more rhythmic intensity, shorter notes."

Since the *corrido* seems to be the form closest to that of the *indita*, it seems appropriate to compare the two. A detailed examination of fourteen *corridos* and four *inditas* from my collection and twenty *corridos* and eight *inditas* transcribed by Mendoza (Mendoza 9d) supplies us with the following information:

	Corridos	Inditas
Total	34	12
With *estribillos*	3	5
Without *estribillos*	31	7
In major mode	31	6
In other mode	3	6
With masculine endings	11	11
With feminine endings	23	1

It is possible to generalize from the above data that, musically speaking:

1. The *indita* often has an *estribillo* or refrain, while the *corrido* usually does not.

2. The *corrido* is almost always in the major mode, while the *indita* is as often as not in some other modal scale.

3. The feminine ending is a usual characteristic of the *corrido*, while the *indita* almost always ends in a masculine cadence.

Rubén Cobos, writing in the Santa Fe *Nuevo Mexicano* (Cobos 4, March 30, 1950), summarized the literary characteristics of his collection of eighty-six *inditas*. The *indita*, he wrote,

is narrative in form, in fact a form of the *corrido;*
consists of a series of four or six line octosyllabic verses;
is usually written in the first person;
resembles the *corrido* in its introductory verse in giving the theme and date of the occurrence;
employs realistic language of the local people;
is given a distinctly New Mexican flavor by the mention of the names of numerous persons associated with the development of the state and of numerous New Mexican towns and topographical features;
is distinguishable from the *corrido* and *romance* by the melody, which contains traces of the music of the Indians of the state.

I am inclined to think that the origin of the *indita* is as natural as the mixture of Spanish and Indian blood by intermarriage. In one instance I encountered what appeared to me to be the missing link itself. It seemed to me to be an electrifying discovery. My friend and informant David Frescas, who told me that he was of mixed Spanish and Indian ancestry, was singing for me in Taos. One of the songs he sang for me he described as a Navajo dance song (F22). It was unmistakably an Indian type of melody, but sung to a mixture of Indian syllables and Spanish words.

Mendoza states that *Una Indita en Su Chinampa* (F12), whose probable origin is Xochimilco, Mexico, is probably the original link, which penetrated into Texas, producing the *Indita Texanita*, and entered New Mexico during the second or third decade of the nineteenth century (Mendoza 9d, p. 455). He states that the capital importance of the style is that the technical musical elements are Indian whereas the literary form and danceable rhythms are derived from the Spanish culture.

For an additional *indita* classified under *cautivos* (songs of captives) see *Indita de Plácido Molina* (N10). Two other *inditas* have been included in Section I. They are *Indita de Ricardo* (I1) and *Indita de Celestino Segura* (I2).

F1. *El Comanchito* (The Little Comanche)
Campa 2 (p. 220), New Mexico, 1946, Campa. Cf. W80, R1236, R1978. See also Appendix A.

<table>
<tr><td>

1
Ahí vienen los indios
por el chaparral.
Ay, nanita, ay, nanita,
me quieren matar.

</td><td>

]
] Bis
]
] Bis

</td><td>

1
Look, there come the Indians
Through the chaparral.
Oh, nanita, oh, nanita,
They want to kill me.

</td></tr>
</table>

Refrán
¡Jeya, jeya, jeya,
jeya, jeya, jeya,
jeya, jeya, jeyaaaaah!

Refrain
Heya, heya, heya,
Heya, heya, heya,
heya, heya, heyaaaaah!

2
Baila el comanchito,
toca el tambor;
baila por buñuelos,
baila por licor.

2
The Comanche dances,
He plays the drum;
He dances for fritters,
He dances for liquor.

Refrán

Refrain

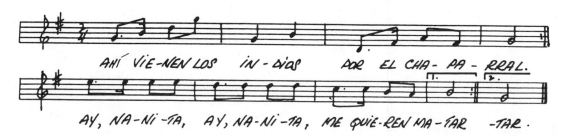

F2. *Indita de Amarante Martínez* (Indita of Amarante Martínez)
R617, N. Trujillo, Bernalillo, N.Mex., 1951, Robb.

I have already published the text of this song, together with a metric translation and an arrangement for piano and voice (Robb 13, pp. 19, 68). The melody and words of verse 1 are included here nevertheless to permit comparison with the music of other *inditas*.

A-ÑO DE MIL NO-VE-CIEN-TOS VIEN-TI-SEIS TAN A-FA-MA-DO, A-ÑO DE MIL NO-VE-CIEN-TOS VEIN-TI-SEIS TAN A-FA-MA-DO. AY IN-DI-TA Y AY PRI-MER-A QUÉ TRA-BA-JO ES TE-NER VI-DA SI LA MUER-TE SE A-PO-DE-RA.

F3. *Indita de Manzano* (Indian Girl of Manzano)
R1405, Edwin Berry, Tomé, N.Mex., 1956, Robb.

Estribillo	*Refrain*
¡Ay! ¡Indita del Manzano!	Oh! Indian girl of Manzano!
Ayuda a sentir	Help us to mourn
pues fuiste tan afamada	For you were so famous
con todo el mundo graciosa.	And benevolent toward all the world.
¡Ay! José Luis,	Oh, with you, José Luis,
y contigo desgraciada.	She was so unfortunate.

1	1
Yo soy José Luis mentado	I am the famous José Luis
entre la flor y decencia.	Between the flower and decency.
Soy el músico afamado	I am the famous musician
del condado de Valencia.	Of the county of Valencia.

2	2
Yo soy José Luis mentado	I am the famous José Luis
entre la gran Competencia.	Among the good ones I was the best.
Hoy va mi cuerpo tomado	Today my broken body goes
al condado de Valencia.	To the county of Valencia.

Indita

¡AY!

¡IN-bi-TA DEL MAN-ZA-NO! A-YU-DAA SEN-TIR

(WHISTLER SINGS)

PUES FUIS-TE TAN A-FA-MA-DA

CON TO-DO EL MUN-DO GRA-CIO-SA. ¡AY! JO-SÉ LUIS,

Y CON-TI-GO DES-GRA-CIA-DA. (SINGER WHISTLES)

421

F4. *Indita de José Luis* (Indian Wife of José Luis)
   Mendoza 9d (pp. 469–70), Amador Abeyta, age 59, Sabinal, N.Mex., 1946, Mendoza.

1

Para cantar esta indita
se necesita tonada,
para que se oiga bonita
con su música arreglada
como la cantó "El Tequita"
un día en la Punta de Agua.

Estribillo
¡Ay, indita de José Luis!
Ven a sentir,
que ¿no eras tan afamada
con todo el mundo graciosa?
¡Ay, José Luis!
y para ti desgraciada.

2

Cuando al Manzano vinieron
y la familia marcharon,
era Sósteno Lobato
él que los acompañaba.

1

To sing this *indita*
A tune is necessary,
So that it may be heard well
With its setting of music
The way "El Tequita" was sung
One day in Punta de Agua.

Refrain
Ah, Indian wife of José Luis!
Come and mourn,
For, were you not famous
And gracious to everyone?
Ah, José Luis!
It was for you that she suffered.

2

When they came to Manzano,
The family walked on foot,
And it was Sósteno Lobato
Who accompanied them.

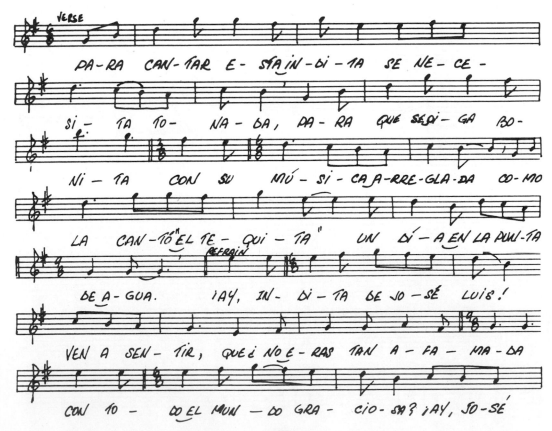

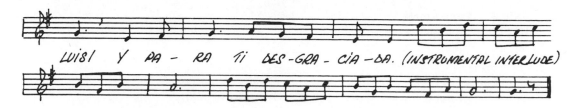

F4a. *Indita de José Luis*

Mendoza 9d (p. 470), Mrs. Juanita Chávez, age 70, San Ignacio, N.Mex., 1937, Lolita Pooler.

Yo soy el Joselín mentado
de tal nombre y competencia,
soy el músico afamado
del condado de Valencia.

I am the famous Joselín
Of great fame and ability,
I am the renowned musician
Of the county of Valencia.

Estribillo
¡Ay, indita de Manzano!
ven a sentir,
que ¿no eras tan afamada
con todo el mundo graciosa?
¡Y ay, Joselín!
y conmigo desgraciada.

Refrain
Ah, Indian woman of Manzano!
Come and mourn,
For were you not famous
And gracious to everyone?
Ah, Joselín!
And with me in misfortune.

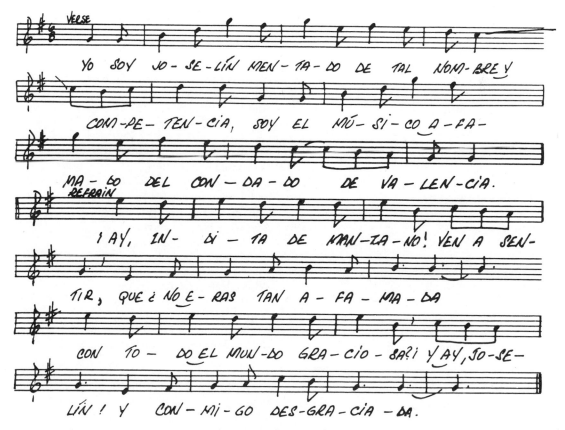

F5. *Indita de Jesús María Sánchez* (Song of Jesús María Sánchez)
R329, Elfego Sánchez, age 63, Tijeras N.Mex., 1950, Robb.

1

Año de mil novecientos
y el uno por lo presente
les encargo a mis amigos
se comuniquen mi muerte,
para que sepan mis hermanos
como me he quedado ausente.

2

Y en las partidas de Joble
y ese caso sucedió
y el treinta y uno de octubre
y en su campo se quedó.
Se quedó haciendo zapatos
la ultima obra que dejó.

3

Y entre las cinco y las seis
salió a topar su ganado;
donde Dios lo llamó a juicio
y en su lugar señalado.
Cuando ya salió del campo
la muerte lo arrebató,
caminó quinientas varas
y una cuchilla subió.

4

Cuando ya se iba muriendo
de un palo se abrazó
pues aquél era su sino
y Dios lo determinó.

5

Y el caporal y pastores
ninguno de ellos lo halló,
éste era un compadre suyo
y Dios se lo concedió;
éste vino a levantarlo
y sepultura le dió.

6

Y adiós, Sierra del Milagro,
donde Jesús quedó allí
¡Quién tal hubiera sabido
y haberme acercado a ti!
Naiden sabe donde muere,
pero donde nace sí.

7

Adiós, madrecita mía,
prenda de mi corazón,

1

In the year of nineteen hundred and one
The present year,
I charge my friends
That they communicate my death,
So that my brothers may know
Why I have been absent.

2

And among the flocks of Hubbell
This is what happened
On the thirty-first of October
In their sheep camp.
He was making shoes,
The last thing that he made.

3

Between five and six o'clock
He went out to meet his flock;
When God called him to judgment
In the appointed place.
When he had just left the camp
Death suddenly grasped him,
He went about five hundred yards
And climbed a knifelike hill.

4

When he was dying
He threw his arms around a tree,
But that was his fate
And God determined it.

5

Neither the foreman nor the shepherds
Were able to find him,
The one who did was a friend of his
and God granted this to him;
This man came and picked him up
And gave him his burial.

6

Farewell, Sierra del Milagro,
Where Jesús remained;
If only I had known
And had found you!
No one knows where he may die
But he does know where he was born.

7

Farewell, my dear mother,
Beloved of my heart,

te encargo a mis dos hijitos,
te los tengas en unión,
porque ya yo y mi esposa
de Dios tenemos perdón.

I entrust my two sons to you,
Keep them with you,
For already I and my wife
Have received the pardon of God.

8

Adiós, compadre Manuel,
dígale a mis hermanitos
quedo muy agradecido
que haigan venido toditos,
que haigan venido a buscarme
y en unión, como hermanitos.

8

Farewell, Manuel, my friend,
Tell my brothers
That I appreciate very much
That all of them have come,
That they have come to search for me,
All together like brothers.

9

Adiós, Plaza de Padilla
donde esperaba volver;
los santos juicios de Dios
nadien puede comprender
pues, este mundo engañoso
sirve para entretener.

9

Farewell, Plaza de Padilla
Where I had hoped to return;
The holy judgment of God
Nobody can understand,
For this deceitful world
Serves only to entertain.

10

Y él que compuso esta indita
la compuso sin poesía
a Jesús María Sánchez
por amor que le tenía;
su nombre, Ramón Barbúa
de la Plaza de Padilla.

10

And he who composed this *indita*
Composed it without knowing poetry
In memory of Jesús María Sánchez
For the love which he bore him;
His name, Ramón Barbúa
Of Plaza de Padilla.

A - ÑO DE MIL NO-VE - CIEN-TOS Y EL U-NO
POR LO PRE - SEN -TE LES EN - CAR-GOA MIS A -
MI - GOS SE CO-MU - NI-QUEN MI MUER-TE,
PA' QUE SE -PAN MIS HER - MA-NOS CO-MO ME HE QUE-DA-DO AU-SEN-TE.

This *indita* is dated October 31, 1901, in its first two verses. The melody to which it is sung is almost identical with that of various versions of the *Corrido de la Muerte de Antonio Maestas* (I17). Like it, this is a memorial of the death of a man, Jesús María Sánchez. It is undoubtedly of New Mexican origin. Padilla is a village south of Albuquerque.

In verse 2 there is a reference to the flocks of Joble (for Hubbell). The Hubbells were for many decades one of the great sheep raising families of New Mexico.

F6. *La Indita Fúnebre* (The Funereal Ballad)
RB98, Romero, Peralta, N.Mex., 1883, Erna Fergusson.

1	**1**
Año de mil ochocientos	It was in the year of 1883,
ochenta y tres desgraciado,	That unfortunate year,
que murió don Manuel B.,	That Don Manuel B. died,
pero murió asesinado.	But died at an assassin's hand.
2	**2**
A don Manuel B. mataron	Don Manuel B. died,
y sin remedio murió,	And died without help,
y con un felomerio	And a coward killed him
un cobarde lo mató.	With a weapon.
3	**3**
El se fué para la Estancia	He went to Estancia
a ver su propiedad	To see his property
Porque un tejano ladrón	For a thief of a Texan
le quería robar.	Wanted to steal it.
4	**4**
El se paró en Punta de Agua	He appeared in Punta de Agua
a esperar a sus cuñados,	To wait for his brothers-in-law
para tratar del asunto	To deal with the matter
que estaba algo apurado.	Which was somewhat sticky.
5	**5**
Llegaron allí a la Estancia,	They came then to Estancia,
él, con su buena intención.	He with good intentions.
Allí estaba el asesino	The assassin was there
y el diablo en su corazón.	And the devil was in his heart.
6	**6**
Le hablaron sobre el asunto,	They talked about the matter,
él no se quiso explicar,	He did not want to explain,
él descargó su pistola	He discharged his pistol
y le dió una herida mortal.	And gave him a mortal wound.
7	**7**
También don Manuel B.	Nevertheless Don Manuel B.
también se portó valiente	Behaved valiantly
ya casi en la agonía	And in agony
al punto vengó su muerte.	Came to the door of death.
8	**8**
El adulón don Fernández	The flatterer Don Fernández
al punto perdió la vida.	At once lost his life.
No hay quien se duela de él	There is no one to mourn for him
porque lo merecía.	For he deserved it.
9	**9**
Whitney, que fué el asesino	Whitney who was the assassin
que no más vino a robar	Who only came to steal

también sacó dos heridas
y luego se hincó a llorar.

Also received two wounds
And presently knelt down weeping.

10
Don Enriques, el doctor,
una herida recibió,
y con un rifle en la mano
a todos los desarmó.

10
Don Enriques, the doctor,
Received a wound,
And with a rifle in his hand
Disarmed them all.

11
Este doctor tan valiente
merece una buena fama
por haberse quedado solo
en el campo de batalla.

11
This doctor so valiant
Deserves a good reputation
For having remained alone
On the field of battle.

12
También don Carlos Armijo
por ser el más advertido
al punto salió a la puerta
para excusar el peligro.

12
Also Don Carlos Armijo,
Being the most clever,
Immediately went out the door
To avoid the danger.

13
El asesino de Whitney
él hizo su diligencia,
pero le hizo una herida
al condado de Valencia.

13
The assassin Whitney
Did his business,
But he inflicted a wound
On the county of Valencia.

14
Oye, bruto y asesino,
serás criminal
por haber matado un hombre
que no te hizo ningún mal.

14
Listen, brute and assassin,
You are a criminal
For having killed a man
Who did you no harm.

15
Pronto vendría la venganza
que del cielo la esperamos;
efetamos en la confianza.

15
Vengeance shall come quickly
Which we await from heaven;
This we maintain in confidence.

16
El en infierno hallarás
la Estancia que andas buscando,
allí tienes a los diablos
que allí te están aguardando.

16
In the inferno you will find
The Estancia land you are searching for,
There you will have the devils
Which are awaiting you there.

17
La venganza ha de venir
que muy pronto la verás
porque el quinto mandamiento
nos dice —No matarás.—

17
Vengeance has to come
Which very soon you will see
Because the fifth commandment
Tells us "Thou shalt not kill."

18
Tú, Whitney, impertinente,
la venganza te llegó
ya porque no puede estar
donde niega una sociedad.

18
You, Whitney, meddling one,
Vengeance already has caught up with you
Because you cannot be
Where society rejects you.

19

Whitney pensó ser valiente
al cometer esa muerte,
pero ahora se halla afianzado.
Veremos cual es suerte.

19

Whitney thought himself brave
To commit this murder,
But now he finds himself under a bail bond.
We shall see what is his fate.

20

El condado de Valencia
perdió un hombre muy valioso,
pero el alma fué a la gloria,
allí tiene su reposo.

20

The county of Valencia
Lost a very brave man,
But his soul went to heaven
Where it has peace.

21

Don Manuel B. fué a la gloria.
Eso es cierto y evidente,
porque ¿quién puede dudar
que el hombre no fuera inocente?

21

Don Manuel B. went to heaven.
This is certain and obvious
Because who can doubt
That he was an innocent man?

22

Su esposa quedó llorando
a exprimentar naturales,
y le quedaron tres niños
para alivios de sus males.

22

His wife remained weeping
To express her natural feelings,
And there remain three baby boys
To alleviate her sorrows.

23

Las lágrimas de su esposa
siempre pedirán venganza,
a Dios le deja el cuidado
y en El pone su confianza.

23

The tears of his wife
Will always beg for vengeance,
On God she lays her cares
And in Him places her confidence.

24

Vamos rogando por él,
que ahora eso necesita,
que Dios a Dios se le haiga llevado
a su mansión infinita.

24

Let us pray for him,
For that is what he needs,
That God may have taken him
To his infinite mansion.

25

Estos versos que aquí asiento
los escribí con mi mano.
Pero lo más especial
que los compuso un anciano.

25

These verses which here I set down
I wrote with my hand.
But the most important thing
Is that an old man composed them.

This ballad commemorates the death of Manuel B. Otero in a gunfight at his ranch in the Estancia Valley of New Mexico. Otero was the scion of a distinguished New Mexico family. The text was given to me by the late Erna Fergusson. The event is fully documented in Miss Fergusson's *Murder and Mystery in New Mexico*, the second chapter of which is entitled "The Ballad of Manuel B."

F7. *Indita de Manuel B. Otero* (Ballad of Manuel B. Otero)
R1416, Edwin Berry, Tomé, N.Mex., 1956, Robb.

Refrán	*Refrain*
¡Ay! Indita de Manuel B.,	Ay! Ballad of Manuel B.,
residente de La Costancia,	A resident of La Costancia,
por defender tus derechos	For defending your rights
sufriste muerte sin causa.	You suffered death unjustly.

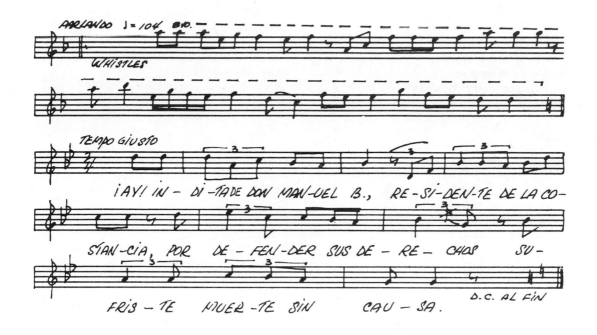

This is the refrain from a different ballad
dealing with the same event as F6.

F7a. *Indita de Manuel B. Otero*
RB905, Andrés, Luján, Torreón, N.Mex., Cobos.

Refrán	*Refrain*
¡Ay! indita de don Manuel B.,	Oh! *Indita* of Don Manuel B.,
residente de la Costancia,	A resident of Costancia,
por librar a tu nación	You suffered death without cause
tú sufriste muerte sin causa.	To free your nation.

1

Dice Manuelito Otero
con su palabra de honor:
—Whittier, enséñame el derecho
para entrar a mi posesión;
que si yo tengo derecho
no quiero tener razón.—

Refrán

2

Ahí Whittier le respondió
de cólera persuadido:
—Derecho no tengo yo,
ni nunca lo he conocido;
tú sólo sales de aquí
o a esta arma estás rendido.—

Refrán

3

Ante Dios pongo mi queja
y al Supremo Tribunal
que se ha de andar mi querella
ante una corte marcial,
que mi muerte fué sin causa
y mi derecho legal.

Refrán

4

Don Anriques por la vida
y en defensa se metió;
¡ay, qué doctor tan valiente,
ni por eso se rindió!

Refrán

5

Doña Isabelita Baca,
y adiós, madre de aflicción;
adiós, Eloisa Lucinda,
tu hermano don Salomón;
tú serás la protegida,
siendo él tu administrador.

6

De Los Lunas y Tomé,
del Torreón y del Manzano,
también los de Punta de Agua
acuden a mi llamado,
a defender esta estancia,
¡qué lugar tan desgraciado!

Refrán

1

Said Manuelito Otero
With his word of honor:
"Whittier, show me the warrant
By which you enter my possessions;
For if the law is on my side
There is no need to argue."

Refrain

2

Then Whittier replied,
Persuaded by his anger:
"I have no law to cite,
Nor have I ever known of one;
Only you leave here
Or by this gun you will be subdued."

Refrain

3

Before God I place my complaint
And before the Supreme Tribunal
That my quarrel should have come
Before a court martial,
And that my death was without cause
And my right legal.

Refrain

4

Don Anriques placed himself on guard
For his life and in defense;
Ah, what a valiant doctor,
Nor would he yield to that man.

Refrain

5

Doña Isabelita Baca,
Farewell, mother of affliction;
Farewell, Eloisa Lucinda,
Your brother Don Salomón;
You will be protected,
With him as your administrator.

6

From Los Lunas and Tomé,
From Torreón and Manzano,
As well as from Punta de Agua
The people came to my call,
To defend this estate,
This so unhappy place!

Refrain

7	**7**
Adiós, Eloisa Lucinda,	Farewell, Eloisa Lucinda,
se acabó todo tu haber,	All that you had is finished,
con una grande fatiga	With great anguish
lo llegaron a saber.	They came to realize it.
Refrán	*Refrain*

Otero had a home in Costancia, near Tomé, New Mexico, according to Edwin Berry.

Costancia is not to be confused with Estancia, where the gunfight took place (see F6).

F8. *El Indio Vitorio* (The Indian Vitorio)
R2418, Juan Griego, age 61, Albuquerque, N.Mex., 1971, Cipriano Griego. Cf. RB743, RB744, RB745, RB746.

1	**1**
Y en una cueva escondida	In a hidden cave
dicen que murió Vitorio,	They say Vitorio died,
le dieron en el fundío	They shot him in the butt
y hasta que gritó muertodío	Until he yelled, I die.
Coro	*Chorus*
Indita que sí	Indian woman, yes
indita que no,	Indian woman, no.
y en ese cerro del humo	In that Cerro del Humo is
donde Vitorio murió.	Where Vitorio died.
2	**2**
Y al incar la rodía	And as he knelt
y a tirarle a ese venado	To aim at the deer
le dice don Juan Dioluna,	Don Juan Dioluna said,
y hoy te llevo retratado.	There, I have taken your photograph.
Coro	*Chorus*
3	**3**
¿Qué es aquello que se miró	What is that which I see
recorriendo los caminos?	Moving down the roads?
Y esos son los remolinos	Those are the dust storms
de esos que el viento levantó.	Which the wind stirs up.
Coro	*Chorus*

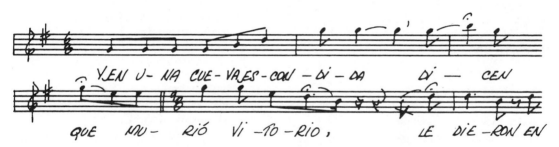

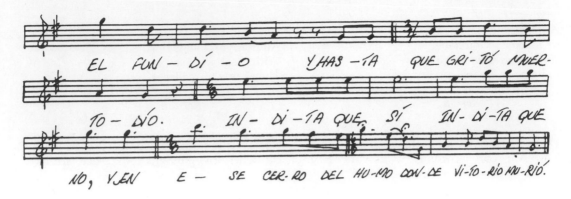

EL FUN-DÍ-O Y HAS-TA QUE GRI-TÓ MUER-
TO-DÍO. IN-DÍ-TA QUE, SÍ IN-DÍ-TA QUE
NO, Y EN E — SE CER-RO DEL HU-MO DON-DE VI-TO-RIO MU-RIÓ.

F9. *Indita de Manuelito* (Indian Wife of Manuelito)
R328, Elfego Sánchez, Tijeras, N.Mex., 1950, Robb.

<table>
<tr><td>

1
Yo soy indio Manuel,
el hermano de Mariano.
Yo con la flecha en la mano
empalmo de a dos y tres.

</td><td>

1
I am the Indian Manuel,
The brother of Mariano.
With an arrow in my hand
I can pierce two or three.

</td></tr>
</table>

1
Yo soy indio Manuel,
el hermano de Mariano.
Yo con la flecha en la mano
empalmo de a dos y tres.

1
I am the Indian Manuel,
The brother of Mariano.
With an arrow in my hand
I can pierce two or three.

2
No importa sea indio o cristiano,   ]
o americano o francés.   ] *Bis*

2
No matter if you are Indian or Christian,
Or American or French.

3
Indita de Manuelito.
¡Con qué sentimiento estás!
En la Sierra de Gallina
te dieron muerte de paz.

3
Indian wife of Manuelito.
What grief you must feel!
They dealt the peace of death
In the Gallina Mountains.

4
No lo mataron al hombre
ni tampoco bien a bien.
Lo mataron a traición
Charles and Capitan Gray.

4
They didn't kill him like a man
Nor even face to face.
Charles and Captain Gray
Killed him by treachery.

5
Charles reclama sus güelles   ]
valido de la ocasión.   ] *Bis*

5
Charles seized his cattle,
Taking advantage of the occasion.

6
Le responde el bocón,
—O, Charles, no me degüelles.
No es ésta tu religión,   ]
ni lo permitan tus leyes.—   ] *Bis*

6
The big mouth replied,
"Oh, Charles, don't cut my throat.
This is not your religion,
Nor should your laws permit it."

7
Indita de Manuelito.
¡Con qué sentimiento estás!
que en el Ojo de la Gallina
te dieron muerte de paz.

7
Indian wife of Manuelito.
What grief you must feel!
For at the Spring of the Gallina
They dealt you the peace of death.

8 Yo soy el indio Manuel que al mundo causó ruina, y hoy me hallo sepultado y en el Ojo de la Gallina.	**8** I am the Indian Manuel Who brought ruin to the world, And here I am today Buried at Gallina Spring.
9 Me hallo sepultado en la Sierra de Gallina por beber un trago de whiskey de una cantina.	**9** They have buried me In the Gallina Mountains Just for having a drink of whiskey In a saloon.
10 Gobierno de Santa Fe, purito café me dabas.] *Bis*	**10** Government in Santa Fe, You gave me nothing but coffee.
11 Gobierno de Santa Fe, purito café me dabas. Y asina me entretuviste en tal de que no me alzara.	**11** Government in Santa Fe, You gave me nothing but coffee. And that's how you kept me So that I would not revolt.
12 Muchas güeyadas robé para que tú las pagaras.] *Bis*	**12** I stole many cattle So you'd have to pay for them.
13 Y un capitán y un doctor se matan en El Bonito sin más achaque y razón que la muerte del indito.] *Bis*	**13** And a captain and a doctor Were killed in El Bonito Without any more reason Than the death of the Indian.
14 Indita de Manuelito se encuentra muy pobrecito.] *Bis*	**14** The Indian wife of Manuelito Finds herself in poverty.
15 Cuenta cinco mil ovejas, quinientas y otras poquitas.] *Bis*	**15** She counts only 5,000 ewes, Five hundred and a few others.

The melody has the characteristic sound of
the *indita*. There is no refrain.

F9a. *Indita del Manuelito*
R1517, Esteban Torres, Tomé, N.Mex., 1957, Robb.

1

Indita, indita, indita,
icon qué sentimiento estás!
que en el ojo de la gallina
te dieron muerte de paz.

2

No te mataron peliando,
ni tampoco bien a bien.
Te mataron a traición
Charles y el Capitán Grey.

3

Yo soy el indio Manuel,
hermanito del Mariano,
que con mi flecha en la mano
empalmo de dos a tres.

4

Yo soy el indio Manuel
que tenía mis ovejitas,
les tenía dada querencia
en ojo de la Lemitar.

5

No eran más de quince mil   ]
quinientas y otras poquitas.   ] *Bis*

6

(Verso 3 se repite)

1

Indita, indita, indita,
What grief you must feel
That at the well of the hen
They dealt you the peace of death.

2

They did not kill you fighting,
Nor did they hand to hand.
They killed you by treachery,
Charles and Captain Gray.

3

I am the Indian Manuel,
Little brother of Mariano,
Who with my arrow in my hand
Pierce two or three at a time.

4

I am the Indian Manuel
Who cared for my ewes,
Who felt affection for them,
At the spring of Lemitar.

5

There weren't more than fifteen thousand
Five hundred and a few more.

6

(Verse 3 repeated)

The range of this *indita* is a perfect fifth.
It is in the Dorian mode (mode of D).

F9b. *Indita de Manuelito*
RB722, Manuel Esquibel, Las Nutrias, N.Mex., 1950, Cobos.

1

Yo soy el indio, Manuel,
el hermano de Mariano;
yo con la flecha en la mano
y empalmo a dos y a tres;
no importa, sea indio, sea cristiano
o americano o francés.

1

I am the Indian, Manuel,
The brother of Mariano;
And with arrow in hand
I have split two or three;
It doesn't matter if you are Indian or Christian
Or American or French.

2

Indita de Manuelito
¡con qué sentimiento está!
que en la Sierra de la Gallina
te dieron muerte de paz;
no te mataron al hombre
ni tampoco bien a bien;
te mataron a traición
Charles y capitán Gray.

2

Indian wife of Manuelito
With what sentiment I relate
How on Gallina Mountain
They gave you the death of peace;
They did not kill you like men,
Nor in hand to hand combat;
They killed you treacherously,
Charles and Captain Gray.

3

Charles reclama su buey,   ]
valido de la ocasión;   ] *Bis*
y le responde el bocón:
—O, Charles, no me degüelles,
no es ésta tu religión,
ni lo permiten tus leyes.—

3

Charles reclaims his ox
Taking advantage of the occasion;
And the talkative man replied:
"Oh, Charles, don't cut my throat,
This is not your religion,
Nor do your laws permit it."

4

Indita de Manuelito
¡con qué sentimiento está!
que en el Ojo de la Gallina
te dieron muerte de paz;
yo soy el indio Manuel   ]
que al mundo le causé ruina.   ] *Bis*

4

Indian wife of Manuelito
With what sentiment I relate
How at the Gallina Spring
They gave you the death of peace;
I am the Indian Manuel
Who brought ruin to the world.

5

Y me hallo asepultado
y en la Sierra de la Gallina,
por ir a beber un trago
de whiskey a una cantina;
gobierno de Santa Fe,
purito café me dabas;
gobierno de Santa Fe,
y asina me entretuviste
y en tal de que no me alzara;
muchas bueyadas robé
para que tú las pagarás.

5

And I find myself buried
There on Gallina Mountain,
Because I took a drink
Of whiskey in a saloon;
Government of Santa Fe,
You gave me pure coffee;
Government of Santa Fe,
Thus you kept me captive
So that I would not be proud;
I have stolen many cattle
So that you will pay.

6

Un capitán y un doctor
matan al Bonito,
sin más achaque y razón   ]
que la muerte de este indito.   ] Bis

6

A captain and a doctor
Killed the Handsome One
Without any more excuse or reason
Than the death of this Indian.

7

Indita de Manuelito   ]
se encuentra muy pobrecito;   ] Bis
cuenta cinco mil ovejas   ]
quinientas y otro poquito.   ] Bis

7

The Indian wife of Manuelito
Is very poor;
She has only five thousand
Five hundred ewes and a few more.

F10. *Indita de Cochití* (Indian Girl of Cochití)
R311, Braulio Prada, Cañada de los Alamos, N.Mex., 1954, Robb.

1

Indita, indita, indita,
indita de Cochití.
No le hace que sea indita,
al cabo no soy para ti.

1

Indita, Indita, Indita,
Indita of Cochití.
It makes no difference that you are Indian,
After all, I am not for you.

2

Mañana por la vereda
me tengo que ir hasta el poso
a ver si esa indita llega,
para agarrarla del reboso.

2

Tomorrow by the pathway
I have to go down to the well
To see if this Indian girl comes,
And seize her by her shawl.

3

Y si sabe cuanto vale
la palabra que me ha dado
que pruebe haber a que sabe
un besito bien tronado.

3

And if one would know the value
Of the word that she has given me
To prove it one would have to have
A nice little kiss.

4

¡Qué bonitas trensas tienes,
indita, hasta la cintura!
se me hace que un día viernes
me quedo con tu hermosura.

4

What lovely braids you have,
Indita, reaching to your waist,
It seems to me that some Friday
I will keep your beauty.

5

Indita, indita, indita—
no le pongas colorado,
mira que nadie no ve
bajo de la palisada.

5

Indita, Indita, Indita—
Don't blush,
See, no one is looking
Beneath the palisades.

6

Si tú te casas conmigo
te compraré tu soguilla,
tu reboso, y tu vestido
adornado con chaquira.

6

If you marry me
I will buy you a headband,
A shawl, and a dress
Adorned with beads.

7

Tus arracadas de plata
y tus botas de charol;
verás que te ves tan guapa
como los rayos del sol.

7

And bracelets of silver
And patent leather boots;
You'll see how well dressed you are,
Like the rays of the sun.

8

Indita te puedes ir,
tu mamá te está esperando,
no sea que vaya a venir
cuando yo te esté abrazando.

8

Indita, you can go,
Your mother is waiting for you,
But you can't go just now
While I am embracing you.

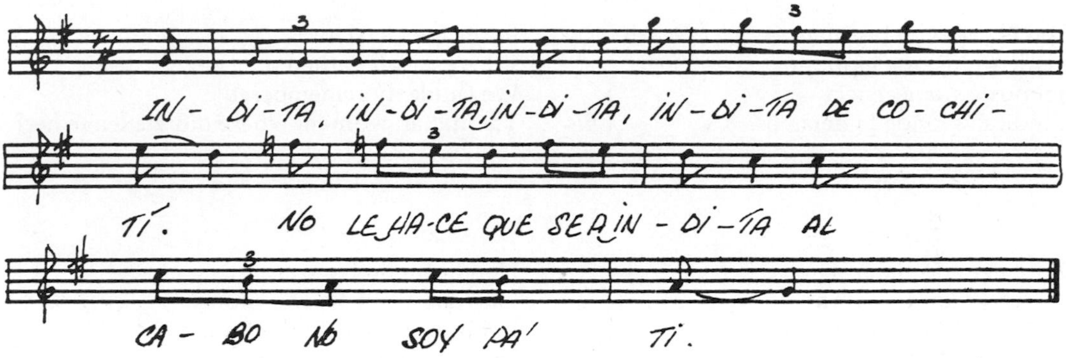

F10a. *Indita de Cochití*
R310, Elfego Sánchez and M. García, Tijeras, N.Mex., 1950, Robb.

¡Ay!
Indita, indita, indita,
indita de Cochití,
que le hace que sea indita,
pero no ha de ser para ti.

Ay!
Indita, Indita, Indita,
Indita of Cochití,
What matter if she be Indian,
But she is not meant for you.

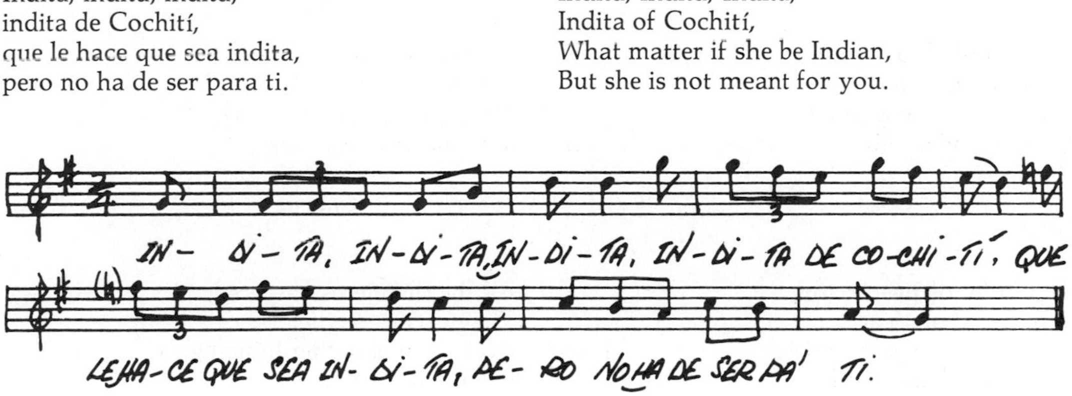

Alternation of eighth-note triplets with two eighth notes is a rhythmic characteristic of some *inditas*, including this one (see also F9).

F10b. *Indita de Cochití*
R2416, Juan Griego, Albuquerque, N.Mex., 1971, Cipriano Griego.

Coro		*Chorus*
Señor:		
Indita, indita mía,		Indian girl, Indian girl mine,
indita de Cochití.		Indian girl from Cochití.
Indita:		
No le hace que sea indita		No matter if I am Indian
si al cabo no soy para ti.		If after all I am not for you.

1		1
Y en el cerro de las Madres		In the Sierra Madres
donde todos nos juntamos		Where we all gathered
hicimos remanecencia	]	We suddenly remembered
la indita, ¿dónde la dejamos?	] *Bis*	The Indian woman, where did we leave her?

Coro   *Chorus*

2		2
Don Segundo Salazar		Don Segundo Salazar
y estando un día solito		One day while he was alone
agarró en brazos a la indita	]	In his arms he held the Indian girl
queriendo darle un besito.	] *Bis*	Wanting to give her a kiss.

Coro   *Chorus*

3		3
Y este el amigo José		This friend José
hombre de mucha razón		A man of great sense
que no más vido la indita	]	When he saw the Indian girl
y hasta les tiró el bordón.	] *Bis*	He even threw away his cane.

Coro   *Chorus*

4		4
Y esta indita vagamunda		This wandering Indian girl
mi covija me robó,		She stole my blanket,
y esa era la consentida,	]	That was my favorite one,
Mamaia me la dió.	] *Bis*	Mamaia gave it to me.

Coro   *Chorus*

5		5
Se juntan los pastorcitos,		All the shepherds gathered,
se ponen a platicar		They began to converse
y esta indita vagamunda	]	And this wandering Indian girl
nos enseñó hasta bailar.	] *Bis*	Even taught us to dance.

Coro   *Chorus*

IN-DI-TA, IN-DI-TA MÍ-A, IN-DI-TA DE CO-CHI-
TÍ, NO LE HA-CE QUE SEA IN-DI-TA SI AL CA-
BO NO SOY PA' TI.

F11. *Las Inditas del Parreal* (The Indian Girls of Parreal)
R279, Macario Leyva, Leyva, N.Mex., 1950, Robb.

1	1
Ahí vienen ya las inditas	There come the Indian girls
de vender Sierra Mojada.	Home from selling in Sierra Mojada.
Toditas vienen diciendo	They all come saying
—Ya venimos de paseada.—	"We are just passing through."

Coro	*Chorus*
Ante nanchi, totema já	Ante nanchi, totema ha
capoti talchi sinimi jue.	Capoti talchi sinimi hue.

2	2
Si fueres a La Mojada	If you ever go to La Mojada
hay muchas cosas que ver;	There are many things to see;
hay inditas muy bonitas	There are pretty Indian maidens
hablando purito inglés.	Speaking nothing but English.

Coro   Chorus

3	3
Las inditas del Parreal	The Indian girls from Parreal
todas usan crinalina;	All are using crinoline
porque la comida es cara,	For food is very dear,
vale un dólar la gallina.	A hen costs a dollar.

Coro   Chorus

4	4
Las Inditas del Parreal	The Indian girls from Parreal
se fueron para La Bonanza;	Went to La Bonanza;
las que no fueron paridas	Those that didn't go already pregnant,
fueron con tamaña panza.	Went with large stomachs.

Coro   Chorus

5

Si fueres a La Mojada
lo primero que verás
las carretas por delante
y los bueyes por detrás.

Coro

5

If you ever go to La Mojada
The first thing you will see
Are the ox carts in front
And the oxen behind.

Chorus

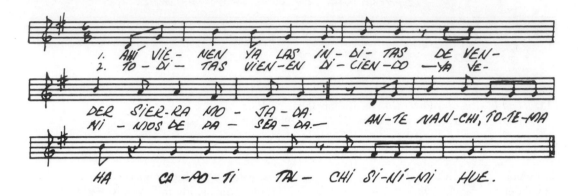

The last line is a relative of the English "cart before the horse" theme and is one of the humorous elements qualifying this as a *disparate*, as well as an *indita*. See also the wry comments about stomachs in verse 4.

F12. *Una Indita en Su Chinampa* (An Indian Girl in Her Garden)
Campa 2 (p. 193), 1946, Campa. Cf. R1201 and RB226 (versions from Arizona and California respectively).

Una indita en su chinampa
estaba cortando flores
y el indio que la cuidaba
le cantaba sus amores:
Chica marica del amasito
bhihuirí ti toho salé.

An Indian girl in her garden
Was cutting flowers
And the Indian that loved her
Was singing to her of his love:
Chica marica del amasito
Bhihuirí ti toho salé.

The word *chinampa* refers to the floating gardens of Xochimilco, Mexico, near Mexico City, where Indian women raise flowers and sell them from canoes to the tourists who tour the lake in gaily named and festooned barges, often with a band of hired musicians.

Chimaca, chinante, chechenaco, and *chinaco* do not appear in the dictionary and, apparently, are all corruptions of *chinampa* (see F12a–12d).

F12a. *Una Indita en Su Chinaco*
R289, Macario Leyva, Leyva, N.Mex., 1950, Robb.

Una indita en su chinaco	]	An Indian girl in her garden
andaba cortando flores	] *Bis*	Was going along cutting flowers
y el indio que la cuidaba	]	And the Indian man who cared for her
le cantaba sus amores.	] *Bis*	Was singing to her of his love.

<table>
<tr><td align="center">*Estribillo*</td><td align="center">*Refrain*</td></tr>
<tr><td>Anda jinda, anda jinda,</td><td>Anda jinda, anda jinda,</td></tr>
<tr><td>ay, ay, ay.</td><td>Ah, ah, ah.</td></tr>
</table>

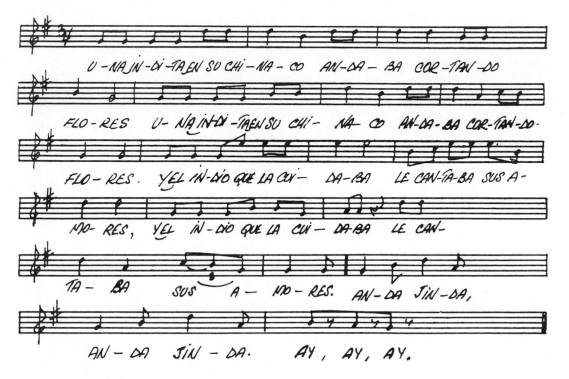

The refrain "Anda jinda . . ." appears to be
in Indian dialect.

F12b. *Una Indita en Su Chimaca*
Campa 2 (p. 193).

<table>
<tr><td align="center">1</td><td align="center">1</td></tr>
<tr><td>Una indita en su chimaca</td><td>An Indian girl in her garden</td></tr>
<tr><td>andaba juntando flores.</td><td>Was going along gathering flowers.</td></tr>
<tr><td>El indio que la rodeaba</td><td>The Indian man who loved her</td></tr>
<tr><td>le cantaba sus amores.</td><td>Was singing to her of his love.</td></tr>
</table>

2

—¿No me lo decías, indita,
que con el amor me amabas,
y que de verme llorabas
a todas horas del día?—

3

—Es verdad, si se lo dije
mientras que tenía dinero.
Hora que no tiene nada,
no, señor, ¡para qué lo quiero!—

4

—Para buscar el dinero,
lo buscaremos los dos.
Si usted sigue la porfía
la seguiremos los dos.—

5

Un consejo a mí me dió,
andando allá en la garita.
Aquí se acaban cantando
los versitos de la indita.

2

"Didn't you tell me, Indian maiden,
That you loved me with all your heart
And that you wept for the sight of me
Every hour of the day?"

3

"It is true, if I said so
When you had money.
Now that you have nothing,
No, sir! Why should I love you?"

4

"Let us go together
And look for money.
If you continue your obstinacy
We will get nowhere."

5

A bit of advice she gave me,
Right then and there.
Here ends the singing
Of the verses of the Indian girl.

F12c. *Una Indita en Su Chinante*
    R2403, Juan Griego, Albuquerque, N.Mex., 1971, Cipriano Griego.

1

Una indita en su chinante,
un día cortando flores.   ] *Bis*
El indito le decía,
—le platique sus amores.   ] *Bis*

2

Indita, indita mía,
indita de Dios, ¿que haré?
en los campos cantaremos,
y en la sierra chiflaré.   ] *Bis*

(Whistled Interlude)

3

El comanche y la comancha
se fueron para Santa Fe
a vender los comanchitos
por azúcar y café.   ] *Bis*

4

Y el comanche y la comancha,
estaban en una porfía,
el comanche que de noche,
y la comancha que de día.

1

An Indian girl in her garden,
One day was cutting flowers.
The Indian man said to her,
"Speak to me of love."

2

"Indian girl, Indian mine,
Indian girl of God, what will I do?
In the country we will sing
And on the mountain I will whistle."

(Whistled Interlude)

3

The Comanche and his woman
Went to Santa Fe
To sell the little Comanches
For sugar and coffee.

4

And the Comanche and his woman
Were persistent,
The Comanche during the night,
And his woman during the day.

5

E-na ta he ha ne ha na
ena ta he ha nan do
he ana, he ana, e a na
he ana he na ya yo.   ] *Bis*

5

E-na ta he ha ne ha na
Ena ta he ha nan do
He ana, he ana, e a na
He ana he na ya yo.

U-NA IN-DI-TA EN SU CHI-NAN-TE, UN DI-A COR-
TAN-DO FLO-RES, UN DI-A COR-TAN-DO FLO-RES.
EL IN-DI-TO LE DE-CI-A, LE PLA-TI-QUE
SUS A-MO-RES, LE PLA-TI-QUE SUS A-MO-RES.

The last verse, in typical Indian chant syllables, is sung to the same melody as that of
the other verses. In this respect and because
it is sung only at the end, it differs from the
usual *estribillo*, or refrain.

F12d. *Indita de Chechenaco* (Indian Girl of Chechenaco)
R531, Francisco S. Leyva, age 81, Leyva, N.Mex., 1951, Robb.

1

Una indita en Chechenaco
andaba juntando flores,
y andaba juntando flores;
y el indio que las regaba
le hablaba de sus amores.   ] *Bis*

1

An Indian girl in Chechenaco
Was gathering flowers,
And was gathering flowers;
And the Indian who sprinkled them
Spoke to her of his love.

2

Indita, yo te daré
correa para tus huaraches
pero has de salir conmigo
y a pelear con los apaches.

2

Indita, I will give you
Leather straps for your huaraches
But you must go out with me
To fight the Apaches.

3

Indita, yo te daré
corales para tu garganta
y una banda colorada
para que seas mi marchanta.

3

Indita, I will give you
Bits of coral for your necklace
And a red colored band
So that you will be my customer.

4

Indita, yo te daré
palma para tu sombrero

4

Indita, I will give you
Palm leaves for your sombrero

pero has de largar la plata
como la largó el cordero.

But you have to give up the money
As the lamb gave up its wool.

5
Y en el cerro de Elemento
son grandes las companías,
ganaron los oficiales
perdió la comanchería.
Largaron sus parapetos
que mi corazón pedían.

5
In the Elemento Mountains
Are large troops,
The soldiers conquered and
The Comanches lost.
They extended their battlefronts
For they were after my heart.

U-NA IN-DI-TA EN CHE-CHE-NA-CO, AN-DA-BA JUN-TAN-DO FLO-RES, AN-DA-BA JUN-TAN-DO FLO-RES, Y EL IN-DIO QUE LAS RE-GA-BA LE HA-BLA-BA DE SUS A-MO-RES, LE HA-BLA-BA DE SUS A-MO-RES.

F13. *Indita de San Luis* (Ballad of Saint Louis)
R312, Helen Little, Elfego Sánchez, and M. García, Tijeras, N.Mex., 1950, Robb.

1
San Gonzalo de Amarante,
aparécete en la mar,
concédeme este milagro
que aquí te vengo a rogar.

1
San Gonzalo de Amarante,
Appear in the sea,
Grant me this miracle
For which here I come to pray.

Estribillo
Yana heyannah heyannah yo,
yana heyanah heyanah yo.

Refrain
Yana heyanah heyanah yo,
Yana heyanah heyanah yo.

2
Dicen que una golondrina
de un volido cruzó el mar,
y aquí me tienes San Luis
que te prometí bailar.

2
They say that a swallow
In one flight crossed the sea,
And here you have me, Saint Louis,
I promised to dance for you.

Estribillo

Refrain

<table>
<tr><td>

3

Indita, indita, indita
de la Sierra de Almirante.
También las inditas dicen
San Luis de mi corazón.

</td><td>

3

Indian, Indian, Indian
Of the mountains of Almirante.
The Indian girls also say
Saint Louis of my heart.

</td></tr>
<tr><td>

Estribillo

</td><td>

Refrain

</td></tr>
<tr><td>

4

Y una mujer de Almirante
y a San Luis le fué a bailar
porque su hijo estuvo ausente
y San Luis se lo hizo lograr.

</td><td>

4

And a woman of Almirante
Went to dance for Saint Louis
Because her son was absent
And Saint Louis made it turn out well.

</td></tr>
</table>

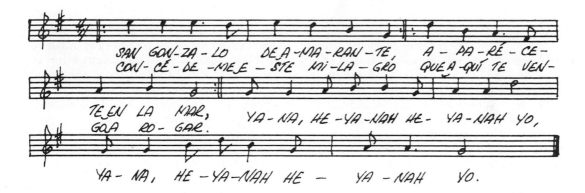

Additional verses are added in profusion,
most of them repetitions of the above verses
varied by the insertion of other names.

F14. *La Indita Vagabunda* (The Roving Indian Girl)
R526, Francisco S. Leyva, age 81, Leyva, N.Mex., 1951, Robb.

This is a *disparate* in the style of an *indita*. I have included it because of its melody. The text, because of its inordinate length, has been omitted, and the following summary substituted.

The first sixteen verses are an account of the amazing travels of the wandering Indian woman, who is represented as having been in all the following places, most of them in New Mexico: Seboyeta, Lemitar, Isleta, Sabinal, Parral, Agua Fria, Mesilla, Algodones, Angostura, Bernalillo, Sandía, Corrales, Pajarito, New York, Placitas, Tejón, Chililí, Torreón, Duranes, Padillas, New Orleans, Mora, Arroyo Seco, San Francisco, Las Vegas, San José, Valencia, Sabino, Independencia (Independence, Missouri?), California, Jerusalem, China, Cañón de Jémez, Belén (or Bethelehem, where, it recites, the Holy Child was born), Nazareth, Galilee, Africa (where she took a steamboat—"estimbote"—for the state of Indiana), Russia, Santa Lucia, Asia, Guasafan, Egypt, Cañoncito, Chiquito (which, it says, is in the land of the Navajos), France, Spain, Mexico, Guadalajara, Chihuahua, Ranchos de Atrisco, and Ranchos de Albuquerque.

God finally called her to judgment and with the advice of all his government destined her to the inferno. In hell everyone observed what a terror she was; even the devils couldn't stand her. So they brought suit against her. It was a famous lawsuit, and God then decided to send her to purgatory.

In purgatory among many blessed souls, she began to steal. The souls in purgatory also brought suit against her, and God decided to send her to the part of heaven where the Holy Fathers were. Undaunted by so much fame, she disturbed the Fathers and stole their cassocks. They, too, were forced to bring suit against her and God decided to send her to Limbo.

Her career continued. In desperation God sent her to Glory, where she so annoyed the angels that God decided to resuscitate her and send her back to earth. When she got back to earth, she married an Indian from the Sandía pueblo. She went hunting and came home with a deer. But she boasted so much that the Sandías held a trial and decreed that she must go to Taos. But people couldn't stand her anywhere, and so she was sent successively to Santa Fe, San Ildefonso, Acoma, Santo Domingo, Albuquerque, Santa Clara, and Zía.

She was finally brought home to Sandía pueblo, starving and in a delicate condition. When the nine months were fulfilled, she gave birth to a boy who was so perverse that he was more of a scoundrel than his mother. The fathers baptized him Felipito. The poor father couldn't stand the mother and child; so he died and went to judgment. As he pleaded his case, he confessed his sins and said that he could not stand his wife or son. God said that he could not stand them either and finally decided to get rid of them once and for all. So he caused an earthquake, and the earth opened up and swallowed them.

F15. *La Indita de Arellana* (The Indian Girl of Arellana)
R1398, Juan Griego, Albuquerque, N.Mex., 1956, Robb. Cf. R2417.

1

Ella:
Soy indita, soy indiana,
soy indita zacatecana,
desertora, desertora
de las tropas de Arellana.

2

El:
Indita, si vas al monte
cuidado con los casadores
no te vayan a matar
por andar entre las flores.

3

El:
Indita, tú me juraste
que de veras me amabas
y a todas horas del día
cuando no me veías llorabas.

4

Ella:
Sí, señor, sí se lo dije,
cuando tenía dinero.
Ahora que no tiene nada,
señor, ¿para qué lo quiero?

5

El:
Voy a buscarte dinero
para tenerte contenta.
Ella:
Mientras que usted lo consigue
yo corro por otra cuenta.

6

El:
Eso de por otra cuenta
a mí no me sale bien.
Ella:
Si le salga o no le salga,
yo mi gusto le a de ser.

7

El:
Allí te dejo estas prendas
para que de ellas te estén dando.

1

She:
I am an Indian girl, an Indian,
I am a Zacatec Indian girl,
Deserter, deserter
From Arellana's troops.

2

He:
Indita, if you go to the wilderness
Look out for the hunters
So they may not kill you
While you walk among the flowers.

3

He:
Indita, you swore to me
That you really loved me
And at all hours of the day
When you didn't see me, you cried.

4

She:
Yes, sir, I did say that,
When you had money.
Now that you have none,
Sir, why would I want you?

5

He:
I'm going to find you money
To keep you happy.
She:
Until you find the money
I will make other plans.

6

He:
That business of other plans,
This does not go well for me.
She:
Whether it goes well for you or not,
I will do as I please.

7

He:
Here I leave you these things
So that you may bargain with them.

Ella:
No, señor, porque dirán
tan bonita y empeñando.

She:
No sir, for they will say
She is so pretty and yet she's pawning things.

SOY IN-DI-TA, SOY IN-DIA-NA, SOY IN-

DIA ZA-CA-TE-CA-NA, DE-SER-TO-RA, DE-SER-

TO-RA DE LAS TRO-PAS DE-JA-RE-LLA-NA.

F16. *La Pablita*
R2414, Juan Griego, age 61, Albuquerque, N.Mex., 1971, Cipriano Griego.

1
Y según dicen por allí
que el anillo le tiró;
pues, éste era un gran presente   ]
que la Pablita le dió.   ] *Bis*

1
They say here and there
That he threw away the ring;
Well, this was a grand present
That Pablita gave him.

2
Y según dicen por allí
que nueve años le aburrieron
de tanto que se quisieron   ]
y ni un besito se dieron.   ] *Bis*

2
They say here and there
That for nine boring years
They loved each other very much
But they never kissed.

3
Y éste, el amigo menor,
no dejaba de chiflar,
dándole vuelta al ganado   ]
vuelta y vuelta para el corral.] *Bis*

3
And this, the youngest friend,
Never stopped whistling,
Rounding up the flock
Again and again toward the corral.

4
Dice el amigo José,
bastante apresurado,
se me hace que ese chiflido   ]
ya es puro calabaciado.   ] *Bis*

4
This friend José says,
Very concerned,
I believe all that whistling
Means there's something going on.

5
Iba Prudencio Luján
por todita la ladera
con una tegua en la mano   ]
pegándose en la cadera.   ] *Bis*

5
Prudencio Luján was going
Along all the ridges
With a shoe in his hand
Slapping his hip.

Y SE-GÚN DI-CEN POR A - LLÍ QUE EL

A -NI-LLO LE TI - RÓ; PUES,

ÉS -TE E-RA UN GRAN PRE - SEN -TE QUE LA PAB-

LI - TA LE DI - Ó.

The melody resembles that of the *Indita de Amarante Martínez* (F2).

F17. *Me Quemaron el Rancho* (They Burned the Ranch)
R2390, Juan Griego, age 61, Albuquerque, N.Mex., 1971, Cipriano Griego.

Coro	*Chorus*
¡Ay! indita, eso no,	Oh, Indian woman, not that,
en el rincón colorado	In the red canyon
la quemazón me rodeó.	The flames surrounded me.
1	1
Decía Santiago López,	Santiago López said,
demostrando sus enojos,	Showing his anger,
—Nestorita de mi vida,	"Nestorita of my life,
ya no puedo de los ojos.—	My eyes can no longer stand it."
Coro	*Chorus*
2	2
Y son tan duras las llamas,	The flames were so hot,
es fuerte el humaredón,	The smoke was so strong,
que no hallaba que hacer	That I did not know what to do
en esa cruel ocasión.	In that cruel situation.
Coro	*Chorus*
3	3
En medio de la montaña,	In the middle of the mountain,
arreando mis ovejitas,	As I drove my sheep away,
pues cuando menos pensé	I stumbled onto a little lake
me encontré una lagunita.	When I least expected it.

Coro

Chorus

4

En medio de la lagunita
una borrega maté
y le quité la zalea
y a toditas las salvé.

4

In the middle of the little lake
I killed a sheep
And removed its hide
And saved them all.

Coro

Chorus

5

Que nos querían quemar,
hicieron una emboscada;
pues con sacos de guangoche
ahí andaba la gringada.

5

They wanted to burn us out,
So they made an ambush;
Then with gunny sacks
The gringo mob was moving around.

Coro

Chorus

6

Les prendieron a los pastos,
a los montes, y a los llanos,
a ver si podían echar
afuera los mexicanos.

6

They ignited the pastures,
The hills, and the fields,
To see if they could drive
Out the Mexicans.

Coro

Chorus

7

Pues para subir al cielo
tiene San Pedro las llaves,
estos versos los compuso
mi sobrino Víctor Chaves.

7

To reach heaven
Saint Peter holds the keys,
These verses were composed
By my nephew Víctor Chaves.

Coro

Chorus

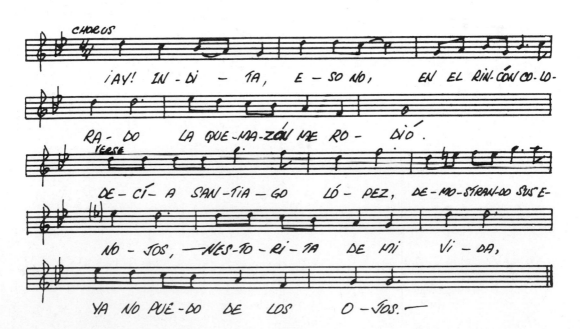

450

The occasional burning of barns or ranches as an incident of violent clashes between the races has continued, even to the present day. Such attacks have been perpetrated by both sides. Only a few years ago the Albuquerque newspapers reported such an incident as occurring in Río Arriba County, New Mexico, in an attempt to burn out an Anglo rancher. In the present *indita*, verses 3 to 5 suggest rather than describe the scene. They indicate that the mob set fire not only to the ranch buildings but also to the vegetation and that to save his sheep from the flames the rancher drove them into the little lake, sheltering himself from the heat with the hide of a sheep.

For clashes in California, Texas, and New Mexico involving Spanish Americans and Anglos, see *Joaquín Murieta* (B35), *Gregorio Cortés* (B49), and *La Indita de Manuel B. Otero* (F7). Verse 5 makes it clear that in the present case it was "gringos" who did the burning.

Of course there were also clashes between the Hispanos and other races, notably the Indians (see *Sandovalito*, F20).

F18. *Indita de Marino Leyba* (Ballad of Marino Leyba)
R318, Elfego and F. G. Sánchez, Tijeras, N.Mex., 1950, Robb.

1	**1**
Año de mil ochocientos	It was the year of eighteen hundred
ochenta y ocho del año	Eighty-eight when they
matán a Marino Leyba	Killed Marino Leyba
el veinte y siete de marzo.	On the twenty-seventh of March.
2	**2**
Indita de Marino Leyba,	Indian wife of Marino Leyba,
escuche mis expresiones:	Listen to what I say:
¡Cómo estará tu mujer	I wonder how your wife will feel
cuando no oiga tus razones!	When she doesn't hear your explanations!
¡Cómo lo habías de oír	How could you hear him
dándote satisfacciones!	Telling you all about it!
3	**3**
Plaza de San Antonito,	Good-bye to all my friends
adiós todos mis amigos.	In the town of San Antonito.
Miren bien como pasó,	Listen carefully how it happened,
la muerte de un desvalido.	The death of a helpless man.
4	**4**
Indita de Marino Leyba,	Indian wife of Marino Leyba,
escuche mis expresiones.	Listen to what I say.
¡Cómo estará tu mujer	I wonder how your wife will feel
de que no oiga tus razones!	Since she doesn't hear your explanations!
5	**5**
Cuando los vido venir,	When he saw them coming,
de sus armas iba a usar.	He started to pull out his gun.
Le grita Joaquín Montoya:	Joaquín Montoya shouts at him:
—¿Por qué me quieres matar?	"Why do you want to kill me?

6

Si porque vengo a tu tierra
te quieres precipitar. —
Atrás llega Tomás Highly,
él que lo iba a traicionar.

7

Indita de Marino Leyba,
escuche mis expresiones:
¡Cómo estará tu mujer
de que no oiga tus razones!

8

No lo mataron peleando
porque no les dió ocasión;
lo mataron platicando
por medio de una traición.

9

Cuando los vido parados,
Margarito es él que acata:
—Hermanito de mi vida,
capéyese que lo matan. —

10

No le acabó de decir
cuando lo vido ir cayendo,
y en las patas del caballo
lo vido estarse muriendo.

11

Margarito se prepara
pues a salir a avisar;
le arrimaron las pistolas,
no lo dejaron caminar.

12

El veintisiete de marzo
sucedió tal avería;
matan a Marino Leyba
como a las nueve del día.

13

Cañada del ojo del indio,
¡qué lugar tan desgraciado!
donde se vido Marino
en su sangre revolcado.

14

Como a las dos de la tarde
lo levantan en el coche;
lo llegaron al real
a las ocho de la noche.

6

"Do you want to start a fight
Because I step on your land?"
Behind him is Thomas Highly,
He who was to double-cross him.

7

Indian wife of Marino Leyba,
Listen to what I say:
I wonder how your wife will feel
Since she doesn't hear your explanations!

8

They didn't kill him in a fight
Because he gave them no reason to;
They killed him as he chatted
By means of treachery.

9

When he saw them standing,
Margarito realizes what's up:
"Dear brother of my life,
Dismount or they'll kill you."

10

He barely said it
When he saw him fall,
And at the horse's hoofs
He saw him dying.

11

Margarito then prepared
To go and tell someone;
They put their guns against
His ribs and stopped him.

12

The twenty-seventh of March
This tragedy happened;
They kill Marino Leyba
Around nine in the morning.

13

In the gully of the Indian well,
What a dreadful place!
There Marino found himself
Bathed in his own blood.

14

Around two in the afternoon
They pick him up in a car;
They took him to the capital
At eight in the evening.

15

Cuando salió su mujer,
salió con el alma partida;
y en sus elementos le dice:
—¡Ay! esposo de mi vida.—

15

When his wife came out,
She came out with a broken heart;
And in her anguish she tells him,
"Oh! Husband of my life."

16

Cuando llegó su mujer
pidiéndoselo de por Dios,
no lo pudo conseguir
para encomendarlo a Dios.

16

When his wife arrived,
Begging them for heaven's sake,
They did not allow her
To commend him to God.

17

Gobierno de Santa Fe:
—Te serví a lo militar;
me echaste un Americano
que me venía a matar.

17

Government of Santa Fe:
"I served you in the Army;
You sent me an American
Who came to kill me.

18

Americanos del Real,
pongan muy bien en su imprenta:
que se va de aquí Marino Leyba
a arreglar con Dios sus cuentas.

18

"Americans of the Capital,
Be sure and print this:
Marino Leyba goes from here
To pay his debts to God.

19

A don Martín Espinoza
como padre yo lo estimo;
¡Ay! les encargo a mi esposa
que solita la he dejado.—

19

"Don Martín Espinoza
I esteem as my own father;
Please look after my wife
Whom I've left all alone."

20

Indita de Marino Leyba,
escuche mis expresiones:
—¡Cómo estará tu mujer
de que no oiga tus razones!

20

Indian wife of Marino Leyba,
Listen to what I say:
"I wonder how your wife will feel
Since she doesn't hear your explanations."

A - ÑO DE MIL O- CHO - CIEN -TOS O-CHEN-TA Y O-
CHO DEL A - ÑO MA-TÁN A MA-RI-NO
LEY - BA EL VEIN-TE Y SIE-TE DE MAR-ZO.

F19. *Indita del 1884* (Ballad of 1884)
R1404, Edwin Berry, Tomé, N.Mex., 1956, Robb.

1		**1**
Año de mil ochocientos	]	In the year of eighteen hundred
ochenta y cuatro ha llegado	] *Bis*	And eighty-four
una creciente varaz	]	There was a growing misfortune
que no la hemos soportado.	] *Bis*	Which we were not able to stand.

Refrán / *Refrain*

¡Ay! indita del Río Grande,	]	Oh! Indita of the Río Grande,
¡Ay! qué ingrata te estás mostrando,	] *Bis*	Oh! How ungrateful you are showing yourself to be.
¡Ay! mira esas pobres mujeres,	]	Oh! See those poor women,
¡Ay! con sus colchones rodando.	] *Bis*	Oh! Roaming about with their mattresses.

2		**2**
El río se nos rompió	]	The river broke its banks
viniendo la luz del día.	] *Bis*	As day was dawning.
Dios me lo perdonará:	]	God may pardon me for saying:
lo rompió Jesús García.	] *Bis*	It was broken by Jesús García.

3		**3**
Salgan todos los correos,	]	All the carriers of news go out,
los de a caballo y de a pie,	] *Bis*	Some on horseback and some on foot.
Lleven pronto la noticia	]	Quickly bring the news
que el río va para Tomé.	] *Bis*	That the river is coming to Tomé.

4		**4**
El señor don Jesús Baca	]	Señor Don Jesús Baca
nos ha dejado confuso,	] *Bis*	Has left us in confusion, saying
si se quedan en Valencia	]	That if we remained in Valencia
allí no se encuentra refugio.	] *Bis*	We would find no refuge.

5		**5**
Toda la gente se fué	]	All the people went
de Valencia para el cerro;	] *Bis*	From Valencia to the mountain;
no se han quedado en la casa	]	No one remained in the house
más que el gatito y el perro.	] *Bis*	Except the kitten and the dog.

6		**6**
Sale el padre Ralliere	]	Father Ralliere goes out
con toda su compatriota,	] *Bis*	With all his compatriots,
todos los días preguntan:	]	All day long they asked:
—¿No se ha caido la parroquia?—	] *Bis*	"Has the parish church fallen?"

7		**7**
A la gente de Peralta	]	People of Peralta,
avísenle desde aquí,	] *Bis*	Notify them from here.
salgan todos de la casa	]	Everyone, get out of your houses
corriendo hasta Picurís.	] *Bis*	And run to Picurís.

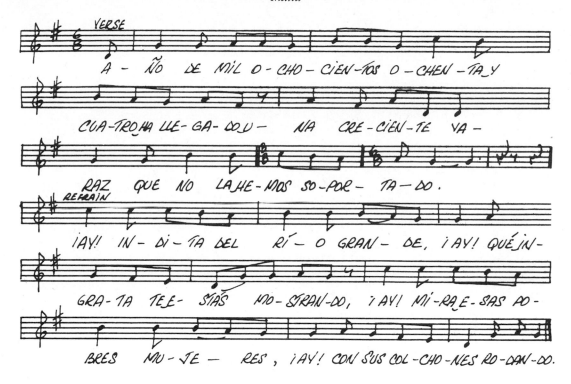

A-ÑO DE MIL O-CHO-CIEN-TOS O-CHEN-TA-Y

CUA-TRO HA LLE-GA-DO U-NA CRE-CIEN-TE VA-

RAZ QUE NO LA HE-MOS SO-POR-TA-DO.

REFRAIN

¡AY! IN-DI-TA DEL RÍ-O GRAN-DE, ¡AY! QUÉ IN-

GRA-TA TE E-SIAS MO-STRAN-DO, ¡AY! MI-RA E-SAS PO-

BRES MU-JE-RES, ¡AY! CON SUS COL-CHO-NES RO-DAN-DO.

The recording of *Indita del 1884* is preceded and followed by comments by the singer. The *indita*, composed by Manuel Vigil, tells the story of the flood of 1884 involving the villages of Tomé, Peralta, and Valencia on the east bank of the Río Grande. Father Ralliere, the famous parish priest of Tomé, is mentioned. See "Tomé and Father J. B. R." (Ellis 4c) for an interesting account of this town; of earlier floods (in 1769, 1780, and 1905); of a Comanche raid in 1777; of Don Julián Zamora (represented in this book by *Kyrie from the Mass of the Angels*, V2, as well as by R1366–1380); and of the fabulous Father Ralliere himself, who served in Tomé for fifty-three years, from 1858 to 1911.

Father Juan B. Ralliere, mentioned in *Indita del 1884* (F19), in Tomé, New Mexico.

F20. *Sandovalito*
RB161, Juanita Chávez González, age 70, San Ignacio, N.Mex., 1937, Lolita Pooler.
Cf. R13 (pp. 20, 76), Mendoza 9d, pp. 461–64.

<table>
<tr><td>

1
Sandovalito, toda tu gente
ya acabó, ya acabó,
ya Calahuasa no más quedó.

</td><td>

1
Sandovalito, all your people
Are bereft, are bereft,
Now Calahuasa alone is left.

</td></tr>
<tr><td>

2
Tú, María Aguila, toda tu gente,
ya acabó, ya acabó,
ya Calahuasa no más quedó.

</td><td>

2
You, María Aguila, all your people
Are bereft, are bereft,
Now Calahuasa alone is left.

</td></tr>
<tr><td>

3
Dominguita, toda tu gente
ya acabó, ya acabó,
ya Calahuasa no más quedó.

</td><td>

3
Dominguita, all your people
Are bereft, are bereft,
Now Calahuasa alone is left.

</td></tr>
<tr><td>

4
Zápiro Largo, toda tu gente
ya acabó, ya acabó,
ya Calahuasa no más quedó.

</td><td>

4
Zápiro Largo, all your people
Are bereft, are bereft,
Now Calahuasa alone is left.

</td></tr>
</table>

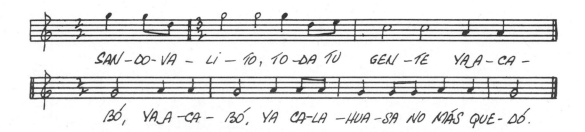

I used this melody as a theme in the third
movement of my Concerto for Piano and
Orchestra.

F21. *Indita de Cleofas Griego* (Ballad of Cleofas Griego)
R2439, Edwin Berry, age 54, Tomé, N.Mex., 1972, Robb.

<table>
<tr><td>

1
El día diez de septiembre
si no estoy equivocado,
entre Cleofas y Polonio
traiban el ganado cortado.

</td><td>

1
On the tenth of September
If I am not mistaken,
Between Cleofas and Polonio
Their flock was short some sheep.

</td></tr>
</table>

Coro	*Chorus*
¡Indita de Cleofas Griego,	Indian woman of Cleofas Griego,
no te vayas a cansar	Don't begin to weaken!
de andar buscando corta	It's foolish to go looking for lost sheep
sin conocer la señal!	Without knowing the earmark.

2	2
Polonio le dice a Cleofas:	Polonio says to Cleofas:
—Ahora sí estoy atrasado,	"Now I am in trouble,
me falta una oveja negra	I am short one black ewe
ya se me cortó el ganado.—	That strayed from my flock."

3	3
Y Cleofas le contestó:	And Cleofas replied:
—¿Cuál es tu reprehensión?	"Why scold me, Polonio?
¡Polonio ya no te acuerdas	You can't even remember
del pintito botijón!—	A black sheep with a fat belly!"

4	4
Entonces observó Polonio:	Thereupon Polonio observed:
—No cabe la menos duda	"There is not the slightest doubt
si ayer tarde yo la vide	That yesterday afternoon I saw
la cabra canjilonuda.—	The goat with a big horn."

5	5
El patrón se lo decía:	The boss was saying:
—Vete por la trincherita.	"Go look in the deep gullies.
Trecientas son las ovejas.	There are three hundred ewes missing.
Allí llevas la cuenta escrita.—	There you have the written count."

6	6
Y le contestó Polonio	And Polonio replied to him
con valor muy suficiente:	With plenty of courage:
—Si no te traigo esa corta	"If I don't find that bunch for you
de mí se rierá la gente.—	May I be the laughing stock to the people."

7	7
Salió de luego Polonio,	Then Polonio set forth,
que le estorba el chaleco,	In a great hurry,
buscando el ganado del Hill.	Looking for the Hill's flock.
Lo encuentra en el Monte Prieto.	He found it on Mount Prieto.

8	8
Y allí se encuentra Nazario	And there he met Nazario
quien le salió a saludar.	Who came out to greet him.
—¿O traes los burros perdidos	"You must be looking for lost burros
o te has venido a pasear?—	Or have you just come for a visit?"

9	9
Polonio le respondió	Polonio responded
(mostrando de andar cansado):	(Showing how tired he was):
—Tres días traigo corridos	"I have been out three days
que se me cortó el ganado.—	Looking for some lost sheep."

10

Nazario le dijo: —Entonces
dime, ¿cuál es la señal?
Aquí se juntó un atajo
de taravia y ramal.—

10

Nazario said to him: "Well,
Tell me, what is the earmark?
Here a bunch are gathered
With a *taravia* and *ramal*."

11

Polonio le contestó:
—Eso puede ser así.
Del ramal, yo no me acuerdo,
de la taravia sí.—

11

Polonio answered him:
"That might be so.
I don't remember the *ramal*
But the *taravia*, yes."

12

Nazario lo aconsejó:
—Allí está un viejo corral.
Mira, a ver como lo arreglas
para que puedas apartar.

12

Nazario advised him:
"There is an old corral.
Go ahead and repair it
So that you can sort them out.

13

Polonio es grande y hombrote,
Polonio no es muchichito.—
¡Si no ha sido por Nazario
no aparta más que el pintito!

13

"Polonio, you're a big man.
Polonio is not a worthless little boy."
If it hadn't been for Nazario
He wouldn't have sorted out more than
    the black one.

14

Nazario las apartaba
y le pegaba otro grito:
—Vete con esas que traes,
vuelve por otro atajito.—

14

Nazario sorted them out
And gave a great shout:
"Go along with those that you have,
Come back for another drove."

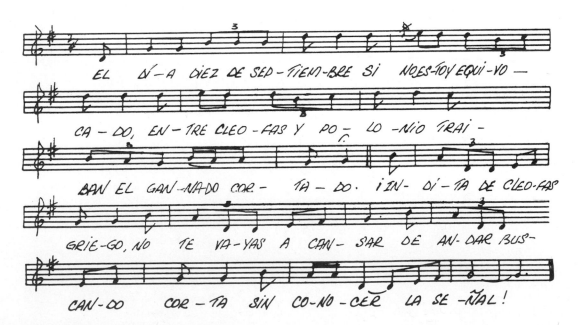

Some identification and definitions may be
necessary: Monte Prieto, a part of the San
Andres Mountains in south-central New
Mexico; *corta*, a group of sheep who have

strayed from the main flock; *taravia*, a semi-circular "bite" out of the lower edge of the ear; *ramal*, an earmark made by splitting the end of the ear into ribbons.

The *indita*, according to Edwin Berry, was composed by Cleofas Griego himself. It could equally well be classified as a shepherd's song in Section I.

F22. *Navajo Dance Song*
R394, David Frescas, age 67, Taos, N.Mex., 1950, Robb.

1
Ana heyana heyana
Ana heyana heyana.
Sin que lasana la hopa.
Sin que lasana la hopa.

1
Ana heyana, heyana
Ana heyana, heyana.
Sin que lasana la hopa.
Sin que lasana la hopa.

2
Sin que lasana la hopa.
Sin que lasana la hopa.
Llegamos . . . ropa (?)
Llegamos . . . segura (?)

2
Sin que lasana la hopa.
Sin que lasana la hopa.
We come . . . cloth
We come . . . secure

Coro
Ay, ay, ay, ay, ay.
¡Navajo!
Ay ya no
¡Navajo!
Ay ya no
Ana hoana haya.
¡Ay, ay, ay, ay, o!

Chorus
Ay, ay, ay, ay, ay.
Navajo!
Ay ya no
Navajo!
Ay ya no
Ana hoana haya.
Ay, ay, ay, ay, o!

(Verso 2 se repite)

(Verse 2 repeated)

Coro

Chorus

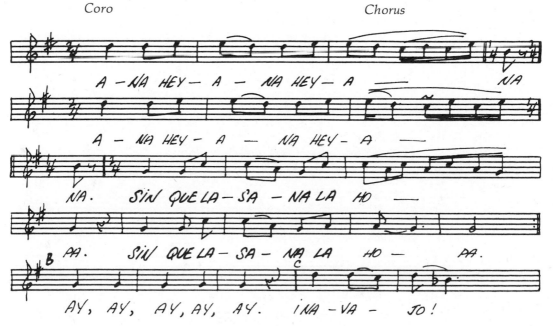

AY YA NO ¡NA-VA— JO!

AY YA NO A-NA HO-A— NA

HAY-A. ¡AY, AY, AY, AY O!

Much of this song consists of meaningless
syllables like those used in Navajo chants.

F23. *La Indita de Ezekiel (Siquio) Lucero* (The Ballad of Ezekiel Lucero)
R797, Severo Montoya, La Jara, N.Mex., 1951, Robb.

1	1
Para cantar esta indita	Before singing this *indita*
pido licencia primero.] Bis	I first ask permission.
2	2
Para año de mil ochocientos	In the year of eighteen hundred
setenta y cinco de cero	And seventy-five
se llegó el terrible día	Came the terrible day
del finado Siquio Lucero.	Of the late Siquio Lucero.
Refrán	*Refrain*
Ti-ri-lai, li-ri-lai-li-lai-la	Ti-ri-lai, li-ri-lai-li-lai-la
Ti-ri-lai, li-ri-lai-li-lo	Ti-ri-lai, li-ri-lai-li-lo
Ti-ri-lai, li-ri-lai-li-lai-la	Ti-ri-lai, li-ri-lai-li-lai-la
Ti-ra-li-ra, lai-li-lo.	Ti-ra-li-ra, lai-li-lo.

Remainder of text undecipherable

VERSE

PA-RA CAN-TAR E-STA IN-DI-TA PI-DO LI-CEN-CIA PRI-

ME-RO, PA-RA CAN-TAR E-STA IN-DI-TA PI-DO

Indita

LI - CEN-CIA ARI - ME - RO . TI-RI-LAI, LI-RI-LAI-LI-

LAI - LA TI - RI -LAI, LI -RI -LAI -LI - LO

TI - RI -LAI, LI -RI - LAI - LI - LAI-LA TI - RA-LI -RA LAI-LI - LO.

G. Trovo

The *trovo* is a type of song contest in which two or more persons sing alternate verses. The word *trova* in Spanish is defined as a metrical composition or a parody. The word, apparently derived from the word *trovador* for versifier, poet, or troubadour, may merely have been given a masculine ending and applied to this particular type of song.

Almost mythical troubadours of New Mexico and of northern Mexico are usually represented as taking part. They are known by such names as "El Zurdo" (the Left-handed one), "El Pelón" (the Bald, or Poor, One), "Chicoria," "El Negrito" (the Little Negro), "Gracia," "Cienfuegos" (One Hundred Fires), and "Taveras." "El Viejo Vilmas" (the Old Vilmas) was probably the most famous of these.

Campa wrote that these troubadours often traveled with the wagon trains from Chihuahua or along the Santa Fe Trail to New Mexico and that not infrequently two wagon trains would meet (Campa 2, pp. 18–20). Arrangements would be made for the two trains to camp together for the night. News would be exchanged and friendships renewed. After the evening meal had been served, the troubadours accompanying the two trains would sit down together in the light of a fire in the midst of a circle of prairie schooners and hobbled oxen and arrange the rules of a song contest. They would sing in turn until they had exhausted their repertories of *décimas de amor*, with a recess for reciting verses of their own composition. Then they would turn to religious *décimas* and to *trovos* improvised on the spot; they would alternately sing to the same tune the improvised verses in the form of *coplas*. In some cases each troubadour would sing his own version of the melody. In the verses they would propound questions to one another and answer them in verse form.

In G1 below several of these *trovadores* are represented as singing to one another. The participants are El Viejo Vilmas, Gracia, Sinjuegas, and Tabera. It will be noted that the spelling of the names is not consistent.

The above spellings come directly from the notebook of the singer, Arvino Martínez. This song (apparently reconstructed from memory) simulates one of these contests with improvised verses in which questions were propounded and answered—at least answered after a fashion, for some of them were unaswerable.

Mendoza suggests that the origin of the *trovos* may be found in the song contests that are known to have taken place in the courts of Spain and Portugal. Famous singers came from remote places to compete in the contests, and the kings themselves were sometimes the judges (Mendoza 9d, p. 350). I have been told by various persons that *trovos* may be heard in many parts of Latin America and in particular in Chile and Peru.

The *trovos* of the present collection sometimes start with lengthy taunts directed by each of the singers at the others and then proceed to questions, usually derived from medieval religious mysticism and often partaking of the nature of a riddle.

Cobos makes numerous interesting observations on the *trovo* (Cobos 4, December 8, 1949). He quotes "Don Agapito," one of his informants, as saying that El Negrito was a Negro who knew Spanish very well. Cobos points out that the contest between Vilmas and El Negrito (G3) is a much more serious contest than the others, for the contestants, in addition to being more profound, were singing in the form of *décimas*, which required them not only to improvise sensible answers but to do so in the very complicated *décima* form. It seems almost incredible that they could improvise in this elaborate poetic form, and, in fact, several of the *décimas* given by Cobos are not complete or contain more than ten lines.

Cobos refers to Taberas, Cienfuegos, and Gracia as frontier poets. He quotes Luis Martínez, of Albuquerque, the well-known poet, as saying that Chicoria came from Los Griegos, now a part of Albuquerque, and that he joined a mule train traveling from Kansas City to Chihuahua in Mexico in the hope of meeting and competing against Gracia. They did in fact meet and compete. See *Principio del Trovo de Chicaria y Gracia* (G4) (Cobos 4, November 17, 1949).

Mendoza states that Gracia came from Chihuahua, that Cienfuegos was from the state of Sonora, and Taveras from Old Mexico. According to Mendoza, however, Chicoria was from San Miguel County, New Mexico (Mendoza 9d, p. 351). Campa has identified two additional *trovadores* of New Mexican origin in El Pelón, who was born in Pojoaque, New Mexico, in 1844 and christened Jesús Gonzales (Campa 2, p. 23), and Apolinario Almanzares, from Las Vegas, New Mexico (Campa 2, p. 18). Little is known about El Viejo Vilmas, but he is referred to in one of the *trovos* by Gracia as *Nuevo México insolente* (insolent New Mexico) (see Campa 2, p. 24).

Campa gives an interesting account of a song contest in which Apolinario Almanzares participated when two caravans met and camped together on the trail from Santa Fe to Chihuahua. The singers were Apolinario Almanzares and El Zurdo, a singer "from the south." During this contest they sang *canciones*, or love songs, followed by *versos* of their own composition with the *trovos*, improvised on the spot, reserved for the last (Campa 2, pp. 19–20).

In the texts for the songs below some of the verses are garbled and make little apparent sense. I have omitted the garbled material. The complete texts in Spanish are of course available by reference to the sources identified in the song headings.

G1. *Trovo del Viejo Vilmas, Gracia, Tabera, y Sinjuegos (Trovo* of Old Man Vilmas, Gracia, Tabera, and Sinjuegos)
R445, Arvino Martínez, Tierra Azul, N.Mex., 1951, Robb. Cf. R1989.

1
Gracia:
Maestro Dimas ¿dónde estás
entre semanas y días
que te han salido a buscar
más de cuatro companías
y no te han podido hallar
entre semanas y días?

2
Viejo:
Nulas son tus fantasías
te acabo de noticiar;
¿dónde son tus companías
que me han salido a buscar
que no me han podido hallar
entre semanas y días?

3
Gracia:
Por la flor de Alejandría
breve lo pondré en mi lista;
Maestro Dimas la menor
él que era de Buena Vista.

1
Gracia:
Master Dimas, where have you been
These weeks and days
For more than four parties
Have gone out to find you
But have not been able to
All these weeks and days?

2
Viejo:
I begin to think
All your fantasies are false;
Where are all these parties
Who have gone out to find me
But have not been able to
All these weeks and days?

3
Gracia:
By the flower of Alexandria
I will add you to my list;
Master Dimas the smallest party
Was the one from Buena Vista.

4

Viejo:
También yo te pondré en mi conquista
para que puedas disurgar.
Me han dicho que tú eres Gracia
conmigo no has de jugar.

5

Gracia:
Maestro, se tiene que dar
como tierra de verano;
¡qué tal chuliaran a Gracia
si le ganaba un anciano!

6

Viejo:
Torpe estás como el gusano,
te acabo de competir;
yo también canto lozano,
no me has de contradecir.

7

Gracia:
Maestro, le voy a aplaudir,
mi trovo no tiene tasa;
si alguna plana me enmienda
ni en la tierra queda Gracia.

8

Viejo:
Gracia fuera que conmigo
Gracia dijiera soy bueno;
y en puntito tan fino
cantarás con eficacia.

9

Gracia:
Breve daremos la traza;
pongan el verso, refleja.
Maestro, aunque, quiera ser bueno
su antiguedad no lo deja.

10

Viejo:
De mi voz naiden se queja,
de lo dicho a lo vulgar;
yo soy como el astro sereno
cuando subo a diversar.

11

Gracia:
Yo soy el Gracia mentado
que ha transitado la aurora;
yo soy el poeta mentado
que alaban mucho en Sonora.

4

Viejo:
I will add you to my conquests
So that you may amuse us.
They have told me that you were Gracia
But you should not play with me.

5

Gracia:
Master, it would be a victory
Of Winter over Summer;
It would make a joke of Gracia
If an old man could beat him.

6

Viejo:
You are dull as a worm,
I have just competed with you;
I too sing proudly,
You needn't contradict me.

7

Gracia:
Master, I shall applaud you
But my trovo is matchless;
If anyone could improve on my verses,
Gracia would not remain here.

8

Viejo:
It would be very gracious
Of Gracia to concede that I am good;
And in such a little point
You would be singing the truth.

9

Gracia:
We shall begin the contest shortly;
Think it over, pick a verse.
Master, even if you want to be good
Your age does not permit it.

10

Viejo:
Of my voice nobody is complaining,
From the sublime to the vulgar;
I am like a serene star
When I start to entertain.

11

Gracia:
I am the famous Gracia,
I have been around;
I am the famous poet
Whom they praise so much in Sonora.

12

Viejo:
Me bajé a la Cantimplora
con satisfacción completa;
y si no, míreme aquí:
el viejo carga paleta.
Mi voz ha sido discreta,
y en todo soy victorioso.
¡Qué tal chuliaran al viejo
si le ganaba un mocoso!

13

Gracia:
Maestro, no se muestre reguroso
que yo canto de noche y día.
Ahora quiero que me cante
textos de filosofía.

14

Viejo:
Si entiendes filosofía
dale a tu discurso vuelo;
Para gobierno del cielo
¿qué cosa mi Dios haría?
Ahora les pregunto yo, poetas
y compositores ¿cuántos fueron
los colores que Dios a la gloria
dió, cuántos jardines plantó,
cuándo su muerte notaría?
Dice la sagrada historia
de esa ciudad solemeda,
¿en qué moda fué formada?
Ahora les pregunto yo
¿acuáles son los querubines,
que un serafín alto y goza?
¿Acuál es la estrella más hermosa
que al mundo da claridad?
¿Qué título se le da al jardín?
Más esencial, ¿acuál es el río
de Jordán donde se paseó María?
Si entiendes filosofía
dale a tu discurso vuelo;
para gobierno del cielo
¿qué cosa mi Dios haría?

15

Gracia:
Maestro, ¿qué quiere que cante
si vengo todo turbado?
¿Cómo quiere que adivine
un punto tan elevado?

16

Viejo:
Van cuatro ¡pongan cuidado!

12

Viejo:
I came down to Cantimplora
With complete confidence;
If you doubt it, look me over:
The old one is ready for combat.
My voice has been discreet,
And in everything I am victorious.
How they would make fun of the old one
If a brat should beat him!

13

Gracia:
Master, don't be nervous
For I can sing all night and day.
Now I want you to sing to me
Texts of philosophy.

14

Viejo:
If you understand philosophy
Give wings to your speech;
As for the government of heaven
How would God proceed?
Now I ask you, poets
And composers, how many were
The colors that God gave to paradise,
How many gardens did he plant,
When he predicted his death?
The sacred story tells
Of the holy city. Only tell me
In what way it was formed?
Now I ask you poets
Which are the Cherubim and
Which the Seraphim, high and rejoicing?
What is the most beautiful star
Which gives clarity to the world?
What title is given to the garden?
More important, what about
The river Jordan where Mary walked?
If you understand philosophy,
Give wings to your speech;
As for the government of heaven,
How would God proceed?

15

Gracia:
Master, why do you want me to sing
If I am as stupid as you have said?
How can you ask me to speculate
About such a high matter?

16

Viejo:
There are four. Be careful!

¡Todo puesto en su lugar!
Oyeme, Gracia mentado,
¿de qué te sirve estudiar
y las tierras que has andado?
Privas por la palomía
no eres el poeta mentado
que pides filosofía.

Every question in its place!
Listen, famous Gracia,
Of what use to you are your studies
And the lands you have traveled?
Deprived of your claque
You are not the famous poet
That asks for philosophy.

17

Viejo:
Y aunque las bellas cuan bellas
tu palmo no es verdadero.
Ya Gracia me la jerro,
respóndela tú, Sinjuegos.

17

Viejo:
And even though beautiful,
Your answer is not correct.
Already Gracia has answered wrong,
Answer it, Sinjuegos.

18

Sinjuegos:
Yo no ha sido de los legos
ni canto con vanidad.
Todos se hacen a la concha
y llegando a Trinidad,
les doy el —cómo les va.—
Y el trobar son mis deseos
y estos cuatro pinacotes
al quince, me las tanteas.

18

Sinjuegos:
I haven't been a mere layman
Nor do I sing with vanity.
All the others hide themselves
When I arrive at Trinidad,
I give them the "How goes it?"
And to sing is my desire
And these four nonentities,
On the fifteenth, you test them against me.

19

Viejo:
Si vajares apaleo
sosiégate tempestad,
y es tanta a la humanidad
que reina en las jerarquías,
y en el nombre de María.
Yo no he sido de los legos.
Oyes, Sinjuegos mentado,
respóndeme la poesía.

19

Viejo:
Just calm down,
Calm your temper,
There is much humanity
That rules in the hierarchies,
And in the name of Mary.
I'm not one of the amateurs.
Listen, famous Sinjuegos,
Answer me in poetry.

20

Sinjuegos:
Yo canto de noche y día
y mi trovo no importuna.
Antes de formar la gloria
pienso que formó la luna.

20

Sinjuegos:
I will sing night and day
And my trovo will not disturb anyone.
Before forming paradise,
I think he formed the moon.

21

Viejo:
Cuéntalos de una en una.
Así tu talento alega.
Ya Sinjuegos la jerró,
respóndela tú, Taberas.

21

Viejo:
Count them one by one.
Is that the best you can do?
Already Sinjuegos has failed,
You answer it, Taberas.

22

Taberas:

A mí en todo la Sonora
no se me ha acabado la cera.
¿Quién diablos habrá metido
en esta bola a Taberas?
Ahí lo tienen, habladores.
Ya llegó él que hace demora
Sinjuegos, no eras gritón,
¿por qué no gritas ahora?

23

Sinjuegos:

Te advierto que en la Sonora
naiden me ha bajado el brío.
¡Qué me quieres espantar
con este viejo tardío!

24

Viejo:

Tápate que trairás frío,
¿o vendrás escalofriado?
Aquí tienes al tardío,
flaco pero no espuellado.
Ya tu maldito pecado
te trajo aquí a mi presencia
y por la mucha omnipotencia
toca el sentimiento, y darle
que con el viejo te sale
floriada tu diligencia.

25

Taberas:

Maestro, ya yo me retiro,
ya vengo de retirado.
Porque Sinjuegos me trata
como si fuera entenado.

26

Viejo:

Con el compás y cuidado,
que tu pecho mara y dice:
—Hazte a los bandos del Viejo
para que naiden te pise.—

27

Taberas:

Yo pregunto a mi memoria,
esencia y sabiduría;
antes de formar la gloria
formaría la luz del día.

22

Taberas:

Let me tell you that in all Sonora
Not one has ever vanquished me.
Who in the devil has put
Taberas in this mess?
There you take it, you braggarts.
You who were so late in arriving,
Sinjuegos, you were yelling then,
Why don't you yell now?

23

Sinjuegos:

I warn you that in Sonora
Nobody ever beat me either.
You want to scare me
With this old grizzled one!

24

Viejo:

Cover yourself. You are cold.
Or have you cold feet?
Here is your grizzled one,
Skinny but not worn out.
It was your cursed vanity
That brought you here to my presence,
And yet your conceit
Fills me with pity. But now that
You have tangled with the old one,
Let your talents flourish.

25

Taberas:

Master, I take my leave,
Now I have to retreat.
Because Sinjuegos treats me
As if I were his stepson.

26

Viejo:

Be serene and careful,
For your heart is saying
"Join the Old Man's group
So that no one will step on you."

27

Taberas:

I consult my memory,
Essence and knowledge;
Before forming paradise
He probably created the light of day.

28

Viejo:
No hay duda por tu victoria
que bien le caís a la ley.
Bien puedes ir a trabajar
a los palacios del rey
si en caso los conocéis.

28

Viejo:
There's no doubt about your victory
That you agree with the law.
You may well go to work
In the palaces of the king
In case you know them.

Remainder undecipherable

The question propounded by El Viejo (The Old Man) in verse 14 perhaps reveals why he was a champion. It is nine questions in one, most of them unanswerable.

The protagonists sing their retorts back and forth with very free variations of the melody.

Martínez told me that he had learned the *Trovo of the Viejo Vilmas* from his grandfather, Arvino Manzanares, who lived and died in the hamlet of Tierra Azul and that the *Trovo of Chicaria* (and presumably also that of *El Negrito*) is sung to the same tune.

G1a. *Principio del Trovo del Viejo Vilmas, Gracia, Sinfuegos, y Tabera* (Beginning of the *Trovo* of Old Man Vilmas, Gracia, Sinfuegos, and Tavera)
R508, Francisco S. Leyva, age 81, Leyva, N.Mex., 1951, Robb.

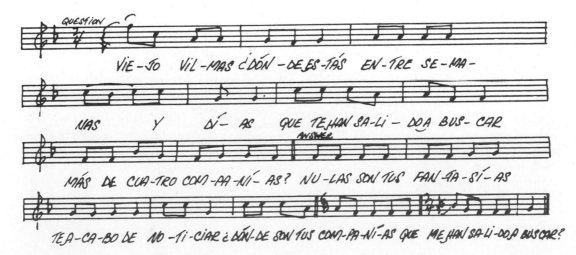

468

This text, a lengthy variant of G1, is omitted for reasons of space, but will be of value to those interested in the study of variants. The melody is quite valuable for purposes of comparison with other *trovo* melodies. Another interesting variant, not included here, is the *Trovo del Viejo Belmas* (R1989). The music was not recorded. These three variants of the same *trovo* with many similar verses are especially interesting because they come from three old men, all in their eighties, from three widely separated villages in New Mexico: Bernalillo, Leyva, and Galisteo.

G2. *Trovo del Viejo Belmas y el Negrito (Trovo* of Old Man Belmas and the Little Negro) R2421, Juan Griego, age 67, Albuquerque, N.Mex., 1971, Cipriano Griego. Cf. R1988.

1

Viejo Belmas:
Salga él que sea prudente
a trovar con la razón.
Que él que es amante no teme
antes busca la ocasión.

Refrán
Tai-da-dai-da,
rai-da,
di-da di-ra.
Tai-da dai-da ri-da da.

2

Negrito Poeta:
Con las fuerzas de Sansón
y las del entendimiento
me ha de refrescar el templo
del rey sabio Solomón.

3

Viejo Belmas:
Hombre si tienes razón
yo te voy a preguntar:
¿dónde está la sepultura
donde fué enterrado Abrán?

4

Negrito Poeta:
Abrán se enterró en Ebrón
en un campo de Almacén
en una cueva, oye bien,
cerca de Jerusalén.

5

Viejo Belmas:
Hombre si tienes razón
y traes memoria y sentido:
¿qué se hicieron las monedas
por quien Cristo fué vendido?

1

Viejo Belmas:
Whoever is prudent, come out
And sing with reason.
He who is a lover, does not fear
But rather seeks the occasion.

Refrain
Tai-da dai-da,
Rai-da,
Di-da di-ra.
Tai-da dai-da ri-da da.

2

Black Poet:
With the strength of Samson
And that of understanding
You must rebuild for me the temple
Of the wise king Solomon.

3

Viejo Belmas:
Well, if you can reason
I shall ask you:
Where was the sepulcher
Where Abraham was buried?

4

Black Poet:
Abraham was buried in Hebron
In a field in Almacen
In a cave, listen well,
Near Jerusalem.

5

Viejo Belmas:
Well, if you can reason
And if you have memory and sense:
What became of the coins
For which Christ was sold?

6

Negrito Poeta:
Aquellos treinta dineros
que en tierra fueron empleados
para que fueran sepultados
peregrinos pasajeros.

6

Black Poet:
Those thirty coins
Were spent on earth
So that traveling pilgrims
Could be buried.

7

Viejo Belmas:
Dime, latrio a quien ya sabes
si el decir eso te atreves:
¿cuál es la culpa más grande
que hace la culpa más breve?

7

Viejo Belmas:
Tell me, wise poet,
If you dare to say:
What is the biggest wrong doing
That makes the smallest sin?

8

Negrito Poeta:
Distinto señor, ya acabo
en esta distinta voz;
quien no venera sus padres
no le ve la cara a Dios.

8

Black Poet:
Distinguished sir, I finish,
Speaking plainly;
He who doesn't love his parents
Will not see the face of God.

SAL-GA ÉL QUE SE-A PRU-DEN-TE A TRO-VAR CON LA RA-ZÓN.

ÉL QUE ES A -MAN-TE NO TE-ME AN-TES BUS-CA LA O-CA-SIÓN.

TAI-DA DAI-DA, RAI-DA DI-DA, DAI-DA DI-DA RA. TAI-DA DAI-DA RI-DA DA.

G2a. *Trovo del Viejo y el Negrito (Trovo* of the Old Man and the Little Negro)
R1491, Samuel Lavadie, Prado, N.Mex., 1957, Robb. Cf. R1988, R2421.

1

Vilmas:
Salga él que fuera prudente
a trovar con la razón.
El que es amante no teme
antes busca la ocasión.

1

Vilmas:
Let him who is wise come forth
To compose verses with his wit.
He who likes to do this has no fear,
He asks the first question.

2

Negrito:
Con las fuerzas de Sansón
y las del entendimiento,
me has de fabricar el templo
del rey sabio Solomón.

2

Negrito:
With the strength of Samson
And that of understanding,
You must build for me the temple
Of the wise King Solomon.

3

Vilmas:
Mira si tengo razón
que te voy a preguntar:
¿Me dirás la sepultura
dónde fué enterrado Adán?

3

Vilmas:
See if I am right
Because I'm going to ask you:
Where is the sepulcher
Where Adam was buried?

4

Negrito:
Adan se enterró en Ebrón
en un campo de Almacén
en una cueva, oye bien,
cercada de Jerusalén.

4

Negrito:
Adam was buried in Hebron
In a field in Almacen,
In a cave, listen well,
Near Jerusalem.

5

Viejo:
Pregunta tú autor, a quien más sabe
que a decirme esto te atreves:
¿cuál es la culpa más leve,
que hace el pecado más grave?

5

Viejo:
Ask yourself, most learned author
If you dare to tell me:
What is the lightest sin
And what makes the worst one?

6

Negrito:
Piensa bien, mi diestra cabe.
Oye mi distinta voz:
Quien no obedece a sus padres
no le ve la cara a Dios.

6

Negrito:
Listen well, for it's my right.
I'll say it plainly:
He who does not obey his parents
Will not see the face of God.

7

Vilmas:
Como inocente pregunto
que nos des conocimiento,
ni ha de saber el asunto,
de tu memoria y talento.

7

Vilmas:
As an innocent, I ask you
That you give us a sample
(You don't have to know everything)
Of your memory and talent.

8

Negrito:
Pues yo en el conocimiento
y diversar con primor;
quieres, compositor,
que tan suficiente te hallas
aguarda, no te vayas
que yo te daré razón.

8

Negrito:
Well, in recognition
I will divert you with entertainment;
You want a composer
That you find adequate.
Wait, don't leave
And I'll give you satisfaction.

9

Vilmas:
Como sabio y entendido
por tu ciencia verdadera
ahora te pregunto yo:
¿cuál es la plana primera?

9

Vilmas:
As a wise and understanding man
Of true knowledge
Now I ask you:
What is the first plane?

10

Negrito:
Como sabio y entendido
yo te voy a contestar:

10

Negrito:
As a wise and understanding man
I will answer you:

Mira, es la plana primera:
fe, esperanza, y caridad.

Look! The first plane is
Faith, hope, and charity.

11

Viejo:
¿Cuál fué Cristo de fineza
de morir crucificado
y quedar sacramentado
dándole al hombre en la mesa.

Viejo:
Which was the Christ of fineness
Who died on the cross
And was made a sacrament
Given to man at the table.

12

Negrito:
Pues si es tanta tu agudeza
y respuesta te he de dar:
que Dios se ha presentado al hombre
en la mesa del altar
el día de su penitencia
cuando subió a comulgar.

Negrito:
Well, if such is your sharpness
Then I will give you my answer:
God has presented himself to man
On the table before the altar
On the day of his repentance
When he went to communion.

13

Viejo:
María parió a Jesús
y Dios a María formó.
Mas todavía no me dices
en que obligación quedó.

Viejo:
Mary gave birth to Jesus
And God created Mary.
But still you don't say
With what obligation she was left.

14

Negrito:
Oye que te digo yo:
desde el huerto hasta la cruz
bien sabes que se obligó
a padecer por Jesús
que nos crió y redimió.

Negrito:
Listen to what I tell you:
From the garden to the cross
You know full well she had
To suffer for Jesus
Who created and redeemed us.

15

Viejo:
Si me sabes entender
o traes memoria o sentido:
¿qué se hicieron las monedas
por que Cristo fué vendido?

Viejo:
If you are able to understand
Or if you have memory or feeling:
What did they do with the money
For which Christ was sold?

16

Negrito:
Aquellos treinta dineros
que en tierra fueron empleados
y, que fueron sepultados
peregrinos pasajeros.

Negrito:
Those thirty coins
Were used for the purpose
Of burying
Traveling pilgrims.

17

Viejo:
Textos de filosofía
te tengo de preguntar:

Viejo:
I am going to ask you for
Texts of philosophy:

¿Cuál es el ave más grande
de la corte celestial?

What is the greatest *ave*[1]
In the celestial court?

18

Negrito:

La contesta te he de dar
pues tienes buena poesía
de la corte celestial:
tan sólo el Ave María
todos hemos de gritar
a todas horas del día.

18

Negrito:

The answer I will give you
For you are quite a poet
In the celestial court:
We must all sing
Only the Ave Maria
All day long.

19

Vilmas:

Te volveré a preguntar
con mi sentido y segundo:

¿Antes de que hubiera Dios,
quién obraría en el mundo?

19

Vilmas:

I will ask you another question
With my second sense (that of
     understanding):
Before there was God,
Who would work in the world?

20

Negrito:

Si de esto no me confundo
yo te pondré en el camino:
antes de que hubiera Dios
ya era espíritu divino.

20

Negrito:

If in this I am not confused
I will put you on the right road:
Before there was God,
The Holy Spirit existed.

21

Vilmas:

Este mundo que formó
para ser su Padre Eterno;
¿cuando tu padre nació,
cómo estabas en su seno?

21

Vilmas:

This world that God formed
In order to be its Eternal Father;
When your father was born
How was it that you were already part
     of him?

SAL-GRÉL QUE FUE-RA PRU-DEN-TE A TRO-VAR CON LA RA-ZÓN.

ÉL QUE ES A-MAN-TE NO TE-ME AN-TES BUS-CA LA D-CA-SIÓN.

In this *trovo* the singer, Samuel Lavadie, of Taos, New Mexico, uses the same basic melody as other *trovo* singers from other parts of New Mexico.

The practice of using one melody for all the *trovos* wherever and by whomever sung is similar to the custom observed in the case of the *décima* (see Section E).

[1] *Ave* has a double meaning here. Viejo seems to be asking: "What is the greatest *bird* of the skies?" Negrito, however, choosing the Latin meaning of *ave* (hail!), delivers the correct answer.

G3. *Trovo del Viejo Vilmas y el Negrito* (Trovo of Old Man Vilmas and the Little Negro)
R1895, Clemente Chávez, Galisteo, N.Mex., 1963, Robb. Cf. RB728.

1

Vilmas:
Hoy que se me hace oportuno
preguntar a tu desvelo,
dime hoy cuantos son los cielos
y los nombres de cada uno;
si por esto te repugno
me explicaré un otro asunto:
¿qué numero es el conjunto
de los huesos de un cristiano?
Respóndeme mano a mano,
todo lo que hoy te pregunto.

2

Negrito:
Once cielos no más cuento,
el sol noble y el astro,
Jupiter, Saturno amante,
y el imperio y firmamento;
memorias medias te aumento,
también la luna en conjunto
y de un cuerpo humano apunto
trescientos huesos y más;
yo te respondo capaz
todo lo que hoy me preguntas.

3

Vilmas:
¿Por qué rumbos corre el viento
que estoy en duda y afán?
Dime también si nacieron
nuestra madre Eva y Adán;
el primero vino y el pan
¿quién fué quien los consagró?

4

Negrito:
Bueno, es por el mundo entero
los rumbos que el viento corre
para que nunca se borre,
y Eva y Adán no nacieron;
del polvo de la tierra fueron,
tal como mi Dios los creó;
el primer vino y el pan,
El fué quien los consagró.

5

Negrito:
Si eres poeta sin igual
yo pregunto a ti ahora:
¿Cuántas horas tiene un año?

1

Vilmas:
Now that I have the chance
To ask while you are paying attention,
Tell me how many heavens there are
And the names of each one;
And if you are reluctant to do this
You can explain another thing:
What is the number of bones
In a Christian?
Answer me one by one
Everything that I ask you.

2

Negrito:
I count only eleven heavens,
The noble sun and the star,
Jupiter, Saturn the lover,
And the empire and firmament;
I will prompt your failing memory,
Likewise the moon in conjunction
And in the human body, I remind you
There are three hundred bones and more;
I answer you capably
Everything that you ask me.

3

Vilmas:
From what direction does the wind blow
That I am in doubt and anxiety?
Tell me also if our mother Eve
And Adam were born;
Who was it that consecrated
The first wine and bread?

4

Negrito:
Well, the wind blows throughout
The whole world from all directions
So that it never ceases,
And Adam and Eve were not born;
They came from the dust of the earth
Just as my God created them;
And it was he who consecrated
The first wine and bread.

5

Negrito:
If you are the poet without an equal
Let me ask you now:
How many hours are there in a year?

474

¿Cuántos grados una hora?
Tu ciencia ¿quién la mejora?
¿Quién capacita tu mente?
¿Qué número es el de gente
que hoy posea por todo el mundo?
Entonces sí sea fácil creer
que eres poeta sin segunda.

How many degrees in an hour?
Your knowledge, who improves it?
Who gives capacity to your mind?
What is the number of people
Which the whole earth possesses?
And then it will be easy to believe
That you are a poet without equal.

6

Vilmas:
Cuento ocho mil setecientas
y ochenta y ocho y un grado;
en dos minutos aumenta
cuantas horas tiene un año;
si no, tú saca la cuenta,
mis trovos están muy ciertos;
treinta grados tiene una hora,
mi ciencia Dios la mejora,
yo capacito mi mente
y el número que no ha muerto
tiene el mundo de vivientes.

6

Vilmas:
I count eight thousand seven hundred
Eighty-eight and one degree;
In two minutes it adds up
To the hours there are in a year;
If not, you figure it out,
My songs are very certain;
An hour has thirty degrees,
My God improves my knowledge,
I charge my own mind
And the number of people who haven't died
Is the number still alive in the world.

7

Vilmas:
Si eres poeta sin igual
tu ciencia resolver pueda;
me dirás que rumbo queda
el Paraíso terrenal;
¿quién mora porfirial
por pendencia y mandamiento?
y Dios ha mandado Elías,
Elías vive ahí honrado;
de noche con gran contento
un ángel por mandamiento
la puerta la está guardando.
Yo también quedo contento
si todo voy explicando.

7

Vilmas:
If you are a poet without equal
Your knowledge can solve this;
You will tell me in what direction
The earthly Paradise lies;
Who lives regally
By will and command?
And God has commanded Elias,
Elias lives there in honor;
At night with great contentment
An angel under orders
Is guarding the door.
I, too, shall remain contented
If I go on explaining everything

8

Negrito:
El Paraíso terrenal
al oriente está situado;
hoy no vive en él más gente
que la que Dios ha mandado;
Elías vive ahí honrado;
de noche con gran contento
un ángel por mandamiento
la puerta le está guardando.
yo también quedo contento
si todo voy explicando.

8

Negrito:
The earthly Paradise
Is situated in the east;
Today only those live there
Whom God has sent there;
Elias lives there in honor;
At night with great contentment
An angel under orders
Is guarding the door.
I, too, remain content
If I am explaining everything.

9

Negrito:
Hoy te quiero preguntar
¿cuánto es lo grueso de la tierra,

9

Negrito:
Now I'm going to ask you
What is the thickness of the earth,

cuántos niños el Limbo encierra,
y arenas tiene el mar?
Y me dirás por qué van
los niños que en Limbo quedan.

How many children there are in Limbo,
How much sand in the sea?
And you will tell me why the children
Who remain in Limbo were sent there.

10

Vilmas:
Cien mil quinientas dos leguas
tiene el grueso de la tierra;

tantos niños el Limbo encierra
como arenas tiene el mar;
y también al Limbo van
los que mueren sin bautismo
porque es el seno de Adán,
un seno sin aguarismo.[2]

Vilmas:
The thickness of the earth
Is one hundred thousand five hundred and
    two leagues;
Limbo holds as many children
As the sands of the sea;
And likewise those go to Limbo
Who die without baptism
For that is the sign of Adam,
A sign that can't be erased.

11

Vilmas:
Si eres poeta sin igual
yo te pregunta a ti ahora:
¿cuántas leguas corre el sol
y en cuántos minutos de una hora,
cuántas leguas la tierra abarca
la tierra de punto a punto?
Responde lo que pregunto
con tu talento eficaz
y si eres hombre capaz
me respondes este asunto.

Vilmas:
If you are a poet without an equal
I will now ask you:
How many leagues does the sun travel
And in how many minutes of an hour,
How many leagues the earth embraces
From point to point?
Answer my question
With your efficient talent
And if you are a capable man
Answer this thing.

12

Negrito:
Los dos minutos de una hora
corre el sol sin hacer brinco
un millón mil ochocientas;
me encomiendas aguas, leguas,
la tierra de punto a punto;
de cierto no sé el conjunto,
si abajo estarán las cuentas
gritando: Cien mil quinientas,

y aquí te explico este asunto.

Negrito:
In two minutes of one hour
The sun travels without leaping
One million, one thousand eight hundred;
You ask me about waters, leagues,
The earth from point to point;
Surely I don't know the total
But the number will be
Shouting: one hundred thousand, five
    hundred
And here I explain to you this business.

13

Negrito:
Pues si tú eres trovador
y de nombre tan sabio privas,

ahora quiero que me digas
las leguas que alumbra el sol,
y con esto soy conforme
que tú eres el mejor autor.

Negrito:
Well, if you are a troubadour
And enjoy the reputation of such a
    wise man,
Now I want you to tell me
How many leagues the sun illumines,
And in this I am in agreement
That you are the better author.

[2]In this verse the informant has written *seno* for *seña*.

14

Vilmas:
Las leguas que alumbra el sol
yo te digo son sin cuenta;
ahora saca tú la cuenta,
si te tienes por mejor,
que en la vida vive autor
que de comprender acabe;
de cierto sólo Dios sabe
la leguas que alumbra el sol.

14

Vilmas:
The leagues that the sun illumines
I can tell you are countless;
Now you count them,
If you consider yourself the better and
That in life there is no author
Whose understanding is endless;
For in fact only God knows
How many leagues the sun illumines.

G4. *Principio del Trovo de Chicaria y Gracia* (Beginning of the Trovo of Chicaria and Gracia)
RB129, Arvino Martínez, Tierra Azul, N.Mex., 1950, Robb. Cf. R1491, R2012.

1

Chicaria:
En el pueblo de Opusura
repicaron las campanas;
cuando yo volví de allá
y era muerto el risguanejo.

1

Chicaria:
In the town of Oposura
The bells were ringing;
When I returned from there
The *risguanejo* (?) was dead.

2

Gracia:
Nuevo México, insolente
entre las cíbolas criado,
dime quien te ha hecho letrado
y a cantar entre la gente
tan roto y despilfarrado.

2

Gracia:
Insolent New Mexican,
Raised among the buffalo,
Tell me who taught you to read
And to sing among the people
So brokenly and so slovenly.

3

Chicaria:
Eres muy inconsecuente,
cantas con mucha eficacia,
aquí te ha caído tierra
y ahora caerás de la gracia
y te faltará memoria.

3

Chicaria:
You are very changeable,
You sing with much efficiency,
But you have gotten into trouble
And now you will fall from grace
And your memory will fail.

4

Gracia:
Si me faltaré memoria
cantaré con libertad.
Dime la entera verdad,
¿eres el poeta Chicaria?

4

Gracia:
If my memory should falter
I will sing with freedom.
Give me the entire truth,
Are you the poet Chicaria?

5

Chicaria:
Esa, si que es necesidad
según yo estoy conociendo;
¿qué más quieras que te diga?
¿pues no te lo estoy diciendo?

5

Chicaria:
That is what is necessary
As I understand it;
What more do you want me to say?
Am I not saying it now?

6

Gracia:
Ahora si voy conociendo,
Chicaria sabes cantar
textos de filosofía,
habías de argumentar.

7

Chicaria:
Gracia, te podré explicar
toda mi sabiduría:
antes de formar la gloria
¿qué cosa mi Dios haría?

8

Gracia:
Hombre, se me hace armonía.
Digo que me corresponde.
Antes de formar la gloria
primero formaría al hombre.

9

Chicaria:
Gracia, no te corresponde.
¿Dime por qué desvarías,
para qué preguntas textos
si has de responder mentiras?

10

Gracia:
Chicaria, no son mentiras,
ahora te voy explicar.
Si no me creyes a mí,
pregunta al padre Julián.

11

Chicaria:
No tengo que preguntar
ni que hacer ningún alarde;
si el padre dice que el hombre
le digo que miente el padre.

12

Gracia:
Hombre, no seas picote,
ahora te voy a decir:
¿cómo quieres desmentir
a un poeta y un sacerdote?

13

Chicaria:
Gracia, te ha de hacer jilote
¿qué ha sido mi vanagloria?
Y desde antes te lo dije
que te iba a faltar memoria.

6

Gracia:
Now if, as I understand it,
Chicaria, you claim to know how to sing
Texts of philosophy,
Then start the argument.

7

Chicaria:
Gracia, I could explain to you
All my wisdom:
Before forming heaven
What would my God do?

8

Gracia:
Man, that's music to my ears.
I tell you my answer.
Before forming heaven
He would form man.

9

Chicaria:
Gracia, that's not the answer.
Tell me why you get delirious,
Why do you ask for philosophy texts
If you have to respond with lies?

10

Gracia:
Chicaria, they are not lies,
Now I will explain to you.
If you don't believe me,
Ask Father Julian.

11

Chicaria:
I don't have to ask
Nor to indulge in bragging;
If the priest says it was man
I say the priest lies.

12

Gracia:
Man, don't be so quarrelsome,
Now I will ask you this:
Why should you want to give the lie
To a poet and a priest?

13

Chicaria:
Gracia, you have to be joking.
In what have I been vainglorious?
And I've already told you
That your memory was going to fail you.

14

Gracia:

Si me faltaré memoria
cantaré muy poco a poco,
pero ¿qué tienes Chicaria?
¿por qué te me has hecho loco?

15

Chicaria:

Gracia, yo he de ser tu coco
y estoy para dar la prueba,
y desde antes te lo dije
no es buena la primer nueva.

16

Gracia:

No es buena la primer nueva,
por eso yo te pregunto.
Por vida tuya, Chicaria,
hazme saber el asunto.

17

Chicaria:

Yo le diera punto al águila
de todo lo que ha pasado.
¿Cómo quieres que sea maestro
y entre las cíbolas criado?

18

Gracia:

Hombre, me había engañado,
perdona la inconsecuencia,
hazme saber el asunto
y el punto con evidencia.

19

Chicaria:

Gracia, te faltó memoria.
Cristo murió en una cruz.
Antes de formar la gloria
primero formó la luz.

20

Gracia:

Mi verdadero Jesús
hizo una resucitoria.
Queden todos albertidos[3]
que Gracia queda rendido
debajo del brazo de Chicaria.

14

Gracia:

If my memory should fail me
I will sing very slowly,
But what is the matter with Chicaria?
Why have you made me crazy?

15

Chicaria:

Gracia, I shall be your bogey man
And now I'll put you to the test,
And as I've already told you
The beginner is not good.

16

Gracia:

The beginner is not good,
Well then, I'll ask you a question.
On your life, Chicaria,
Pick a subject.

17

Chicaria:

Now I'll give you the point
Of everything that has taken place.
How do you expect me to be a master
If I've been raised among the buffalos?

18

Gracia:

Sir, I was mistaken,
Excuse the irrelevance,
Explain the subject
And the point with evidence.

19

Chicaria:

Gracia, your memory failed you.
Christ died on a cross.
Before forming heaven
He created light.

20

Gracia:

My true Jesus
Made a reappearance.
Let all be advised
That Gracia has been vanquished
By the arm of Chicaria.

---

[3] *Albertidos* for *advertidos.*

21

Chicaria:
En el pueblo de Opusura
allí hubo una torna boda
ya Gracia para mí no hubo.
Ya Gracia torció la cola.

21

Chicaria:
In the town of Opusura
A double wedding was held.
There was no grace *(gracia)* for me
For Gracia twisted my tail.

Cobos' version of this song (Cobos 4, 11/17/49) is prefaced by an interesting note in Spanish, part of which I have translated as follows:

Mr. Luis Martínez, the poet of Martínez, now a part of Albuquerque, states that Chicoria was once persuaded to join a mule train which was carrying merchandise from Kansas City to Chihuahua, Mexico. According to Mr. Martínez, Chicoria was from Los Griegos [now a part of Albuquerque]. When the mule train passed through Albuquerque, Chicoria joined it as a muleteer. What the friends of Martín Chicoria really wanted was to take him to Chihuahua so that he could engage in a *trovo* or song contest with Gracia, a popular poet of that area. Poor Chicaria did not know of this plot until he arrived in Chihuahua. His friends told him there was to be a wedding and that the poet Gracia would be singing there and that they wanted Chicoria to compete against him in a song contest. Chicoria was nervous at first but was losing his fear as they arrived at the wedding. It appears that each poet had heard the other sing and both seem to have been very apprehensive about facing one another in a song contest. This item purports to be the *trovo* which they sang.

Another version of this *trovo* (RB129) ends with the following inscription:

Copiado por mi mano este día
de hoy enero quince de 1860.

Copied by my hand this
Fifteenth day of January, 1860.

This text is from a notebook loaned to me in 1951 by Arvino Martínez, who was at that time a young man. The note at the end indicates that the song was copied about ninety years before by some unidentified person. The notebook itself may have been handed down to Arvino, or the song slavishly copied footnote and all by Arvino, or possibly by his uncle, José Gallegos (see I17).

H. *Cuando*

Occasionally one encounters a song text in which each verse ends with the word *cuando*. These songs are called *cuandos* by the singers, and despite their relative rarity I am including the examples below under that heading.

So few examples have been available to me that it is difficult to generalize. One example, *Cuando de Pecos*, also known as *Cuando de los Galisteos* (H1), is clearly in the form of a *décima* and thus can be considered a hybrid form. It adheres not only to the ten-line verse form of the *décima* but also to the typical rhyme scheme (abbaacc-ddc) of the classical form of *décima* known as the *espinela* (see *Décima* above).

Other *cuandos*, however, employ an eight-line verse, like *A Nuestra Señora de Guadalupe* (R6). Some of the *cuandos* appear to be quite obviously degenerations of the form of the *décima*, as for example *Cuando de Pecos* (H1a).

H1. *Cuando de Pecos*, or *Cuando de los Galisteos*
R1985, Clemente Chávez, Galisteo, N.Mex., 1956, Robb.

1

Las vísperas de San Juan
quince Pecos escogidos
con caballos muy lucidos
contra los Taños están
ya traen formado su plan.
Otro día van llegando
muy ansiosos y apurando.
Vienen echándonos el fallo
que van a llevarse el gallo.
¿Pero que lo llevan cuándo?

1

On the Eve of San Juan
Fifteen chosen men of Pecos
With fancy horses chosen
To compete against the Taños[1]
Have already formed a plan.
The next day they're arriving
Very anxious and in haste.
They are giving us the verdict
That they're going to take the rooster.
But when are they going to do it?

2

Don Ambrosio, con prudencia,
a sus amigos llamó
y él muy despacio ensilló
con muchísima paciencia
a pesar de la violencia
con que le están atizando.
Ya la hora se está pasando
de poner mano a la obra
como de mala obra,
¿pero que lo llevan cuándo?

2

Don Ambrosio cautiously
Called his friends
And very slowly saddled up
With great patience
In spite of the excitement
With which they're urging him.
The time is now passing
To get started
To do the dirty work,
But when are they going to do it?

[1] The Taños are the people of Galisteo, where there was formerly a pueblo of the Taño Indians.

3

Quien primero rompió el juego
fué un Encarnación Gonzales
para alivio de sus males;
no se sacó el gallo luego
a tres veces de rejuego.
Se agachó y lo fué sacando.
Pablo Padilla animando
dijo: —éstos no valen pito,
ya se les así ha visto.—
¿Pero que lo llevan cuándo?

3

He who first started the game
Was a certain Encarnación Gonzales
To make matters worse;
He didn't get the rooster
Although he tried three times.
He bent down and reached for it.
Pablo Padilla, urging him,
Said, "These guys are worthless,
I've seen it happen before."
But when are they going to do it?

4

Venían con gran empeño
y muy crecida esperanza
porque traían la confianza
en Ursino, el afuereño,
agarró el gallo halagüeño.
Levantó al cielo la voz:
—Adiós, Galisteos, adiós,
me voy a Pecos volando.—
Cuando ya lo fué alcanzando
el músico Marcelino:
—Dime ¿quién es ese Ursino?—
¿Que ya se lo llevan cuándo?

4

They came with great plans
And with lots of hope
Because they had confidence
In Ursino, the man from out of town,
He seized the handsome rooster.
He raised his voice to heaven:
"Good-bye, Galisteos, good-bye,
I'm flying back to Pecos."
When he was reaching down for it
Marcelino, the musician, said:
"Tell me, who's that Ursino?"
But when are they are going to do it?

5

Ahí nos traían tres Luceros
para anunciarnos el día,
aquí les salió la guía
a los tales caballeros;
tres Chávez muy placenteros
se les fueron aprontando;
a Santiaguito abrazando
dijo Víctor, con honor,
—Suélteme el gallo, señor.—
¿Que ya se lo llevan cuándo?

5

Now they bring on three Luceros
To celebrate the day,
But those gentlemen
Found their match here;
Three Chávezes very pleasantly
Approached them;
While embracing little Santiago
Victor said courteously,
"Let go of the rooster, sir."
But when are they going to do it?

6

Los Vigiles muy decentes
también vienen en la danza
aliados de la confianza
porque son inteligentes;
Los Madriles suficientes
Señor Davis ayudando,
Jesús Lovato animando.
José Manuel Sandoval
dice que quedamos mal.
Pero ¿que podemos cuándo?

6

The Vigils very decently
Also joined in the dance,
Alive with confidence
Because they're intelligent;
The Madriles also,
Señor Davis helping,
Jesús Lovato urging them on.
José Manuel Sandoval
Says that we made a poor showing.
But when can we do it?

7

También Albino Roybal
vino haciendo su papel,
Manuel Gurulé con él,
que no lo hacía muy mal

7

Albino Roybal also
Came putting on his act,
Manuel Gurulé with him,
Who didn't do so badly

pero perdieron cabal,	But they lost fairly,
que venían vaneando,	They were talking vainly,
también venían pensando	They were also thinking
que ganaban su trofeo	They could win the prize
arruinando a Galisteo,	By ruining Galisteo.
pero ¿qué lo arruinen cuándo?	But when will they ruin it?

8

En la Punta de Cristón	At the Punta de Cristón
tenían el mejor caballo	They had the best horse,
esperando a los del gallo	Hoping to win the rooster
cuando vuelva el escuadrón,	When they arrived,
pero se volteó el chirrión	But their plan backfired,
él que allí los está esperando,	The one who was awaiting them there,
los vido que iban andando	He saw them on foot
con un crecido pesar	Very unhappy
que ellos estaban pensando	For they were thinking
alzar bandera encarnada	Of raising the red flag of victory
pero les salió floreada	But it turned out to be a flowered flag of defeat
porque con los Taños ¿cuándo?	For, win against the Taños, when?

9

En la bajada de la mesa	At the foot of the mesa
ahí tenían sus equipajes,	There they had their gear
ahí tenían sus carruajes	And their carriages
para llegar con presteza.	Ready to roll.
Los de atrás con ligereza,	The ones in back, hurrying,
otros iban galopando;	Others galloping;
era que venían pensando	Because they were thinking
que ganaban su trofeo	That they'd win the prize
arruinando a Galisteo,	By ruining Galisteo.
¿pero que lo arruinen cuándo?	But when will they ruin it?

10

Oiga, don Ambrosio Pino,	Listen, Don Ambrosio Pino,
campeón entre los campeones,	Champion among champions,
ahí le mando estos renglones.	Here I send you these verses.
Oiga, amigo Federino,	Listen, friend Federino,
conozco mi desatino	I know it may be improper
en hacer lo que no sé.	To do what I am not good at.
Yo lo hago de buena fe,	I do it in good faith,
usted debe de estar elegiando.	You deserve to be praised.
Muchos amigos tendré	I may make many friends
pero otro más fino ¿cuándo?	But a finer one, when?

Pues se acabó este cuando,	Well, to make a long story short,
que querían los Tañitos	The Tañitos wanted
arruinar a los de Pecos	To ruin the people of Pecos,
y también a Santiaguito.	And also little Santiago.

A feature of frontier life in the Spanish villages was the "rooster pull." A rooster would be buried in sand with only his head and neck showing. Competing horsemen would ride past at a gallop and reaching down would try to pull the rooster out of the sand, a very difficult feat requiring excellent horsemanship. The above *cuando* tells the story of a rooster pull between the rival villages of Galisteo and Pecos, New Mexico.

It takes the form of a *décima espinela* without a *planta* (see Section E).

H1a. *Cuando de Pecos*
R529, Francisco S. Leyva, age 81, Leyva, N.Mex., 1951, Robb.

Cuando se verá ese cuando	When this *cuando* is sung
que Santiaguito desea:	It is what little Santiago desires:
que con los Pecos se vea	That the people of Pecos see themselves
de los Galisteos triunfando.	Triumphing over those of Galisteo.

1

Las vísperas de San Juan		On the Eve of San Juan
quince Pecos escogidos		Fifteen chosen Pecos riders
con caballos muy lucidos		With fancy horses
junto a los Taños están.		Approach the Taños.
Y traen formado su plan.		They have already formed a plan.
otro día van verando		The next day they are arriving
muy ansioso y apurando		Very tense and impatient,
siempre echándonos el fallo		Constantly throwing it up to us
que van a llevarse el gallo	]	That they are going to win the rooster pull,
¿pero que lo llevan cuándo?	] *Bis*	When will they do it?

2

Don Ambrosio con prudencia		Don Ambrosio with foresight
a sus amigos llamó		Called together his friends
y su caballo ensilló		And saddled up his horse
con muchísima paciencia		With much patience
A pesar de violencia		In spite of the violent feeling
con que le están apurando;		That stirs his blood;
ya la hora se está pasando		Already the time has come
de poner mano a la obra.		To get down to work.
Ya se les echan la obra	]	Already they are working at it
¿pero que lo llevan cuándo?	] *Bis*	But when will they win?

3

Para comenzar el juego	To commence the game
pasó Encarnación Gonzales	Encarnación Gonzales made the first run
para alivio de sus males;	To make matters worse;
no se sacó el gallo luego.	He didn't get the rooster on that try
A tres veces de rejuego	After trying three times
se atenta y se fué sacando	In vain, he gave up,
de todos animando;	Cheered by everyone;
dijo: —éstes no valen pito	He said: "These are worthless,
y se les así ha visto.—	As has been seen before."
¿Pero que lo llevan cuándo?	But when will they win?

4

Venían con gran empeño	They were coming along boldly
y muy crecida esperanza	And with high hopes

——— la confianza
en Ursino, el afuereño.
Que agarró el gallo halagüeño
y al santo llevó la voz:
—Adiós, Galisteos, adiós,
a poco my voy volando.—
Y ——— lo fué alcanzando
el músico Marcelino
le dijo: —¿Quién es ese Ursino?—
¿Que ya se lo llevan cuándo?

Because they were counting
On Ursino, the out-of-towner.
He grasped the handsome rooster
And praised his saint:
"Good-bye, Galisteans, good-bye.
I'll be on my way."
And when he grabbed it
Marcelino, the musician, said,
"Tell me, who is that Ursino?"
Well, they take it, but when?

5

Ahí los traían tres Luceros
para anunciarnos el día.
Aquí les salió la guía
a tres tales caballeros.
Tres Chávez muy placenteros
se les fueron aprontando
a Santiaguito abrazando,
dijo Victor Chávez con honor:
—Suélteme el gallo, Señor.—
¿Que ya se lo llevan cuándo?

Along come three Luceros
To celebrate the day.
But here those three gentlemen
Were shown who guided them.
Three of the Chávez men
Were approaching them very pleasantly
And embracing little Santiago,
Victor Chávez said courteously,
"Hand me that rooster, sir!"
But when are they going to do it?

6

Los Vigiles muy urgentes
también vienen en la danza
aliados de la confianza
porque son inteligentes.
Los Madriles suficientes.
Jesús Lovato llorando,
Señor Davis animando,
y José Manuel Sandoval
dicen que quedamos mal,   ]
¿pero que podemos cuándo?   ] *Bis*

The Vigils very urgently
Also joined in the dance
Alive with confidence
Because they are intelligent.
The men from Madrid were good, too.
Jesús Lovato was weeping,
Señor Davis was cheering him up,
And José Manuel Sandoval says that
We made a poor showing.
But when can we win it?

7

También Albino Royal
vino haciendo su papel,
Manuel Gurulé con él
que no le hacía tan mal.
Pero perdieron cabal,
eran que vienen vaneando,
porque venían pensando
que ganaban su trofeo,
arruinando a Galisteo   ]
¿pero que lo arruinan cuándo?   ] *Bis*

Albino Royal also came
Doing his stuff,
Manuel Gurulé came with him
And didn't do too badly.
But though they came bragging,
They lost fairly and squarely,
For they came thinking that
They could win the prize,
And ruin Galisteo,
But when will they ruin Galisteo?

8

En la Punta de Cristón
tenía el mejor caballo
esperando a los del gallo
cuando vuelva el escadrón.
Pero se volteó el chirrión
él que allí los está esperando
los vido que iban a andando

In Punta de Cristón
They had the best horse
And hoped to win the rooster
When their turn came.
But the plan backfired
And the one who was waiting for them
Saw they were walking slowly

con un crecido pesar.	And with heavy sadness.
Que ellos estaban pensando	For they had been hoping
alzar bandera encarnada	That they could raise the victory flag
pero los salió floreada	But they left with flowers of defeat
porque con los Taños ¿cuándo?	For win against the Taños, when?

<table>
<tr><td colspan="2" align="center">9</td></tr>
</table>

En la bajada de la mesa	At the foot of the mesa,
ahí tenían sus carruajes,	There they had their carriages,
ahí tenían sus equipajes	There they had their gear
para volver con presteza,	To return home speedily,
de ahí atrás con ligereza	The ones in back hurrying,
otros iban galopeando	Others galloping,
—————— venían paseando	Because they thought that
que —————— su trofeo,	They would win the prize,
arruinando a Galisteo	Ruining Galisteo,
¿pero que lo arruinan cuándo?	But when do they ruin it?

<table>
<tr><td colspan="2" align="center">10</td></tr>
</table>

Oiga, don Ambrosio Pino,	Listen, Don Ambrosio Pino,
campeón entre los campeones,	Champion among champions,
oiga, amigo Federino,	Listen, friend Federino,
ahí le mando estos renglones.	Here I send you these lines.
Conozco mi desatino	I recognize my foolishness
en hacer lo que no sé,	In doing what I know nothing about,
yo lo hago de buena fe,	But I do it in good faith,
no puede ser disputando.	You cannot dispute it.
Muchos amigos tendré	I will have many friends
¿pero otros más finos cuando?	But when will I have others finer?

<table>
<tr><td colspan="2" align="center">11</td></tr>
</table>

Aquí se acabó este cuando	Here ends this *cuando*
que querían los Tañitos	About how the Galisteans wanted
arruinar los de Pecos	To ruin those of Pecos
y también a Santiaguito.	And also little Santiago.

This *cuando* and H1 above came from aged informants, Clemente Chávez from Pecos, New Mexico, and Francisco Leyva from the neighboring town of Leyva. Although no date is given for the event described, a rooster pull, it seems probable that one or both of these men were present at the time.

H2. *Cuando de 1905*
Cobos 4 (6/15/50, RB764), José I. Vigil, Mosquero, N.Mex., 1950, Cobos.

De mil novecientos cinco
algo tenemos que hablar,
que este maldito gusano
no nos deja cosechar.

About 1905
We have something to say,
That this accursed worm
Ruined our harvest.

1

En el principio del año
tuvimos muy buen invierno,
pues lo esperábamos bueno
hasta que llegó el verano;
pero el maldito gusano
ya no nos deja labor;
todito el maíz y el frijol
hasta las hierbas del llano
también las está arruinando;
la hormiga le está ayudando
junto con el chapulín;
éste sí no tiene fin,
con todo viene acabando;
habrá otro animal sutil
pero ya como éste, ¡cuándo!

1

At the beginning of the year
We had a very mild winter
And we had high hopes
Until summer came;
But the accursed worm
Does not let us work;
All the corn and beans,
Even the weeds of the plain,
Are being ruined;
The ants and the locusts
Are aiding them;
There is no end to this,
Everything is becoming destroyed;
There may be other cunning animals,
But animals like these—when?

2

Se juntan grandes reuniones
de gusanos y hormiguitas
caminan por las lomitas
que parecen formaciones;
en altos, planos, y ancones
se detienen muy de prisa,
y si hallan una hortaliza
allí se van amachando
y poco a poco dejando
la tierra limpia y sin nada;
habrá otra epidemia mala
pero ya como ésta, ¡cuándo!

2

There are great conventions
Of worms and ants,
They travel over the hills
In what look like formations;
In high places, plains, and roads
They move in quickly
And if they find a garden
They go in and stubbornly stay there
And little by little they leave
The earth clean of vegetation;
There may be other bad epidemics
But one like this—when?

3

Las mujeres, ¡pobrecitas!
esto tienen que decir:
—Ya me comió la hormiguita
los coles y el cebollín;
pero ahí viene el chapulín
no lo había visto yo,
cuanto sembré se me acabó;
este maldito animal
fué de tan mal natural
que hasta el chile se comió;
unas matas me dejó,
ahora las estoy regando,
parece que ya salió,
pero que se vaya, ¡cuándo!

3

The women—poor things—
Have this to say:
"The ant has eaten
The cabbage and the young onions,
But here come the locust in swarms
Such as I had not seen before,
And what I planted was soon finished;
This accursed animal
Was of such a bad nature
That it even ate the chile peppers;
It left me some small bushes,
Now I am watering them,
It seems they'd go away,
But they will go—when?"

4

—Mi hortaliza se acabó,
comadrita, yo me espanto;
¿sabe lo que me dejó?
un poquito de culantro;
ya no hallo yo que santo
hacerle mi aplicación,
pedirle de corazón
que retire este animal,
pues nos hizo tanto mal
que se acabó mi alberjón;
y la chinche y el pulgón
parece que van llegando
para acabar el frijol
que el gusano está dejando,
y nos dejará lo peor
eso será menos ¡cuándo!—

4

"My garden is finished,
My friend, I am frightened;
Do you know what they left me?
A tiny bit of coriander;
Now I don't know
What saint to pray to,
To ask from the heart
That he take away this animal,
For he has done us such damage
That my alberjón (?) is finished;
And the bedbug and the louse
It seems are coming
To finish off the beans
That the worm is leaving,
And will leave us worse off.
A worse thing will happen—when?"

5

Las habas y el alberjón,
las papas y los tomates,
éstos sí los dejó a rapis,
que no les dejó ni flor;
qué animal tan sabedor
parece que sabe leer;
cuando él se empieza a mover,
viene muy poco a poquito
que no se echa de ver;
ya se empieza a destender
por las matitas brincando
en traje de cazador;
si nos dejará labor,
pero no se sabe cuando.

5

The garden beans and the alberjón, (?)
The potatoes and tomatoes,
They have indeed ravished
And haven't left even a flower;
These animals are so smart
It seems as if they can read;
When they decide to move,
It is so very slowly
That you can't even see them moving;
Then they decide to spread out
Jumping over the small bushes
Like hunters after game;
If they would only leave us our work!
But no one knows when.

6

Padre mío San Luciano,
líbranos en esta esfera
del chapulín y el gusano,
que no dejen las hueveras,
porque en la otra primavera
volveremos a sembrar;
si nos viene a castigar
como lo estamos mirando
pues nos vendrá atormentado
para hacernos padecer;
así debemos de creer
que Dios la va a retirar
con su infinito poder,
porque de otro modo, ¡cuándo!

6

My father Saint Lucian,
Save us in this world
From the locust and the worm,
Let them not lay eggs,
So that next spring
We can sow our crops;
If they come to punish us
As we are seeing them do now,
Do not let them come to torment us
And make us suffer;
We have to believe
That God will take them away
With his infinite power,
For if there is another way—when?

I. OCCUPATIONS

Unlike the foregoing song texts, which have been classified on the basis of their form, the songs included in this section are grouped together here primarily because of their subject matter. The occupations represented include shepherd, soldier, railroader, cowboy, sailor, wagoner, coal miner, shoemaker, farmer, laborer, and miller.

SHEPHERD

I1. *La Indita de Ricardo* (The Ballad of Ricardo)
R218, Celestino Segura, age 66, Canjilón, N.Mex., 1949, Robb.

<table>
<tr><td>

1
Voy a cantar esta indita,
señores, pongan cuidado,
de los pastores de Fulton,
de lo que les ha pasado:
que el año noventa y nueve
le acabaron el ganado.

</td><td>

]
] *Bis*

</td><td>

1
I'm going to sing this *indita*,
Gentlemen, pay attention,
About the shepherds of Fulton,
About what befell them:
About how in 1899
They lost their flock.

</td></tr>
<tr><td>

2
Y esto no fué por descuido
les notaré en esta indita;
él ensilló su burrito;
fué a buscar su venadita.

</td><td>

]
] *Bis*
]
] *Bis*

</td><td>

2
And this was not for lack of care
As I will make plain in this song;
He saddled his donkey;
Went looking for his doe.

</td></tr>
</table>

Herding sheep between Taos and Mora, New Mexico, about 1949.

3

Le dice don Harry Fulton,
cuando acaba de contar,   ] Bis
—Ricardo, ¿cuándo has perdido?
dame la suma total.—
Le dice que mil quienientas,
Fulton se quiso desmayar!

3

Don Harry Fulton says to him,
When he finished counting,
"Ricardo, how many have you lost?
Give me the total count."
He answered, "One thousand five hundred,"
And Fulton nearly fainted.

4

Ya les pega a los caballos   ]
para seguro más rico.   ] Bis
Pero que no se te olviden   ]
trescientas que te dió tu hijo.   ] Bis

4

Now he whips the horses,
Here he vents his rage.
But do not forget the three hundred
Your son gave you.

5

Le dice don Harry Fulton   ]
que Ricardo es él que manda;   ] Bis
y a reportar una corta   ]
de trescientas que ya le anda.   ] Bis

5

Don Harry Fulton says to him
That Ricardo is the boss;
And now he must report a loss
Of three hundred who have strayed.

6

Le dice don Harry Fulton:]
—Ricardo, pues bien, refleja,   ] Bis
cuatro años me has trabajado
no has perdido ni una oveja,
ahora traes setecientas
por irte a ver a tu vieja.—

6

Now says Don Harry Fulton:
"Ricardo, look here, see here,
In four years of service
You never lost one sheep,
Now you've lost seven hundred
By going to see your old woman."

7

La gente del Cañon Diablo   ]
ya le tiene por refrán;   ] Bis
y el burrito de don Ricardo   ]
murió aventado de pan.   ] Bis

7

The people of Canyon Diablo
Now gossip freely;
And Don Ricardo's donkey
Died of overeating bread.

8

También don Leandro Lucero   ]
le presentó a Dios sus quejas;   ] Bis
y el día del revillión
salió bien con las ovejas,
nada más que a su burrito
se le helaron las orejas.

8

Don Leandro Lucero also
Presented his complaints to God;
On that stormy day
He never lost one sheep,
Only his donkey
Froze his ears.

9

De que esta cantada pase   ]
de Cubero para Corrales,   ] Bis
toda la gente dirá:
—Van cambiando mis pesares.—

Y los pastores de Fulton
ya hacen corvas regulares.

9

When this song goes
From Cubero to Corrales,
All the people will say:
"My troubles are taking a turn for the
      better."
And Fulton's shepherds
Come in for plenty of criticism.

10

Conozcan a don Ricardo,   ]
ya es un hombre anciano y viejo,   ] Bis

10

Know Don Ricardo,
He is an ancient and an old man,

no echó menos la cachucha	]	He did not miss his cap
hasta que no se vió en el espejo.	] *Bis*	Until he looked in the mirror.

11

Tengo que tomar la pluma	]	I must take up the pen
y el papel con el tintero,	] *Bis*	Also paper and ink,
para notar esta indita,		In order to write this *indita*,
que lo sepa el mundo entero		That the world may know
que don Ricardo ha perdido		That Don Ricardo has lost
la cachucha y el sombrero.		His cap and hat.

12

Si quieren saber, señores,	]	Gentlemen, if you want to know
quien compuso esta cantada	] *Bis*	Who composed this song,
él que perdió el sombrero,	]	It was he who lost his hat,
la cachucha, y la venada.	] *Bis*	His cap, and his deer.

VOY A CAN-TAR ES-TA IN-DI-TA, SE-ÑOR-ES, PON-GAN CUI-DA-DO; VOY
A CAN-TARES-TA IN-DI-TA, SE-ÑO-RES, PON-GAN CUI-DA-DO.

This song was sung for me at a sheep camp on the mountain called El Mogote near Canjilón, New Mexico, by the cook, Celestino Segura. It deals with the loss of a flock of sheep at Canyon Diablo, near Seligman, Arizona, in the year 1899. (For an amusing note on the singer, see *Indita de Celestino Segura*, I2.)

In verse 4 Harry Fulton "whips his horse" in a rage. For another instance of "taking it out on a horse," see verse 18 of the *Corrido de la Muerte de Antonio Maestas* (I17), see Robb 13, verse 18, at p. 55.

I1a. *Indita de Ricardo*
R616. Napoleón Trujillo, Bernalillo, N.Mex., 1951, Robb.

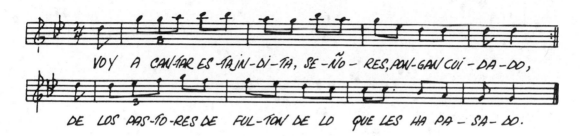

VOY A CAN-TAR ES-TA IN-DI-TA, SE-ÑO-RES, PON-GAN CUI-DA-DO,
DE LOS PAS-TO-RES DE FUL-TON DE LO QUE LES HA PA-SA-DO.

In view of the similarity of the texts of I1 and I1a, the latter text is omitted here. However, the music of I1a is included for comparison with the melody of I1.

12. *Indita de Celestino Segura* (Ballad of Celestino Segura)
RB907, Abrán Sánchez, Cuba, N.Mex., Cobos.

1

¡Qué condado tan desgraciado
es éste de Sandoval!
Son muchas las anécdotas
que de él se pueden contar.
Con esto he de principiar
dando fin a la escritura,
y aquí voy a representar
y a Celestino Segura.

2

Muy cerca de treinta días
por mí no se conmovieron,
pensando sería verdad
la última razón que dieron.
Ya me salen a buscar
sin que nadien les quebrante,
le pagan a un navajó
porque haga su pujacante.

3

Cuando el indio concluyó
lo que declaró primero:
—Fue muerto de tres balazos
que le dió su compañero.—
Basilio, que ausente estaba
cuando el indio ha declarado,
dice que en medio del rodeo
y estaba el cuerpo enterrado.

4

¡Madrecita de mi vida!
sé que bien me va a sentir
de ver con la grande infamia
con que fuí y vine a morir.
Me ha enterrado en un rodeo
para sécula sin fin,
pensando ocultar mi muerte
desde el principio hasta el fin.

5

¡Quién podía haberlo pensado
que Satanás lo tentara
y que de aquella manera
conmigo determinara!

6

Ya llegan los alguaciles
con su reporte legal,
dicen, —Ni vivo ni muerto,
lo pudimos encontrar.

1

What an unfortunate county
Is this county of Sandoval.
There are many anecdotes
Which could be told about it.
With this remark I must begin,
Finishing with the formalities,
And now I am going to tell
The story of Celestino Segura.

2

For close to thirty days
They didn't hear from me,
They thought that probably
The worst had happened.
They go out to look for me
Without finding a trace,
They pay a Navajo
To follow the trail.

3

When the Indian finished
The first thing he said was:
"He is dead with three bullets
With which his companion shot him."
Basilio, who was absent
When the Indian made his statement,
Says that the body was buried
In the rodeo ground.

4

Little mother of my life!
I know well that you will weep for me
To see such a great infamy
As caused my death.
They have buried me in a rodeo ground,
For centuries without end,
Thinking that they could conceal my death
From the beginning to the end.

5

Who could have thought
That Satan would tempt him
And that in this way
It would be ordained for me?

6

The constables come
With their legal report,
They say, "We've been unable to learn
Whether he's alive or dead."

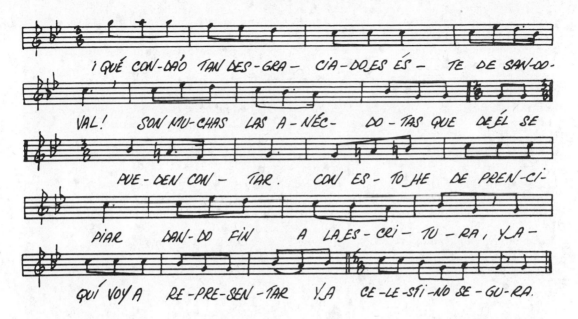

¡ QUÉ CON-DÁO TAN DES-GRA — CIA-DO ES ÉS — TE DE SAN-DO-VAL! SON MU-CHAS LAS A-NÉC — DO-TAS QUE DE ÉL SE PUE-DEN CON — TAR. CON ES-TO HE DE PREN-CI-PIAR DAN-DO FIN A LA ES-CRI — TU-RA, Y A-QUÍ VOY A RE-PRE-SEN-TAR Y A CE-LE-STÍ-NO SE-GU-RA.

This indita was composed in memory of Celestino Segura who had been missing for some time and was presumed dead. A Navajo Indian, as the song relates, had been hired to follow his trail and reported that he had been shot with three bullets by his companion and had been buried in the "rodeo ground." However, to everyone's consternation, he turned up alive and well.

When photographed in 1949 (see p. 528), Celestino was the *cocinero* (cook) in a sheep camp where he bashfully came out of the cook tent and sang some songs including *La Indita de Ricardo* (I1).

Another song in which the dead man tells the story of his death is *Indita de Amarante Martínez* (F2).

I3. *El Borreguero* (The Shepherd)
R226, Juan Luján, Santo Niño, N.Mex., 1949, Robb. See Appendix A.

1	**1**
Pues hay un dicho vulgar	Well, there is a common saying,
que es proverbio verdadero,	A saying that's true as true can be,
que no hay trabajo en el mundo	That there isn't any calling
—yugar, yugar—	Yugar, yugar,
como andar de borreguero.	Like herding, as most will agree.
2	**2**
Que no hay hoy que manaña,	Today and tomorrow don't exist
ni un santo ni a quien rezarle,	Nor even a saint to whom to pray,
y para tender la cama	And as for a place to make your bed
—yugar, yugar—	Yugar, yugar,
no hay lugar que le cuadre.	Upon the hard ground your head must lay.
3	**3**
Pues es una vida triste	It's quite a sad life, I'll tell you that,
¡ay! andando de llano en cerro.	Alone in the mountains or the plain.

No halla de aquí desviarse
—yugar, yugar—
ni aunque traiga buen perro.

It is so easy to lose your way
Yugar, yugar,
No matter how well your dog you train.

4

Pues la vida del pastor
es una vida pesada,
con su zalea y colchón
—yugar, yugar—
chaqueta de almohada.

4

The life of a shepherd is dreary
His bed he must carry in a sack,
His mattress is only a sheepskin,
Yugar, yugar,
His pillow's the jacket off his back.

5

Gorrita achucharrada,
toda rota y descosida;

de ese modo va pasando
—yugar, yugar—
el pobre pastor su vida.

5

His cap is a shapeless rag of cloth,
All tattered and stained and smudged and
      torn,
And this is the way his life passes,
Yugar, yugar,
No wonder a shepherd looks forlorn.

6

En la plaza llega a bajar
con sus burros por delante.
Unos lo tratan de trampe,
—yugar, yugar—
otros tratan de animal.

6

He goes from the ranges into town
His burros, ahead, expect a feast.
Some people will treat him just like a tramp,
Yugar, yugar,
While others will treat him as a beast.

7

—Pachequita, ten paciencia,—
le dice su compañero,
—Verás como te aquerencia,
—yugar, yugar—
y sigues de borreguero.—

7

"Be patient my friend, Pacheco,"
Says the shepherd in bidding adieu,
"You'll see how this job will grow on you,
Yugar, yugar,
And you will remain a shepherd, too."

8

—No me enreda, no me enreda;
lo digo por mi experencia,
y ahí están ya tus ovejas
—yugar, yugar—
Yo ya perdí la paciencia.—

8

"Don't kid me, old man, I've had my fill,
I've seen for myself. You'll not trap me,
Take back all your sheep and keep them,
Yugar, yugar,
I've had it—that's how it's going to be."

PUES HAY UN DI-CHO VUL-GAR QUE ES PRO-VER-BIO VER-DA-DE-RO, QUE NO HAY TRA-BA-JO EN EL MUN-DO-YU-GAR, YU-GAR-CO-MO AN-DAR DE BOR-RE-GUE-RO.

This is an *indita* in the form of a *canción*. It is a beautiful melody. As the songs of the Anglo settlers of the Southwest were largely about the life of the cowboy, his horses, and cattle, the songs of the Spanish and Mexican settlers were often about the life of the shepherd, for before the coming of the Americans, there were many more sheep than cattle in New Mexico. Some of these men traveled long distances to accept jobs as herders in other states. Próspero Baca, for instance, once herded sheep in Wyoming. Garcilón Pacheco, of Córdova, New Mexico, worked as a shepherd in Colorado. Celestino Segura did the same in Arizona.

The melody of this song was employed as the opening theme of the second movement of my Concerto for Piano and Orchestra.

14. *La Vida de los Borregueros* (The Life of the Shepherds)
R1395, Juan Griego, age 46, Albuquerque, N.Mex., 1956, Robb.

1

Un día veintiocho de enero
que bajamos a La Sal.
Matamos una borrega
cansada de andar.

1

On the day of January twenty-eighth
We went to La Sal.
We killed a ewe
That was too tired to walk.

2

Mediante el desastre
no la hizo andar el herrero.
Como contra de una carta
más el gasto de dinero.

2

Such was the disaster that not even
The blacksmith could make it walk.
To make matters worse, the ewe
Was an expensive one.

3

De ron de don Pacheo
le dimos a la seca.
Muchachos a la muñeca
le sacaron la manteca.

3

We gave Don Pancho's rum
To the thirsty ewe.
The boys from the ewe
Milked all the milk.

4

Si en el paso se conoce,
y en el andar y en el traje,
que por muy humilde que seas;
siempre pareces salvaje.

4

If one is known by his step,
His manner of walking and costume,
Your humility doesn't matter;
You always look savage.

5

Si uno tiene becerro
que es lo mucho que le place,
que devuelva la que traiga,
y que la pobre se agache.

5

If one has a calf
This is his great delight,
For it returns his affection
And is playful.

6

Sí la vida del pastor
es una vida pesada,
ponga leña de colchón
y una chaqueta de almohada.

6

Indeed the shepherd's life
Is a hard life,
He uses wood for a mattress
And his jacket for a pillow.

7

Cucharita apachurrada,
toda rota y encogida,
como por irla pasando
en recovecos de la vida.

7

Little spoon all smashed,
Broken and shrunken,
As if barely surviving
In the labyrinth of life.

8

Ya pasaron veinte días,
ya guardando mi mochila,
cada vez que va a la casa
hace un romance de aldea.

8

Twenty days passed while
I carried my knapsack,
Every time a shepherd goes home
He has a village love affair.

9

Yo le dije a mi compañero:
—Ya te hice una hamaca.
Reuniremos el ganado,
y mataremos una pata.

9

I said to my companion:
"I made a hammock for you.
We will round up the flock,
And then we'll kill a duck."

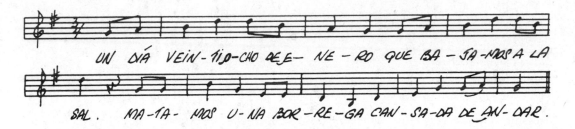

UN DÍA VEIN-TIO-CHO DE E-NE-RO QUE BA-JA-MOS A LA SAL. MA-TA-MOS U-NA BOR-RE-GA CAN-SA-DA DE AN-DAR.

Juan Griego advised the author that he himself wrote the words of this song. His mother got sick and he borrowed money to put her in the hospital. He had to go to work for the lender, to pay him back, herding sheep in eastern New Mexico. He got the tune from another song.

15. *La Vida del Campero* (The Life of the Camper)
R1381, Juan Griego, Albuquerque, N.Mex., 1956, Robb.

1

Escuchen amigos
y amigas que tengo,
si saber desean
mi triste pasión.
La vida, la vida
que pasa el campero,
que pasa el campero
con gran atención.

1

Listen, my friends,
Ladies and gentlemen,
If you wish to know
Of my sad passion.
The life, the life
That the shepherd lives,
That the shepherd lives
Pay close attention.

2

Yo vivo en los campos,
mi casita es fea;
está hecha de ramas,
no tiene azotea.

2

I live in the open,
My house it is ugly;
It's made of boughs,
It has no roof.

El techo se ocupa
con la chiminea;
cuando no cae agua
que no se gotea.

3

La puerta es de cuero.
Tiene dos armellas
y ventanas tiene
como cielo y estrellas.
Y para sombría
tengo dos zaleas
que ya los ratones
me comen por ellas.

4

Y allí mis vecinos
que son los coyotes,
que bonitas piezas
tocan a las noches.
Ellos tocan cunas,
cuadrillas, y chotes,
y los pobres zorrillos
valsean al trote.

5

Y llego a mi campo
rendido y cansado
y debajo de mi armada
yo oigo estar tocando.
Las víboras pasan
casi galopiando.
Debajo de mi cama
forman su fandango.

6

No tengo más gusto
cuando hecho tortillas,
unas salen crudas,
otras bien cocidas,
unas muy redondas
y otros con esquinas,
unas cuadraditas,
y otras con esquinas.

7

Pues ésta es la vida
que pasa el campero
que para amasar
usa su sombrero,
y de charolada,
una garra de cuero,
que eche sus galletas
dentro el cenicero.

The roof is wide open
And serves as a chimney;
When there is no rain
It doesn't leak at all.

3

The door is of rawhide.
It has two hinges
And it has many windows
Like the sky and stars.
And for shade
I have two sheepskins
Which the rats
Are always trying to eat.

4

Here my neighbors
Who are the coyotes,
Such beautiful pieces
They play in the night.
They play *cunas*,
Quadrilles, and schottisches,
And the poor skunks
Waltz and do the fox trot.

5

Worn out and tired
I come to my camp
And under my pillow
I hear them playing.
The rattlesnakes pass
As if at a gallop.
Under my bed they
Perform a fandango.

6

I have no more pleasure
In making tortillas,
Some come out half-baked,
Others are over-cooked,
Some come out round
And others with corners,
Some square,
And others with corners.

7

Well, this is the life
That the shepherd lives,
Who, to make dough,
Uses his hat,
And for a dish holder,
An old piece of leather,
To put his biscuit pan
Into the hot ashes.

8

Y en un rincón yo tengo
mi puela colgada
porque los ratones
la usan de guitarra
sin dudas, en bailes
sin dudas con ella,
porque ahí en la harina
se sigue la juella.

8

And up in a corner
My skillet is hanging
Because the rats
Use it for a guitar
Without doubt, without doubt,
They dance to it,
Because here in the flour
I find their footprints.

9

Mi patio es lujoso
¡Qué cosa tan fina!
está hecho de arena y
ceniza de harina;
por mi buena suerte.
No hay ni una gallina
que sino peor fuera
de piso mi ruina.

9

My patio's luxurious
What a fine thing!
It's made of sand
Mixed with flour;
For my good luck.
There is not even a hen
But that might be worse
For the floor of my ruin.

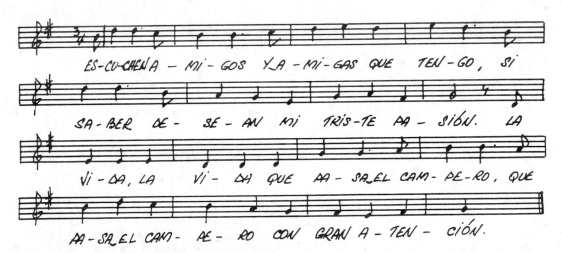

ES-CU-CHEN A - MI-GOS Y A-MI-GAS QUE TEN-GO, SI
SA-BER DE - SE-AN MI TRIS-TE AA - SIÓN. LA
VI - DA, LA VI - DA QUE AA - SA EL CAM-PE-RO, QUE
AA - SA EL CAM - PE - RO CON GRAN A - TEN - CIÓN.

This song is a variant of I19 below, although the latter is sung as relating not to the life of a shepherd but to that of a cowboy.

Juan Griego, singer of *La Vida del Campero* (I5), and his family, in Albuquerque, New Mexico, 1956. Standing at his father's left is Cipriano Griego, who recorded a number of his father's songs for me.

I6. *Año de 1895*, or *Teófilo Vigil* (In the Year of 1895)
R628, Nicolás Martínez, age 75, Chimayó, N.Mex., 1951, Robb. Cf. R1995.

1

Año de mil ochocientos
noventa y cinco es decir
de lo que sucedió
¡ay! el día cinco de abril.

1

In the year 1895,
This is the story
Of what happened,
Alas, on April fifth.

2

¡Qué desgracia sucedió!
¡ay! el día cinco de abril.
En el Ojo del Carrizo
¡ay! ¿cómo les voy a decir?

2

What a misfortune occurred
Alas, the day of April fifth
At Carrizo Spring,
(Alas, how am I going to tell you?)

3

Estos eran dos pastores
lo que hace les sucedió,
eran llena de dolores
¡ay! cuando el rebelión llegó.

3

There were two shepherds
To whom this happened,
They were filled with sorrow,
Alas, when the storm came.

4

Estos eran dos pastores
y amigos de buena fe.
los dos eran paisanitos.
¡ay! reciben Señor.

4

There were two shepherds
And friends of good faith.
The two were fellow countrymen.
Alas, protect them, O Lord!

5

Estos eran dos pastores,
¿cómo les voy a decir?
uno era David González
¡ay!, el otro Teófilo Vigil.

5

There were two shepherds,
How am I going to tell you?
One was David González,
Alas, the other Teófilo Vigil.

6

Le dieron el agua a su ganado
y le dan agua a su partida.
le dice David González
¡ay!, voy a hacerte la comida.

6

They gave water to the cattle
And they gave water to the sheep.
David González tells him,
Oh, I'm going to fix dinner for you.

7

A poco que caminaron
llegó un viento torbellino
que no los dejaba ver
¡ay!, y perdieron el camino.

7

They walked a short while
And a whirlwind came
That didn't let them see,
Alas, and they lost their way.

8

Cuando David llegó al campo
previno la provisión;
luego en el mismo momento
¡ay!, lo ha pescado el rebelión.

8

When David arrived at camp
He got the provisions ready;
Then at the same time,
Alas, the blizzard hit them.

9

Agarró la dirección
que oriente en el puro llano

9

He took the direction
That led across the plains

donde lo encontraron muerto
ante un soterrano.

Where they found him dead
Before an underground shed.

10

Quince millas caminó
llevando esa dirección
y el viento que le llevaba
¡ay!, su cuerpo está sepultado.

10

Fifteen miles he walked
Going in that direction
And the wind that carried him,
Alas, his body was buried.

11

Pobre de David González
jugó en tan afamado
en el Ojo del Carrizo
¡ay!, su cuerpo está sepultado.

11

Poor David González
Played such a famous role!
At Carrizo Spring,
Alas, his body is buried.

12

Pobre de David González
jugó en tan afamado;
ya no pudo caminar
¡ay!, viendo éste tan fatigado.

12

Poor David González
Played such a famous role!
He wasn't able to walk anymore,
Alas, he was so tired.

13

Yo fuí otro compañero
agarro acá mi dirección
camino para el sur
¡ay!, empujado del rebelión.

13

I was another companion,
I take my direction here
I walk toward the south,
Alas, driven by the blizzard.

14

Cuando ya supo donde estaba
luego hizo reminiscencia
y le da gracias a Díos
¡ay!, a la divina providencia

14

When he found out where he was
Then he remembered
And gave thanks to God,
Alas, to divine Providence.

15

Caminó por el poniente
llevando esa dirección
donde se pudo encontrar
¡ay!, con la casa del patrón.

15

He walked to the west
Taking that direction
That would bring him,
Alas, to the house of the patron.

16

Dió plena satisfacción
de lo que había pasado;
él mismo les informó
¡ay! que había dejado el ganado.

16

He fully informed them
Of what had happened;
He himself told them,
Alas, that he had left the flock.

17

El sábado en la mañana
salió en busca de su partida;
unas se encontraban muertas
¡ay!, otras se encontraban vivas.

17

Saturday morning
He left to look for his flock;
Some sheep he found dead,
Alas, others he found alive.

18

La pérdida que sería
serián como unas mil

18

The number that were lost
Was about a thousand

y el pastor que las halló ¡ay!, era Teófilo Vigil.	And the shepherd who found them, Alas, he was Teófilo Vigil.

<table>
<tr><td>19</td><td>19</td></tr>
<tr><td>Pobrecito de su papá,
del joven David González
quizás así sería mi hijo
¡ay!, comido de los animales.</td><td>Poor father
Of the young man David González
Perhaps my son,
Alas, would be food for the animals.</td></tr>
<tr><td>20</td><td>20</td></tr>
<tr><td>Unos vaqueros que andaban
en busca de sus animales
hallaron el cuerpo muerto
¡ay!, del joven David González.</td><td>Some cowboys who were passing
In search of their animals
Found the dead body,
Alas, of the young man David González.</td></tr>
<tr><td>21</td><td>21</td></tr>
<tr><td>Los hombres que allá le hallaron
tuvieron grande ternura;
luego se determinaron
¡ay!, a darle su sepultura.</td><td>The men that found him there
Were very tender;
Then they decided,
Alas, to bury him.</td></tr>
<tr><td>22</td><td>22</td></tr>
<tr><td>Porbrecita su mamá
del joven David González;
quizás así sería mi hijo
¡ay!, comido de los animales.</td><td>Poor mother
Of the young man David González;
Perhaps my son,
Alas, would be food for the animals.</td></tr>
<tr><td>23</td><td>23</td></tr>
<tr><td>Adiós todos mis amigos,
compadres todos iguales,
todos deben de sentir
¡ay!, la muerte de David González.</td><td>Good-bye all my friends,
All equal compadres,
All of you should regret,
Alas, the death of David González.</td></tr>
</table>

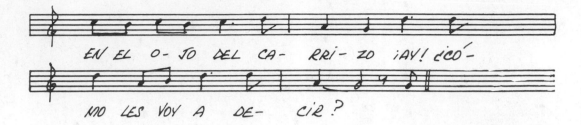

EN EL O- JO DEL CA- RRI- ZO ¡AY! ¿CÓ-

NO LES VOY A DE- CIR ?

Not all of the shepherds' songs were light-hearted. Death occasionally came to the shepherds during their lonely vigils which lasted for months.

Año de 1895 is about two shepherds, one of whom, David Gonzales, froze to death. Nicolás Martínez, of Chimayó, learned it about 1906 from a Chimayó man, José Cruz. It is about a place called Ocotea, New Mexico. The death happened April 5, 1889, in a place called Carrizo.

Another ballad of the lonely death of a shepherd is the *Indita de Jesús María Sánchez* (F5), whose protagonist was apparently the victim of a heart attack far from any help.

A similar song dealing with the perils of sheepherding is the *corrido Manuel Tenorio* (R737), composed by Manuel Tenorio, of Galisteo. He was the foreman of a sheep camp for Ortiz, of Galisteo, and had three men under him. They were going to Lincoln County with four thousand sheep in December (*ca.* 1898) when a storm caught them near Pino, New Mexico. They lost their camp and the sheep, and they themselves got lost. At eleven in the morning they built a fire and had to kill a goat, a *castrado*. Tenorio is dead now.

SOLDIER

17. *Ya Se Llegó* (The Time Has Come)
R66, Juan Sandoval, Chimayo, N.Mex., 1945, Robb. Cf. Mendóza 9d (pp. 327–28).

1

Ya se llegó mi partida
ya sin remedio me voy,
y voy sintiendo vencer
los días que he de tener.
Tengo esperanza en volver
en prestándome Dios vida;
ésta es mi patria querida
y esto no puede evitarse.
Con el corazón partido
me voy sintiendo el dejarte.

1

The time has come for me to go
Now I must go,
And I know I must conquer
My future days.
I hope to return
If God gives me life;
This is my beloved country
And this duty cannot be evaded.
With a broken heart
I suffer leaving you here.

2

... [undecipherable]
Si cumples con tu deber
yo me veré en la confianza
que dejo una mujer;
más no des en que conocer
que él que amas se halla ausente—
mira que dirá la gente;

2

...
If you live by your duty
I'll live with confidence
That I can trust a woman;
Do not let anyone know
That your lover is absent—
Think what people may say;

procura no estar a luz,	Keep yourself out of sight,
y estas palabras te doy;	This advice I give you;
y al dividirnos los dos,	And now at parting
llorando gotas de sangre	Bloody tears do fall
dame tu mano y adiós.	Give me your hand and good-bye.

YA SE LLE-GÓ MI PAR-TI-DA YA SIN RE-ME-DIO ME VOY, Y VOY SIN-TIEN-DO VEN-CER LOS DÍ-AS QUE HE DE TE-NER. TEN-GO ES-PE-RAN-ZA EN VOL-VER EN PRE-STÁN-DO-ME DIOS VI-DA; É-STA ES MI PA-TRIA QUE-RI-DA Y E-STO NO PUE-DE E-VI-TAR-SE. CON EL CO-RA-ZÓN PAR-TI-DO ME VOY SIN-TIEN-DO EL DE-JAR-TE.

18. *Soldado Razo* (Private Soldier)
R1220, Tom Dickerson, age 20, Albuquerque, N.Mex., 1954, Robb.

1	1
Me voy de soldado razo,	I am enlisting as a private soldier,
voy a ingresar a las filas	I am going to enter the ranks
con los muchachos valientes	With the brave boys
que dejan madre querida,	Who leave a beloved mother,
que dejan novias llorando,	Who leave a weeping fiancée,
llorando su despedida.	I leave behind me this farewell.

503

2

Voy a la guerra contento,
ya traigo lista pistola;
ya volveré de sargento
cuando se acabe la bola;
no más una cosa siento:
dejar a mi madre sola.

Coro

Virgen morena,
mándame tu consuelo
y nada más permita
que me la robe el cielo.

3

Virgen Guadalupana,
porteged a mi bandera
y cuando me halle en campaña
muy lejos ¡ay! de mi tierra
les probaré que mi raza
sabe morir dondequiera.

Coro

2

I go to war content,
I already have my arms ready;
And I will return a sergeant
When the game is over;
I only regret one thing:
Leaving my mother alone.

Chorus

Dark Virgin,
Send me your consolation
and grant only
That heaven take me.

3

My Guadalupan Virgin,
Protect my flag
And when I find myself in a campaign
A long way, alas, from my country
I will prove to everyone that my race
Knows how to die anywhere.

Chorus

504

I8a. *El Soldado Razo*
R75, Elisa Montoya, Los Griegos, Albuquerque, N.Mex., 1946, Robb.

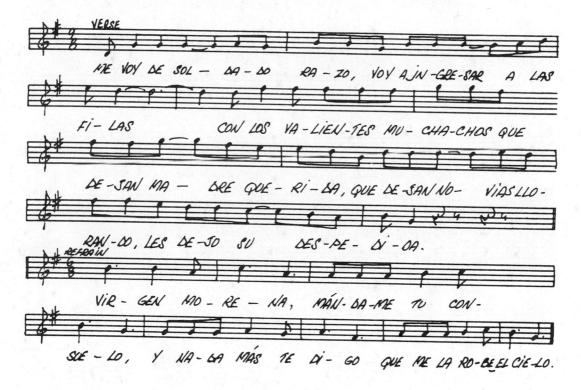

VERSE

ME VOY DE SOL — DA-DO RA-ZO, VOY A IN-GRE-SAR A LAS FI-LAS CON LOS VA-LIEN-TES MU-CHA-CHOS QUE DE-SAN MA — DRE QUE-RI-DA, QUE DE-SAN NO— VIAS LLO-RAN-DO, LES DE-JO SU DES-PE- DI-DA.

REFRAIN

VIR-GEN MO-RE—NA, MAN-DA-ME TU CON-SUE-LO, Y NA-DA MÁS TE DI-GO QUE ME LA RO-BE EL CIE-LO.

The text of this song is omitted since it is virtually identical with verses 1 through 3 of I8.

I9. *Soldado de Levita* (Soldier in Full Uniform)
R133, Vidal Valdez, age 26, Albuquerque, N.Mex., 1947, Robb.

1
Soy soldado de levita
de esos de caballería,
de esos de caballería
soy soldado de levita.

1
I am a soldier in full uniform
Of the cavalry,
Of the cavalry
I am a soldier in full uniform.

2
Me incorporan a las filas
por una mujer bonita,
por una mujer bonita
que burla la vida mía.

2
They put me in the front lines
Because of a beautiful woman,
Because of a beautiful woman
Who ruins my life.

3
Corazón apasionado,
disimula tus tristezas;
disimula tus tristezas,
corazón apasionado.

3
Passionate heart,
Conceal your sadness;
Conceal your sadness,
Passionate heart.

<table>
<tr><td>4</td><td>4</td></tr>
</table>

4	4
El que nace desgraciado	He who is born unfortunate
desde la cuna comienza;	Commences in the cradle;
desde la cuna comienza	Commences in the cradle
a vivir martirisado.	A life of martyrdom.

SOY SOL-DA-DO DE LE-VI-TA DE E-SOS DE CA-BA-LLE-RÍ-A, DE E-SOS DE CA-BA-LLE-RÍ-A, SOY SOL-DA-DO DE LE-VI-TA. SOY SOL-DA-DO DE LE-VI-TA ¡AY! DE E-SOS DE CA-BA-LLE-RÍ-A, DE E-SOS DE CA-BA-LLE-RÍ-A ¡AY! SOY SOL-DA-DO DE LE-VI-TA.

This is an example of formal construction where the form as well as the substance attracts one's interest. Note that each verse opens with two lines *(ab)*, which are then repeated in reverse order *(ba)*. For another example see *El Sombrerito* (C71).

I10. *¿Tecolote, Dónde Vienes?* (Owl, Where Do You Come From?)
R165, Adolfo Maes, Canjilon, N.Mex., 1949, Robb. Cf. Mendoza 9d (p. 504), R713, R838.

1		1
—Tecolote ¿dónde vienes?—	] *Bis*	"Little owl, where do you come from?"
—Del pueblo de Colorido. ¡Ay!	] *Bis*	"Colorido is the place, sir. Ay!
Vengo a traerte una noticia,	] *Bis*	And I come to bring you warning,
que tu amor está perdido ¡Ay!—	] *Bis*	That your love isn't in mourning. Ay!"

Estribillo		*Refrain*
Pájaro, cu, cu, cu,	] *Bis*	Pájaro, cu, cu, cu,
pobrecito animalito,		The life of an animal is trying,
tiene hambre el tecolotito ¡Ay!		Poor little owl. For hunger it's crying. Ay!

2		2
—Tecolote ¿dónde vienes?	] *Bis*	"Little owl, where do you come from?
tan fresco y tan de mañana ¡ay!—	] *Bis*	For the day is hardly breaking, ay!"
—Vengo de hacer ejercicio,	] *Bis*	"With the troops of Santa Ana,
en las tropas de Santa Ana. ¡Ay!—	] *Bis*	Exercise I have been taking. Ay!"

Estribillo		*Refrain*

3		3
—Tecolote ¿dónde vienes?—	] *Bis*	"Little owl, where do you come from?"
—De arriba de una sotea ¡Ay!	] *Bis*	"I've been up there on the housetop. Ay!
Vengo de ver un borracho,	] *Bis*	I could see you drinking whiskey,
empinarse la botella ¡Ay!—	] *Bis*	Drinking whiskey's very risky. Ay!"

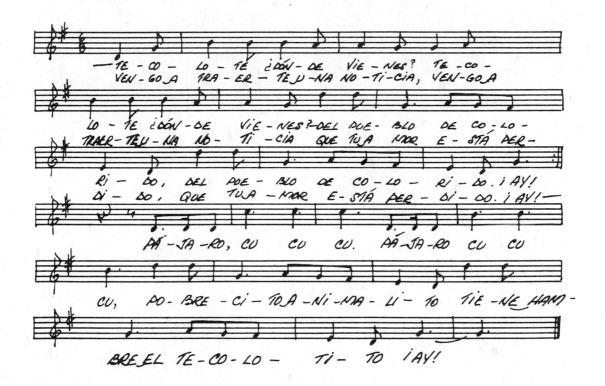

I10a. *El Tecolote* (The Owl)
R209, Tomás Archuleta, age 55, Abiquiu, N.Mex., 1949, Robb.

1		1
Tecolote ¿qué haces? ¡ay!	] *Bis*	Owl, what are you dong? oh!
Arriba de una azotea ¡ay!	] *Bis*	On top of a flat roof, oh!

2		2
Mirando a los borrachitos,	] *Bis*	Watching the drunks,
empinarse la botella ¡o, o!	] *Bis*	Tip up the bottle, oh, oh!

Coro		Chorus
Tecolotito, tecolotón,		Little owl, big owl,
toma tu vara y trae mi cotón, io, o!	] Bis	Take your stick and bring me my wrap,
		oh, oh!

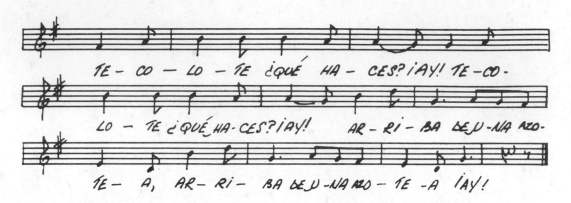

I10b. *El Tecolote*
R1218, Tom Dickerson, age 20, Albuquerque, N.Mex., 1954, Robb.

1		1
El tecolote ya no baila	] Bis	The owl no longer dances
Porque no tiene camisa,		Because he has no shirt,
Porque no tiene calzones,		Because he has no pants,
pájaro cu cu cu,	] Bis	Bird cu cu cu,
Porque no tiene camisa,		Because he has no shirt,
Porque no tiene calzones,		Because he has no pants,
vuelva, vuelva mañana.	] Bis	Come back tomorrow.

2		2
Con la pluma de una gallina	] Bis	With the feathers of a chicken
Van a tejerle una camisa,	] Bis	They are going to knit him a shirt,
pájaro cu cu cu,	] Bis	Bird cu cu cu,
Ya no le falta una camisa,	] Bis	He no longer needs a shirt,
vuelva, vuelva mañana.	] Bis	Come back tomorrow.

3		3
Con la cola de una vaca	] Bis	With the tail from a cow
Van agarrarle una corbata,	] Bis	They are going to make him a necktie,
pájaro cu cu cu,	] Bis	Bird cu cu cu,
Que van atarle una corbata,	] Bis	They are going to tie his necktie
vuelva, vuelva mañana.	] Bis	Come back tomorrow.

4		4
El tecolote no tiene padrino,	] Bis	The owl hasn't any godfather,
¿Qué será de tecolotito?	] Bis	What will become of the little owl?
pájaro cu cu cu,		Bird cu cu cu,
¿Qué será de tecolotito?		What will become of the little owl?

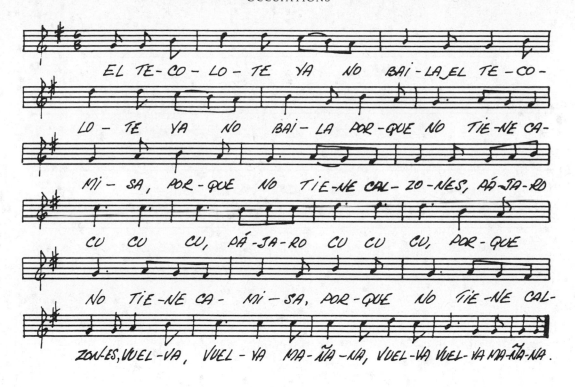

I10c. *¿Tecolotito, Dónde Vienes?* (Little Owl, Where Do You Come From?)
R1423, David Frescas, age 70, Taos, N.Mex., 1956, Robb.

¿Tecolote, dónde vienes?	] *Bis*	Little owl, where do you come from?
Del pueblo de Colorido ¡ay!	] *Bis*	From the village of Colorido, ah!
Vengo a traerte una noticia,	] *Bis*	I come to bring you this news,
que tu amor está perdido, ¡ay!	] *Bis*	That your love is lost, ah!

Refrán		Refrain
¡Pájaro, cur, cur, cur!		The bird sings cur, cur, cur.
Estás así en la botella,		This news I'll drown in the bottle,
esperando al borrachito,	] *Bis*	Waiting to get a little drunk,
que se empine la botella ¡ay!		As I hit the bottle, ah!

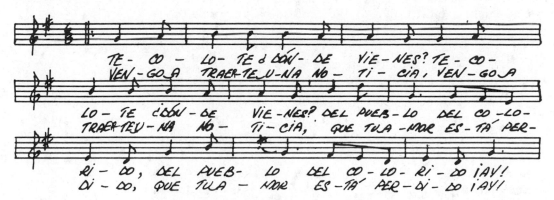

509

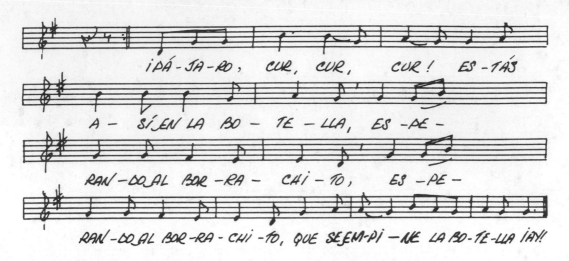

I10d. *El Tecolote*
Mendoza 9d (p. 505), Amador Abeyta, age 58, Sabinal, N.Mex., 1898, Cobos.

1		1
Tecolitito mañoso,	] *Bis*	Clever little owl,
pájaro madrugador.	] *Bis*	Bird of the dawn.
Estribillo		*Refrain*
Pájaro cu, cu, cu;	] *Bis*	Little bird cu, cu, cu,
pobrecito animalito,		Poor little animal,
tiene hambre el tecolotito.		The little owl is hungry.
2		2
El tecolote, señores,		The owl, gentlemen,
el tecolote, señoras,		The owl, ladies,
metió la mano en la ollita.	] *Bis*	Put his claw in the vase.
Estribillo		*Refrain*
3		3
Como estaba tan caliente	] *Bis*	Since it was so hot
se le quemó la manita.	] *Bis*	He burned his claw.
Estribillo		*Refrain*
4		4
Todo cabe en un jarrito,	] *Bis*	Everything fits in a little jug,
sabiéndolo acomodar.	] *Bis*	You have to know how to arrange it.
Estribillo		*Refrain*
5		5
El tecolote nochero,	] *Bis*	The nighttime owl,
le dice al madrugador:	] *Bis*	Said to the morning owl:

6
Que le diga al carpintero   ] *Bis*
que le arregle su cajón.   ] *Bis*

6
Go tell the carpenter
To get his coffin ready.

Estribillo   *Refrain*

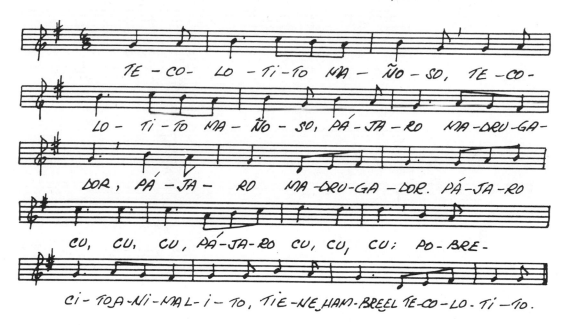

TE - CO - LO -TI -TO MA - ÑO - SO, TE -CO-
LO - TI - TO MA - ÑO - SO, PÁ - JA - RO MA -DRU-GA-
DOR, PÁ - JA - RO MA -DRU-GA - DOR. PÁ-JA-RO
CU, CU, CU, PÁ-JA-RO CU, CU, CU; PO-BRE-
CI - TO A -NI-MAL-i - TO, TIE-NE HAM-BRE EL TE-CO-LO-TI -TO.

I10e. *Tecolote de Aguardaña*
R336, Henry Fountain, Mesilla Park, N.Mex., 1950, Robb. Cf. R1965.

1
Tecolote de aguardaña,
pájaro madrugador,   ] *Bis*
que tuviera tus alitas,   ]
que tuviera tus alitas,   ]
que tuviera tus alitas   ]
para ir a ver mi amor.   ] *Bis*

1
Owl, with a scythe,
Early bird,
Would that I had your little wings,
Would that I had your little wings,
Would that I had your little wings
So that I could go and see my love.

Coro
Y cu-i, cu-i, cu-i, cu-i,
y cu-i, cu-i, cu-i, cu-i,
y cu-i, cu-i, cu-i, y cu-i,
pobrecito tecolotito
ya se cansa de volar.

Chorus
And cu-i, cu-i, cu-i, cu-i,
And cu-i, cu-i, cu-i, cu-i,
And cu-i, cu-i, cu-i, and cu-i,
Poor little owl
He's tired of flying.

2
Si yo fuera tecolote no me ocupa en
    volar;   ] *Bis*
me queda en mi nidito,   ]
me queda en mi nidito,   ]

2
If I were an owl I wouldn't bother to fly;

I would stay in my little nest,
I would stay in my little nest,

me queda en mi nidito]   I would stay in my little nest
ya acabándome de criar.   ] *Bis*   And finish growing up.

Coro   *Chorus*

I10f. *Tecolote de Guadaña* (Owl of Guadaña)
     R2369, Vincent F. Gallegos, age 72, Albuquerque, N.Mex., 1970, Robb.

1   1

Tecolote de Guadaña,   ]   Owl of Guadaña,
pájaro madrugador,   ] *Bis*   Bird of the morning,
que tuviera tus alitas,   Would that I had your wings,
que tuviera tus alitas,   Would that I had your wings,
que tuviera tus alitas   Would that I had your wings
para ir a ver a mi amor.   So that I could go and see my love.

512

Coro

Ti curi curi curi cu,
y curi curi curi cu,
y curi curi curi cu,
que tuviera tus alitas
para ir a ver a mi amor.

Chorus

Ti curi curi curi cu,
And curi curi curi cu,
And curi curi curi cu,
Would that I had your wings
So that I could go and see my love.

2

Tecolote ¿qué haces ahí
arrimado a la pared?
Esperando a mi tecolota,
esperando a mi tecolota,
esperando a mi tecolota
que me traiga de comer.

2

Owl, what are you doing
Up there on the wall?
I am waiting for my girl friend,
I am waiting for my girl friend,
I am waiting for my girl friend
Who's bringing me something to eat.

Coro

Chorus

I10g. *Tecolote de Guadaña*
R1965, Frank McCullough, age 35, Albuquerque, N.Mex., 1964, Robb.

1

Tecolote de Guadaña,   ]
pájaro madrugador   ] *Bis*
que tuviera tus alitas   ] *Bis*
para ir a ver a mi amor.

Coro

y cu-i, cu-i, cu-i, cu-i,
y cu-i, cu-i, cu-i, cu-i,
y cu-i, cu-i, cu-i, cu-i,
pobrecito tecolotito,
ya se cansa de volar.

1

Owl of Guadaña,
Bird of the morning,
Would that I had your wings
To fly to my love.

Chorus

And cu-i, cu-i, cu-i, cu-i,
And cu-i, cu-i, cu-i, cu-i,
And cu-i, cu-i, cu-i, cu-i,
Poor little owl,
It's tired of flying.

514

I11. *La Partida Militar* (The Soldier's Farewell)
R518, Francisco S. Leyva, age 81, Leyva, N.Mex., 1951, Robb.

1

Un joven militar	A young soldier boy
al tiempo de partir	When he has to go
deja a su madre	Was to leave his mother
y se va a marchar	And go away
como joven singular, y le dice:	And he's a very special young man, so she says to him:

2

Quédate en paz,	God be with you,
O ilustrado joven,	O intelligent youth,
íntima fuente	Intimate fountain
de la mar inmenso;	Of the deep blue sea;
todo se acabó . . .	Everything's finished . . .
Ya acerca un fuego intenso,	A hot flame is coming near,
un fuego al viento	A fire fanned by the wind
y me labora el corazón.	And my heart labors.

3

¿Qué quieres que haga,	What can I do
si el destino me manda abandonarte?	If fate orders me to leave you?
tomaré la línea	I will get in line
y marcharé hacia el puerto	And march to the port
y solo allí	And when I am alone there
y no desespere el muerto;	I will not be afraid of death;
y un foco bien tener	And my heart labors
me labora mi corazón.	To keep a proper focus.

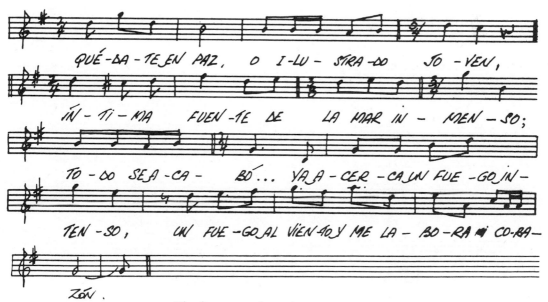

QUÉ-DA-TE EN PAZ, O I-LU-STRA-DO JO-VEN,
IN-TI-MA FUEN-TE DE LA MAR IN-MEN-SO;
TO-DO SE A-CA-BÓ . . . YA A-CER-CA UN FUE-GO IN-
TEN-SO, UN FUE-GO AL VIEN-TO Y ME LA-BO-RA MI CO-RA-
ZÓN.

The first verse is spoken, not sung.

112. *La Partida Militar*
R520, Francisco S. Leyva, age 81, Leyva, N.Mex., 1951, Robb.

1

La partida militar ya me exige
a dejar una juventud que adoro.
Es mi placer y mi tesoro
y mi gloria y mi dicha formó.

2

Pues, escucha el clarín ya, vieja;
de la carga ya soy el sonido
de una voz que resuena en mi oído
que me anuncia que voy a partir.

3

No permita mi Dios que yo parta
ni abandone el placer de la vida,
pues a Dios yo he siempre querido.
Pues ya voy al servicio militar.

1

The call of the army compels me
To leave the youth which I adore.
It is my pleasure and my treasure
And I seek glory and happiness.

2

Listen to that bugle now, old lady;
It is the voice of the charge
Which echoes in my ear
And announces my departure.

3

God will not permit me to leave
Nor to abandon the pleasure of life,
For I have always loved God.
Now I go into the military service.

I13. *Recordarás Cada Noche* (You Will Remember Every Night)
R519, Francisco S. Leyva, age 81, Leyva, N.Mex., 1951, Robb.

1

Recordarás cada día que anochece
Yo marcharé a los campos con valor
como un soldado al frente de una batalla;
el sueño del soldado es el amor.

2

Y ahora me temo,
me falta la metralla
y al monte trueno
de camino aterredor.
Como un soldado al frente de una batalla;
el sueño del soldado es el amor.

1

You will remember every day at evening
I will march to the fields with courage
Like a soldier to the battlefront;
The dream of the soldier is love.

2

And now I am afraid,
I lack ammunition
And I fear the terrible road
To Thunder Mountain (?).
Like a soldier at the battlefront;
The dream of the soldier is love.

RAILROADER

114. *Yo Soy Rielera* (I Am a Railroad Woman)
    R2409, Juan Griego, age 61, Albuquerque, N.Mex., 1971, Cipriano Griego. Cf. R2441,
Mendoza 9g (p. 340).

Coro	*Chorus*
Yo soy rielera.	I am a railroad woman.
Tengo a mi Juan.	I have my John.
El es mi vida	He is my life
y yo soy su querer.	And I am his love.
Cuando me dicen	When they tell me
que va saliendo el tren:	That the train is leaving:
—Adiós, mi querida,	"Good-bye, my love,
ya se va tu Juan.—	Your John is leaving."

1	1
Dicen que los ingenieros	They say that engineers
no pueden tener mujer	Cannot have a wife
porque la vida la tienen	Because they spend their life
entre las ruedas del tren.	On the wheels of the train.

Coro   *Chorus*

2	2
Allí vienen los ingenieros	There come the engineers
con sus paños colorados	With their red handkerchiefs
y sus cachuchas chiquitas	And their little hats
quedándoles de lado.	Worn sideways.

Coro   *Chorus*

3	3
Dicen que lo negro es triste,	They say that black is sad,
yo digo que no es verdad;	I say it is not true;
tú tienes los ojos negros	For you have black eyes
y eres mi felicidad.	And you are my joy.

Coro   *Chorus*

4	4
Tengo mis zapatos blancos	I have my white shoes
con mi naguita de olán	With my skirt
y mi túnico de seda	And my silk dress
que me regaló mi Juan.	Which John gave me.

Coro   *Chorus*

VI - DA Y YO SOY SU QUE - RER. CUAN - DO ME DI - CEN QUE VA

SA - LIEN - DO EL TREN: --- A - DIÓS, MI QUE - RI - DA, YA

VERSE 1

SE VA TU JUAN. --- DI - CEN QUE LOS IN - GE - NIE - ROS

NO PUE - DEN TE - NER MU - JER POR - QUE LA VI - DA LA

TIE - NEN EN - TRE LAS RUE - DAS DEL TREN.

For four different songs about railroads, see
El Ferrocarril (C91–91b) and Lummis, p. 180
(this last without music).

I14a. *La Rialera* (The Railroad Woman)
R2441, Edwin Berry, age 54, Tomé, N.Mex., 1972, Robb.

1	1
Yo soy rialera	I am a railroad woman
y tengo mi Juan.	And I have my John.
El es mi vida,	He is my life,
y yo soy su querer.	And I am his love.
2	2
Cuando me dicen	When they tell me
que ya viene el tren,	That the train is leaving,
Adiós mi querido	Good-bye my sweetheart
ya me voy también.	For I'm going too.
3	3
Tengo mi par de pistolas	I have my pair of pistols
con sus cachas de marfil,	With their handles of ivory,
para pelear mis balazos	To fire my bullets
con los del ferrocarril.	With those of the train.
4	4
(Verso 1 se repite)	(Verse 1 repeated)
5	5
(Verso 2 se repite)	(Verse 2 repeated)

Coro

Pobrecitos ingenieros,
no pueden tener mujer
porque su vida la pasan
entre la llega del tren.

Chorus

Poor engineers,
They can't have wives
For all their life is spent
Between the comings of the train.

6
(Verso 1 se repite)

6
(Verse 1 repeated)

YO SOY RIAL-E-RA Y TEN-GO MI JUAN.

ÉL ES MI VI-DA, Y YO SOY SU QUE-RER.

CUAN-DO ME DI-CEN QUE YA VIE-NEEL

TREN, A-DIÓS MI QUE-RI-DO YA

ME VOY TAM-BIÉN. Fin TEN-GO MI

PAR DE PIS-TO-LAS CON SUS CAR-

CHAS DE MAR-FIL, PA-RA PE-

LEAR MI BA-LA-ZOS

CON LOS DEL FE-RRO-CA-RRIL.

I15. *El Pasajero* (The Passenger Train)
R2440, Edwin Berry, age 54, Tomé, N.Mex., 1972, Robb. Cf. C91–91b.

¡Ju! ¡Ju! ¡Ju!   Whoo! Whoo! Whoo!

1   1
¡Atísenle, atísenle!   Stoke up, stoke up
a ese pasajero,   That passenger train,
que ya mi amor va rendido.   For my love is very tired.
Llegamos a una estación   We came to a station
que le llaman Alamillo.   That is called Alamillo.

2   2
Cuando subimos al tren   When we boarded the train
había asiento y buenas camas   There were seats and good beds
y allí pasó un americano   And an American went by saying
¿pues, qué no compran bananas?   "Why don't you buy my bananas?"

(Verso 1 se repite)   (Verse 1 repeated)

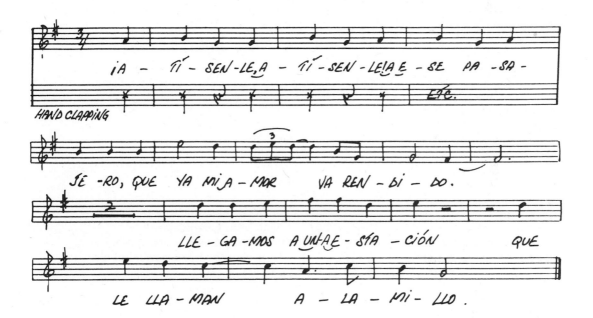

Before starting to sing, the singer cleverly imitates the whistle, the hiss of escaping steam, and, with his hands, the sound of the train on the rails.

521

COWBOY

I16. *Miguel Romancayo*
R1394, Juan Griego, age 46, Albuquerque, N.Mex., 1956, Robb.

1	1
Año de mil ochocientos	Year of one thousand eight hundred,
año de noventa y dos	Year of ninety-two (1892)
murió Miguel Romancayo,	Miguel Romancayo died,
un caballo lo mató.	A horse killed him.
Coro	*Chorus*
¡Ay! Dios de mi alma,	Oh! God of my heart,
no me quisiera acordar,	I do not like to remember,
lo arrastró quinientas varas	It dragged him five hundred varas
por un duro pedregal.	Over hard rocks.
2	2
Miguel venía llegando.	Miguel had just arrived.
Se tenía que era buen gallo,	He was confident of his skill,
cuando le partió el novillo	Then a young bull charged
se le destantó el caballo.	And frightened his horse.
Coro	*Chorus*
3	3
El novillo no era grande,	The bull was not big,
de un año que iba en dos.	One year, going on two.
Era de la noviada	It belonged to the herd
de Margarito Muiño.	Of Margarito Muiño.
Coro	*Chorus*
4	4
El caballo no era de allí.	The horse was not from there.
Era de Guadalajara.	It was from Guadalajara.
El pagó quinientos pesos	He had paid five hundred pesos
no más para que lo matara.	Just so that the horse could kill him.
Coro	*Chorus*
5	5
Y el caballo no era prieto,	Miguel's horse was not a black,
no es pinto, ni colorado.	Nor a pinto, nor a bay.
Es un caballo tordillo	It is a gray one
de un hijo de un licenciado.	Which belonged to the son of a lawyer.
Coro	*Chorus*
6	6
Y luego llega su padre:	Then his father arrived:
¿Pues qué hubo? ¿qué ha sucecido?	What is it? What has happened?
Cuando se paró en la puerta	As he stood at the door
allí vido a su hijo tendido.	He saw his son lying dead.

Coro

Chorus

7

¡Ay, Dios y válgame Dios!
Madre mía de los dolores.
Si mi Miguel reviviera
te ponía tu arco de flores.

7

Oh, God, help me, God!
My Mother of sorrows.
If my Miguel would revive
I would make you a crown of flowers.

Coro

Chorus

8

(Verso 1 se repite)

8

(Verse 1 repeated)

Coro

Chorus

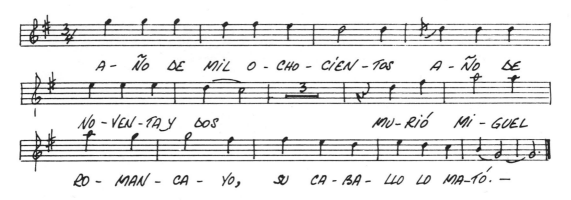

A - ÑO DE MIL O - CHO - CIEN - TOS A - ÑO DE NO - VEN - TA Y DOS MU - RIÓ MI - GUEL RO - MAN - CA - YO, SU CA - BA - LLO LO MA - TÓ. —

I17. *Corrido de la Muerte de Antonio Maestas* (Ballad of the Death of Antonio Maestas) R77, José Gallegos, Abiquiu, N.Mex., 1946, Robb. Cf. Robb 13 (pp. 16, 50); Robb 13a, R159, R216, R224, R428, R444.

1

Año de mil ochocientos
ochenta y nueve pasó,
que el día cinco de julio,
mi Dios lo determinó,
que al finado Antonio Maestas
un caballo lo mató,
en el lugar de "El Mogote,"
ese lugar escogió.

1

In the year of eighteen hundred
And eighty-nine in July,
On the fifth day God determined
Antonio Maestas must die,
That he should be thrown from his mount
And meet his death on the ground,
Near the ridge of El Mogote,
And there his body was found.

2

Del "Rancho de los Ingleses"
salió el hombre bueno y sano
a dar rodeo a las reses
según la orden de su amo.
Joven, alegre, y lozano,
fué resignado a su suerte;
salió a recibir la muerte
en el lomo de un caballo.

2

From the ranch owned by the English
Antonio rode at dawn
To round up a herd of cattle
Which from their range had gone.
Though young and handsome and happy,
Antonio to fate was resigned;
To die like a man and a cowboy
Was in Antonio's mind.

3

En su cama verdadera
se presentó en su agonía,
faltó de su compañía,
no despertó al cocinero,
un amigo verdadero
que él en el fondo tenía;
se dijo que el mismo día
en visión vió el caballero.

3

For as he slept in the bunkhouse
Antonio had a dream,
A dream of death in the mountains,
By humankind unseen.
The cook he did not waken,
Who was his bosom friend;
And who, they say, in a vision
Foresaw Antonio's end.

4

Otro día en la mañana
salen todos a buscarlo,
recorren montes y valles
y sótanos y cañadas;
por último, de las cansadas,
lo dejan para otro día.
Se ausentó la compañía,
y el muerto quedó tirado.

4

The next morn all went searching,
They searched the land in vain,
They searched the mountain forests,
They searched the sagebrush plain;
They searched from early morning
Until the darkness fell,
But finding nothing, departed
Although they had hunted well.

5

A "La Cebolla" volando
vino el despacho improviso,
dándole a la gente aviso
de lo que estaba pasando;
la gente salió llorando
de compasión alarmada,
y toda muy empeñada
al muerto siguen buscando.

5

To La Cebolla came flying
The unexpected word,
To give the people notice
Of what had just occurred;
The people came out crying
With pity and alarm,
And everyone was fearful
Antonio had suffered harm.

6

Mi Dios, que todo lo mira
y todo pone en acuerdo,
orillas de una colina
hizo que gorjear un cuervo
diciendo: —Aquí está tu siervo
entre esos zacatonales;
hombres, sean razonales,
observen lo que yo observo.—

6

But God who watches and knows
The thing that the searchers seek,
Caused a crow who stood on the hill
These bitter words to speak:
"Below me lies your servant
Among the grasses tall;
Observe the thing that I see,
It's here your friend did fall."

7

El día siete de julio
toda la gente lo halló
al finado Antonio Maestas,
un caballo lo mató.
La gente se estremeció
viendo con asombro el cuerpo
hinchado y desfigurado
y casi todo deshecho.

7

July the seventh they found him,
And all with sorrow were filled,
As they viewed Antonio's body,
Who by a horse was killed.
They turned away in horror,
The blood within them froze,
For the boy, swollen and rotting,
Was disfigured by carrion crows.

8

Llegó Bernabel Trujillo
y mirando tal espanto,
de ternura formó el llanto

8

Then came Bernabel Trujillo
And saw him where he lay,
In tenderness he lamented,

diciéndole: —Hermano mío
¿por qué te hallas tan mustio?
¿Qué es lo que yo estoy mirando,
un hermano de mi vida
en estos campos tirado?—

And crying out did say:
"My brother, what has befallen,
And what is this I see,
So dead and still in the meadow,
Can this thing really be?"

9

Ya salió Ambrosio Espinosa
que es un joven vigilante,
a darle a su gente parte
de muerte tan lastimosa;
y como ágil mariposa
voló en el viento veloz,
con la voluntad de Dios,
en noche tan tenebrosa.

9

Ambrosio Espinosa,
A strong and vigilant youth,
Was sent to bear to the family
The stern and dreadful truth;
And like the agile butterfly
He flew through the winds of the night,
And the will of God sustained him
With courage and with might.

10

Al llano llegó por fin,
donde su padre vivía,
y le dice: —Qué avería
le causé a don Agustín;
padrecito, usted por fin
se tomará este trabajo,
y váyase para abajo;
dé parte a don Agustín.—

10

At last he came to the valley
In which his father dwelt,
And thus he spoke of the matter,
And full of sadness he felt:
"Please go, my dearest father,
And tell Don Agustín
His son lies dead in the mountains,
But gently please begin."

11

Don Benito se salió
y para abajo se fué:
—Buenos días tenga usted,
¿cómo le va, amiguito?—
—Apéese, don Benito,—
le dice don Agustín;
aunque sin saber el fin
se enterneció ¡pobrecito!

11

Don Benito did as requested,
To bear the news he went:
"Good day, little friend. How goes it?
With a message I am sent."
"Dismount, my friend Don Benito,"
Don Agustín calmly did speak;
But though, poor man, he knew nothing,
He suddenly felt weak.

12

—Dispense usted mi venida,
amigo, tan de mañana,
del hijo de sus entrañas
vengo a traerle una noticia.—
Y Maestas, muy asustado
le dice: —¿Qué sucedió?—
Don Benito, recatado
de este modo respondió:

12

"Forgive me for coming so early,
I come to bring you word
Of your beloved Antonio,
Which I have just now heard."
And Maestas, greatly excited,
Exclaimed, "What happened, I pray?"
And Don Benito responded
To Don Agustín this way:

13

—Que al finado Antonio Maestas
un caballo lo mató
en el lugar de "El Mogote,"
ese lugar escogió.—

13

"The late Antonio Maestas"—
Don Agustín's heart was chilled,
"On the mountain called 'El Mogote'
By a bronco has been killed."

14

Maestas el llanto soltó,
desesperado lloró:

14

Maestas cried out in anguish,
"I've lost my only joy;

—Perdí todo mi caudal,
perdí todo mi tesoro,
y sólo a mi Dios imploro.—
Le dice a la Martinita
—Ya murió tu esposo, hijita,
ya se acabó tu decoro.—

I pray to God in my sorrow
That he may take my boy."
He went to tell Martinita
(She felt a sense of dread),
"Your happiness is finished,
Your husband dear is dead."

15

La joven se desmayó
asustada y macilenta
de noticia tan violenta
que así a sus oídos llegó.
Su pecho en llanto rompió
y entre sollozos decía:
—¡Ay, esposo del alma mía,
qué es lo que te sucedió!

The poor young woman fainted
From shock, surprise, and fears,
At the violent news he related
Which thus had reached her ears.
And sighs and moanings of anguish
Came forth from this breast so true:
"Oh, husband dear of my spirit,
What has become of you!

16

¡Ay, padrecito Atilano,
ay, padrecito Agustín,
ay, hermanos de mi vida,
amado Antonio, hasta el fin!
¿Qué más te podré decir,
esposo y fiel verdadero?
En Dios mi remedio espero,
¡ay, Antonito, hasta el fin!—

"My father Atilano,
And father Agustín,
Oh, brothers of my childhood,
My grief is very keen.
Beloved husband Antonio,
My husband and faithful friend,
In God is my only comfort,
Antonio, till the end."

17

Sale don Agustín Maestas
para "La Cebolla" violento,
cubierto de sentimiento
para traer a su hijo al fin.

Don Agustín saddled his horse,
Consumed with passionate grief,
To give his son the last honors
Would be his only relief.

18

Salen don Agustín Maestas
y don Atilano Herrera
y repasando la Sierra,
pues ya no vían las cuestas;
ni cansancio para las bestias
este día no se sintió.
Al finado Antonio Maestas
un caballo lo mató.

Don Agustín rode northward
With Don Atilano his friend,
Went up to the town of Cebolla
Where the cowboy met his end;
And as they climbed the steep mountain,
The father lashed at his steed.
"I've no pity for horses,
For a horse has done this deed."

19

Llegaron a "La Cebolla"
en donde hallaron el cuerpo,
Antonito preguntando
si lo sucedido es cierto;
más dormido que despierto
don Agustín le decía:
—¡Ay hijo del alma mía!
¿qué de veras estás muerto?—

They came at last to Cebolla
Where the cowboy had been brought,
And gazing down at his body,
The anguished father thought:
"Am I awake? Am I sleeping?
Is this a dream in my head?
An evil dream I am dreaming,
Or are you really dead?"

20

Agustín triste y confuso
a su hijo lo remiraba,
y más ternezas le echaba,
viendo su cuerpo difunto.
Y entre tanto, se dispuso
a ponerlo en el cajón,
y traerlo sin dilación
a su país como es el uso.

20

Don Agustín, sad and bewildered,
Looked down at the corpse of the lad,
And many a deep sigh escaped him,
And these are the thoughts that he had:
"I must take him home in a coffin,
I must take his body down,
And give him a Christian burial
In his own native town."

21

Mas mirando el cuerpo hinchado
indisponible al intento,
sufre nuevo sufrimiento
y lo deja sepultado,
deciéndole a su hijo amado
sus padres enternecidos:
—Adiós, hijito querido
que te nos has ausentado.—

21

But seeing the swollen body
Which would not go in a case,
He knew he must bury the body
At once in that very place.
"Good-bye, beloved Antonio,
Good-bye, my dear little boy;
Alas, alas, you have left us
And taken all our joy."

22

Un grande acompañamiento
lo ha llevado al camposanto
y todos con tierno llanto
le dan sepultura al muerto.

22

In great and solemn procession,
The people from miles around
Accompanied him to the graveyard
And laid him there in the ground.

23

Ahí fueron las ternuras
al golpe de las paladas,
y atravesaban espadas
el pecho de esas criaturas;
despidiéndose muy puras
de este atinado arancel,
a quien un caballo cruel
condujo a la sepultura.

23

And then like swords of anguish,
The heavy spadefuls fell,
And shudders ran through the people
Who had known Antonio well;
They said farewell full of sorrow,
With pity they were filled,
At the memory of poor Antonio
Whom a wild horse had killed.

24

En fin, todo terminó
y hasta sus casas volvieron,
y todos se convinieron
que Antonio Maestas murió;
con más ternura lloró
doña Martinita Herrera
porque ni muerto siquiera
a verlo jamás volvió.

24

At last, when all had been finished
And they to their homes had returned,
And all of the young man's relations
His tragic fate had learned;
Antonio's wife Martinita
Raised up her voice in pain:
"I shall never see my husband
Returning home again."

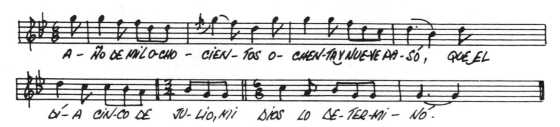

527

Tracing the *corrido*, El Mogote, New Mexico. Celestino Segura is at the left, Mrs. John D. Robb in the center.

Preparing to leave for the site of Maestas' death.

Shepherds pointing to cairn of stones heaped up to mark the spot where Maestas' body was found on the mountain called El Mogote.

Antonio Maestas, subject of the *corrido*.

Don Agustín Maestas, Antonio's father, who figures in the ballad.

Epimenio Chacón, fellow cowboy of Antonio Maestas in 1889 who joined in the search for his body. This photograph was taken in 1947, when Chacón was eighty years old, at Cebolla, New Mexico.

Pedro Trujillo y Chacón, another fellow cowboy of Maestas, in Cebolla, New Mexico, 1947.

Higinio V. Gonzales, composer of the *Corrido de la Muerte de Antonio Maestas.*

José Gallegos (left), singer of the *Corrido de la Muerte de Antonio Maestas,* with Vicente T. Mendoza, in Tierra Azul, New Mexico, 1946.

I18. *Los Vaqueros de Kansas* (The Cowboys of Kansas)
R150, Adolfo Maés, Canjilón, N.Mex., 1949, Robb. Cf. R217, R282, R736, R1453, R1891, RB501, RB753, I29.

<table>
<tr><td>

1

Cuando salimos para Kansas
Con aquella novillada,
¡Ay! ¡qué trabajos pasamos   ]
Por aquella llanada!   ] *Bis*

</td><td>

1

When we went to Kansas
With that herd of cattle,
Ah, what work we had
On that journey!

</td></tr>
<tr><td>

2

Quinientos eran los novillos
Los que íbamos a llevar;
Entre cinco mexicanos
No los pudimos dominar.

</td><td>

2

The cattle numbered five hundred
Which we had to take;
Among five Mexicans
We could not control them.

</td></tr>
<tr><td>

3

Como las nubes eran tan prietas
Y sin alcanzar el corral.
Los truenos eran tan recios   ]
Que nos hacían llorar.   ] *Bis*

</td><td>

3

The clouds were very black
And we were without shelter.
The thunder was so loud
That it made us weep.

</td></tr>
<tr><td>

4

Bajamos al Río Grande.
No había barco en que pasar.
El caporal nos decía
Muchachos, se van a ahogar.

</td><td>

4

We went down to the Río Grande.
There was no boat in which to cross.
The foreman said to us
Boys, you're going to drown.

</td></tr>
<tr><td>

5

Los vaqueros le responden
Todos en general
—Si somos del Río Grande,
De los buenos para nadar.—

</td><td>

5

The cowboys replied
All together
"But we are from the Río Grande,
Let the good ones swim it."

</td></tr>
<tr><td>

6

En el valle de palomos
Salió un novillo huyendo
El caporal lo lazaba   ]
En su caballo berrendo.   ] *Bis*

</td><td>

6

In the valley of doves
A steer went astray
The foreman lassoed him
On his spotted horse.

</td></tr>
<tr><td>

7

La madre de un vaquero
Le pregunta al caporal
¿Qué razón me das de mi hijo,
que no lo he visto llegar?

</td><td>

7

The mother of a cowboy
Asked the foreman
What news can you give me of my son
For I have not seen him arrive.

</td></tr>
<tr><td>

8

Señora, yo le dijera
Pero ha de querer llorar,
Su hijo lo mató un novillo
En las trancas de un corral.

</td><td>

8

Lady, I will tell you
But it will make you weep,
A steer killed your son
Against the logs of a corral.

</td></tr>
</table>

9	9
Si seguimos como vamos	If we keep on as we go
Y como vamos seguimos,	And go as we keep on,
Aquí se acabó cantando	Here is ended the singing
Los versitos de un vaquero.	Of the verses of a cowboy.

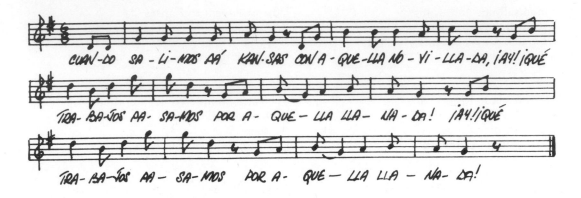

CUAN-DO SA-LI-MOS AA' KAN-SAS CON A-QUE-LLA NO-VI-LLA-DA, ¡AY! ¡QUÉ

TRA-BA-JOS AA-SA-MOS POR A-QUE-LLA LLA-NA-DA! ¡AY! ¡QUÉ

TRA-BA-JOS AA-SA-MOS POR A-QUE-LLA LLA-NA-DA!

I19. *Cowboy Song*

R266, Garcilán Pacheco, Córdova, N.Mex., 1950, Robb. Cf. I5, "Greer County" (R759), "Little Old Sod Shanty" (R760), RB780.

This text, being almost the same as *La Vida del Campero* (I5), is omitted here. The melody, however, is included for comparison with the melody of I5, from which it differs considerably.

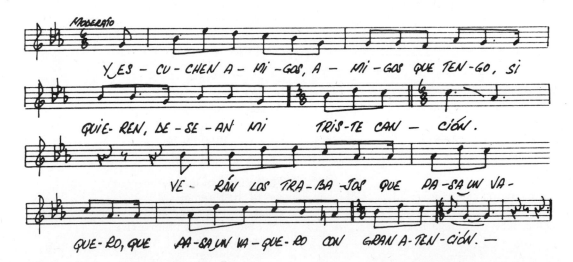

Y ES-CU-CHEN A-MI-GOS, A-MI-GOS QUE TEN-GO, SI

QUIE-REN, DE-SE-AN MI TRIS-TE CAN-CIÓN.

VE-RÁN LOS TRA-BA-JOS QUE PA-SA UN VA-

QUE-RO, QUE AA-SA UN VA-QUE-RO CON GRAN A-TEN-CIÓN. —

The singer, Garcilán Pacheco, composed this song when he was wrangling cattle in Wyoming shortly after leaving a sheep camp in Slater, Wyoming. He described it as a lonely song and yet said that it was written to "make the cowboys laugh." It has to do with loneliness and rattlesnakes and making tortillas and getting wet because the roof of the cow camp leaked (cf. I5 on the life of a shepherd). For more on Pacheco, see *Huapango* (C4).

SAILOR

For a remarkable *romance* from Spain dealing with a sailor, see *El Marinero* (Matos 8a, Parte Literaria, p. 47). It has a Faustian theme, telling of a drowning sailor who, when tempted by the devil, refuses to sell his own soul but is willing to sell anything else, even his wife, in exchange for his life.

I20. *La Cubanita* (The Little Cuban Girl)
R1742, Próspero S. Baca, age 70, Bernalillo, N.Mex., Robb. Cf. R1488.

1
Salí de Cuba con rumbo a España
en una barca de Nuevo León;
de señas traigo una Cubanita,
linda y hermosa como el sol.

1
I left Cuba heading for Spain
In a ship from Nuevo León;
As proof I bring a Cuban girl,
Lovely and beautiful like the sun.

2
La Cubanita vivía en la isla,
y el marinero la enamoró;
la Cubanita lloraba triste
de ver la suerte que le tocó.

2
This Cuban girl was living on the island
And the sailor fell in love with her;
But the Cuban girl wept sadly
On seeing what fate had done to her.

3
La Cubanita lloraba triste
de verse sola en tan ancho mar;
el marinero la consolaba:
—Cubana hermosa, no te has de ahogar.

3
The Cuban girl wept sadly
At seeing herself alone on the high seas;
The sailor tried to console her:
"Beautiful Cuban, you will not drown.

4
Si tú no tienes, Cubana hermosa,
vente conmigo, yo te daré
corales finos, perlas de Oriente,
y todo el oro que yo gané.

4
"If you have nothing, beautiful Cuban,
Come with me. I will give you
Fine corals, pearls of the Orient,
And all the gold that I have earned.

5
Si no me quieres, Cubana hermosa,
Hoy porque vivo en tan ancho mar,
toma mi mano, toma la tuya,
Cubana, ven a tomar.—

5
"If you don't love me, beautiful Cuban,
Today because I live on the high seas,
Put your hand in mine,
Cuban girl, come and enjoy life."

6
El marinero le daba fuerza
a su barca para salir;
la Cubanita lloraba triste:
—¡Por Dios eterno, voy a morir!—

6
The sailor made his ship ready
To leave the harbor;
The Cuban girl wept sadly:
"By the eternal God, I am going to die!"

7
Muy bien se veía pues del barquillo
cuando el trapillo empezaba a arder.
—Marino ingrato, tú me sacaste,
que yo a mis padres no volví a ver.—

7
One could see the ship very well
When they began to hoist the sail.
"Ungrateful sailor, you kidnapped me,
And I never again saw my parents."

8	**8**
Mañana linda,	Beautiful morning,
mañana hermosa del mes de abril;	Lovely April morning;
la Cubanita lloraba triste	The Cuban girl was weeping sadly
de ver la barca que iba a partir.	As the ship was leaving.

I20a. *La Cubanita*
 R1488, Samuel N. Lavadie, age 86, Prado, N.Mex., 1957, Robb. Cf. R1252 (Saltillo, Mexico, 1954).

1	**1**
De Cuba vengo, con rumbo a México	I come from Cuba, to Mexico
en la barquilla de Nuevo León.	In a boat of Nuevo León.
De señas traigo una Cubanita,	To prove it I bring a Cuban girl,
linda y hermosa como es el sol.	Pretty and lovely as the sun.
2	**2**
La Cubanita lloraba triste	The Cuban girl was weeping sadly
de verse sola en tan ancho mar.	At being alone on the wide sea.
El marinero la consolaba:	The sailor tried to console her:
—no llores triste, no te has de ahogar.	"Don't cry so sadly. You'll not drown."
3	**3**
El marinero le daba vuelo	The sailor raised the sail
a su barquilla para salir.	On his boat to leave.
La Cubanita lloraba triste:	The Cuban girl was weeping sadly:
—¡Dios de mi vida, voy a morir!	"God of my life, I am going to die."

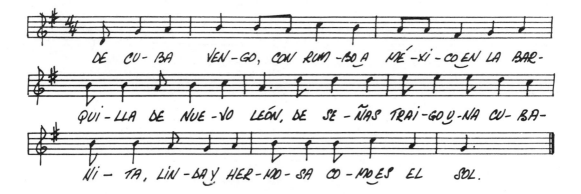

I21. *La Lola y el Buque Maine* (Lola and the Battleship Maine)
 R524, Francisco S. Leyva, age 81, Leyva, N.Mex., 1951, Robb.

1	**1**
Cuando en las playas	When my pretty Lola
mi bella Lola	Goes strolling on the beaches
su lindo talle luciendo va,	Showing off her figure,
los marineros se vuelvan locos	The sailors go crazy
y hasta el piloto perdió el compás.	And the pilot lost his compass.

Coro

¡Ay, qué placer sentía yo!
cuando de las playas sacó
un pañuelo y me saludó.
Luego, después,
se acercó a mí,
me dió un abrazo
y en aquel lazo
sentí que iba a morir.

Chorus

Oh, what pleasure I used to feel
When she took out her handkerchief
And waved at me.
Then afterward
She approached me,
And gave me a hug
And in her embrace
I thought I'd die.

2

El Buque Maine se fué para España
a ver si hallaba lo que perdió;
se encontró con los españoles;
vido a la reina y se sospendió.

2

The battleship Maine went to Spain
To see if it could find what it had lost;
It had an encounter with the Spaniards;
Saw the queen and was astonished.

Coro

Chorus

3

Los españoles, no usan altirantes,
y ni saber comer jamón,
pero en tiempo de una batalla
¡qué bien se fajan el pantalón!

3

The Spaniards don't use suspenders,
Nor do they know how to eat ham,
But in time of battle
They give a good account of themselves.

4

Después de un año de no ver tierra
porque la guerra me lo impidió,
me fuí para el puerto donde se hallaba
la que anhelaba mi corazón.

4

After a year of seeing no land
Because the war kept me from it,
I came to port to see the girl,
The girl that my heart longed for.

Coro

Chorus

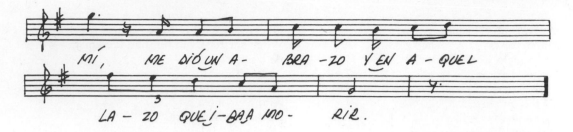

MÍ, ME DIÓ UN A- BRA -ZO Y EN A-QUEL LA - ZO QUE I-BAA MO- RIR.

I22. *La Embarcación* (The Embarkation)
R1722, Próspero S. Baca, age 70, Bernalillo, N.Mex., 1945, Robb. Cf. Mendoza 9g (p. 578).

1	1
Ya se va la embarcación	Now is the time of embarkation.
en una nube ligera;	There are light clouds in the sky.
ya se va, ya se la llevan	Now she is going, they are taking her away,
a la dueña de mi amor.	The one who owns my love.

2	2
Cuando te vayas de aquí	When you go from here
de señas me dejarás;	These tokens you leave me;
un lunar de dos que tienes,	One beauty spot of two that you have,
para atormentarme más.	To torment me the more.

3	3
No lloro porque te vas,	I am not weeping because you are going,
ni lloro porque te alejas;	Nor because you are going far away;
lloro sí porque me dejas	I weep because you leave me
herido del corazón.	With a wounded heart.

4	4
Adiós, jardín de Chihuahua,	Farewell, garden of Chihuahua,
ya terminó la función.	Now the party is over.
Adiós, muchachas bonitas,	Good-bye, pretty girls,
ya se va la embarcación.	Now is the time of embarkation.

WAGONER

I23. *Corrido de Wingate* (Ballad of Fort Wingate)
R738, Francisco S. Leyva, age 81, Leyva, N.Mex., 1951, Robb.

1		1
Para Wingate salimos	]	We started out for Wingate
con cien mil libras de flor.	] *Bis*	With a hundred thousand pounds of flour.

2

Nos dice el gobernador —Echen buñuelos muchachos; que será en su favor.—	] *Bis*

2

The boss says to us:
"Make fritters boys;
That will be to your credit."

3

Nos dice don Manuel Chávez
—Enmelados a mí,
que enmelados son mejores
y agarraron mejor sabor.—

3

Don Manuel Chávez tells us
"Put honey on mine.
They're better that way
And taste better."

Coro

Ahí dirán que sí,
y después que no;
para Wingate con flete,
les da consejos que no.

Chorus

Now you say yes,
Later you'll say no.
On to Wingate with the freight,
We went despite those who said no.

4

Como a las once del día llegamos a La Parida. se volvió Francisco Chávez malo de la rabadilla.	]] *Bis*

4

At about eleven in the morning
We came to La Parida.
Francisco Chávez turned up
With a bad backache.

Coro

Chorus

5

Como a las tres de la tarde
llegamos a La Jornada;
se volvió Francisco Chávez
porque le entró la forzada.

5

At about three in the afternoon
We came to La Jornada;
Francisco Chávez turned up
With a case of loose bowels.

Coro

Chorus

6

La cuestecita de La Nutria
tiene cosa de una milla;
que cortándose una manea
pierden los hombres la vida.

6

The little hill of La Nutria
Is about a mile long;
If the brakes fail here
Men may lose their lives.

Coro

Chorus

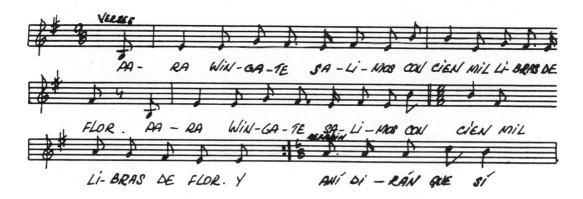

Y DES-PUÉS QUE NO; DA — RA WIN-GA-TE CON

FLE-TE, LES DA CON-SE-JOS QUE NO.

This was one of many songs sung for me by the late Francisco Leyva at Leyva, New Mexico, in 1951. Leyva's grandfather had moved to Leyva, New Mexico, in 1882. Francisco was relatively well-to-do. He told me that he owned three thousand acres of land. This *corrido* was composed by Eustacio Espinosa, later of Cerrillos, New Mexico, who then lived in Galisteo, New Mexico.

Leyva's father owned about ten ox-drawn wagons, each of which could carry 4,000 to 5,000 pounds of freight. He was in partnership with Francisco's uncle and cousin. In 1889, Francisco's father took 100,000 pounds of flour to Fort Wingate. *El Corrido de Win-gate* is about this trip. It was a dry year and they ran out of water and almost died of thirst. Francisco Chávez, of Galisteo, who had three wagons, was afraid and turned back. Most of the oxen died and coming back there was only one team for each two wagons.

Francisco's father, Canuto, the hero of the Fort Wingate trip, often went on long trips with his wagons—as far as Kit Carson, Kansas—and sometimes these trips took six months. He died in 1934 at the age of eighty-eight.

The melody is in the minor mode and resembles that of an *indita*.

COAL MINER

124. *El Buey* (The Ox)
R1490, Samuel M. Lavadie, Prado, N.Mex., 1957, Robb.

1
El buey con ser animal, mamá,
llora de ver el arado;
¿cómo no he de llorar yo, mamá,
si estoy lejos de tu lado?

2
El bucy con ser animal, mamá,
llora por ir a la sierra;
¿cómo no he de llorar yo mamá
si estoy lejos de mi tierra?

3
El primer amor que yo tenga, mamá,
ha de ser de un carbonero;
aunque lo vean tiznado, mamá,
pero ganando dinero.

1
The ox, being an animal, mama,
Weeps at the sight of the plow;
Why should I not weep, mama,
At being so far from your side?

2
The ox, being an animal, mama,
Weeps as he goes to the mountain;
Why should I not weep, mama,
If I am far from my homeland.

3
The first love that I have, mama,
Must be a coal miner;
Although he may get dirty, mama,
He would be earning a living.

538

4

Estoy de noble, mamá,
me voy con un carbonero;
aunque lo vean tiznado, mamá,
pero ganando dinero.

5

Voy hacer una casita, mamá,
con piedritas de ormiguero,
donde me vaya a vivir yo, mamá,
junto con el carbonero.

4

I am of a noble family, mama,
But I go with a coal miner;
Although he may get dirty, mama,
He would be earning money.

5

I am going to build a little house, mama,
With little stones from an ant hill,
Where I am going to live, mama,
Together with the coal miner.

EL BUEY CON SER A-NI-MAL, MA-MÁ, LLO-RA DE VER EL A-RA-DO; ¿CÓ-MO NO HE DE LLO-RAR YO, MA-MÁ, SI E-STOY LE-JOS DE TU LA-DO?

SHOEMAKER

125. *El Zapatero* (The Shoemaker)
   R90, Arthur L. Campa, Chimayó, N.Mex., 1946, Robb. Cf. RB209 (Lummis, California, 1904).

Yo le dije a un zapatero
que me hiciera unos zapatos,
con los piquitos redondos
como los tienen los patos.

Refrán
¡Malhaya zapatero,
o, cómo me engaño!
Me hizo los zapatos,
y el piquito no.

I told an old shoemaker
To make me a pair of shoes,
With the toes all nicely rounded
Like the bill of a duck.

Refrain
O wretched old shoemaker,
How could he cheat me so!
He made me a pair of shoes, yes,
But toes like a duck bill? No!

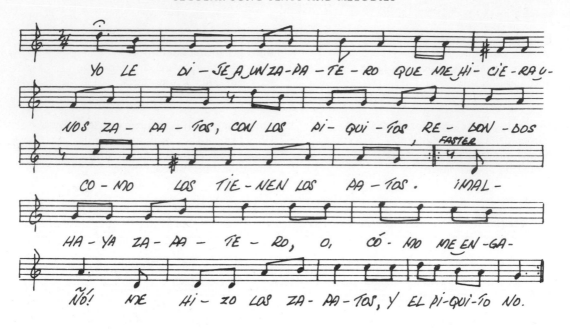

126. *El Zapatero*
R726, Francisco S. Leyva, age 81, Leyva, N.Mex., 1951, Robb.

1	1
El zapatero va a misa,	The shoemaker goes to mass and
no hay algo que rezar,	Having nothing to pray for,
a los santos les pedía	From the saints he asks
chancletas para remendar.	Slippers to mend.

2	2
Hello, my friend,	Hello my friend,
good evening and good night,	Good evening and good night,
palabras misteriosas,	Mysterious words,
Compuesto, ya es *all right.*	They're fixed now, it's all right.

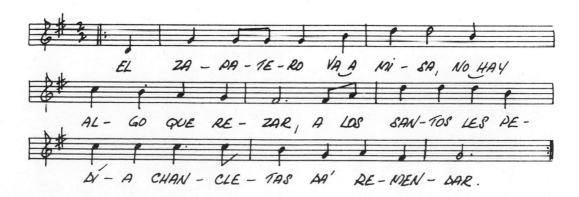

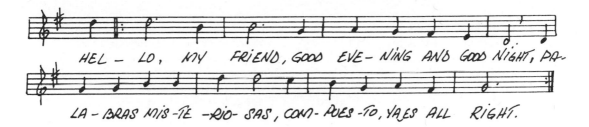

HEL - LO, MY FRIEND, GOOD EVE-NING AND GOOD NIGHT, PA-

LA-BRAS MIS-TE-RIO-SAS, COM-PUES-TO, YA ES ALL RIGHT.

FARMER

I27. *Punta y Punta* (Point by Point)

Mendoza 9d (p. 457), Eduardo Ulibarrí, age 78, Las Vegas, N.Mex., 1945, Cobos. Cf. H2 (a plague of locusts).

Punta y punta,
punta y punta,
cobaitine
yebaitine ya
hfú, hfú, hfú,
hfú, hfú, hfú.

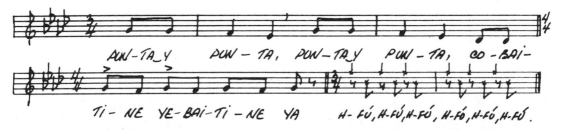

PUN-TA Y PUN-TA, PUN-TA Y PUN-TA, CO-BAI-

TI-NE YE-BAI-TI-NE YA H-FÚ, H-FÚ, H-FÚ, H-FÓ, H-FÚ, H-FÚ.

Threshing wheat in Trampas, New Mexico, in the 1940's.

Threshing wheat in Andalucía, Spain, in 1970.

This song text from Mendoza bears the initials of Virginia Rodríguez Rivera, wife of Vicente Mendoza, and was apparently transcribed by her from the Cobos recording. Mendoza describes it as an Indian wheat-threshing song used, as he told me, when the wheat was tossed into the air on a windy day so that the chaff would be blown away.

The words *cobaitine* and *yebaitine* are possibly of Indian origin, while the word *hfú* simulates the sound of the wind.

The musical transcription of Vicente T. Mendoza is followed by this comment: "Es canción antigua. Se usaba en 1867" (It is an old song. It was used in 1867).

128. *La Mata de Maíz* (The Cornfield)
R724, Francisco S. Leyva, age 81, Leyva, N.Mex., 1951, Robb.

<table>
<tr><td>

1
Yo tengo una mata de maíz,
la siembré en el puro llano.
Con lo caliente del país
y el fuego del verano
la mata no tuvo raíz
ni lo tiene otro grano.

(Verse 1 se repite)

</td><td>

1
I have a cornfield,
I sowed it on the open prairie.
With the warming of the country
And the drought of summer
The field did not take root
Nor did the other grain crops.

(Verse 1 is repeated)

</td></tr>
</table>

Verses 2 and 3 undecipherable

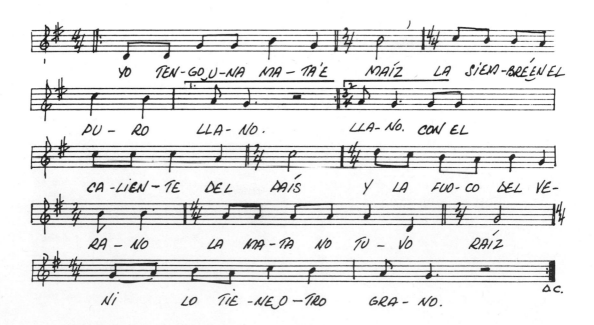

542

LABORER

129. *Los Reenganchados a Kansas* (Contract Laborers to Kansas)
   "Corridos of the Mexican Border," by Brownie McNeil, in Boatright, Texas 18 (vol. 21, p. 13), Texas, 1946, Brownie McNeil.

1

Un día tres de septiembre
¡Qué día tan señalado!
que salimos de Laredo
para Kansas reenganchados.

2

Cuando salimos de Laredo
me encomendé al santo fuerte
porque iba de contrabando
por ese lado del puente.

3

Uno de mis compañeros
gritaba muy afanado:
—Ya nos vamos reenganchados
a trabajar al contado.—

4

Corre, corre, maquinita,
por esa línea del Quiri,
anda a llevar este enganche
al estado de Kansas City.

5

Salimos de San Antonio
con dirección a Laguna,
le pregunté al reenganchista
que si íbamos para Oklahoma.

6

Respondió el reenganchista:
—Calle, amigo, no suspire,
pasaremos de Oklahoma
derechito a Kansas City.—

7

Ese tren a Kansas City
es un tren muy volador,
corre cien millas por hora
y no le dan todo el vapor.

8

Yo les digo a mis amigos:
—El que no lo quiera creer,
que monte en el Santa Fe,
y verá donde está él amanecer.—

1

One day the third of September,
Oh, it was the appointed day!
We left Laredo
Signed up for Kansas.

2

When we left Laredo
I committed myself to the strong saint
Because I was traveling illegally
On that side of the bridge.

3

One of my companions
Shouted very excitedly:
"Now we are going under contract
To work for cash."

4

Run, run, little machine,
Along that Katy line,
Carry this party of laborers
To the state of Kansas City.

5

We left San Antonio
In the direction of Laguna,
I asked the contractor
If we were going through Oklahoma.

6

The contractor replied:
"Quiet, friend, don't even sigh,
We shall pass through Oklahoma
Right straight to Kansas City."

7

That train to Kansas City
Is a flying train,
It goes one hundred miles per hour
And they don't give it all the steam.

8

I say to my friends:
"Let him who doesn't want to believe it
Get aboard the Santa Fe
Just to see where he will be by morning."

9
Al llegar a Kansas City
nos queríamos regresar,
porque nos dieron el ancho
con las veras de alinear.

10
Decían los americanos
con muchísimo valor:
—Júntense a los mexicanos
para meterlos en la unión.—

11
Nosotros le respondimos:
—Lo que es la unión no entramos,
ésta no es nuestra bandera
porque somos mexicanos.

12
Si nos siguen molestando
nos vamos a regresar
para el estado de Texas
donde hay en que trabajar.—

13
Agarramos un volante,
trabajamos noche y día,
no más daban de comer
sólo purita sandía.

14
Vuela, vuela, palomita,
párate en ese manzano,
estos versos son compuestos
a todos los mexicanos.

15
Ya con ésta me despido
por la flor del granado,
aquí se acaba cantando
los versos de los reenganchados.

9
On arriving at Kansas City
We wanted to return,
Because they gave us a raw deal
With the aligning bars.

10
The Americans said
With a great deal of bravery:
"Round up the Mexicans
So as to put them in the union."

11
We replied to them:
"We will not join this thing called union,
This is not our flag
Because we are Mexicans.

12
"If you continue to bother us
We will go back
To the state of Texas
Where there is work."

13
We got in a gang.
We worked night and day,
All they gave us to eat
Was plain watermelon.

14
Fly, fly, little dove,
Light on that apple tree,
These verses are composed
For all the Mexicans.

15
Now with this I bid farewell
By the flower of the pomegranate,
Here one stops singing
The verses about those under contract.

MILLER

I30. *El Molinero* (The Miller)

R723, Francisco S. Leyva, age 81, Leyva, N.Mex., 1951, Robb. Cf. R1487; Schindler 14a (Parte Musical, no. 63, no. 64).

1		**1**
Por todo este llano	]	I have a fine field where
tengo que sembrar	] *Bis*	Each season I grow
maíz y trigo blanco	]	Both wheat and fine corn from
para mi molinar.	] *Bis*	The seed that I sow.
Coro		*Chorus*
Quite, quite, quite,	]	Take it, take it, take it,
yo lo quitaré;	] *Bis*	I'll take it away.
soy molinerinerito	]	To grind out the flour in
yo lo harinarinaré.	] *Bis*	My own special way.
2		**2**
Por todo este llano	]	Each year I must clean out
tengo que sacar	] *Bis*	The ditch in my land
una acequia jonda	]	And make it a deep one
para mi molinar.	] *Bis*	And clean out the sand.
Coro		*Chorus*
3		**3**
Por toda esta mesa	]	I search on the mesa
tenemos que andar	] *Bis*	And search with a will
buscando metates	]	For rock for metates
para mi molinar.	] *Bis*	To use in my mill.
Coro		*Chorus*
4		**4**
Por todo este monte	]	I go to the mountains
tenemos que andar	] *Bis*	To cut wooden pegs
buscando clavijas	]	To use in my mill
para mi molinar.	] *Bis*	Though it's hard on my legs.
Coro		*Chorus*

I have given a rather free translation of this song. Literal translations, though more faithful, miss the lilt and gaiety of the rhymed originals. Rather than a dreary series of literal translations, I have in a number of cases compromised in order to preserve a song's spirit, while retaining at least the general idea of its actual sense.

J. PATRIOTISM, HISTORY, POLITICS

Patriotism. It is heartening to know that there are those so filled with love and gratitude to our country and the freedoms it protects that they have felt impelled to compose and sing songs inspired by that love and gratitude. This patriotism coupled with an interest in history as seen through local eyes and a really consuming interest in politics are reflected in the song texts that I have included in this section.

A number of the songs appearing here—and many in the other categories classified by subject matter—could also logically be listed under other headings. Some of the patriotic songs, for instance, might have been included in Section I under "Soldier." Likewise, scattered through other sections of this book are song texts which, though classified by form under other headings, attest a deep feeling of patriotism for our great country. For instance the twelfth verse of *Los Islas Hawaiianas* (B41) translates:

> We are not composers
> Or inclined to being poets.
> We composed these verses
> To teach patriotism.

Political. One of the manifestations of popular music among New Mexicans of Hispanic origin is the writing of popular songs with texts in Spanish in behalf of candidates in political campaigns or in favor of or in opposition to certain measures, such as constitutional amendments to be voted on by the people. A typical example of these is the really rousing *corrido* sung by the Mexican singer Tito Guizar that was broadcast daily during the 1952 election campaign in behalf of Dennis Chávez, candidate for United States senator from New Mexico on the Democratic ticket.

Some of these ballads are of considerable age. Because of their rather topical character they do not, however, enjoy the general popularity of songs of a more general character and tend to die out as their *raison d'être* ceases. Nevertheless they possess a folk quality because their composers, steeped in the folk music of the people as it has developed, naturally adopt in their compositions the idioms of folk music.

At least some *corridos* are commissioned by the candidates or their campaign managers. Others are commissioned by organizations interested in the passage or defeat of some measure to be submitted to the people on the ballot. Others are composed simply because of the interest of the composer in some candidate or issue.

For an interesting and well-documented political ballad dealing with the Republican state convention of 1920, at which Governor Larrazolo was denied renomination, see *Corrido de Larrazolo* (R560). Larrazolo's career is documented in *Octaviano Larrazolo, A Political Portrait* (Bulletin No. 32, Albuquerque: Division of Research, Department of Government, University of New Mexico, 1952).

PATRIOTIC

J1. *Hymn to the Statehood of New Mexico*
R513, Francisco S. Leyva, age 81, Leyva, N.Mex., 1951, Robb.

1

Gloria a Dios en las alturas,
y al hombre en la tierra paz.
¡Gloria! ¡Viva la libertad!
Dios bendijo a sus criaturas
concediéndoles la igualdad.
¡Gloria! ¡Viva la libertad!

1

Glory to God in the highest,
And to men, peace on earth.
Glory! Long live liberty!
God blessed his creatures
Granting them equality.
Glory! Long live liberty!

Coro	Chorus
¡La Unión para siempre!	The Union forever!
Viva proclamada	Let it be proclaimed
teniendo presente	Maintaining always
la Unión de igualdad.	A Union of equality.
Pues los Nuevo Mexicanos	Now the New Mexicans
gozan de felicidad.	Rejoice in happiness.
¡Gloria! ¡Viva la libertad!	Glory! Long live liberty!

2	2
Gloria a los hombres que hicieron	Glory to the men who drafted
tan buena Constitución.	Such a good Constitution!
Gloria! Viva la libertad!	Glory! Long live liberty!
Pues unidos ellos vieron	Well, united, they saw
la necesidad de unión.	The necessity of union.
¡Gloria! ¡Viva la libertad!	Glory! Long live liberty!

Coro	Chorus

3	3
Cuando se reunió el Congreso	When Congress came to order
en su sesión regular,	At its regular session,
Gloria! Viva la libertad!	Glory! Long live liberty!
trabajaron en exceso	They worked excessively hard
para conseguir la paz.	To maintain peace.
¡Gloria! ¡Viva la libertad!	Glory! Long live liberty!

Coro	Chorus

4	4
Finalizó la sesión	The session ended
no podiendo acordinar	Without an agreement
Gloria! Viva la libertad!	Glory! Long live liberty!
y Taft de buen corazón	And Taft out of goodness of heart
llamó una sesión especial.	Called a special session.
¡Gloria! ¡Viva la libertad!	Glory! Long live liberty!

Coro	Chorus

5	5
Agosto día veintiuno	On the twenty first day of August
finalizó la sesión,	The session ended,
Gloria! Viva la libertad!	Glory! Long live liberty!
y con un voto oportuno	And by an opportune vote
se firmó nuestra admisión.	They signed our admission.
¡Gloria! ¡Viva la libertad!	Glory! Long live liberty!

6	6
Lo que nos falta paisanos	Countrymen what we must learn
es ver en primer lugar	Is, in the first place
¡Gloria! ¡Viva la libertad!	Glory! Long live liberty!
como buenos ciudadanos	To be good citizens
quien nos ha de gobernar	Who must govern ourselves,
¡Gloria! ¡Viva la libertad!	Glory! Long live liberty!

Coro	Chorus

J2. *La Patria Idolatrada* (The Beloved Country)
R515, Francisco S. Leyva, Leyva, N.Mex., 1951, Robb.

1

O patria idolatrada,
tu nacional bandera
rompe la idea ligera
y el grito nacional.

1

O beloved country,
Your national flag
And the national cry of loyalty
Are not to be taken lightly.

2

¡Vivan valientes!
héroes que patria no negaron
y que con sangre compraron
la cara libertad.

2

Hail to the valiant men
Who did not deny our country
And who bought with their blood
Our precious liberty.

3

Marchemos al progreso
por bien de la Unión;
tres meses de él es eso
de la constitución.

3

Let us march forward in progress
For the good of the Union;
It took us three months
To get our constitution.

NAL BAN-DE-RA ROM-PE LA I-DEA LI-GE-RA Y EL GRI-TO NA-CIO-NAL. ¡VI-VAN VA-LIEN-TES! HÉ-ROES QUE PA-TRIA NO NE-GA-RON Y QUE CON SAN-GRE COM-PRA-RON LA CA-RA LI-BER-TAD.

J3. *A Los Soldados de Cuarenta y Dos* (To the Soldiers of Forty-two)
R39, Próspero S. Baca, age 70, Bernalillo, N.Mex., 1942, Robb.

1
San Lorenzo, santo amado,
te pido de corazón,
ayuda a nuestros soldados
a defender la nación.

1
Saint Lorenzo, blessed saint,
I implore thee from my heart,
Help our soldiers
To defend the nation.

2
Con tu escudo verdadero
y tu santa voluntad
que peleyen con esmero
y reine la libertad.

2
That with thy shield of truth
And thy holy will
They may fight skillfully so
That liberty may reign.

3
Libértalos de la muerte
!O dulcísimo Jesús!
Con una escala más fuerte
que es la de la Santa Cruz.

3
Save them from death,
O sweetest Jesus,
With the strongest shield,
That of thy holy cross!

4
Defiéndelos en la lucha
que peléen con lealtad;
pues a ti el Señor te escucha,
te pido la libertad.

4
Defend all those
Who fight with loyalty;
Accept our prayer, O Lord,
As we pray for liberty.

5
A esta América del Norte
y también a sus aliados
les van a echar una buena parte
para todos sus soldados.

5
To this North America
And to its allies
Deign to give great support
For all thy soldiers.

6

Todos estén bien unidos
y que peleyen con valor
para que vivan reunidos
bajo la ley del Señor.

6

That they may fight with valor
For the United States
So that they may live united
Under the law of the Lord.

7

Con gran júbilo y gloria
que vuelvan a sus hogares,
la palma de la victoria
a poner en tus altares.

7

With great joy and glory
May they return to their homes,
To place the palm of victory
Upon your altars.

8

San Lorenzo, gran patrón,
vuelve a las madres su hijo,
con tu santa bendición
y con un gran regocijo.

8

Saint Lorenzo, great patron,
Restore the son to his mother,
With thy holy benediction
And with great rejoicing.

9

A las esposas su esposo
devuélvelos a su lado,
con gran libertad y gozo
!O Jesús Sacramentado!

9

The husband to his wife
Restore in his turn
With great liberty and joy
O Jesus, Holy One.

10

En nombre de nuestro patrón
Jesús con divina mano
échanos tu benedición
a este pueblo americano.

10

In the name of our patron
Jesus with thy divine hand
Grant thy blessing
To the American people.

11

El pueblo triste sigue
de ver la guerra en la Europa.
San Antonio lo proteja
con las celestiales tropas.

11

The sad people turn
Toward the war in Europe.
Saint Anthony, protect them
With the celestial armies.

12

Devotas de San Antonio,
pídanle a Dios infinito
que con su poder inmenso
hoy se acabe este conflicto.

12

Followers of Saint Anthony,
Pray to the infinite God
That he, with his immense power,
Today may end this conflict.

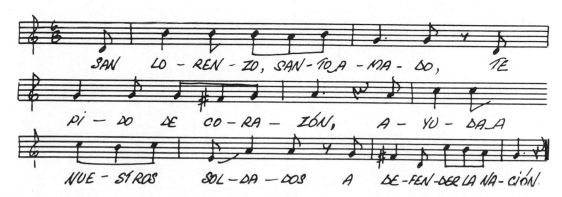

SAN LO-REN-ZO, SAN-TO A-MA-DO, TE PI-DO DE CO-RA-ZÓN, A-YU-DA A NUE-STROS SOL-DA-DOS A DE-FEN-DER LA NA-CIÓN.

J4. *Cuba en Guerra* (Cuba in the War)
RB783, Eleuto Medina, Taos, N.Mex., Cobos.

1

Cuba es, la que por su guerra
fué causa que esta nación
se levantara en armas
para defender la Unión.

1

Cuba, because of its war,
Was the cause that this nation
Took up arms
To defend the Union.

2

Estos eran dos amigos
que por su patria y Unión
fueron a perder sus vidas
en los campos de honor.

2

There were two friends
Who for their fatherland and Union
Were to lose their lives
On the fields of honor.

3

Uno tenía a su madre,
el otro tenía a su amor;
se despiden de su patria
dándole el último adiós.

3

One of them had a mother,
The other had a sweetheart;
They bade farewell to their country
Giving it their last good-bye.

4

Adiós le dice el amante
y con canción le rogó
que le diera mil abrazos
y en sus labios la besó.

4

Good-bye says the lover
And with a song he prayed
That she'd give him a thousand embraces
And a kiss upon the lips.

5

Adiós, estimada prenda,
adiós, adorada flor;
me pesa el haber nacido
y experimentado el amor.

5

Good-bye, esteemed sweetheart,
Farewell, adored flower;
I mourn the fact that I was born
And learned what love is.

6

Cuando se iba a despedir
el amante de su amor
ella le regaló un diamante
y a sus labios lo besó.

6

When the time came to leave
The sweetheart gave a diamond
To her beloved
And kissed him on the lips.

7

Adiós, prenda querida,
dueña de mi corazón;
ruégale a Dios que con vida
vuelva a formar nuestra unión.

7

Farewell, my beloved betrothed one,
Mistress of my heart;
Pray to God that I may return alive
To consummate our union.

8

Adiós, madre querida,
que ésta sí es separación;
no te culpo que me llores
si soy de tu corazón.

8

Good-bye, beloved mother,
Now I really must go;
Don't blame yourself for weeping
For you love me in your heart.

9

Sus desdichas y amarguras
la prometida lloró,
de ver que a su fino amante
a verlo jamás volvió.

9

The promised one wept
In misfortune and bitterness,
Realizing that her fine lover
Would never return to see her again.

J4a. *Cuba*
R730, Francisco S. Leyva, age 81, Leyva, N.Mex., 1951, Robb.

1

Cuba es la que por su guerra
fué causa que esta nación
se levantara en armas
para defender la Unión.

1

Cuba is the one that
Was the cause that this nation
Took up arms
To defend the Union.

2

Y estos eran dos soldados
que por su patria y Unión
salen a perder la vida
por los campos de honor.

2

And there were two soldiers
Who for their country the Union
Left to lose their lives
On the fields of honor.

3

Y uno tenía a su madre
y el otro tenía a su amor.
Con su fusil y su sable
se presentan con valor.

3

And the one had his mother
And the other had his lover.
With their rifle and their sword
They present themselves with courage.

4

Y él que tenía a su madre
con caricia la abrazó
y la estrechó en sus brazos
y en la boca la besó.

4

And the one who had a mother
With a caress embraced her
And held her tightly in his arms
And kissed her on the mouth.

5

Y él que tenía a su amante
al darle el último adiós
El le regaló un diamante,
y ella brindó una flor.

5

And the one who had a lover
To say his last good-bye
He gave her a diamond,
And she offered him a flower.

553

J5. *Natalicio de Washington* (Washington's Birthday)
R1486, Samuel M. Lavadie, age 86, Prado, N.Mex., 1957, Robb.

1

Hoy conmemoramos
el día de Washington,
cantando por las calles
en grande batallón.

Coro

¡Que viva la nación,
que viva la nación,
que flote la bandera
en el campo de honor!

Tarram, tarram, tarram,
tarram, tarram, tarram,
con pitos y tambores
hoy día de Washington.

2

El primer presidente
de nuestra grande unión
fué un hombre muy valiente
llamado Washington.

Coro

3

Fusiles disparemos
en conmemoración
de feliz nacimiento
de George Washington.

Coro

4

La bandera de la unión
denota nuestro honor;
así fué preservada
por toda la nación.

Coro

1

Today we commemorate
Washington's birthday,
Singing through the streets
In a great battalion.

Chorus

Long live the nation,
Long live the nation,
Long float the flag
In the field of honor!

Tarram, tarram, tarram,
Tarram, tarram, tarram,
With fife and drum
This day is Washington's.

2

The first president
Of our grand union
Was a very brave man
Called Washington.

Chorus

3

We fire off guns
In commemoration
Of the happy birth
Of George Washington.

Chorus

4

The flag of the union
Is the symbol of our honor;
So it was preserved
For all the nation.

Chorus

BA-TA-LLÓN. ¡QUE VI-VA LA NA-CIÓN, QUE VI-VA LA NA-CIÓN, QUE FLO-TE LA BAN-DE-RA EN EL CAM-PO DE HO-NOR! TA-RRAM, TA-RRAM, TA-RRAM, TA-RRAM, TA-RRAM, TA-RRAM CON PI-TOS Y TAM-BO-RES, HOY DÍA DE WA-SHING-TON.

POLITICAL

J6. *Corrido de Clyde Tingley*
R313, Salomón Ruiz, age 40, Tijeras, N.Mex., 1950, Robb.

1
Desde que nació la aurora
brilló en aquel pensamiento
de un hombre que el pueblo adora
y aprecia cada momento.

1
With the birth of day
A certain mind was inspired,
That of a man the people adore
And appreciate each moment.

2
Desde el este llegó un día,
y nadie se daba cuenta.
Demostró su simpatía
al pueblo que hoy representa.

2
From the east he came one day,
And no one noticed him at first.
Soon he demonstrated his sympathy
For the people he now represents.

3
Tingley fué de los primeros
así lo quiso su suerte
de los buenos caballeros
que vinieron a Albuquerque.

3
Tingley was one of the first,
So did his luck direct him,
Of the good gentlemen
Who came to Albuquerque.

4
Asina el pueblo se basa,
gozando de lo mejor
con el vato de la rosa
llegó a ser governador.

4
And so the people form their opinion,
And he enjoyed the best;
With that rose which became his trademark
He went on to become governor.

5

Cuando en su administración
hizo su cuenta cabal
le nació de corazón
ponernos un hospital.

5

When his administration made its report,
He saw fit
And found the means
To give us a hospital.

6

Con toda cordialidad
demostró su amor sincero,
le ha formado a la ciudad
un parque de lo primero.

6

With all cordiality
He demonstrated his sincere love,
And he gave to the city
A fine and first-rate park.

7

Tingley demostró su nombre
y se cumplió su deseo
para que el pueblo se asombre
formó un bono de recreo.

7

Tingley made a name for himself
And his wish came true
And that all may wonder more
He created a bond issue for recreation.

8

Entre desmantes y cobres,
Aquella perlita fina.
El amigo de los pobres
que al pueblo oscuro ilumina.

8

Conservative yet progressive,
He remained a fine pearl.
The friend of the poor,
He enlightens the humble and obscure.

9

Así queremos señores,
a decirlo me resuelvo
de los buenos servidores
que se paran por el pueblo.

9

And so we wish to speak, gentlemen,
And I resolve to speak
About all good civil servants
Who stand up to defend their people.

10

Amigos, pues no se sientan.
La verdad se las presento.
Hay muchos que representan
el veinte y cinco por ciento.

10

My friends, do not take offense.
I present the truth to you.
But there are many who represent
Only twenty-five percent.

11

Hago mis cuentas cabales
y les hablo a lo presente.
Políticos no formalas
que desprecian a su gente.

11

I think simply and count clearly
And now I speak in like manner.
There are many insincere politicians
Who despise their own people.

12

Prometen torres de viento;
hablan con mucha franqueza;
jurando ya están en el asiento
hacen falsa su promesa.

12

They promise castles in the air;
They speak very smoothly;
But once they take office
Their promises prove false.

13

Por eso con libertad
les dirijo lo presente.
Yo les hablo on realidad
para que lo sepa la gente.

13

And so as a free man
I direct my words today.
I speak in reality
That the people may hear and know.

This song is a political ballad composed by Salomon Ruiz out of admiration for the late Clyde Tingley, one of the composer's political heroes and one of the most colorful politicians of New Mexico's history. Tingley, who became mayor of Albuquerque and later governor of New Mexico, was a somewhat unlettered man whose homespun grammar and malapropisms became locally famous. On one occasion when he was showing a visitor from the East some of the monuments to the name of Tingley in Albuquerque, his guest remarked, "If you don't watch out, they'll be canonizing you." Tingley thrust out his jaw and replied: "Let them try it. That's what them damned Republicans have been trying to do for years."

When, as governor during World War II, Tingley insisted on being taken in to see President Franklin D. Roosevelt by his political associate, Senator Dennis Chávez—an interview to which the president had consented with great reluctance in view of the harassing burdens of the war—the president showed his displeasure by sitting back in silence, forcing the senator and governor to talk to one another. Senator Chávez, in desperation for something to say, remarked that he had heard that Tingley's secretary was about to get married. Tingley replied, "It looks that way. She's gettin' her *torso* ready." At this President Roosevelt sat up, and his whole demeanor changed to one of charmed interest.

Once when Tingley was hunting geese from a blind in the Río Grande he shot one and it fell in the river. As it started drifting downstream, Tingley did as any true hunter would: he stripped to the skin and plunged into the icy waters. As he approached the goose, which had only been winged, it paddled to the shore and waddled down the main street of the village of Los Chávez with the unabashed Tingley stark naked in hot pursuit.

Many old-timers remember Tingley with admiration, although at times his actions were as outrageous as his speech. On occasion he arrogantly took advantage of his political muscle.

J7. *Elfego Baca*
R1625, two girls from Belén, N.Mex., Albuquerque, N.Mex., 1959, Robb.

1	1
¡Escúchenme ciudadanos!	Hear me citizens!
El día cuatro de noviembre,	On November fourth
voten por Elfego Baca	Vote for Elfego Baca,
de Nuevo México siempre.	Who is always for New Mexico.

Coro	*Chorus*
¡Elfego, Elfego Baca!	Elfego, Elfego Baca!
¡Voten por Elfego Baca!	Vote for Elfego Baca!
¡Elfego, Elfego Baca!	Elfego, Elfego Baca!
Teniente Gobernador.	Lieutenant Governor.

2	2
Hombre de honor y cultura,	A man of honor and culture,
Valencia es su condado.	Valencia is his county.
Voten por Elfego Baca,	Vote for Elfego Baca,
hijo nativo y honrado.	An honored native son.

Coro	*Chorus*

Elfego Baca, a relative and namesake of the more famous gunman-sheriff of earlier days, was a handsome, urbane gentleman who, as I remember it, was at the time of this song sheriff of Valencia County, New Mexico. This song was used during his campaign in 1958, when he was a candidate for lieutenant governor of the state.

J8. *Corrido of the Big Five*
R1666, Eduardo Gallegos, age 45, Albuquerque, N.Mex., 1960, Robb.

1

Lo que les quiero decir
no se vayan a olvidar
porque éste es uno
hombre honesto y buena gente
Que siga marchar al frente,
¡Mechem para Gobernador!

1

What I want to tell you
You must not forget
Because this is an
Honest and fine man.
Follow him and march to the front,
Mechem for Governor!

2

Ya acompaña un compañero,
hombre honrado y muy sincero,
para servir nuestro estado
no hay otro mejor.
Le tendremos que ayudar
pero vamos a votar,
buena gente Tom Bolack
Teniente Gobernador.

2

He has a comrade,
An honorable, sincere man,
To serve our state
There isn't a better one.
We have to help him
By going to vote,
Tom Bolack is a good fellow
For Lieutenant Governor.

3

¡Ay, ay, ay, ay!
No tienes que te engañen
por honesto y por buen gallo
En el día diez de mayo
por Ed Mechem y Tom Bolack
tendremos que votar.

3

Ay, ay, ay, ay!
Don't cheat yourself
For an honest and a he-man
On the tenth day of May
We all have to vote
For Ed Mechem and Tom Bolack.

4

Spoken:
Que vivan los *Big Five* honestos
The *Big Five*—heh—ohoy,
viva Bill Colwes
y también Dean Robb
así como de Ed Balcomb
el quinteto más famoso
y sé que es muy cierto
que siempre van a triunfar.

(Verso 1 se repite)

4

Spoken:
Long live the Big Five honest men
The Big Five—heh—ohoy,
Long live Bill Colwes
But also Dean Robb
And Ed Balcomb also,
The most famous quintet
And it is very certain
That they are always going to triumph.

(Verse 1 repeated)

LO QUE LES QUIE-RO DE-CIR NO SE
VA-YAN OL-VI-DAR POR-QUE ÉS-
TE ES U-NO HOM-BRE HO-NES-TO Y BUE-NA
GEN-TE QUE SI-GA MAR-CHAR AL FREN-TE,
¡ME-CHEM PA' GO-BER-NA-DOR! ¡AY.
AY, AY, AY! NO TIE-NES QUE TE EN-GA-
ÑAR POR HO-NE-STO Y POR BUEN GA-LLO
EN EL DÍ-A DIEZ DE MA-YO
POR ED ME-CHEM Y TOM BO-LACK
TEN-DRE-MOS QUE VO-TAR.

This song of relatively recent and well-known origin was composed by the late Eduardo Gallegos for the political campaign of 1960. Nevertheless, it has the true style and flavor of the New Mexican *corrido*. The Big Five were the five Republican candidates for governor, lieutenant governor, United States senator, and two congressmen-at-large.

As a candidate for the United States House of Representatives, the author is mentioned in the song with four words: "y también Dean Robb."

J9. *Corrido de Dan R. Sedillo*
RB3, Manuel Cantú and Roberto Gali, Albuquerque, N.Mex., 1948, Robb.

Coro	*Chorus*
¡Ay! Te deseamos la suerte.	Ah, we wish you well.
¡Ay! Que tengas buen destino.	Ah, may you have a good destiny.
¡Ay! Que ni la misma muerte	Ah, may death itself
Pueda tracar tu camino.	Not cross your path.

1

A todo mi pueblo	To all my people
le digo cantando,	I say in song,
si puedo trovar	In simple language
en lenguaje sencillo	If I can find it,
por un amigo	There is a friend
que estimo y lo quiero,	Whom I esteem and cherish,
amigo de todos,	A friend of all,
ese es Dan Sedillo,	This one is Dan Sedillo,
amigo sincero.	A sincere friend.

2

Nació en la frontera	Born on the frontier
al sur del estado,	In the south of the state,
un joven brillante	A brilliant young man
que es muy afamado;	Who is very famous;
él con sus amigos	He with his friends
pues nunca se raja	Indeed never quarreled
y para servirles	And in order to serve
él siempre trabaja,	He always worked,
no lo hallan cansado.	He was never found wanting.

3

Condado de Lincoln	The counties of Lincoln
y también Doña Ana,	And also Doña Ana,
tierra de los hombres	A land of men
que fueron valientes,	Who were brave,
sientan un orgullo	Felt a pride
por Danny Sedillo	In Danny Sedillo
que fué de su ambiente	Who was in his country
joven distinguido	A distinguished young man
y hombre "del mañana."	And a man "of tomorrow."

4

Ahora el destino	Now destiny
lo puso en la cumbre	Lifts him to the heights of
de un puesto importante	An important post
de gran precaución,	Of great responsibility,
pidiéndole al cielo	Imploring the heavens
que siempre lo alumbre	That they shall always enlighten him

y dar buen servicio	That he may give good service
con mucha atención	With much diligence
como de costumbre.	As is his custom.

Coro   *Chorus*

Dan R. Sedillo was a Democratic candidate
for corporation commissioner.

J10. *Corrido de Roosevelt*
RB131, Arvino Martínez, age 35, Tierra Azul, N.Mex., 1951, Robb.

1

Año de mil novecientos
treinta y cinco fué por cierto
que el Presidente Roosevelt
puso el mundo en movimiento.

2

Todo el mundo le comprende
lo dice de corazón
que Roosevelt no es presidente,
él nos dió la desención.

3

Otras naciones lo alumaron
por todo el globo terrestre
que nunca se había visto
un presidente como éste.

4

Cuando se separó Hoover
ya estábamos entendidos
que lo hacía para la gente
que tenía Estados Unidos.

5

Repartió a los mexicanos
cerca de tres cientos mil,
no sabiendo que algún día
alguno le había de servir.

6

Luego preparó Roosevelt
como el sol con resplendor.
El tomó su administración
y con todos sus senadores.

7

Al mes de ser presidente
el soñó un sueño profundo
que todos tienen derecho
de vivir en este mundo.

8

De este país no salga nadie,
ni un negrito, ni un blanquito,
que se ha de llegar el día
que a todos los necesita.

1

It was certain that
In the year of 1935
President Roosevelt
Set the world in motion.

2

All the world understands
And says from the heart
That Roosevelt is not president,
What he gave us was dissension.

3

Other nations were illuminated
Throughout the terrestrial globe
For never had there been seen
A president like this one.

4

When Hoover left
We understood
What he would do for the people
Of the United States.

5

He distributed to the Mexicans
About three hundred thousand,
Not realizing that one day
Someone would have to pay.

6

Then Roosevelt prepared
With a splendor like the sun.
He took office
With all his senators.

7

In the month when he became president
He dreamed a profound dream
That everyone had the right
To live in this world.

8

Let no one leave this country,
Be he black or white,
For the day is bound to come
When everyone will be needed.

9

Pensó de día de noche
y para formar su plan
que se ha de llegar el día
que todos trabajarán.

10

Les dijo a las millionarias,
compañías, y commerciantes
que tenían que cooperar
para los necesitantes.

11

Señor, le vengo a decir
que necesito de hacer.
Yo tengo mucha familia
y no tengo que comer.

12

En este mes de septiembre,
no es mentira lo que cuento,
estamos recibiendo cheques
sin trabajar un momento.

13

Ahora sí va diferente
por valles y serranías;
todos con su pico y pala
parecen infanterías.

14

Se presentan las mujeres,
todititas muy pintadas,
diciendo que son solteras
y duermen acompañadas.

15

Las verán el día del pago
en las cantinas borrachas,
muy echas del permanente
diciendo que son muchachas.

16

De los hombres no les digo
porque a mí me causa pena.
Que un día después del pago
siempre está la cárcel llena.

17

Algunos gastan el cheque,
se olvidan que están casados,
y amanecen en la cárcel
muy crudos y desvelados.

9

He thought day and night
In order to formulate his plan
So that the day could come
When everyone will have a job.

10

He said to the millionaires,
Companies, and merchants
That they had to cooperate
In doing what was necessary.

11

Sir, I come to tell you
What I need.
I have a large family
And I have nothing to eat.

12

In this month of September,
It is no lie that I tell you,
We are receiving checks
Without working for a moment.

13

Now everything is different
In the valleys and hills;
Everyone has a pick and shovel
And they look like infantry.

14

There are women,
All of them rouged,
Saying that they are single
And don't sleep alone.

15

You see them on payday
Drunk in the saloons,
With their new permanents
And saying that they are girls.

16

I don't say these things about the men
Because sorrow overcomes me.
One day after payday
The jail is always full.

17

Some cash their checks,
Forgetting that they are married,
And wake up in jail
Hung over and tired out.

18

A las diez de la mañana
luego llegó la mujer.
Ellas con aquella pena
no la quisieran ver.

18

At ten in the morning
The women come.
They are so upset that
They don't want anyone to see them.

19

Luego los sentencia el juez
y se muestran muy sinceros:
—Tiene usted sesenta días
por andar de parrandero.—

19

Then the judge sentences them
And they are sincerely repentant:
"You get sixty days
For disorderly conduct."

20

Ya con esto me despido,
yo se las puedo probar.
Con el cuento de *relief*
ya no quieren trabajar.

20

Now with this I say farewell,
I can prove these things.
With the relief payments
Nobody wants to work.

21

Estos versos son compuestos
arriba de aquel relis.
Son compuestos por el hombre
que se llama José Ortiz.

21

These verses are composed
Up above that landslide.
They are composed by the man
Who calls himself José Ortiz.

This *corrido* of 1939 is a rather surprising satire on the programs of the New Deal instituted by President Franklin D. Roosevelt. It recalls the interesting fact that during the years preceding the election of Franklin D. Roosevelt, and during the heyday of Senator Bronson Cutting, a very large proportion of the Spanish Americans of the Southwest were Republicans of conservative leanings. Some, although not very many, retain that stance today.

J11. *Corrido de Montoya*
RB820, Los Reyes de Albuquerque, Albuquerque, N.Mex., 1970.

1

Hay un hombre que todos conocemos,]
ciudadano de calibre major,] *Bis*
y su nombre es Joseph M. Montoya]
y no menos que el futuro senador.] *Bis*

1

There is a man whom everyone knows,
A citizen of high quality,
And his name is Joseph M. Montoya,
Our next U.S. senator he'll be.

2

¡Ay, Montoya, vanguardia de la patria!
amante de la justicia y libertad,
un asiento te espera en el Senado.
Te llevaremos a nuestra Capital.

2

Ah, Montoya, leader of our country!
Lover of justice and liberty,
A seat awaits you in the Senate.
In the election you'll see victory.

Instrumental Interlude
"Erviva"

3

No se crean de palabras zabameras
ni promesas (¡quizas cuándo vendrán!)
Hombres sinceros no crecen como yerbas
y aquí hay un hombre que dice la verdad.

3

Words of flattery do not convince,
Nor do promises when bought and sold.
Honest men do not grow on bushes.
The truth Montoya has always told.

4

El partido democrático le alumbra
y en sus alas al triunfo volará.
No olvidemos a los hombres de batalla

y por Montoya todo el mundo votará.

4

The Democratic party has chosen
To ride his wings to triumph for us all.
Let's remember the ones who have helped
    him
And we'll vote for Montoya in the fall.

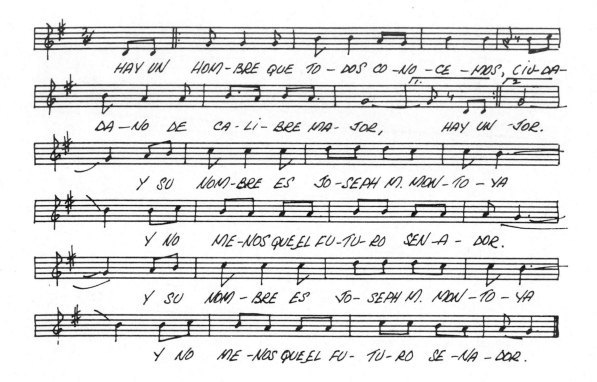

The *Corrido de Montoya* was composed by Lautaro Vergara. The recording is from a commercial disk, Peralta-Ramos Records, ASR, 217642.

K. COURTSHIP AND MARRIAGE

The most frequently encountered songs on the subject of courtship and marriage are the *entregas de novios*, or delivery of the newlyweds. Rubén Cobos has described other wedding songs, including *despedidas* and some songs relating to baptism (Cobos 4, 10/20/49). K4 is one of these.

This much may be said about the *entrega de novios*. In the Spanish villages of New Mexico the wedding is followed by a dance. After the dance is over, the bridegroom, bride, parents, and other relatives of the newly married couple go to the home of the bride or to the couple's new home. They are preceded by "the music," consisting usually of a fiddle and a guitar. At the entrance the bride is delivered to her parents-in-law and the groom to his. The actual *entrega* is sung by the godfather or, if he does not know the verses, by the local *poeta*. These verses have a very tender meaning for the young couple, signifying the inception of the marriage, pointing out its responsibilities and joys. I am told that the young brides particularly sometimes ask to hear it sung on other occasions. The words and the melodies differ in the different villages. One old musician told me that "any old waltz will do for the *entrega*."

Alex Chávez has recorded charming music of the *casorios* (weddings) of the San Luis Valley, Colorado (RB972ff.).

K1. *Entrega de Novios* (Delivery of the Newlyweds)
R431, Félix Ortega, Chimayó, N.Mex., 1951, Robb. See Appendix A.

1
Es un ser infinito
y más un ser verdadero,
pues el mismo Jesucristo
nos lo ha dado a entender.

1
It is an infinite being
And also a true being,
Because Jesus Christ himself
Has made us understand it.

2
Estando el mundo formado
. . . [undecipherable]
con el nombre de Adán,
el mismo que el verdadero.

2
The world being already formed
. . .
With the name of Adam,
The same as the true one.

3
Ya volvieron de sus sueños
con una voz admirable;
te recibo por esposa
para obedecer al Padre.

3
They came back from their dreams
With an admirable voice;
I receive you as my wife
In order to obey the Father.

4
Le hizo que Adán se durmiera
en un hermoso vergel
y le dió una compañera
que se estuviera con él.

4
Now he made Adam go to sleep
In a beautiful garden
And gave him a companion
That should always be with him.

5

Por ser hueso de mi hueso,
por ser carne de mi carne,
te recibo por esposa
para obedecer al Padre.

6

Ya de la iglesia salieron
con muchísima alegría;
ya quedaron esposados
como San José y María.

7

Piensan los malos casados,
piensan a Dios engañar;
ellos son los engañados;
no se vayan a equivocar.

8

Atiéndame, el esposado,
lo que le voy a mentar;
ya no hay padre, ya no hay madre,

ahora lo que hay es mujer.

9

Atiéndame la esposada,
de amor muestre su cariño;
ya no hay padre y no hay madre

ahora lo que hay es marido.

10

Los padrinos de estos novios
ya saben su obligación:
de entregar a sus ahijados
y echarles la bendición.

11

Los padres de estos novios
que ha de aumentar su cariño,
ya aquí están sus dos hijos
siguiéndoles por el camino.

5

To be bone of my bone,
To be flesh of my flesh,
I receive you as my wife
In order to obey the Father.

6

They came out from the church
With the greatest joy;
Already married
Like Joseph and Mary.

7

Bad spouses think
That they can cheat God;
They are the ones that are cheated;
Do not be mistaken.

8

Hear, o groom,
What I am going to say;
Now you have no father, you have no
      mother,
What you have now is a wife.

9

Hear me, o bride,
And show your love;
Now you have no father, you have no
      mother,
What you have now is a husband.

10

The godparents of these newlyweds
Know their duty:
To give away their children
And give them their blessing.

11

The parents of these newlyweds
Must increase their love,
Here are your two children
Following in your path.

ES UN SER IN-FI-NI-TO Y MÁS UN SER VER-DA-DE-RO, PUES EL MIS-MO JE-SU-CRIS-TO NOS LO HA DA-DO A EN-TEN-DER.

K2. *Entrega de Novios*
R327, Elfego Sánchez, age 63, Tijeras, N.Mex., 1950, Robb. Cf. Cobos 4 (10/20/49).

1

Y Ave María dijo el ave
para comenzar a volar;
y Ave María digo yo
para comenzar a cantar.

1

The bird said Ave Maria
Just before he took flight;
And Ave Maria, I say,
Just before I start to sing.

2

Hizo que Adán se durmiera,
y en un hermoso vergal;
Dios le dió una compañera
para que estuviera con él.

2

He made Adam go to sleep
In a beautiful garden;
God gave him a companion
To be with him.

3

Para empezar a cantar
a Dios le pido memoria
para que nos conserve
como a San Pedro en la gloria.

3

In order to start singing
I ask the Lord for a good memory
So that he will keep us
Like Saint Peter in glory.

4

¡De la sala ya van saliendo
de mañana cuatro rosas!
El padrino y la madrina
y el esposado y su esposa.

4

Early in the morning
Four roses are coming out.
The maid of honor and the best man,
The husband and his wife.

5

¿Qué significan las velas
cuando las van a encender?
Significa un mismo cuerpo
que allí va a permanecer.

5

What do the candles symbolize
When they are going to light them?
They stand for one and the same
Body that the two will be.

6

¿Qué significan las arras
cuando las van a echar?
Significa el matrimonio
y el anillo pastoral.

6

What do the pieces of silver signify
As they are being placed?
They symbolize the pledge of
Matrimony and the pastoral ring.

7

Entre suegros y consuegros
no debe de haber enojos
porque hoy se han conservado
las dos niños de sus ojos.

7

There should not be any
Misunderstanding between in-laws,
Because their two dearest children
Have become one today.

8

Todo este río para abajo
corre la agua cristalina
donde se lavan las manos
el padrino y la madrina.

8

All the length of this Río Abajo
The water runs crystal clear
Where the best man and the
Maid of honor wash their hands.

9

El padrino y la madrina
ya saben su obligación

9

The best man and the maid of honor
Already know their obligation

de entregar a sus hijados
y echarles la bendición.

To give their godchildren in
Marriage and to bless them.

YA - VE MA-RÍ - A DI-JO EL A - VE PA'
CO - MEN- ZAR A VO - LAR; YA - VE MA-RÍ-
A DI-JO YO PA' CO - MEN-ZAR A CAN-TAR.

This same melody, here sung in parallel thirds, appears to be used widely throughout New Mexico for *entregas*, somewhat in the manner of the *décima* melody, on which I have commented above. The *entregas* appear to be usually if not always in 3/4 or 6/8 time.

K3. *Entrega de Novios*
R451, Arvino Martínez, age 25, Abiquiu, N.Mex., 1951, Robb. Cf. Cobos 4 (11/3/49).

1
Este novio y esta novia
ya se fueron a casar
a la iglesia de Logan
al pie de un bendito altar.

1
This bridegroom and this bride
Have just been married
In the church of Logan[1]
At the foot of the blessed altar.

2
De la iglesia va saliendo
un automóbil con rosas.
El padrino y la madrina,
el esposado y la esposa.

2
From the church there is going away
An automobile festooned with roses.
The godfather and the godmother,
The groom and the bride.

3
Dios les conceda la fe
y el poder de su eficacia
y les dé estado de gracia
como a María y San José.

3
God has granted them the faith
And the power of its efficiency
And gave them a state of grace
As he did to Mary and Joseph.

4
Han recibido las arras
y el anillo pastoral.
Es una prueba paterna
que es matrimonio legal.

4
They have received the *arras*[2]
And the pastoral ring.
It is a paternal proof
That the marriage is legal.

[1] Logan is a town in New Mexico.
[2] *Arras* is a pledge of thirteen pieces of money given by the bridegroom to the bride during the wedding.

5	5
Al darles los buenas días y al saber como les va, ya quedaron desposados, haga Dios su voluntad.	As we greet them And know that they are going, They have gone from us, God's will be done.
6	6
El estado no es por un rato ni por un día ni dos; es por una eternidad mientras vivos sean los dos.	Marriage is not for a while, Nor for a day or two; It is for eternity While both are alive.
7	7
Atiéndame, el esposado, lo que le voy a mentar. Esta cruz que se ha echado— no la vaya a abandonar.	Listen, newlyweds, To what I have to tell you. This cross which you have undertaken, Don't abandon it.
8	8
Ya me dirijo a la novia, téngalo siempre advertido ya no hay padre ya no hay madre. Lo que hay ora es su marido.	Now I say to the bride, Always remember There is no longer a father or mother. What there is now is your husband.
9	9
Ya me dirijo al padrino, le hablo con todo cuidado. No olvide usted los consejos que debe darle a su ahijado.	Now I say to the godfather, Speak to him with all care. Don't forget the advice Which you ought to give to your godson.
10	10
Y hablándole a la madrina, con todo muy buen sentido, pues que enseñe a su ahijada que respeta a su marido.	And speaking to the godmother, With the best of wishes I say, Teach your goddaughter To respect her husband.
11	11
A los padres de esta novia: los siento con gran dolor. Ya se les va su hijita, la prenda de su amor.	To the parents of this bride: I know of their great sorrow. They have lost their daughter, The darling of their love.
12	12
No los reciban llorando, recíbanlos con valor, que es una casa sagrada que nos la dotó el Señor.	Do not receive them weeping, Receive them with courage, For this is a sacred house Which God gave us.
13	13
Los compadres y comadres, reciban los desposados; ya la iglesia los unió, ya ellos están casados.	Godfathers and godmothers, Receive the bridal couple; Now the church has united them, Now they are married.

14

El padrino y la madrina
ya saben su obligación:
de entregar a sus ahijados
y echarles la bendición.

14

The godfather and godmother
Know their duty:
It is to deliver the newlyweds
And give them their blessing.

ES-TE NO-VIO Y ES-TA NO-VIA YA SE FUE-

RON A CA-SAR A LA I-GLE-SIA DE

LO-GAN AL PIE DE UN BEN-DI-TO AL-TAR.

K4. *Principio de la Entrega de Bautismo* (Beginning of the Delivery of Baptism)
RB155, Arvino Martínez, age 35, Abiquiu, N.Mex., 1951, Robb.

1

Mi corazón se ha partido
en millones de redosos.
Reciban esta criatura.
Estréchenla en sus brazos.

1

My heart is broken
Into millions of pieces.
Receive this girl I have raised.
Hold her tightly in your arms.

2

Recíbete prenda querida
que de la iglesia saliste
con los santos sacramentos
y el agua que recibiste.

2

Receive this beloved girl
As you come out from the church
With the holy sacraments
And the water which you received.

3

Gracias, compadre y comadre.
Gracias les doy yo presente,
gracias en una palabra
a la atención de la gente.

3

Thanks, godfather and godmother.
I hereby give thanks to you,
Thanks in one word
In the presence of the congregation.

K5. *Entrega de Novios*
Cobos 4 (11/3/49) Pablita Galindo, Las Colonias, N.Mex., 1949, Cobos.

1

Atención pido a la gente
y a este público honrado
para celebrar el enlace
de los recién esposados.

1

Ladies and gentlemen,
I ask for your attention
In order to celebrate the union
Of the newlywed couple.

2

Muy de mañana salieron,
cuatro flores para la iglesia,
el padrino y la madrina,
el esposo y la princesa.

3

El padre les preguntó:
—¿Si quieres casarte di?—
y la iglesia les oyó
que ambos dijeron que sí.

4

El padre con el manual
los pasa por el altar,
les echa las santas arras
y el anillo pastoral.

5

Reciben las santas arras
y el anillo pastoral,
enseña que es una prueba
de un matrimonio legal.

6

Ya de la iglesia salieron
con muchísima alegría
en un estado de gracia
con José y María.

7

Dios los conserve en su gracia,
Dios los conserve en su fe;
los haga buenos casados
como a María y José.

8

El Señor los ha juntado
con su santo matrimonio;
procuren vivir muy bien,
no le den gusto al demonio.

9

Miren que es estar casados
no es para un día ni dos;
es para una eternidad,
mientras que vivan los dos.

10

Ahora óigame usted, la novia,
que ha de aumentar su cariño;
ahora no es padre ni madre,
ahora es su esposo querido.

2

They started early in the morning,
Four flowers for the church,
The godfather and godmother,
The groom and the princess.

3

The priest asked them:
"Do you want to get married?"
And the church heard them
As both of them said "Yes."

4

The priest with the manual
Led them to the altar,
The holy dower was given
As was the pastoral ring.

5

They receive the holy dower
And the pastoral ring,
Which serve as proof
Of a legal marriage.

6

Now they have come out of the church
With the greatest happiness
In a state of grace
With Joseph and Mary.

7

God holds them in his grace,
God holds them in his faith;
He makes them good spouses
Like Mary and Joseph.

8

The Lord has united them
In his holy matrimony;
They endeavor to live a good life
And not to please the devil.

9

Note well that being married
Is not for a day or two;
It is for an eternity,
As long as both shall live.

10

Now let the bride listen to me,
She must increase her tenderness;
Now it is neither father nor mother,
Now it is her beloved husband.

11

Ahora dígame usted, el novio,
lo que le voy a mentar,
que esa cruz que Dios le ha dado
no la vaya a abandonar,
que es un cargo que se ha echado
ante el justo tribunal.

11

Now let the bridegroom hear
What I am going to tell him,
That this cross that God had given him
He must never abandon,
For it is a responsibility
Which the just tribunal has imposed.

12

Si la dejarás por otra,
ella pegará un suspiro;
esa carga usted se ha echado
ante el justo tribunal.

12

If you should leave her for another,
She will weep;
This charge you have been given
Before the just tribunal.

13

Adán con sabiduría
y Dios con su gran poder
de una costilla del hombre
de ahí se formó la mujer.

13

Adam with knowledge
And God with his great power
From the rib of a man
Formed woman.

14

Viéndose con compañía
al momento despertó,
la recibió como esposa
porque Dios se la mandó.

14

Coming before this company
In the early morning,
You received her as your wife
Because God ordained it.

15

Los padres de los esposos
que aumenten su cariño;
reciban a sus dos hijos,
guíenlos por buen camino.

15

The parents of the spouses
Should increase their love;
Take care of the two children,
Guide them to a good life.

16

Lo que la Escritura nota
lo manda la ley divina,
de entregar a sus ahijados
el padrino y la madrina.

16

That which the Scriptures say
The divine law demands,
That the godfather and godmother
Deliver their godchildren.

17

Del cielo viene cayendo
una agua muy cristalina,
donde se lavan las manos,
el padrino y la madrina.

17

From heaven is falling
A pure crystalline water
In which the godfather and godmother
Wash their hands.

18

El padrino y la madrina
ya saben su obligación,
de entregar a sus ahijados
y echarles la bendición.

18

The godfather and godmother
Know well their obligation,
To deliver their godchildren
And give them their benediction.

K6. *Consejos acerca del Matrimonio* (Advice about Marriage)
R43, Jacinto Ortiz, Chimayó, N.Mex., 1945, Robb.

1

Es proverbio verdadero
y merece la atención
que antes de entrar en unión
debe pensar el soltero.
Este es el paso primero
que debe considerar:
que si se quiere casar
debe reflejarlo bien,
porque después no halla quien
se lo pueda remediar.

1

It is a true proverb
And merits attention
That before getting married
The bachelor ought to think twice.
This is the first thing
That he ought to consider:
That if he wants to get married
He ought first to think it over
Because afterward there is no one
That can help him.

2

Más para elegir su enlace
y que no le salga mal,
una mujer muy igual
en edad debe registrarse,
condición que igual abrace
siendo una mujer prudente,
laboriosa, inteligente,
dócil, casta en sus deberes,
sobria, tímida en placeres,
y a su paso muy decente.

2

Furthermore, to choose his bride
And be sure that it won't turn out badly,
He should pick a woman
Of his own age,
And equally important she should be
A prudent woman,
Industrious, intelligent,
Good-natured, chaste,
Sober, not fond of wild pleasures,
And, in a word, decent.

3

Una compañera en todo,
temerosa del Señor,
de gran conducta y honor
y virtudes a su modo,
caritativa y que en todo
le consuele en su desgracia
y que cuide de la casa,
librando de sus fatigas;
difícil es que consigas
mujer tan de buena masa.

3

A companion in everything,
Standing in fear of the Lord,
Honorable and of good conduct
And virtuous in her mode of living,
Charitable, and one who always
Comforts you in your misfortune
And who cares for the house,
Making light of her fatigue;
It is not easy to find a woman
Made of such fine mettle.

4

Todas estas cualidades
hace al hombre hacer esfuerzo,
si tú sabes a comienzo
evitar dificultades,
en tu mano están las llaves
de su pecho candoroso,
y si vivir con reposo
en esta vida prefieres,
abandona los placeres
y serás sabio y dichoso.

4

All these qualities
Make a man do his best,
And if you know from the start
How to avoid difficulties,
Then you hold the key
To her loving heart,
And if you prefer in this life
To live in peace,
Give up worldly pleasures
And you will be wise and respected.

Consejos acerca del Matrimonio was spoken, without music. It has the textual form of a *décima* with the rhyme scheme of an *espinela* (see Section E).

K7. *En Trinidad Me Casé* (I Was Married in Trinidad)
RB777, Amador Abeyta, Sabinal, N.Mex., Cobos.

1

En Trinidad me casé,
de allá me vine en un tren;
¡Ay! si mis padres supieran,   ] *Bis*
los trabajos que pasé.

1

I was married in Trinidad,
From there I came in a train;
Ah, if my parents only knew,
The hardships I have suffered!

2

Mi marido es un borracho;
no se acuerda ni de mí.
Se mantiene en las tabernas   ]
sin apuro y sin cuidado.   ] *Bis*

2

My husband is a drunkard;
He never thinks of me.
He hangs out in the bars
Without anguish or care.

3

A media noche me cae,
pidiéndome de cenar,
sabiendo que no me tiene   ]
ni un centavo que gastar.   ] *Bis*

3

He comes home at midnight,
Begging me to get supper,
Knowing that I don't have
Even one cent to spend.

4

¡Alma mía de mis chiquitos!
De verlos da compasión;
de verlos encueraditos   ]
sin ninguna educación.   ] *Bis*

4

My heart goes out to my children!
To see them engenders pity;
To see them dressed in scraps of hides
Without any education.

En Trinidad Me Casé was spoken, without
music.

K8. *Mi Boda* (My Wedding)
Mendoza 9d (p. 720), collectors: Armendáriz and Campa. Cf. Campa 2 (p. 188);
Mendoza 9d (pp. 219, 222).

1

El día que yo me case
debe de ser un día muy feliz;
habrá muchos invitados,
un banquete, y un baile al fin.

1

The day when I marry
Will be a very happy day;
There will be many invited,
A banquet, and at the end a dance.

Estribillo

Por esta calle
me verán pasar,
con vestido blanco
y corona de azahar.

Refrain

They will see me passing
Along this street,
In my white gown
And crown of orange blossoms.

EL DÍ-A QUE YO ME CA-SE DE-BE DE SER UN DÍA MUY FE-LIZ; HA-BRÁ MU-CHOS IN-VI-TA-DOS, UN BAN-QUE-TE Y UN BAI-LE AL FIN. POR E-STA CA-LLE ME VE-RÁN PA-SAR, CON VES-TI-DO BLAN-CO Y CO-RO-NA DE A-ZA-HAR.

Note that the verse alternates between minor and major (rather than the relative major). This is an instance not of modulation from key to key in the modern sense of the word but of so-called true modulation from mode to mode in the medieval sense. For a discussion of such survivals as the use of medieval modes, see *Hispanic Folk Songs of New Mexico* under the heading "Modality" (Robb 13, p. 6).

L. SOCIAL COMMENTARY

Many of the songs of this type are the reflections of old men who react savagely to changes of custom, which to me (now eighty-seven) seem to be innocent. Certainly the use of bustles today does not appear to be as vicious a practice as it appears to be in *Las Caderas* (L4). In comparison with the innovations of more recent younger generations in matters of sex, drugs, disruption of education, and the like, our parents and grandparents appear to have been paragons of circumspection.

However the very evils against which these songs inveigh have the advantage for us of suggesting the dates of origin of the songs. Some go well back into the nineteenth century. It must have been some time ago when men of the Spanish-American villages all wore *chongos* (long hair tied up behind the head), when high heels were introduced, and when bustles came into style.

And perhaps it should be comforting to us to realize that people have in the past become wrought up about conditions that, after all, did not completely undermine the decency of society, however disruptive they appeared at the time.

For additional songs belonging in the category of social commentary see *Vale Más Volverse Loco* (E19), *Guerras, Pleitos Sucediendo* (E20), *Ya el Mundo Está Caducante* (E21), and *Los Padres Consentidores* (E22).

L1. *Don Simón*
R63, Juan M. Sandoval, age 57, Chimayó, N.Mex., 1945, Robb. Cf. R41, R70, R207, R427, R1710, RB171, RB393, RB512, L1a–1c (all twelve being variants of this same song).

<table>
<tr><td>

1

Don Simón, los ochenta he cumplido.
Bueno estoy y doy gracias a Dios,
y en el mundo fatal, corrompido,
presenciando el escándalo atroz.

</td><td>

1

Don Simón, I am eighty years old.
I am well and give thanks to God,
But in this fatal, corrupted world
I see an atrocious scandal.

</td></tr>
<tr><td>

2

En mis tiempos las señoras grandes
se vestían con moderación:
usaban vestidos oscuros,
muy honestos, señor don Simón.

</td><td>

2

In my day the great ladies
Dressed with moderation:
They wore dark clothes, and were
Very decent, Don Simón.

</td></tr>
<tr><td>

3

Hoy se ponen vestidos chillones,
un botín con tamaño tacón,
y se pintan lunares y ojeras;
¡Rabos verdes, señor don Simón!

</td><td>

3

Today they wear loud clothes,
Shoes with high heels,
And paint their eyes and faces;
Very fresh, Don Simón.

</td></tr>
<tr><td>

4

En mi tiempo para ir a la iglesia,
iban todas con gran devoción;
sólo llevaban las señoras grandes
un rosario o alguna oración.

</td><td>

4

In my day when they went to church
They all went with great devotion;
The great ladies took only a
Rosary and a prayer book.

</td></tr>
</table>

5

Hoy las vemos llevando a toditas
su almohada, y catre, y colchón,
y en el tiempo que empieza la misa,
¡Hasta roncan, señor don Simón!

5

Today we see them all carrying
Their pillow, cot, and mattress,
And when the mass begins
They even snore, Don Simón!

6

En mi tiempo los hombres usaban
chongo[1] largo, pantalón rabón;
trabajaban de día y de noche
con la pala y con el cavador.

6

In my day the men wore
Knotted hair and short pants;
They worked night and day
With the spade and the hoe.

7

Hoy los vemos tomando a toditos,
enamorando y en toda reunión,
les echan flores a pollas y a viejas,
¡ah, qué tiempos, señor don Simón!

7

Today we see everyone drinking,
And making love at all gatherings,
They flirt with young and old,
Oh, what times, Don Simón!

DON SI- MÓN, LOS O- CHEN-TA HE CUM- PLI- DO. BUE-NO ES-

TOY Y DOY GRA-CIAS A DIOS, Y EN EL

MUN-DO FA- TAL, COR-ROM-PI-DO, PRE-SEN-

CIAN-DO EL E - SCÁN-DA - LO A - TROZ.

Juan Sandoval, singer of *Don Simón*, and his wife,
in Chimayó, New Mexico, about 1945.

[1] *Chongo* is an Indian word meaning long hair
tied in an Indian knot.

L1a. *Don Simón*
R122, Próspero S. Baca, age 72, Bernalillo, N.Mex., 1947, Robb.

1

Don Simón los ochenta cumplidos
bueno y sano, doy gracias a Dios
y en el tiempo fatal corrompido
presenciando el escándalo atroz.

1

Don Simón, having reached eighty
Well and sane, I give thanks to God
But in these fatally corrupted times
I am witnessing atrocious scandal.

2

En mis tiempos las señoras grandes
se vestían con moderación;
usaban vestidos oscuros
pero muy honestas, señor don Simón.

2

In my time the great ladies
Dressed with moderation;
They wore dark clothes
And were very modest, Don Simón.

3

Hoy se ponen vestido a la moda
y botines con tremendo tacón
y se pintan lunares y ojeras.
¡Rabos verdes, señor don Simón!

3

Today they dress in style
And walk on tremendous high heels
And paint their faces and eyes.
Very offensive, Don Simón.

4

En mis tiempos para ir a la iglesia
iban todas con gran devoción,
y llevaban todas las señoras
un rosario y alguna oración.

4

In my days when they went to church
They all went with great devotion,
And all the ladies carried
A rosary and some prayerbook.

5

Hoy las vemos llevando a toditas
una almohada y catre y colchón,
y en el acto que pasa la misa
¿qué hacen? ¡Hasta roncan, don Simón!

5

Today we see them all carrying
A cushion, a cot, and a mattress,
And during the mass itself
What do they do? They even snore, Don
  Simón!

6

Cuando yo era muchacho los hombres
se portaban con admiración,
buenos hijos y buenos maridos
y cumplían palabra de honor.

6

When I was a boy the men
Conducted themselves with pride,
Good sons and good husbands,
And their word was one of honor.

7

Hoy ya fuman y toman sus copas
y enamoran en toda región,
echan flores a pollas y viejas.
¡Ay, qué grande, señor don Simón!

7

Today they smoke and they drink
And make love all over the county,
They flirt with the chicks and old women.
Oh, how great, Don Simón!

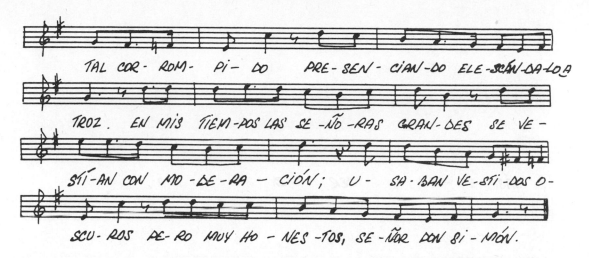

TAL COR-ROM-PI-DO PRE-SEN-CIAN-DO ELE-SCÁN-DA-LO A
TROZ. EN MIS TIEM-POS LAS SE-ÑO-RAS GRAN-DES SE VE-
STÍ-AN CON MO-DE-RA-CIÓN; U-SA-BAN VE-STI-DOS O-
SCU-ROS PE-RO MUY HO-NES-TOS, SE-ÑOR DON SI-MÓN.

L1b. *Don Simón*
R1493, M. Lavadie, age 86, Prado, N.Mex., 1957, Robb.

1	1
Don Simón, don Simón de mi vida,	Don Simón, my lifelong friend,
ya usted sabe que en gracia de Dios	You know by the grace of God that
valía más morir que haber visto,	It's better to have died than to see
tanto, tanto como he visto yo.	As much, as much as I have seen.

1

Don Simón, don Simón de mi vida,
ya usted sabe que en gracia de Dios
valía más morir que haber visto,
tanto, tanto como he visto yo.

1

Don Simón, my lifelong friend,
You know by the grace of God that
It's better to have died than to see
As much, as much as I have seen.

2

En mis tiempos los hombres usaban
chongo largo y pantalón rabón;
hoy los vemos usando chaleco
y botines con alto tacón.

2

In my days men used to wear
A large *chongo* and short pants;
Today they are wearing vests,
Spats, and high heels.

3

En mis tiempos los jóvenes eran
muy celosos por la educación;
hoy los vemos más bien educados,
¡Ay, qué tiempos, señor don Simón!

3

In my time the young people were
Very anxious for education;
Today they come better educated but—
Ah, what times, Señor Don Simon!

4

En mis tiempos las niñas usaban
por adorno su gran peinetón;
hoy las vemos con chinos y rizos
y con grandes rosas de listón.

4

In my time the girls used
To wear a large comb as adornment;
Today they wear curlicues and curls
And large roses made of tape.

5

Las señoras con sus mojonatas
sus enaguas de medio color;
les colgaban hasta la rodilla
con plomitos por alrededor.

5

The ladies with their pompadours,
Their shirtwaists of neutral color;
They hung to the knee
With weights all around.

L1c. *Don Simón*
RB210, Charles F. Lummis, California, 1905, Lummis.

The words, originally recorded on a wax cylinder and later dubbed onto tape by the Southwestern Museum in Los Angeles, are largely undecipherable. However the melody is distinguishable, and it is included for purposes of comparison with the other variants.

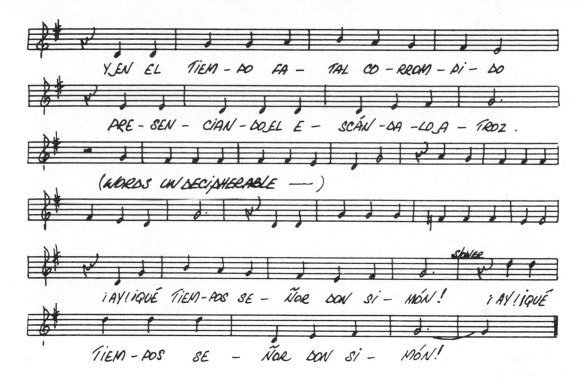

L2. *Los Pollos de la Capital* (The Roosters of the Capital)
Campa 2 (p. 199), Aureliano Almendariz, Mesilla, N.Mex., 1946, Campa. Cf. R277, L2a.

1
Yo conozco algunos pollos
de varia condición;
que desean ser casados
sin salir del cascarón.

1
I know some young roosters
Of varied condition
Who wish to be married
Even before being hatched.

2
A la solita
a la solita
y estos son los pollos
de la Capital.

2
To the lonely one
To the lonely one
These are the young roosters
From the capital city.

3
También hay pollitas chicas
que sienten el amor;
a pesar de ser tan chicas
les palpita el corazón.

3
Also there are young hens
Who feel the pangs of love;
In spite of being so young
Their hearts beat fast.

4
Si viene algún pollito
y les hace quiriquiquí
corriendo van y dicen:
—venga por aquí.—

4
If there comes a chick (boy)
And whistles cocka-deedle-dee
They run and say to him:
"Baby, you come with me."

5

También hay gallinas viejas
que sienten el amor;
que a pesar de ser tan viejas
les palpita el corazón.

5

Also there are old hens
Who feel the pangs of love;
In spite of being so old
Their hearts beat fast.

6

Si ven algún gallote
se hacen caracacá,
corriendo van y dicen:
—venga para acá.

6

If they see a big rooster
Who whistles cocka-doodle-doo,
They run to him and say:
"You come this way with me."

L2a. *Los Pollos de la Capital*
R559, Francisco S. Leyva, age 81, Leyva, N.Mex., 1951, Robb.

Yo conozco algunos pollos
de variada condición
que quieren hacer conquistas
sin salir del cascarón.
Y si ven que alguna polla
por la calle sola va
descienden a la solita
le comienzan a pillar.

I know some young roosters
Of various stations in life
Who want to make conquests
Before they're out of the shell
And if a young hen
Comes down the street alone
They go down to the lonely one
And commence to make love (?)

Remainder largely undecipherable

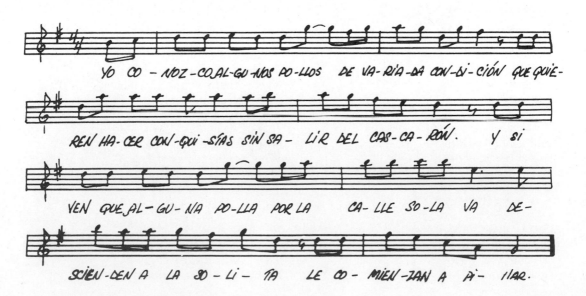

YO CO-NOZ-CO AL-GU-NOS PO-LLOS DE VA-RIA-DA CON-DI-CIÓN QUE QUIE-
REN HA-CER CON-QUI-SÍAS SIN SA-LIR DEL CAS-CA-RÓN. Y SI
VEN QUE AL-GU-NA PO-LLA POR LA CA-LLE SO-LA VA DE-
SCIEN-DEN A LA SO-LI-TA LE CO-MIEN-ZAN A PI-LLAR.

L3. *A Cantar Cuantos Versos* (Let's Sing a Few Verses)
R211, Tomás Archuleta, age 55, Tierra Azul, N.Mex., 1949, Robb.

1

A cantar vamos y unos cuantos versos
de lo que ahora se usa por aquí.
Cuánto más valiera que se usiera todo

como en el rancho donde yo nací.

1

Let's sing a few verses
About the things they do here these days.
How much better it would be if all were
    done
The same as on the ranch where I was born.

2

Por aquí todos van en automóbil,
matando gente pasan por aquí.
Cuánto más valiera cada esta con huellas
como en el rancho donde yo nací.

2

Here everyone rides in an automobile,
They go by here killing people.
How much better to go on foot
As on the ranch where I was born.

3

Por aquí todos presumen bisoños,
andan diciendo —*Sweetheart*, dí, dí, dí, —

Cuánto más valiera —dame un beso—
como en el rancho donde yo nací.

3

Here all act like greenhorns,
They go about saying "sweetheart, I give,
    I give you all."
How much better "give me a kiss"
As on the ranch where I was born.

4

Por aquí todas con qué mil colores,

se ponen bellas como un maniquí.
Cuánto más valiera ordeñando vacas
como en el rancho donde yo nací.

4

Around here the girls all wear a thousand
    colors,
They adorn themselves like a manikin.
How much better to milk cows
As on the ranch where I was born.

5

Por aquí todos estilo borrego,
mascando chicle pasan por aquí.
Cuánto más valiera no tragarán saliva
como en el rancho donde yo nací.

5

Around here all do like the sheep,
They go by chewing gum.
How much better not to swallow saliva
As on the ranch where I was born.

6

Por aquí todas al estilo mula,
bien tusaditas pasan por aquí.
Cuánto más valiera con chicas trenzotas
como en el rancho donde yo nací.

6

Around here the girls all like the mule style,
With short hair they walk by.
How much better if they wore braids
As on the ranch where I was born.

7

Por aquí todas pasan muy rabonas,
pues enseñando y hasta por aquí.
Cuánto más valiera muy bien tapaditas
como en el rancho donde yo nací.

7

Around here the girls all wear short dresses,
They show off a lot around here.
How much better to keep covered
As on the ranch where I was born.

8

Por aquí todas con chicos escotes
y atrás abiertos y hasta por aquí.
Cuánto más valiera con chaqueta de
    hombre
como en el rancho donde yo nací.

8

Around here all wear deep necklines
And in back open down to here.
How much better to wear men's coats

As on the ranch where I was born.

A CAN-TAR VA—MOS Y U-NOS CUAN-TOS VER-SOS DE LO QUE A-
HO-RA SEU-SA POR A- QUI. CUAN-TO MÁS VA-LI-ERA
QUE SEU-SIE-RA TO-DO CO-MUENEL RAN-CHO DON-DE YO NA-CÍ.

L4. *Las Caderas* (The Bustles)

R2179, Vincent F. Gallegos, age 68, Albuquerque, N.Mex., 1966, Robb.

<table>
<tr><td>

1

Se acabó la religión
de las modas estranjeras.
Quien ha venido a ser caso
de las malditas caderas.

</td><td>

1

People have forgotten religion
Because of new, strange customs.
Everyone has begun to notice
The accursed bustles.

</td></tr>
<tr><td>

2

Viejitas quijadas huecas
capotito encenizado
presumiendo las caderas
aunque les queden de lado.

</td><td>

2

Even the toothless old ladies
Whose hair is white as ashes
Are making use of bustles
Even those that stick out sideways.

</td></tr>
<tr><td>

3

Ya también las cocineras
ya van agarrando el uso
de ponerse de caderas
más que sea un trapo sucio.

</td><td>

3

Even the women in the kitchens
Have now adopted the custom
Of putting on these bustles
Even if it's a dirty cloth.

</td></tr>
<tr><td>

4

Las indias con tantas jetas
se visten de coqueteras.
Parecen fardos de lana
presumiendo las caderas.

</td><td>

4

The Indian women, with their heavy lips,
Now dress up as flirts.
They look like bales of wool
Making use of bustles.

</td></tr>
</table>

SE A-CA- BÓ LA RE-LI- GIÓN DE LAS
MO-DAS E-STRAN-JE-RAS. QUIEN HA VE-NI-
DO HA-CER CA-SO DE LAS MAL-DI-TAS CA—DE—RAS.

586

L5. *Muchacha con Muchos Novios* (Girl with Many Lovers)
  R2508, Edwin Berry, age 54, Tomé, N.Mex., 1972, Robb. Cf E29, R795, R798, R1472, RB697.

<table>
<tr><td>

1

Voy a cantarles la moda
de estos malores muchachos
que no quieren trabajar
nomás andar de borrachos.

</td><td>

1

I am going to sing you
About these malodorous youths
Who don't know how to work
And are drunk all the time.

</td></tr>
<tr><td>

2

Se visten a lo pipín
y se creen muy galanes
con su pantalón balún
como las enaguas de olanes.

</td><td>

2

They dress outrageously
And think that they are very stylish
With their baggy pants
Like those worn by the men of Holland.

</td></tr>
<tr><td>

3

Muchachas con muchos novios
no se dejen engañar.
Ellos dicen que trabajan
nomás quieren vacilar.

</td><td>

3

Girls with many fiances
Never stop cheating.
They say that they work
When in fact they are playing around.

</td></tr>
<tr><td>

4

También los hombres casados
que andan en su vacilada,
paseando mujeres de otro,
no le hace que sean casados.

</td><td>

4

The married men, too,
Who play around with them,
Running around with married women,
Even though they have their own wives.

</td></tr>
<tr><td>

5

También aquellos casados
que andan en nuevo placer
con sus queridas en carros
se olviden de su mujer.

</td><td>

5

Furthermore these married men
Who go looking for new pleasures
With their sweethearts in cars
Forget about their wives.

</td></tr>
<tr><td>

6

Ya con esto me despido;
con ésta les hago ver
que no juegen con el hecho
si quieren tener mujer.

</td><td>

6

Now with this I say good-bye;
With this I admonish you:
Don't play around
If you want to keep your wife.

</td></tr>
</table>

VOY A CAN - TAR - LES LA MO - DA DE E - STOS MAL -
O - RES MU - CHA - CHOS QUE NO QUIE - REN TRA - BA -
JAR NO - MÁS AN - DAR DE BO - RRA - CHOS.

M. POPULAR SONGS

Scholars usually draw a line between so-called popular songs, written and performed by professionals for money, and folk music, conceived of as a spontaneous expression of the thoughts and feelings of a people in reaction to their environment or to events of interest to that people, without commercial motivation. There are, of course, professional singers, really a part of the entertainment world, who are advertised as folk singers because they employ folk melodies. In my definition they are no such thing. The tunes are so often dressed up in the style of the contemporary popular music, including even elaborate orchestrations and sometimes clichés of the contemporary commercial music, as almost to obliterate the simple folk quality of the melody.

In this section, however, I shall be dealing with a different phenomenon: songs that first saw the light of day as popular songs but have been adopted and transformed by the folk singers for their own purposes. The modifications that have taken place in the process of adoption are interesting and, as one would expect, tend to move from the style of their origin toward the style of the Hispanic folk music of the region. For instance, there is a tendency to substitute the metric signature of 6/8 for that of 2/4.

A similar process of adoption and change is observable in the instrumental melodies, many of which have been taken over from other cultures.

M1.   *Susanita*
R73, Julianita Trujillo, Chimayó, N.Mex., 1949, Robb. Cf. R202.

<table>
<tr><td>

1
Susanita se embarcó
en un buque de vapor,
y sospirando decía,
— ¿por qué se me fué mi amor?—

</td><td>

1
Suzanita went a-traveling
On a steamship one fine day,
But with sadness she was sighing,
"Why has my love gone away?"

</td></tr>
<tr><td>

Refrán
¡Ay, Susana!
no llores por mí
que me voy para Alta California
a traer oro para ti.

</td><td>

Refrain
Oh, Suzanna!
Don't you cry for me
For I'm off to Upper California
To bring back gold to thee.

</td></tr>
</table>

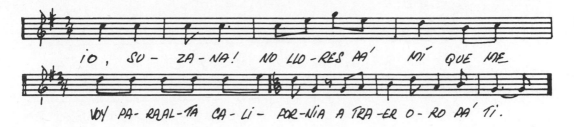

¡O, SU-ZA-NA! NO LLO-RES AA' MI' QUE ME

VOY PA-RAAL-TA CA-LI- FOR-NIA A TRA-ER O-RO AA' TI.

Originally composed by Stephen Foster (1826–1864) and thus well over a hundred years old, *Oh! Susannah* is richly documented. It differs from the Negro dialect songs like *Swanee River*, for which Foster is most famous. They were cleverly designed to exploit the commercial market created by the then immensely popular minstrel shows, of which the Christy Minstrels were the most famous.

The present fragment is an offshoot, admiringly adapted by and for a special part of the public who viewed the American scene through the colored glasses of their Spanish-American heritage.

M2. *La Luna Se Va Metiendo* (The Moon Is Setting)
R566, Alfred Campos, age 21, and Edwin Lobato, age 20, Albuquerque, N.Mex., 1961, Robb.

1
La luna se va metiendo
y el sol empieza a brillar
Apenas te estoy queriendo
como te podré olvidar.
Bien sabes que yo te quiero
y sin ti no puedo estar
dame solo una esperanza
para podernos casar.

1
The moon it is slowly setting
And the sun begins to shine.
I am beginning to love you
And to think of you as mine.
You know well that I love you,
Life without you I can't see.
Give me just a little hope
That one day my wife you'll be.

2
La luna se va metiendo
y el sol empieza a brillar
Apenas te estoy queriendo
como te podré olvidar.
Bien sabes que mis canciones
Alegran los corazones
Si es que te encuentro triste
Yo te vengo a consolar.

2
The moon it is slowly setting
And the sun begins to shine.
I am beginning to love you
And to think of you as mine.
You know my songs bring gladness
And drive away care and fear.
If you're ever sad and lonely,
You will know that I'll be near.

Refrán
Paloma que alegre canta,   ] *Bis*
llégate junto al balcón.
Canta, canta alegre canta   ] *Bis*
Mi rendido corazón.

Refrain
Oh pigeon who sings so sweetly,
Now come to my true love's door
A-singing, so gladly singing,
To the one that I adore.

Refrán

Refrain

This song, sung to the accompaniment of two guitars, was recorded at Albuquerque, New Mexico, on February 14, 1951, by Alfred Campos and Edwin Lobato. It is another Mexican *huapango* like C4 above. The *huapango* derives its name from its characteristic rhythm, rather than from its subject matter. The musicians informed me that they had heard this song over the radio and learned it by ear.

These two young men rival the excellent professional singers and guitar players who perform daily and nightly in the bars in the border towns such as Juárez and Nogales. Unlike the musicians of Old Mexico, who are thoroughly organized as professionals into trade unions and often bargain frankly before playing, the village singers of New Mexico, as a whole, are amateurs who make their living by other means (see Campa 2, p. 25). Some of them make a supplementary income by playing at dances and other functions.

La Luna Se Va Metiendo is a good example of recent Mexican popular music adopted by folk musicians but as yet not very much changed. It is in the characteristic 6/8 meter interspersed with measures in 3/4—like the hemiola rhythm of the early baroque period

in Europe—and other rhythmic subtleties and employs the customary eight-syllable line.

The songs *La Luna Se Va Metiendo* (M2) and *Cuatro Caminos* (M3) are popular songs of considerable charm. Their beauty, however, is of a more sophisticated type than that usually found in folk music. It depends more upon complex elements such as the fine two-guitar accompaniments.

The original recording appears as part of a Folkways album, *Spanish and Mexican Music of New Mexico* (Robb 13r).

M3. *Cuatro Caminos* (Four Roads)
R562, Alfred Campos, age 21, and Edwin Lobato, age 20, Albuquerque, N.Mex., 1961, Robb.

1

Es imposible que yo te olvide,
Es imposible que yo me vaya.
Por dondequiera que voy te miro,
yo ando con otra y por ti suspiro,
Es imposible que todo acabe,
yo sin tus ojos me arranco el alma
si ando en mi juicio no ando contento,
si ando borracho, ¡para qué te cuento!

Refrán
Cuatro caminos hay en mi vida.
¿Cuál de los cuatro será el mejor?
tú que me viste llorar de angustia,
dime, paloma, por cual me voy.

2

Tú que juraste que amor del bueno
siempre en tus brazos yo encontraría,
ya no te acuerdas cuando dijiste
que yo era tuyo y que tú eras mía.
Si es que te marchas, paloma blanca,
alza tu vuelo poquito a poco,
llévate mi alma bajo tus alas
y dime adiós, a pesar de todo.

1

It is impossible for me to forget you.
It is impossible for me to go away.
Wherever I go I always see you.
I go with another and sigh for you,
It is impossible that all should end.
Without your eyes I root out my soul,
If I rely on my reason, I am not contented,
If I get drunk, I still think of you.

Refrain
There are four roads in my life.
Which of the four will be the best?
You who see me weeping in anguish,
Tell me, o dove, which way to go.

2

You who swore that I should always find
Love in your arms,
You don't remember when you said
That I was yours and you were mine.
If you are going, white dove,
Raise your wings gently,
Carry my heart beneath your wings
And tell me farewell, in spite of all.

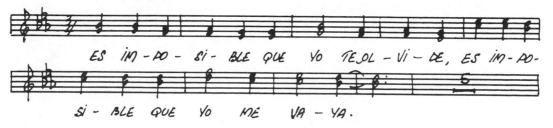

591

POR DON-DE- QUIE-RA QUE VOY TE MI-RO,

YO AN-DO CON O-TRA Y POR TI SUS-PI-RO,

ES IM-PO- SI-BLE QUE TO-DO A CA-BE,

YO SIN TUS O-JOS ME A-RRAN-CO EL AL-MA

SI AN-DO EN MI JUI-CIO NO AN-DO CON-TEN-TO,

SI AN-DO BO-RRA-CHO ¡AA' QUÉ TE CUEN-TO!

REFRAIN

CUA-TRO CA-MI-NOS HAY EN MI

VI-DA. ¿CUÁL DE LOS CUA-TRO SE-RÁ EL ME-JOR?

TÚ QUE ME VI-STE LLO-

RAR DE AN-GUS-TIA, DI-ME, PA-LO-MA, POR

CUAL ME VOY.

The text of this song as sung for me in Albuquerque is identical with that published in a *cancionero* I bought some twenty years ago in Mexico. It is entitled *Cancionero Occidental No. 120*, edited by Bruno Carrillo, Anguilla 137, Guadalajara, Mexico. In the *cancionero* it is described as a *canción ranchero*, although it contains no reference to ranch life, and the authorship is attributed to J. Alfonso Jiménez. Note the unusual tensyllable line. Like M2, it is sung in thirds.

N. MISCELLANEOUS SECULAR

In this section I have included the secular songs that are, so to speak, left over. The relatively few examples given here are included largely to call attention to the ramifications of the subject of Hispanic folk music that might well be explored further.

The first of this group are miscellaneous song texts associated with dances or other social gatherings. *Indio Comanche* (N6) is a surviving fragment of a secular folk play which so far as I can ascertain has become virtually extinct. (See also *Los Comanches* [R1982], the text of a folk play, and R2219–2221, three dance songs from *Los Comanches*.) For social dance music without words, see Section X.

Coplas de Circunstancias (N7) is an example of the pleasant custom of the older singers to sing improvised *coplas* in honor of persons present.

The game of the pipes, *Juego de los Canutes* (N8), a gambling game similar to the moccasin game of the Navajo Indians, was formerly played at social gatherings between two teams who would try to guess in which of three *canutes* (decorated pipes) a certain object had been concealed by the other team. This game was presented in a charming manner at the 1972 meeting of the New Mexico Folklore Society and was recorded by the Taos Historical Society. It is possible that Taos Recordings and Publications will publish an album covering this game.

The *cautivos* (N9 and N10) can be traced back to Spain where they tell of captives taken by the Moors. In the New World the *cautivos* are about captives taken by Indians.

A number of southwestern game songs of children have been collected and published in the *Spanish American Song and Game Book* (WPA 19). A number of others are scattered through this book, including the *romances Canción del Fraile* (A1), *Delgadina* (A2), *Las Señas del Esposo* (A7b), *Don Gato* (A16), *Hilito de Oro* (A8), and *Los Diez Perritos* (D28) (see in this connection Matos 8a, Parte Literaria, pp. 74–99).

N1. *Versos para el Vals Chiqueado* (Verses for the Chair Waltz)
R1428, David Frescas, age 70, Ranchos de Taos, N.Mex., 1956, Robb.

1
Muchacho:
En el llano está una yerba
que le nombran cargosanto.
Ya conozco a la Feliz.
No me la pondrán tanto.

1
Boy:
On the plain there grows an herb
That they call *cargosanto*.
I already know Feliz.
Don't exaggerate so much.

2
Muchacha:
En la puerta de tu casa
está una águila pintada.
¡Qué más águila que tú,
correo maleta aguada!

2
Girl:
On the door of your house
Is painted an eagle.
Since you are even more of an eagle
I go with my suitcase empty.

3

Muchacho:
En el día que te fuiste
no hay cosa que a mí me cuadre;
ni el dinero me consuela,
ni la fresca de las tardes.

4

Muchacha:
Dices que te vas mañana.
Dime adiós para mi consuelo.
Adiós lámpara lucida!
Adiós pedacito del cielo!

5

Muchacho:
¡Qué bonito es la alema
que cerca estará la marsa!
A que usted no me la divina
cual de esas dos es mi chata.

6

Muchacha:
Si la de la frente china
o la coqueta reflata.   ]
                                     ] *Bis*

7

Muchacho:
Limoncito verde, verde,
ya yo me voy a retirar,
porque estás malo del genio, iay!
No me vayas a pegar.

3

Boy:
On that day when you went away
There was nothing that pleased me;
Money did not comfort me,
Nor the freshness of the afternoons.

4

Girl:
You say you are going away tomorrow.
Say good-bye to console me.
Farewell clear shining lamp!
Farewell little fragment of the sky!

5

Boy:
How pretty is the irrigated field
That is near the marsh!
I bet you can't even guess
Which of those two is my choice.

6

Girl:
Should I turn him down cold
Or flirt a little?

7

Boy:
Green, green little lemon,
Now I am going to retire,
Because you have a bad disposition, ah!
Don't hit me.

Chiqueado, or, according to Cobos, *chiquiao*, means coaxing. The girl is seated in a chair in the middle of the dance floor, and the boy coaxes her to dance with him by singing verses which he is supposed to improvise. She replies in like manner. If rebuffed, he may end with a sarcastic verse, all presumably in the spirit of fun. For further information see Cobos' article, "The New Mexican Game of 'Valse Chiquiao.'" (Cobos 4a).

N2. *Valse de Silla* (Chair Waltz)
R1387, Boleslo Gallegos, age 72, Albuquerque, N.Mex., 1956, Robb. Cf. X3.

1

El:
Vieja no muy vieja
¡qué aborrecida te tengo!
con pretextos y mentiras
pero siempre te mantengo.

1

He:
Old woman but not too old
Whom I hold in abhorrence
With pretexts and lies,
But still I always keep you.

2

Ella:
Vieja o no vieja
ya me tiene que querer
y cien años más
me tendrás que mantener.

2

She:
Old woman or not
You always want me
And for one hundred years more
You will have to keep me.

3

El:
¡Ah, qué música tan bonita
qué bonito están tocando!
de deveritas parece
que yo me ando casando.

3

He:
Oh, what beautiful music it is
That they are playing so beautifully!
In truth it appears
That I am going to marry you.

4

Ella:
Anda viejo alburusero
ya que te has de casar,
aunque te quieras hacer muchacho,
a otra no vas a engañar.

4

She:
Go on, you old fibber,
Since you must get married,
Although you want to act like a boy,
You won't fool another one.

5

El:
Si a regarme vinites
yo no me he de dejar
y hasta que la panza me duele
esta noche he de bailar.

5

He:
If you come to throw cold water on me
I don't have to leave
And although my belly pains me
I've got to dance tonight.

6

Ella:
Me dices que estás enfermo
y que no puedes trabajar;
para bailar el bambito
naiden te ha de ganar.

6

She:
You tell me that you are sick
And that you cannot work;
But nobody outdoes you
Dancing the *bambito*.

7

El:
Pues que sea como tú dices
y seguiremos gustando
y este baile tan bonito
lo seguiremos bailando.

7

He:
Well, even if it's as you say
We'll go on having a good time
And this dance is so beautiful
Let's go on dancing.

Valse de Silla was spoken, without music.

N3. *Valse Chiqueado* (Chair Waltz)
R1925, Rubén Cobos, Albuquerque, N.Mex., 1963, Robb.

The host speaking:
De estos dos que andan bailando.
Si mi vista no me engaña
anda bailando la reina
con el príncipe de España.

See those two who are dancing.
If my eyes do not betray me
It is the queen who dances
With the prince of Spain.

Young man speaking:
Estrellita reluciente,
fina perla de la mar,
levántate de ese asiento
con licencia de la gente
dos abrazos te he de dar
como soy hombre prudente,
güerita, ven a bailar.

Radiant star so bright,
Fine pearl of the sea,
Stand up from your chair
With permission of the people
I give you two embraces
For I am a prudent man,
Little blonde, come and dance.

En orillas de una laguna
prendí una vela al momento;
si quieres bailar conmigo,
levántate de ese asiento.

Beside the waters of a lake
At this moment I light a candle;
If you want to dance with me,
Get up from your chair.

He sings:
¡Qué bonita estás creciendo
como una mata de trigo!
Ya me estoy apreviniendo
para casarme contigo.

How beautiful you are growing
Like a wheat plant!
I am ready and waiting
For the time when we may wed.

She sings:
¡Qué bonita estás creciendo
como una mata de mostaza!
Ya me estoy apreviniendo
para darte calabazas.

How beautiful you are growing
Like a mustard plant!
I am ready and waiting
To give you the slip.

N4. *Versos por los Bailadores* (Verses for the Dancers)
R290, Macario Leyva, age 78, Leyva, N.Mex., 1950, Robb.

1
Allí viene saliendo el sol,
viene tocando la Diana.

]
] *Bis*

1
Now the sun is coming out,
Diana is playing.

2
Mamá, gritan los toditos,
¡Que viva él de la manzana!

]
] *Bis*

2
Mama, everyone cries,
Long live he of the apple!

3
En blanco papel te escribo
porque blanca fué mi suerte.

]
] *Bis*

3
I write you on white paper
For white was my lucky color.

4

Y entre más estoy contigo
más ganas me dan de verte.

] Bis

4

The longer I am with you
The more I want to see you.

5

El águila para volar
busca la tierra caliente.

] Bis

5

The eagle in its flight
Seeks the hot country.

6

El hombre para enamorar
busca la mujer decente.

] Bis

6

A man when he falls in love
Looks for a decent woman.

7

Quisiera escribir en el agua
y dibujar en el viento.

] Bis

7

I would like to write on the water
And paint on the wind.

8

Dicen que me han de quitar
este loco pensamiento.
Coraje le he de dar
que yo he de seguir mi intento.

(Versos 5 y 6 se repiten)

8

They say that I must give up
This crazy thinking.
But I'll have to take the consequences
Of doing what I want to do.

(Verses 5 and 6 repeated)

9

Ya el águila se voló
y el nido quedó cimbreando;
busquen quien lo repeye
que se está desilachando.

9

The eagle took off
And left his nest shaking;
Look for someone to salvage it
For it is coming apart.

10

Dale cuerda a tu reloj
hasta llegar a Sonora.

] Bis

10

Wind your watch
Until you get to Sonora.

11

Que él que no conoce a Dios
y en cualquier monito adora.

] Bis

11

For he who doesn't believe in God
Worships any old imitation.

12

Dicen que me han de quitar
que toda la noche andando;
primero se han de morir
y yo he de querer andar.

12

They tell me I have to quit
Running around all night;
They'll go to their graves
Before I stop making love.

13

Yo soy aquel cantador
que canta en los Algodones.

] Bis

13

I am the singer
Who sings in Algodones.

14

Si quieres cantar conmigo
fíjate bien los calzones.

] Bis

14

If you want to sing with me
Tighten your belt.

15

De las estrellas del cielo
tengo de bajarte dos.

] Bis

15

From the stars in the sky
I have to bring down two for you.

16

Una para despedirme
y otra para decirte adiós.

] Bis

16

One to take my leave
And the other to say good-bye.

ALLÍ VIE - NE SA - LIEN - DO EL SOL, VIE-

NE TO - CAN - DO LA DIA - NA, ALLÍ VIE-

NE SA - LIEN - DO EL SOL, — VIE - NE TO-

CAN - DO LA DIA - NA.

This example is somewhat different from the others, apparently intended to be sung by a member of the dance orchestra to amuse the dancers. Algodones is a small village about twenty miles north of Albuquerque, New Mexico.

N5. *Valse de Honor* (Waltz of Honor)
RB776, Teresa M. Gurulé, Alameda, N.Mex., 1950, Cobos.

1

Sobre los llanos del norte se ha visto
una ciudad de alta extensión,
donde sacaron la fiesta florida
del dicho valse de honor.

1

Upon the plains of the north
There is a city of a large area,
Where they hold the flowery festival
Of the happy waltz of honor.

2

Hasta los indios que bailan tombé
mirar desean con su corazón
de conocer esta pieza florida
del dicho valse de honor.

2

Even the Indians who dance
Show that they live with all their hearts
To learn this flowery piece
Of the happy waltz of honor.

3

Hasta las monjas que están en colegio
aprecian y miran su corazón;
de conocer esta pieza en retrato
del dicho valse de honor.

3

Even the nuns who are in the college
Like it and show what is in their hearts;
As they learn this piece by watching
The happy waltz of honor.

4

Todas las gentes del mundo se admiran,
sienten, y dicen con grande y honor;
—Hoy se resuena la música fina
con el dicho valse de honor.—

4

All the people of the world admire it,
Feel it, and say it with greatness and honor;
"Today resounds the fine music
Of the happy waltz of honor."

5

Gusto me ha dado y a todos señores,
hoy bailaremos con grande atención,
para apreciar este hermoso valse
del dicho valse de honor.

5

It has pleased me and all the people,
Today we dance with great attention,
To appreciate this lovely waltz,
The happy waltz of honor.

Note the unusual syllabification of 11, 10, 11, 7, as well as the almost literal repetition in each verse of the last line of verse 1, a feature observed in some of the *décimas*.

N6.   *Indio Comanche* (Comanche Indian)
      R286, Macario Leyva, age 78, 1950, Robb. Cf. R1425, R1426, R1982, R2219–2221.

1

. . . el acero mío
en toda la nación;
es tanta la valentía
que siento en el pecho mío.

1

. . . my steel
Over the entire nation;
I feel so much courage
In this breast of mine.

2

Se levanta mi bandera,
con el viento giro a giro,
con el viento atribulado
. . . ya mi pecho
¿quién es y cómo se llama?

2

My flag rises,
It flutters in the wind,
Troubled by the wind
. . . already my heart
Who is it and what is its name?

3

¿A la orden de quién esperas,
indio infiel?
que soy de tan noble brillo
que vengo en mi caballo
a cuidar de este castillo.

3

Whose order do you await,
Infidel Indian?
I am of noble spirit
And I come upon my horse
To guard this castle.

4

No es ya menester que apeles,
ya tu valentía se ha huído;
dime tu nombre
para quedar de todo entendido.

4

There is no need for appeal,
Already your courage has fled;
Tell me your name
In order to have an understanding.

5

Y para ahorrarme de palabras
ɔasta con lo que te he dicho;
¡A orden de quién esperas
A dar tu servicio
ɍ enbravecer tu soverbia?

5

To save words
What I have said is enough;
Whose order do you await?
Whom do you serve?
Do you intend to inflame your hatred?

6

Qué no sabes que en la España
l señor que nos gobierna,
l señor soberano
ue a todo el mundo gobierna?

6

Don't you know that Spain is
The lord which governs us,
The sovereign lord
Who rules all the world?

7

Y en todos los cuatro polos
que circunden la tierra
brilla su soberanía.

8

Al oír su nombre tiemblan,
Alemanes, Portugueses,
Turquía y la Inglaterra;
porque dicen "españoles"
todas las naciones tiemblan.

7

And in all four poles
Which surround the globe
His sovereignty shines.

8

Upon hearing the name all tremble,
Germans, Portuguese,
Turkey and England;
When they hear the word *Spaniard*
All nations tremble.

The folk play *Los Comanches* in Albuquerque, New Mexico.

This is an intriguing fragment in the form of a speech without music from the folk play *Los Comanches*, as recited by Macario Leyva, of Leyva, New Mexico, in 1950. The cross references cited in the song heading are an attempt to piece together the sources in my possession regarding this folk play:

Los Comanches (R1982) is a seventeen-page copy of the manuscript of *Los Comanches* from a handwritten notebook of Clemente Chávez of Galisteo, New Mexico.

R2219–2222 are three dance songs from *Los Comanches*, performed and danced in

Two young warriors with stolen crèches in *Los Comanches.*

The old drummer from *Los Comanches.*

Dancer and women singers from *Los Comanches.*

costume at Albuquerque in the home of Felix Torres in 1969.

Finally, I have a 1956 memorandum containing a description by David Frescas of a performance of *Los Comanches* at Taos in December, 1955.

These sources from various localities indicate that the play was known throughout New Mexico.

Frescas' memorandum gives the following description of *Los Comanches*. The play is performed in commemoration of an actual battle between the Comanches, who frequently raided the Spanish settlements, and the Spanish settlers of Tomé, New Mexico. The battle took place "possibly" between 1800 and 1848. The 1955 performance was given in a big field south of Taos, opposite the Sagebrush Inn. The two competing armies, Indians and Spanish, lined up facing

each other. All the actors were mounted on horseback except for the Nana, watching the children, Baruga Dulce (Sweet Belly), a comic character, and the children. The Spanish had an imaginary "castle" and the Indians a camp nearby. The Comanches had spies who infiltrated the castle, left a shield as an excuse for returning, and finally returned and took *cautivos* (captives). The Spanish tried to retrieve the captives. The Indian chief Cuerno Verde (Green Horn), and the Spanish leader, Don Carlos, boasted and hurled taunts at one another (reminiscent of the *trovos*). The Spanish defenders circled their castle in one direction, while the Comanches, outside, circled it in the opposite direction singing war chants (R1425 and 1426). Finally the Comanches made a dash for the castle, while presumably the Spanish tried to ride them off. If three Indians were able to get inside, they would win.

N7. *Coplas de Circunstancias* (Improvised Couplets)
R49, Antonio Medina, Chimayó, N.Mex., 1945, Robb. Cf. RB701.

1
Su atención pido a toditos
en el nombre de Ficacia,
en nombre de Pedro Trujillo
que estamos aquí en su casa.

1
I beg all of you to pay attention
In the name of Ficacia,
In the name of Pedro Trujillo
For we are here in his house.

2
Gracia le doy a don Pedro
Fino, amado, Polito,
destinguido caballero,
también a doña Pablita.

2
We render thanks to Don Pedro
And fine, beloved Polito,
A distinguished gentleman,
Also to Doña Pablita.

3
¡Qué bonito es lo bonito,
y en esto no hay que dudar!
El nombre de Pedro queda;
finas gracias debo le dar.

3
He is a very good man,
And of this there is no doubt.
The name of Pedro stands;
We ought to give him our thanks.

4
Yo no he sido cantador,
pero soy aficionado
como me sobra valor
todo el mundo tengo andado,
por el mar y sus orillas
y en el centro del condado.

4
I have not been a singer,
But I am a fan
As I have valued it highly
And have gone all over the world,
By the sea and its shores
And in the center of the county.

5	5
Señora, *give me san wada*	Lady, give me some water
que ya me abraso de sed;	For I am burning up with thirst;
aquí en el pomito de mi cuero.	Put it in this bottle in my jerkin.
¿Por qué en su boca me di	Why don't you say something
no me ande con *wat su mada*	Don't answer with "What's the matter?"
ni tampoco *wat yu se.*	Or even "What did you say?"

Occasionally during the years of my collecting, a singer has felt impelled to compose verses, usually simple *coplas*, in honor of the host of the evening or others present. There is a feeling of warmth and cordiality about these verses, which are sometimes accompanied by a bit of sly humor that justifies including this example. I was present on the occasion when these verses were improvised.

N8. *Juego de los Canutes* (Game of the Pipes)
R2422, Juan Griego, age 61, Albuquerque, N.Mex., 1971, Cipriano Griego.

1	1
El mulato y el cinchado	The mulatto and the *cinchado*
van a poner un jurado,	Will set up a jury,
el uno de juez de paz,]	The first as justice of the peace
y el dos para licenciado.] *Bis*	And the second as advocate.

2	2
Allí vienen los canuteros	There come the players
los que no conocen miedo	Who have no fear
pero de aquí llevaron]	But from here they have taken
Atolito en el sombrero.] *Bis*	Gruel in their hats.

3	3
Allí vienen los canuteros	There come the players
que pasaron de cupidos	Who passed as cupids
a ver si podían llegar]	To see if they could find
donde está el clavo escondido.] *Bis*	Where the nail is hidden.

4	4
La flor de la calabaza	The squash blossom
Santa Rita la enverdece;	Santa Rita makes green;
la palabra de los hombres]	The honor of man's word
se ha perdido y no aparece.] *Bis*	Has been lost and will not return.

5	5
Voy al otro lado del río	I am going across the river
y a traí sebo de berrendo	To bring back deer meat
para hacerles un caldillo]	To make broth
a los contentos y ardiendos.] *Bis*	For the happy and the envious.

EL MU-LA-TO XEL CIN-CHA-DO VAN A PO-NER

UN JU-RA-DO, EL U-NO DE JUEZ DE PAZ,

XEL DOS PA-RA LI-CEN-CIA-DO.

N9. *Marcelina*

R2392, Juan Griego, age 61, Albuquerque, N.Mex., 1971, Robb. Cf. Schindler 14a (Parte Musical, nos. 455, 561, 697) for Spanish *cautivos*.

Coro	*Chorus*
¡Ay, mamá, qué dulce es el amor,	Oh, mother, how sweet love is,
que me llevan cautiva	They are taking me captive
para el río de Huicho!] *Bis*	To the Río Huicho region.

1	1
La cautiva Marcelina	Marcelina, the captive,
ya se va, ya se la llevan,	She is leaving, they are taking her
ya se va, ya se la llevan,	She is leaving, they are taking her
ya se va, ya se la llevan,	She is leaving, they are taking her
a comer carne de yegua.] *Bis*	To eat horse meat.

Coro	*Chorus*

2	2
Y al pasar el Puertecito	As she passed by Puertecito
voltea sospirando y dice,	She looked back, sighed, and said
voltea sospirando y dice,	She looked back, sighed, and said

voltea sospirando y dice,	She looked back, sighed, and said
¡Ay, alma mía de mi hermanito!] *Bis*	Oh, little brother of my heart!

Coro   *Chorus*

3   3

Al pasar el Río Grande	As I passed the Río Grande
me caí y no me mojé.] *Bis*	I fell but did not get wet.
Como el hilo no se corte,	If the thread of my life is not cut
yo a mis tierras volveré.] *Bis*	I will return to my land.

Coro   *Chorus*

Captive songs of the New World have their Spanish counterparts in songs having to do with Spanish captives of the Moors, which presumably date back to the period before the reconquest of Spain in 1492. See for ex-ample the children's song *Las Tres Cautivas* (Matos 8a, Parte Literaria, p. 91–92).

Marcelina is the best known of the *cau-tivos*, or songs dealing with captives.

N9a. *La Cautiva Marcelina* (The Captive Marcelina)
Mendoza 9d (p. 472), Amador Abeyta, 58, Sabinal, N.Mex., 1898, Cobos.

<table>
<tr><td>

1
La cautiva Marcelina
ya se va, ya se la llevan,
ya se va, ya se la llevan,
ya se van, ya se la llevan,
a comer carne de yegua.   ] *Bis*

</td><td>

1
Marcelina, the captive,
She is leaving, they're taking her,
She is leaving, they're taking her,
She is leaving, they're taking her
To eat horse meat.

</td></tr>
<tr><td>

2
Por eso en el mundo
no quiero más amor;
de mi patria querida
me van a desterrar.   ] *Bis*

</td><td>

2
Therefore never again in this world
Will I fall in love;
From my beloved fatherland
They are taking me away.

</td></tr>
</table>

N10. *Indita de Plácido Molina*
Mendoza 9d (p. 393), Pascual Martínez, age 65, Taos, N.Mex., 1929, Campa.

<table>
<tr><td>

1
El que compuso esta historia
habla como un caballero
que vive en la Rinconada
nueve millas de Cubero.

</td><td>

1
He who composed this history
Speaks like a gentleman
Who lives in Rinconada
Nine miles from Cubero.

</td></tr>
<tr><td>

2
Llegué al Ojito Salado
con aquel dolor ardiente
como es para jimeta,
allí esperaba la gente.

</td><td>

2
I came to Ojito Salado
With that burning pain
Like a man pierced by a spear;
I was waiting there for the people.

</td></tr>
</table>

3

Adiós, Cubero afamado,
se te acabó lo valiente;
caminando para el Socorro
vide que mataron dos.
Uno se llamaba Ignacio
y el otro Juan de Dios.

4

Adiós, esposo querido,
José Domingo Gallegos,
quizá no tienes amigos
ni parientes en Cubero;
que tus huesos se quedaron
tirados en un gallinero.

5

A Dios le pido licencia
como Dios lo determine
al componer esta historia
a Plácido Molina.

6

Se me secaron los ojos
de ver para ese llano
para ver si veía venir
a mi padre o a mi hermano.

7

Adiós, madrecita de mi vida,
que mal lo noticiaré
que a mi esposo lo mataron
y a mí me llevó el nané.

8

Mi Señora de la Luz
fué la que reinó en Cubero
pídanle al Niño Jesús
que salga de cautiverio.

9

El día que ya salimos
de esa sierra desgraciada,
las piedras se enternecieron,
los palos brotaron agua
de ver los islamentos
que sus hijitos le echaba.

10

El miércoles por la mañana
cosa de las seis del día,
una cosa así seria;
mataron a don Domingo,
y también a José María.

3

Farewell, famous Cubero,
The brave man is lost to you;
Traveling to Socorro
I saw two men killed.
One was named Ignacio
And the other Juan de Dios.

4

Farewell, beloved husband,
José Domingo Gallegos,
You leave behind in Cubero
No friends or relatives;
And your bones lie exposed
For the chickens to pick at.

5

I beg permission from God,
As he may decide,
To compose this story
About Plácido Molina.

6

My eyes were dry
From looking at that plain
To see if my father or brother
Were coming.

7

Farewell, dear mother,
What bad news I must send you,
That they killed my husband
And took my nurse from me.

8

My Lady of the Light
Who reigned in Cubero
Beg of the Child Jesus
To save me from captivity.

9

The day when we went out
From this unfortunate mountain,
The rocks were moved to pity,
The trees gushed water
To see the kidnapping
Of the children.

10

On Wednesday morning
At about six o'clock
It happened;
They killed Don Domingo
And also José María.

11

Adiós, madrecita mía,
tú sentirás mi desgracia;
adiós, padre Pedro Molina,
adiós, madre Marucacia.

11

Good-bye, dear mother of mine,
You will sorrow for my misfortune;
Farewell, father Pedro Molina,
Good-bye, mother Marucacia.

12

Llegué a la Mesa del Oro,
allí vide que mataron tres:
uno se llama Severo,
y el otro se llama José.
Y a él que se llevan cautivo
se llama Antonio José.

12

I came to the Mountain of Gold,
There I saw they killed three men:
One was named Severo,
And the other was called José.
And one whom they took captive
Was called Antonio José.

Cubero, mentioned several times in *Indita de Plácido Molina*, is a village in New Mexico.

Part II: RELIGIOUS SONG TEXTS AND MELODIES

CONTENTS

O. Alabado

The *alabados* are associated with the religious sect commonly known as the Penitentes, although they prefer to be known by the title of Hermanos de Nuestra Padre Jesús. In fact when I used the word "Penitente" in speaking to one of them, he reproved me gently, saying that it was a "hurting word." Penitente is the word usually used in describing the sect, however, and the longer designation is cumbersome and unfamiliar to the public. I use the word without the slightest feeling of disrespect, but on the contrary with great respect and affection for members of the group whom I know. For these reasons I trust that no one will take offense at my frequent use of the word Penitente in these pages.

The Penitente practices of flagellation and crucifixion, described by Charles F. Lummis in *The Land of Poco Tiempo* and by Alice Corbin Henderson in her *Brothers of Light* (two excellent books that I highly recommend), were abandoned after several years of persistent effort by the Roman Catholic archbishop of New Mexico. His prohibition was directed against *public* demonstrations of penance and suffering, and members of the group have informed me that flagellation is still carried on in the privacy of the *moradas*, or chapels, of the sect.

To be fully appreciated as a deep and sincere religious expression the *alabados* should be heard in one of the villages during Holy Week, especially during the nocturnal processions or evening services such as the Tenievoles, the Good Friday service in the village church. They are a deeply impressive outpouring of sorrow for the fate of the Savior and of guilt and remorse for personal sins, conceived of as the cause of the Crucifixion. As the humble procession, preceded by a member reading from a notebook by the light of a lantern, comes down the path from the *morada* to the village church under the light of the moon singing these mournful chants, there is a sense of awe and mystery rarely felt in more conventional religious observances. Added to all this is the *pitero*

walking at the head of the procession and playing fascinating traditional arabesques on the *pito*, or vertical flute. That is enough to engrave the scene on anyone's memory forever. Before the archbishop's edict took effect, I witnessed several times the added drama of penitents dressed in long white drawers with black hoods over their heads, dragging huge crosses or whipping themselves over the shoulders and back with yucca whips until the blood ran down to their heels.

The villagers of the Southwest both Indian and Hispanic have inherited a genius and a zest for ritual pageantry, combining with seemingly infinite variations their deepest beliefs, their music, their own ideas of costuming and dancing in settings as diverse as a sunlit plaza or a mountain canyon but somehow always almost incredibly dramatic.

The music of the *alabado* is in the main unmeasured, like the plainsong of the medieval church. Some examples are in the medieval modes and employ practices that were peculiar to the music of the sixteenth century and were largely abandoned with the coming of the tonal system. The *alabados* are sung in unison without accompaniment except for arabesques played on the *pito* and the occasional use of a *matracas*, or rattle.

While it has been the custom in the Southwest to use the word *alabado* to describe a wider range of religious folk poetry, I have preferred to follow the practice of the Mexican authority Vicente Mendoza, who during his stay as visiting professor at the University of New Mexico always used it in the more limited sense of a folk poem relating to the Passion of Christ, employing the term *alabanza* to describe the songs of praise to the Virgin Mary and the saints.

Musically speaking, the *alabado* covers a considerably wider range than that of songs commemorating the Passion of Christ, the limited sense in which I have used it for the purpose of classifying the song texts. Again musically speaking, the *alabado* might be defined as a style of unaccompanied singing distinguished by phrases without formal musical or mathematical meters but rather following the rhythm of the words. There is, however, frequent use of melismas (a number of notes sung to one syllable). It is sung in slow tempos and is associated with the religious and other ritual observances of the Penitentes.

In this broader musical sense, therefore, the *alabado* may be said to include, in addition to songs commemorating the Passion, a number of the *alabanzas* (songs of praise for holy personages), some songs of religious exhortation to be found in Section V (V3–V4), and certain others when they are sung in the unique style of the *alabado*. I shall refer to such examples as being "in the style of the *alabado*" rather than as *alabados* proper.

The subject of the *alabado* has been covered in an authoritative manner by Juan B. Rael in his book *The New Mexico Alabado*. I reviewed Rael's book and expressed some ideas about the *alabado* in an article in the *New Mexico Historical Review* (Robb 13l).

Many, if not most, of the *alabados* in Rael's monograph come from Colorado, and many of them have their counterparts in New Mexico. The San Luis Valley of Colorado and the Río Grande Valley of New Mexico are separated politically by the state boundaries, but culturally they are one area. Alex Chávez was born and reared in the San Luis Valley, where he learned many of the songs he sings (Discography, Chávez 26 and 27); some of these songs are well known in New Mexico.

It would be redundant to publish here the very large numbers of *alabados* that are merely variants of those already published by Rael. Rael has not as a rule published English translations, however. And, for purposes of comparison, it should be useful to make available some of the variants of the texts and melodies. For these reasons I have decided to include here a limited group from among the large number available in my collection and the collections of others.

Attention is called to the fact that, where several versions from different villages are reproduced below, the words tend to follow a common pattern while the melodies differ, each village having its own recognizable tune. Since the words of the *alabados* often differ only slightly from village to village and the emphasis of this study is on the music, and for the further reason that printing several nearly identical texts would require many pages whereas the music can be condensed into two or three pages, I have omitted many of the variant texts while including the melodies (See O1a–d, O2a–b, O4a). The sources in which the omitted texts can be found are given in the song headings.

One of my informants, Jorge López, was reluctant to sing more than the first three or four verses of his songs and his examples are therefore only fragments. Fortunately most of the texts are verifiable in their complete form by reference to the copy of the singer's handwritten notebook (López 8).

O1. *Por el Rastro de la Cruz* (By the Trail of the Cross)
R154, Tomás Archuleta, age 55, Tierra Azul, N.Mex., 1949, Robb. Cf. R79, R1002, R1048, R1058, RB112, RB738, Rael (p. 24).

1	1
Por el rastro de la cruz	Following the trail of the cross
que Jesucristo llevaba	Which Jesus Christ carried
camina la Virgen Pura	The Pure Virgin goes forth
en una fresca mañana.	One cool morning.

2	2
De tan de mañana que era	It was so early in the morning
que la Virgen caminaba	That as the Virgin went along
las campanas de Belén	The bells of Bethlehem
que tarde tocaban el alba.	At last rang the dawn.

3

Encontró a San Juan Bautista
y de esta manera le hablaba:
¿Ha pasado por aquí
un hijo de mis entrañas?

4

Por aquí pasó señora
antes que el gallo cantara;
llevaba Cristo un garrote
en sus sagradas espaldas.

5

Cuando la Virgen oyó esto
cayó en tierra desmayada.
San Juan, como buen sobrino,
procuraba levantarla.

6

Levántese, tía mía,
que no es tiempo de tardanza;
allá en el monte calvario
tristes trompetas sonaban.

7

Llevaba una cruz en sus hombros
de madera muy pesada;
tres clavos lleva en sus manos
con que ha de ser clavado.

8

Una soga en su garganta
con lo que ha de ser atado;
corona de espinas lleva
con que ha de ser coronado.

9

¡Ay, Jesús, mi padre amado!
Que por mi estás de esta suerte;

ya te llevan a la muerte
a remediar los pecados.

3

She met Saint John the Baptist
And in this manner spoke to him:
Has a son of my womb
Passed through here?

4

He passed through here, my lady
Before the rooster crowed;
Christ carried a scaffold
Upon his sacred shoulders.

5

When the Virgin heard this
She fell to the ground in a faint.
Saint John, like a good nephew,
Attempted to help her up.

6

Get up, my aunt,
There is no time to lose;
Over on Mount Calvary
Trumpets are sadly sounding.

7

He carried a cross upon his shoulders
Of a very heavy wood;
In his hands he had three nails
With which he was to be nailed.

8

A cord with which he was to be tied
Was around his throat;
He carried a crown of thorns
With which he was to be crowned.

9

Ah, Jesus, my beloved father!
Alas! that for me you are undergoing this
      fate;
They are taking you to die
To redeem our sins.

POR EL RA-STRO DE LA CRUZ QUE JE-SU-CRIS-
TO LLE-VA-BA CA-MI-NA LA VIR-GEN PU-
RA EN U-NA FRES-CA MA-ÑA-ÑA.

O1a. *Por el Rastro de la Cruz*
R1002, Tranquilino Luján, Santa Fe, N.Mex., 1952, Reginald and William R. Fisher.

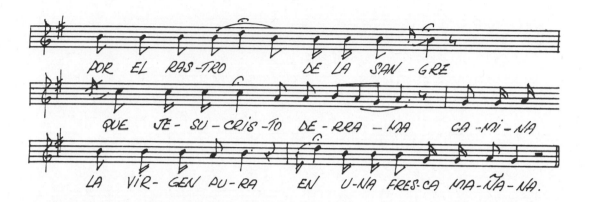

The late Reginald Fisher and the late William R. Fisher (who was at the time, 1952, a student of mine) were father and son. William R. Fisher, as a student honors project, made a large number of recordings of *alabados* with the enthusiastic assistance of his father, many of which are referred to herein.

Some of the *alabados* that follow are included for the purpose of comparing the melodies from various villages as set forth in Appendix B. The examples for which only the music is included may be found complete with text by consulting the sources (in this instance R1002).

O1b. *Por el Rastro de la Sangre* (By the Trail of Blood)
R1058, Group from Pecos, N.Mex., 1952, Reginald and William R. Fisher.

See note to O1a.
Each verse of this *alabado* is sung by the leader, and then verse 1 is sung, responsorially, as a refrain by a chorus of men.

O1c. *Por el Rastro de la Cruz*
R1018, Jorge López, age 52, Córdova, N.Mex., 1952, Reginald and William R. Fisher.

POR EL RAS — TRO DE LA CRUZ QUE JE — SU — CRIS-TO LLE -VA-BA, CA-MI-NA-BA LA VIR-GEN PU- RA EN U — NA FRES-CA MA-ÑA — NA.

See note to O1a.

O1d. *Por el Rastro de la Cruz*
R79, Juan M. Ortega, Chimayó, N.Mex., 1946, Robb.

POR EL RA-STRO DE LA CRUZ QUE JE — SU — CRIS-TO LLE — VA CA- MI-NA LA VIR-GEN PU-RA EN U- NA FRES- CA MA — ÑA — NA.

See note to O1a.

O2. *Mi Dios y Mi Redentor* (My God and My Redeemer)
R249, Jorge López, age 50, Córdova, N.Mex., 1950, Robb. Cf. R1003, R1032, R1060, R2159; Rael (p. 49), Ralliere d (p. 36).

1	1
Mi Dios my mi Redentor	My God and my Redeemer
en quien espero y confío	In whom is my hope and trust
por tu pasión, Jesús mío,	By your passion, my Jesus,
abrazadme a vuestro amor.	Embrace me with your love.

1

Mi Dios my mi Redentor
en quien espero y confío
por tu pasión, Jesús mío,
abrazadme a vuestro amor.

1

My God and my Redeemer
In whom is my hope and trust
By your passion, my Jesus,
Embrace me with your love.

2

Escucha con atención
lo que padeció Jesús
desde el huerto hasta la cruz.
En su sagrado pasión
lágrimas de devoción
nos dé a todos el Señor.

2

Listen with attention
To what Jesus suffered
From the garden to the cross.
In his sacred passion
Tears of devotion
The Lord shed for us all.

3

Aflijido y angustiado
lo vemos en la oración,
sangre en el huerto ha sudado.
Hasta la tierra ha llegado.
Lo copioso del sudar.

3

Afflicted and in anguish
We see him at prayer,
His blood was shed in the garden.
The abundance of it
Stained the earth.

4

A la mejilla inocente
con mano de hierro armada
dan tan riesa bofetada
que hacen que en sangre revienten.
Mi Dios pues que el alma siente
ser causa de tal rigor.

4

To the innocent cheek
With steel in hand
They gave such a beating
That the blood rushed out.
My God then, what must his soul feel,
To be the cause of such cruelty.

5

Por tu pasión, Jesús mío,
abrazadme a vuestro amor.
Con furia y rabia es llevado
de uno a otro tribunal,
y lo miraron tal mal
que de loco lo trataron
y con Barrabás mirado
dicen que es Jesús peor.

5

By your passion, my Jesus,
Embrace me with your love.
With fury and madness he is carried
From one tribunal to the other,
And they looked at him so badly
That they treated him as a madman
And when they looked at Barrabas
They said Jesus was worse.

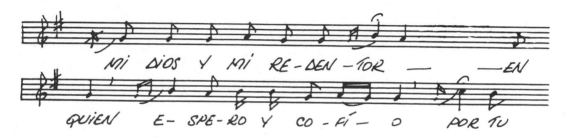

PA - SIÓN JE-SÚS MÍ — — O A - BRA -ZAO-

ME A VUES — — TRO_A- MOR.

This *alabado* is sometimes known as *Por Tu Pasión, Jesús Mío.*

Jorge López, singer of several *alabados* in Section O, and his wife, in Chimayó, New Mexico.

O2a. *Mi Dios y Mi Redentor*
R1003, Tranquilino Luján, Santa Fe, N.Mex., 1952. Reginald and William R. Fisher.

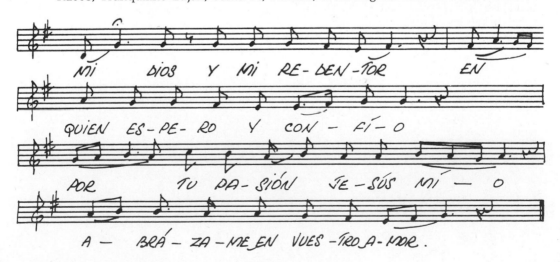

MI DIOS Y MI RE-DEN-TOR EN

QUIEN ES-PE-RO Y CON-FÍ—O

POR TU PA-SIÓN JE-SÚS MÍ — O

A — BRÁ — ZA-ME_EN VUES -TRO_A-MOR.

See note to O1a.

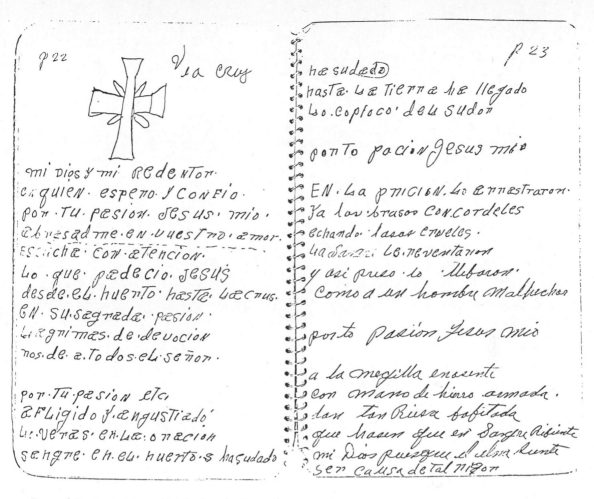

Page of Penitente Manual in the handwriting of Jorge López.

O2b. *Mi Dios y Mi Redentor*
R1032, Jorge López, age 52, Córdova, N.Mex., 1952, Reginald and William R. Fisher.

See note to O1a.

The singer follows the musical phrase-ology, sometimes to the point of breaking off in the middle of a word, as in *abrazadme*.

O3. *Bendito el Santo Madero* (Blessed Be the Holy Wood)
R260, Jorge López, age 50, Córdova, N.Mex., 1950, Robb. Cf. R1019, R2156; Rael (pp. 36–40).

1 Bendito el santo madero, árbol de la santa cruz en quien fuimos redimidos con sangre de mi Jesús.	**1** Blessed be the holy wood, The tree of the holy cross On which we were redeemed By the blood of Jesus.
2 En la cruz mi Redentor con tres clavos fué clavado. Allí se quedó enarbolado el cuerpo de mi Jesús.	**2** To the cross my Redeemer Was nailed with three nails. There hung, crucified, The body of my Jesus.
3 Oíd, Cristiano pecador, la muerte de mi Jesús, que por tenernos amor quiso morir en la cruz.	**3** Hear, Christian sinner, Of the death of my Jesus, Who, because he loved us, Wanted to die on the cross.
4 Cristo murió por nosotros para que vivamos en la luz y dejó en nuestra defensa a la santísima cruz.	**4** Christ died for us So that we might live in the light And he left us for our defense The most holy cross.
5 Se verá un árbol tan fuerte como este santo madero preocupó el mundo entero, Cristo en él tuvo su muerte.	**5** Never was there a tree as strong As this holy wood Which filled the entire world, On it Christ met his death.
6 Este divino estandarte, este saberno teño, en el muerte nuestro dueño y Cristo por rescatarte.	**6** This blood stained symbol, This divine standard, On it died our master And our Christ, to save you.
7 Si el enemigo y la culpa te tenían prisionero, Cristo en el santo madero de muerte eterna te indultó.	**7** If the devil and your sin Held you prisoner, Christ on the holy cross Saved you from eternal death.
8 Allégate al confesor, Cristiano, busca la luz y el madero de la cruz será nuestra defensor.	**8** Go to confession, Christian, seek the light And the wood of the cross Will be our defender.
9 Este sagrado estandarte a Cristo le fué el suplicio.	**9** This sacred standard For Christ was the scaffold.

Ya parecerá el día de juicio
cuando Dios venga a Jualja.

It will appear on the day of judgment
When God comes to Jualja.

10

La santísima cruz
es la señal del Cristiano
y en ella de pies y manos
clavaron a mi Jesús.

10

The holiest cross
Is the symbol of the Christian
And to it they nailed
The hands and feet of my Jesus.

11

En fin santísima cruz,
no me despido de usted.
Cuando Dios me llame a juicio
ruega a mi Creador por mí.

11

Finally, holiest cross
I shall never give you up.
When God calls me to judgment
Before my Creator, pray for me.

12

La cruz está en la custodia
y la hostia en la cruz está
y en el juicio universal
la cruz con Cristo vendrá.

12

The cross is in the host
And the host is in the cross
And in the universal judgment
The cross will come with Christ.

13

Si la cruz es mi abogado
cuando cuenta le dé a Dios
a me se ofera me voz (sic)
dano el más santificado.

13

If the cross is my advocate
When I give account to God
My voice is raised
To the most holy one.

14

¡Con qué gusto, con qué luz
mi alma estará en ese día,
sagrada Virgen María
con la santísima cruz!

14

With what joy, with what light
Will my soul be illumined on that day,
Sacred Virgin Mary
With the holy cross.

15

Alaben al santo madero,
yo adoro a la santa cruz.
En ella murió mi Jesús
nuestro Mesías verdadero.

15

Let us praise the holy wood,
I pray to the holy cross.
On it my Jesus died,
Who was our true Messiah.

16

Adoremos a Jesús
todos postrados al suelo
y la santísima cruz
abra las puertas del Cielo.

16

Let us all adore Jesus,
Lying prostrate on the earth
And may the holiest cross
Open the gates of Heaven.

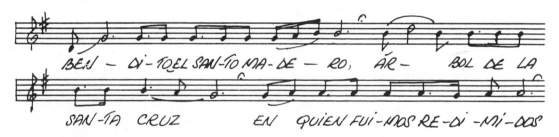

BEN-DI-TO EL SAN-TO MA-DE-RO, ÁR-BOL DE LA SAN-TA CRUZ EN QUIEN FUI-MOS RE-DI-MI-DOS

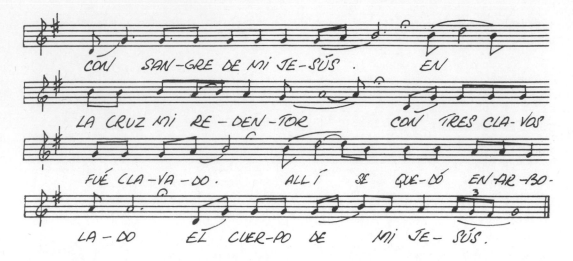

CON SAN-GRE DE MI JE-SÚS. EN
LA CRUZ MI RE-DEN-TOR CON TRES CLA-VOS
FUÉ CLA-VA-DO. ALLÍ SE QUE-DÓ EN-AR-BO-
LA-DO EL CUER-PO DE MI JE-SÚS.

O4. *La Ultima Cena* (The Last Supper)

R25, Francisco Chávez, La Jara, N.Mex., 1944, Robb. Cf. R1028, R1054, R1061, R1083, R1084; Rael (pp. 77–83); Campa 2d (pp. 18–23).

1 Con mansedumbre y ternura y señas de fino amor, le previenen sus discípulos la última cena al Señor.	**1** With meekness and tenderness And signs of fine love, His disciples prepared The last supper of the Lord.
2 Y por mucha caridad que en los mortales ves después ya de haber cenado, les lavó humilde los pies.	**2** And for all the benevolence That was in these mortals, After having supper, He humbly washed their feet.
3 Luego consagró su cuerpo, y con cariñoso afán se les dió muy escondido entre accidentes de pan.	**3** Then he consecrated his body And he showed his solicitous love By dividing the bread Among them.
4 Por este medio dispuso aquel Nuevo Testamento sacrificándose así para desterrar el viejo.	**4** By this means he dispensed this New Testament Thus sacrificing the Old Testament for it.

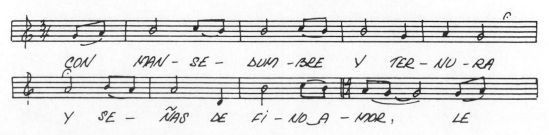

CON MAN-SE-DUM-BRE Y TER-NU-RA
Y SE-ÑAS DE FI-NO_A-MOR, LE

PRE-VIE-NEN SUS DI-SCÍ-PU-LOS

LA ÚL-TI-MA CE-NA AL SE-ÑOR.

I have included only the opening verses of this almost interminable *alabado* since the full text has been published by Juan B. Rael, who includes 133 verses (Rael, pp. 77–83), and by Arthur L. Campa (Campa 2d, pp. 18–23). In fact, the singer referred to the Campa text, which I had brought with me, while singing in order to refresh his recollection.

Rhythmically, this example departs from the unmeasured style of the *alabado*. In its steady 3/4 meter it resembles the *himno*.

O4a. *La Ultima Cena*
R1028, Jorge López, age 52, Córdova, N.Mex., 1952, Reginald and William R. Fisher.

CON MAN-SE-DUM-BRE Y TER-NU-RA

Y SE-ÑAS DE UN FI-NO A-MOR. LES

PRE-VIE-NE A SUS DI-SCÍ-PU-LOS LA ÚL-

TI-MA CE-NA AL SE-ÑOR.

See note to O1a.

O5. *Jesucristo Me Acompañe* (May Jesus Be with Me)
R2154, Jorge López, age 66, Córdova, N.Mex., 1966, Robb. Cf. Rael (p. 35); R1021.

1	1
Jesucristo me acompañe	May Jesus be with me
y el santo ángel de mi guarda	And my guardian angel
para hacer el ejercicio	As I perform the ceremony
del sermón y las tres caídas.	Of the sermon and three falls.

2	2
Recuerda padre querido	Remember dear father
con tan fina voluntad,	With such a fine willpower,

porque éste es el primer paso
y la primera caída que da.

Because this is the first step
And the first fall he takes.

3

Segundo padecimiento
de Jesús Sacramentado,
hoy lo vemos sin alientos,
herido y ensangrentado.

3

Second suffering
Of Jesus, Consecrated,
Today we see him breathless,
Wounded and bloody.

JE - SU - CRI - STO ME A - COM - PA - ÑE

Y EL SAN - TO ÁN - GEL DE MI GUAR - DA PA - RA HA - CER

EL E - JER - CI - CIO DEL SER -

MÓN Y LAS TRES CAÍ - DAS.

For the full text (20 verses) of this *alabado* and others in the facsimile handwriting of the singer, see López 8. Note that the modulation from the Ionian (major) mode to the Aeolian mode, is accomplished by altering the B-natural to B-flat in two places. This is a survival of a medieval practice.

O5a. *Jesucristo Me Acompañe*
R1021, Jorge López, age 52, Córdova, N.Mex., 1952, Robb.

1

Jesucristo me acompañe
y el santo ángel de mi guarda
para hacer el ejercicio
del camino y las tres caídas.

1

May Jesus Christ accompany me
And my guardian angel
As I perform the ceremony
Of the road and the three falls.

2

Recuerde Padre querido
con tu fina voluntad
porque éste es el primer paso
y la primera caída que da.

2

Remember beloved Father
With your fine goodwill
For this is the first step
And the first fall he takes.

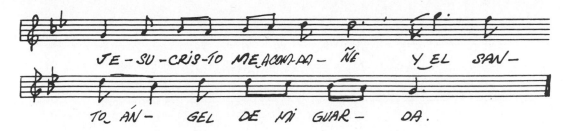

JE-SU-CRIS-TO ME ACON-PA-ÑE Y EL SAN-

TO AN- GEL DE MI GUAR- DA.

This is the same *alabado* as O5, although this version was sung fourteen years earlier (in 1952) by the same singer; note the differences.

O6. *Estaba Junto al Madero* (She Stood Close to the Wood)
R1000, Tranquilo Luján, Santa Fe, N.Mex., 1952, Reginald and William R. Fisher. Cf. Rael (p. 52); R1064.

Refrán	*Refrain*
Estaba junto al madero	She stood close to the wood
de la cruz dolorosa;	Of the sad cross;
Madre de Jesús llorosa	The Mother of Jesus wept
viendo pendiente al Cordero.	At the sight of the Lamb hanging there.

1	1
Cuya alma triste gemía,	Her soul grieved in sadness,
traspasada por el rigor	Transfixed by the keen sharpness
de la espada del dolor	Of the sword of sorrow
de la antigua profecía.	Long ago foretold.

2	2
¡Cuán triste! ¡Con qué aflicción!	Oh, how sad and how afflicted
aquella Madre bendita	Was that blessed Mother
del Unigenito imita	Of the only begotten Son
compasiva la cruel Pasión.	Sharing sadly the cruel Passion.

3	3
Tiembla ya la mujer fuerte	Now the strong Mother trembles
al ver al ínclito yo	To see her illustrious Son
luchando en el leño fijo,	Fighting, nailed to the timbers,
con la más terrible muerte.	With this most terrible death.

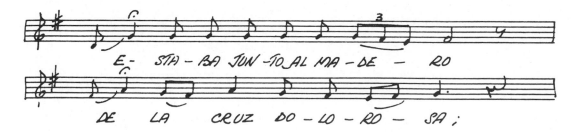

E- STA- BA JUN-TO AL MA-DE - RO

DE LA CRUZ DO - LO - RO - SA;

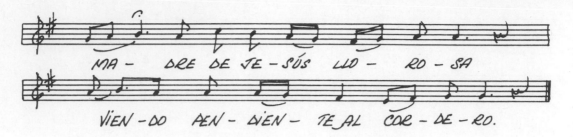

MA - DRE DE JE - SÚS LLO - RO - SA

VIEN - DO PEN - DIEN - TE AL COR - DE - RO.

O7. *Mi Dulce Jesús* (My Sweet Jesus)
R246, Jorge López, age 50, Córdova, N.Mex., 1950, Robb. Cf. R1065.

1 Mi dulce Jesús, dulce padre mío, pésame Señor de haberte ofendido.	**1** My sweet Jesus, My sweet father, I am sorry, Lord, For having offended thee.
2 Madero en los hombros y cruelmente escupido pésame Señor de haberte ofendido.	**2** With the cross on thy shoulders And cruelly spat upon, I am sorry, Lord, For having offended thee.
3 La cruz y corona para Jesús ha sido; pésame Señor de haberte ofendido.	**3** The cross and crown For Jesus were fashioned; I am sorry, Lord, For having offended thee.
4 Corona de espinas que lo lleva vencido; pésame Señor de haberte ofendido.	**4** A crown of thorns Which brought him to submission; I am sorry, Lord, For having offended thee.
5 Una soga gruesa lo lleva vencido; pésame Señor de haberte ofendido.	**5** A thick rope Leads him along; I am sorry, Lord, For having offended thee.
6 Pésame Señor de haberte ofendido.	**6** I am sorry, Lord, For having offended thee.

slow

MI DUL - CE JE - SÚS,

DUL - CE PA - DRE MÍ - O

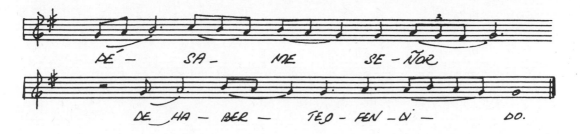

DÉ — SA — ME SE — ÑOR

DE HA — BER — TED — FEN — DI — DO.

O8. *Soy Esclavo de Jesús* (I Am a Slave of Jesus)
   R1005, Tranquilo Luján, Santa Fe, N.Mex., 1952, Reginald and William R. Fisher.
Cf. Rael (p. 86).

1	1
Soy esclavo de Jesús.	I am a slave of Jesus.
Creo en su santa doctrina.	I believe in his holy doctrine.
Creo en su divina estampa	I believe in his divine imprint
de la bandera divina.	And the divine flag.

2	2
Ahí viene ya la bandera	Here it comes now,
de nuestro amado Jesús;	The flag of our beloved Jesus;
es el mismo que clavaron	It is the same that they nailed
en la santísima cruz.	To the holiest cross.

3	3
Esta es la santa bandera	This is the holy flag
de Jesús de Nazareno	Of Jesus of Nazareth.
en ella vemos	In it we see
a un Dios tan justo y tan bueno.	Our God, so just and so good.

4	4
Los creyentes, los cristianos	Those believers, those Christian
que creen en Dios del cielo	Who believe in God in heaven
vengan a ver la bandera	Will come to see the flag
de Jesús de Nazareno.	Of Jesus of Nazareth.

5	5
Por esta bandera santa	By this holy flag
de mi Padre celestial	Of my eternal Father,
por el amor de María	By the love of Mary,
no me vayas a olvidar.	I shall not forget.

6	6
Mi Jesús, mi Padre amado,	My Jesus, beloved Father,
hijo del eterno Padre,	Son of the eternal Father,
nos dejó de intercesora	Left us as an intercessor
a su santísima Madre.	His holiest Mother.

7	7
No olviden la devoción;	Don't forget your devotions;
miren bien que es el camino,	Note well that this is the road,

de seguir esta bandera
de Jesús, pastor divino.

To follow the flag
Of Jesus, the divine shepherd.

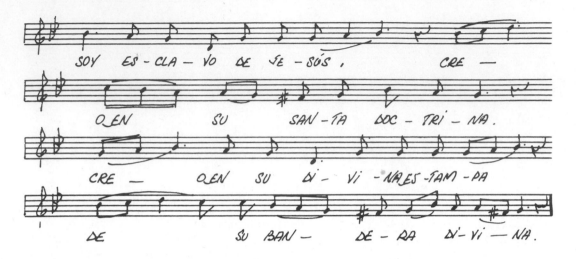

SOY ES-CLA-VO DE JE-SÚS, CRE —
O EN SU SAN-TA DOC-TRI-NA.
CRE — O EN SU DI-VI-NA ES-TAM-PA
DE SU BAN — DE-RA DI-VI-NA.

O9. *Considere, Alma Perdida* (Consider, Lost Soul)
R1076, V. Padilla, Santa Fe, N.Mex., 1952, Reginald and William R. Fisher. Cf. Rael (p. 70).

1
Considere, alma perdida,
en aqueste paso fuerte;
dieron sentencia de muerte
al redentor de la vida.

1
Consider, lost soul,
This stern fact;
They condemned to death
The Redeemer of life.

2
Alvierte lo que cuesta,
hijo ingrato, del Creador,
pues por ser tu redentor
cargó con la cruz a cuestas.

2
Observe, ungrateful son,
What it cost your Creator,
For to redeem you
He accepted death on the cross.

3
El que a los cielos creó
y a la tierra dió el ser,
por su amor quiso caer
al tercer paso que dió.

3
He who created the heavens
And gave the earth its being,
For love of you chose to fall
On the third step which he took.

4
Considera cual sería
en tan recíproco amor,
la pena del Salvador
y el martirio de María.

4
Consider how great would be the pain,
In such a mutual love,
The pain of the Savior
And the martyrdom of Mary.

5
Perdió la ira y el compás
cuando dispuso, severa
que algo menos padeciera
porque padeciera más.

5
He lost his anger and desire for revenge
When he arranged, in a severe decision
That you should suffer somewhat less
Because he would suffer more.

6

El que luz al mundo dió
con semblante sereno
por estar de sangre lleno
en un lienzo se imprimió.

7

Tus culpas fueron la causa
y el peso que le rindió,
pues, segunda vez cayó,
en tu llanto no hagas pausa.

8

Si a llorar Cristo te enseña
y no aprendes la lección,
o no tienes corazón
o serás de bronce o peña.

9

Considera cuán tirano
serás con Jesús rendido
si en tres veces que ha caído
no le das ni aún la mano.

10

A la misma honestidad
los verdugos desnudaron
y sus llagas renovaron
con inhumana crueldad.

11

En medio de los ladrones
en la cruz lo enarbolaron
y su cuerpo descoyuntaron
al clavarle los sayones.

12

Aquí murió el Redentor;
Jesus, ¿cómo pueda ser
que tanto amor llegó a ver
y que viva el pecador?

13

Los clavos ¡qué compasión!
y espinas que le quitaron,
y segunda vez traspasaron
de María el corazón.

6

He who gave light to the day
With its serene aspect,
Because he was covered with his blood,
Imprinted his face on a linen cloth.

7

Your sins were the cause
And the weight which overwhelmed him,
Then for a second time he fell,
In your weeping let there be no pause.

8

If Christ teaches you to weep
And you don't learn the lesson,
Either you have no heart
Or you are made of bronze or stone.

9

Consider what a tyrant
You would be, with Jesus exhausted,
If in the three times he fell
You didn't even give him a hand.

10

Offending his innate modesty
The executioners undressed him
And reopened his wounds
With inhuman cruelty.

11

They fastened him to the cross
Between the thieves
And they disjointed his body
While driving in the nails.

12

Here died the Redeemer;
Jesus, how could it be
That I should live to see so much love
And that the sinner still lives?

13

The nails and thorns
That compassion removed
Pierced the heart of Mary
For the second time.

CON — SI-DE-RA AL-MA PER-DI-DA,   EN A —

QUES-TE   PA —   SO FUER — TE;   DIE — RON SEN —TEN-

Each verse is followed by a brief instrumental interlude on the *pito*, or vertical flute, a characteristic feature of the Penitente processions.

O10. *Jesucristo Se Ha Perdido* (Jesus Christ Is Lost)
R2157, Jorge López, age 66, Córdova, N.Mex., 1966, Robb.

1
Jesucristo se ha perdido.
María lo anda buscando:
¿No ha pasado por aquí
una estrella relumbrando?

1
Jesus Christ is lost.
Mary is out looking for him:
Has there not passed by here
A shining star?

2
Por aquí pasó, Señora,
tres horas antes del alba.
Lleva una túnica blanca
que de sangre va manchada.

2
Lady, he passed by here
Three hours before dawn.
He was wearing a white robe
Which was stained with blood.

3
Una cruz lleva arrastrando
de madera muy pesada;
una soga lleva arrastrando
de los pies a la garganta.

3
He was dragging a cross
Of very heavy wood;
He was dragging a rope
From head to foot.

4
Comencemos a caminar
para llegar a Calvario.
Tres clavos lleva en las manos
con los que ha de ser clavado.

4
Let us start our journey
And go to Calvary.
He was carrying three nails in his hands
With which he would be nailed.

5
San Juan y la Magdalena
se agarran de la mano.
De tanto que caminamos
ya lo habrán crucificado.

5
Saint John and the Magdalene
Hold each other by the hand.
We have walked so long
They will already have crucified him.

6
El que este alabado canta
todos los viernes del año
saca una ánima de penas
y la suya de pecado.

6
He who sings this *alabado*
All the Fridays of the year
Rescues a soul from Purgatory
And his own from sin.

7

Señor mío, Jesucristo,
yo te ofrezco este alabado
por las ánimas benditas
y los que están en pecado.

7

My Lord, Jesus Christ,
I offer you this *alabado*
For the blessed souls
And for the sinners.

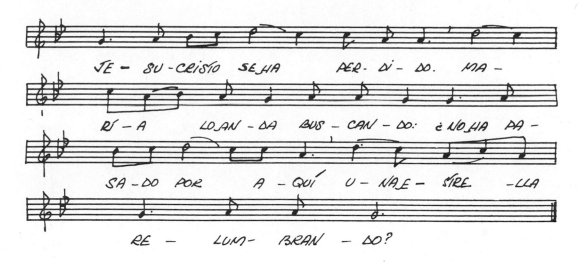

JE - SU - CRIS-TO SE HA PER-DI-DO. MA -
RI - A LO AN - DA BUS - CAN - DO: ¿NO HA PA -
SA - DO POR A - QUÍ U - NA E - STRE - LLA
RE - LUM - BRAN - DO?

O11. *Míralo, Va Caminando* (See Him, He Is Walking)
R2148, Jorge López, age 66, Córdova, N.Mex., 1966, Robb.

1

Míralo, va caminando
mi Jesús Sacramentado.
En la mesa del altar
sea bendito de alabado.

1

See him, he is walking,
My Consecrated Jesus.
At the table of the altar
Let him be blessed in song.

2

Ya lo llevan para el Calvario
a Jesús Sacramentado.
Ya lo ponen en la cruz.
Sea bendito de alabado.

2

They are taking Consecrated Jesus
To Calvary.
Now they are putting him on the cross.
Let him be blessed in song.

3

Pilatos lo sentenció
a Jesús Sacramentado.
Ya le remacharon los clavos.
Sea bendito de alabado.

3

Pilate sentenced
Consecrated Jesus.
Now they are hammering in the nails.
Let him be blessed in song.

4

Corazones afligidos
de Jesús Sacramentado
y le ponen su corona.
Sea bendito de alabado.

4

Hearts are afflicted
For Consecrated Jesus
And they crown him.
Let him be blessed in song.

5

El rostro de mi Jesús
en un lienzo fué estampado.
En la mesa del altar
sea bendito de alabado.

5

The face of my Jesus
Was stamped in a linen cloth.
At the table of the altar
Let him be blessed in song.

6

El sepulcro de Jesús
se quedó purificado.
En la mesa del altar
sea bendito de alabado.

6

The sepulcher of Jesus
Remained purified.
In the table of the altar
Let him be blessed in song.

7

De la llaga del costado
de Jesús Sacramentado
vierte sangre y agua pura.
Sea bendito de alabado.

7

From the wound in the side
Of Consecrated Jesus
Flows blood and pure water.
Let him be blessed in song.

8

Del corazón de Jesús
se compuso este alabado.
Me dejaste en el mundo.
Sea bendito de alabado.

8

From the heart of Jesus
This *alabado* was composed.
You left me in the world.
Let him be blessed in song.

9

Pendiente al pie de la cruz,
mi Jesús Sacramentado,
donde llorara su madre.
Sea bendito de alabado.

9

Waiting at the foot of the cross,
His mother wept,
My Consecrated Jesus.
Let him be blessed in song.

10

Ya lo llevan al Calvario
a que reciba su cruz.
Su corazón fué partido,
de nuestro Padre, Jesus.

10

They are taking him to Calvary
To receive his cross.
The heart of our Father, Jesus,
Was broken.

11

El rostro de mi Jesús
de Jesús, Sacramentado,
en la mesa del altar.
Sea bendito de alabado.

11

The face of my Jesus,
Of Consecrated Jesus
Is present at the table of the altar.
Let him be blessed in song.

12

Dulcísimo Jesús mío,
yo te doy mi corazón
para que cuides de mi alma
y yo tenga perdón.

12

My sweetest Jesus,
I give you my heart
So that you will care for my soul
And I may receive pardon.

13

Dulcísimo Jesús mío
yo te ofrezco este alabado
por la corona de espinas
y la llaga del costado.

13

My sweetest Jesus
I offer you this *alabado*
For the crown of thorns
And the wound in your side.

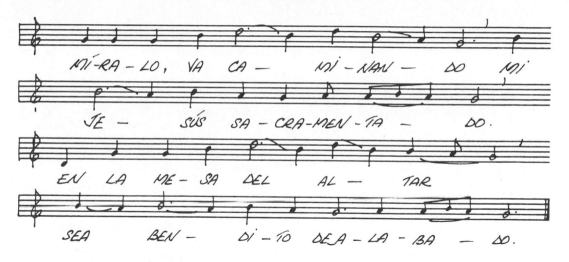

MÍ-RA-LO, VA CA — MÍ-NAN — DO MÍ

JE — SÚS SA-CRA-MEN-TA — DO.

EN LA ME-SA DEL AL — TAR

SEA BEN — DI-TO DEA-LA-BA — DO.

O12. *¡Ay! Mi Jesús Nazareno* (Ah, My Jesus of Nazareth)
R2150, Jorge López, age 66, Córdova, N.Mex., 1966, Robb.

<table>
<tr><td>

1
¡Ay! mi Jesús Nazareno,
por tu pasión tan pesada,

Refrán
San Pedro me abra sus puertas
para entrar en su morada.

2
Cuando a Jesús lo vendió
por plata falsificada,

3
Con un beso de traición
en su mejilla encarnada,

4
Fué la seña que le dió.
En el templo lo tomaba.

5
Al momento lo prendieron
con una muy grande armada.

6
Le ataron los pies y manos
y la soga que le echaron.

7
Ya lo sacan a empellones
y al pretorio lo llevaban.

</td><td>

1
Ah! My Jesus of Nazareth,
By your heavy load of suffering,

Refrain
Saint Peter, open your gates to me
That I may enter your dwelling.

2
When Jesus was sold
For counterfeit silver,

3
With a traitor's kiss
On his rosy cheek,

4
This was the sign of betrayal.
They took him to the temple.

5
At that moment they took him
With a very large armed force.

6
They tied him hand and foot
And put a rope upon him.

7
Now they push him and take him away
To the governor's palace.

</td></tr>
</table>

<table>
<tr><td>

8

En el pretorio lo veían,
los Judíos y sus guías.

9

De ahí lo llevan a Pilatos
para que lo sentencien.

10

Pilatos lo sentenció
de muerte y muy cruel lanzada.

11

De ahí lo sacan al encuentro
donde su madre lo esperaba.

12

Su madre lo agarra en brazos,
y afligida y angustiada.

13

Ya lo quitan de sus brazos
y al Calvario lo llevan.

14

Ya lo tienden en la cruz
y los clavos remachaban.

15

Cuando estaba agonizando
los Judíos burlaban.

16

El día del juicio vendrá
a donde los muertos estaban.

17

Ya lo llevan a la cruz
donde la Reina lo esperaba.

18

Ya lo llevan al sepulcro
y todos lo acompañaban.

19

Su madre como afligida
al sepulcro lo acompañaba.

20

Adiós, hijo de mi vida,
mi bendición te acompaña.

21

Al tercer día vendrá
a donde los muertos estaban.

</td><td>

8

In the palace they looked at him,
The Jews and their rulers.

9

From there they took him to Pilate
For sentencing.

10

Pilate sentenced him to death
And very cruel lance thrusts.

11

From there they took him to the place
Where his mother was waiting for him.

12

His mother embraces him,
Afflicted and in anguish.

13

Now they take him from her arms
And take him to Calvary.

14

Now they place him on the cross
And hammer in the nails.

15

When he was in agony
The Jews made fun of him.

16

The day of judgment will come
In the place of the dead.

17

Now they take him to the cross
Where the Queen was waiting.

18

Now they are taking him to the grave
And everyone is following him.

19

His mother in deep affliction
Accompanied him to the sepulcher.

20

Farewell, son of my life,
May my benediction go with you.

21

On the third day he will come again
From the place of the dead.

</td></tr>
</table>

22

El subió al cielo glorioso
y nadie lo perturbaba.

22

He ascended into heaven in triumph
And no one disturbed him.

22

He ascended into heaven in triumph
And no one disturbed him.

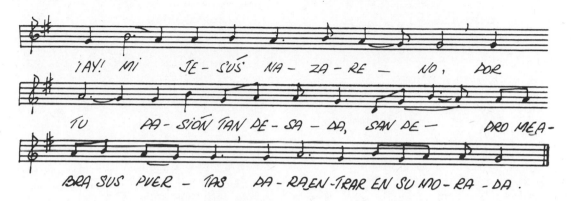

¡AY! MI JE-SÚS NA-ZA-RE — NO, POR
TU PA-SIÓN TAN PE-SA — DA, SAN PE — DRO MEA-
BRA SUS PUER — TAS PA-RAEN-TRAR EN SU MO-RA-DA.

The refrain is intended in actual ceremonies
to be repeated as the last half of each verse.

O13. *Estaba Orando en el Huerto* (He Was Praying in the Garden)
R2149, Jorge López, age 66, Córdova, N.Mex., 1966, Robb.

1

Estaba orando en el huerto
todo lleno de amargura
obedeciendo el precepto
de mi Señor de Esquipula.

1

He was praying in the garden
Full of bitterness
Obeying the precept
Of my Lord of Esquipula.

2

Y Judas que lo vendió
por una falsa locura
por treinta monedas falsas
a mi Señor Esquipula.

2

Judas betrayed him
Out of sheer madness
And for thirty false coins,
He sold my Lord Esquipula.

3

Hoy se lo entregó
con una señal segura,
con un beso que le dió
a mi Señor Esquipula.

3

Today he delivered him
With a certain signal,
A kiss that he gave
To my Lord Esquipula.

4

Los sayones lo amarraron
con una cuerda tan dura;
la sangre le reventaron
a mi Señor Esquipula.

4

The executioners tied him up
With a rope so tight
That it drew forth the blood
Of my Lord Esquipula.

5

A Anás se lo presentaron
y este atrevido asegura
de que han de crucificar
a mi Señor Esquipula.

5

They took him to Annas
And this insolent man asserted
That they must crucify
My Lord Esquipula.

6

En casa de Caifás
¡qué bofetada tan dura
le dió marcas en su rostro
a mi Señor Esquipula!

6

In the house of Caiaphas
They struck such heavy blows that
They left marks on the face
Of my Lord Esquipula.

7

Del tribunal lo sacaron.
Van con el preso, aseguran.
A Pilatos lo llevaron,
a mi Señor Esquipula.

7

From the tribunal they took him.
They take the prisoner manacled.
They took him to Pontius Pilate,
My Lord Esquipula.

8

Pilatos les ordenó
que lo aten a una columna.
Cinco mil azotes dieron
a mi Señor Esquipula.

8

Pilate ordered them
To tie him to a column.
They gave five thousand lashes
To my Lord Esquipula.

9

Herido se lo llevaron
y lo juzgan a la cruz.
Se lo vuelven a Pilatos
a mi Señor Esquipula.

9

They took him away wounded
And sentence him to the cross.
They turn him over to Pilate,
My Lord Esquipula.

10

Dos mil azotes sufrió
por salvar a los cristianos.
Todo el mundo redimió
a mi Señor Esquipula.

10

Two thousand lashes he suffered
To save the Christians.
He redeemed the whole world,
My Lord Esquipula.

11

Le ayuda el Cirneo
con aflicción y ternura.
Este le quita el madero
a mi Señor Esquipula.

11

The Cyrenian helps him
With sadness and tenderness.
He takes away the cross
Of my Lord Esquipula.

12

Una piadosa mujer
con aflicción y ternura
limpió su divino rostro
a mi Señor Esquipula.

12

A pious woman
With sadness and tenderness
Sponged the divine face
Of my Lord Esquipula.

13

Una mujer piadosa
con aflicción y ternura
mirando como lo llevan
a mi Señor Esquipula.

13

A pious woman
With sadness and tenderness
Watches them taking away
My Lord Esquipula.

14

Cuando lo crucificaron
hubo una grande tremora.
Toda la gente lloraba
a mi Señor Esquipula.

14

When they crucified him
There was a great trembling.
All the people wept
For my Lord Esquipula.

<table>
<tr><td>

15

Colocaron en su templo
con una bella ternura
donde van todos a ver
a mi Señor Esquipula.

</td><td>

15

They placed him in his temple
With beautiful tenderness
Where everyone goes to see
My Lord Esquipula.

</td></tr>
<tr><td>

16

Todos los necesitados
que llegan con amargura;
alegres salen de aquí con
mi Señor Esquipula.

</td><td>

16

All those in need
Who come there with bitterness
Go away from here happy, with
My Lord Esquipula.

</td></tr>
<tr><td>

17

Con su poderosa mano
a todos enfermos nos cura.
Quiera Dios Padre que sea
a mi Señor Esquipula.

</td><td>

17

With his powerful hand
He cures all of us who are sick.
I beg God the Father that he be
With my Lord Esquipula.

</td></tr>
<tr><td>

18

Echanos tu bendición.
Por su divino padre;
le pido de corazón
a mi Señor Esquipula.

</td><td>

18

Give us your blessing.
For the divine father;
I pray with all my heart
To my Lord Esquipula.

</td></tr>
</table>

O14. *Después de Haber Azotado* (After Having Whipped)
R2160, Jorge López, age 66, Córdova, N.Mex., 1966, Robb.

1	1
Después de haber azotado al más inocente Abel, que fuese crucificado ordena Pilato cruel.	After having whipped This most innocent Abel, "Let him be crucified" Ordered cruel Pilate.

2	2
Desnudaron al Señor.	They undressed the Lord.
Lo hacen salir a un balcón.	They made him come out on a balcony.
Por hombre tan inhumano	The sentence was carried out
la sentencia se llevó.	By such inhumane men.
3	3
En la segunda estación	In the second station of the cross
con gran prisa caminaba	He walked with great urgency
a la puerta de Pilato	To the door of Pilate
donde la sentencia estaba.	Where the sentencing took place.
4	4
En la tercera estación	In the third station
cayó el divino Jesús	The divine Jesus fell
en la tierra la primera vez	To the ground for the first time
con el peso de la cruz.	With the weight of the cross.
5	5
En la cuarta estación	In the fourth station
volaba más que caía,	He fell less often,
atisba Nuestro Redentor	Our Redeemer sees
su dulce madre, María.	His sweet mother, Mary.
6	6
¡Ay, qué terrible dolor	Ah, what terrible sorrow
los dos amantes pasaron	The two beloved persons felt,
y cuál pena padecieron	And what pain they suffered
al tiempo que se encontraron!	When thus they met!
7	7
En la quinta estación	At the fifth station
al Cirineo obligaron	They compelled the Cyrenian
pero con mala intención	But with bad intentions
y pronto así lo ayudaron.	And thus quickly they helped him.
8	8
Pues por su ciega razón	Because of their blind reasoning
vinieron a descubrir	They came to discover
que el negar es necesario	That to say no is necessary, for
el alivio de morir.	The alleviation of death.
9	9
En la sexta estación	At the sixth station
unas mujeres querían	Some women wanted
enjugar al Redentor	To sponge from the Redeemer
el polvo, sangre, y saliva.	The dust, blood, and saliva.
10	10
En la séptima estación	At the seventh station
y cayó la vez segunda.	He fell for the second time.
Aquellos viles sayones	Those vile executioners
que mi amado hijo siguiera.	Kept following my beloved son.

<table>
<tr><td>

11

En la octava estación
unas mujeres seguían
y al verlas, Jesús, llorar,
con amor las convertían.

</td><td>

11

At the eighth station
Some women were following
And on seeing them weep
Jesus lovingly converted them.

</td></tr>
<tr><td>

12

En la novena estación
cayó de boca en el suelo,
tan herido y lastimado
que vino a dar en el suelo.

</td><td>

12

At the ninth station
He fell on his face,
So wounded and hurt
That he couldn't get up.

</td></tr>
<tr><td>

13

En la décima estación
a Cristo lo desnudaron.
Hiel y vinagre le dieron
que de vino no alcanzaron.

</td><td>

13

At the tenth station
They disrobed Christ.
They gave him gall and vinegar
Instead of wine.

</td></tr>
<tr><td>

14

Lo clavaron de pies y mano
a Nuestro Padre, Jesús,
los judíos inhumanos
en el árbol de la cruz.

</td><td>

14

They nailed him by the hands and feet,
Our Father, Jesus,
On the tree of the cross,
Those inhumane Jews.

</td></tr>
<tr><td>

15

En la undécima estación,
enarbolado en la cruz
al punto cayó el madero
y el cuerpo de buen Jesús.

</td><td>

15

At the eleventh station
As he hung there on the cross,
Suddenly the cross fell
And with it the body of the good Jesus.

</td></tr>
<tr><td>

16

En la duodécima y última estación
fué el entierro de Jesús;
allí lloraba María
y de tinieblas la luz.

</td><td>

16

At the twelfth and last station
The burial of Jesus took place;
Mary was there weeping
And light turned into darkness.

</td></tr>
<tr><td>

17

En esta última estación
todos vamos ofreciendo
por los siglos y de los siglos
por siempre, Jesús, amor.

</td><td>

17

At this last station
All of us come offering
For centuries and centuries,
Forever, Jesus, our love.

</td></tr>
</table>

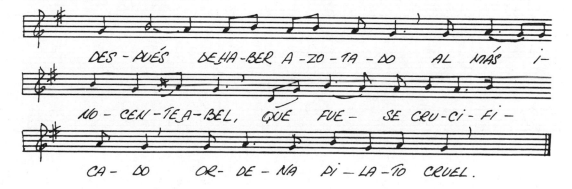

DES-PUÉS DE HA-BER A-ZO-TA-DO AL MÁS I-
NO-CEN-TE A-BEL, QUE FUE- SE CRU-CI-FI-
CA- DO OR-DE-NA PI-LA-TO CRUEL.

These are verses for the stations of the cross.

O15. *Padre Jesús, Nazareno* (Father Jesus of Nazareth)
R1059, Group of Singers from Pecos, N.Mex., 1952, Reginald and William R. Fisher.

1	**1**
Padre Jesús, Nazareno,	Father Jesus of Nazareth,
que queréis hacer de mí,	Do what you will with me,
alabando tu poder	For I hail thy power
y suspirando por ti.	And sigh for thee.
2	**2**
Ya lo estiran de los brazos	They stretched out his arms
para clavarlo mejor;	In order better to nail them;
le remacharon los clavos	And drove the nails
a nuestro Padre Jesús.	Into our Father Jesus.
3	**3**
Le ponen en la cabeza	They placed on his head
una corona de espinas;	A crown of thorns;
se le clavaron las puntas	They drove the spines
en esas sienes divinas.	Into those divine temples.
4	**4**
Ya le echan la soga al cuello	Now they tie a rope around his neck
y lo llevan estirado	And they drag him along,
a nuestro padre, Jesús,	Our Father, Jesus,
ya lo van atormentando.	Tormenting him.

O15a. *Padre Jesús, Nazareno*
R1026, Jorge López, age 52, Córdova, N.Mex., 1952, Robb.

Padre Jesús, Nazareno,	Father Jesus, Nazarene,
que queréis hacer de mí,	Do what you wish with me,
alabando tu poder	As I praise thy power
y suspirando por ti.	And sigh for thee.

PA - DRE   JE - SÚS, NA - ZA - RE — NO, QUE

QUE- RÉIS HA - GA DE MÍ, A - LA - BAN - DO

TU PO - DER Y SU — SPI - RAN - DO POR TI.

O16. *Ayudad, Alma Querida* (Help, Beloved Soul)
R1023, Jorge López, age 52, Córdova, N.Mex., 1952, Reginald and William R. Fisher.
Cf. Rael (p. 29).

1	1
Ayudad, alma querida,	Help, beloved soul,
a sentir a nuestro Padre	To reach our Father
que es Jesús Nazareno	Who is Jesus of Nazareth
hijo de la Virgen Madre.	Son of the Virgin Mother.

2	2
El Jueves Santo en la tarde	On Holy Thursday in the afternoon
cuando a mi Jesús lo prendieron,	When they took Jesus,
caminaba la Virgen Madre	The Virgin Mother went
hasta el Calvario y la cruz.	To Mount Calvary and the cross.

A - YU-DAD, AL - MA QUE - RÍ — DA,

A   SEN-TIR   A NUES -TRO PA - DRE QUE ES JE-SÚS

NA – ZA – RE – NO HI –
JO DE LA VIR – GEN MA – DRE.

O17. *Al Pie de Este Santo Altar* (At the Foot of This Holy Altar)
R1022, Jorge López, age 52, Córdova, N.Mex., 1952, Reginald and William R. Fisher. Cf. Rael (p. 23).

<table>
<tr><td>

1

Al pie de este santo altar
la Virgen fué llorando
por Jesús, su hijo divino,
y en su pasión contemplando.

</td><td>

1

At the foot of this holy altar
The Virgin was weeping
For Jesus, her divine son,
To see his suffering.

</td></tr>
<tr><td>

2

En su santísimo llanto
llama y dice —Ay mi Jesús!
¿Qué haré sola en este monte?
¿Quién lo baja de la cruz?

</td><td>

2

In her holiest complaint
She cried out and said, "O my Jesus!
What will you do alone on this hill?
Who will lower you from the cross?"

</td></tr>
</table>

AL PIE DEES-TE SAN – TO AL – TAR LA
VIR-GEN FUÉ LLO-RAN-DO POR JE-SÚS, SU HI-JO DI-VI-
NO, Y EN SU PA – SIÓN CON TEM-PLAN-DO.

O18. *Venid Pecadores* (Come Sinners)
R372, Group of Women, Chimayó, N.Mex., 1946, Robb.

<table>
<tr><td>

Venid Pecadores,
venid con su cruz
a adorar la sangre
de dulce Jesús.

</td><td>

Come sinners,
Come with your cross
To adore the blood
Of sweet Jesus.

</td></tr>
</table>

642

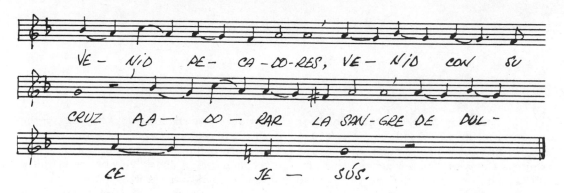

VE — NID PE — CA — DO — RES, VE — NID CON SU

CRUZ AA — DO — RAR LA SAN — GRE DE DUL —

CE JE — SÚS.

O19. *Pito Melody* (no words)
R947, Vicente Padilla, Santa Fe, N.Mex., 1952, Reginald Fisher. Cf. R948.

P. *Alabanza*

The *alabanza* may generally be defined for our purposes here as a song in praise of the Virgin Mary, a saint, or other holy figure. Whereas the *alabados* are generally distinguishable by their characteristic unmeasured melodic line and melismas, the *alabanzas* are found in a number of musical styles and textual forms. This fact I think justifies grouping the *alabados* together as one class separate from the *alabanzas*, not only because of their common subject matter—the Passion of Christ—but also because musically the melodies differ markedly from those of most other religious or secular songs. The lack of a common musical style makes the classification of the *alabanzas* more difficult. For instance, there are songs that, musically, fall somewhere in between the *alabanzas* and the *himnos*, or hymns, although the latter tend to resemble Protestant hymns in their metrical regularity and simplicity, which result in a high proportion of melodies of great beauty. Others occupy the borderland between *alabanza* and *rogativo*, the latter placing emphasis on prayer rather than praise. Classification therefore cannot be exact. Nevertheless, it has the virtue of facilitating the comparison of similar examples and permitting some more or less accurate generalizations.

This section, then, is devoted to representative examples of songs of praise for holy figures. The selections were made on the basis of subject matter rather than on the basis of formal structure of the texts or music. They consequently appear in various forms, each of which might logically have been assigned to other sections of this book. They include, for instance, a number of *alabados*, *décimas*, and *himnos*.

The *alabanzas* that have been available to me, other than those in praise of the Virgin, usually have one of the following as subject: Jesus, Joseph and Mary, Saint Joseph, Saint Anthony, Saint Ignatius de Loyola, Saint Isidor, San Ramón de Nonato, the Holy Sacrament, and a particularly cherished shrine, the Sanctuary of Chimayó, New

Mexico. There are also songs in praise of the Lord in his aspects as Lord of Esquipula and the Holy Child of Atocha. Each of these has its counterpart in the naively beautiful *bultos* (hand-carved and painted statues) and *retablos* (paintings on wood) of Jesus, Mary, and the saints created by the nineteenth-century *santeros* of New Mexico, which have become a treasured chapter in the history of art in America.

The great preponderance of *alabanzas* below are devoted to praise of the Virgin Mary, who enjoys in the Southwest a greater popularity and prestige than in other Latin countries, where the figure of Christ, as for instance in El Salvador, overshadows that of all other holy personages. The patron saint of Mexico is the Virgin of Guadalupe, and for New Mexico a similar position is beginning to be occupied by the Conquistadora, whose cherished image is housed in the cathedral in Santa Fe.

The Southwest has its favorite saints, selected usually from the Catholic iconography by virtue of their relationship to the vicissitudes of frontier life. The reasons for their popularity become self-evident when the saints' backgrounds are known: San Ramón de Nonato is the patron of captives, to whom the prisoners of raiding Indians naturally turned; San Juan Nepomuceño was martyred for refusing to reveal secrets of the confessional and is thus a natural favorite of the secret society of Penitentes; San Ysidro is the patron of agriculture to whom the settlers prayed for protection from locusts and the weather; and El Santo Niño de Atocha, according to tradition, rescues people from all kinds of danger.

Human beings, secular heroes of the people, have been canonized in a way in the patriotic and political songs, the *corridos* and *inditas* and other secular forms, although most people would probably feel competent to select a better list of heroes. In fact, some of these sung heroes have been characters whose only redeeming feature was courage, a virtue that understandably

644

dedico el presente retablo a la Virgen santicima del refucio en acción de gracias por verme concedido el milagro de que enkontrara una llegua que ya la consideraba perdida, viendo yo que todo lo que ise por enkontrarla fue inutil le pedi a nuestra señora del refugio que me concediera enkontrala yyo le publikaria su milagro en cambio de su beneficio como prueva de gratitud por el grandicimo veneficio que me iso al oir mi ruego, lleno de angustia, (la llegua la enkontre en AGUACATITLAN, MEXICO, doy grasias a la santicima Virgen del refugio (Justa Gallegos) de PUEBLO NUEVO ESTANCIA DE SOLIZ MEXICO

Mexican *retablo*, painted on tin, dedicated to Our Lady of Refuge in recognition and gratitude for a miracle.

SAINTS

Retablo of San Ramón de Nonato, patron saint of captives — a favorite saint in a region where many captives were carried off by marauding Indians.

Retablo of San Juan Nepomuceño, patron saint of secret societies.

Below: *Bulto* of San Ysidro made by the famous wood carver Jorge López.

Above: *Retablo* of El Santo Niño de Atocha, repainted on an old board.

was highly prized in the dangerous days of the expanding frontier.

There can be little controversy, however, over most of the ecclesiastical heroes who have been made the subject of the *alabanzas*. They are revered if not worshiped by a large segment of the people, as evidenced by these songs.

Perhaps the most useful source book relating to the subject of this section is Ral-liere's collection of *Cánticos Espirituales* (Ralliere a–d). Originally published in Las Vegas, New Mexico, in the nineteenth century, it has been reprinted in a number of editions. The earliest editions were merely a collection of texts; later editions contain references to hymnbooks or entries such as "aire nacional," indicating a popular origin; and finally the 1944 edition includes music but lacks some of the texts (see Bibliography).

P1. *¡Dios Te Salve, Luna Hermosa!* (God Save Thee, Beautiful Moon!)
R2188, Vicente T. Gallegos, age 69, Albuquerque, N.Mex., 1967, Robb. Cf. Rael (p. 94).

1

¡Dios te salve, luna hermosa!
¡Dios te salve, luz del día!
¡Dios te salve, sol y estrellas!
¡Y Dios te salve, María!

1

God save thee, beautiful moon!
God save thee, light of the day!
God save thee, sun and stars!
And God save thee, Mary!

2

Los ángeles en el cielo,
los hombres en alabanzas
la boca llena digamos
—Virgen, llena eres de gracia.—

2

The angels in the sky,
Mankind with songs of praise
Declare with a loud voice
"Virgin, thou art full of grace."

3

Muy rendido a tus plantas
Reina, mercedes te pido;
concédemelas, Señora,
pues el Señor es contigo.

3

Here at thy feet
Queen, I beg for mercy;
Grant me this, my lady,
For the Lord is with you.

4

Más hermosa que la luna
y más linda que el sol eres
desde el principio del mundo,
Señora, bendita tú eres.

4

More beautiful than the moon
And lovelier than the sun art thou
Since the beginning of the world,
My lady, thou art blessed.

5

Pues tu fuiste la escogida
sagrada Virgen bien puedes
tenerte por la mejor
entre todas las mujeres.

5

Since thou wert chosen
Sacred Virgin, thou mayest well
Regard thyself as the best
Among all women.

6

Los ángeles y los santos
tengan gloria con gran gusto
en el nombre de Jesús,
digan, bendito es el fruto.

6

The angels and the saints
Rejoice with great happiness
In the name of Jesus,
And say, blessed is the fruit.

7

Del oriente nació el sol
dando al mundo hermosa luz;
de tu boca nació el alba,
y de tu vientre, Jesús.

7

In the east the sun arose
Giving beautiful light to the earth;
From thy mouth was born the dawn,
And from thy womb, Jesus.

8

Quien, dichoso, mereciere
ser tu esclavo, madre mía,
con un letrero en el pecho
diciendo, Santa María.

8

The fortunate one who deserves
To be thy slave, mother of mine,
Wears an inscription on his chest
Which reads, "Holy Mary."

9

Pues te dió el rey celestial,
———— gracias;
eres hija de Dios Padre
y santa madre de Dios.

9

For the celestial king
Bestowed on thee all graces (?);
Thou art the daughter of God the Father,
And the holy mother of God.

10

Desde que te coronaron
de diamantes y de flores,
te suplicamos, Señora,
ruega por los pecadores.

10

Since thou wert crowned
With diamonds and flowers,
We implore thee, Lady,
Pray for the sinners.

11

Eres torre de David,
de Jacobo escala fuerte;
danos tu mano ahora
y en la hora de nuestra muerte.

11

Thou art the tower of David,
The strong ladder of Jacob;
Give us thy hand now
And in the hour of our death.

12

En fin, divina Señora,
postrado a tu amparo y luz,
misericordia te pido,
diciéndote, Amén, Jesús.

12

Finally, divine Lady,
Prostrate before thy favor and light,
I beg for mercy,
Saying, Amen, Jesus.

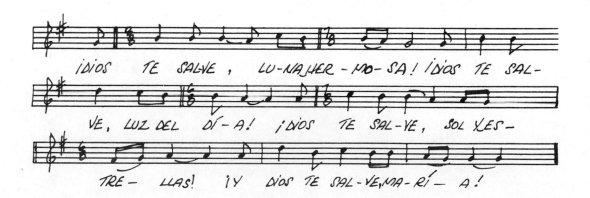

The verses of this *alabanza* are sung solo
with verse 1 repeated by the chorus after
each verse.

P1a. *¡Dios Te Salve, Luna Hermosa!*
R1033, Jorge López, age 52, Córdova, N.Mex., 1952. Reginald and William R. Fisher.

1
¡Dios te salve, luna hermosa!
¡Dios te salve, luz del día!
¡y Dios te salve, gran Señora,
y Dios te salve, María!

1
God save thee, beautiful moon!
God save thee, light of day!
And God save thee, great lady,
And God save thee, Mary!

2
Los ángeles en el cielo,
los hombres en alabanza
la boca llena digamos
—Virgen, llena eres de gracia.

2
The angels in heaven,
Mankind in songs of praise
Say with a loud voice
"Virgin, thou art full of grace."

P1b. *Dios Te Salve, Luz Hermosa* (God Save Thee, Beautiful Light)
R1062, Group of Singers, Pecos, N.Mex., 1952, Reginald and William R. Fisher.

1
Dios te salve, luz hermosa,
Dios te salve, luz del día,
Dios te salve, sol y estrellas,
y Dios te salve, María.

1
God save you, beautiful light,
God save you, light of the day,
God save you, sun and stars,
And God save you, Mary.

2
Los ángeles en el cielo,
los hombres en alabanzas,
la boca llena digamos
—Virgen, llena eres de gracia.—

2
The angels in the sky,
And men with songs of praise,
In full voices we declare
"Virgin, you are full of grace."

3
Voy rendido a tus plantas
y una merced te pido
concédemela Señora
pues el Señor es contigo.

3
I come humbly to your holiness
And a mercy I beg,
Grant it, Lady,
For the Lord is with you.

4

Más hermosa que la luna
y más linda que el sol eres;
desde el principio del mundo
Señora bendita tú eres.

4

More beautiful than the moon
And lovelier than the sun are you.
From the beginning of the world
Lady, you have been blessed.

Each verse of this *alabanza* is sung solo with
the chorus singing verse 1 again after each
verse.

P1c. *Dios Te Salve, Luna Hermosa*
   R1039, Chorus from Sociedad Folklórica, Santa Fe, N.Mex., 1952, Reginald and
William R. Fisher.

1

Dios te salve, luna hermosa,   ]
Dios te salve, luz del día,   ]
Dios te salve, sol y estrella,   ]
Dios te salve, María.   ] *Bis*

1

God save thee, beautiful moon,
God save thee, light of day,
God save thee, sun and star,
God save thee, Mary.

2

Los ángeles en el cielo,
los hombres en alabanza,
la boca llena, proclamamos
—Virgen, llena eres de gracia.—
Dios te salve, luz del osa,[1]
Dios te salve, luz del día,
Dios te salve, sol y estrella,
y Dios te salve, María.

2

The angels in the sky,
Mankind with songs of praise,
Lifting our voices, we proclaim
"Virgin, thou art full of grace."
God save thee, light of the bear,
God save thee, light of day,
God save thee, sun and star,
And God save thee, Mary.

[1] *Luz del osa*, or light of the she-bear, may refer to the constellation Ursa Major, the Great Bear.

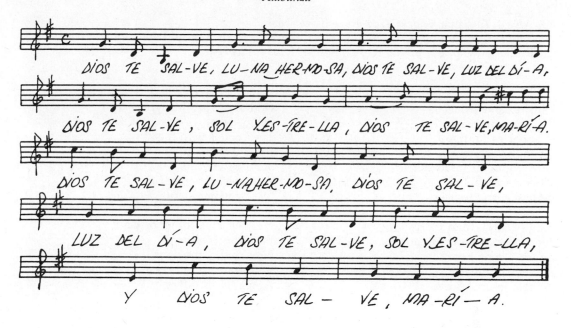

DIOS TE SAL-VE, LU-NA HER-MO-SA, DIOS TE SAL-VE, LUZ DEL DÍ-A,

DIOS TE SAL-VE, SOL Y ES-TRE-LLA, DIOS TE SAL-VE, MA-RÍ-A.

DIOS TE SAL-VE, LU-NA HER-MO-SA, DIOS TE SAL-VE,

LUZ DEL DÍ-A, DIOS TE SAL-VE, SOL Y ES-TRE-LLA,

Y DIOS TE SAL—VE, MA-RÍ—A.

P2. *Dios Te Salve, Dolorosa* (God Save You, Sad Lady)
R1025, Jorge López, age 52, Córdova, N.Mex., 1952, Reginald and William R. Fisher, Cf. Rael (p. 100).

1
Dios te salve, dolorosa,
Madre de nuestro consuelo.
¡Tú nos defiendas, señora,
de las penas del infierno!

2
Por aquel puñalamiento
que tienes atravesado,
no permitas, gran señora,
que mi alma muera en pecado.

1
God save you, sad lady,
Mother of our consolation.
Defend us, lady,
From the pangs of hell!

2
By this dagger thrust
Which you have suffered,
Do not permit, great lady,
That my soul die in sin.

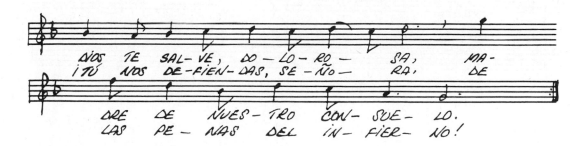

DIOS TE SAL-VE, DO-LO-RO-SA, MA-DRE DE NUES-TRO CON-SUE-LO.
¡TÚ NOS DE-FIEN-DAS, SE-ÑO-RA, DE LAS PE-NAS DEL IN-FIER-NO!

P3. *Dios Te Salve, María* (God Save Thee, Mary)

R1017, Jorge López, age 52, Córdova, N.Mex., 1952, Reginald and William R. Fisher.
Cf. Ralliere d (no. 82, p. 78); R1012, R1038, R1056, R1078.

Dios te salve, María,	God save thee, Mary,
llena eres de gracia,	Full of grace,
el Señor es contigo,	The Lord is with thee,
y bendita tú eres	Blessed art thou
entre todas las mujeres,	Among women,
y bendito es el fruto	And blessed is the fruit
de tu vientre, Jesús.	Of thy womb, Jesus.
Santa María, Madre de Dios,	Holy Mary, Mother of God,
ruega por nosotros pecadores,	Pray for us sinners,
ahora y en la hora	Now and at the hour
de nuestra muerte,	Of our death,
así sea. Jesús, María.	Amen. Jesus, Mary.

P4. *Dios Te Salve, Virgen* (God Save You, Virgin)
R1006, Tranquilo Luján, Santa Fe, N.Mex., 1952, Reginald and William R. Fisher. Cf. Rael (p. 99).

Refrán
Dios te salve, Virgen pura,
quien humilde y recibida
fuiste de Dios tan querida
que no quiso otra criatura.

Refrain
God save you, pure Virgin,
Who, humble and receptive,
Was so loved by God
That he loved no other living creature.

1
Por eso Virgen María
verdadera imitadora
de Jesús que el alma implora,
siendo nuestro amparo y guía.

1
It is through this Virgin Mary,
True imitator of Jesus,
That the soul implores,
She being our protection and guide.

Refrán

Refrain

2
La que por todo elegiste
la mejor sagrada rosa,
también fuiste mariposa
que a las alturas subiste.

2
Since you were chosen from all the world
The best, most sacred rose,
Likewise you were a butterfly
Who ascended to the heavens.

Refrán

Refrain

3
Dentro de una hermosa nube
los ángeles te ———
y ellos mismos preguntaban,
—¿cuál es la aurora que sube?—

3
Behind a beautiful cloud
The angels ——— you
And they asked themselves,
"What is this dawn which is coming up?"

Refrán

Refrain

4
Tanto ha estado su humildad
entre coloquios y aromas
del Señor las tres coronas,
Santísima Trinidad.

4
So great has been her humility
Between talks and odors
Of the Lord three crowns,
Holiest Trinity.

Refrán

Refrain

5
Mas mirando el resplendor
todos te cantamos una
hermosa más que la luna,
reluciente más que el sol.

5
But seeing this splendor
Everyone sings to you of a
Beauty surpassing that of the moon,
More brilliant than the sun.

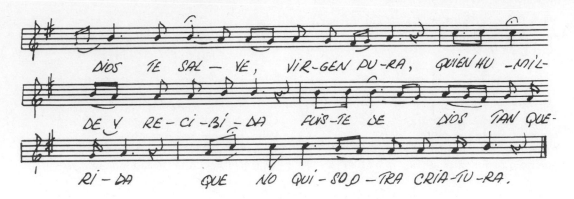

DIOS TE SAL — VE, VIR-GEN PU-RA, QUIEN HU —MIL-
DE Y RE-CI-BÍ —DA FUIS-TE DE DIOS TAN QUE-
RI-DA QUE NO QUI-SO O-TRA CRIA-TU-RA.

P5. *Dios Te Salve, Dolorosa* (God Save You, Lady of Sorrows)
R2155, Jorge López, age 66, Córdova, N.Mex., 1966, Robb. Cf. Rael (p. 100).

<table>
<tr><td>

1
Dios te salve, dolorosa
traspasada madre
en tribulaciones
¡o, madre agradable!

</td><td>

1
God save you, Lady of Sorrows,
Mother pierced with pain
And tribulations
Oh, adorable Mother!

</td></tr>
<tr><td>

2
Del puñal agudo
de aquel venerable
tradujo en su pecho:
se cumplió el dictamen.

</td><td>

2
By the sharp dagger
Thrust in the breast
Of that holy one
The sentence was fulfilled.

</td></tr>
<tr><td>

3
Suspiros ardientes
de tu pecho salen.
¡Ay! que mis entrañas
pueden aliviarte.

</td><td>

3
Ardent sighs
Come from your breast.
Oh, may my heart
Comfort you!

</td></tr>
<tr><td>

4
Los ojos divinos
fueron unos mares;
dales a los míos
lágrimas de sangre.

</td><td>

4
The divine eyes
Were like oceans;
Give to mine
Tears of blood.

</td></tr>
<tr><td>

5
Las piedras se quiebran
y braman los mares a
los ejecutivos.
Los sepulcros se abren.

</td><td>

5
The rocks broke
And the sea roared at
The executioners.
The tombs were opened.

</td></tr>
<tr><td>

6
Cuando tu cabeza
Virgen, coronaste
suspiros tenían
como dulce madre.

</td><td>

6
When your head,
Virgin, was crowned
There were sighs,
Sweet Mother.

</td></tr>
</table>

7

Tú sola padeces
tus penas iguales
al pie de la cruz
constante.

8

Viuda y sin esposo,
huérfana y sin padre,
triste y sin el hijo,
sola y sin amante.

9

Virgen poderosa
¡Ay! que aquí te alaben
con la voz del hombre
al eterno Padre.

10

O Madre piadosa
O inocente Madre
tortolita triste
Amén, salve, salve.

7

You alone suffer
Along with him
Beside the cross
Constantly.

8

Widow, without a husband,
Orphan, without a father,
Sad, without her son,
Alone, without a lover.

9

Powerful Virgin
May they praise you here
With the voice of man
To the eternal Father.

10

O merciful Mother,
O innocent Mother,
Sad turtledove
Amen, hail, hail.

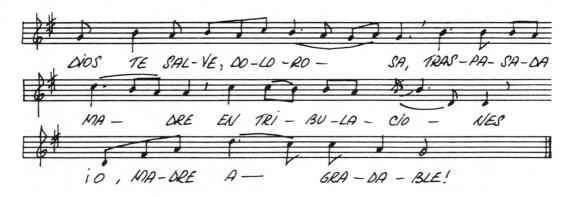

P6. ¡*O María*! ¡*Madre Mía*! (O Mary, My Mother!)
R203, Julianita Trujillo, Chimayó, N.Mex., 1949, Robb. Cf. Ralliere a (p. 73).

1

¡O María! ¡Madre mía!
¡O consuelo del mortal!
Amparadme y guíadme
a la patria celestial.

2

Con el Angel de María
la grandeza celebrad
transportando de alegría
por mí —— es cantar.

1

O Mary, my Mother!
O consolation of mankind!
Shelter me and guide me
To the celestial fatherland.

2

With the Angel of Mary
We celebrate her greatness
And transported with happiness
For me it is —— to sing.

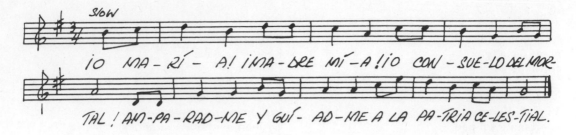

¡O MA-RÍ-A! ¡MA-DRE MÍ-A! ¡O CON-SUE-LO DEL MOR-TAL! AM-PA-RAD-ME Y GUÍ-AD-ME A LA PA-TRIA CE-LES-TIAL.

This is an *alabanza* in form of a *himno* (hymn).

P7. *¡Ave María Purísima!* (Hail Purest Mary!)
R1067, Group of Singers from Pecos, N.Mex., 1952, Reginald and William R. Fisher. Cf. R2381, R2382, R2384; Rael (p. 103).

1
¡Ave María purísima!
¡Ave María poderosa!
¡Ave María prodigiosa!
¡dulce Ave María santísima!

1
Hail purest Mary!
Hail powerful Mary!
Hail prodigious Mary!
Sweet and most holy Mary!

2
Siempre de Dios benditísima
eres refulgente aurora,
seno con Dios protectora,
dulce Ave María santísima.

2
Always the most blessed of God
You are the glowing dawn,
The protective womb of God,
Sweet and most holy Mary!

3
De aquella sierpe cruelísima
que nos quiere devorar,
de ella nos has de librar,
dulce Ave María santísima.

3
From the most cruel serpent
That wants to devour us
You have to deliver us,
Sweet and most holy Mary!

4
Pues eres excelentísima
Virgen Reina y sin igual,
siempre diré sin cesar
dulce Ave María santísima.

4
Since you are the most excellent
Virgin without an equal,
I shall always say without ceasing
Sweet and most holy Mary!

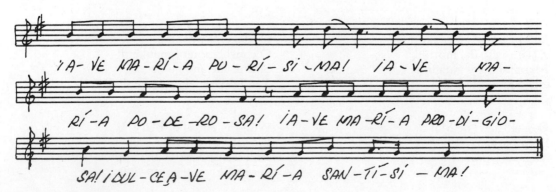

¡A-VE MA-RÍ-A PU-RÍ-SI-MA! ¡A-VE MA-RÍ-A PO-DE-RO-SA! ¡A-VE MA-RÍ-A PRO-DI-GIO-SA! ¡DUL-CE A-VE MA-RÍ-A SAN-TI-SI-MA!

P8. *Tañita de Galisteo* (Tañita of Galisteo)
R556, Francisco S. Leyva, age 81, Leyva, N.Mex., 1951, Robb.

Planta
Tañita de Galisteo
sabia, valerosa, y fuerte
favorece nuestra gente
es todo nuestro deseo.

1
Hija del eterno Padre,
del santo espíritu esposa,
del hijo madre amorosa,
y patrona de este valle,
hermosa y respetable
de los ángeles recreo.
Y en tu patrocinio creo y
nos tengas en su memoria
Y hasta vernos en la gloria
Tañita de Galisteo.

2
Ante vuestro catamiento
piden tus Taños postrados
los permita el aliento
de valerosos soldados
para que como sus criados
que sirven rendidamente
piadosa y omnipotente
que nos ayuda de fuerza
pues eres tú, providencia
sabia, valerosa, y fuerte.

Planta
Tañita of Galisteo
Wise, brave, and strong,
All we want is that you look
With favor on our people.

1
Daughter of the eternal Father,
Wife of the Holy Spirit,
Loving mother of the Son,
And patron of this valley,
Beautiful and respectable
Joy of the angels.
I believe in your patronage.
May you remember us
Until you see us in heaven,
Little Taño of Galisteo.

2
Before your glance
Your prostrate Taños beg
That you grant them the vigor
Of brave soldiers
So that like your servants
They may serve you humbly,
Holy and omnipotent one
Who helps us with your strength,
For you are our protector,
Wise, brave, and strong.

Three remaining verses are undeciphered.

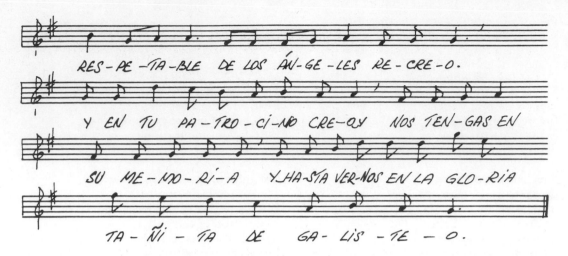

RES-PE -TA-BLE DE LOS ÁN-GE-LES RE-CRE-O.

Y EN TU PA-TRO-CÍ-NO CRE-OY NOS TEN-GAS EN

SU ME-MO-RÍ-A Y HA-STA VER-NOS EN LA GLO-RÍA

TA- ÑI - TA DE GA- LIS -TE - O.

The church at Galisteo was formerly dedicated to La Tañita. After reconstruction it was rededicated to a new patron, San José del Cadillal (see P11; also T5, a different song with the same title as this; also P8).

P9. *Madre de Dolores* (Mother of Sorrows)
R1001, Tranquilo Luján, Santa Fe, N.Mex., 1952, Reginald and William R. Fisher. Cf. R1027, R1045, R1050, R1069, R1081; Rael (p. 40).

Refrán	*Refrain*
Madre de dolores,	Mother of sorrows,
madre de tormentos	Mother of torment,
¡ay, dulce madre,	Oh, Sweet Mother,
qué sentimiento!	What sadness!

1	1
Vuestro hijo hermoso,	Your handsome son,
vuestro lucero,	Your morning star,
sudando sangre	Is in the orchard
está en el huerto.	Sweating blood.

Refrán	*Refrain*

2	2
Mortales ansias	Mortals anxious
de mi remedio	For my help,
hacen que sude	May you exude
licor tan bello.	A liquid as beautiful as that.

Refrán	*Refrain*

3

Luz escogida,
en tanto aprieto,
lo dejan solo,
dados al sueño.

Refrán

4

Ya vino Judas,
traidor perverso,
con los sayones
para prenderlo.

3

The chosen one, light of the world,
They left you alone
In such a crisis,
They gave themselves up to sleep.

Refrain

4

Then Judas came,
That perverse traitor,
With the executioners
To arrest him.

P9a. *Madre de Dolores*
R1027, Jorge López, age 52, Córdova, N.Mex., 1952, Robb.

The words are identical with those of P9 except that the refrain is sung only at the beginning and the singer sang only three verses.

Musically this is a cross between the unmeasured *alabado* style and the metered style of the *himno*.

P10. *Jesús, María, y José* (Jesus, Mary, and Joseph)
R1470, Esteban Torres, age 62, Tomé, N.Mex., 1957, Robb.

1	1
Daremos gracias con fe	We give thanks with faith
y crecidas esperanzas	And growing hope
cantando las alabanzas	Singing the praises
de Jesús, María, y José.	Of Jesus, Mary, and Joseph.
2	2
Cantan dulces serafines,	The sweet seraphim sing,
Ellos le saludaré,	I shall salute them,
cantando las alabanzas	Singing the praises
de Jesús, María, y José.	Of Jesus, Mary, and Joseph.
3	3
Tres padres caritativos	Three fathers of charity
para pedirles merced	Come to beg mercy
las tres divinas personas	Of the three divine persons
de Jesús, María, y José.	Of Jesus, Mary, and Joseph.
4	4
Hoy preparen tus gargantas	Today prepare your throats
en pregon para quien	To proclaim to everyone
cantando las alabanzas	In song the praises
de Jesús, María, y José.	Of Jesus, Mary, and Joseph.
5	5
Las tres divinas personas	The three divine persons,
(¡cómo las adoraré!)	(How I adore them!)
las rosas matutinas	Are the roses of morning
de Jesús, María, y José.	Jesus, Mary, and Joseph.
6	6
Muy bien demuestra consuelo	Well proven comfort
al instante se ven	Comes immediately
los tres pilares del cielo	From the three pillars of the sky
de Jesús, María, y José.	Jesus, Mary, and Joseph.
7	7
Por unos lindos candores	When I enter the church
cuando por la iglesia entré	It is only to see among the flowers
sólo por ver entre flores	These pure and beautiful ones
a Jesús, María, y José.	Jesus, Mary, and Joseph.
8	8
¡Qué tronos tan encumbrados!	What elevated thrones!
¡qué elevado me quedé!	How elevated I am!
de ver en tan lindos prados	To see in such beautiful meadows
a Jesús, María, y José.	Jesus, Mary, and Joseph.
9	9
Ví tres luces encendidas	I saw three glowing lights,
y luego al punto me hinqué	And at once I knelt before

las tres rosas de Castilla,
de Jesús, María, y José.

10
Permite, Sangre preciosa,
que en nuestros labios esté
la miel pura y deliciosa
de Jesús, María, y José.

11
La Trinidad soberana
me permita esta merced
que yo para siempre alabe
a Jesús, María, y José.

12
¿Para la hora de mi muerte
a quién me encomendaré?
A los dulcísimos nombres
de Jesús, María, y José.

13
El que quisiera salvarse
y quiera pedir merced,
cantando las alabanzas
de Jesús, María, y José.

14
Las nubes y los relámpagos
y las estrellas también
todos rinden obediencia
a Jesús, María, y José.

15
Bendito seas Padre Eterno
él que nos hizo este bien
de darnos todo el consuelo
en Jesús, María, y José.

16
¿Para las puertas del cielo,
qué padrinos llevaré?
Serán San Miguel Arcángel
y Jesús, María, y José.

17
Desde el sur hasta el norte
frío hasta el oriente también
todos rinden obediencia
a Jesús, María, y José.

18
Por aquel día postrero,
ésta mi Dios te diré:

The three roses of Castile,
Jesus, Mary, and Joseph.

10
Grant, precious Blood,
That on our lips may be
The pure and delicious honey
Of Jesus, Mary, and Joseph.

11
The sovereign Trinity
Permits me this mercy
That forever I may praise
Jesus, Mary, and Joseph.

12
In the hour of my death
To whom shall I commend myself?
To the sweetest names
Of Jesus, Mary, and Joseph.

13
He who would save himself
And would beg for mercy,
Should sing the praises
Of Jesus, Mary, and Joseph.

14
The clouds and the lightning
And the stars as well
All give obedience
To Jesus, Mary, and Joseph.

15
Blessed be Thou Eternal Father,
Thou who hast made us,
For giving us all the consolation
Of Jesus, Mary, and Joseph.

16
At the gates of heaven
What godfather will I have?
It will be the Archangel Michael
And Jesus, Mary, and Joseph.

17
From the south to the cold north
And to the east as well
All give obedience
To Jesus, Mary, and Joseph.

18
On the last day
This, My God, I will say to you:

me amparen los dulces nombres
de Jesús, María, y José.

May the sweet names protect me,
Of Jesus, Mary, and Joseph.

19
Canten en su son las aves
mejor de lo que pensé
declaren las alabanzas
de Jesús, María, y José.

19
The birds in their song
Sing better than I thought
And proclaim the praises
Of Jesus, Mary, and Joseph.

DA-RE-MOS GRA-CIAS CON FE Y CRE-CI-DAS ES-PE-RAN-ZAS CAN-TAN-DO LAS A-LA-BAN—ZAS DE JE-SÚS, MA-RÍA y JO-SÉ.

P10, an unusually beautiful text, is an *alabado* in the form of a *himno*. Like P7, it is characterized by the repetition of the same words as the last line of each verse.

P11. *San José del Cadillal* (Saint Joseph of the Cadillal)
R557, Francisco S. Leyva, age 81, Leyva, N.Mex., 1951, Robb. Cf. P8.

Planta
Salve, patriarca supremo,
salve, esposo de María;
padre eres del Hijo eterno,
de los cielos alegría.

Planta
Hail, supreme patriarch,
Hail, husband of Mary;
You are father of the eternal Son,
Joy of the heavens.

1
San José, vara florida,
inmaculado varón,
dame paz en esta vida
y en la muerte salvación;
ten de mi alma compasión
hoy te suplica tu siervo;
líbranos del fuego eterno
para ensalzar todo el orbe;
San José, tu santo nombre,
salve, patriarca supremo.

1
Saint Joseph, flowering staff,
Immaculate man,
Give me peace in this life
And in death, salvation;
Have compassion for my soul,
Your servant begs you today;
Deliver us from the eternal fire
To extol you throughout the world;
Saint Joseph, your holy name we
Hail, supreme patriarch.

2
San José, vara de plata,
escogido entre millares
para esposo de la más santa;
de los sagrados altares
Dios te escogió entre pilares;

2
Saint Joseph, rod of silver,
Chosen from among thousands
To be the husband of the holiest woman;
From the sacred altars
God chose you to be three pillars;

Jesús, José, y María,
grande es tu soberanía;
ángeles con dulce canto
publican tu nombre santo,
salve, esposo de María.

Jesus, Joseph, and Mary,
Great is your sovereignty;
Angels with sweet song
Publish your holy name,
Hail, husband of Mary!

3

Padre del linaje humano,
amparo de pescadores,
no nos dejes de tu mano;
esperamos tus favores;
líbranos de los rigores
de las penas del infierno;
te pide tu pueblo tierno,
pues tu favor singular
en el trono celestial,
padre eres del Hijo eterno.

3

Father of the human lineage,
Guardian of fishermen,
Do not withhold your helping hand;
We hope for your favors;
Save us from the rigors
Of the punishments of hell;
Your humble people beg
For your special favor
Before the heavenly throne,
For you are the father of the eternal Son.

4

San José del Cadillal,
de Galisteo patrón,
tú eres el fuerte pilar
de la Católica Unión;
tú sostienes la cuestión
contra la cruel herejía;
en el nombre de María
tú destierras el error
de tus siervos defensor,
de los cielos alegría.

4

Saint Joseph of the Cadillal,
Patron of Galisteo,
You are the strong pillar
Of the Catholic Union;
You uphold the arguments
Against cruel heresy;
In the name of Mary
You refute all errors
As the defender of your servants
And the joy of the heavens.

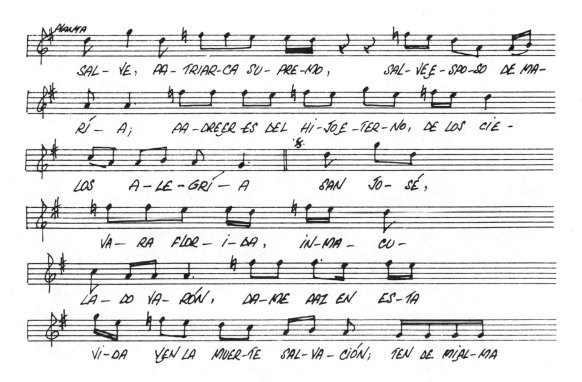

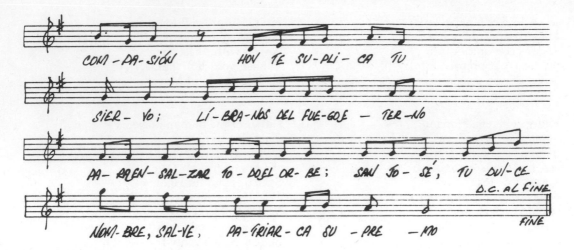

This is an *alabanza* in both the literary and musical form of a *décima*. The Cadillal is an area near the town of Galisteo, New Mexico, the subject of nineteenth-century litigation. See *Tañita de Galisteo* (T5), a prayer for victory in that litigation.

A fifth verse heard on the recording remains undeciphered.

P12. *Milagros de San Antonio* (Miracles of Saint Anthony)
R245, Jorge López, age 50, Córdova, N.Mex., 1950, Robb. Cf. R373.

1	1
Y si mi lengua me ayuda	If my tongue will help me
y me escucha mi auditorio	And my audience will listen
le cantaré los milagros	I will sing them the miracles
del glorioso San Antonio.	Of glorious Saint Anthony.

2	2
Yo soy nacido en Lisboa	I was born in Lisbon
y criado en la misma playa	And raised in the same place
y en la capilla del Rey	And in the chapel of the King
la fe de Cristo tomaba.	I accepted the faith of Christ.

3	3
Yo nací de padres nobles	I was born of noble parents
como así lo diré yo,	Just as I will tell you,
de Doña María de Atodeo	Of Doña María de Atodeo
y Don Diego de Agodoy.	And Don Diego de Agodoy.

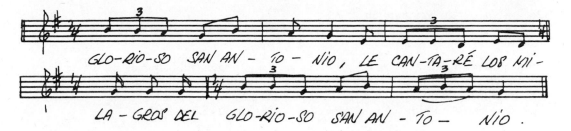

GLO-RIO-SO SAN AN - TO - NIO, LE CAN-TA-RÉ LOS MI-
LA - GROS DEL GLO-RIO-SO SAN AN - TO - NIO.

This appears to be a religious *romance* of Portuguese origin (note the reference to Lisbon). Note also the assonated sixteen-syllable line, characteristic of the *romance*.

Saint Anthony is the patron of things lost, to whom devout believers pray for the restoration of lost objects.

Bulto of San Antonio carrying a lost child in his arms.

Retablo of San Antonio, again with a lost child.

P12a. *Milagros de San Antonio*
R373, Julianita and Eusebia Trujillo, Chimayó, N.Mex., 1946, Robb.

Si mi lengua me ayuda,	If my tongue will help me
si me escucha mi auditorio	If my audience will listen
para cantar los milagros	I shall sing the miracles
del glorioso San Antonio.	Of glorious Saint Anthony.

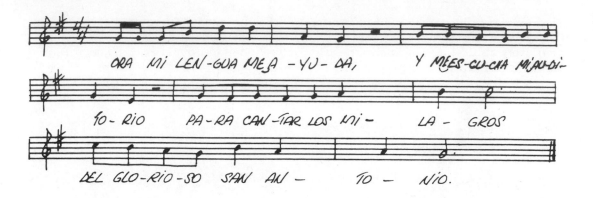

P13. *Por Vuestros Grandes Favores* (By Your Great Kindness)
R1009, Tranquilo Luján, Santa Fe, N.Mex., 1952, Reginald and William R. Fisher.
Cf. Ralliere d (p. 195).

1

Por vuestros grandes favores	By your great kindness
dan de quien sois testimonio.	Give to everyone a testimony.

Coro

Milagroso San Antonio	Miraculous Saint Anthony
rogad por los pecadores.	Pray for all sinners.

2

Vuestra palabra divina	Your divine words
forzó a los peces del mar	Compelled even the fish of the sea
que saliesen a escuchar	To come out to listen
vuestro sermón y doctrina	To your sermon and doctrine
y pues fué tan peregrina	And it was so perfect
que extirpó diez mil errores.	That it wiped out ten thousand errors.

Coro

3

Vos sois de la tempestad	You are our miraculous defense
el amparo milagroso	Against the tempests
del incendio rigoroso;	And raging fires;
agua de la claridad,	You are the pure waters,
puerto de seguridad	The gateway of security
del mal y de sus rigores.	Against evil and its rigors.

Chorus

Chorus

666

Coro   Chorus

4   4

Sanáis mudos y tullidos   You heal the dumb and the crippled,
paralíticos, leprosos;   Paralytics and lepers;
a endemoniados furiosos   To those possessed by demons
restituyen los sentidos,   You restore their senses.
volvéis los bienes perdidos   You bring back lost loved ones
y curáis todos dolores.   And cure all afflictions.

Coro   Chorus

DAN DE QUIEN SOIS TES-TI-MO-NIO.

This is an *alabanza* in the style of an *alabado*.

P13a.   *Pues Vuestros Grandes Favores*
R1008, Tranquilo Luján, Santa Fe, N.Mex., 1952, Reginald and William R. Fisher.

Pues vuestros grandes favores,   In view of your great favors,
dan de quien sois testimonio,   Gift of him whose witness you are,
milagroso San Antonio   Miraculous Saint Anthony,
rogad por los pecadores,   Pray for all sinners,
rogad por los pecadores.   Pray for all sinners.

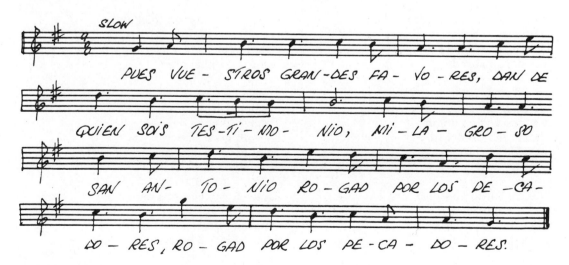

This is an *alabanza* in the style of a *himno*.   cept that each verse ends with the last three
Additional verses remain undeciphered, ex-   lines of the above text.

P14. *San Ysidro, Labrador* (Saint Isidor, Laborer)
R244, Jorge López, age 50, Córdova, N.Mex., 1950, Robb. Cf. R1927, R2544.

1	**1**
San Ysidro, Labrador	Saint Isidor, Laborer,
patrón de la labor,	Patron of labor,
liberta nuestro sembrado,	Deliver our cornfields,
San Ysidro, Labrador.	Saint Isidor, Laborer.
2	**2**
Por el gran merecimiento	For the great merit
con que te adoro, el Señor,	With which I adore you, Lord,
liberta nuestro sembrado,	Deliver our cornfields,
San Ysidro Labrador.	Saint Isidor, Laborer.
3	**3**
Por el sudor y trabajo	By the sweat and labor
con que fuiste fatigado,	With which you were fatigued,
liberta nuestro sembrado,	Deliver our cornfields,
San Ysidro Labrador.	Saint Isidor, Laborer.
4	**4**
Porque está comisionado	Because you were announced
por patrón de la labor,	By God as patron of labor,
liberta nuestro sembrado,	Deliver our cornfields,
San Ysidro Labrador.	Saint Isidor, Laborer.
5	**5**
Porque fuiste anunciado	Because you were announced
de Dios por trabajador,	By God as a worker,
liberta nuestro sembrado,	Deliver our cornfields,
San Ysidro Labrador.	Saint Isidor, Laborer.
6	**6**
Del ladrón acostumbrado	From the customary thief and
y sin temer al Señor,	From fear, O Lord,
liberta nuestro sembrado,	Deliver our cornfields,
San Ysidro Labrador.	Saint Isidor, Laborer.
7	**7**
En ti esperamos	In you we trust
llevar cosecha en unión	To give us good harvest
por tu gran misericordia,	By your great mercy,
San Ysidro Labrador.	Saint Isidor, Laborer.
8	**8**
Adiós mi Santo Glorioso,	Farewell, my glorious saint,
cortesano del Señor,	Courtier of the Lord,
hasta el año venidero,	Until next year,
San Ysidro Labrador.	Saint Isidor, Laborer.

SAN Y- SÍ- DRO, LA- BRA- DOR — PA-
-TRÓN DE LA LA- BOR, LI-
BER-TA NUES-TRO SEM- BRA- DO
SAN Y- SI- DRO LA- BRA- DOR

This *alabanza* is in the style of an *alabado*.

San Ysidro is a favorite saint in the Southwest, where he is regarded as the patron of farmers and relied on to protect crops. There are many *bultos* of the saint in the rural communities and, it is said, when crops fail, his *bulto* is put into a dark closet as a punishment.

P14a. *San Isidro, Labrador*

R1016, Tranquilo Luján, Santa Fe, N.Mex., 1952, Reginald and William R. Fisher. Cf. R82, R244, R1041; Ralliere d (p. 197).

Coro	*Chorus*
San Isidro, labrador,	Saint Isidor, laborer,
patrón de los labradores,	Patron of the laborers,
liberta nuestros sembrados	Deliver our fields
de langostas y temblores.	From locusts and earthquakes.

1	1
Por el gran merecimiento	By the great merit
con que te adoro y el Señor,	With which I adore you and the Lord,
liberta nuestros sembrados,	Save our fields,
San Isidro, labrador.	Saint Isidor, laborer.

2	2
Cuando el Señor por castigo	When the Lord as punishment
nos mande mal temporal,	Sends us temporal evils,
con tu poderoso abrigo	Sheltered by your powerful protection
nos vemos libres de mal.	We see ourselves free from harm.

Coro	*Chorus*

3

Adiós mi santo glorioso,
contigo saludo el Señor
hasta el año venidero,
San Isidro, labrador.

3

Farewell my glorious saint,
With you I hail the Lord
Until the coming year,
Saint Isidor, laborer.

This *alabanza* is in the style of a *himno*.

P14b. *San Isidro, Labrador*
R82, Adela Romero, San Antonio, Socorro County, N.Mex., 1946, Robb.

San Isidro, Labrador,
patrón de los labradores,
liberta nuestros sembrados
de langostas y temblores.

Saint Isidor, Laborer,
Patron of laborers,
Deliver our cornfields,
From insects and earthquakes.

P14c. *San Ysidro, Labrador*
     R1041, Sociedad Folklórica Chorus, Santa Fe, N.Mex., 1952, Reginald and William R. Fisher.

1	**1**
San Ysidro, Labrador,	Saint Isidor, Laborer,
patrón de los labradores,	Patron of workers,
que nos libres de favor	Kindly deliver us
de langostas y temblores.	From locusts and earthquakes.
2	**2**
En tu ——— confiado	Trusting in your ———
te pido de corazón,	I beg from the heart,
levantes a mis sembrados	Save my fields
. . . [undecipherable]	. . .
3	**3**
Adiós, o santo glorioso,	Farewell, O glorious saint,
el cortiso del Señor,	Courtier of the Lord,
hasta el año venidero,	Until next year,
San Ysidro, Labrador.	Saint Isidor, Laborer.

This *alabanza* is in the style of a *himno*.

P15. *San Ignacio de Loyola* (Saint Ignatius of Loyola)
     R2151, Jorge López, age 66, Córdova, N.Mex., 1966, Robb.

1	**1**
San Ignacio de Loyola	Saint Ignatius of Loyola
conquista fraternidades;	Conquers fraternities;
pues que reuniendo los concilios,	He gathers together the councils,
sellando las hermandades.	Sealing the brotherhoods.

2

San Ignacio de Loyola,
pues tú has sido inventor
de concilios y hermandades;
tú fuiste conquistador.

3

Coronado de imperiales,
fuiste príncipe hacendado;
menospreciaste tus bienes
por ser fraterno cofrado.

4

De Jesús fuiste dotado
para formar fraternidades,
estableciendo cofradías
también, grandes hermandades.

5

Entre fieras y montañas
allí pasaste los días
disciplinando tu cuerpo
para cumplir tus profecías.

6

Pues en el huerto dejaste
un calvario y direcciones;
son catorce los Vía Cruces
hoy lamentos de estaciones.

7

De tu vida y de tu muerte
en la historia sea hallada;
la conquista de hermandades
con tu sello está firmada.

8

San Ignacio de Loyola,
fiel esclavo de Jesús;
en tu historia está firmado
toda hermandad de Jesús.

9

San Ignacio de Loyola,
quedaste por grandes siglos
para reunir las hermandades
a los centros de concilios.

10

Al templo de Jesucristo
fué San Ignacio llegado
con cantos y melodías,
de sesenta acompañado.

2

Saint Ignatius of Loyola,
You have been the inventor
Of councils and brotherhoods;
You were the conqueror.

3

Honored by monarchs,
You were a prince, a landowner;
You scorned your wealth
To become a fraternal brother.

4

Jesus endowed you
With forming fraternities,
Establishing associations
Also, great brotherhoods.

5

Among wild animals and mountains
There you spent your days
Disciplining your body
In order to accomplish the prophesies.

6

In the garden you left
A calvary and instructions;
Fourteen are the stations
Of the cross, which we lament today.

7

Of your life and your death
In history it has been found;
The conquest of brotherhoods
With your seal is signed.

8

Saint Ignatius of Loyola,
Loyal servant of Jesus;
In your history is affirmed
All the brotherhoods of Jesus.

9

Saint Ignatius of Loyola,
You remained for many centuries
To unite the brotherhoods
To the council centers.

10

At the temple of Christ
Saint Ignatius has arrived
With songs and melodies,
By sixty accompanied.

11

San Ignacio de Loyola
del templo se ha separado
y en la misa del altar
su nombre quedó grabado.

11

Saint Ignatius of Loyola
Got away from the temple
And in the mass at the altar
His name became engraved.

12

Y para salir del templo
de rodillas adorando
con sesenta seis cofrados,
a Dios salieron cantando.

12

And on going out from the temple
On their knees, praying,
With sixty-six brothers,
To God they began to sing.

13

Tu fraternal cofradía
todo el mundo se divisa;
presenta un templo de luz
el miércoles de ceniza.

13

Your fraternal brotherhood
All over the world is seen;
It presents a temple of light
On Ash Wednesday.

This *alabanza* is in the style of an *alabado*.

P16. *En Este Ultimo Momento* (At This Last Moment)
R2147, Jorge López, age 66, Córdova, N.Mex., 1966, Robb.

1

En este último momento
que en este lugar estamos,
santísimo sacramento;
adiós, adiós, ya nos vamos.

1

At this last moment
In this place we are here,
Holy Sacrament;
Good-bye, good-bye, we are going.

2

Adiós, celestial consuelo,
lucero hermoso del mar,
santísimo sacramento,
ya me voy a caminar.

2

Good-bye, heavenly comfort,
Beautiful star of the sea,
Holy Sacrament,
Now I'll be on my way.

3

Echanos tu bendición,
padre lleno de clemencia,
santísimo sacramento,
donde hice penitencia.

4

Adiós, adiós, dulce encanto,
Señor mío, en la corona,
me voy de tu templo santo,
adiós, preciosa hermosura.

5

Adiós, que he nombrado
el patriota San José
en donde fué aposentado
nueve días que duró.

6

Ya me voy con mucho dolor
¡sabe Dios si volveré!
santísimo sacramento
y Jesús, María, y José.

7

Adiós, Madre de la iglesia
donde no hay tribulación,
ya me voy para mi tierra;
échame la bendición.

8

Santísimo sacramento
que con grande devoción
nos explica la doctrina,
dame vuestra bendición.

9

Adiós, mi hermosa capilla
de mi madre y de la luz.
Piden pan los pecadores
a Nuestro Padre, Jesús.

10

Adiós, linda procesión
que por la noche salió;
santísimo sacramento,
dame vuestra bendición.

11

Adiós, mi dulce pastor,
tu bendición me has de dar;
santísimo sacramento,
ya me voy a caminar.

3

Give us your blessing,
Father of all clemency,
Holy Sacrament,
Where I made my penitence.

4

Good-bye, good-bye, sweet delight,
My Lord, in your crown,
I'm going from your holy temple,
Good-bye, most precious sanctity.

5

Good-bye, I have named
Saint Joseph, the patriot,
For the nine days he endured,
During which he was sheltered.

6

I am going with much pain,
God only knows if I'll return,
Holy Sacrament
And Jesus, Mary, and Joseph.

7

Good-bye, Mother of the church
Where there is no tribulation,
Now I'm going to my land;
Give me your blessing.

8

Holy Sacrament
That with great devotion
Explains the doctrine to us,
Give me your blessing.

9

Good-bye, my beautiful chapel
Of my mother and of the light.
Sinners ask for bread
From Our Father, Jesus.

10

Good-bye, beautiful procession
Which went out at night;
Holy Sacrament,
Give me your blessing.

11

Good-bye, my dear shepherd,
Your blessing you must give me;
Holy Sacrament,
Now I go on my way.

12

Adiós, casa celestial,
que es día de mi salida;
seré sustento en comida,
ya me voy a caminar.

12

Good-bye, celestial house,
It is time for me to leave;
I'll be sustained with food,
Now I go on my way.

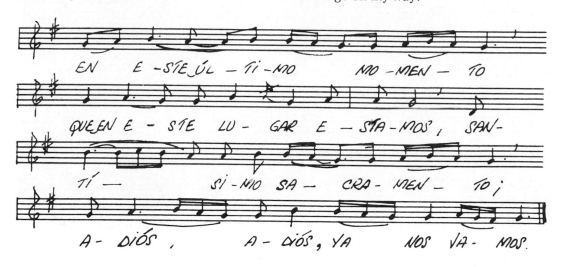

EN E-STE ÚL-TI-MO MO-MEN-TO QUE EN E-STE LU-GAR E-STA-MOS, SAN-TÍ-SI-MO SA-CRA-MEN-TO; A-DIÓS, A-DIÓS, YA NOS VA-MOS.

This *alabanza* is in the style of an *alabado*.

P17. *Alabado Sea* (Let Him Be Praised)
R1911, Edna Garrido de Boggs, Albuquerque, N.Mex., 1963, Robb.

1

Alabado sea, alabado sea,
en este momento, alabado sea,
santo sacramento, alabado sea,
santo sacramento.

1

Let him be praised, let him be praised,
At this moment, let him be praised,
Holy Sacrament, let him be praised,
Holy Sacrament.

2

Abranme la puerta,
ábranme la puerta,
que estoy en la calle
y mira la gente,   ]
que esto es un desaire.   ] *Bis*
Alabado sea, en este momento,   ]
alabado sea, santo sacramento.   ] *Bis*

2

Open the door for me,
Open the door for me,
For I'm in the street
And the people are looking;
This is a rebuff.
Let him be praised, at this moment,
Let him be praised, Holy Sacrament.

Refrán

La la la la la la.
La la la la la la.
La la la la la la.
La la la la la la.

Refrain

La la la la la la.
La la la la la la.
La la la la la la.
La la la la la la.

P17a. *Alabado Sea*
R1046, Female Chorus, Santa Fe, N.Mex., 1952, Reginald and William R. Fisher.

Alabado sea el santísimo	Be thou praised,
sacramento del altar	Holiest Sacrament of the altar
en los cielos y en la tierra]	In the heavens and on earth
aquí en todo lugar.] *Bis*	Here and everywhere.

This *alabanza* is in the style of a *himno*. Two
additional verses of the recording remain undeciphered.

P18. *Al Señor de Esquipula* (To Our Lord of Esquipula)
R61, Jacinto Ortiz, Chimayó, N.Mex., 1945, Robb. Cf. K6, T3.

Planta
El dieciocho de febrero
llegué con grande cordura
a la sagrada presencia
de mi Señor de Esquipula.

Planta
On the eighteenth of February
Feeling great confidence
I arrived at the sanctuary
Of my Lord of Esquipula.

1
¡Qué dichoso territorio
este lugar de "El Potrero"
que viniera el Rey del Cielo
a vernos con tan buen modo!
Es el más rico tesoro
y profeta verdadero;
éste es él que tiene el fuero
y él que nos ha de juzgar.
¡Cuándo se me ha de olvidar
el dieciocho de febrero!

1
A blessed area is
This "colt pasture"
For the King of Heaven
Has seen fit to visit us here!
He is indeed the greatest treasure
And the true prophet.
He is the law and
He shall judge us.
How could I ever forget
The eighteenth of February!

2
Dios Soberano y Eterno
y tú eres mi padre amado
por mí que soy pecador
se quedó sacramentado
en ese cáliz sagrado;
es patente y con dulzura.
¡Soberana Virgen, Madre
del Divino Redentor!
Por esta divina flor
me presento con cordura.

2
Sovereign and Eternal God
You are my beloved father,
For me, a sinner,
You chose to remain here
Consecrated in this sacred chalice;
This is the sweet, manifest truth.
Sovereign Virgin, Mother of the
Divine Redeemer!
Before this divine flower
I present myself with confidence.

3
¡Señor y Redentor mío,
Padre de la Omnipotencia,
es el astro más luciente
y sólo en tu amor confío;
a tus banderas me humío,
lo digo sin resistencia
. . . [undecipherable]
. . .
llévame, Padre amoroso,
a tu sagrada presencia.

3
My Lord and Redeemer,
Omnipotent Father,
You are the brightest star
And I trust in you alone;
I humble myself before your banners,
I surrender without reserve
. . .
. . .
Take me, oh loving Father,
Into your sacred presence.

4
Te saludo, Padre amado
con la mayor distinción,
te ofrecí mi corazón
¿y por qué no lo has tomado?

4
Father, I salute you
With the greatest distinction,
I offered you my heart
Why have you not taken it?

Yo te estimo, Padre amado,
Cordero y noble criatura,
por tu infinita dulzura,
sé bien que no te quebrantas
yo me postraré a tus plantas
¡O mi Señor de Esquipula!

I esteem you, beloved Father,
Lamb of God, noble creature,
I love your sweetness,
I shall always trust in you
And now I kneel at your feet,
Oh my Lord of Esquipula!

P19. *El Santo Niño de Atocha* (The Holy Child of Atocha)
R81, Julianita, Eusebia, and Tila Trujillo, Chimayó, N.Mex., 1946, Robb. Cf. V9
(a *cuando* to the holy child).

1

Santo Niñito de Atocha,
mi dulzura y mi placer,
en la hondura de la gloria,
¡cuándo te volveré a ver!

1

Little Holy Child of Atocha,
My sweetness and my pleasure,
In the fullness of glory,
When shall I see thee again!

<table>
<tr>
<td>

2

Adiós, Niñito de Atocha,
mi dulzura y mi placer,
hermosura de la gloria,
¡cuándo te volveré a ver!

</td>
<td>

2

Good-bye, Child of Atocha,
My sweetness and my pleasure,
Beauty of heaven,
When shall I see thee again!

</td>
</tr>
<tr>
<td>

3

Naciste divino Niño
en la ciudad de Belén
trono de dominaciones
¡Cuándo te volveré a ver!

</td>
<td>

3

Thou wast born, divine Child,
In the town of Bethlehem,
Throne of all dominions,
When shall I see thee again!

</td>
</tr>
<tr>
<td>

4

Por tus santísimos padres
por tu divino poder,
gloria de los mismos tronos
¡cuándo te volveré a ver!

</td>
<td>

4

By thy most holy parents,
By thy divine power,
Glory of these same thrones,
When shall I see thee again!

</td>
</tr>
<tr>
<td>

5

Es posible Dios de mi alma,
que yo no te pueda ver
dentro de una sepultura
donde mi casa ha de ser.

</td>
<td>

5

It is possible, God of my soul,
That I shall not be able to see thee
Within a grave
Where surely my last abode shall be.

</td>
</tr>
<tr>
<td>

6

Adiós Niñito de Atocha,
ya con ésta me despido
con amor y tierno llanto.
Dame un lugar en tu gloria
para cantar Santo, Santo.

</td>
<td>

6

Farewell, Holy Child of Atocha,
Now with this verse I say good-bye
With love and tender tears.
Give me a place in thy glory,
That I may sing "Holy, Holy."

</td>
</tr>
</table>

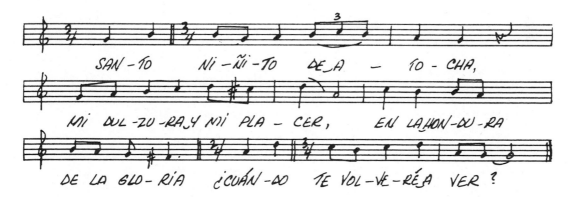

Although only the first verse was sung, this was enough to provide the melody. The remaining verses were supplied by the singers at the time. Note the repetition of the last line of verse 1 in verses 2, 3, and 4. The repetitive use of the word *cuando* relates it to the *cuandos* in Section V. However, despite the nearly identical titles, it is an entirely different text from that of V9.

Q. *Décima a lo Divino*

The *décima a lo divino* differs from the ordinary secular *décima* primarily in its religious subject matter. See Section E for the history and formal structure of the *décima*.

Q1. *En una Redoma de Oro* (In a Golden Flask)
R371, José M. Gallegos, Abiquiu, N.Mex., 1947, Robb.

Planta
En una redoma de oro
traigo almendras de cristal
para darle cuando llore
al pajarillo cardinal.

Planta
In a golden flask
I carry crystal seeds
To give to the cardinal bird
When it weeps.

1
¡Qué lucido resplendor,
él de la Virgen María,
en aquel dichoso día
cuando nació el Redentor!
De aquella divina flor
nació el más fino tesoro,
donde con tanto decoro
su gracia y todo lo creado
en una redoma de oro
se quedó sacramentado.

1
What lucid splendor,
That of the Virgin Mary,
On that great day
When the Redeemer was born.
From this divine flower
Was born the finest treasure,
Wherefore with much honor
Her grace and all the creation
In a golden flask
Remained consecrated.

2
Donde que resplendeció
en el mundo su belleza,
fué tan celestial pureza
que hasta el infierno tembló.
La eterna gloria se abrió
con alegría espiritual,
y por su amor maternal
la Trinidad en alta voz
dice para el mismo Dios,
—Traigo almendras de cristal.—

2
Wherever in the world
Her beauty radiated,
The purity was so celestial
That even hell trembled.
Eternal glory opened up
With spiritual happiness,
And by her maternal love
The Trinity in a loud voice
Said for God himself,
"I carry crystal seeds."

3
Mil parabienes te alaban
las imágenes más bellas
. . . [undecipherable]
el sol, la luna, y estrellas
para Belén caminaban,
y de Jerusalén brotaban,
honrado en su Santo Nombre,

3
There remained a thousand
Most beautiful images,
. . .
The sun, the moon, and stars
Were going to Bethlehem,
And from Jerusalem they came forth,
Honoring her Holy Name,

María, en su Santo Misterio,
coge a agua bautisterio
para darle cuando llore.

Mary, in her Holy Mystery,
Drawing water from the baptismal font
To give to him when he cries.

4

4

Más mirando el nacimiento
del dulce Jesús estaban;
a su majestad le daban
gracias del aves del viento;
que el gallo en aquel momento
dió el aviso en general
que del vientre virginal
había nacido el Mesías
a darle los buenos días
al pajarillo cardinal.

Many witnessed the birth
Of sweet Jesus;
To his majesty the birds of the wind
Were giving thanks;
And the rooster at that moment
Gave notice to the world
That the Messiah had been born
From the virgin womb
To say good day to
The cardinal bird.

DÓ   SA - CRA - MEN - TA - DO.

This *décima* is sung by José Gallegos to the same melody (subject to minor variations) as that to which Próspero S. Baca sang all his *décimas* and as that used by Francisco S. Leyva and others in singing *décimas*.

See Section E and Table E1 above.

Q2. *Ni el Ladrón ni el Asesino* (Neither the Thief nor the Assassin)
R1787, Próspero S. Baca, age 70, Bernalillo, N.Mex., 1945, Robb.

Ni el ladrón ni el asesino,
ni el perjurio y adulón,
ni el chucho ni el abatido
de Dios tendrán salvación.

Neither the thief nor the assassin,
Nor the perjurer and flatterer,
Nor the tattle-tale nor the vile
Will receive salvation from God.

1

No hay razón para robar,
¿cuándo Dios lo ha requerido?
no lo hay para asesinar,
pues esto está bien sabido;
y aquél que a Dios ha ofendido—
mal será su paradero,
y mi Dios que es justiciero
luego le dará destino;
porque no podrán salvarse
ni el ladrón ni el asesino.

1

There is no reason to steal,
When has God requested it?
Nor is there reason to assassinate,
For this is well known;
And he who has offended God—
His resting place will be bad,
And my God who is judge
Will then give him his destiny;
Because salvation will be possible
To neither the thief nor the assassin.

2

Pues yo a ninguno acrimino
y a nadie deseo mal,
pero entre los criminales
el perjurio es sin igual;
esto nadie ha de negar
que es cosa espantable y fea
que entre la gente se vea
ese terrible borrón,
que causan con su ignominia
el perjurio y adulón.

2

I accuse no one
And I wish no one ill,
But amongst criminals
The perjurer has no second;
This no one can deny
That it is a horrible and ugly thing
That among the people one may see
That terrible stigma,
And the public disgrace caused by
The perjurer and flatterer.

3

¿Quién que tenga corazón
puede negar lo que he dicho?
sólo uno de la pacota,
un botorate, un bicho;
pues juntos tienen su nicho,
y es tanta su alevosía
que se junta una pandilla
de esos del pecho podrido

3

Who that has a heart
Can deny what I have said?
Only an adventurer,
A blusterer, a mischief maker;
For together they make their niche,
And so great is their perfidy
That they get together a gang
From those with rotten hearts

que entre la gente se llaman
el chucho y el abatido.

Who among the people are called
The tattle-tale and the vile.

4
A varios les ha podido
que se sepa lo que son;
el mundo está corrompido
causa de tanto bribón;
se sabe que sin razón
se viven vociferando
como estarán esperando;
pregunto a mi corazón
si pensarán algún día
de Dios tener Salvación.

4
For some it has been possible
That they know what they are;
The world is corrupt
Because of so many scoundrels;
It is known that they live
Vociferous without reason
As they await their doom;
I ask my heart
If they will think that some day
They will receive salvation from God.

As was his practice, Próspero Baca sang this *décima* to the well-known *décima* melody (see E1). See also Q4, Francisco S. Leyva singing a *décima* to a variant of the same tune.

Q3. *De un Nopal y Sus Verdores* (From a Prickly Pear Tree and Its Fruit)
R1788, Próspero S. Baca, age 70, Bernalillo, N.Mex., 1945, Robb.

Planta		*Planta*
De un nopal y sus verdores	a	From a prickly pear and its fruit
nacen flores peregrinas,	b	Pilgrim flowers are born,
que las más hermosas flores	a	For the most beautiful flowers
suelen andar entre espinas.	b	Grow among thorns.

1		1
Sentado al lado del rey	a	Seated at the side of the
de los cielos poderoso,	b	Powerful king of the skies,
dijo demás fervoroso,	b	He said too fervently,
Dominus, menentor mei;	a	*Dominus Menentor Mei;*
luego lo admitió a su ley	a	Then the Lord admitted to his law
él que por los pecadores	c	Him who for the sins of others
padeció crueles rigores.	c	Suffered such cruel hardships.
Causa en sus sienes divinos	d	They pierced his divine temples
traspasaron las espinas	d	With thorns
de un nopal y sus verdores.	c	From a prickly pear and its fruit.

2		2
Crucificado en la cruz	a	Nailed to the cross
por satisfacer al padre,	b	To satisfy the Father,
Cristo le dijo a su madre,	b	Christ said to his mother,
mabilus anfilio a tuo;	a	*Mabilus anfilio a tuo;*
no dulcísimo Jesús,	a	No, sweetest Jesus,
estas penas abominan	c	These sufferings are abominable
por librarnos de las ruinas.	c	Though they save us from ruin.
Por mi culpa ofrezco el alma	d	For my sin I offer you my soul
y de María sacra palma	d	And from Mary's sacred palm tree
nacen flores peregrinas.	c	Pilgrim flowers are born.

3

Viendo a María suspirar	a	Seeing Mary sigh
empezar tan de prodijio	b	At such a prodigious thing, he said,
dadmentuo in mater, dijo	b	*Dadmentuo in mater*,
en medio de su pesar;	a	In the midst of his suffering;
luego quiso perdonar	a	Then he wished to forgive
al hombre tantos errores	c	Man's many sins
y con ansias y dolores	c	With anxiety and sorrow,
por que Cristo padeció;	d	That is why Christ suffered;
y más ejemplo nos dió	d	He gave us a better example
que las más hermosas flores.	c	Than the most beautiful flowers.

4

Pendiente de clavos tres	a	Hanging from three nails
se vió en aquel madero,	b	He was seen on this cross,
y con angustia el cordero	b	And with anguish the Lamb
dijo, *consumatins deis;*	a	Said, *consumatins deis;*
hombre tan ciego no estéis	a	Man, don't be so blind as to
en tinieblas divertido.	c	Enjoy yourself in dark places.
Sigue con ansias tan finas	c	Behave with eagerness as fine as
como el sol y las estrellas;	d	The sun and the stars;
porque las flores más bellas	d	Because the most beautiful flowers
suelen andar entre espinas.	c	Grow among thorns.

De un Nopal y Sus Verdores is an excellent example of the *décima glosada* form, each of the four *décimas* ending with the correspondingly numbered line of the *planta*. Furthermore, it closely follows the rhyme scheme of the *espinela*. To clarify this scheme, I have added after each line of the Spanish text a letter corresponding to the rhyme or assonance of the final two syllables of the line.

Q4. *Una Mujer Lo Tenía* (There Was a Woman)
R516, Francisco S. Leyva, age 81, Leyva, N.Mex., 1951, Robb.

Planta	*Planta*
Una mujer lo tenía	There was a woman in a stable
todito de paja lleno	Half full of straw
y no lo comiste bueno;	And she did not eat well.
infanto de mediodía.	At noon she gave birth to a child.

1

Ya—el mediodía en que nací	My godparents told me
me dijeron mis padrinos	That at that noon when I was born
antes de hacerme cariños	Even before they caressed me
una prisma recibí	I received a prism
el nombre de Cristo allí	With the name of Christ on it
y también él de María.	And also that of Mary.
La agua bendita sentía	I felt the holy water
cuando estaba en el sagrario	When I was in the sanctuary.
y había un niño de Dios humanado.	There was a son of God made human.
Una mujer lo tenía.	A woman bore him.

2

. . . [undecipherable]

. . .

. . .

. . .

. . .

Si vas con intento bueno
y no es para dar veneno,
en un pesebre nació
y su madre lo acercó
todito de paja lleno.

3

Entré a un magnífico templo
ya confesaba mi pecado.
Allí ví un gran ejemplo
a Jesús sacramentado;
ví un vaso consagrado
de formas estaba lleno
y ¡cómo era tan ameno!
El padre lo levantó
de allí sacó uno en medio
ya me da comida ¡qué bueno!

4

En fin cuando los sayones
perseguían a Jesús,
lo llevaban con la cruz
por las calles y mesones,
gozan de aceptar pendones
y le daban con la perfida
y naiden en sí contra el día.
Al dedo crucificado
lo llegaron al Calvario
en punto de mediodía.

2

. . .

. . .

. . .

. . .

. . .

If you come with good intentions
And not to poison,
He was born in a manger
And his mother is nearby
And everything is covered with straw.

3

I entered a magnificent temple
And was confessing my sin.
There I saw a great example,
Sanctified Jesus himself;
I saw a consecrated tumbler
Filled to the brim and
How delightful it was!
The priest raised it high
And took a bit of biscuit
And gave it to me to eat. How good!

4

Finally, when the executioners
Persecuted Jesus,
They took him with the cross
Past the streets and inns,
They were glad to lead the procession
And they perfidiously betrayed him
And no one spoke out for him that day.
They took him to Calvary
In the middle of the day
To be crucified.

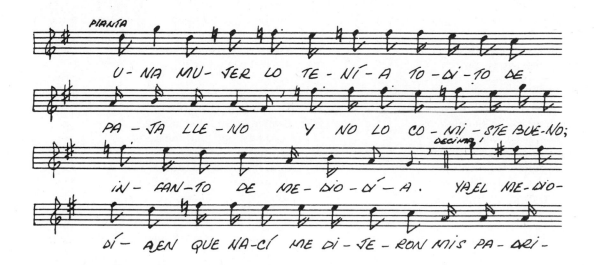

NOS AN-TES DE-HA-CER-ME CA-RI-ÑOS U-NA

PRIS-MA RE-CI-BÍ EL NOM-BRE DE CRIS-TO A-

LLÍ Y TAM-BIÉN ÉL DE MA-RÍ-A.

LA A-GUA BEN-DI-TA SEN-TÍ-A CUAN-DO E-STA-

BA EN EL SA-GRA-RIO Y HA-BÍ-A UN NI-ÑO

DE DIOS HU-MA-NA-DO. U-NA MU-

JER LO TE-NÍ-A.

Q5. *El Pobre Lázaro* (The Poor Lazarus)
R2129, Carlos Marambia, Melipilla, Chile, 1965, Ester Grebe.

Cuarteta		*Quartet*
Tengo, y no te quiero dar,	a	I have plenty, but I don't care to give it to you,
porque tienes quien te dé;	b	Because you have someone else to give to you;
cuando te dejen de dar,	a	When they stop giving it to you,
entonces, yo te daré.	b	Then, I shall give to you.

1		1
El pobre Lázaro hambriento	a	Poor hungry Lazarus
se apoyaba en sus muletas,	b	Leaned upon his crutches,
y se paraba en la puerta	b	And he stopped at the door
de aquel rico avariento.	a	Of that rich miser.
Y le pidió el alimento,	a	And he asked for food
para su hambre sustentar	c	To assuage his hunger, even
de las migajas de pan	c	The crumbs of bread
que caen sobre su mesa.	d	That fell from his table.
Le respondió con gran priesa:	d	He answered right away:
—¡Tengo, y no te quiero dar!—	c	"I have plenty, but I don't care to give it to you!"

2

Cuando el Lázaro llegó
adonde aquel rico estaba,
en su puerta se paraba
y alimento le pidió.
El rico le respondió
con la mayor altivez:
—¡Anda, vete y déjame,
porque me causa un pudor!
Tengo pan y no te doy,
porque tienes quien te dé.—

3

El rico era sin conciencia:
no tenía corazón,
ni tenía compasión
para los que sufren dolencias.
Era tanta la opulencia,
sólo faltaba el "Irán."
Le negó un pedazo de pan
a aquel mendigo llagado:
—Yo te daré pan sobrado
cuando te dejen de dar.—

4

Al mirar a aquel llaguiento,
volvió el rico las espaldas;
pero los perros sus llagas
las lamieron con respeto.
Al mirar el sufrimiento,
le dijo Dios, a su vez:
—Muy pronto te llevaré
para darte la corona;
¡Hasta el reino de la gloria,
entonces, yo te daré!

a
b
b
a
a
c
c
d
d
c

a
b
b
a
a
c
c
d
d
c

a
b
b
a
a
c
c
d
d
c

2

When Lazarus arrived
Where that rich man lived,
He stood at his door
And asked for food.
The rich man replied
With his haughtiest manner:
"Go, go away and leave me,
Because you embarrass me!
I have bread that I won't give you,
Because you have someone else to give to
  you."

3

The rich man was without conscience:
He had no heart,
Nor had he compassion
For those who sadly suffered.
He had so much opulence,
But he lacked the generosity.
He denied a piece of bread
To that leprous beggar, saying:
"I'll give you bread to spare
When others stop giving you."

4

Upon looking at the leper,
The rich man turned his back;
But the dogs licked
His sores with respect.
Upon seeing his suffering,
God said to him:
"Very soon I'll take you away
To give you a crown;
Then in the kingdom of heaven
I'll give it to you!"

This is one of a number of *décimas* from Chile which Ester Grebe sent me in trade for a number of New Mexican *décimas* from my own collection (for the others see R2130–2136). They are accompanied by guitar and are of unusual musical interest. This example is a good specimen of the *décima glosada* rhymed (or frequently assonated) in the style of the *espinela*. The singer omitted the singing of the *cuarteta* (or *planta*). The fascinating melody, with its sad descending cadences, has a remote resemblance to the traditional New Mexican *décima* melody in its slow descent from the highest point of the melody to the lowest.

The melody is in the Dorian mode (mode of D) but seems to modulate (by "true modulation" in the medieval sense rather than by transposition) to the Mixolydian mode. (See Robb 13, pp. 6–7.)

The strange descending parallelism of the guitar accompaniment has a Spanish flavor. The most striking characteristic of the melody is the slow, sad, descending melismas at the cadences.

That the melodies from Chile and New Mexico have the same remote roots and are derived from the same tradition is indicated not only by the resemblance mentioned above but also by the fact that these Chilean *décimas*, like their New Mexican counterparts, are all sung to more or less varied versions of the same melody. This is surely more than mere coincidence.

The closest analogy to this practice that occurs to me is the Psalm Tones of the Liber Usualis of the Roman Catholic Church, where the much simpler variation technique of setting different texts to repetitions of a single tone followed by florid cadences is practiced.

Q6. *Los Sabios para Cantar* (The Wise Men Before They Sing)
R2132, Carlos Marambia, Melipilla, Chile, Ester Grebe.

1

Los sabios para cantar,
estudian varios días,
se encomiendan a María,
y adoran su memorial.
El primer hombre fué Adán
que cantó con Querubin;
no le pudo dar el fin
porque es de naturaleza;
de dos clavijas inglesas
tengo que hacer un violín.

1

The wise men before they sing,
Practice several days,
Entrust themselves to Mary,
And adore her memory.
The first man was Adam
Who sang with the Cherubim;
He could not finish it
Because it is of nature;
I have to make a violin
With two English pegs.

2

Bajará un ángel del cielo
a ver lo que están cantando;
San Pedro estaba tocando
en un instrumento bueno.
Baja Santo Nicodemo
a repique de campanas;
le pide a su prima hermana
una vihuela divina
con espejos en las esquinas
y la encordadura romana.

2

An angel will come down from heaven
To see what they are singing;
Saint Peter was playing
On a fine instrument.
Down comes Saint Nicodemus
To the chime of bells;
He asks his lady cousin
For a divine guitar
With mirrors on the corners
And Roman strings.

This additional Chilean *décima* is included for two reasons: first, to make possible side-by-side comparisons of *décimas* Q5 and Q6, and, second, because the portrayal in the text of the revered figures of Adam, Saint Peter, and Saint Nicodemus all singing or playing on various musical instruments summons up a lovelier, or at least a more richly varied, picture of the hereafter than the customary stereotype, which holds out little hope or allurement for musicians other than those fortunate enough to play the harp. It also conjures up the charming text that accompanies the last movement of Gustav Mahler's Fourth Symphony.

As to the first of these reasons, the other Chilean *décimas* in my collection are closer musically to Q5, indeed to the point of being virtually identical.

S. *Himno*

The *himno* is the familiar country hymn as sung in the village churches. In contrast to the unmeasured and melismatic music of the *alabados*, it is syllabic (with one syllable per note) and measured in duple or triple meter or mixtures of the two. It is simple, singable music and includes a high proportion of beautiful melodies. It is music of the church rather than of the *morada*.

Some of the *himnos* are included in various editions of Ralliere's *Cánticos Espirituales* under such headings as "aire nacional," apparently to indicate that the source was local folk music and to distinguish them from hymns derived from other hymnals (Ralliere a–d).

Some of the *himnos* are known in Latin American countries. I heard one of these, *Bendito Sea Dios* (S2), sung in El Salvador in Central America in 1962. For purposes of comparison I have included a hymn—*Viva Cristo Rey* (S11)—sung by the Caballeros de Cristo Rey (Horsemen of Christ the King) of El Salvador which I recorded there in 1962.

Other *himnos* could be included here, including many in the various editions of Ralliere and others from my collection that, for various reasons (the chief one being the undecipherability of the recordings), have been omitted. The following constitute a representative collection.

S1. *O Jesús, O Buen Pastor* (O Jesus, O Good Shepherd)
R5, Próspero S. Baca, age 69, Bernalillo, N.Mex., 1944, Robb.

1
O Jesús, o Buen Pastor,
dueño de mi vida,
ven a mí con santo amor
dulce Redentor.

1
O Jesus, O good shepherd,
Guardian of my life,
Come to me with holy love,
Sweet Savior.

2
Eres tierno padre,
Tú el buen pastor
eres verbo eterno,
nuestro Salvador.

2
Thou art a tender father,
Thou, good shepherd,
Art the eternal word,
Savior of mankind.

3
Una santa llama
en la comunión
por tu amor se inflama
en mi corazón.

3
During the communion
A holy flame
Of love for thee burns
Within my heart.

4
Con amor te imploro,
Dios de majestad;
en silencio adoro
tu Divinidad.

4
Lovingly I pray to thee,
God of majesty;
Silently I adore
Thy Divinity.

5

O Jesús de mi alma,
fuente de dulzor,
quiero en santa calma
meditar tu amor.

6

Yo en ti espero
aumentar mi fe;
con amor sincero
te recibiré.

7

O Divino Amante,
venme a visitar,
ven en este instante
mi alma a consolar.

8

Madre, acompañe,
oye, por favor,
que Jesús reciba
siempre con fervor.

9

Hijo ingrato he sido
dulce Redentor,
mas ya arrepentido
heme aquí, Señor.

5

O Jesus of my soul,
Fountain of sweetness,
In holy calm I desire
To contemplate thy love.

6

In thee I hope
To increase my faith;
With true love
I will receive thee.

7

O Divine Lover,
Come and visit me,
Come this very moment
To comfort my soul.

8

Mother, stay with us,
Hear us, please,
That Jesus may receive us
Always fervently.

9

I have been a faithless son,
Sweet Redeemer,
But now I have repented,
I am here, Lord.

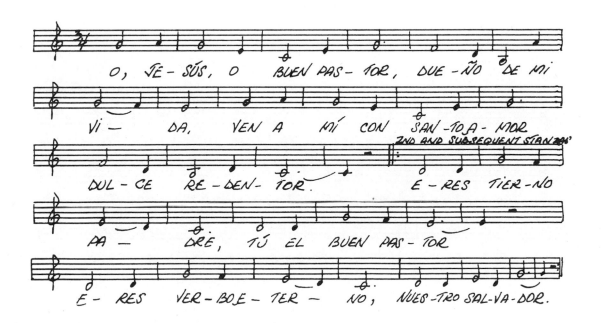

S2. *¡Bendito Sea Dios!* (Blessed Be God!)

R38, Próspero S. Baca, age 67, Bernalillo, N.Mex., 1942, Robb. Cf. R1034, R1043, R1073. See also Appendix A.

1	1
¡Bendito, bendito,	Blessed, blessed,
bendito sea Dios!	Blessed be God!
Los ángeles cantan]	The angels sing
y alaban a Dios.] *Bis*	And praise the Lord.

2	2
Yo creo Dios mío	I believe, my God,
que estás en el altar,	That you are in the altar,
oculto en la hostia.]	Hidden in the host.
Te vengo a adorar.] *Bis*	I come to adore you.

3	3
Adoro la hostia,	I adore the host,
el cuerpo de Jesús,	The body of Jesus,
su sangre preciosa]	His precious blood
que dió por mí en la cruz.] *Bis*	Which he gave for me on the cross.

4	4
Jesús de mi alma,	Jesus of my soul,
te doy mi corazón.	I give you my heart.
En cambio te pido]	In exchange I beg you
tu santa bendición.] *Bis*	That you give me your blessing.

5	5
En este santuario	In this sanctuary
te dejo y me voy.	I leave you and I go.
Adiós, Jesús mío,]	Good-bye, my Jesus,
adiós, adiós, adiós.] *Bis*	Good-bye, good-bye, good-bye.

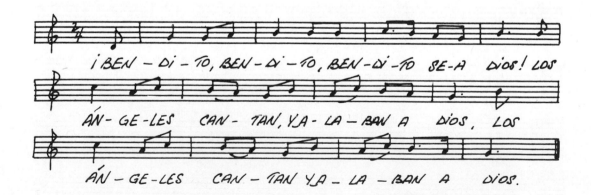

The melody of this hymn was arranged for orchestra and chorus and employed as the finale of the Prologue of my opera *Little Jo.*

S3. *Salve, Corazón Abierto* (Hail, Open Heart)
R223, Tomás Archuleta, age 55, Tierra Azul, N.Mex., 1949, Robb.

1		1
Salve, corazón abierto,	]	Hail, open heart,
santa y dulce habitación.	] *Bis*	Holy and sweet habitation.

Coro		*Chorus*
Adiós, Jesús de mi vida,	]	Good-bye, Jesus of my life,
dadnos vuestra bendición.	] *Bis*	Give us your blessing.

2		2
Salve, corazón cargado	]	Hail, heart, weighted down
con la cruz de tu pasión.	] *Bis*	With the cross of your passion.

Coro   *Chorus*

3		3
Salve, corazón punzado	]	Hail, heart pierced
con nuestro olvido y traición.	] *Bis*	By our thoughtlessness and treason.

Coro   *Chorus*

4		4
Adiós, amante y querido,	]	Good-bye, my dear beloved,
dueño de mi corazón.	] *Bis*	Master of my heart.

Coro   *Chorus*

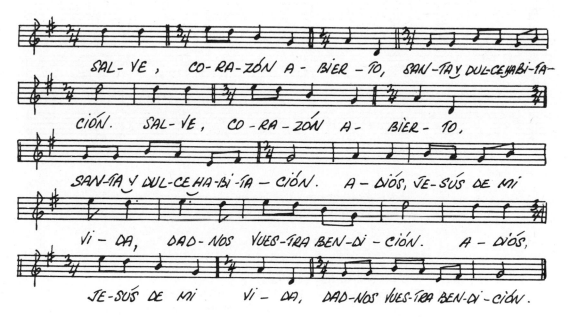

I used the melody of this hymn as the principal theme of the second movement of my Symphony No. 2 in C Major.

S3a. *Salve, Corazón Abierto*
R1383, Celina Griego, Albuquerque, N.Mex., 1956, Robb.

1	1
Salve, corazón abierto,	Save us, open heart,
santa y dulce habitación.	Holy and sweet abode.
Adiós, Jesús de mi vida,	Farewell, Jesus of my life,
dadme vuestra bendición.	Give me your blessing.

2	2
Salve, corazón cargado	Save us, open heart burdened
con la cruz de tu pasión.	With the cross of your passion.
Adiós, Jesús de mi vida,	Farewell, Jesus of my life,
dadme vuestra bendición.	Give me your blessing.

3	3
Salve, corazón punzado	Save us, heart wounded
con nuestro olvido y traición.	With our neglect and treason.
Adiós, Jesús de mi vida,	Farewell, Jesus of my life,
dadme vuestra bendición.	Give me your blessing.

4	4
Adiós, amante querido,	Farewell, beloved,
dueño de mi corazón.	Patron of my heart.
Adiós, Jesús de mi vida,	Farewell, Jesus of my life,
dadme vuestra bendición.	Give me your blessing.

This is a rather unusual case of a hymn sung
to two entirely different tunes, this and S3.

S4. *O María, Madre Mía* (O Mary, My Mother)
Recollection of J. D. Robb, Albuquerque, N.Mex., 1973, Robb.

O María, Madre mía,	O Mary, my Mother,
o consuelo del mortal,	O consolation of mankind,
amparadme y guíadme	Help me and guide me
a la patria celestial.	To the heavenly fatherland.

O, MA-RÍ-A, MA-DRE MÍ-A, O, CON-SUE-LO DEL MOR-TAL

AM-PA-RAD-ME Y GUÍ-AD-ME A LA PA-TRIA CE-LES-TIAL.

I have searched my records in vain for the source of this song. In desperation I wrote it down from memory. S4a (a text without music) will supply a number of verses missing from my recollected version.

S4a. *O María, Madre Mía*
R1986, Notebook of Clemente Chávez, age 88, Galisteo, N.Mex., 1954, Robb.

<table>
<tr><td>

1

O María, madre mía,
o consuelo del mortal,
amparadme y guíadme
a la patria celestial.

</td><td>

1

O Mary, my mother,
O consolation of mortal man,
Help me and guide me
To the heavenly home.

</td></tr>
<tr><td>

2

Salve, júbilo del cielo,
del excelso dulce imán;
salve, hechizo de este suelo,
triunfadora de Satán.

</td><td>

2

Hail, joy of heaven,
The charm of paradise;
Hail, enchantment of this earth,
Conqueror of Satan.

</td></tr>
<tr><td>

3

Quien a ti ferviente clama
halla alivio en el pesar,
pues tu nombre luz derrama,
gozo y bálsamo sin par.

</td><td>

3

He who fervently cries to you
Finds relief from guilt,
Your name sheds light,
Joy and balm without equal.

</td></tr>
<tr><td>

4

De sus gracias tesoreras
te ha nombrado el Redentor;
con tal madre y medianera,
nada temas, pecador.

</td><td>

4

From his treasured graces
The Redeemer has named you;
With such a mother and mediator,
Fear nothing, sinner.

</td></tr>
<tr><td>

5

Pues te llamo con fe viva,
muestra, o madre, tu bondad
y a mí vuelve compasiva
esos ojos de piedad.

</td><td>

5

I call you with living faith,
Show, o mother, your kindness
And look on me compassionately
With your eyes of pity.

</td></tr>
<tr><td>

6

Con el ángel de María
las grandes os celebran,
transportado de alegría
sus finezas publican.

</td><td>

6

With the angel of Mary
The great ones celebrate you,
Transported with happiness
They proclaim your greatness.

</td></tr>
</table>

S5. *El Alba* (The Dawn)
R1926, Rubén Cobos, Albuquerque, N.Mex., 1963, Robb.

1	1
Ahí viene el alba,	Oh! The dawn is coming.
Ahí viene el día.	Oh! The day is coming.
Cantemos todos	Let us all sing
Ave María.	Hail Mary.

2	2
Quien canta el alba,	Whoever sings this morning song
muy de mañana	At the break of day
indulgencias	Gains indulgences
al cielo gana.	To enter heaven.

3	3
Cantemos el alba.	Let us sing the dawn.
Ahí viene el día.	Oh! The day is coming.
Daremos gracias.	Let us give thanks.
Ave María	Hail Mary.

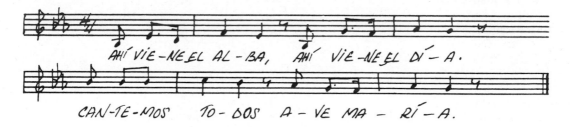

I employed the melody of this hymn in the
second movement of my Concerto for Viola
and Orchestra.

S6. *Pan del Cielo* (Bread of Heaven)
R1015, Tranquilo Luján, Santa Fe, N.Mex., 1952, Reginald and William R. Fisher.
Cf. R1014, Ralliere d (p. 67).[1]

¡O, pan del cielo admirable!	Oh, admirable bread of heaven!
¡O, dulcísimo alimento!	Oh, sweetest of foods!
Tú eres la vida del hombre	You are life to mankind
y la salud del enfermo.	And health to the sick.

[1] R2014 is a version of the same text but in the musical-style of an *alabado*. The Ralliere version contains eighteen verses.

¡O, PAN DEL CIE-LO AD-MI-RA-BLE!O, DUL-CÍ-SI-MO A-LI-
MEN-TO! TÚ E-RES LA VI-DA DEL HOM-BRE Y LA
SA-LUD DEL EN — FER-MO.

S7. *Al Cielo* (To Heaven)
R2383, Cipriano Griego, Albuquerque, N.Mex., 1971, Robb. Cf. R1004,[2] R1100.

1	**1**
Si al cielo quieres ir	If you want to go to heaven
a recibir tu palma,	To receive your palm,
a Dios con cuerpo y alma	You must love and serve God
has de amar y servir.	With body and soul.
Coro	*Chorus*
Al cielo, al cielo,]	To heaven, to heaven,
al cielo quiero ir.] *Bis*	I want to go to heaven.
2	**2**
Si al cielo quieres ir,	If you want to go to heaven
jurar en falso evita	You must not agree to give
y a más toda maldita	False testimony
no debes proferir.	Or do other accursed things.
Coro	*Chorus*

SI AL CIE-LO QUIE-RES IR A RE-CÍ-
BIR TU PAL-MA, A DIOS CON CUER-PO Y AL-
MA HAS DE A-MAR Y SER-VIR.   *CHORUS*   AL
CIE-LO, AL CIE-LO, AL CIE-LO

[2]R1004 is musically in the style of an *alabado*.

QUIE-RO IR; AL CIE-LO, AL
CIE-LO, AL CIE-LO QUIE-RO IR.

S8. *María, María* (Mary, Mary)

R1042, Sociedad Folklórica, Santa Fe, N.Mex., 1952, Reginald and William R. Fisher. Cf. Ralliere c (p. 117) for four additional verses.

María, María,	Mary, Mary,
nombre de gracia y favor,	Name of grace and favor,
o Madre querida,	O beloved Mother,
tú eres mi amor.	You are my love.
El nombre de María	The name of Mary
hemos de celebrar;	We must celebrate;
niñez con armonia	May your voice speak
sea vuestro trinar.	To childhood with harmony.

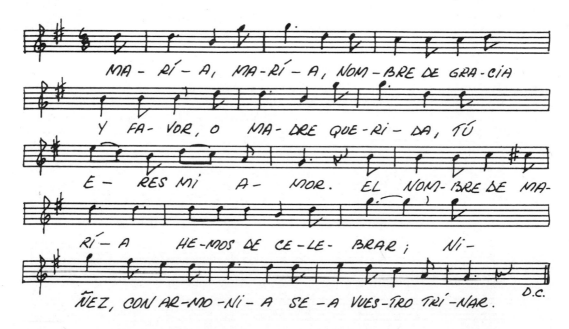

MA - RÍ - A, MA-RÍ - A, NOM - BRE DE GRA -CIA
Y FA - VOR, O MA-DRE QUE-RI - DA, TÚ
E - RES MI A - MOR. EL NOM-BRE DE MA-
RÍ - A HE-MOS DE CE -LE- BRAR; NI-
ÑEZ, CON AR-MO-NI - A SE -A VUES-TRO TRÍ -NAR.
D.C.

S9. *Madre Dolorosa* (Sorrowing Mother)

R1045, Sociedad Folklórica, Santa Fe, N.Mex., 1952, Reginald and William R. Fisher.

Ay, madre dolorosa,	Ah, sorrowing mother,
madre de la cruz llorosa,	Weeping mother at the cross,
donde colga [?] el Redentor.	Where hangs the Redeemer.

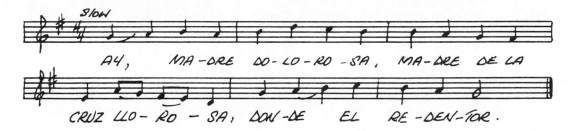

This *himno* departs from the usual form of four musical phrases and somewhat surprisingly is limited to three.

S10. *Alaben, Cristianos* (Christians, Let Us Praise)
R1066, Group of Singers, Pecos, N.Mex., 1952, Reginald and William Fisher. Cf. Rael (p. 97).

1	1
Alaben, Cristianos,	Christians, let us praise
por Dios concebida	The light of the heavens
la luz de los cielos	Conceived by God
y una Ave María.	And an Ave Maria.

2	2
Por mi dulce fuego	For my sweet fire
que fuego sería	That fire would be
fuiste milagrosa	You were miraculous, Lady,
y una Ave María.	And an Ave Maria.

Each verse is first sung by the leader and then verse 1 is repeated responsorially as a refrain by the group of men. Note the unusual six-syllable line, which is also found in a number of other *himnos*. This musical setting is an interesting departure from the strict syllabic setting, typical of the *himno*, since it incorporates two characteristics of the Penitente *alabados*: melismas and alterations without transposition of the scale or mode (B-natural to B-flat).

S11. *Viva Cristo Rey* (Long Live Christ the King)
R1668, Male Chorus, Ilobasco, El Salvador, 1962, Robb.

1

¡O Cristianos! un Padre tenemos
que nos dió de la patria la unión.
A ese Padre gozosos cantemos
empuñando con fe su pendón.　　] *Bis*

Coro

¡Que viva mi Cristo!
¡Que viva mi Rey!
¡Que impere do'quiera³ triunfante su
　ley!　　] *Bis*
¡Viva Cristo Rey!
Grito: ¡Viva!
¡Viva Cristo Rey!

2

El formó con voz hacedora
cuanto existe debajo del sol;
de la inercia y la nada incolora
formó luz en candente arrebol.　　] *Bis*

Coro

3

Nuestra patria, la patria querida
que arrulló nuestra cuna al hacer

a él le debe cuanto es en la vida,
sobre todo él que sepa querer.　　] *Bis*

Coro

4

Es en vano que cruel enemigo
nuestra Cristo pretenda humillar;
de ese Rey llevarán el castigo

los que intenten su nombre ultrajar.　　] *Bis*

Coro

1

O Christians, we have a Father
Who gave us the union of the fatherland.
Let us sing songs of praise to that Father,
Seizing with faith his standard.

Chorus

Long live my Christ!
Long live my King!
May he rule wherever he wishes, his law
　triumphing!
Long live Christ the King!
Shouted: Viva!
Long live Christ the King!

2

He formed with his creative voice
Whatever exists under the sun;
From inertia and colorless nothing
He formed light in the incandescent sunset.

Chorus

3

Our fatherland, the beloved fatherland
Which rocked our cradle when we were
　born,
To him is owed whatever is in life,
Above all, to the one who knows how to
　love.

Chorus

4

It is in vain that the cruel enemy
Pretends to humiliate our Christ;
From this King those who try to kill his
　name
Will receive the punishment they deserve.

Chorus

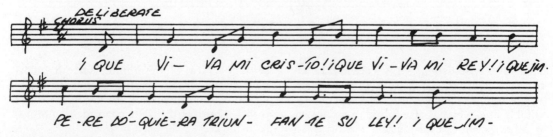

³*Do'quiera* for *dondequiera* (everywhere).

PE - RE DO' - QUIE - RA TRIUN - FAN - TE SU LEY!

slower

¡VI - VA CRIS - TO REY! ss ¡VI - VA! (SHOUTED) ¡VI - VA

VERSE 1

CRIS - TO REY! ¡O CRIS - TIA - NOS! UN PA - DRE TE -

NE - MOS QUE NOS DIÓ DE LA PA - TRIA LA U - NIÓN. A E - SE

PA - DRE GO - ZO - SOS CAN - TE - MOS EM - PU -

ÑAN - DO CON FE SU PEN - DÓN, EM - PU -

ÑAN - DO CON FE SU PEN - DÓN.

T. *Rogativa*

Rogativa in Spanish means prayer, and accordingly grouped under this heading are those religious song texts in the nature of prayers. They include prayers of various types. *Salgan, Salgan, Salgan* (T4–4b), for example, is of a special type known as the *deprecación*, or prayer for the souls in purgatory.

T1. *Ayúdame, Buen Jesús* (Help Me, Good Jesus)
R2163, Jorge López, age 66, Córdova, N.Mex., 1966, Robb.

1
Ayúdame, buen Jesús,
que vengo necesitado
a buscar el alimento
de Jesús Sacramentado.

1
Help me, good Jesus,
For I come by necessity
To seek the nourishment
Of Jesus the Consecrated.

2
Al ángel de nuestra guardia
le pido por su clemencia
con un candil encendido
alumbrando esta mesa.

2
I pray to our guardian angel
For his clemency
With a lighted candle
Lighting this table.

3
Al ángel de la custodia
le pido por su clemencia
que me ha dado el sustento
con su sabrosa comida.

3
I pray to the angel of custody
For his clemency
For he has given me sustenance
With delicious food.

4
A mi padre celestial
le pido por su clemencia
él que me dé su comida
en la mesa del altar.

4
I pray to my heavenly father
For his clemency,
That he give me his food
At the table of the altar.

5
Ayúdame, buen Jesús,
que siempre lo encomiendo
con el nombre de María
para que nos des la luz
y sea ella nuestra guía.

5
Help me, good Jesus,
That I may always trust
In the name of Mary
So that you may give us light
And she may be our guide.

6
Al santo ángel de mi guardia
siempre tengo en mi memoria.
Libre, nos libre del mal
y sea ella nuestra guía.

6
To my holy guardian angel I say
I have you always in my thoughts.
Save, oh save us from evil
And may she be our guide.

7

Y que siempre te pedimos,
El Santísimo Sacramento
en esta mesa de flores,
nos has de dar tu socorro.

7

As we always pray to you,
Holy Sacrament
On this table of flowers,
You must give us your succor.

8

Como santo milagroso
al confesor con frecuencia,
acúsate tus pecados,
y de allí saldrás perdonado.

8

As to a miraculous saint,
Go often to confession,
Confess your sins,
And you will go out from there pardoned.

9

Ayúdame con amor.
Dame, Padre Celestial,
las migajas que has perdido
de la mesa del altar.

9

Help me with love.
Give me, Heavenly Father,
The crumbs that you have lost
From the table of the altar.

10

Ayúdame, buen Jesús,
con el santo de mi nombre
en el nombre de María
el santo de mi nombre sea nuestra guía.

10

Help me, good Jesus,
With my name saint
And in the name of Mary,
May my name saint be our guide.

11

Oye, Jesús Nazareno,
e hijo de la Virgen María.
Adiós, Padre Celestial,
Adiós, hijo de María.

11

Listen, Jesus of Nazareth,
Son of the Virgin Mary.
Farewell, Celestial Father,
Farewell, Son of Mary.

12

Echamos tu bendición,
hijo del divino padre,
hijo de la Virgen María,
Dios por los siglos, Amén.

12

Give us your blessing,
Son of the divine father,
Son of the Virgin Mary,
God for the centuries, Amen.

T2. *Tened Piedad* (Have Pity)
R1029, Jorge López, age 52, Córdova, N.Mex., 1952, Robb.

1

Tened piedad, Dios mío,
suma bondad eterna,
de mí, según la grande
misericordia vuestra.

1

Have pity on me, my God,
Embodiment of eternal goodness,
According to the greatness
Of Thy mercy.

2

Según la muchedumbre
de tus piedades tiernas,
borra, Señor, mis culpas
del libro de la cuenta.

2

According to the multitude
Of Thy tender mercies,
Erase, Lord, my faults
From the book of accounts.

T3. *Al Señor Esquipula* (To the Lord of Esquipula)
R80, Julianita Trujillo et al., Chimayó, N.Mex., 1946, Robb. Cf. P18.

Nuestro Señor de Esquipula,
nuestro amor y protección,
hoy postrados a tus plantas
pedimos tu bendición.

Our Lord of Esquipula,
Our love and protection,
Today kneeling at thy feet
We beg thy blessing.

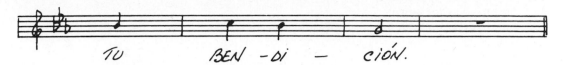

TU   BEN -DI — CIÓN.

T4. *Salgan, Salgan, Salgan* (Come Out, Come Out, Come Out)
    R1013, Tranquilo Luján, Santa Fe, N.Mex., 1952, Reginald and William R. Fisher.
Cf. R87, R1044, R1070; Rael (p. 126).

Coro	*Chorus*
Salgan, salgan, salgan,	Come out, come out, come out,
ánimas de penas.	Souls in pain.
Que el rosario rompe	May the rosary break
grillos y cadenas.	Their fetters and chains.
1	**1**
Atended, cristianos,	Listen, Christians,
católicos pechos,	Catholic hearts,
allí hay dolor que pueda	Is there a sorrow
compararse al nuestro.	Comparable to ours?
Coro	*Chorus*
2	**2**
Los que transitáis	You who are passing
del mundo los cercos,	Through the world,
mirad nuestras penas,	Look and see our pains,
oíd nuestros lamentos.	Hear our lamentations.
Coro	*Chorus*
3	**3**
Son tantas las penas	Our pains are so great
y tan largo el tiempo,	And the time so long
que aquí son mil años	That a moment in the world
del mundo un momento.	Seems here a thousand years.

SAL- GAN, SAL-GAN ,   SAL-GAN,   Á-NI-MAS DE
PE — NAS.   QUE EL RO-SA-RIO ROM — — AE
GRI-LLOS   Y   CA — DE- NAS.

T4a. *Salgan, Salgan, Salgan*
R87, Adela Romero, San Antonio, Socorro County, N.Mex., 1946, Robb.

Salgan, salgan, salgan,	Come out, come out, come out,
ánimas de pena.	Souls in punishment.
Que el rosario rompe	May the rosary break
grillos y cadenas.	Your bars and chains.

T4b. *Salgan, Salgan, Salgan*
R1044, Sociedad Folklórica, Santa Fe, N.Mex., 1952, Reginald and William R. Fisher.

Text identical with T4a above.

T5. *Tañita de Galisteo*
R1990, Clemente Chávez, Galisteo, N.Mex., 1963, Robb. Cf. H1, P8, R557.

1	1
Tañita de Galisteo,	Tañita of Galisteo,
sabia, valerosa, y fuerte,	Wise, brave, and strong,
remedio de nuestros males,	Remedy for our misfortunes,
favorece a vuestra gente.	Be kind to your people.

2	2
Pues eres Sol refulgente	For you are the shining sun
que alumbras las jerarquías.	Which illuminates the hierarchies.
Mira tus Taños postrados;	Look upon your Taños, prostrate before you;
todos están de rodillas.	They are all upon their knees.

3

Pues en la cuestión del día,
que es del cerco del Cadillal,
te piden como abogada
para poderlo ganar.

4

Pues eres buena abogada
en la cuestión principal,
piden tus Taños postrados
no los has de abandonar.

5

A San José en el lugar
como segundo patrón,
lo piden como abogado
todos en esta cuestión.

6

Todos tus Taños postrados
te piden de corazón
que seas fuerte pilar
por ser segundo patrón.

7

Tañita de Galisteo,
la patrona de este valle,
eres madre equitativa,
remedio de nuestros males.

8

Eres madre equitativa,
patrona del Cadillal,
y abogada de los Taños
en la cuestión principal.

9

Desde el año de catorce
que se vinieron los Taños,
te pusieron de patrona
y reina del Pueblo Taño.

10

Desde el año de catorce
en tu templo colocada
piden tus Taños postrados
que seas su abogada.

11

A San José aclamaremos
porque es querido de Dios,
es esposo de María
y padre del niño Dios.

3

For in the question of the day,
Which concerns the border of the Cadillal,
They beg you as advocate
That they may triumph.

4

Because you are a good advocate
In the chief question,
Your kneeling Taños
Beg you not to abandon them.

5

Saint Joseph in the place
Of second patron,
They beg to act as their advocate
In this question.

6

All your kneeling Taños
Implore you from their hearts
That you will be a strong support
Acting as their second patron.

7

Tañita of Galisteo,
The patron of this valley,
You are a just mother,
The remedy for our misfortunes.

8

You are a just mother,
Patron of the Cadillal,
And advocate of the Taños
In the question of the day.

9

Since the year of fourteen (1814?)
When the Taños came,
They made you their patron
And queen of the Taño pueblo.

10

Since the year fourteen
Your Taños, kneeling before you
In your own church,
Beg you to be their advocate.

11

We acclaim Saint Joseph
Because he is the beloved of God,
The husband of Mary
And father of the child God.

12

Todos te aclamábamos
porque estamos apurados.
Los del Pueblo de los Taños
hoy se ven atribulados.

12

We all acclaimed you
For we are destitute.
Those from the village of the Taños
Today find themselves in tribulation.

13

San José es buen abogado,
él que le ha ayudado a Clansy
que tumbaron el enllonso
que había sometido Panty.

13

Saint Joseph is a good advocate,
He who has aided Clansy
To overthrow the complaint
Which Panty had filed.

14

Qué plaza tan desgraciada
será el Pueblo de los Taños
si les ganan la cuestión
los echaron de la mano.

14

What an unfortunate place
Will be the village of the Taños
If they gain the victory
And the Taños get thrown out.

15

Yo le pediré a San Ramos
y a la corte celestial
que entren todos de abogados
para que puedan ganar.

15

I beg San Ramos
And the celestial court
That they will be all our advocates
So that they may win for us.

16

San José es nuestro patrón
como lo están contemplando;
bendice a la comisión
y a los Pueblos de Taños.

16

Saint Joseph is our patron
As they are considering the matter;
Bless the commission
And the Taño people.

17

San José, nos dé la mano
en toda tribulación,
que es el mejor abogado
que defiende la cuestión.

17

Saint Joseph, lend us a hand
In all our tribulation,
For he is the best advocate
And defends our position.

18

Guerita tápalo grande,
estrellado como el cielo,
con él cubres a los Taños
de la Plaza de Galisteo.

18

Great shawl,
Starry like the sky,
With it you cover the Taños
Of the town of Galisteo.

19

Eres hermoso lucero.
En tu templo colocada
te piden los Galisteos
que tú has de ser su abogada.

19

You arc the beautiful star.
Assembled in your church
The people of Galisteo beg you
To be their advocate.

20

Todos tus Taños postrados
te piden de corazón
que les prestes larga vida
y les des tu bendición.

20

All your Taños kneeling
Beg you from their hearts
That you will give them long life
And your benediction.

21

Me acuerdo de mis amigos
y de su antigua amistad.
Si quieren saber mi nombre
soy Leyva Natividad.

Galisteo, New Mexico
Domingo, 15 de noviembre
Año de Nuestro Señor, 1942
   Clemente Chávez

21

I remember my friends
And their long-standing friendship.
If you wish to know my name
I am Natividad Leyva.

Galisteo, New Mexico
Sunday, November 15
Anno Domini, 1942
   Clemente Chávez

This song comes from Galisteo and is a prayer to the Virgin Mary, former patron saint of the village, known locally as the Tañita (little Taño girl) of Galisteo. The Taños were a tribe of Indians who lived just north of Galisteo but abandoned their pueblo, possibly in fear of the Comanches who frequently raided the area. In this song the people of Galisteo ask the aid of Mary and of Joseph of the Cadillal, the present patron of Galisteo, in the matter of a hearing or lawsuit involving the Cadillal, a large area east of the Ortiz Mountains, named after a weed called *cadillal* that grows there.

Verse 15 refers to San Ramos, an obvious misspelling of the name Ramón. San Ramón (Saint Raymond Nonatus), "protector of captives and those oppressed by the infidel," had a special meaning for the colonists who lived under the menace of Indian raids, in which many were taken captive and held in slavery.

U. *Despedimento*

Cobos in one of his articles in *El Nuevo Mexicano* expresses the conviction that at least one of the *despedimentos, Adiós Acompañamiento* (U1), was brought from Spain in the seventeenth century (Cobos 4, 5/4/50). This opinion finds some confirmation in the song's use of a sixteen-syllable line rhymed or assonated at the end of each sixteen syllables, in which respect it follows the form of the Spanish *romance*. That this is a well-known song with numerous variants argues that it is very old. In my own collection I have no less than six variants (R1010, R1030, R1052, R1071, R1080, RB758).

On the other hand, there are other *despedimentos*, for instance examples U2 and U3, which, like the *corrido*, refer to the recent death of a named person and even to a specific day, month, and year. These two were published in Spanish-language newspapers of the state of New Mexico in 1903, when, it is known, it was the custom of local *poetas* to compose and publish in the papers such memorials to the dead. Furthermore, melodically most of the *despedimentos* are found in the style of the *alabados*, florid and unmeasured, and not in the more objective, measured style of most of the *romances*. They are usually couched in the form of an address in the first person by the deceased to his parents, relatives, and others, a peculiar characteristic rarely if ever encountered in the *romance*. And the *romance* is typically a narrative form, whereas the *despedimentos* resemble much more closely the introspective character of the *canción*. Finally, the *despedimentos* are often sung by brothers of the Penitente *cofradías* and seem to be specifically appropriate to, if not designed for, wakes or, as they are called, *velorios* of the *cofradía*.

While the *despedimento* may originally have been introduced into the New World from the Iberian Peninsula, it has been adapted as a form by the people of the villages for their own purposes, refashioned into something different from any European source and completely consistent with the cultural pattern of Hispanic colonization in the Southwest.

It may be added that a song text in which a dead person speaks in the first person to relatives and friends is not found exclusively in the *despedimentos*. It occurs in other forms of Hispanic folk poetry as well. A good example of this is the *Indita de Amarante Martínez* (F2):

> On the twenty-sixth, September
> At about the hour of two,
> From this world I then departed
> Unto God to pay his due.

In fact the same convention is observed in certain Indian funeral ceremonies. An example of this is the following moving song text from the Santo Domingo Indian pueblo collected and transcribed by Frances Densmore in her excellent book *The Music of the Santo Domingo Pueblo*:

> All the white cloud eagles
> Lift me up with your wings and take me to shipap . . .
> 'Way down in the Southwest where our fathers and mothers have gone.
> Put me there with your wings. (p. 68)

U1. *Adiós, Acompañamiento* (Farewell, My Friends)
R1010, Tranquilo Luján, Santa Fe, N.Mex., 1952, Reginald and William R. Fisher. Cf. R1071, RB758 (with twenty-seven verses but no music).

1	1
¡Adiós, acompañamiento,	Farewell, my friends
donde me estaban velando;	Who are sitting up with me;
ya se llegó la hora y tiempo	Now the hour and time are coming
de que me vayan sacando!	When they will take me away!

2

¡Adiós, mis amados padres,
que conservaron mi vida;
ya se llegó la hora y tiempo;
ya se llegó mi partida!

(Verso 1 se repite)

3

¡Adiós, amado Jesús!
¡Adiós, esposo querido!
¡Adiós, mi acompañamiento,
ya yo voy para la otra vida!

(Verso 1 se repite)

4

¡Adiós, todos mis parientes!
¡Adiós, mi dulce morada!
¡Adiós, acompañamiento,
que ya voy en la jornada!

(Verso 1 se repite)

5

Adiós, acompañamiento,
se llegó la hora postrera;
acompáñame al sepulcro,
que es mi casa verdadera.

2

Farewell, my beloved parents,
Who saved my life;
Now the hour and time are coming;
Now comes my hour of parting!

(Verse 1 repeated)

3

Farewell, beloved Jesus!
Farewell, beloved husband!
Farewell, my friends,
Now I go to the other life.

(Verse 1 repeated)

4

Farewell, all my relatives!
Farewell, my sweet morada!
Farewell, my friends,
For I'm going on that journey!

(Verse 1 repeated)

5

Farewell, my friends,
Now my last hour comes;
Accompany me to the grave,
Which is my true home.

U1a. *Adiós, Mi Acompañamiento* (Farewell, My Friends)
R1030, Jorge López, age 52, Córdova, N.Mex., 1952, Robb.

1

¡Adiós, mi acompañamiento,
de que me están velando,
ya se llegó la hora y tiempo
de que me vayan sacando!

2

¡Adiós, mis amados padres,
que conservaron me vida,
ya se llegó la hora y tiempo,
ya se llegó mi partida!

1

Farewell, my friends,
Who have been keeping watch for me,
Now the hour and time have come
When they will be taking me away!

2

Farewell, my beloved parents,
Who raised me;
Now the hour and time have come,
The hour of my departure!

3
¡Adiós, amado Jesús!
¡Adiós, esposo querido!
¡Y adiós, mi acompañamiento,
que ya voy en la jornada!

3
Farewell, beloved Jesus!
Farewell, beloved husband!
And farewell, my friends
For now I go on the journey!

U2. *Despedimento de Eloisa Pacheco* (Farewell of Eloise Pacheco)
RB759, Abundio Pacheco, 1903, Cobos. (Published in *La Voz del Pueblo*, Las Vegas, N.Mex., Sept. 19, 1903.)

1
Día diez y seis de julio
año novecientos tres
me fuí con mi papá Félix
y con mis tías también.

1
On the sixteenth of July
In the year of 1903
I went with my papa Felix
And with my aunts also.

2
Me llevan con gran placer
y también con mucho amor;
adiós mis padres y abuelos
échenme su bendición.

2
They took me with great pleasure
And also with much love;
Farewell my parents and grandparents
Give me your benediction.

3
Adiós suelo en que nací,
en que me crié con anhelo
puesto que ahora quiere el cielo
que me despida de ti.

3
Farewell my native soil,
In which I was born in desire
For I now seek heaven
And must say good-bye to you.

4
Virgen, tú eres mi consuelo,
tú te has de doler de mí;
adiós mis padres amados,
nunca se olviden de mí.

4
Virgin, you are my consolation,
You must have pity for me;
Farewell my beloved parents,
Don't ever forget me.

5

San Pedro es mi protector
yo lo aclamo con esmero,
para que ahora se presente
a abrirme la puerta del cielo.

5

Saint Peter is my protector,
I acclaim him in particular,
For now he is coming
To open the gate of heaven for me.

6

También a ti, madre mía,
Virgen, reina del dolor,
te aclamo, pues, recibidme
en tu regazo de amor.

6

Also to you, my mother,
Virgin, queen of sorrow,
I acclaim you, so receive me
On your lap of love.

7

San José, patriarca amado,
prestadme tu protección,
y desde el cielo mandadme
vuestra santa bendición.

7

Saint Joseph, beloved patriarch,
Lend me your protection,
And send me from heaven
Your holy benediction.

8

Adiós, mi papá, Librado,
adiós, mamá Rafaelita,
también adiós, papá Félix,
adiós, mi mamá Juanita.

8

Farewell, my papa, Librado,
Farewell, mama Rafaelita,
Also farewell, papa Felix,
Farewell, my mama Juanita.

9

Adiós, tías queriditas,
échenme su bendición;
ya me voy con Clotildita,
el encanto de mi amor.

9

Farewell, beloved aunts,
Give me your benediction;
Now I go with little Clotilda,
The enchantment of my love.

10

Adiós, todos mis hermanos,
pedazos del alma mía;
también adiós, mis hermanas,
ya llegó mi último día.

10

Farewell, all my brothers,
Beloved of my life;
Also farewell, my sisters,
My last day arrives.

11

Adiós, mis demás parientes,
mis tíos, primos, sobrinos;
acompáñenme sus preces
ante los ojos divinos.

11

Farewell, my other relatives,
My uncles, cousins, nephews and nieces;
May your prayers accompany me
Before the divine eyes.

12

A mis padres aconsejo
que vivan por vida mía,
mirándose en el espejo
de San José y María.

12

I counsel my parents
To live in memory of my life,
Mirroring the life
Of Saint Joseph and Mary.

13

Y, al romper mi alma agobiada
los muros de su prisión,
me acompañe en mi jornada
su paternal bendición.

13

And, that my oppressed spirit
May break the walls of its prison,
Accompany me on my journey
With your paternal blessing.

U3. *Despedimento de Valentín C. de Baca* (Farewell of Valentín C. de Baca)
RB760, Cobos. (Published in *La Voz del Pueblo*, Las Vegas, N.Mex., December 5, 1903.)

1

Día diez y nueve de junio
de mil novecientos tres,
me despedí de este mundo
por la postrimera vez.

2

Adiós, suelo en que nací,
donde me crié con anhelo;
y me despido de ti
para poder ir al cielo.

3

A mis padres les suplico
que no se olviden de mí;
que a Dios del cielo ruegen
por su caro Valentín.

4

Adiós, papá Valentín,
adiós, mamacita fina;
así lo tenía ordenado
la Providencia Divina.

5

Adiós, mi hermanita, adiós,
prenda de mi corazón;
acompáñenme tus preces
ante los ojos de Dios.

6

Princesa eres de mi amor,
encanto y prenda notoria;
triunfante estás en la Gloria
rogando por mí al Señor.

7

Imagen de tu Creador,
templo de vida y victoria;
alma eres de mi memoria
y símbolo de mi amor.

8

O Dios santo y eternal,
ya no quiero más amar;
comprendo que he de acabar,
sólo Dios es immortal.

9

Cuál Fénix resplandeciente
al cielo fuiste volando,

1

On the nineteenth of June
In nineteen hundred and three
I took leave of this life
At last.

2

Farewell, land in which I was born,
Where I was created in desire;
Now I take leave of you
In order to go to heaven.

3

I beg my parents
Not to forget me;
And that they pray to God in heaven
For their beloved Valentín.

4

Farewell, papa Valentín,
Farewell, fine mother;
So it has been ordained
By Divine Providence.

5

Farewell, my little sister, farewell,
Darling of my heart;
May your prayers accompany me
Before the eyes of God.

6

You were the princess of my love,
Well-known enchantment and sweetheart;
You are triumphant in heaven
Praying to the Lord for me.

7

Image of your Creator,
Temple of life and victory;
You were the soul of my memory
And the symbol of my love.

8

O holy and eternal God,
I no longer wish to love;
I understand that I have to end,
Only God is immortal.

9

What a resplendent Phoenix
You were while flying to heaven,

714

señas en el aire dejando	Leaving signs in the air
de tu huella reluciente.	Of your shining trail.

10	10
En fin, ya para acabar,	Finally to come to the end,
hijo de mi corazón,	Son of my heart,
recibe mi bendición	Receive my blessing
por toda la eternidad.	For all eternity.

U4. *Despedimento de Facundo González* (Farewell of Facundo González)
RB761, Cobos. (Published in *El Nuevo Mexicano*, Santa Fe, N.Mex., September 3, 1931.)

1	1
Aquí me siento a anotar	I seat myself here to write,
a anotar esta memoria,	To write this memorial,
en nombre de Facundo González	In the name of Facundo González
que Dios lo tenga en la Gloria.	Whom God has received in heaven.

2	2
Novecientos treinta y uno	In nineteen hundred thirty-one
de este siglo tan mentado,	Of this famous century,
murió Facundo González	Facundo González died
en el Denver, Colorado.	In Denver, Colorado.

3	3
El día ocho de agosto	On the eighth day of August,
día sábado en la tarde,	It was a Saturday afternoon,
dejó de existir González	Facundo González lost his life
por manos de un cobarde.	At the hands of a coward.

4	4
Con los trastes en las manos	With his tools in hand
muy contento él andaba;	He started out contentedly;
no sabía que atrás de la puerta	He did not know that behind the door
Albert Davis lo esperaba.	Albert Davis was waiting for him.

5	5
Pobrecito de Facundo	Poor Facundo González
en un hotel trabajaba;	Was working in a hotel;
y su compañero Davis	And his companion Davis
con recelo lo miraba.	Regarded him with suspicion.

6	6
El día de la desgracia	On the unfortunate day
este diablo lo traicionó;	This devil betrayed him;
cuando menos lo esperaba	When he least expected it
un cuchillo le clavó.	He was stabbed with a knife.

7	7
Decían sus padres llorando:	His parents, in tears, said:
—Adiós, hijito querido;	"Beloved little son, farewell;

recibe la bendición
de tu padre adolorido.

Receive the benediction
Of your aggrieved father."

8
—Adiós, querido Facundo—
decían todos juntitos;
—que Dios te lleve al cielo
y ruegues por tus hijitos.—

8
"Farewell, beloved Facundo,"
Said everyone together;
"May God take you to heaven
And may you pray for your children."

9
Seis hermanos que tenía
hoy lloran su separación;
pero le ruegan a la Virgen
lo tenga en su mansión.

9
Six brothers that he had
Today lament his passing;
But they pray to the Virgin
That she receive him in her mansion.

10
Triste doce de agosto
cuando fuiste sepultado,
aquí, lejos de tu tierra,
en el Denver, Colorado.

10
It was a sad twelfth of August
When you were buried,
Here, far from your home,
In Denver, Colorado.

11
Jesucristo te acompañe
en esta larga jornada;
de bendiciones te bañe
y te lleve a la morada.

11
May Jesus Christ accompany you
On that long journey;
Bathe you with blessings
And take you to your home.

12
Adiós, mi querido esposo,
yo te amaba con anhelo;
encomiendo a Dios tu alma,
te dé cabida en el cielo.

12
Farewell, my beloved husband,
I loved you dearly;
I commend your soul to God,
May he grant you a place in heaven.

13
Las gracias doy a la gente
a todos en general;
tuvo mucho acompañamiento
y muy bonito funeral.

13
I give thanks to the people,
To each and every one;
There were many who came,
It was a very nice funeral.

14
Siento mucho a los dolientes,
siento mucho su pesar;
que el alma de Facundo
Dios la lleve a descansar.

14
I am sorry for the mourners,
I regret their suffering;
May God give rest
To the soul of Facundo.

V. MISCELLANEOUS RELIGIOUS

I suppose that it might be possible to find and classify a number of other types of Hispanic folk songs that have flourished or may be emerging in the American Southwest. I believe, however, that the foregoing represent all the most important types. The following are grouped together largely because there are not enough examples of each type to justify separate classification or because they are difficult to classify as part of more important groups.

There are several fragmentary examples of plainsong, originally, no doubt, taught by the padres. Some of these are at least partly transformed into the folk-song idiom. Then there are several songs that are mainly related to one another in that they sermonize or exhort. There are two variants of the only religious *cuando* that I have collected, together with one from the collection of Rubén Cobos. The last three are sung in the musical style of the *alabado*, but, though one of them was labeled an *alabado* by the singer, I have included them here because they do not relate to the Passion of Christ and are thus excluded from my definition of the *alabado*.

PLAINSONG

V1. *Santo, Santo, Santo* (Holy, Holy, Holy)
R29, Group of Indian Women, 1939, Francis M. Kercheville.

Santo, santo, santo,
Señor Dios de los ejércitos,
Llenos están los cielos y la tierra
  de vuestra gloria.
¡Gloria al Padre!
¡Gloria al Hijo!
¡Gloria al Espíritu Santo!

Holy, holy, holy,
Lord God of the heavenly hosts
Heaven and earth are full of thy
  glory.
Glory to the Father!
Glory to the Son!
Glory to the Holy Spirit!

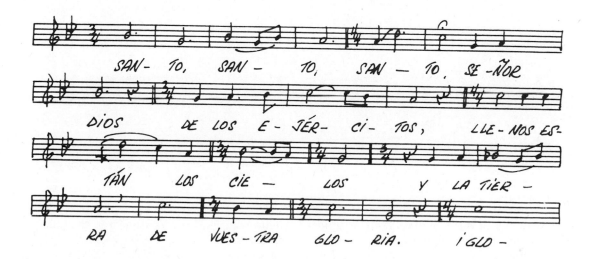

SAN-TO, SAN-TO, SAN-TO SE-ÑOR DIOS DE LOS E-JÉR-CI-TOS, LLE-NOS ES-TÁN LOS CIE-LOS Y LA TIER-RA DE VUES-TRA GLO-RIA. ¡GLO-

RIA AL   PA — DRE!   IGLO — RIA AL

HI — JO!   IGLO — RIA AL ESPÍ — RI — TU   SAN — TO!

This song was dubbed from a 1939 recording and presented to the author by Francis Ker-cheville.

V2. *Kyrie from the Mass of the Angels*
R1368, Julián Zamora, age 83, Tomé, N.Mex., 1956, Robb. Cf. R1377, R1368, and R1369 for other examples of plainsong by the same singer.

Kyrie eleison.   God have mercy.
Christe eleison.   Christ have mercy.
Kyrie eleison.   God have mercy.

KY — RI-E,   E —   E —

E —   E — —   LE — i- SON.   REPEATED

CHRIS -TE —   ,   E — —   ,

E — —   LE — i - SON ·

KY — RI - E — —   ,   E — —   ,

E — —   LE — i SON.   SUNG THREE TIMES

In the practice of the church each line is sung three times. The singer does not adhere to this practice.

This recording draws aside for the moment the curtain of time and gives us a momentary glimpse of a vivid past. It is sig-

718

nificant as a surviving recollection of the work of the famous priest Juan B. Ralliere, who was active in Tomé, New Mexico, from 1858 to 1911. See Florence Hawley Ellis' engrossing account of the career of Father Ralliere and life in the village of Tomé from 1858 for several decades, in the *New Mexico Historical Review*, April, 1955 (Ellis 4c, pp. 103–114). The singer, the late Julián Zamora, was a choirboy under Father Ralliere and learned what he knew of plainsong from him. Here then we hear him at the age of eighty-three singing one of the Kyries as he remembered it.

Example V2 is a faithful version of the Kyrie from the Mass of the Angels as found in plainsong notation on page 37 of the *Liber Usualis*, edited by the Benedictines of Solesmes, Desclée and Co., Tournai, Belgium, 1934.

Julián Zamora (front center), singer of *Kyrie from the Mass of the Angels* (V2), in Tomé, New Mexico, in 1956.

RELIGIOUS EXHORTATION

V3. *Mira, Mira, Pecador* (Consider, Sinner)
R1007, Tranquilo Luján, Santa Fe, N.Mex., 1952, Reginald and William R. Fisher. Cf. Rael (p. 136).

Coro	*Chorus*
Mira, mira, pecador,	Consider, sinner, and see
que si vives en pecado	That if you live in sin
puedes anochecer bueno	You can go to bed well
y amanecer condenado.	And awake condemned.

1	1
Mira que es breve tu vida,	See how short is your life,
y que vas muy a la posta	And that you are moving
caminando hacia la muerte;	Rapidly toward death;
piénsalo bien que te importa.	Think well what it means.

Coro	*Chorus*

2	2
Triste, turbado, y confuso,	Sad, perturbed, and confused,
temeroso y aun temblando,	Fearful and even trembling,
entre batallas y penas	You will agonize
estarás agonizando.	Midst struggles and pains.

Coro	*Chorus*

3	3
Piénsalo bien que te importa,	Think well how it matters to you,
para que enmiendes tu vida.	So that you will amend your life.

Y lo hagas cuanto antes,	And do it as soon as you can,
porque ya está de partida.	For already death is near.

<table>
<tr><td align="center">*Coro*</td><td align="center">*Chorus*</td></tr>
<tr><td align="center">4</td><td align="center">4</td></tr>
</table>

Cuando agonizando estés	When you are in agony
y roncándote ya el pecho,	And your breast is already roaring,
y con la vela en la mano,	And you are ready for the last sacrament,
¿qué quisieras haber hecho?	What will you wish that you had done?

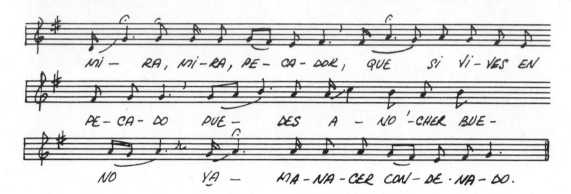

MI - RA, MI - RA, PE - CA - DOR, QUE SI VI - VES EN PE - CA - DO PUE - DES A - NO'-CHER BUE - NO YA - MA - NA - CER CON - DE - NA - DO.

This example and the following through V5 are musically in the florid unmetered style of the *alabado* and are sung at Penitente ceremonies. The most elaborate melismas are usually reserved for the cadences or phrase endings—note the ending of the musical phrases of example V3a.

V3a. *Mira, Mira, Pecador*
R1923, Group of Men, Albuquerque, N.Mex., 1963, Cobos. Cf. R155.

<table>
<tr><td align="center">1</td><td align="center">1</td></tr>
<tr>
<td>*Leader:*
Mira, mira, pecador,
que si vives en pecado,
en pecado,</td>
<td>*Leader:*
Consider, sinner, and see
That if you live in sin,
in sin,</td>
</tr>
<tr><td align="center">2</td><td align="center">2</td></tr>
<tr>
<td>*Group:*
Puedes anochecer bueno
y amanecer condenado,
condenado.</td>
<td>*Group:*
You may end one day well
And begin the next condemned,
Condemned.</td>
</tr>
<tr><td align="center">3</td><td align="center">3</td></tr>
<tr>
<td>*Leader:*
Mira que es breve tu vida,
y que vas muy a la posta,
a la posta,</td>
<td>*Leader:*
Observe that your life is short,
And that you are going rapidly,
Rapidly,</td>
</tr>
</table>

4

Group:
Caminando hacia la muerte,
piénsalo bien que te importa,
que te importa.

4

Group:
Traveling toward death,
Think well, for it concerns you,
It concerns you.

5

Leader:
Triste, temoroso, y confuso,
temoroso aun temblando,
aun temblando,

5

Leader:
Confused, sad, and frightened,
Frightened even to trembling,
Even to trembling,

6

Group:
Quien se va ya está sin pena,
esperando agonizando,
agonizando,

6

Group:
He who has gone is without worry,
But as you wait, agonizing,
Agonizing,

7

Leader:
Piénsalo que te importa,
para que limpies tu vida,
que limpies tu vida.

7

Leader:
Think well, for it concerns you,
So that you may cleanse your life,
Cleanse your life.

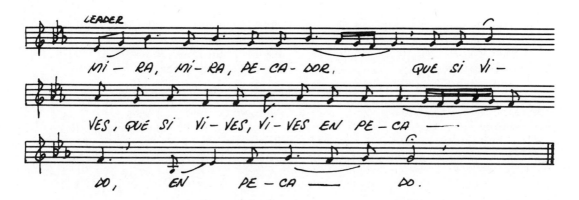

The echo effect in V3a at the end of each verse lends solemnity to the religious adjuration, as, for example, in verse 2: "*condenado, condenado.*"

V4. *Recuerda, Si Estás Dormido* (Wake Up, If You Are Asleep)
R2164, Jorge López, age 66, Córdova, N.Mex., 1966, Robb.

1

Recuerda, si estás dormido,
deja de vivir atroz,
que por vivir divertido,
hombre, has olvidado a Dios.

1

Wake up, if you are asleep,
Stop living atrociously,
For while having a good time,
Man, you have forgotten God.

2

Recuerda el año y el mes
y el día de tu promesa;
engañaste a Jesucristo,
juraste con ligereza.

2

Remember the year and the month
And the day of your conversion;
You deceived Jesus Christ,
You swore heedlessly.

3

Recuerda el año y el mes
en aquel templo de Cristo;
allí diste tu juramento
y engañaste a Jesucristo.

3

Remember the year and the month
In Christ's own temple;
There you took the oath
And deceived Jesus Christ.

4

Recuerda en aquel día
allí en aquel templo de Cristo,
allí levantaste la mano derecha
y engañaste a Jesucristo.

4

Remember on that day,
There in Christ's temple,
There you raised your right hand
And deceived Jesus Christ.

5

Busca la vida de Cristo.
Estúdiala con amor.
Puede que así te arrepientas
de ese tu vivir atroz.

5

Seek the life of Christ.
Study it with love.
Maybe you will thus repent
Of your atrocious way of life.

6

Deja de vivir atroz,
examina tu conciencia,
vuelva a la casa de Dios,
cumple con la penitencia.

6

Stop living atrociously,
Examine your conscience,
Return to the Lord's house,
Fulfill your penitence.

7

Hombre, no tientes a Cristo,
porque serás condenado;
recuerda el juramento
que a Dios en vano has jurado.

7

Man, do not tempt Christ,
Because you will be condemned;
Remember the oath
That to God in vain you have sworn.

8

Piensa bien lo que te importa,
no vivas desarreglado;
y llega al templo de Dios,
reconcilia tu pecado.

8

Think of what matters to you,
Do not live a disorganized life;
Go to God's temple and
Confess your sin.

9

Hombre, llega arrepentido,
con humildad y devoción,
reconcilia con la iglesia,
que es el remedio mejor.

9

Man, come repentant,
With humility and devotion,
Be reconciled with the church,
Which is the best medicine.

10

Si vas bien arrepentido,
hecho examen de conciencia,
allí serás recibido
de Cristo en su santa mesa.

10

If you come repentant,
And have examined your conscience,
You will be received there
By Christ at his holy table.

11

Mira lo que es el descuido,
el vivir desarreglado,
un discípulo de Cristo
del demonio fué tentado.

12

Es Cristo tan verdadero,
lo que te digo y advierto;
Judas por treinta monedas
entregó al divino maestro.

13

Como vives engañado.
Hombre, despierta y advierte;
entre las horas del día
te acercas más a la muerte.

14

No seas escandaloso
en tu vida temporal;
y a mi Dios has olvidado.
Mira que te ha de pesar.

15

Si de esa suerte comienzas
sin llegarte a comulgar,
¿cómo puedes alcanzar
el don que el Señor te asigna?

16

Vuelve, vuelve, pecador,
vuelve, vuelve, arrepentido,
vuelve a la casa de Dios
en vez de Cristo, tu amigo.

17

Allí recibirás la gracia
y el sacramento divino.
Mira a Cristo en esa misa,
hombre ingrato, entretenido.

11

Look what it is to be careless,
To live a disorganized life,
One of Christ's disciples
Was tempted by the devil.

12

Christ is so true,
I tell you and I warn you;
Judas for thirty coins
Betrayed the Divine Master.

13

You are living a deception.
Man, wake up and take notice;
During the hours of each day
You approach nearer to death.

14

Don't live scandalously
In your temporary life;
You have forgotten our God.
Listen or you will be sorry.

15

If thus you begin
Without going to communion,
How can you reach
The gift that the Lord has in store for you?

16

Come back, come back, sinner,
Come back, come back, repentant.
Come back to the Lord's house
In time, to Christ, your friend.

17

There you will receive grace
And the Holy Sacrament.
Look at Christ in the mass,
Ungrateful, distracted man.

RE-CUER - DA, SI ES-TÁS DOR-MI-DO, DE- JA DE
VI- VIR A - TROZ, QUE POR VI- VIR DI-VER - TI - DO,

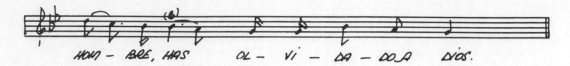

One of the fascinating features of the *alabado* style is the development by each singer of his own special style or type of melismas, in addition to those features on which there is more or less general agreement. Jorge López, for instance, often groups or ties together as at *(A)* in the above example an eighth note, a dotted quarter note, and an eighth note. Another melisma, characteristic of this singer, is *(B)*—after a dotted quarter note (with or without a hold) one or two eighth notes as in the example above.

V5. *En la Noche Perennal* (In Perpetual Night)
R2279, Edwin Berry, Tomé, N.Mex., 1969, Robb.

1

En noche perennal gemido
por siglos la prole de Adán,
aguardando ansiosa al Mesías
que nacer debe de Abrán.

Coro
Rorate coeli desuper
Et nubes pluant justum.

2

¡Qué triste la suerte del justo!
En tierra llorar, padecer;
y en el limbo después del muerto
no gozar tampoco el placer.

Coro

3

La culpa que el hombre rebelde
cometió por su vanidad
las puertas tenía cerradas
de la seráfica ciudad.

Coro

4

Para abrirlas el mismo Verbo
del cielo hubo de bajar
y tomando la carne humana
la sangre por nos derramar.

Coro

1

In perpetual night moaning
For centuries, the offspring of Adam
Were waiting anxiously for the Messiah
Who should be born of Abraham.

Chorus
Rorate coeli desuper
Et nubes pluant justum.

2

How sad is the fate of the just!
On earth to weep, to suffer;
And not even in limbo after death
To rejoice in pleasure.

Chorus

3

The fault that rebel man
Committed through his vanity
Kept closed the gates
Of the seraphic city.

Chorus

4

To open them the Word itself
Had to descend from heaven
And taking on a human body
To pour out its blood for us.

Chorus

<table>
<tr><td>

5

¡Qué dicha, qué bien, qué ventura,

gozas, tierra, en esta ocasión!
Canta la iglesia, —Feliz culpa,
que mereció tal Redentor!—

</td><td>

5

What happiness, what blessing, what good
    fortune,
You, earth, enjoy on this occasion!
The church sings, "Happy fault,
That merits such a Redeemer!"

</td></tr>
<tr><td>

Coro

</td><td>

Chorus

</td></tr>
</table>

<table>
<tr><td>

Note that the singer ignores the elision of the
last two words, "de Abrán." The Latin words

</td><td>

of the chorus are probably a legacy of the
teaching of Father Ralliere.

</td></tr>
</table>

V6. *La Iglesia* (The Church)
R512, Francisco S. Leyva, age 81, Leyva, N.Mex., 1951, Robb.

<table>
<tr><td>

1

Descendamos con fuerza a la iglesia.
No proteste jamás nuestra fe,
en auxilio de la sagrada empresa
el Jesús, la María, y José.
De la iglesia San Pedro es la piedra,
donde el templo de él significó,
donde el hombre pecado se enmienda
y por esto el pecado perdonó.

</td><td>

1

Let us descend in force upon our church.
Let no one ever deny our faith,
And helping in this sacred undertaking
Will be Jesus, Mary, and Joseph.
Saint Peter is the rock on which is built
His temple where
A sinful man can go
And have his sins forgiven.

</td></tr>
</table>

2

Y él dirá que arrepentido
de sus faltas y sus culpas confiesa,
él se debe tal bien persuadido
que recibe el perdón por la iglesia.
¡O! el santo bendice este día
pero vuelve tu cielo a su fe
renunciando a la idolatría
por Jesús, por María, y José.

2

And if he will only go and say
That he repents of his sins and confesses,
He should be well persuaded
That he will receive pardon from the church.
Oh, may the saint bless this day
And put heaven back into the faith,
Renouncing idolatry
For Jesus, Mary, and Joseph.

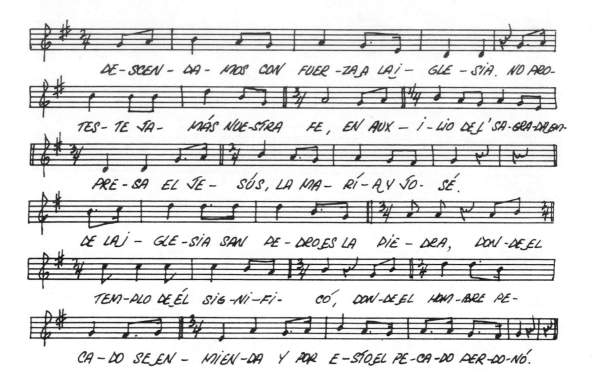

"Por Francisco S. Leyva." The singer ends with these words. Señor Leyva is credited with composing a number of songs, and the text of this may be one of them.

This melody is borrowed from an Anglo source (see "Anglo" in Definitions). It is freely varied from the original, the well-known hymn *In the Sweet Bye and Bye* and a parody of about 1905, *There's a Hole in the Bottom of the Sea.*

V7. *Mira, Mujer* (Regard, Woman)
R731, Francisco S. Leyva, age 81, Leyva, N.Mex., 1951, Robb.

1

Mira, mujer, el Dios que has ofendido.
Tú ya no tienes conciencia y corazón.
Ese gran Dios de ti tendrá clemencia
y te dará su eterna salvación.

1

Regard, woman, the God you have offended.
You no longer have conscience or heart.
Yet the great God will have mercy on you
And will give you eternal salvation.

726

2
Mas en el mundo, ofendiste su nombre,
y si lo encuentras, pídele perdón.
Mas él te quiere, te dirá su nombre,
Y si no mujer que te bendiga Dios.

2
But in the world, you offended his name,
And if you find him, ask his pardon.
But he loves you, he will tell you his name,
And if not woman—may God bless you.

(Each verse is repeated.)

RELIGIOUS *CUANDO*,

V8. *A Nuestra Señora de Guadalupe* (To Our Lady of Guadalupe)
R6, Próspero S. Baca, age 69, Bernalillo, N.Mex., 1944, Robb. Cf. Section H.

1
¿Cuándo llegará ese cuando
que mi fino amor disea
que otro México se vea
en otro imperio formado?
Sí había reinas en Las Indias
pero otra Guadalupana, ¡cuándo!

1
When will there be another *cuando*
Which tells of my fine love,
Which foresees another Mexico
Formed in another empire?
Other queens may rule the Indies
But another Guadalupe, never.

2

Este cuando se compuso
a la Reina Soberana
la que bajó de los cielos
a la ciudad Mexicana,
Madre mía Guadalupana,
mi alma se vive implorando.
Sí había reinas en Las Indias
pero otra Guadalupana, ¡cuándo!

2

This our *cuando* is composed
To our great and sovereign queen
Who descended from the heavens
To our City of Mexico,
My mother, Guadalupe,
Hear the voice of supplication.
Other queens may rule the Indies
But another Guadalupe, never.

3

Eres la Madre Divina,
Guadalupana María,
que en ti cuanto estamparte
las estrellas principales,
y digan los nacionales
de corazón y cantando,
sí había reinas en Las Indias
pero otra Guadalupana, ¡cuándo!

3

You are the divine mother,
Mary of Guadalupe,
Who has so much impressed
The most radiant stars of heaven,
And the citizens declare
With their hearts and voices singing,
Other queens may rule the Indies
But another Guadalupe, never.

4

La luna a tus pies pusiste
y allí te sirvió de peana.
Ni en la América, ni en Francia,
ni en las potencias de España
no habrá otra Guadalupana
que nos esté acompañando.
Sí había reinas en Las Indias
pero otra Guadalupana, ¡cuándo!

4

At your feet the moon abases itself
And comes to serve you with paean.
Neither in America, nor in France,
Nor in the dependencies of Spain
Is there another Guadalupe
Like her who has come to us.
Other queens may rule the Indies
But another Guadalupe, never.

5

Entre dos luces del día
Tú le hablaste a Juan Diego
y en aquel dichoso cerro
donde se vió aquel portento
y allí le diste las flores
que las llevara al convento,
sí había reinas en Las Indias
pero otra Guadalupana, ¡cuándo!

5

In the twilight of the day
You appeared to Juan Diego
And on that happy hill
Where the vision appeared
And you gave him the flowers
Which he carried to the convent,
Other queens may rule the Indies
But another Guadalupe, never.

6

En el rigor del invierno
cuando el suelo está nevado,
y en aquel triste lugar
allí las flores se han dado
y ni el aire, ni el calor,
ni el frío las ha marchitado.
Sí había reinas en Las Indias
pero otra Guadalupana, ¡cuándo!

6

In the rigors of the winter
When the earth with snow was covered,
And in that sad place
There the flowers blossomed,
And neither the air, nor the heat,
Nor the cold had withered them.
Other queens may rule the Indies
But another Guadalupe, never.

7

En México sucedió
el prodigioso milagro.
Los obispos y ministros
se te van arrodillando;

7

And in Mexico transpired
The prodigious miracle.
The bishops and ministers
Came kneeling to you;

las monjas de los conventos
toditas salen cantando.
Sí había reinas en Las Indias
pero otra Guadalupana, ¡cuándo!

And the nuns from the convents
All assembled and were singing.
Other queens may rule the Indies
But another Guadalupe, never.

8

Esas tus divinas niñas,
esas tus ojos sagrados
son las que a mí me consuela,
y tus labios sacrosanctos
y tus dos manos unidas
abogan por mis pecados.
Sí había reinas en Las Indias
pero otra Guadalupana, ¡cuándo!

8

Your divine children,
Your sacred eyes
Give me comfort,
And your lips so pure and holy
And your hands clasped in prayer
Make entreaty for my sins.
Other queens may rule the Indies
But another Guadalupe, never.

9

El día doce de diciembre,
tu día se te ha llegado;
todo el mundo festeja
y todo ese reino indiano,
digamos todos cantando
a la Virgen alabando.
Sí había reinas en Las Indias
pero otra Guadalupana, ¡cuándo!

9

The twelfth of December,
Your day has arrived;
All the world celebrates
And all this Indian kingdom,
We all join in singing
To the virgin, lifting praises.
Other queens may rule the Indies
But another Guadalupe, never.

10

¿Cuándo se verá otro imperio
ni otro México formado,
ni otra Reina en el cielo
que nos esté acompañando?
Porque en ninguna potencia,
porque en este mundo cuando.
Sí habrá Reina en Las Indias
pero que haiga otra Guadalupana, ¡cuándo!

10

When will we see another realm
Or another Mexico formed,
Or another Queen in heaven
Who has come to be with us?
Because in no power,
Because in this world never.
Other queens will rule the Indies
But there'll be another Guadalupe, never.

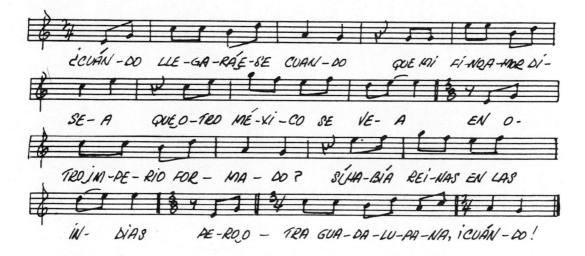

This melody is in the Mixolydian mode (mode of G). A subtle but charming musical feature of this text and melody is that, though each of the preceding seven lines of each verse contains eight syllables, the last line of each verse is unexpectedly prolonged to ten syllables. The result is intriguing both rhythmically and melodically. As in other instances where the last line of each verse is reiterated, the effect is almost hypnotic, driving home a belief or conviction as conclusive.

V8a. *Cuando a Nuestra Señora* (*Cuando* to Our Lady)
R1415, Edwin Berry, age 38, Tomé, N.Mex., 1956, Robb.

This text is almost identical with that of verses 1, 3, 4, and 5 of V8.

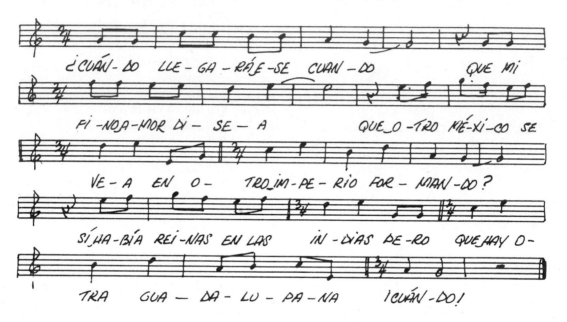

V9. *Cuando al Santo Niño de Atocha* (*Cuando* to the Holy Child of Atocha)
RB763, Vicente Sánchez, Las Lagunitas, N.Mex., 1950 or earlier, Cobos. Cf. P19.

Planta	*Planta*
¡Cuándo! se verá ese cuando	When this *cuando* is seen
que deseya toda criatura,	Let every living creature
en comprender su hermosura	Understand his beauty
y sus prodigios mirando.	And take note of his miracles.
1	1
Don José María Delgado	Don José María Delgado
de la suidá de Fresnillo[1]	Of the city of Fresnillo
logró el favor de este Niño;	Won the favor of this Holy Child;

[1]Ciudad de Fresnillo is a town in the state of Zacatecas, Mexico.

mirándose acongojado,
con un sable fué pasado
y estando el alma entregando
al Niño estaba invocando
su agoniya sin cesar;
la herida fué muy mortal
pero que muriera, ¡cuándo!

Seeing that he was afflicted,
Having been transfixed by a sword,
And on the point of giving up his soul
In the midst of his agony
He invoked the aid of the Holy Child.
The wound was mortal
But if he should die—when?

2

Doña Juliana Agodines
de la suidá de Jerez[2]
un dolor fuerte una vez
la causaba mucha ruina;
la providencia divina
de este Niño le fué dando,
su entera salud gozando
luego las gracias le da;
dice: —Médicos habrá
pero otro de Atocha, ¡cuándo!—

2

Doña Juliana Agodines
Of the city of Jerez
At one time developed a severe pain
Which caused her much damage;
But divine Providence
In the person of this Child
Restored her health,
Wherefore she gives thanks,
Saying, "There may be doctors
But another of Atocha—when?"

3

Galistro Aguirres se llama
quien declara con fervor,
sanar de parte interior
cuando al Santo Niño aclama;
y que con fervor le aclama
sus auxilios proclamando;
dice con mucho fervor,
sus lágrimas derramando,
dice: —Médicos habrá,
pero otro de Atocha, ¡cuándo!—

3

There is a man called Galistro Aguirres
Who declares with fervor
That he was cured of internal injuries
When he called upon the Holy Child;
Promising that in return for his help
He would announce to the world his aid;
He did so with much fervor
With tears streaming down,
Saying, "There may be doctors,
But another of Atocha—when?"

4

En una cierta ocasión
Jorge García fué minero
y lo agarró por entero
una panza de cañón;
al Niño en su corazón
sus auxilios proclamando
y al instante le fué dando
auxilios, pues lo invocó;
la salud le concedió
pero él que muriera, ¡cuándo!

4

On a certain occasion
Jorge García, a miner,
Was seized with a very bad
Pain in his belly;
With the Child in his heart
He begged that he would help
And immediately he received aid
As he had requested;
In good health now,
Someday he will die but—when?

5

María Eleuteria estaba
un día en su puerta sentada,
llegó un hombre decedido
tirándole puñaladas;
María Catarina estaba
esta desgracia mirando;

5

María Eleuteria one day
Was sitting at her doorstep
When a man possessed came along
Stabbing people with a knife;
María Catarina was watching this;
Thereupon she prayed to the Child

---

[2] Ciudad de Jerez (de la Frontera) is a town in Andalucía, Spain. This reference suggests the possibility of Spanish origin, as the reference to Fresnillo suggests additions from Mexico.

al Niño estaba invocando
la librase de aquel mal;
la herida fué muy mortal
pero que muriera, ¡cuándo!

To deliver them from this misfortune.
The wound was mortal and
She must die someday, but
The question is—when?

6

María Maximiana Esparza
por su recia condición
se vido en una prisión
sin la más leve esperanza,
y del Santo Niño alcanza
su libertad ya gozando;
dice con mucho fervor,
sus lágrimas derramando:
—Otro defensor habrá,
pero otro de Atocha, ¡cuándo!

6

María Maximiana Esparza
To her misfortune
Found herself in prison
Without the slightest hope,
And the Holy Child obtained
Her freedom which she now enjoys;
She declares with great fervor,
The tears streaming down her cheeks:
"There may be other defenders
But another of Atocha—when?"

These *décimas* relating to holy personages are the musical counterparts of the *retablos* painted on tin and presented to various churches in Mexico in gratitude for favors granted by the saints, which are regarded as miracles.

V9 exhibits a rather subtle rhythmic effect in the irregular alternation of seven-syllable and eight-syllable lines, resulting in "masculine" (strong beat) and "feminine" (weak beat) endings.

ADAM AND EVE

V10. *Adán y Eva* (Adam and Eve)
R510, Francisco S. Leyva, age 81, Leyva, N.Mex., 1951, Robb.

1

Inmenso Dios
que en el éter divino;
le diste el hombre
al mundo vivir,
y le dejaste
libre aquel camino
hasta el momento
que deje de existir.

1

Great powerful God,
In your ethereal heavens;
You put man on
The earth to live,
And you left open
All his choices
As long as
You let him live.

2

Pero pensando
que jamás la muerte
lejos va
un día de tocar,
quiso gozar
del todo de su suerte
y la delicia
siempre desultar.

2

Thinking that
Death would
Nevermore
Play with him,
Man wanted to enjoy
All that luck brought
And all the delights
That came his way.

<table>
<tr><td>

3

También le viste
segundo la mujer
y la hermosura
para deleitar.
Y la pusiste
libre en el Edén
dándole vista
para falsionar.

</td><td>

3

And then you left him
To follow woman
With her loveliness
To delight in.
And you left her
Freely to roam in Eden,
Giving a mind
To go and deceive.

</td></tr>
<tr><td>

4

Y siempre astuta
la mujer traidora
al hombre encantó
fácil engañó.
Con la manzana
a la misma hora
que la serpiente
—¿Comes tú, señor?

</td><td>

4

The treacherous woman
Is always astute,
It's easy to fool
A man that's bewitched.
Influenced by the serpent,
She comes with an apple
And says to Adam:
"Won't you have a bite, sir?"

</td></tr>
</table>

IN-MEN-SO DIOS QUE EN EL É-TER DI- VI-NO; LE DI-STEEL HOM-BRE AL MUN-DO VI-VIR, Y LE DE-JA-STE LI-BRE A-QUEL CA-MI-NO HAS-TA EL MO-MEN-TO QUE DE-JE DE EX-IS-TIR.

CREED

V11. *El Credo* (The Creed)
R1031, Jorge López, age 53, Córdova, N.Mex., 1952, Robb. Cf. Rael (p. 120).

<table>
<tr><td>

1

Creo en Dios, Padre, poderoso
creador del cielo y la tierra,
protector universal,
donde todo el bien me encierra.

</td><td>

1

I believe in God the Father,
Powerful creator of heaven and earth,
Universal protector,
Who surrounds me with all good things.

</td></tr>
<tr><td>

2

Siempre creo en Jesucristo,
su único Hijo y verdadero,
Padre de misericordia,
que te alaba el mundo entero.

</td><td>

2

I always believe in Jesus Christ
His true and only Son,
The Father of mercy,
Whom the entire world praises.

</td></tr>
</table>

3
Creo en el Espíritu Santo
que es un solo Señor nuestro,
también que fué concebido
por obra del Espíritu Santo.

3
I believe in the Holy Spirit
Who is our only Lord and
Who was also conceived
By the work of the Holy Spirit.

CRE-O EN DIOS, PA-DRE, PO-DE-RO-SO CRE-A-
DOR DEL CIE-LO Y LA TIE-RRA, PRO-TEC-TOR U-NI-VER-
SAL, DON-DE TO-DO EL BIEN ME EN-CIE-RRA.

This is sung in the musical style of an *ala-bado*.

THE VIRGIN AND THE DEVIL

V12.   *Orillas de un Ojo de Agua* (By the Edge of a Spring of Water)
R1401, Juan Griego, Albuquerque, N.Mex., 1956, Robb.

1
Orillas de un ojo de agua,
estaba un ángel llorando
de ver que se condenaba
el alma que traiba a su cargo.

1
By the edge of a spring of water,
There an angel was crying
To see condemned
The soul which was in his charge.

2
La Virgen le dice al ángel:
—No llores, ángel varón,
que yo rogalé con mi hijo
que esta alma alcance perdón.—

2
The Virgin says to the angel:
"Don't cry, archangel,
I shall plead with my son
So that this soul may receive pardon."

3
La Virgen le dice a Cristo:
—Hijo de mi corazón,
por la leche que mamaste,
que esta alma alcance perdón.—

3
The Virgin says to Christ:
"Son of my heart,
By the milk that you sucked,
Grant pardon to this soul."

4
Cristo le dice a la Virgen:
—Madre de mi corazón,
¿cómo quieres esta alma,
si en tanto nos ofendió?—

4
Christ says to the Virgin:
"Mother of my heart,
Why do you want this soul,
If he has offended us so?"

5

La Virgen le dice a Cristo:
—Hijo de mi corazón,
pastoreando sus ovejas,
un rosario me rezó.—

6

Cristo le dice a la Virgen:
—Madre de mi corazón,
si tanto quieres esta alma
sácala de fuego ardor.—

7

La Virgen como piadosa
a las llamas se metió,
con su santo escapulario
su devoto lo sacó.

8

El diablo cómo enojado
a Jesucristo le habló:
—El alma que me has dado,
tu madre me la quitó.

9

—Quítate de aquí, Malino,
no te heche una maldición,
pues lo que mi madre hiciere
por hecho lo dejo yo.

5

The Virgin says to Christ:
"Son of my heart,
While keeping his sheep
He prayed a rosary to me."

6

Christ says to the Virgin:
"Mother of my heart,
If you want this soul so much
Take him out of the fiery flames."

7

The Virgin so merciful
Entered the flames
With her holy scapulary and
She rescued her devotee.

8

The devil, angered,
Spoke to Jesus Christ:
"The soul that you gave me
Your mother took away."

9

"Leave here, you evil one,
Before I place a curse on you,
For what my mother does
I leave as done."

Part III: INSTRUMENTAL MELODIES

CONTENTS

X48. *San Antone*
X49. *Round Waltz*

Leyva, New Mexico, 1950

X50. *Polka*
X51. *El Rancho Grande*
X52. *Jacolitos*
X53. *Cielto Lindo*
X54. *Polka*
X55. *Valse de Cadena*
X56. *Polka*
X57. *Polka*
X58. *Schottisch*
X59. *Cuna*

Llano de San Juan, New Mexico, 1950

X60. *Valse*

X61. *Cuna*
X62. *Cotillo*
X63. *Valse*
X64. *Cotillo*
X65. *Polka*
X66. *Polka*
X67. *Vals*

Y. OTHER INSTRUMENTAL MELODIES

Y1. *Grasshopper Waltz*
Y2. *Scissors Grinders Street Call*
      (Oaxaca, Mexico)
Y3. *Scissors Grinders Street Call*
      (Seville, Spain)

A NOTE ON THE FORMAT OF PART III

I have grouped the instrumental melodies largely by village. Although the villages represented are merely a sample, this method of grouping emphasizes the richness and diversity in an era now passing away of the musical literature of the villages (see Appendix B). Including these instrumental numbers enriches the portrait of that era. This seems to me more important than grouping all the various forms such as polkas together, although separate studies might reveal interesting comparisons.

This emphasis on individual villages conforms with the practice of fiction writers, who in dealing with the Hispanic people of the Southwest tend to write about specific villages. For example, Willa Cather wrote about Acoma in *Death Comes for the Archbishop*; Robert Bright wrote about Talpa in *The Life and Death of Little Jo*.

Pride and love are in the hearts of the people for their villages and their village cultures, their heroes and customs and songs, each to some extent unique and to some extent shared with other villages, even with other races. Grouping the music by villages brings this out. It also helps convey more vividly the atmosphere of village social occasions where joy predominated, though tragedy often lurked just outside in the darkness.

W. *Matachines* DANCE AND RELATED FORMS

The tradition of ritual dancing in the Spanish villages of the Southwest, like the folk play *Los Pastores*, is engaged in a struggle for survival, possibly a losing struggle. It tends to die out in a village and then to be revived. This has happened in San Antonio, Bernalillo County, New Mexico, and in Bernalillo, New Mexico, to cite two instances. In other places all that is left of the dances are the melodies lingering in the memories of old fiddlers, guitarists, or singers. And since many of the musicians are now dead, these pages may contain the only surviving record of this music. Some ritual dances are already moribund or dead. "The Dance of the Moors and Christians" seems to be *spurlos versenkt* in the Southwest, leaving only a few literary or musical traces. Those of Hispanic, Mexican, and mestizo inheritance will ultimately decide the fate of these dances—whether they are to live or die or perhaps be resuscitated, like Don Gato in the well-known romance (A16b).

Actually the ritual-dance tradition in the Spanish-speaking villages (many of them, like Los Griegos, now engulfed by the expanding cities) has nowhere near the vitality of the corresponding tradition of the Indian villages of the Southwest, where many different ritual dances are still enjoying a life of healthy vigor. In fact, the corn dances of 1979 at Santo Domingo Indian Pueblo, New Mexico, were by far the finest, at least in numbers of dances and singers, that I have seen over a period of thirty years. The number of dancers in each clan had doubled from about 125 to 250, and the chorus had increased from about 50 men to nearly 100.

I have already published many of my findings about the *matachines* dance (Robb 13e), and much of what I have written can be incorporated by reference here. Nevertheless, the subject warrants further attention in these pages. Like the Indian dances of the Southwest, the *matachines* dances, usually performed outdoors in the bright sunlight, combine in a multifaceted art form simple but somehow fascinating melodies, colorful costumes, and interesting dance steps and formations of dancers. They also incorporate aspects of the village religious ritual, comedy in the antics of the *abuelo* (grandfather) and the bull, and a dramatic enactment of the triumph of good over evil.

These dances cast a spell upon any sensitive observer and enrich the lives of the villagers, who silently observe the dances from the periphery of the plaza. Certainly part of the intense love shown by Spanish-surnamed villagers for their villages and their culture derives from their childhood experience of such village customs. Absorbed like the catechism, the Lord's Prayer, and the Twenty-third Psalm, they exert a lifelong influence. These dances are a manifestation of the love of beauty inherent in man, beauty not only in its physical forms but also in its aspects of neighborliness, loyalty, character, hospitality, and love of one's own microcosmic environment.

The format I have followed up to now has been modified slightly for this section. Grouped by village and date, the examples do not include this information in their headings. Also two different dances (or two separate entries in my collection) are sometimes danced to the same melody. In such cases the melody is entered only once, though it is given a double heading (see W26, for example).

The music itself needs some explaining. When a *matachines* dance consists of several musical phrases, the musicians take liberties, and literal repetitions cannot be taken for granted. Though the musician frequently returns to the beginning, he may pick out certain phrases for subtle alteration so that the repetitions are varied. This is not mere caprice on the part of the fiddler, for the melody must coordinate with the steps and evolutions of the dancers. Musicians who furnished unaccompanied violin music for the dances employed many double stops. I have annotated a few of these but merely to indicate their use, for this is not a part of the present study.

The procession preceding the *matachines* dance, San Antonio, Bernalillo County, New Mexico, June 13, 1949.

Matachines dance, Santa Clara Indian pueblo, New Mexico. Indian dancers in Indian costumes.

Matachines dance, Santa Clara Indian pueblo, New Mexico.

MATACHINES DANCES

Matachines dance, Santa Clara Indian pueblo, New Mexico.

Matachines dance, Santa Clara Indian pueblo, New Mexico.

Matachines dance, Bernalillo, New Mexico, June 9, 1967.

Matachines dance, Bernalillo, New Mexico, June 9, 1967.

Matachines dance, Tortugas, New Mexico, 1953.

The Maypole, *matachines* dance, Tortugas, New Mexico, 1953.

MATACHINES DANCES

San Antonio, Bernalillo County, New Mexico, 1949

W1. *Matachines Dance*, R227.
Matachines Dance, R237n.

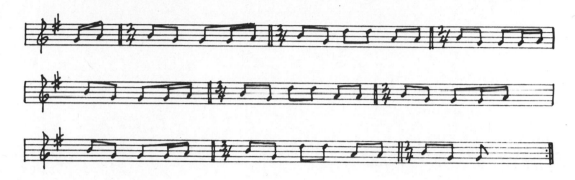

W2. *Matachines Dance*, R228.

W3. *Matachines Dance*, R229.

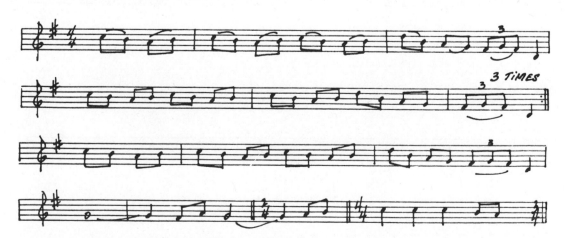

W4. *Matachines Dance, R230.*

W5. *Matachines Dance, R231.*

W6. *Matachines Dance, R232.*

San Antonio, Bernalillo County, New Mexico, 1954

W7. *La Dala del Pie* (Put Your Foot Forward), R1275. Cf. W1, W2.

W8. *La Malinche*, R1276. Cf. W3.

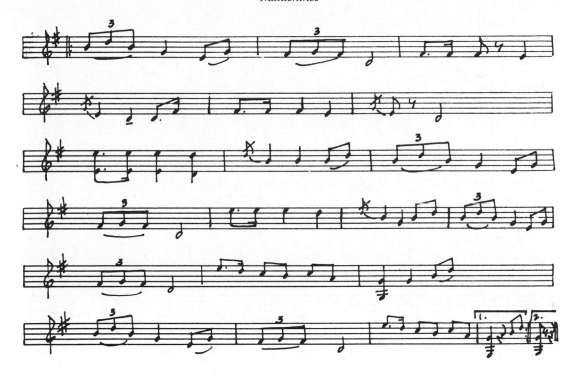

W9. *La Toreada del Toro* (Fighting the Bull), R1277. Cf. W4.

W10. *Contra* (Counter Dance), R1278. Cf. W15, W27.

W11. *La Correrita* (The Little Run), R1279. Cf. W5.

ETC. WITH VARIATIONS

San Antonio, Bernalillo County, New Mexico, 1962

W12. *Matachines Dance, R76a. Cf. W1.*

W13. *Matachines Dance, R76b.*
Matachines Dance, R76c.

W14. *Matachines Dance, R76d.*

W15. *Matachines Dance, R76e. Cf. W10.*

W16. *Matachines Dance, R76f.*

W17. *Matachines Dance*, R76g.

Bernalillo, New Mexico, 1951

W18. *General Dance*, R807.

W19. *Dance in Pairs*, R808.

W20. *Bull and Malinche,* R809.

W21. *General Dance,* R810. Cf. W3.

W22. *Monarca's Dance,* R811.

W23. *Monarca and Bull,* R812.

W24. *Monarca and Malinche,* R813. Cf. W9.

W25. *Matachines Dance,* R814. Cf. W19.

W26. *Matachines Dance,* R815. Cf. W11.
Grandmothers' Dance, R816.

W27. *Final Dance,* R817. Cf. W10, W15.

Bernalillo, New Mexico, 1967

W28. *La Malinche,* R2201. Cf. W20.

W29. *La Tejida* (Make the Turn), R2202. Cf. W21.

W30. *La Batalla* (The Weaving), R2203. Cf. W22.

W31. *La Vuelta* (The Return), R2204. Cf. W23.

W32. *Mata el Toro* (Kill the Bull), R2205. Cf. W24.

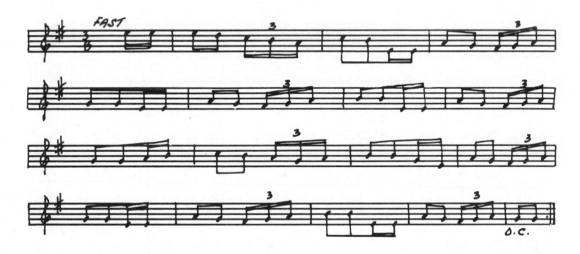

W33. *La Cruz* (The Cross), R2206. Cf. W25.

W34. *La Tendita* (The Spread Out), R2207. Cf. W26.

W35. *La Promesa* (The Promise) or *La Paterita* (The Little Kick), R2208. Cf. W3.

W36. *La Carera* (The Dear One), R2209.

Llano de San Juan, New Mexico, 1952

W37. *Matachines Dance*, R957.

W38. *Matachines Dance, R958.*

SIX TIMES

W39. *Matachines Dance, R959.*

W40. *Matachines Dance, R960.*

REPEATED WITH VARIATIONS

Tortugas, New Mexico, 1953

W41. *La Entrada* (The Entrance), R1143.

W42. *La Batalla* (The Battle), R1144.

W43. *La Mudanza* (The Mutation), R1145.

W44. *La Ese* (The Letter S), R1146.

W45. *Guajes* (Rattles), R1147.

W46. *Los Paños* (The Silk Handkerchiefs), R1148.

W47. *El Son de la Malinche*, R1149.

W48. *La Entre Tejida* (The Woven Entrance, or Maypole Dance), R1150.
La Trenza (The Braid), R1151.

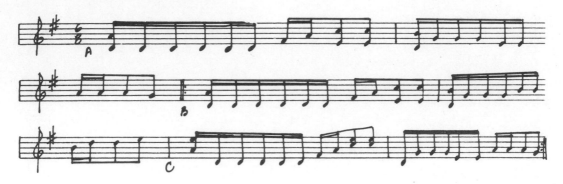

W49. *La Procesión* (The Procession), R1152.

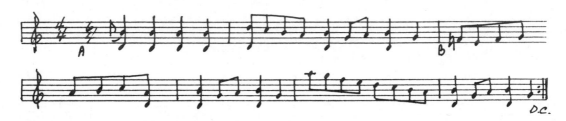

W50. *El Toro* (The Bull), R1153.

W51. *La Escondida* (The Hidden Girl), R1154.

W52. *Matachines Dance*, R2124.

W53. *Matachines Dance*, R2125.

W54. *Matachines Dance*, R2126.

D.C.

W55. *Matachines Dance, R2127.*

W56. *Matachines Dance, R2128.*

Tierra Amarilla, New Mexico, 1957

W57. *La Paseada* (The Stroll), R1586.

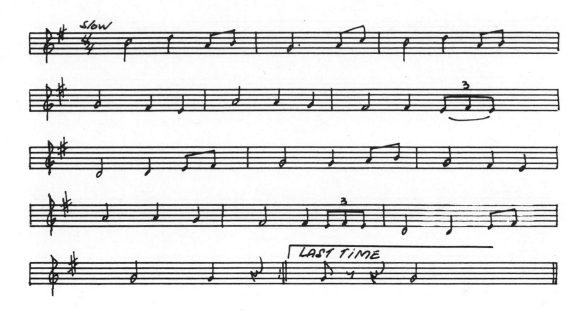

W58. *La Vuelta* (The Twist), R1587.

W59. *La Paseada* (The Stroll), R1588.

W60. *La Malinche,* R1590.

W61. *La Cruz* (The Cross), R1591.

W62. *El Toro* (The Bull), R1592.

W63. *La Vaquiadita* (The Little Heifer),[1] R1593.

[1]This is described in FTR (4/21/57) as "the going backward, slow."

W64. *La Paseada* (The Stroll), R1594.[2]

W65. *La Vuelta*, R1595.

[2] The melodies W64–69 are those played by the same two musicians from Tierra Amarilla when they play at San Juan, the Indian pueblo.

W66. *La Malinche,* R1596.

W67. *La Cruzada* (The Crossing), R1597.

W68. *La Vaquiadita* (The Little Heifer), R1598.

W69. *El Torito* (The Little Bull), R1599.

San Juan Indian Pueblo, New Mexico, 1959

W70.   *Matachines Dance, R1659.*

W71. *Matachines Dance*, R1660.

W72. *Matachines Dance*, R1661.

W73. *Matachines Dance, R1662.*

W74. *Matachines Dance, R1663.*

W75. *Matachines Dance*, R1664.

Matachines Dances From Old Mexico

W76. *Matachines Dance*, R1974.

W77. *Matachines Dance,* R1975.

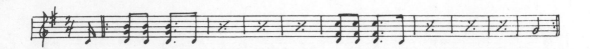

W78. *Matachines Dance,* R1976.

W79. *Matachines Dance,* R1977.

W80. *Matachines Dance,* R1978 (Ahí Vienen los Indios).

W81. *El Toro*, RB35.

W82. *El Zapateado* (The Stamping Dance), RB36.

W83. *La Malinche*, RB37.

This melody is difficult to hear due to the guitar which often drowns out the fiddle.

W84. *La Tejada* (The Woven Pattern), RB38.

W85. *La Procesión*, R39.

W86. *El Monarca*, R40.

W87. *La Corona* (The Crown), RB41.

RELATED DANCES

Tortugas, New Mexico, 1953

W88.   *Aztecas Dance, R1126.*

W89.   *Aztecas Dance, Part II, R1127.*
Aztecas Dance, R1130.
Aztecas Dance, R1141.

Aztecas Dance, Part II

Aztecas Dance, Part III. Same as Part II but with this arrow rhythm:

W90. *Aztecas Dance, R1128.*

W91. *Aztecas Dance,* R1131.

W92. *Aztecas Dance,* R1133.
Aztecas Dance, R1142.

W93. *Aztecas Dance,* R1136.
Aztecas Dance, R1203.

W94. *Aztecas Dance*, R1137.
Aztecas Dance, R1138.

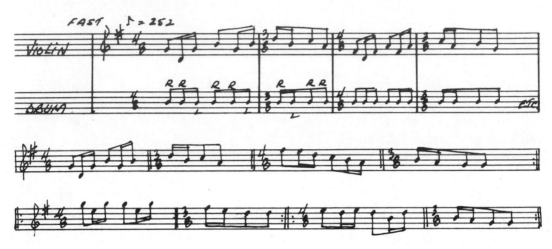

W95. *Aztecas Dance*, R1139.
El Monarca, R1205.

W96. *Aztecas Dance*, R1140.

Tortugas, New Mexico, 1954

Introductory material preceding several of the following pieces:

W97. *Mata al Viejo* (Kill the Old Man), R1204.

W98. *Los Indios Vienen* (The Indians Are Coming), R1206.

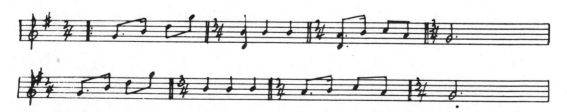

W99. *La Caminata,* R1207.

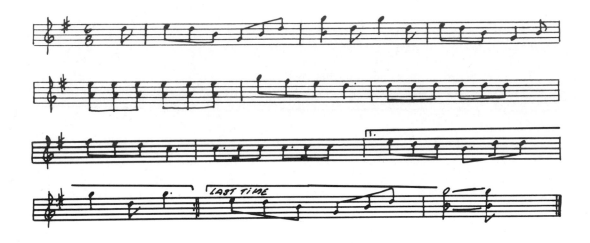

W100. *Bow Dance,* R1208.

W101. *La Cruz*, R1209.

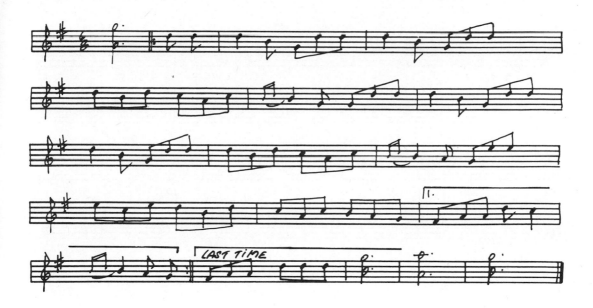

W102. *Perriquito* (Puppy), R1210.

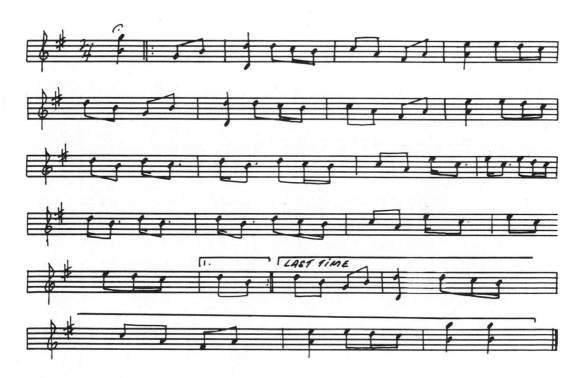

W103. *El Redoblado*, R1211.
Ring Dance, R1216.

W104. *La Mudanza*, R1212.

W105. *El Azteca*, R1213.

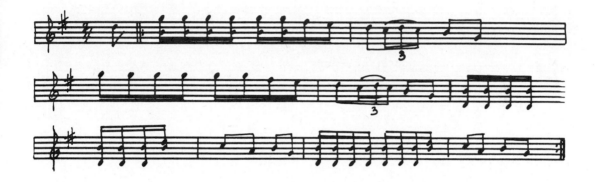

W106. *Redoblado*, R1214.

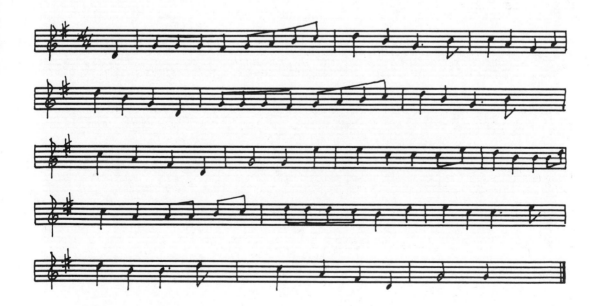

W107.   *Los Nanos,* R1215.

W108.   *War or Flechas Dance,* R1217.

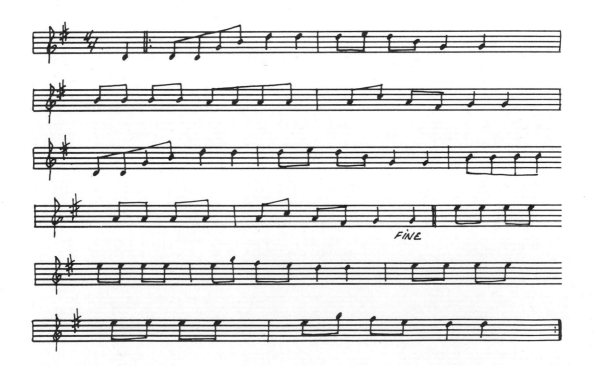

X. SOCIAL DANCES

Under this heading I have included an assorted group of the tunes, almost invariably fiddle tunes, to which the Spanish-American villagers danced. They were recorded by the fiddlers themselves, usually old men. The younger musicians seem to be more attracted to the instruments and music of the city dance bands, complete with "traps," or of the Mexican mariachi orchestras. Such groups usually learn their repertory by ear over the radio or from records, rather than from the older singers and the handwritten notebooks laboriously copied from generation to generation. This book may therefore be the last large, authentic collection of the old tunes to be assembled, since many if not most of the older musicians who made these recordings are now dead.

Américo Paredes says that the dance played little part in Texas-border folkways and that many border families were prejudiced against dancing because it brought the sexes too close together and gave rise to quarrels and bloody fights (Paredes 10, p. 14). That this prejudice was justified is evidenced by a number of *corridos* telling how a girl was shot to death on the spot for impugning the honor of a young man by refusing to dance with him. See *Jesús Cadenas* (B17–B17b), *Rosita Alvírez* (B19–B19b), and *El Día de San Juan* (B20–20a).

The social dances, as Paredes says and as their names imply, were largely a modern importation reflecting non-Spanish European vogues. But many were also drawn from contemporary Mexican and American sources.

A group of melodies (all but two of which are represented in this book) were arranged attractively for the tipica orchestra of Santa Fe High School by Pablo Mares, its director, and published as *Santa Fe Tipica Orchestra Folio* (see Bibliography, Mares). The arrangements are for strings and guitars.

Albuquerque, New Mexico

X1. *Cuadrilla* (Quadrille), R1384.

X2. *Polka*, R1385.

X3. *Mazurka, Valse de Silla* (Mazurka, Chair Waltz), R1386. Cf. N2.

This is of course misnamed for the meter is neither that of the mazurka nor of the waltz.

X4. *Chile Amarilla*, R1388.

X5. *Después del Baile* (After the Ball), R1389.

X6. *Galopa de Cuadrilla, R1390.*

Galopa de Cuadrilla, Part II.

X7. *Polka de Cuadrilla*, R1391.

X8. *El Vaquero* (The Cowboy), R1891.

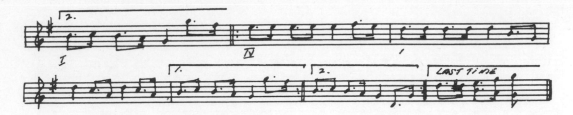

This version is transcribed from a piano solo
by the late Nato Hernández, accompanied
by hand clapping.

X9. *La Camilla,* R1892.

X10. *El Chote* (Schottisch), R1893.

X11. *Polka*, R1894.

Arroyo Hondo, New Mexico, 1951

X12. *Cotillo*, R464.

The fiddler kept time by beating audibly
with his foot.

X13. *Valse,* R465.

X14. *Corrido de una Pelea* (Ballad of a Fight), R466.

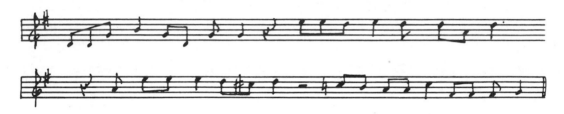

X15. *Cotillo,* R467.

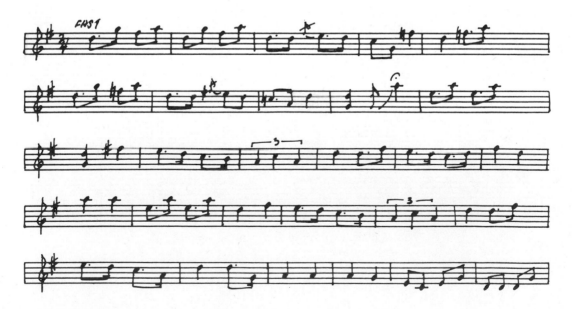

X16. *Hay Poder en Jesús* (There Is Power in Jesus), R468.

X17. *Polka*, R469.

FINE

D.C. AL FINE

X18. *Cuna* (Cradle), R470.

FAST

D.C.

X19. *Valse Chiqueado*, R471.

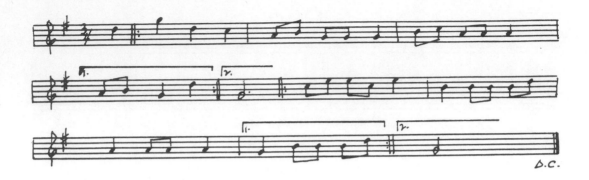

X20. *La Muerte* (The Death), R472.

Imagine dancing to a tune called La Muerte (death). Perhaps this has something to do with the day of death as celebrated in Mexico and Central America. The fiddler uses many double stops.

X21.   *Vals*, R473.

X22.   *Varsoviana*, R474.

Bernalillo, New Mexico

X23. *Cuna* (Cradle), R623.

X24. *Old Polka*, R624.

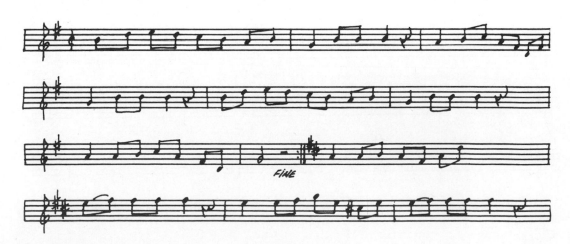

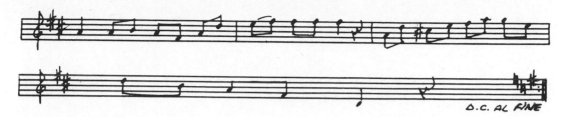

X25. *Camilla, R625.*

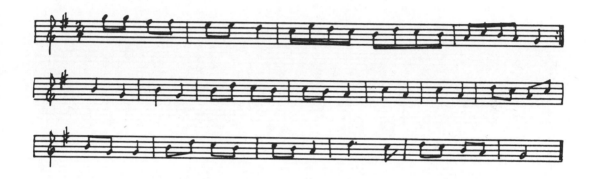

X26. *Square Dance, R626.*

Chilili, New Mexico, 1963

X27. *Polka*, R1914.

X28. *La Marcha*, R1915.

X29. *Varsoviana*, R1916.

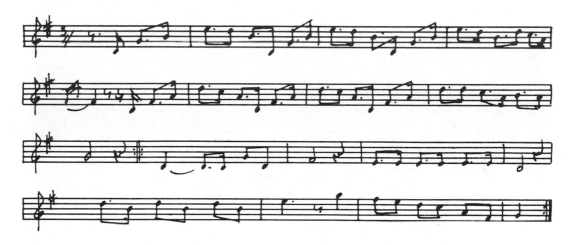

X30. *La Raspa*, R1917.

X31. *El Venadito* (The Little Deer), R1918.

X32. *Polka,* R1922.

Córdova, New Mexico

X33. *Chiapanecas,* R253.

X34. *Varsoviana, R254.*

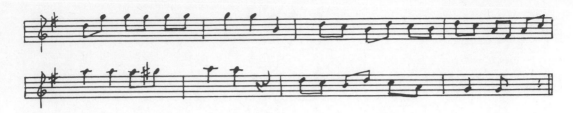

X35. *Zacatecas*, R268.

La Jara, New Mexico, 1951

X36. *La Finada Pablita*, R791.

X37. *Cuadrilla*, R793.

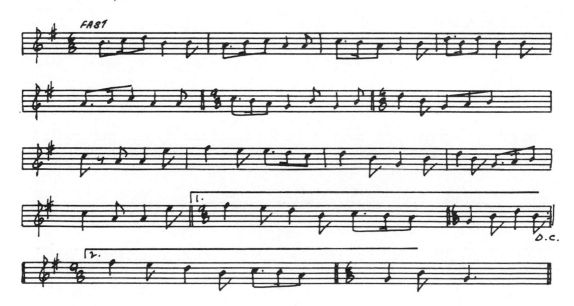

X38. *Polka,* R794.

La Puente, New Mexico

X39. *Varsouvien,* R1458.

X40. *Varsouvien,* R1459.

X41. *Polka*, R1460.

X42. *Cuna* (Cradle), R1461.

X43. *La Virgencita* (The Little Virgin), R1462.

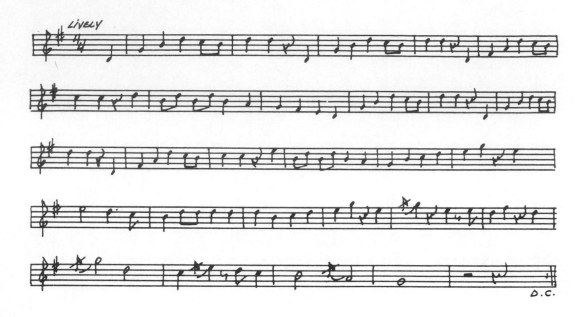

X44. *Indita* (Indian Girl), R1463.

X45. *Valse de Cadena* (Chain Waltz), R1464.

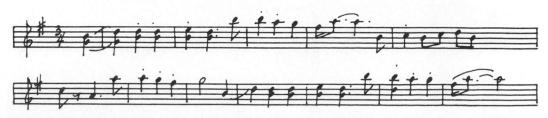

X46. *Valse de Cadena* (Chain Waltz), R1465.

X47. *Man or Two*, R1466.

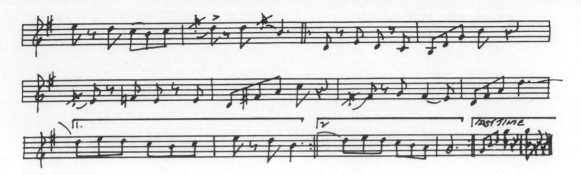

X48. *San Antone, R1467.*

X49. *Round Waltz, R1468.*

Leyva, New Mexico, 1950

X50. *Polka,* R292.

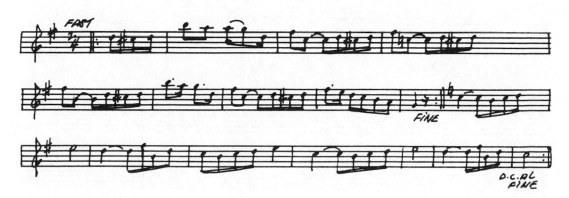

X51. *El Rancho Grande* (The Big Ranch), R293.

The fiddler indulges in a number of double
stops and variations in subsequent verses.

X52. *Jacolitos*, R294.

X53. *Cielto Lindo*, R295.

X54. *Polka*, R296.

X55. *Valse de Cadena* (Chain Waltz), R887.

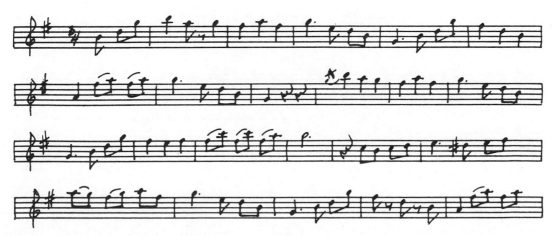

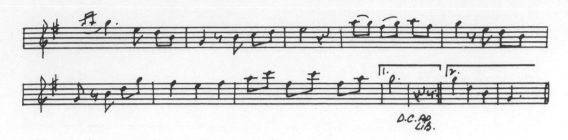

X56. *Polka*, R888.

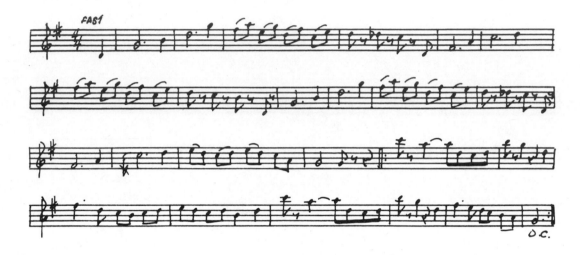

X57. *Polka*, R889.

X58. *Schottisch,* R890.

X59. *Cuna* (Cradle), R892.

Llano de San Juan, New Mexico, 1950

X60. *Valse*, R299.

X61. *Cuna* (Cradle), R300.

X62. *Cotillo*, R301.

X63. *Valse*, R484.

A.C.

X64. *Cotillo*, R485.

X65. *Polka*, R487.

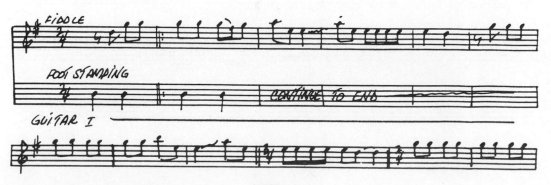

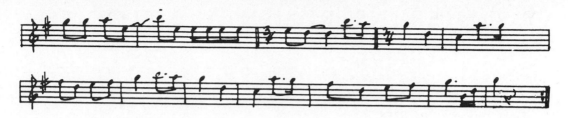

X66. *Polka, R488.*

X67. *Vals, R961.*

Y. OTHER INSTRUMENTAL MELODIES

Y1. *Grasshopper Waltz, R128.*

Y2. *Scissors Grinder's Street Call, R999.*

The actual sound is two octaves higher.

Y3. *Scissors Grinder's Song*, R2313, Seville, Spain.

Talking with a scissors grinder in Seville, Spain, 1970.

APPENDICES

A. PIANO-VOCAL ARRANGEMENTS
OF SELECTED SONGS

In the course of an interview in Rio de Janeiro, Heitor Villa-Lobos, who was known in his country as "Mr. Folklore," told me: "I am not a folklorist. I use folklore to form my musical personality." I confess that I have something of this feeling too, and the result has been that I have made arrangements of folk songs and have used them as thematic materials in many of my musical compositions.

In addition to the twelve piano-vocal arrangements included here, in my earlier *Hispanic Folk Songs of New Mexico* (Robb 13) I have already published such arrangements of the following songs:

Selections from *Los Pastores* as performed at Los Griegos, New Mexico: *Pedimento de las Posadas*, p. 24; *Cuando por el Oriente*, p. 28; *De la Real Jerusalén*, p. 30; *La Levantada de Bartolo*, p. 32; *Ofrecimiento de los Pastores*, p. 34.
Other Christmas carols sung in New Mexico: *Vamos Todos a Belén*, p. 38; *A la Ru*, p. 40.
Secular songs: *Corrido de Elena*, p. 44; *Co-rrido de la Muerte de Antonio Maestas*, p. 50; *Palomita Que Vienes Herida*, p. 58; *Sierra Nevada*, p. 61; *El Muchacho Alegre*, p. 66; *Indita de Amarante Martínez*, p. 68; *Sandovalito*, p. 76; *Mi Carro Ford*, p. 78.

Sheet music and recordings of other (unpublished) folk songs that I have arranged are available at the Fine Arts Library of the University of New Mexico in Albuquerque, New Mexico.

The following songs are included here:

Canción del Fraile (A1)
Don Gato (A16)
En la Cantina de Denver (B53)
Senaida (C32)
Cuatro Palomitas Blancas (C39)
Leonor (D6)
El Comanchito (F1)
El Borreguero (I3)
Entrega de Novios (K1)
Bendito Sea Dios (S2)
Tun Tun (Christmas Carol)
Adiós José, Adiós María (Christmas Carol)

Canción del Fraile (A1)

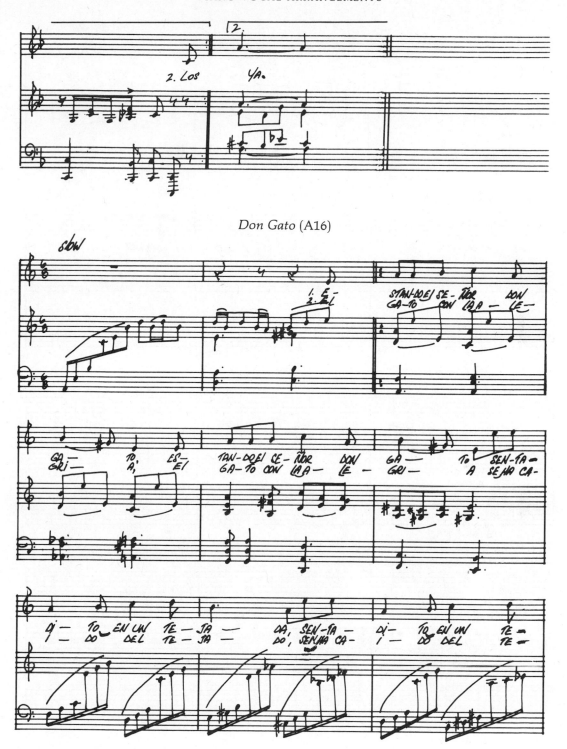

Don Gato (A16)

En la Cantina de Denver (B53)

NI-ÑA: — NO SE VA-YA TAN TEM-PRA-NO; NO SE VA-YA

TAN TEM-PRA-NO, TO-DA-VÍA NO SON LAS SIE-TE. NO SE VA-YA

TAN TEM-PRA-NO, TO - DA-VÍA NO SON LAS SIE-TE.

Senaida (C32)

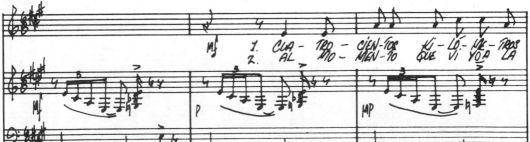

1. CUA - TRO - CIEN-TOS KI-LÓ-ME-TROS
2. AL MO - MEN-TO QUE VI YO A LA

Cuatro Palomitas Blancas (C39)

Leonor (D6)

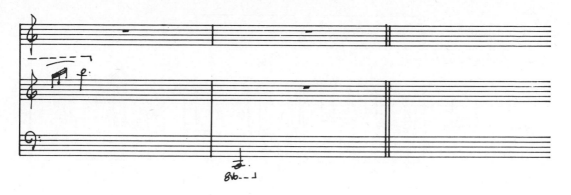

El Comanchito (F1)

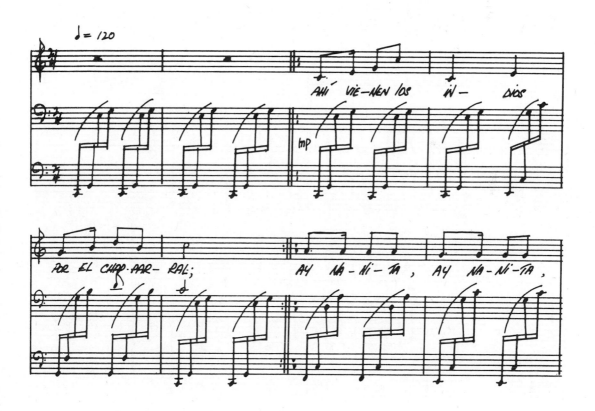

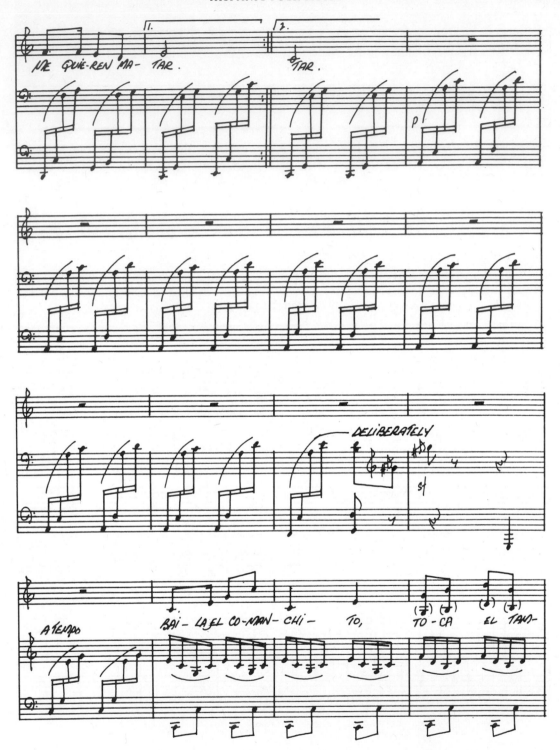

El Borreguero (13)

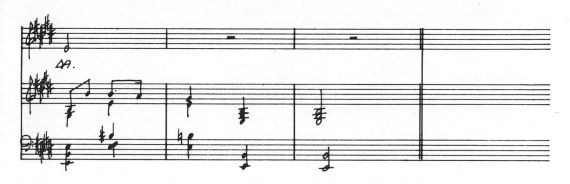

Entrega de Novios (K1)

853

Bendito Sea Dios (S2)

Tun Tun (Christmas Carol)

This is a Venezuelan carol that I introduced into New Mexico where it is now sung every year at Christmas. Perhaps one can call it New Mexican by adoption.

Adiós José, Adiós María (Christmas Carol)

A-DIÓS JO— SÉ A-DIÓS MA — RÍA,   A- DIÓS JO— SÉ A-DIÓS MA-

RÍ-A, A-DIÓS NI— ÑO CHI-QUI-TI-TO,   A-DIÓS NI— ÑO CHI-QUI-

TI-TO.

8vo- - - -

B.   SONG LITERATURE OF THE VILLAGES

One striking feature of village life in the South-west is the corpus of songs that circulate in a particular region telling of well-known local characters and noteworthy local events both recent and remote. It is easy to identify the narrative poems such as the *corrido* and the *indita*, for they are written in a factual way with special attention to dates and often to places. With some exceptions I believe these facts are reliable; in many cases I have verified them.

I have omitted from this table many well-known *corridos* dealing with places in Mexico. Many of these also circulate in the Southwest.

For ritual and social dance tunes from various villages, see Sections W and X.

Title	Source	Subject	Date
ARIZONA			
Allá en Arizona	(C65)	Homesickness	Undated
Canyon del Diablo			
Indita de Ricardo	(I1a)	Loss of a flock	1899
(Composed by "Ricardo")		of sheep	
Tucson			
El Merino	(B36)	Racehorse	Undated
CALIFORNIA			
Ya Me Voy para California	(D38)	Travel	Undated
Joaquín Murieta	(B35)	Racial strife	1850
COLORADO			
Pagosa Springs			
Indita of Amarante Martínez	(F2)	Automobile death	1926
(Composed by Leandro Lucero)			
KANSAS			
Los Reenganchados a Kansas	(I29)	Mexican day labor	Undated
NEW MEXICO			
Albuquerque			
Carlos Briley	(B26)	A drowning	1955
(Composed by Boleslo Gallegos, grandfather of the deceased)			

Title	Source	Subject	Date
Adiós de Fernández Gallegos	(C76)	Accidental death	Undated
Words composed by Boleslo Gallegos, father of the deceased. The tune by the singer, Mary Inez Jaramillo)			
Lucila Ramírez	(B29)	Murder	1948
Albuquerque	(C89)	Praise of city	1960
(Composed by Vincent Saucedo)			
Bernalillo			
Año de 1837	(E23)	Disorder in New Mexico	1837
Canjilón			
Corrido de la Muerte de Antonio Maestas	(I17)	Death of a cowboy	1889
(Composed by Higinio V. Gonzales)			
Chimayó			
Los Chimayoses	(C87)		
Año de 1895, or *Teófilo Vigil*	(I6)		1895
Cochití			
Cochití	(C86)		
Cuba			
Indita de Celestino Segura	(I2)	A lost shepherd	Undated
Federico Chávez	(B32)	Murder	
Estancia			
La Indita Fúnebre	(F6)	Death in a land dispute	1883
Indita de Manuel B. Otero	(F7)		1883
Galisteo			
Cuando de Pecos, or *Cuando de los Galisteos*	(H1)	Rooster pull	June 24, 1875
Gallina Springs			
Indita de Manuelito	(F9)	Death of Indian chief	Undated
Las Cruces			
Toribio Huertas	(B11)	A hanging	April 26, 1801 (probably 1901)
Leyva			
La Vaca del Condado	(D17)	Spoils system	Undated
Corrido de Wingate	(I23)	Freighting by wagon	Undated

861

Title	Source	Subject	Date
Manzano, Valencia County			
Indita de José Luis	(F4)	Death of beloved musician	Undated
Indita de Manzano	(F3)	Death of beloved musician	Undated
Moriarty			
Andrés Mora y Lola Chávez (Composed by Luisito Antonio Sánchez) (Probably from Moriarty, cf. FTR 5/31/63)	(B31)	Murder	1917
Mosquero			
Cuando de 1905	(H2)	A pest of insects	1905
Padilla			
Indita de Jesús María Sánchez (Composed by Ramón Barbúa)	(F5)	Death of a shepherd	1901
Pecos			
Cuando de Pecos	(H1a)	A rooster pull	June 24, 1875
Rivera			
Rubén Leyva	(B18)	Death at a dance	February 5, ———
San Antonio, Bernalillo County			
Corrido de José Apodaca	(B55)	A dancer	Undated
San Marcial			
San Marcial (Words by Ramón Luna, music by Eddie Gallegos)	(B52)	A flood	August 20, 1929
Santa Fe			
Santa Fe (Composed by Vincent Saucedo)	(C88)	Praise of city	1970
Silver City			
Luisito Núñez	(B7)	A hanging	1895
Socorro			
Carlos Saiz	(B10)	A hanging	January 11, 1907
Tomé			
Indita del 1884	(F19)	A flood	1884
Indita de Cleofas Griego	(F21)	Loss of flock of sheep	September 10, ———
Truchas			
Pedro Sandoval	(B34)	Suicide	June 21, ———

	Miscellaneous		
La Enfermedad de los Fríos	(D7)		Undated
(Various towns in New Mexico)			
La Indita Vagabunda	(F14)	A catalogue of New Mexico and other place names	Undated

TEXAS

	El Paso		
El Contrabando de El Paso	(B47)	Lament of a captured bootlegger	ca. 1919
	Laredo Area		
Gregorio Cortés	(B49)	Praise of an outlaw	
	Unspecified		
Luis Arcos	(B4)	An execution	November 6, 1930

C. SAMPLING OF *Despedidas*

A charming feature of a number of folk songs, especially prominent in the *corridos*, is the *despedida*, or final verse. It may serve as a moral to the story (as in B17b, *Jesús Cadenas*), a simple farewell (S2, *Bendito Sea Dios*), a mere conclusion (A5b, *Elena*), or a disclosure of authorship (I1, *Indita de Ricardo*, B8, *Bonifacio Torres*), among other uses. Many of these final verses start with the words *vuela, vuela, palomita* (fly, fly, little dove) (see for example A5, B1a, B5, B21).

Here are a few of these *despedidas* translated into English:

A2a. *Delgadina.*

Delgadina has died
And gone to heaven
And her lustful father
Has gone to the depths of hell.

A5. *La Esposa Infiel.*

Fly, fly, little dove,
Stop at that fig tree.
Here ends the *corrido*
Of Helen, the unfaithful.

B1. *Guadalupe Rayos.*

The little doves flew away
Saying, with a very harmonious voice,
"To be brave is very costly.
Take care in your bad hours."

B17b. *Jesús Cadenas.*

Said the gossip Antonia,
Said the gossip Juana,
"Take care, girls,
Life does not bloom twice."

B19. *Rosita Alvírez.*

Rosita is in heaven
Giving her accounting to the Creator;
And Pólito is in the jail
Making his statement,
Making his statement.

B21. *Reyes Ruiz.*

Fly, fly, little dove,
Go to other regions,
Go tell my mama
That I want her blessings.

B38. *María.*

This song was composed by a fine
    Mexican.
Two times seven make fourteen,

Three times seven, twenty-one.
There may be beautiful songs,
But none equal to this one.

B43. *Corrido de Cananea.*

Now with this I leave you   ]
Through the leaves of a pomegranate
    tree.   ] *Bis*
And here the ballad is finished   ]
Of this cock so free.   ] *Bis*

B47. *El Contrabando de El Paso.*

Ah! my little mother, I send you
A sigh and an embrace.
Here end the tomorrows
Of the bootlegger of El Paso.

C37. *La Mancornadora.*

I do not know how to say good-bye,
My farewell will be this song,
The farewell which I know how to give
When I leave this town.

I1. *La Indita de Ricardo.*

Gentlemen, if you want to know   ]
Who composed this song,   ] *Bis*
It was he who lost his cap,   ]
Also his deer.   ] *Bis*

P14. *San Ysidro Labrador.*

Farewell, my glorious saint,
Courtier of the Lord,
Until next year,
Saint Isidor, Laborer.

P19. *El Santo Niño de Atocha.*

Farewell, Holy Child of Atocha,
Now with this verse I say good-bye
With love and tender tears.
Give me a place in thy glory,
That I may sing "Holy, Holy."

D. SONGS WITH CHORUS OR REFRAIN

One of the most artful and attractive features which, as is shown below, is common to many of the types of songs described in this book is the *coro* (chorus) or *refrán* (refrain). It can consist of meaningless syllables (for example, A6, D17), syllables expressive of grief such as *ay, ay, ay* (D13), interpolated syllables of Indian dialect (F11, F13), a suggestion of tolling bells (A2), and the like.

The chorus or refrain also serves the purpose of framing the verses of a long ballad, of creating a mood such as gaiety or sadness, of adding an element of contrast or variety, and of avoiding monotony, especially when the melody of the refrain is different from that of the verses. For these and other reasons the chorus or refrain is a world-wide feature of folk songs, and it therefore seems appropriate to call attention to a few of the songs included in this volume that display this feature.

A2.	*Delgadina*	D17.	*La Vaca del Condado*
A6.	*Firo Liro Li*	D19.	*San Fernándico*
B14.	*Roberto y Simón*	D36.	*Tango, Tarango, Tango*
C2.	*Juanita*	F2.	*Indita de Amarante Martínez*
C5.	*Las Estrellas*	F8.	*El Indio Vitorio*
C12.	*Las Fuentes*	F11.	*Las Inditas del Parreal*
C21.	*Ya Tú No Soplas*	F12a.	*Una Indita en Su Chinaco*
C23.	*La Tumba*	F12c.	*Una Indita en Su Chinante*
C39.	*Cuatro Palomitas Blancas*	F13.	*Indita de San Luis*
C40.	*La Paloma y el Palomo*	I8.	*El Soldado Razo*
C49.	*El Durazno*	I10f.	*Tecolote de Guadaña*
C54.	*El Palo Verde*	I23.	*Corrido de Wingate*
D3.	*Yo No Me Quiero Casar*	I25.	*El Zapatero*
D6.	*Leonor*	M2.	*La Luna Se Va Metiendo*
D13.	*Doña Clara*	M3.	*Cuatro Caminos*
D16.	*En Capricho*		

E. FORM FOR ANALYSIS
OF FOLK MELODIES

The following form is suggested for the use of those interested in the analysis of the melodies.

Serial no. _____ Title _____

Place recorded _____

Date recorded _____

Informant _____

Place of origin (if identifiable) _____

Classification (*romance, corrido,* etc.) _____

           Religious or Secular _____

1. Number of phrases   Total

    _____ _____ _____ _____ _____ _____

    _____ _____ _____ _____ _____ _____

2. Cadences (M = masculine, F = feminine)

    _____ _____ _____ _____ _____ _____

    _____ _____ _____ _____ _____ _____

3. Last two notes—degrees of scale 1 to 8
    (each cadence)

    _____ _____ _____ _____ _____

    _____ _____ _____ _____ _____

4. Principal meter (duple, triple, compound, unmetered) _____
5. Metric signature (2/4, 3/8, 6/8, etc.) _____
6. Heterometric (Yes or No)   _____

    If yes, what other meters?

    _____   _____   _____   _____

7. Use of triplets, etc., including hemiola rhythm _____
8. Modality (Major, Minor, Dorian, Phrygian, etc.) _____
9. Style of text setting:

    Syllabic—One note per syllable   _____

    Neumatic—Two or three notes per syllable   _____

    Melismatic—Several notes per syllable   _____

10. "Borrowed" melody source _____
11. "Borrowed" text source _____
12. Variants of

        Melody __ __ __ __ __ __ __ __ __ __

        Text   __ __ __ __ __ __ __ __ __ __

13.   Singing in parallel intervals (Yes or No)   _____
        What interval?   _____
14.   Miscellaneous comments:

DEFINITIONS

Alabado A unique type of religious folk song developed by the Penitentes of New Mexico to commemorate the Passion of Christ.

Alabanza A religious song of praise to a holy personage or object.

Anglo A term widely used in the Southwest to designate anyone except a person of Hispanic, Mexican, or Indian ancestry. As so used, it therefore refers not only to a person of English extraction but also to a white person of any of a number of different ethnic or national origins.

Assonance In Spanish poetry coincidence of vowel sounds at the conclusion of a line, as distinguished from *rhyme*, which requires the coincidence of both vowels and consonants.

Examples: Assonance encontra*da*
llam*aba*
Rhyme encontr*ado*
ilustr*ado*

Auto A folk play.

Ay, ay, ay A type of folk song originating in Andalucía, Spain, marked by the use of the words *ay, ay, ay*.

Baile A social dance, as distinguished from a *danza*, or ritual dance.

Bulto A hand-carved wooden figurine of a saint or holy personage, sometimes painted.

Cadence The ending of a musical phrase.

Canción A folk song of a romantic or introspective nature.

Canción de cuna A lullaby, often characterized by an *estribillo*. Synonym: *arrullo*.

Cautiva A folk song relating to captives.

Copla A stanza of four eight-syllable lines, the second and fourth rhyming *(abcb)*, that is characterized by a completely rounded thought. Sometimes the rhyme scheme varies, the first line rhyming with the third and the second with the fourth *(abab)*, or the first rhyming with the fourth and the second with the third *(abba)*, as in the *glosa* of the *espinela*. *Coplas* with eight-line stanzas are known as *double coplas*. Other variations also occur. Synonym: *verso*.

Coro A refrain interpolated between verses of a song. Synonyms: *refrán, estribillo*.

Corrido A narrative folk song, ordinarily composed of *coplas*, dealing with the lives of ordinary people. It is derived from the *romance* but features rhyme rather than assonance and a line of eight syllables rather than sixteen.

Cotillo A type of folk-dance tune resembling the *cuadrilla*.

Cuando A form of folk song in which each stanza ends with the word *cuando*. The *cuando* may be in the form of a *décima* and may be secular or religious.

Cuna A dance usually in duple time. The word means "cradle." To be distinguished from *canción de cuna*, or cradle song.

Danza A ritual dance, as distinguished from a social dance.

Décima A folk song consisting of ten-line stanzas. The lines are usually octosyllabic. Many forms of the *décima* are found throughout Latin America. In Panama the *décima* is known as the *mejorana*, in Cuba as the *guajira*, in Mexico as the *valona*, in Venezuela as the *canta*, in Veracruz as the *zapatero*. The most common form of *décima* encountered in New Mexico is the *espinela*.

Décima a lo divino A religious *décima*.

Décima a lo humano A secular *décima*.

Décima de amor A *décima* whose theme is love.

Décima glosada A forty-four-line *décima* opening with a four-line *copla* known as the *planta* (also known as the *cuarteta, redondilla,* or *glosa*) followed by four ten-line stanzas. The first ten-line stanza ends with the first line of the *planta*, the second with the second line of the *planta*, etc. Various rhyme schemes are employed, the most common of which is that of the *espinela*.

Deprecación A type of religious folk song in which souls are called from purgatory.

Despedida The final verse or verses of conclusion or farewell, usually in the form of the *copla*, added at the end of the song.

Días Songs or serenades sung or played on the saint's day or name day of a particular person. Synonyms: *mañanitas, Manueles*.

Disparate A song featuring exaggeration or absurdity. Synonym: *mentira*.

Duodécima A verse form employing stanzas of twelve lines. A variant of the *décima*.

Entrega de novios A term meaning delivery of the newlyweds, describing verses sung or recited after the wedding ball in which the bride is delivered over to her parents-in-law and the groom to his. Usually sung to a waltz tune.

Espinela A form of *décima glosada* named after the sixteenth-century Spanish writer Vicente

Espinel in which the usual rhyme scheme is *abbaaccddc*, though it frequently varies. This is the most common form of the *décima* in New Mexico.

Estribillo 1. A refrain introduced between the verses of a song. Sometimes it consists of meaningless syllables or of onomatopoetic syllables suggesting sounds of nature, such as the tolling of a bell or a bird's call. Because it is used to introduce variety into a monotonous rhythmic pattern, it often has a different rhythmic pattern or a different number of syllables to the line. 2. The repetition of the same phrase as the last line of each of the stanzas of a *décima* or other song.

Glosa The introductory *copla* of a *décima glosada*. Synonyms: *redondilla, planta, cuarteta*.

Gozo A religious song of praise, usually in the form of a *décima*.

Himno A hymn.

Indita A song combining the elements of Spanish and Indian music (usually a Spanish text with a melody showing Indian origin or influence) and often identified in the text by the word *indita*. Frequently includes a refrain of meaningless syllables. Said to be derived from the *tonadilla*, which has for the song portion a duple meter and for the dance portion a fast triple meter.

Letras 1. A generic term for the words of a song. 2. The sung portions of an *auto*.

Letrilla A *décima* in which the lines of the verses have fewer than eight syllables.

Mañanitas Synonym of *días*.

Manueles Synonym of *días*, but sung only to a person named Manuel.

Melisma A melodic ornamentation consisting of several notes sung to a single syllable of text.

Milagro A religious folk song dealing with a miracle.

Morada 1. A private chapel of a *cofradía*, or group of Penitentes. 2. Synonym of *habitación* (habitation).

Penitente A member of a secret *cofradía*, or brotherhood, known as the Hermanos de Nuestro Padre Jesús (Brothers of Our Father, Jesus).

Planta The opening four-line verse of a *décima*. Synonyms: *glosa, redondilla, cuarteta*.

Polka A dance in quadruple meter characterized by a strong third beat and a rest on the fourth. It originated in Bohemia about 1830.

Quintilla A form of the *décima glosada* with a *planta* of five lines and five ten-line verses.

Relación A humorous narrative folk song often containing a long list of names of places or people, usually in the form of *coplas*.

Retablo A picture of a saint or holy personage painted on a wooden board.

Romance A form of narrative ballad, derived from Spain, having a heroic subject. Characterized by a sixteen-syllable line with rhyme or assonance at the end of each line. Sometimes found with an *estribillo*.

Schottisch A dance of the mid–nineteenth century in duple meter, similar to the polka but slower.

Seguidilla A four-line verse form similar to the *copla* but with alternating lines of seven and five syllables. Sometimes followed by an *estribillo* of three lines with five, seven, and five syllables, respectively.

Son A lyric-choreographic form characterized by mimicry of animal sounds or human types and by the alternation of 3/4 and 6/8 rhythms.

Tinievolas One of the Holy Week ceremonies of the Penitentes.

Tonada The melody of a folk song.

Tonadilla A song-and-dance form, the sung portion in 2/4 time and the danced portion in a faster 3/8 time. Rarely found in New Mexico. See *indita*.

Trovos *Coplas* linked in dialogue in which two or more persons sing alternate verses. Originally, it is said, the *trovos* were improvised by famous singers. Apparently only the words were improvised, however, with the same music accompanying each verse. Sometimes each singer would sing his own somewhat different version of the tune.

Valona A generic term used to describe all the various forms of the *décima*.

Valse A dance in triple meter.

Valse chiqueado A dance in which verses, usually *coplas*, are interpolated. The verses sometimes consist of an invitation to dance sung by the man and a reply sung by the lady.

Valse de escoba A waltz in which an extra man dances with or is left with a broom instead of a partner. When he wishes to dance, he offers the broom to the partner of the desired lady, who must take it and find another partner in the same way.

Valse de silla A form of dance in which a chair is placed in the middle of the floor or elsewhere and, as a couple dances past the chair, the young lady, if so inclined, sits down in it until her partner sings a satisfactorily complimentary verse.

Verso 1. A general term for poetic stanzas. 2. Synonym for *copla*.

BIBLIOGRAPHY

Except as otherwise indicated, the materials listed are published. Unpublished materials marked with an asterisk (*) may be consulted in the Library of the University of New Mexico in Albuquerque. Unpublished materials marked with a dagger (†) are available in Xerox copies at the University of New Mexico Fine Arts Library.

The abbreviations enclosed in parentheses after each entry are those used in the text to cite sources and to refer the reader to sources of further information.

Books and Articles

Anaya, Rudolfo A. *Heart of Aztlán*. Berkeley, Calif.: Editorial Justa Publications, Inc., 1976. (Anaya)

Baca, Próspero S. "One Hundred Twenty-one Décimas and Other Folk Songs." Unpublished. (Baca 1)*

——. "Fifty-three New Mexican Folksongs." Unpublished. (Baca 1a)*

——. "Thirteen Folksongs of New Mexico." Unpublished. (Baca 1b)*

Bartók, Béla. *Hungarian Folk Music*. London: Oxford University Press, 1931. (Bartók)

Boatright, Mody C., ed. *Mexican Border Ballads, and Other Lore*. Publications of the Texas Folklore Society, vol. 21. Austin: Texas Folklore Society, 1946. (Texas 18)

Boyd, E. *Saints and Saint Makers*. Santa Fe, N.Mex.: Laboratory of Anthropology, 1946. (Boyd 1c)

Bukofzer, Manfred F. *The Music of the Baroque Era*. New York: W. W. Norton, 1947. (Bukofzer)

Campa, Arthur L. *Spanish Folk Poetry in New Mexico*. Albuquerque: University of New Mexico Press, 1946. (Campa 2)

——. *Spanish Religious Folktheatre in the Spanish Southwest, First Cycle and Second Cycle*. Albuquerque: University of New Mexico Press, 1934. (Campa 2a)

——. "Folksongs." Unpublished. (Campa 2b)*
This unpublished notebook, presented to me in the early 1940's, contains words and melodies of twenty-two songs.

——. "Spanish Religious Folktheatre in the Southwest, Cycle I." *University of New Mexico Bulletin*, 1934. (Campa 2c)

——. "Spanish Folksongs in the Southwest." *University of New Mexico Bulletin* (Modern Language Series), vol. 4, no. 1 (1933). (Campa 2d)

Chávez, Clemente. "Notebook of Clemente Chávez." Unpublished. (Chávez 2b)* Through permission of Mrs. Antonio Mendonca, Moriarty, N.Mex.

Cobos, Rubén. "El Folklore Nuevo Mexicano." *El Nuevo Mexicano* (Santa Fe, N.Mex.), October 9, 1949, to November 16, 1950. (Cobos 4)

——. "The New Mexican Game of 'Valse Chiquiao'." *Western Folklore*, vol. 15, no. 2 (April, 1956). (Cobos 4a)

Córdova, Gilbert Benito. *Abiquiú and Don Cacahuate*. Cerrillos, N.Mex.: San Marcos Press, 1973. (Córdova)

Corridos Mexicanos. Guanajuato, Mexico: Editorial Olimpia, 1950. (Olimpia 4b)
This contains thirty-five song texts, many of which are sung in the border states.

Curtin, Leonora. Volume of Fifty-nine Texts. Edited by Arthur L. Campa. Unpublished. (Curtin 4)†

——. Volume of Corresponding Music. Transcribed by A. Armendariz. Unpublished. (Curtin 4a)†

Dobie, J. Frank, ed. *Publications of the Texas Folklore Society*, vol. 4. Austin: Texas Folklore Society, May, 1925. (Texas 18)

Densmore, Frances. *The Music of the Santo Domingo Pueblo*. Los Angeles: Southwestern Museum Papers, no. 12, 1938. (Densmore)

Ellis, Florence Hawley. "Tomé and Father J.B.R." *New Mexico Historical Review*, vol. 30, no. 2 (April, 1955), no. 3 (July, 1955). (Ellis 4c)

Espinosa, Aurelio M. "Romancero Nuevomejicano." *Revue Hispanique*, vol. 33 (1915), pp. 446–560. (Espinosa 5)

——. "Traditional Spanish Ballads in New Mexico." *Hispania*, vol. 15, no. 2 (March, 1932) pp. 89–102. (Espinosa 5a)

García, Bonifacio Gil. *Cancionero Popular de Extremadura*. Badajoz, Spain: Imprensa de la Extremadura Diputación, 1956. (García 5b)

Hague, Eleanor, ed. *Spanish-American Folksongs*. New York: American Folklore Society, 1944. (Hague 6)

Hansen, Terrence L. "Corridos in Southern California." *Western Folklore*, vol. 18, nos. 3 and 4 (July and October, 1959). (Hansen 6a and 6b)

Lea, Aurora Lucero-White. *Literary Folklore of the Hispanic Southwest*. San Antonio, Texas: Naylor, 1953. (Lea 7)

Libro Español. *Método de Guitarra*. Seminario no. 14. Mexico City. (Libro 7a)
This Mexican *cancionero* contains two hundred song texts, many of which are sung in the border states.

López, José Dolores. "Penitente Manual." Unpublished. (López 8)†

Lummis, Charles F. *The Land of Poco Tiempo*. Albuquerque: University of New Mexico Press, 1952. (Lummis)

Matos, Vicente T. *Cancionero Popular de la Provincia de Madrid*. Madrid: Instituto Español de Musicología, 1951. Vol. 1 (Matos 8a), vol. 2 (Matos 8b), vol. 3. (Matos 8c)

———. *Antología del Folklore Musical de España*. Madrid: Hispavox, 1960. (Matos 8d)

Mendoza, Vicente T. *La Canción Hispanomexicana en Nuevo México*. Organo de la Universidad de México, vol. 1, no. 2 (November, 1946). (Mendoza 9)

———. *Cincuenta Romances*. Mexico City: EDIPSA, 1940. (Mendoza 9a)

———. *Fifty Corridos Mexicanos*. Mexico City: Secretaría de Educación Pública, 1944. (Mendoza 9b)

———. *La Décima en México*. Buenos Aires: Ministerio de Instrucción Pública, 1947. (Mendoza 9c)

———. "Estudio y Clasificación de la Música Tradicional Hispánica de Nuevo México." Unpublished. (Mendoza 9d)†

———. *Lírica Narrativa de México—El Corrido*. Mexico City: Instituto de Investigaciones Estéticas, 1964. (Mendoza 9e)

———. *El Romance Español y El Corrido Mexicano*. Mexico City: Imprenta Universitaria, 1939. (Mendoza 9f)

———. *La Canción Mexicana*. Mexico City: Instituto de Investigaciones Estéticas, Universidad Nacional Autónoma de México, 1961. (Mendoza 9g)

Mingote, Angel. *Cancionero Musical de la Provincia de Zaragoza*. Zaragoza, Spain: Institución Fernando el Católico, 1967. (Mingote)

Nef, Karl. *An Outline History of Music*. New York: Columbia University Press, 1935. (Nef)

Neruda, Pablo. *Fulgor y Muerte de Joaquín Murieta*. Santiago, Chile: Zig Zag Press, 1967.

Paredes, Américo. *With His Pistol in His Hand*. Austin: University of Texas Press, 1958. (Paredes 10)

———, with George Foss. *The Décima on the Texas-Mexican Border*. Austin: University of

Texas, Institute of American Studies, 1966. (Paredes 10a)

Rael, Juan B. *The New Mexico Alabado*. Palo Alto: Stanford University Press, 1951. (Rael)

Ralliere, Juan B. *Cánticos Espirituales*. Las Vegas, N.Mex.: Revista Católica, 1908. (Ralliere a)
8th ed. El Paso, Texas: Revista Católica, 1928. (Ralliere b)
9th ed. 1933. (Ralliere c)
"Tercera" ed. Con Musica. 1944. (Ralliere d)

Ridge, John Rollin. *The Life and Adventures of Joaquín Murieta*. Norman: University of Oklahoma Press, 1955.

Robb, John D. *Hispanic Folk Songs of New Mexico*. Albuquerque: University of New Mexico Press, 1954. (Robb 13)

———. "The Origins of a New Mexico Folksong." *New Mexico Folklore Record*, vol. 5 (1950–51). (Robb 13a)

———. "The J. D. Robb Collection of Folk Music Recordings." (Robb 13b)*
New Mexico Folklore Record, vol. 7 (1952–53), lists the first 1096 of the over 3000 items of this collection.

———. "H. V. Gonzales: Folk Poet of New Mexico." *New Mexico Folklore Record*, vol. 13 (1973–74), pp. 1–6. (Robb 13c)

———. "The Music of Los Pastores." *Western Folklore*, vol. 16, no. 4 (October, 1957). (Robb 13d)

———. "The Matachines Dance." *Western Folklore*, vol. 20, no. 2 (April, 1961). (Robb 13e)

———. "The Relación in the United States." *New Mexico Folklore Record*, vol. 11 (1963–64). (Robb 13f)

———. "Folk Poets of New Mexico." *New Mexico Magazine*, December 25, 1966. (Robb 13g)

———. "Songs of the Western Sheep Camps." *New Mexico Folklore Record*, vol. 12 (1969–70). (Robb 13h)

———. "Sheep Shearing in New Mexico 1956." *New Mexico Historical Review*, October, 1956, p. 357. (Robb 13i)

———. Foreword to "One Hundred and Twenty-One Décimas and Other Folk Songs," by Próspero S. Baca. Unpublished. (Robb 13j)*

———. "Field Trip Reports." Unpublished. (Robb 13k)*

———, Review of *The New Mexico Alabado*, by Juan B. Rael. *New Mexico Historical Review*, vol. 26, pp. 250–55. (Robb 13l)

———. "A Pocket Without Money." *Western Folklore*, vol. 33, no. 3 (July, 1974), pp. 247–53. (Robb 13m)

———. "Rhythmic Patterns of the Santo Domingo Corn Dance." *Ethnomusicology*, vol. 8, no. 2 (May, 1964). (Robb 13n)

Sachs, Curt. *The Rise of Music in the Ancient World, East and West*. New York: W. W.

Norton and Company, 1943. (Sachs)

Schaeffer, Myron. "La Mejorana." *Bulletin of the Institute of Folklore Research* (Inter-American University, Panama), vol. 1, no. 2 (November, 1944). (Schaeffer 14)

Schindler, Kurt. *Folk Music and Poetry of Spain and Portugal.* New York: Hispanic Institute in the United States, 1941. (Schindler 14a)

Sedillo, Mela. *Mexican and New Mexican Folkdances.* 2d. ed. Albuquerque: University of New Mexico Press, 1938. (Sedillo 15)

Stark, Richard B. *Music of the Spanish Folk Plays in New Mexico.* Santa Fe: Museum of New Mexico Press, 1969. (Stark 16)

Texas Folklore Society, Publications of. (Texas 18) See Boatright and Dobie, above.

Toor, Frances. *A Treasury of Mexican Folkways.* New York: Crown Publishers, 1947. (Toor)

Van Stone, Mary. *Spanish Folksongs of New Mexico.* Chicago: Ralph Seymour Fletcher, 1928. (Van Stone 17)

This gives song settings of twenty-three songs.

Velázquez, Mariano. *New Revised Spanish and English Dictionary.* Chicago, New York: Follett Publishing Co., 1959. (Velázquez 17a).

Works Progress Administration. *Spanish American Song and Game Book.* New York: A. S. Barnes & Co., 1924. (WPA 19)

Published Music

Mares, Pablo. *Santa Fe Tipica Orchestra Folio.* New York: Carl Fischer, Inc., 1947. (Mares) This is a group of melodies (all but two of which are represented in this book) arranged for strings and guitars.

The following publications are based on melodies represented in this book or in the J. D. Robb Collection:

Rhoads, William E. *Música Simpática.* New York: Carl Fischer, Inc., 1958. Melodies arranged for band.

Robb, John D. *Hispanic Folk Songs of New Mexico.* Albuquerque: University of New Mexico Press, 1954. This includes fifteen selected songs, collected, transcribed, and arranged for voice and piano.

———. *Little Dove (Palomita Que Vienes Herida): Madrigal for Mixed Voices.* New York: Broadcast Music, Inc., 1946. Now out of print.

DISCOGRAPHY

Both the Bibliography and the Discography are limited to items to which I have referred in the text. Many recordings by others have been assigned serial numbers in the B series of the J. D. Robb Collection and are referred to in the text by the capital letters RB followed by the appropriate serial number.

Chávez, Alex. "Duérmete Niño and Other Songs." Albuquerque: University of New Mexico. (Chávez 26)

————. "El Testamento and Other Songs." Albuquerque: University of New Mexico. (Chávez 27)

Robb, John D. "The J. D. Robb Collection of Folk Music Recordings." Unpublished. (Robb 13q) Contains 3,364 titles. Tapes of most of these are available for listening at the Music Library, University of New Mexico, Albuquerque.

————. *Spanish and Mexican Folk Music of New Mexico* (Folkways Album FE4426). New York: Folkways, 1961. (Robb 13r)

————. *Peter Hurd Sings Ranchera Songs* (Folkways Album FA2204). New York: Folkways, 1966. (Robb 13s)

————. *Cowboy Ballads* (Folkways Album FP22). New York: Folkways, 1952. (Robb 13t)

The following are available from Taos Recordings and Publications, care of Jenny Wells Vincent, Taos, New Mexico (for sale), or from the University of New Mexico Fine Arts Library, Albuquerque, New Mexico (for listening).

Taos Recordings and Publications. "Taos Spanish Songs." Taos, N.Mex. (Taos 22)

————. "New Mexican Alabados." Taos, N.Mex. (Taos 23)

————. "Taos Matachines Music." Taos, N.Mex. (Taos 24)

————. "Buenos Días, Paloma Blanca." Taos, N.Mex. (Taos 25)

————. "Taos Matachines Music." Taos, N.Mex. (Taos 25a)

INDEX OF TITLES

INDEX OF FIRST LINES

GENERAL INDEX

(See also Index of Song Titles
and Index of First Lines.)